Eighth Edition

Public Speaking

Michael Osborn
University of Memphis

Suzanne Osborn
University of Memphis

Randall Osborn
University of Memphis

PEARSON

Boston New York San Francisco
Mexico City Montreal Toronto London Madrid Munich Paris
Hong Kong Singapore Tokyo Cape Town Sydney

Editor-in-Chief: Karon Bowers
Series Editorial Assistant: Jessica Cabana
Associate Editor: Jenny Lupica
Marketing Manager: Suzan Czajkowski
Production Editor: Claudine Bellanton
Editorial Production Service: Progressive Publishing Alternatives
Composition Buyer: Linda Cox
Manufacturing Buyer: JoAnne Sweeney
Electronic Composition: Progressive Information Technologies
Interior Design: Deborah Schneck
Photo Researcher: Lisa Jelly Smith
Cover Administrator: Kristina Mose-Libon

For related titles and support materials, visit our online catalog at www.ablongman.com

Between the time website information is gathered and then published, it is not unusual for some sites to have closed. Also, the transcription of URLs can result in typographical errors. The publisher would appreciate notification where these errors occur so that they may be corrected in subsequent editions.

Library of Congress Cataloging-in-Publication Data
Osborn, Michael.
    Public speaking / Michael Osborn, Suzanne Osborn, Randall Osborn. — 8th ed.
        p. cm.
    Includes bibliographical references and index.
    Student Edition ISBN-13: 978-0-205-58456-7
    Student Edition ISBN-10: 0-205-58456-X
    Instructor's Annotated Edition ISBN-13: 978-0-205-58284-6
    Instructor's Annotated Edition ISBN-10: 0-205-58284-2
    1. Public speaking. I. Osborn, Suzanne. II. Osborn, Randall. III. Title.

PN4129.15.O83 2009
808.5'1—dc22

                                                          2007038979

Printed in the United States of America
10 9 8 7 6 5   V011   10
Credits appear on page 522, which constitutes an extension of the copyright page.

Why You Need This New Edition

Strengthened by the insights of a new author and by the enthusiastic support of a new publisher, we approached the eighth edition of *Public Speaking* with a sense of renewal and rededication to our central purpose: offering a quality book that helps today's student develop communication skills and sensitivities. The eighth edition is our latest attempt to seek answers to the core questions first posed by Aristotle and Plato: *What is the nature of the art of public speaking? How can one master this art? And, can one be an ethical speaker and still be effective?*

During the revision of this book, we have made some valuable discoveries and changes. These include:

Transformation of Chapter 1. Reconceptualizing and refocusing the introductory chapter has improved it as a "gateway" chapter into the rest of the book.

Sharper focus on the definition of public speaking. The idea of public speaking as "an interactive, dynamic procsss" has helped unify important concepts in the first chapter.

Greater simplicity and clarity. Clarity and simplicity are cardinal virtues of textbook writing. We have revised with our undergraduate readers constantly in mind.

Introduction of the narrative design early in the text. Discussing this innovative concept earlier in the book (Chapter 3) helps students benefit from its insights throughout the course.

Focused discussion of audience analysis. Chapter 5 now deals more precisely with issues speakers must confront in adapting to their listeners.

Simpler and more functional approach to informative speaking. Our discussion of the forms of informative speaking in Chapter 14 is now grounded in three basic human impulses: our desires to expand our awareness, enhance our abilities, and satisfy our curiosity.

More emphasis on the ethics of persuasive speaking. By reversing the order of arrangement in Chapters 15 and 16, we have made it easier for students to apply *argumentative persuasion* as an ethical standard in their decisions concerning persuasive strategy.

An abundance of particular improvements. We have enriched the fabric of our book in many specific ways. These detailed changes include new speeches, references to new research, improvements to particular sections and sub-sections, new vignettes, new examples and illustrations, and new pedagogical features. These materials make the book more informative, relevant and engaging.

You can learn more about these and other new features on pages x–xxii of the Preface.

We were also pleased to discover that adding a new author can add new insights. Dr. Randall Osborn brings to our writing team both a rich teaching background and a sense of family pride in the book's success. With practical teaching skills honed by teaching the basic course at the University of Arkansas, Dyersburg State Community College, University of Indiana, University of Indiana–South Bend, University of Memphis, and the University of Nevada Las Vegas, he has refreshed our knowledge of the contemporary classroom and of its pressures and needs. He has also brought us some wonderful new examples of student speaking.

4 Becoming a Better Listener   70

5 Adapting to Your Audience and Situation   94

6 Finding Your Topic   120

7   Researching Your Topic   142

8   Supporting Your Ideas   168

9 Structuring Your Speech 194

10 Outlining Your Speech 222

11 Presentation Aids 246

12 Using Language Effectively 282

13 Presenting Your Speech 310

PART FOUR   Types of Public Speaking   340

14 Informative Speaking 340

Preface

From ancient times, educators have recognized that the study and practice of public speaking is the core of a liberal education. What other discipline requires students to think clearly, be attuned to the needs of listeners, organize their thoughts, select and combine words artfully and judiciously, and express themselves with power and conviction, all while under the direct scrutiny of an audience? The challenge to teach such a complex range of abilities has always been difficult, but today it is especially so, as people struggle to define what it means to be human against a backdrop of global inhumanity. This book represents our best effort to help teachers rise to this challenge. Another core objective of our book is to illuminate the role of public speaking in a diverse society. Adjusting to a diverse audience is a challenge ancient writers could not have anticipated. The increasing cultural diversity of our society adds to the importance of public speaking as a force that can counter division. Thus, cultural diversity is a theme that remains constant in our book.

We continue to believe that a major goal of the public speaking course is to make students more sensitive to the impact of speaking on the lives of others. Because of the pervasive importance of values and ethics, we discuss ethical considerations throughout the book. For example, we direct the attention of students to ethical concerns as we consider listening, audience analysis and adaptation, cultural variations, topic selection, research, ways of structuring speeches, presentation aids, use of language, and the consequences of informing and persuading others. Often we use an Ethics Alert!, to highlight these concerns.

Ethics *Alert! 12.1*

The Ethical Use of Powerful Language

To use the power of words in ethical ways, follow these guidelines:

1. Avoid depictions that distort reality: Let your words illuminate the subject, not blind the listener.

2. Use words to support sound reasoning, not substitute for it.

3. Use language to empower both traditions and visions.

4. Use images to renew appreciation of shared values.

5. Use language to strengthen the ties of community, not divide people.

6. Use language to overcome inertia and inspire listeners to action.

7. Be cautious about melodramatic language that reduces complex issues and the people in disputes into good versus evil.

The persuasion chapters develop an ethical concept, *argumentative persuasion*, that emphasizes the centrality of reasoned proofs. This concept is advanced as an antidote to that *manipulative persuasion* evident in much of contemporary communication. The development of argumentative persuasion extends a moral axiom that has characterized our book since its inception: the speaker's obligation to offer listeners *responsible knowledge*.

For all these reasons, we continue to believe that a college course in public speaking should offer both practical advice and an understanding of why such advice works. We emphasize both the *how* and the *why* of public speaking—*how* so that beginners can achieve success as quickly as possible, and *why* so that they can manage their new skills wisely. Our approach is eclectic: we draw from the past and present and from the social sciences and humanities to help students understand and manage their public speaking experiences.

The Roman educator Quintilian held forth the ideal of "the good person speaking well" as a goal of education. Two thousand years later, we join him in stressing the value of speech training in the development of the whole person. In addition, understanding the principles of public communication can make students more resistant to unethical speakers and more critical of the mass-mediated communication to which they are exposed. The class should help students become both better consumers as well as producers of public communication.

What's New in the Eighth Edition?

*I*n the seventh edition of *Public Speaking*, we offered a number of innovations: new models and figures to clarify communication concepts; new chapters on controlling communication anxiety, selecting and evaluating topics, and researching these topics; substantial revision of the persuasion chapters, including development of a new theme, *argumentative persuasion*; development of the concept of narrative, including narrative design; and development of the concept of *integrated communication* to focus our chapter on presentation. This new edition offers a chance to consolidate, polish, and improve these innovations and to develop other improvements. These latest changes fall into two large categories: *macro changes* that required reconceiving and restructuring important sections of the book, and *micro changes* that involved refining and refreshing specific details.

Macro Changes

Revisions that reconceive and restructure significant sections of the book occur in Chapter 1 ("Public Speaking and You"), Chapter 14 ("Informative Speaking," and the two persuasion chapters (Chapter 15, "Building Powerful Arguments," and Chapter 16, "Persuasive Speaking").

Changes in Chapter 1. We have revised Chapter 1 with the following objectives in mind: (A) We wanted a simpler, more welcoming introduction to the study of public speaking; (B) We wanted to clarify the logical connection between major concepts within the chapter; and (C) We wanted to emphasize major themes that develop throughout the book, underscoring its conceptual cohesiveness.

In pursuit of these objectives, we decided to restructure the chapter around two major headings: *What does this course offer you?* and *What does this course ask of you?* We next revised and renamed the models of communication so that they develop a single conception that defines our approach: *public speaking is an interactive, dynamic process.* Finally, we refocused our discussion of the rhetorical tradition in order to bring out major questions about the subject that have resonated through the ages: *What is the nature of the art of public speaking? How can it be practiced more successfully? And How can it be practiced more ethically?*

Changes in Chapter 14. We have developed a simpler, more functional approach to informative speaking grounding the major forms of such speaking in three basic impulses: (1) the impulse to expand our awareness of the world around us (speeches of description); (2) the impulse to develop practical or enjoyable skills (speeches of demonstration); and (3) the impulse that drives curiosity (speeches of explanation). This more functional approach allows us to focus more precisely on useful advice to the developing public speaker.

Changes in the Persuasion Chapters. Several reviewers pointed out that if we reversed the order of emphasis in Chapters 15 and 16, we might make it easier for students to apply *argumentative persuasion* as an ethical standard when they decide on persuasive strategies in planning their speeches. This advice, consistent with our concern for ethical issues throughout the book, also proved useful in helping us rearrange the logical development of these chapters.

Other Changes.   Additional macro improvements in the 8th edition include: (1) seeking closer, more cohesive connections between structuring (Chapter 9) and outlining (Chapter 10); (2) refocusing our discussion of audience analysis (Chapter 5) more precisely on the major concerns speakers must address in adapting to their listeners; and (3) revising the chapter on structure (Chapter 9) in order to achieve better balance, to reduce unnecessary theoretical materials, and to introduce the major speech designs. These changes should result in a more useful book for students.

Micro Changes

A wealth of specific changes has enriched our book. These changes include new speeches, references to new research, improvements to particular sections and sub-sections, new vignettes, new examples and illustrations, and new pedagogical features.

New Speeches.   Two speeches in particular add color and interest to the new edition. John Bakke's ceremonial speech redefining Martin Luther King's concept of nonviolence, pointing up its relevance in a troubled world, is a rich source of illustration. Sabrina Karic's student speech, "A Little Chocolate," tells how she managed to survive the ethnic cleansing that took place in Bosnia and Herzegovina when she was a child. Her speech becomes a plea to help protect the lives and innocence of children from the world's ongoing inhumanity.

New Research.   The new edition offered the opportunity to update and refine our advice to speakers in light of recent research discoveries. These discoveries concern, for example,

> the role of language intensity in persuasive efforts.
>
> the value of rehearsing before "live" audiences.
>
> the comparative value of statistical and narrative forms of evidence.
>
> the relationship of the use of colorful language to a speaker's ethos.
>
> the way one should address reluctant audiences.
>
> the importance of ethics in persuasion.
>
> how humor can advance or inhibit speech effectiveness.

Improvements to Particular Sections and Sub-sections.   Much of the creative enjoyment of textbook writing comes from discovering that we can improve sections and sub-sections of chapters. The following improvements are among many that might illustrate the point:

- Developing succinct advice on how to cope with a diverse audience (Chapter 5).
- Rewriting and rearranging the mind-mapping technique of topic exploration (Chapter 6).
- Developing new material on information literacy (Chapter 7).
- Adding focus to the discussion of facts and statistics and enrichment to the explanation of narratives (Chapter 8).
- Offering more advice on the use of key-word outlines (Chapter 10).

- Rewriting and reordering sections on clarity and conciseness (so that they are more clear and concise!) (Chapter 12).
- Reorganizing and reordering discussion of video presentations (Chapter 13).
- Adding liveliness to the discussion of helping listeners learn (Chapter 14).
- Introducing a new ethical issue: the contamination of expert testimony by special interests (Chapter 15).

New Vignettes, Examples, and Illustrations. The book abounds with new and fresh illustrations. In particular, we point to

new and heavily revised introductory vignettes, as in Chapters 7, 9, 10, 11, and 16, which offer fresh and updated perspectives on the issues addressed within these chapters.

the new figures and visual examples that refresh Chapter 11's discussion of presentation aids.

the new examples that update the discussion of speech structure (Chapter 9) and that offer striking illustrations of language techniques (Chapter 12).

New Pedagogical Features. The new edition introduces two new pedagogical features:

1. a *running glossary*, which identifies and defines key terms at the bottom of pages in which they are introduced. This feature helps students focus their reading, and helps them prepare for examinations on the material.
2. "Explore and Apply the Ideas in this Chapter," provided after the summary of each chapter, encourages students to reflect on the relevance of the discussion to their lives and interests.

"We invite you to encourage your students to submit the texts of excellent speeches for possible use in later editions of *Public Speaking*. Send these materials to osbornso@gmail.com.

Distinctive Features of Our Book

textbook is a rhetorical product: it must constantly adapt to the changing times and needs of its student audience. Nevertheless, some features have remained constant and distinctive across the many editions of our book.

- *Responsible knowledge as a standard for public speaking.* In order to develop a standard for the quality and depth of information that should be reflected in all speeches, we offer the concept of *responsible knowledge*. This concept is developed in detail in Chapter 7, in which we discuss the foundation of research that should support speeches.
- *Special preparation for the first speech.* As teachers we realize the importance of the first speaking experience to a student's ultimate success in the course. Yet much useful advice must be delayed until later chapters as the subject of public speaking develops systematically over a semester. Having experienced this

frustration ourselves while teaching the course, we decided to include an overview of practical advice early in the book that previews later chapters and prepares students more effectively for their first speeches. This overview is provided in Chapter 3.

- *Communication ethics.* We have always discussed ethical issues as they arise in the context of topics. The *Ethics Alert!* feature helps highlight these concerns as they develop chapter-by-chapter within the situations to which they apply.

- *Internet research.* We offer a comprehensive introduction to research on the Internet, including, for example, discussion of "the invisible Web." We also emphasize standards to help students evaluate what they may find in such explorations, and help them develop a plan to use such material judiciously.

- *InterConnections.LearnMore,* offered in most chapters, highlight online learning opportunities throughout the book.

- *The importance of narrative in public speaking.* We discuss narrative as an important form of supporting material and as a previously neglected design option. We also identify appeals to traditions, heroic symbols, and legends—all built upon narrative—as an important emerging form of proof (*mythos*) in persuasive speaking.

- *Improving language skills.* We introduce students to the power of language, help them apply standards so that this power is not diminished, and demonstrate special techniques that can magnify this power at important moments in speeches. Among the standards is learning how to avoid grammatical errors that make listeners cringe.

- *Enhanced understanding of ceremonial speaking.* We provide coherence and respect for the study of ceremonial speaking by pointing out the importance of such speaking in society, and by indicating how two powerful concepts, one offered by Aristotle and the other by Kenneth Burke, can combine to generate successful ceremonial speeches, especially speeches of tribute and inspiration.

Plan of the Book

*P*ublic Speaking is designed to help beginning students build cumulative knowledge and skills. Positive initial speaking experiences are especially important. For this reason, Chapter 2 helps apprehensive students control communication anxiety as they stand to speak for the first time. Chapter 3 offers an overview of advice to help students design and present successful first speeches.

In the chapters that follow, students learn how to listen critically and constructively; analyze their audiences; select, refine, and research speech topics; develop supporting materials; arrange these materials in appropriate structures; and create effective presentation aids. They also learn how to manage words and present their messages. Students become acquainted with the nature of information and how to present it, the process of persuasion and how to engage it, and the importance of ceremonial speaking in its various forms. Appendix A, "Communicating in Small Groups," describes how to use public communication skills to participate effectively in small group interactions.

Teachers may adapt the sequence of chapters to any course plan, because each chapter covers a topic thoroughly and completely.

Detailed Plan of the Book

Part One, "The Foundations of Public Speaking," provides basic information that students need for their first speaking and listening experiences. Chapter 1 defines public speaking, highlights the personal, social, and cultural benefits of being able to speak effectively in public, and emphasizes the ethical responsibilities of speakers. Chapter 2 helps students come to terms with communication anxiety, so that they can control this problem early in the course. Chapter 3 offers practical advice for organizing, practicing, and presenting first speeches. Chapter 4 identifies common listening problems and ways to overcome them, helps students sharpen critical-thinking skills, and presents criteria for the constructive evaluation of speeches.

Part Two, "Preparation for Public Speaking," introduces the basic skills needed to develop effective speeches. Chapter 5 emphasizes the importance of the audience, indicating how to adapt a message and how to adjust to factors in the speaking situation. Chapter 6 provides a systematic way to discover, evaluate, and refine speech topics. Chapter 7 shows how to research these topics, emphasizing the importance of acquiring *responsible knowledge*. Chapter 8 identifies the major types of supporting materials gathered from such research, including facts and statistics, examples, testimony, and narratives. The chapter shows how to bring supporting materials to life through comparison, contrast, and analogy. Chapter 9 shows how to develop simple, balanced, and orderly speech designs; how to select and shape main points; how to use transitions; and how to prepare effective introductions and conclusions. Chapter 10 explains how to develop working outlines, refine them into formal outlines, and derive key-word outlines for use during presentation.

Part Three, "Developing Presentation Skills," brings the speaker to the point of presentation. Chapter 11 explains the preparation of presentation aids, including PowerPoint presentations. Chapter 12 provides an understanding of the role of language in communication and offers practical suggestions for using words effectively. Chapter 13 offers exercises for the improvement of voice and body language and helps students develop an extemporaneous style that is adaptable to most speaking situations.

Part Four, "Types of Public Speaking," discusses informative, persuasive, and ceremonial speaking. Chapter 14 covers speeches designed to share information and increase understanding. The chapter discusses the types of informative speeches and presents the major designs that can structure them. In Chapter 15, we develop the concept of argumentative persuasion, helping students develop strong, reasoned cases to support their positions. The chapter also identifies the major forms of fallacies so that student speakers can avoid them and detect them in the messages of others. Chapter 16 describes the persuasive process, focusing on how to meet the many challenges of persuasive situations. Chapter 17 explains how to prepare effective ceremonial presentations, including speeches of tribute and inspiration, speeches introducing others, eulogies, after-dinner speeches, and speeches presenting and accepting awards. The chapter explains the narrative design, often used in ceremonial speeches.

Appendix A, "Communicating in Small Groups," introduces students to the problem-solving process and to the responsibilities of both group leaders and group participants. This appendix also provides guidelines for managing informal and formal meetings, and explains the basic concepts of parliamentary procedure. Appendix B provides a number of student and professional speeches for additional analysis.

Learning Tools

To help students master the material, we offer a number of special learning tools.

- We open each chapter with a table of contents and learning objectives that prepare students for efficient and productive reading.

- The epigrams and vignettes that start each chapter help point up the topic's significance and motivate readers.

- We use contemporary artwork and photographs to illustrate ideas, engage student interest, and add to the visual appeal of the book.

- Examples illustrate and apply the content in a clear, lively, and often entertaining way.

- Speaker's Notes, Ethics Alert!, and InterConnections.LearnMore features help students focus on the essentials, apply what they are learning to ethical issues, and pursue additional information using the Internet.

Speaker's Notes 13.1

Handling Questions and Answers

Strengthen your message during the question-and-answer time by observing the following guidelines:

1. Practice answering tough questions before an audience of friends.

2. Repeat or paraphrase the question you are asked.

3. Maintain eye contact with the audience as a whole as you answer.

4. Defuse hostile questions by rewording them in unemotional language.

5. Don't be afraid to say, "I don't know."

6. Keep answers short and to the point.

7. Handle nonquestions politely.

8. Bring the question-and-answer session to a close by reemphasizing your message.

Ethics Alert! 5.1

The Ethical Adaptation of Messages

Ask yourself, Will I have any special ethical problems in adapting my message to my audience? To counter possible problems, keep in mind the following guidelines:

1. Change your strategies, not your convictions.

2. Appeal to shared needs, values, and beliefs to help bridge cultural differences.

3. Respect individual differences among listeners.

4. Resist stereotypes that lead you to misjudge or derogate others.

5. Avoid using slang terms to refer to racial, gender, ethnic, or religious groups.

6. Suppress any impulse toward ethnocentrism.

InterConnections.LearnMore 15.2

Fallacies

Fallacy Files
http://fallacyfiles.org

   An interactive site containing an extensive collection of fallacies and bad argument, with definitions and examples; well organized and entertaining as well as educational (see especially "Stalking the Wild Fallacy"); developed by Gary N. Curtis.

Watch Out for these Common Fallacies
www.coping.org/write/percept/fallacies/content.htm

   Offers good discussion and often striking examples of fallacies in everyday reasoning; developed by James J. Messina and Constance M. Messina.

Soyouwanna Avoid Common Logical Errors?
www.soyouwanna.com/site/syws/logic/logic.html

   Discusses the logical rules that govern the making and evaluation of arguments from a philosophical perspective.

Fallacies Drawn from Aristotle's *Rhetoric*
www.cc.utah.edu/~sms5/wrtg3700/bgtexts/fallacies.htm#Appeals

   A discussion of common fallacies as they are developed in Aristotle's Rhetoric, one of the first books on public communication and perhaps the greatest.

- A Running Glossary develops through the book, helping students focus on key terms as they are introduced.

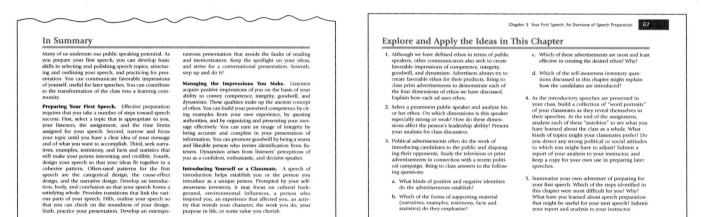

- **Receiver (or audience):** listeners who receive the message—those for whom the message is intended and in anticipation of whom the message is shaped. We develop advice for analyzing your audience in Chapter 5.

source The originator of a message.
encoder The speaker's voice.

message The words, nonverbal cues, and presentation aids that convey the speaker's ideas, motives, and feelings toward a subject.

channel Air or medium through which the message flows.
receiver The audience; those for whom the message is intended and in anticipa-

- We end each chapter with In Summary and Explore and Apply the Ideas in This Chapter features that further reinforce learning.

In Summary

Many of us underrate our public speaking potential. As you prepare your first speech, you can develop basic skills in selecting and polishing speech topics, structuring and outlining your speech, and practicing for presentation. You can communicate favorable impressions of yourself, useful for later speeches. You can contribute to the transformation of the class into a learning community.

Preparing Your First Speech. Effective preparation requires that you take a number of steps toward speech success. First, select a topic that is appropriate to you, your listeners, the assignment, and the time limits assigned for your speech. Second, narrow and focus your topic until you have a clear idea of your message and of what you want to accomplish. Third, seek narratives, examples, testimony, and facts and statistics that will make your points interesting and credible. Fourth, design your speech so that your ideas fit together in a cohesive whole. Provides transitions that link the various parts of your speech. Fifth, outline your speech so that you can check on the soundness of your design. Sixth, practice your presentation. Develop an extempo-

raneous presentation that avoids the faults of reading and memorization. Keep the spotlight on your ideas, and strive for a conversational presentation. Seventh, step up and do it!

Managing the Impressions You Make. Listeners acquire positive impressions of you on the basis of your ability to convey competence, integrity, goodwill, and dynamism. These qualities make up the ancient concept of ethos. You can build your perceived competence by citing examples from your own experience, by quoting authorities, and by organizing and presenting your message effectively. You can earn an image of integrity by being accurate and complete in your presentation of information. You can promote goodwill by being a warm and likeable person who invites identification from listeners. Dynamism arises from listeners' perceptions of you as a confident, enthusiastic, and decisive speaker.

Introducing Yourself or a Classmate. A speech of introduction helps establish you or the person you introduce as a unique person. Prompted by your self-awareness inventory, it may focus on cultural background, environmental influences, a person who inspired you, an experience that affected you, an activity that reveals your character, the work you do, your purpose in life, or some value you cherish.

Explore and Apply the Ideas in This Chapter

Chapter 3 Your First Speech: An Overview of Speech Preparation **67**

1. Although we have defined ethos in terms of public speakers, other communicators also seek to create favorable impressions of competence, integrity, goodwill, and dynamism. Advertisers always try to create favorable ethos for their products. Bring to class print advertisements to demonstrate each of the four dimensions of ethos we have discussed. Explain how each ad uses ethos.

2. Select a prominent public speaker and analyze his or her ethos. On which dimensions is this speaker especially strong or weak? How do these dimensions affect the person's leadership ability? Present your analysis for class discussion.

3. Political advertisements often do the work of introducing candidates to the public and disparaging their opponents. Study the television or print advertisements in connection with a recent political campaign. Bring to class answers to the following questions:

   a. What kinds of positive and negative identities do the advertisements establish?

   b. Which of the forms of supporting material (narratives, examples, testimony, facts and statistics) do they emphasize?

   c. Which of these advertisements are most and least effective in creating the desired ethos? Why?

   d. Which of the self-awareness inventory questions discussed in this chapter might explain how the candidates are introduced?

4. As the introductory speeches are presented in your class, build a collection of "word portraits" of your classmates as they reveal themselves in their speeches. At the end of the assignment, analyze each of these "autobios" to see what you have learned about the class as a whole. What kinds of topics might your classmates prefer? Do you detect any strong political or social attitudes to which you might have to adjust? Submit a report of your analysis to your instructor, and keep a copy for your own use in preparing later speeches.

5. Summarize your own adventure of preparing for your first speech. Which of the steps identified in this chapter were most difficult for you? Why? What have you learned about speech preparation that might be useful for your next speech? Submit your report and analysis to your instructor.

- Sample classroom speeches found at the ends of many chapters illustrate important concepts. The annotated speech texts show how the concepts apply in actual speaking. Appendix B contains additional speeches for analysis that cover an interesting array of topics, contexts, and speakers.

Supplementary Materials

*T*o learn more about our supplements and view sample materials, please visit www.mycoursetoolbox.com. Contact your Pearson representative for ordering information about all of these supplements (or for an access code to download materials).

The following materials are available to adopters of *Public Speaking*:

For Instructors

Print

- An *Instructor's Annotated Edition*, with annotations written by the authors, includes general and ESL teaching tips for every chapter.

- *Classroom Kit, Volumes I and II*. Our unparalleled Classroom Kit includes every instruction aid a public speaking professor needs to manage the classroom. We have made our resources even easier to use by placing all of our book-specific print supplements in two convenient volumes, and electronic copies of all of our resources on one CD-ROM, available separately.

Organized by chapter, each volume contains materials from the Instructor's Manual and Test Bank, as well as slides from the PowerPoint Presentation Package that accompanies this text. Electronic versions of the Instructor's Manual, Test Bank, PowerPoint, images from the text, and select video clips—all searchable by key words—are made easily accessible to instructors on the accompanying Classroom Kit CD-ROM.

- The *Instructor's Manual* material has been completely updated and revised by Randall Osborn of the University of Memphis. Part I of the manual includes sections on the purpose and philosophy of the course, preparing a syllabus, various sample syllabi, an assortment of speech assignment options, a discussion of evaluating and grading speeches, and a trouble-shooting guide with teaching strategies for new instructors. Part II offers a chapter-by-chapter guide to teaching *Public Speaking*, including learning objectives, suggestions for teaching, lecture/discussion outlines, classroom activities, and transparency/handout masters. This comprehensive manual can be used as a text for training teaching assistants.

- The *Test Bank*, also prepared by Randall Osborn, contains multiple choice, true/false, and short answer questions. Answers are provided for each question.

- *Great Ideas for Teaching Speech (GIFTS)*, 3/e by Raymond Zeuschner. This instructional booklet provides descriptions of and guidelines for assignments successfully used by experienced public speaking instructors in their classrooms.

- *New Teachers Guide to Public Speaking*, 3/e by Calvin Troup, Duquesne University. This guide helps new teachers teach the public speaking course effectively. It covers topics such as preparing for the term, planning and structuring your course, evaluating speeches, utilizing the textbook, integrating technology into the classroom, and much more.

- *Public Speaking Transparency Package, Version II*. One hundred full-color transparencies created with PowerPoint™ software provide visual support for classroom lectures and discussions.

Electronic

- *MySpeechLab*. Where students learn to speak with confidence! MySpeechLab is an interactive and instructive online solution for introductory public speaking. Designed to be used as a supplement to a traditional lecture course, or to completely administer an online course, MySpeechLab combines multimedia, video, speech preparation activities, research support, tests and quizzes to make teaching and learning fun! Students benefit from a wealth of video clips that include student and professional speeches with running commentary, questions to consider, and helpful tips—all geared to help students learn to speak with confidence. Visit www.myspeechlab.com (access code required).

- *Classroom Kit CD-ROM*. This exciting new supplement for instructors will bring together electronic copies of the Instructor's Manual, the Test Bank, the PowerPoint presentation, images from the text, and select video clips for easy instructor access. This CD-ROM is organized by chapter and is searchable by key term.

- *TestGen EQ: Computerized Test Bank*. The user-friendly interface enables instructors to view, edit, and add questions, transfer questions into tests, and print tests in a variety of fonts. Search and sort features allow instructors to locate questions quickly and arrange them in preferred order. Available through our Instructor's Resource Center at www.ablongman.com/irc (access code required).

- *PowerPoint Presentation Package,* by Suzanne Osborn of University of Memphis. This text-specific package consists of a collection of lecture outlines and graphic images keyed to every chapter in the text. Select sample speech video clips are also included. Available on the Web at www.ablongman.com/irc (access code required).

- *Communication Digital Media Archive, Version 3.0.* The Digital Media Archive CD-ROM contains electronic images of charts, graphs, maps, tables, and figures, along with media elements such as video, audio clips, and related web links. These media assets are fully customizable to use with our pre-formatted PowerPoint™ outlines or to import into instructor's own lectures. Available in Windows and Mac formats.

- *Lecture Questions for Clickers* by William Keith, University of Wisconsin–Milwaukee. An assortment of questions and activities covering a multitude of topics in public speaking and speech delivery are presented in PowerPoint. These slides will help liven up your lectures and can be used along with the Personal Response System to get students more involved in the material. Available on the Web at www.ablongman.com/irc (access code required).

- *PowerPoint Presentation for Public Speaking.* This course-specific PowerPoint outline adds visual punch to public speaking lectures with colorful screen designs and clip art. Our expanded Public Speaking PowerPoint™ package now includes 125 slides and a brief User's Guide. A book-specific PowerPoint™ presentation also is available for this text. Available on the Web at www.ablongman.com/irc (access code required).

- *VideoWorkshop for Public Speaking Version 2.0.* Written by Tasha Van Horn of Citrus College and Marilyn Reineck of Concordia University, St. Paul, *VideoWorkshop for Public Speaking* is more than just video footage you can watch. It's a total learning system. Our complete program includes quality video footage on an easy-to-use dual platform CD-ROM plus a Student Learning Guide. The result? A program that brings textbook concepts to life with ease that helps your students understand, analyze, and apply the objectives of the course.

- *A&B Contemporary Classic Speeches DVD.* This exciting supplement includes over 120 minutes of video footage in an easy-to-use DVD format. Each speech is accompanied by a biographical and historical summary that helps students understand the context and motivation behind each speech. Speakers featured include Martin Luther King Jr., John F. Kennedy, Richard Nixon, the Dalai Lama and Christopher Reeve.

- *A&B Public Speaking Video Library.* Allyn & Bacon's Public Speaking Video Library contains a range of videos from which adopters can choose. The videos feature different types of speeches delivered on a multitude of different topics, allowing you to choose the speeches best suited for your students. Please contact your Pearson representative for details and a complete list of videos and their contents to choose which would be most useful in your class.

For Students

Print

- *The Classical Origins of Public Speaking.* Written by Michael Osborn of the University of Memphis, this supplement offers a concise overview of classical Greek theory on the nature and importance of public speaking.

- The *Speech Preparation Workbook* by Suzanne Osborn of the University of Memphis, contains forms to help students prepare a self-introductory speech, analyze the audience, select a topic, conduct research, organize supporting materials and outline speeches.

- *Speech Preparation Workbook* by Jennifer Dreyer & Gregory H. Patton of San Diego State University. This workbook takes students through the stages of speech creation—from audience analysis to writing the speech—and includes guidelines, tips, and easy to fill-in pages.

- *The Speech Outline: Outlining to Plan, Organize, and Deliver a Speech: Activities and Exercises,* by Reeze L. Hanson & Sharon Condon of Haskell Indian Nations University. This brief workbook includes activities, exercises, and answers to help students develop and master the critical skill of outlining.

- *Study Card for Public Speaking.* Colorful, affordable, and packed with useful information, Pearson's Study Cards make studying easier, more efficient, and more enjoyable. Course information is distilled down to the basics, helping you quickly master the fundamentals, review a subject for understanding, or prepare for an exam. Because they're laminated for durability, you can keep these Study Cards for years to come and pull them out whenever you need a quick review.

- *Multicultural Activities Workbook,* by Marlene C. Cohen and Susan L. Richardson, both of Prince George's Community College, Maryland. This workbook is filled with hands-on activities that help broaden the content of speech classes to reflect the diverse cultural backgrounds of the class and society. The book includes checklists, surveys, and writing assignments that all help students succeed in speech communication by offering experiences that address a variety of learning styles.

- *Public Speaking in the Multicultural Environment,* 2/e by Devorah Lieberman of Portland State University. This two-chapter essay focuses on speaking and listening to a culturally diverse audience and emphasizes preparation, delivery, and how speeches are perceived.

- *Preparing Visual Aids for Presentations,* 4/e by Dan Cavanaugh. This brief booklet provides a host of ideas for using today's multimedia tools to improve presentations, including suggestions for how to plan a presentation, guidelines for designing visual aids and storyboarding, and a walkthrough that shows how to prepare a visual display using PowerPoint.

- *ResearchNavigator.com Guide: Speech Communication.* This updated booklet, by Steven L. Epstein of Suffolk County Community College, includes tips, resources, and URLs to aid students conducting research on Pearson Education's research website, www.researchnavigator.com. The guide contains a student access code for the Research Navigator database, offering students unlimited access to a collection of more than 25,000 discipline specific articles from top-tier academic publications and peer-reviewed journals, as well as the *New York Times* and popular news publications. The guide introduces students to the basics of the Internet and the World Wide Web, and includes tips for searching for articles on the site, and a list of journals useful for research in their discipline. Also included are hundreds of web resources for the discipline, as well as information on how to correctly cite research.

Electronic

- *MySpeechLab.* Where students learn to speak with confidence! MySpeechLab is an interactive and instructive online solution for introductory public speaking. Designed to be used as a supplement to a traditional lecture course, or completely administer an online course, MySpeechLab combines multimedia, video, speech preparation activities, research support, tests and quizzes to make teaching and learning fun! Students benefit from a wealth of video clips that include student and professional speeches with running commentary, questions to consider, and helpful tips—all geared to help students learn to speak with confidence. Visit www.myspeechlab.com (access code required).

- *Public Speaking Website.* This open access website contains six modules students can use along with their public speaking text to learn about the process of public speaking and help prepare for speeches. Focuses on the five steps of speech preparation: Assess Your Speechmaking Situation, Analyze Your Audience, Research Your Topic, Organize and Write Your Speech, Deliver Your Presentation, and Discern Other Talks. Interactive activities aid in speech preparation. "Notes from the Instructor" provide additional details on selected topics. Visit www.ablongman.com/pubspeak.

- *Public Speaking Study Site.* This course-specific website features public speaking study materials for students, including flashcards and a complete set of practice tests for all major topics. Students also will find web links to sites with speeches in text, audio, and video formats, as well as links to other valuable sites. Visit www.abpublicspeaking.com.

- *News Resources for Speech Communication Access Code Card.* News Resources for Speech Communication with Research Navigator is one-stop access to keep you abreast of the latest news events and for all of your research needs. Highlighted by an hourly feed of the latest news in the discipline from the *New York Times*, students will stay on the forefront of currency throughout the semester. In addition, Pearson's Research Navigator™ is the easiest way for students to start a research assignment or research paper. Complete with extensive help on the research process and four exclusive databases of credible and reliable source material including the EBSCO Academic Journal and Abstract Database, *New York Times* Search by Subject Archive, and *Financial Times* Article Archive and Company Financials, Research Navigator helps students quickly and efficiently make the most of their research time.

- *Speech Writer's Workshop CD-ROM, Version 2.0.* This speechwriting software includes a Speech Handbook with tips for researching and preparing speeches, a Speech Workshop which guides students step-by-step through the speech writing process, a Topics Dictionary which gives students hundreds of ideas for speeches, and the Documentor citation database that helps them to format bibliographic entries in either MLA or APA style.

- *VideoLab CD-ROM.* This interactive study tool for students can be used independently or in class. It provides digital video of student speeches that can be viewed in conjunction with corresponding outlines, manuscripts, notecards, and instructor critiques. A series of drills to help students analyze content and delivery follows each speech.

- *VideoWorkshop for Public Speaking Version 2.0* by Tasha Van Horn of Citrus College and Marilyn Reineck of Concordia University, St. Paul. *VideoWorkshop for Public Speaking* is more than just video footage you can watch. It's a total learning system. Our complete program includes quality video footage on an easy-to-use dual platform CD-ROM plus a Student Learning Guide. The result? A program that brings textbook concepts to life with ease that helps your students understand, analyze, and apply the objectives of the course.

To Our Students

As you prepare for the adventure of public speaking, we hope you will be an opportunistic reader of our book. Of course you will want to read the chapters in the order suggested by your instructor. But this is also the time to browse through the book so that you have some idea of the resources it offers you. You can then call upon these resources as you need them. For example,

- Suppose you are preparing your first speech following the guidelines in Chapter 3. You are trying to decide on an appropriate introduction for your speech. At this point you could jump ahead to Chapter 9, and survey the different options for introducing speeches.
- Or perhaps you are feeling uncomfortable about presenting your first speech. Chapter 2 offers sound advice on controlling your anxiety so that it generates positive energy to spark your speech.
- After your first speech, your instructor suggests that you should work on developing greater vocal variety. Chapter 13 can help guide your efforts.

As you travel along the way, you will also discover some boxed materials that offer special help or highlight major ideas.

- SPEAKER'S NOTES present concise summaries of important information. Many of them contain checklists to help ensure that you go through the necessary steps in your work.
- ETHICS ALERT! boxes remind you of the ethical importance and consequences of public communication. Understanding these principles can help you resist unethical speakers and develop a healthy skepticism for manipulative communication.
- SAMPLE SPEECHES show public speaking strategies in action. Throughout the book, excerpts from speeches illustrate the ideas discussed.
- INTERCONNECTIONS.LEARNMORE direct you to Internet materials that expand on the ideas in this book. Note: If a URL provided doesn't open for you, type the name of that website into a search engine to see if it has moved. Or, simply wait a while and try the URL again.
- RUNNING GLOSSARY. Each subject has its own vocabulary of technical terms. The key terms of public speaking are printed in boldface type throughout the text and defined at the bottom of the pages on which they occur.

We wish for you a successful adventure. Long ago, we entered our own public speaking class, slightly terrified by what was to come. Now many years later, we don't remember the speeches we made, but we do remember how it felt to finally taste some success in speaking. And, we do remember at least one speech given by a classmate, and how it opened our eyes. We also remember forming friendships that would last well beyond the class.

May you too savor such success and make such friends. Bon voyage!

We invite you to submit texts of successful speeches for possible inclusion in later editions of *Public Speaking*. Send these materials to osbornso@gmail.com

Acknowledgments

Many people have helped improve *Public Speaking* over its more than two decades of existence. For this edition, we especially thank Hilary Jackson, development editor, for her suggestions, kind encouragement, and perceptive readings of the manuscript. Karon Bowers, Editor-in-Chief of Communication at Allyn & Bacon, has been a positive and helpful friend during the transition period as we joined Allyn & Bacon. We have met many people in publishing over the past twenty years, and Hilary and Karon are both extraordinary. We also want to thank Suzan Czajkowski, our aggressive marketing manager, who rides her motorcycle around the countryside seeking new friends for Osborn, Osborn, and Osborn. Finally, we wish to thank Mary Finch, our previous sponsoring editor for communication at Houghton Mifflin, who was considerate and supportive during our final years with that company.

We are grateful to our colleagues listed below whose critical readings have sparked the improvements in the Eighth Edition.

Kenneth Albone, Rowan University

LaKesha N. Anderson, George Mason University

Dave Berg, Weber State University

Jennifer Bieselin, Florida Gulf Coast University

Dorothy Collins, Texas A&M University

Susan Dobie, Humboldt State University

Melissa A. Dreyer, Oklahoma State University–Okmulgee

Gray Matthews, University of Memphis

Marjorie Keeshan Nadler, Miami University

Linda J. Nelson, Davenport University–Merrillville, IN

Mabry M. O'Donnell, Marietta College

Stephanie Nicole Patterson, Western Kentucky University

Soterios C. Zoulas, Eastern Nazarene College

1

Public Speaking and You

This chapter will help you

- appreciate what a public speaking course can do for you
- understand what a public speaking course asks of you in return

The ability to make a good speech is a
great gift to the people from their Maker,
Owner of all things.

—Oglala Sioux

Emily was more than a little upset about having to take public speaking. She just wanted to be a marine biologist—what did this course have to offer her? She never had been much of a speaker: would she be able to survive with her GPA intact? "Just shut up, quit worrying, and go to class," said her weary roommate. At the first class meeting, Emily saw twenty-five others who looked about as uncomfortable as she felt. But she decided to stick it out.

Her first oral assignment was a speech of self-introduction. As she prepared her speech, it dawned on her why she found her major so fascinating. When she spoke, her enthusiasm for her topic helped relieve some of her nervousness. Although her speech was not perfect, she did some things very well. She had begun to build credibility for her later informative and persuasive speeches on the fate of the oceans.

As she listened to her classmates, Emily began to care about them and to take pleasure in their successes. As she researched her speeches, she sought out facts, expert opinions, examples, and stories that they would find useful and interesting. Toward the end of the term, it dawned on her: She was becoming a speaker! She believed she could meet the challenges of oral communication whenever they should arise in her life beyond the classroom.

Our Emily represents many students whom we have taught over our teaching career. You too may wonder why you are taking this course, even whether you can make it through the semester, let alone be successful. To become an "Emily," you must first make a commitment. You must decide that you want to learn more about this complex art of public speaking, that you will select meaningful topics, that you will invest the time needed to develop them, that you will treat listeners ethically, and that you will listen constructively to others. This chapter explains why your public speaking course deserves your commitment: what it offers you and what it asks of you in return.

What Public Speaking Has to Offer You

Welcome to public speaking! And welcome to the many benefits this course can offer you. As much as anything else, the ability you cultivate here to communicate in public settings will distinguish you as a competent and well-educated person. What's more, learning to present yourself and your ideas effectively can help prepare you for some of the more important moments in your life: times when you need to speak to protect your family's interests, when your values are threatened by the action or inaction of others, or when you need approval to undertake some important project. Finally, the principles you learn in this class will make you a more astute consumer of public messages. They will help you sort through the barrage of information and misinformation that bombards us on a daily basis.

Beyond these vital considerations, the public speaking course offers practical, personal growth and knowledge benefits that can have profound importance throughout your life.

Practical Benefits

The public speaking course offers three practical benefits of fundamental importance. You will develop an array of basic skills. You will become a more successful person. And you will become a better citizen.

You Will Develop an Array of Basic Skills. The chapter titles in this book reflect this extensive range of skills:

- Learning how to control your communication anxiety in public settings.
- Learning how to present your best side in the impressions you make on others.
- Learning how to listen effectively and constructively.
- Learning how to "read" an audience and to adapt your messages accordingly.
- Learning how to develop ethical sensitivity for what speeches can do both *for* and *to* listeners.
- Learning how to select subjects that listeners will find vital and fascinating.
- Learning how to conduct research that produces *responsible knowledge*.
- Learning how to design, structure, and outline messages that accomplish the goals of communication.
- Learning how to support your points with well-selected data, testimony, examples, and stories.
- Learning how to use presentation aids that make your speeches clear and striking.
- Learning how to manage language so that your words work for rather than against your message.
- Learning how to express your ideas before audiences with power, confidence, and conviction.
- Learning the special skills of informative, persuasive, and ceremonial speaking.

Will you become an *expert* in all thirteen of these fundamental skills over the course of a semester? Probably not. But if you take this course seriously and invest your time and energy in it, you should advance in your knowledge of many of them, perhaps strikingly in some of them. And in the process, you will be growing as a person as well as developing abilities that will serve you throughout your life.

You Will Become a More Successful Person. Developing the kinds of basic skills we have just described will help you succeed both in school and in your later professional life. Each year, the National Association of Colleges and Employers (NACE) surveys hundreds of corporate recruiting specialists. According to the organization,

> Employers responding to NACE's *Job Outlook 2007* survey named communication skills and honesty/integrity as a job seeker's most important skills and qualities. "Communication skills have topped the list for eight years." NACE advises: "Learn to speak clearly, confidently, and concisely."[1]

The skills you learn in your public speaking class can help you in many ways. Learning to present yourself well can be an asset in job interviews.

Paul Baruda, who serves as an employment expert for the jobs site Monster.com, agrees that "articulating thoughts clearly and concisely will make a difference in both a job interview and subsequent job performance."

> The point is, you can be the best physicist in the world, but if you can't tell people what you do or communicate it to your co-workers, what good is all of that knowledge? I can't think of an occupation, short of living in a cave, where being able to say what you think cogently at some point in your life isn't going to be important.[2]

So unless you plan to live in a cave, what you learn in this course can be absolutely vital to your success in life.

You Will Become a Better Citizen.   As social creatures, all of us feel compelled to "speak out" in defense of our vital interests and core values from time to time. Developing your public speaking skills will equip you to more effectively and more ethically do just that. For instance, you might find yourself wanting to speak at a school board meeting about a proposal to remove "controversial" books such as *The Catcher in the Rye*, the Harry Potter series, or *The Adventures of Huckleberry Finn* from your local school, or you may wish to speak for or against attempts to rezone your neighborhood at a city council meeting. On campus, you might find yourself speaking for or against attempts to alter your college's affirmative action policy, the firing of a popular but unorthodox professor, or allowing religious groups to stage protests and distribute literature on school grounds. In your class, you might speak for or against stronger immigration laws, the policy of preemptive warfare as it relates to the "war on terror," allowing gay people to marry or serve openly in the military, and even whether notorious hate groups such as the Ku Klux Klan should be allowed to stage public rallies.

As you take part in such controversies, both speaking and listening, you will be enacting the role envisioned for you as a citizen by those who framed the Constitution of the United States:

> Congress shall make no law...abridging the freedom of speech, or of the press; or the right of people peaceably to assemble, and to petition the government for a redress of grievances. (*First Amendment to the Bill of Rights*)

The political system of the United States is built on faith in open and robust public communication. If we citizens are the repositories of political power, then our understanding must be nourished constantly by a full and free flow of information and exchange of opinions so that we can make good and wise decisions on such matters as who should lead us and which public policies we should endorse.

Speaker's Notes *1.1*

Practical Benefits of the Public Speaking Course

This course can help you in many vital ways:

■ Help you present yourself as a competent, well-educated person.

■ Help you prepare for important moments in your life.

■ Help you become a more critical consumer of public information.

■ Help you develop basic communication skills.

■ Help you control your communication anxiety.

■ Help improve odds that you will succeed in college and career.

■ Help you become a more effective citizen.

Public speaking classes therefore become laboratories for the democratic process.[3] Crafting, presenting, and listening to speeches—even classroom speeches—is a valuable way to develop your citizenship skills. Preparation for your role as citizen is a benefit that serves not just you but the society in which you live.

Personal Growth Benefits

Some benefits of this course are invisible but nevertheless can be vital to the quality of your life. Such benefits include learning more about yourself, becoming acquainted with the intellectual tradition of public speaking, and expanding your cultural horizons.

Learning More about Yourself. In a very real sense, we are the sum of our communication experiences with other people. As you put together speeches on topics that you care about, you will explore your own interests and values, expand your base of knowledge, and develop your skills of creative expression. In short, you will develop your own "voice" as a unique individual.

InterConnections.
LearnMore 1.1

Freedom of Speech

Thomas Jefferson Center for the Protection of Free Expression
www.tjcenter.org/about.html
A unique nonpartisan organization devoted to the defense of free expression in all its forms.

Philosophers and Freedom of Speech
www.sjsu.edu/faculty/Brent/190/speechlinks.html
San Jose State University Web site offering a variety of links to freedom of speech sites, many containing texts of historical documents.

The Freedom Forum
www.freedomforum.org
A nonpartisan international foundation dedicated to free press, free speech, and free spirit for all people.

Public speaking is vital to the maintenance of a free society. The right to assemble and speak on public issues is guaranteed by the Bill of Rights.

As you tailor your voice to diverse audiences, you will develop a heightened sensitivity to the interests and needs of others—an important part of what has been called an "other-orientation." The public speaking class invites us to listen to one another, to savor what makes each of us unique and valuable, and to develop an appreciation for the different ways people live. Your experiences should bring you closer to meeting one of the major goals of higher education: "to expand the mind and heart beyond fear of the unknown, opening them to the whole range of human experience."[4]

Finally, as you learn to speak and listen, you will gain a richer and more sophisticated appreciation of the world around you. You will be encouraged to seek out and consider multiple perspectives on controversial issues before committing yourself. Public speaking classes are unique in that they make you an active participant in your own education. You don't just sit in class, absorbing lectures. You communicate. And as you communicate, you help your class become a learning community. It is no accident that the words *communication* and *community* are closely connected.

Learning More about the Intellectual Tradition of Public Speaking. Some people are surprised to discover that the study and practice of public speaking rests upon a rich intellectual history that extends back over two thousand years to the ancient Greeks—the same people credited with introducing democracy to Western civilization. In an age long before the printing press, Internet, and 24-hour cable-news service, public speaking served as the major means of disseminating ideas and information, resolving legal disputes, and debating political issues. Oratory even served as popular entertainment.

In those long-ago years, there were no professional lawyers and politicians, and citizens were expected to speak for themselves in legal proceedings and as active participants in the deliberations that shaped public policy. Most of all, the Greeks considered the power and eloquence of the spoken word as necessary to virtuous behavior.[5] One of their greatest leaders, Pericles, reflects this attitude in a much celebrated speech:

> For we alone think that a man that does not take part in public affairs is good for nothing, while others only say that he is "minding his own business." We are the ones who develop policy, or at least decide what is to be done, for we believe that what spoils action is not speeches, but going into action without first being instructed through speeches. In this too we excel over others: ours is the bravery of people who think through what they will take in hand, and discuss it thoroughly; with other men, ignorance makes them brave and thinking makes them cowards.[6]

We are heirs to this tradition and shall draw upon it constantly in this book. We are concerned especially with two themes: first, the effort to understand the nature and practicality of communicating through the public speech, and second, the ethical issues that can arise in connection with the public speech.

The ancient Greek who organized and systematized the study of public speaking was the famous philosopher Aristotle. In his *Rhetoric*, Aristotle described the type of reasoning used in public speaking. He recognized that unlike pure logic, reasoning on public problems usually involves uncertainties and probabilities. Thus, the public speaker helps her or his listeners arrive at an informed judgment on issues. On such issues, the speaker works from what we call *responsible knowledge*. Responsible knowledge is not perfect or exact, but it is the best that might reasonably be expected given the situation.

Aristotle described three prominent forms of speaking: political, legal, and ceremonial. We still write about and teach these forms today. Finally, he identified three major forms of persuasive proof: appealing to reason, appealing to audience emotions, and appealing to the speaker's own personal qualities of character, competence, and good will. Again, we still discuss these forms today.

Aristotle's *Rhetoric* laid the groundwork for the Romans, who would further explore the role of public speaking in legal and then religious settings.[7] Cicero, one of the most celebrated orators of antiquity, described rhetoric as "an art made up of five great arts." In his greatest work, *De Oratore*, he concentrated on how to think through and defend positions, how to arrange and organize arguments, how to use language effectively, how to store ideas in the mind for recall during speaking, and how to present a speech effectively.[8] He stressed that the ideal speaker would be broadly educated and would understand the culture and values of those to whom she or he speaks.

Raphael's painting shows "The School of Athens" where rhetorical skills were part of the basic curriculum.

The second great theme of the ancient intellectuals is concern for the power of public speaking and how it should be managed ethically. Here the leader was Plato, who wrote two classic dialogues that deal specifically with the power of the public oration.

InterConnections.

LearnMore 1.2

Classical Origins of Public Speaking

Aristotle's *Rhetoric*
http://classics.mit.edu/Aristotle/rhetoric.html

> *The first, and some still think finest, comprehensive inquiry into how public speaking can shape the public mind. The W. Rhys Roberts translation of the full text of this document is made available through the Massachusetts Institute of Technology.*

Plato's *Phaedrus*
http://ccat.sas.upenn.edu/jod/texts/phaedrus.html

> *Offers Plato's vision of the ethical foundations of rhetoric. Also offers his account of the art of the oration. The B. Jowett translation is made available through the University of Pennsylvania.*

Plato's *Gorgias*
http://philosophy.eserver.org/plato/gorgias.txt

> *Plato's dark reflection of the public speaking he saw practiced around him in the Athens of his day. Offers disturbing similarities to some of the public communication of our own time.*

Rhetoric and Composition
http://eserver.org/rhetoric/

> *Offers a variety of resources relevant to classical rhetoric, including texts of Plato's Gorgias and Phaedrus, Aristotle's Rhetoric, and selections from Cicero. The Gorgias is Plato's scathing indictment of the public mind and how it distorts the search for truth.*

Quintilian's Institutes of Oratory
http://honeyl.public.iastate.edu/quintilian/index.html

> *Offers the masterwork of the greatest teacher of speech of the Roman world and perhaps of all time. Quintilian developed his thoughts on educating the ideal orator from cradle to old age in twelve books.*

The first, the *Gorgias*, expresses Plato's dark vision of the subject. He noted that the statesmen of his time too often pandered to the ignorance and prejudices of the masses instead of advancing their own visions of what was right. These orators too often told their listeners what they *wanted* to hear rather than what they *needed* to hear in order to advance the speakers' own self-centered and often tragically misguided agendas.[9]

The second dialogue, the *Phaedrus*, paints Plato's ideal of the virtuous speaker, one whose words will help his or her listeners become better citizens and people.[10] But how can one avoid the cynical, depressing reality of the one vision and nurture the second ideal into being? Plato left this question as a puzzle and challenge for the ages that would follow.

Quintilian, perhaps the greatest speech teacher of all time, offered one answer to this challenge. This Roman writer insisted that immediate effect and gratification fade quickly, and the career of the speaker who builds on such shifting sands will soon collapse. To be a good speaker whose influence endures, he argued, *one must also be a good person.*[11] We strongly agree.

These two themes from antiquity, focusing on "What works?" and "What's right?", will occupy us throughout this book.

Expanding Cultural Horizons.　A third personal growth benefit is what you gain from direct exposure to various cultures and lifestyles in the public speaking classroom. Today's typical classroom audience is increasingly diverse, often offering

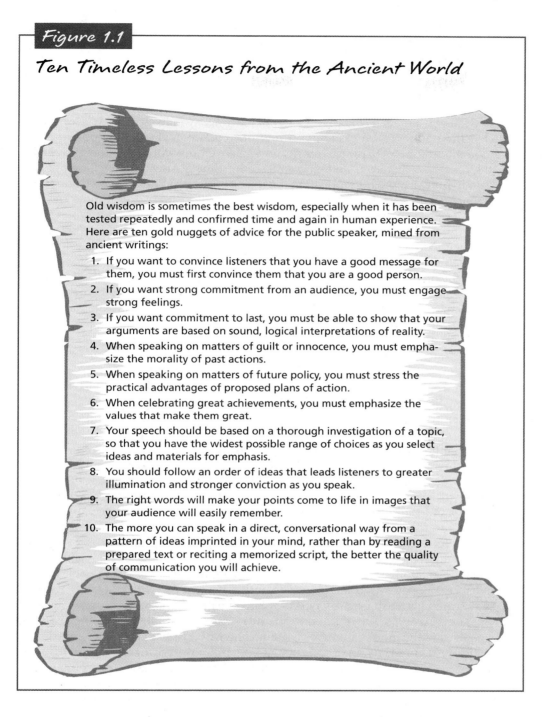

Figure 1.1

Ten Timeless Lessons from the Ancient World

Old wisdom is sometimes the best wisdom, especially when it has been tested repeatedly and confirmed time and again in human experience. Here are ten gold nuggets of advice for the public speaker, mined from ancient writings:

1. If you want to convince listeners that you have a good message for them, you must first convince them that you are a good person.
2. If you want strong commitment from an audience, you must engage strong feelings.
3. If you want commitment to last, you must be able to show that your arguments are based on sound, logical interpretations of reality.
4. When speaking on matters of guilt or innocence, you must emphasize the morality of past actions.
5. When speaking on matters of future policy, you must stress the practical advantages of proposed plans of action.
6. When celebrating great achievements, you must emphasize the values that make them great.
7. Your speech should be based on a thorough investigation of a topic, so that you have the widest possible range of choices as you select ideas and materials for emphasis.
8. You should follow an order of ideas that leads listeners to greater illumination and stronger conviction as you speak.
9. The right words will make your points come to life in images that your audience will easily remember.
10. The more you can speak in a direct, conversational way from a pattern of ideas imprinted in your mind, rather than by reading a prepared text or reciting a memorized script, the better the quality of communication you will achieve.

a sampling of various races, religions, and cultural backgrounds. We have much to teach each other!

What barriers may stand in the way of expanding our cultural horizons as we listen to others in classroom speeches? Problems may originate, as Shakespeare observed, "not in our stars, but in ourselves." One such problem may be **ethnocentrism**, the tendency to presume that one's own culturally defined way of

ethnocentrism The tendency of any nation, race, religion, or group to believe that its way of looking at and doing things is right and that other perspectives have less value.

seeing and doing things is essentially correct and is the standard against which other cultural worldviews and behaviors are to be judged. There is nothing inherently wrong, of course, with being a proud American, a proud Mexican American, or even a proud Southerner. But when we allow these feelings of pride to manifest themselves as cultural arrogance that belittles outsiders, they block communication in a multicultural society.

Had you attended college just a few decades ago, you likely would have encountered the unquestioned assumption that this country is a "melting pot" that has fused the cultures of various minority and native groups into a superior alloy called "the American character." Still encountered in some quarters, the melting pot may seem harmless enough in providing the image of the ideal American. The problem, of course, is the way this metaphor projects ethnocentrism. Its "ideal American" has too often been painted with a white male face. At least historically, women and minority groups have not been admitted as equal participants to public discussions, and their distinct identities and contributions are depreciated by the presumption that there is a single dominant American character. No less important to our purposes, the melting pot metaphor simply fails to adequately characterize the diversity of audiences you will encounter both in school and in later life. Elizabeth Lozano summarizes the shortcomings of the melting pot and proposes an alternative view of American culture:

> The "melting pot" is not an adequate metaphor for a country which is comprised of a multiplicity of cultural backgrounds.... [W]e might better think of the United States in terms of a "cultural bouillabaisse" in which all ingredients conserve their unique flavor, while also transforming and being transformed by the adjacent textures and scents.[12]

A public speaking class is an ideal place to savor this rich broth of cultures. As we hear others speak, we often discover the many flavors of the American experience. And as you examine your own identity and that of the people around you, you may well discover that most of us in this country are indeed "multicultural." In either case, if you want to speak effectively and ethically before American audiences, then a sensitivity toward and appreciation for cultural diversity is increasingly necessary.

A second barrier rises in the form of **stereotypes**, generalized assumptions that supposedly represent the essential character of races, genders, religious affiliations, sexual orientations, and so on. Before we get to know the individual members of our audience, we may invoke stereotypes to anticipate how they will react to our words. Even seemingly positive stereotypes—Asian Americans are good at math, Mexican Americans have a strong devotion to family—can be hurtful if they block us from experiencing the unique humanity of someone who just happens to be an Asian or Mexican American. As a general rule, nobody likes to feel that he or she is being addressed as an "other" by another "other." So pack your stereotypes away as you enter the public speaking class. You may discover that they are not that useful after all.

One of our favorite metaphors for the complex culture of the United States was introduced in the conclusion of Abraham Lincoln's first inaugural address, as Lincoln sought to hold the nation together on the eve of the Civil War:

> **The mystic chords of memory, stretching from every battlefield, and patriot grave, to every living heart and hearthstone, all over this broad land, will yet swell the chorus of the Union, when again touched, as surely they will be, by the better angels of our nature.[13]**

stereotypes Generalized pictures of a race, gender, or group that supposedly represent its essential characteristics.

Lincoln's image of America as a harmonious chorus implied that the individual voices of Americans will not only survive but will create a music more beautiful than that of any one voice alone. Lincoln's vision holds forth a continuing dream of a society in which individualism and the common good can not only survive but can also enhance each other.

In your class and within these pages, you will hear many voices: Native Americans and new Americans, women and men, conservatives and liberals, Americans of all different colors and lifestyles. Despite their many differences, all of them are a part of the vital chorus of our nation. Public speaking gives you the opportunity to hear these voices and add yours to the chorus.

Powerful Knowledge

In addition to significant practical and personal growth benefits, your public speaking class offers you the opportunity to develop knowledge of communication as an interactive and dynamic force in shaping our lives. Knowledge of the public speaking process arises from the rich rhetorical tradition we have sketched, going back to the time of Aristotle and Plato. But it also arises from more recent quests for knowledge.

Public Speaking as an Interactive Process. At times, beginning speakers think of a speech as though it were a product or object that one produces on occasion to receive the admiration of onlookers. Just a little reflection, however, convinces us that this is the wrong approach. Instead, *a speech is an interactive process that attempts to do some work on a specific occasion: to introduce the speaker to listeners, to share knowledge with them, to convince them of the rightness or wrongness of certain attitudes and actions, or to celebrate with them some special moments.* The speech is not so much a product as it is an act performed with and for the sake of listeners. The speech realizes its purpose when the audience responds in accordance with its message.

The interactive nature of speaking becomes clear when we realize that there can be no speech without a speaker, a listener, an occasion that calls it forth, and a situation in which it is presented. A speech is a dynamic interplay of all these factors and others. To help us grasp this complexity of interacting factors, we turn to some groundbreaking work performed by scientists at the Bell Telephone Laboratory around the middle of the twentieth century. As this work has been applied and adapted by scholars of communication, it identifies the following factors:[14]

- **Source (or speaker):** the originator of the message. The importance of establishing yourself as a credible person is discussed in Chapter 3.

- **Encoder (or transmitter):** the speaker's voice. We deal with developing the speaker's voice as an instrument of communication in Chapter 13.

- **Message (or speech):** the words, nonverbal cues, and presentation aids that convey the speaker's ideas, motives, and feelings toward a subject. We discuss message factors throughout this book.

- **Channel (or medium):** air or medium through which the message flows; becomes important only when there is a problem (bad acoustics in room, microphone not working, etc.). We consider such problems in Chapters 5 and 13.

- **Receiver (or audience):** listeners who receive the message—those for whom the message is intended and in anticipation of whom the message is shaped. We develop advice for analyzing your audience in Chapter 5.

source The originator of a message.
encoder The speaker's voice.

message The words, nonverbal cues, and presentation aids that convey the speaker's ideas, motives, and feelings toward a subject.

channel Air or medium through which the message flows.
receiver The audience; those for whom the message is intended and in anticipation of whom the message is shaped.

■ **Decoder:** works when listeners can hear and understand the speaker's words. We talk about problems of translating technical language in Chapter 13.

■ **Noise (or interference):** can indicate a range of problems from physical noise, such as distracting sounds in the room, to psychological noise (stereotypes, distractions, cultural barriers, etc.) in listeners that interferes with and possibly distorts the reception of the message. We cover coping with interference problems in Chapters 4 and 13.

■ **Feedback (or response):** how audience members react to the speaker's message both during and after its presentation. The nods, frowns, and puzzled looks that audience members sometimes provide during a presentation allow speakers to make on-the-spot adjustments and give their messages a better chance to receive a favorable hearing. Speeches sometimes conclude with a question-and-answer session that gives audience members a chance to offer feedback directly. We discuss these issues in Chapter 13.

In addition to these factors, public speaking occurs within a physical and psychological **setting** that often affects the way messages are constructed, presented, and received. The *physical setting* includes such factors as the actual place where the speech is to be presented, the time of day the speech is given, and the size and arrangement of the audience. Plato's *Phaedrus* takes place in a woodland setting that frames and colors its message appropriately. In this lovely pastoral context, Socrates envisions an ideal communication that promotes the spiritual growth of listeners and speakers alike.

The *psychological setting* of a speech includes such factors as the occasion for speaking, the expectations that audiences members bring to the speaking situation, and the context of recent events. When audience members expect an informative presentation on investing in the stock market but are instead subjected to a sales pitch for mutual funds, they may feel exploited and come away with a negative impression of both speaker and speech.

Finally, recent events can change the psychological setting of a speech. For instance, if you have planned a speech attacking oppressive campus security measures, and right before your speech a frightening and well-publicized crime is committed on your campus, the setting for your speech may suddenly be less receptive.

A typical critique we might write for a student speech illustrates the interplay of these various factors and the usefulness of grasping the interactional nature of the speech process:

> You were right to emphasize your personal experience with this subject at the beginning of your speech [*establishing the validity of the source*]. However, you need to speak louder so that listeners in the back of the room can hear clearly [*improving the quality of encoding*]. Your speech is well organized and makes effective use of examples [*praising the quality of the message*]. You did need to explain more clearly some of the technical terms you used [*to help listeners decode*].

This charismatic speaker seems dynamic and likeable.

decoder Process by which the listener determines the meaning of the speaker's message.

noise Sometimes called interference, this can indicate a range of problems from physical noise such as distracting sounds in the room to psychological noise (stereotypes, distractions, cultural barriers, etc.) in listeners that can distort or even block the reception of the message.

feedback Speaker's perception of how audience members react to the message both during and after its presentation.

setting Physical and psychological context in which a speech is presented.

To overcome the objection that a man could hardly understand the problems of women, you need to introduce expert testimony to strengthen your perception as a fair, informed, and credible speaker [*overcoming psychological noise*]. When listeners look puzzled or shake their heads, provide an example or show what you're talking about on the chalkboard [*reacting to feedback*]. Finally, on such a warm spring day, be more energetic in your presentation and use more colorful language [*adapting to the setting*].

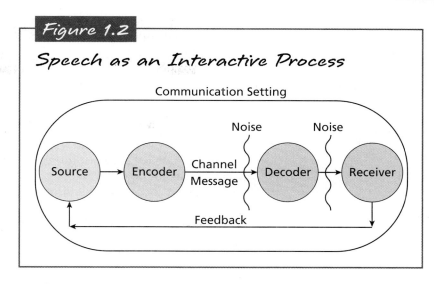

Figure 1.2

Speech as an Interactive Process

Figure 1.2 offers a visual model of the interactional process.

Public Speaking as a Dynamic Process.   Kenneth Burke, one of the major communication theorists of our time, suggested that speakers are constantly confronting the problem of listeners who feel divided and weak and who lack effective definition as groups. The challenge that speakers must meet is to bring these listeners together into action communities who know what they are and what they wish to become. In the process, speakers also define themselves.

The first day you enter your public speaking class, you encounter twenty-five or so other individuals. Perhaps a few of them know each other, but most are strangers. Many are secretly frightened about the "ordeal" they believe they will soon have to endure. So on the day you first stand to speak, your main task may be to tear down all those invisible walls that separate people, to bring listeners together around your ideas and personality. You will have begun Burke's work of **identification**, creating the feeling among people that they share the speaker's experiences, values, fears, desires, and dreams and that they are, in effect, bound together in community.[15]

Public speaking, when it is successful, changes the relationships among people—the distances that separate them disappear, the boundaries that confine them are lifted. *This is why public speaking is a dynamic process: it changes people and the relationships among them.*

Figure 1.3 offers a picture of this process when it works successfully. In

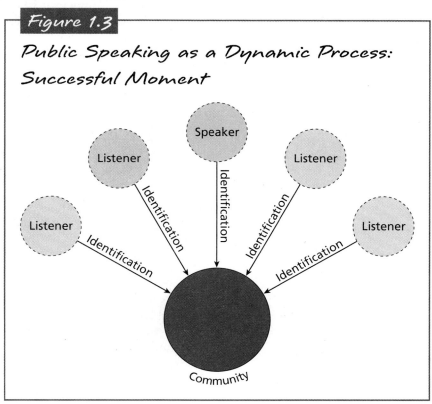

Figure 1.3

Public Speaking as a Dynamic Process: Successful Moment

identification   The feeling of closeness between speakers and listeners that may overcome personal and cultural differences.

it, we see a mythical speaker and group of listeners as they are before the successful speech has worked its magic upon them. They are separate from each other and vaguely defined. Their pastel colors hint of their weakness in isolation from each other. But during the dynamic process of successful speaking, they are drawn together by the speaker's identification appeals. They are joined finally in a larger circle of inclusion, a community, in which they enjoy both definition and expanded power. Note the use of the power color, royal blue, to reinforce this impression of greater collective strength (see Chapter 11 for more about the meaningfulness of color). The speaker also shares in this new sense of identity and power. When this new group takes action, following the speaker's leadership, they will have a much greater chance of achieving their purpose than had they acted alone.

Burke's concept of identification is one of those rich conceptions we draw upon throughout this course, because it explains so much. For example, it helps explain the power of the appeal offered in Anna Aley's speech protesting slum housing in her town of Manhattan, Kansas:

> . . . What can one student do to change the practices of numerous Manhattan landlords? Nothing, if that student is alone. But just think of what we could accomplish if we got all 13,600 off-campus students involved in this issue! Think what we could accomplish if we got even a fraction of those students involved! [See Anna Aley's speech at the end of Chapter 16.]

Anna, a Kansas State student, helped her listeners realize that they were victims of slum housing. In other words, she pointed out their *identity*. And she offered a new, dynamic vision of themselves acting together to correct these abuses. Similarly, much of the power of Vanderbilt student Ashlie McMillan's tribute to her dwarf cousin is that Tina is so small physically but so large spiritually. Tina becomes an example listeners can identify with, and listeners themselves become larger as they take her life as a lesson:

> The next time a large obstacle stands in your way, remember Tina, my small cousin who has achieved such noteworthy things. You too may seem too short to grasp your stars, but you never know how far you might reach if you stand upon a dream. [See Ashlie McMillan's speech at the end of Chapter 17.]

Finally, identification helps us explain the power of public speaking on the wider stage of public affairs. Effective politicians typically offer voters new visions of themselves. They may have been *victims of bad policy*, but now they can become a *force for change*. When Martin Luther King Jr. strove to change racial practices in America, he offered an answer for the legacy of humiliation and segregation that continued to divide Americans in his time. In his celebrated speech, "I Have a Dream," King offered a vision of identification as an answer to the old racial divisions:

> I have a dream that . . . one day right there in Alabama little black boys and black girls will be able to join hands with little white boys and white girls as sisters and brothers. I have a dream today.[16]

Throughout the course of the civil rights movement King led from 1956 to 1968, he repeatedly identified himself with Moses as a leader. He spoke as though he had been destined by God to lead his followers out of their Egypt of semi-slavery. Those who responded, many of whom had suffered from degrading identities assigned to them for generations, were redefined by his rhetoric as the "Children of Israel."[17] Through the many battlefields of the civil rights movement, where they would be beaten, jailed, and some of them killed, these people saw themselves as moving toward a new Promised Land. King was still offering visions of that land on the night before he was assassinated.

As his leadership emerged over those years, King's own image seemed to grow and expand. And his followers were also transformed into heroic figures as they marched through one ordeal after another. These transformations indicate how people can grow and enlarge when they interact in ethical communication that inspires and encourages the humanity of listeners. In contrast, deceitful and dishonest communication that is designed to manipulate or browbeat listeners or that misuses source material can reduce the humanity of listeners.

Plato, of course, told us long ago in the *Phaedrus* that ethical communication that respects the humanity of listeners and nourishes it with responsible knowledge encourages the spiritual growth of both speaker and listeners. This connection between Kenneth Burke and Plato, identification and ethical communication, leads us into the next section.

What This Course Asks of You

Hopefully by now you are convinced that this course has much to offer in terms of practical benefits, personal growth, and knowledge of an interactive, dynamic process. Now it is time to consider: what does this course ask of you in return?

Obviously, the course asks that you make a commitment of time and energy. But beyond this commitment, the course asks that you take seriously your ethical responsibilities as a communicator. Public speaking can be a powerful tool in shaping the attitudes and actions of listeners. As such, it requires great respect for and sensitivity to your responsibilities as a speaker.

Because just about every aspect of putting together and presenting speeches can raise ethical questions, you will encounter relevant discussions and "Ethics Alert!" features throughout this text. In addition, the code of ethics of the National Communication Association, the "Credo for Ethical Communication," is reprinted at the end of this chapter. In this final section, we discuss three major considerations that underlie ethical public speaking: *respect for the integrity of ideas and information, a genuine concern for consequences, and the shared responsibilities of listeners.*

Respect for the Integrity of Ideas and Information

Respect for the integrity of ideas and information requires that you speak from responsible knowledge, use communication techniques carefully, and avoid plagiarism.

Speaking from Responsible Knowledge. No one expects you to be an expert as you speak in class. You should, however, make an effort to acquire **responsible knowledge** of your subject. As we discuss in detail in Chapter 7, responsible knowledge of a topic includes

- knowing the main points of concern.
- understanding what experts believe about them.

responsible knowledge An understanding of the major features, issues, information, latest developments, and local applications relevant to a topic.

- being aware of the most recent events or discoveries concerning them.
- realizing how these points affect the lives of listeners.

Responsible knowledge requires that you know more about a topic than your audience so that your speech has something useful to give them.

Consider how Stephen Huff, one of our students at the University of Memphis, acquired responsible knowledge for an informative speech. Stephen knew little about earthquakes before his speech, but he knew that Memphis was on the New Madrid fault and that this location could mean trouble. He also knew that a major earthquake research center was located on campus. Stephen arranged for an interview with the center's director. During the interview, he asked a series of well-planned questions:

> *Where* was the New Madrid fault, and what was the history of its activity?
> *What* was the probability of a major quake in the area in the near future?
> *How* prepared was Memphis for a major quake?
> *What* kind of damage could result?
> *How* could his listeners prepare for it?
> *What* readings would the director recommend?

All these questions were designed to gain knowledge that would interest and benefit his listeners. Armed with knowledge from the interview, Stephen went to the library and found the readings suggested by the director. He was well on his way to giving a good speech.

You should follow Stephen's example. Acquiring responsible knowledge takes time and effort, but it is well worth the work.

Careful Use of Communication Techniques.
Some of the most useful techniques for communicating ideas and information can also be misused by speakers to confuse or mislead an audience or to hide the speaker's agenda. Consider, for instance, the practice called **quoting out of context**. In Chapter 8, we encourage you to cite experts and respected authorities to support important and controversial assertions. However, this becomes ethically troublesome when speakers distort the meanings of such statements to support their own positions.

Many social activists, for instance, argue that certain leaders routinely invoke Martin Luther King's "dream" of a color-blind society to roll back the progressive social reforms that he helped to inspire. In his famous "I Have a Dream" speech, for example, King offered his vision of a world in which we would judge people "not by the color of their skin but by the content of their character." One state official offered these words to justify ending scholarships to the state's college and universities targeted for black students. A prominent governor used the same dream to explain why he was appointing only white men to the board running the university system in his state. A well-known theater critic in New York invoked King's wisdom to condemn the formation of black theatrical companies.[18]

The problem, of course, is that these people were using King's own words to defeat the kinds of things he wanted to encourage. King wanted to remove the massive barriers of segregation that had too long constrained the advancement of black people. These manipulators of his words applied his principles *out of the context* of that purpose to attack programs and policies specifically designed to help black people recover from a history of oppression.

Environmentalists also point to an example of quoting out of context, which they feel may have grave consequences for our planet's future. They allege that the

quoting out of context An unethical use of a quotation that changes or distorts the original speaker's meaning or intent by not including parts of the quote.

Bush administration distorted a National Academy of Sciences report in 2001 to justify not taking decisive action sooner to counter global warming. After pointing out alarming signs of climate change, the report had concluded: "The changes observed over the last several decades are likely mostly due to human activities, but we cannot rule out that some significant part of these changes are also a reflection of natural variability." In responding to the report, government representatives focused on the "natural variability" qualifier to make the claim that the report was inconclusive as to whether global warming was caused by humans.[19]

To avoid such ethical problems, be sure you are representing experts' positions fairly when you cite them in your speeches. Throughout this text, we discuss the potential misuse of evidence, reasoning, language, visual aids, and other powerful communication techniques. You should avoid such practices like the plague!

Avoiding Academic Dishonesty.   For a variety of reasons, rates of academic dishonesty are apparently rising on college campuses.[20] Most colleges consider this increase a serious threat to the integrity of higher education, and they stipulate penalties ranging from a major grade reduction to suspension or even expulsion from the university. You can probably find your university's policy in your student handbook or on your college Web site. Your communication department or instructor may have additional definitions and rules regarding academic dishonesty.

The most blatant form of such dishonesty is **plagiarism**, *presenting the ideas or words of others as though they were your own*. Related abuses include "parroting" an article or speech from a newspaper, magazine, or Internet site as if it were your own creation; "cutting and pasting" passages verbatim from multiple sources and splicing them together as *your own* speech; "collusion," or working with another student to present the same speech in different sections of the public speaking course, and the willful misuse or fabrication of sources of information.

We strongly discourage you from committing academic dishonesty in this or any other college classes. Instructors are better at spotting academic dishonesty than some students may realize. Many departments keep files of speeches and speech outlines, instructors do talk to each other, and there are Internet resources that instructors can use for looking up "stock" speeches that have been pulled or purchased from the Internet. If you misrepresent information, you are only cheating yourself regardless of whether you get caught. You likely will not "speak well" when you do not prepare and present your own work. You end up compromising all the benefits we have described.

A Concern for Consequences

Recognizing the power of communication leads ethical speakers to a genuine concern for how their words might affect the lives of others. Serious speeches most often convey moral visions or dreams of communities that speakers want to promote. Speakers must reflect upon the larger consequences of making these dreams into reality.

Another related concern is the impact of our speaking on the quality and integrity of public communication itself. There can be occasions that tempt us, times when the right ends might seem to justify unethical means. In the final days of a heated political campaign, for example, when we know that "we're right" and "they're wrong," it might seem acceptable for our preferred candidates to rely on ugly character attacks, shameless fear-mongering, and fallacies such as we discuss in

plagiarism   Presenting the ideas and words of others without crediting them as sources.

Ethics *Alert 1.1*

Avoiding Plagiarism

Avoiding plagiarism is a matter of faith between yourself, your instructor, and your classmates. Be especially alert to the following:

1. Don't present or summarize someone else's speech, article, or essay as though it were your own.

2. Draw information and ideas from a variety of sources, then interpret them to create your own point of view.

3. Don't parrot other people's language and ideas as though they were your own.

4. Always provide oral citations for direct quotations, paraphrased material, or especially striking language, letting listeners know who said the words, where, and when.

5. Credit those who originate ideas: "John Sheets, director of secondary curriculum and instruction at Duke University, suggests there are three criteria we should apply in evaluating our high schools."

6. Identify your sources of information: "According to *The 2008 American Almanac*, tin cans were first used in 1811 as a means of preserving food"; or "The latest issue of *Time* magazine notes that : . . . ."

7. Introduce your sources as lead-ins to direct quotations: "Studs Terkel has said that a book about work 'is, by its very nature, about violence—to the spirit as well as the body. '"

8. Allow yourself enough time to research and prepare your presentation.

9. Take careful notes as you do your research so that you don't later confuse your own thoughts and words with those of others.

Constructive listeners encourage speakers, listen to speeches with open minds, and emphasize the positive values of messages.

Chapter 15. But we need to always ask ourselves whether short-term benefits are worth the long-term damage of creating a communication climate in which such blatantly unethical practices are now seen to be "justifiable under certain circumstances." Public communication in democratic societies should foster informed and rational decision making while reinforcing a commitment to open, tolerant, and civil discussion of issues.[21]

The Shared Responsibilities of Listeners

Finally, no discussion of public speaking ethics would be complete without considering the shared responsibilities of listeners. Often we talk to people who have grown disenchanted with the quality of public discourse and the very prospect of democracy. It is disheartening to hear them cite their cynicism as an excuse for "tuning out" and ignoring public issues altogether. Nothing does more to reinforce dishonesty and demagoguery in public discussions than ignorance born of cynical indifference among otherwise "good" and "intelligent" citizens. Listeners are the ultimate arbiters of communication transactions. If public speaking is to be ethical, then listeners must play the critical and constructive roles we discuss further in Chapter 4.

When one reflects upon it, playing an honorable role as speaker and listener is a small price to pay for the cornucopia of benefits described in this chapter. At the outset, therefore, we offer a toast: Here's to a successful adventure as you develop into a public speaker!

In Summary

Your public speaking class offers you many benefits. First, it helps you develop an array of practical skills ranging from techniques for the control of communication anxiety to learning how to express yourself with power and conviction. It increases your chances of success both in school and in your later professional life. It also helps you to become a better citizen, ready to participate in the communication life of a democratic society.

Second, the class offers important opportunities for personal growth. It helps you understand better your own strengths and limitations and introduces you to a rich tradition of learning, the wisdom concerning public speaking that has accumulated since the time of Plato and Aristotle. It also helps you expand your cultural horizons by exposing you to the variety of backgrounds represented in the typical public speaking class.

Third, the class helps you develop knowledge of an interactive, dynamic process that can enrich many dimensions of your life. As an interactive process, public speaking touches upon such factors as source, message, medium, encoding and decoding, interference, receiver, feedback, and communication setting. As a dynamic process, public speaking helps replace division among people with identification among them. It helps people overcome the barriers that separate them, and it encourages their spiritual growth in communities.

The public speaking class asks several things from you in return. First, it asks for an appropriate commitment of time and energy. Second, it asks that you treat the power of speech with respect and ethical sensitivity. You must speak from responsible knowledge, and avoid the misuse of public speaking techniques and the temptations of plagiarism. You should cultivate concern for how your words might affect others. You should also take seriously your role as a critical and constructive listener for classroom speeches.

Explore and Apply the Ideas in This Chapter

1. Visualize yourself as the speaker you hope to become by the end of this class. What specific skills will you have to acquire to make this ideal a reality?

2. Bring to class examples of advertisements that you think are ethical and unethical, and explain why.

3. Do you agree that it is better to think of American culture as a "bouillabaisse" or "chorus" rather than as a "melting pot"? Can you think of other desirable metaphors for American identity?

4. Begin keeping a speech evaluation diary in which you record comments on effective and ineffective, ethical and unethical speeches you hear both in and out of class. As you observe speeches, ask yourself the following questions:

(1) How did the speaker rate in terms of credibility?

(2) Was the speech well adapted to its listeners' needs and interests?

(3) Did the speech take into account the cultural complexity of its audience?

(4) Was the message clear and well structured?

(5) Did the medium pose any problems?

(6) Was the language and presentation of the speech effective?

(7) How did listeners respond, both during and after the speech?

(8) Did the setting have any impact on the message?

(9) Did the speech overcome interference to achieve its goal?

(10) Did the speech promote identification between speaker and listeners?

(11) Did the speaker demonstrate responsible knowledge and an ethical use of communication techniques?

(12) Did listeners meet their responsibilities as critical, constructive listeners?

At the end of the term, conclude what you have learned about the ethics and effectiveness of speech-making, and submit the record of your observations and conclusions to your teacher.

5. The National Communication Association has adopted a code of ethics concerning free expression. As you read this code, think of a recent political, religious, or social controversy in which one or more of the principles affirmed here was violated. Be prepared to report on these violations in class.

Credo for Ethical Communication

Questions of right and wrong arise whenever people communicate. Ethical communication is fundamental to responsible thinking, decision making, and the development of relationships and communities within and across contexts, cultures, channels, and media. Moreover, ethical communication enhances human worth and dignity by fostering truthfulness, fairness, responsibility, personal integrity, and respect for self and others. We believe that unethical communication threatens the quality of all communication and consequently the well-being of individuals and the society in which we live. Therefore we, the members of the National Communication Association, endorse and are committed to practicing the following principles of ethical communication.

- We advocate truthfulness, accuracy, honesty, and reason as essential to the integrity of communication.

- We endorse freedom of expression, diversity of perspective, and tolerance of dissent to achieve the informed and responsible decision making fundamental to a civil society.

- We strive to understand and respect other communicators before evaluating and responding to their messages.

- We promote access to communication resources and opportunities as necessary to fulfill human potential and contribute to the well-being of families, communities, and society.

- We promote communication climates of caring and mutual understanding that respect the unique needs and characteristics of individual communicators.

- We condemn communication that degrades individuals and humanity through distortion, intimidation, coercion, and violence and through the expression of intolerance and hatred.

- We are committed to the courageous expression of personal convictions in pursuit of fairness and justice.

- We advocate sharing information, opinions, and feelings when facing significant choices while also respecting privacy and confidentiality.

- We accept responsibility for the short- and long-term consequences for our own communication and expect the same of others.[22]

2 Managing Your Fear of Speaking

This chapter will help you

- realize you are not alone in your fear of public speaking
- understand the nature of communication anxiety
- learn ways to manage communication anxiety

Bravery is being the only one who knows you're afraid.

—David Hackworth

Professor, could I talk with you for a few minutes? I'm supposed to graduate this semester, and I've put off taking this course until now. Well, actually, I started it twice before and dropped it after the first couple of classes. I've got to make it through this time or I won't graduate. But the idea of speaking to a group makes me so nervous, I don't think I can handle it. Everyone else seems more confident than I am. Can you help me?"

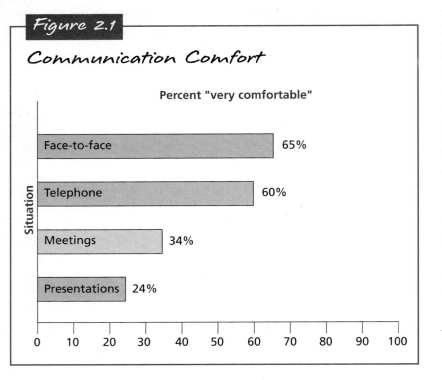

Figure 2.1

Communication Comfort

Percent "very comfortable"

Would it help to know you're not alone? For years, survey after survey has placed public speaking at or near the top of the list of people's fears.[1] Jerry Seinfeld once observed that since most people prefer death to public speaking, almost anyone would rather be in the coffin than delivering the eulogy at a funeral. For many of us, however, this is no laughing matter. The National Communication Association recently commissioned the Roper Starch polling organization to conduct a nationwide survey to determine how comfortable and effective people feel communicating in different situations.[2] Figure 2.1 shows that most of us are more comfortable with one-on-one interactions or talking on the phone than we are with speaking up in meetings or giving a speech. Indeed, most people are *not comfortable* speaking up at a meeting, and even more are not comfortable giving a presentation or speech.

Almost all college students are uncomfortable when they have to address a class. International students and students from marginalized cultural groups often have a great deal of apprehension. Once, when we were teaching a public speaking course in summer school, a student confessed that she was enrolled at another college but was taking the course with us so that if she didn't do well, it wouldn't spoil her GPA and keep her out of medical school. Her fears were unfounded. The text of her excellent first speech, "My Three Cultures," has been a staple in all previous editions of our text and is included in Appendix B.

Many celebrities also suffer from performance anxiety. Michael Jackson delayed the start of the World Music Awards for 30 minutes because he was suffering from "stage fright."[3] Barbara Streisand, Sir Laurence Olivier, Kim Bassinger, Joaquin Phoenix, and Nicole Kidman are reported to be fellow sufferers.[4] Prominent sports figures also have such fears. "Pro-golfer Annika Sorenstam was so afraid of public speaking that she said there were times when she would intentionally finish second to avoid giving a victory speech!"[5]

Your speech instructor may even have some communication anxiety, but you probably won't be able to detect it. Even your authors have experienced this problem. Here is their story:

A Confession

As college professors and authors, we have done a lot of speaking both in and out of the classroom. Being the authors of a public speaking text puts even more pressure on you. When you earn your bread and butter by telling others how to do something, they expect you to be able to do it yourself—and do it much better than most other people. Even with all our experience, every time we face a new group—a class of undergraduates, citizens in community meetings, or our professional colleagues at conventions—we feel the burden of this pressure.

Surprised? Still think that everyone else is more confident than you are? The late Edward R. Murrow, a famous radio and television commentator, once said:

"The best speakers know enough to be scared. . . . The only difference between the pros and the novices is that the pros have trained the butterflies to fly in formation."

The first step in controlling communication apprehension is understanding it. In this chapter, we first discuss the nature of this fear and then tell you some things you can do to manage it. Our goal is not to rid you of communication anxiety but to help you train your butterflies to fly in formation.

Understanding Communication Anxiety

You may have noticed that earlier in this chapter we put the words *stage fright* in quotation marks to indicate our reservations about using these words to describe public speaking fears. *Stage* suggests theater, and *theater* suggests performance. However, a public speech is not a performance but an interactive, dynamic communication event.[6] If you think of your speeches as performances, you cast yourself as an actor and your messages become soliloquies rather than authentic attempts to communicate. You may also see the audience as critics you must please.

A better way to discuss this problem is to call it **communication anxiety**. Communication anxiety encom-

Pro golfer Annika Sorenstam once avoided press conferences because she suffered from communication anxiety.

passes the range of unpleasant sensations you may experience before or during a presentation. The fears associated with public speaking are rooted in the risks involved in true communication: In public speaking, you open your hearts and minds to the scrutiny of others. This experience can result in personal growth and self-enhancement. But it also involves risk—which can cause anxiety. When you open your hearts and minds to others, you subject yourself to criticism. We begin by examining the symptoms of communication anxiety, the reasons you might feel anxious when you stand up to speak, and the specific things people are concerned about.

Symptoms of Communication Anxiety

It's the night before your first speech. You go to bed, but instead of going to sleep, you toss and turn. You try reciting the alphabet backward. That doesn't work, so you just lie in bed worrying. The more you think about your speech, the more tense and irritable you feel. You hear music, so you get up, tramp down the hall, burst into the room, and yell, "Will you turn that down! I've got to give a speech tomorrow, so I have to have a good night's sleep!"

Finally, morning dawns. You're in class waiting for your turn. You don't really listen to the speeches before yours because you feel miserable. You hear your name called. Your stomach drops. Your hands begin to sweat. Your heart races.

communication anxiety The range of unpleasant sensations and fears you may experience before or during a presentation.

Visible signs of communication anxiety can be controlled using the techniques described in this chapter.

Your ears feel hot. Your mouth feels dry. You plod to the podium and look up at the audience. Your knees start to shake. You grab hold of the lectern for support.

Any of these symptoms sound familiar? What you are experiencing is a natural "adrenaline rush." It's the same type of reaction you might have if you suddenly encountered a bear in the woods or a mugger on a dark street. These are the physical symptoms you usually associate with fear. They make up the "fight-or-flight" readiness that can help you cope with a difficult situation. But when it's your turn to speak, neither fight nor flight is appropriate. You can't punch your instructor and you can't run out the door. You have to give that speech.

Most likely, you won't have *all* of these symptoms of communication anxiety, but you may well have some of them. If you didn't, you wouldn't be normal. *Moreover, a little bit of communication anxiety is a good thing*. It can "psych" you up for your presentation. However, too much nervousness can be paralyzing and is a cause for real concern.

You may be surprised to learn that a little bit of communication anxiety is a good thing. Why is this true? The absence of any nervousness may suggest that you don't care about your audience or your message. We recently taught a student who announced to the class that she never had any "stage fright" because she had won many high school speech contests and was used to "performing" (her words). She didn't understand why she had to take this course. She was indifferent to learning what the course had to offer. She never really listened when others were speaking, because she didn't think she could learn anything from her classmates. She also didn't listen to her instructors, because she felt she already knew all she needed to know about public performances. After all, she had the trophies to prove how good she was! Perhaps because of this attitude, her classroom speeches sounded as though they had been dredged up from her high school files. They didn't really fit her audience or the assignment. Although her delivery was smooth, she never connected in any meaningful way with her audience. *She never truly communicated with them*.

Where do you stand in terms of your personal communication anxiety? One way to estimate how much communication anxiety you have is to complete the questionnaire in Figure 2.2. You may be surprised to find that you didn't score as high on this scale as you thought you might. If your score is higher than 120, you should arrange a meeting with your instructor to discuss the problem.

Why Public Speaking Can Be Frightening

Right about now you may be thinking, "Well, perhaps I'm not alone, but I'm still pretty uptight about giving a speech. I'm afraid I'll do or say something stupid. Or, I'll forget something important. Or, my classmates will make fun of me." These are very common concerns, so let's investigate why speaking before a group can be frightening. As we cover these concerns, we'll do some reality testing.

Figure 2.2

A Gauge of Communication Anxiety

Directions: Assume that you have to give a speech within the next few weeks. For each of the statements below, indicate the degree to which the statement applies to you within the context of giving a future speech. Mark whether you strongly agree (SA), agree (A), are undecided (U), disagree (D), or strongly disagree (SD) with each statement. Circle your SA, A, U, D, or SD choices. Do not write in the blanks next to the questions. **Work quickly: just record your first impression.**

____ 1. While preparing for the speech, I would feel uncomfortably tense and nervous. — SA_5 A_4 U_3 D_2 SD_1

____ 2. I feel uncomfortably tense at the very thought of giving a speech in the near future. — SA_5 A_4 U_3 D_2 SD_1

____ 3. My thoughts would become confused and jumbled when I was giving a speech. — SA_5 A_4 U_3 D_2 SD_1

____ 4. Right after giving the speech I would feel that I'd had a pleasant experience. — SA_1 A_2 U_3 D_4 SD_5

____ 5. I would get anxious when thinking about the speech coming up. — SA_5 A_4 U_3 D_2 SD_1

____ 6. I would have no fear of giving the speech. — SA_1 A_2 U_3 D_4 SD_5

____ 7. Although I would be nervous just before starting the speech, after starting it I would soon settle down and feel calm and comfortable. — SA_1 A_2 U_3 D_4 SD_5

____ 8. I would look forward to giving the speech. — SA_1 A_2 U_3 D_4 SD_5

____ 9. As soon as I knew that I would have to give the speech, I would feel myself getting tense. — SA_5 A_4 U_3 D_2 SD_1

____ 10. My hands would tremble when I was giving the speech. — SA_5 A_4 U_3 D_2 SD_1

____ 11. I would feel relaxed while giving the speech. — SA_1 A_2 U_3 D_4 SD_5

____ 12. I would enjoy preparing for the speech. — SA_1 A_2 U_3 D_4 SD_5

____ 13. I would be in constant fear of forgetting what I had prepared to say. — SA_5 A_4 U_3 D_2 SD_1

____ 14. I would get uncomfortably anxious if someone asked me something that I did not know about my topic. — SA_5 A_4 U_3 D_2 SD_1

____ 15. I would face the prospect of giving the speech with confidence. — SA_1 A_2 U_3 D_4 SD_5

Figure 2.2

A Gauge of Communication Anxiety (Continued)

___ 16. I would feel that I was in complete possession of myself during the speech. SA_1 A_2 U_3 D_4 SD_5

___ 17. My mind would be clear when giving the speech. SA_1 A_2 U_3 D_4 SD_5

___ 18. I would not dread giving the speech. SA_1 A_2 U_3 D_4 SD_5

___ 19. I would perspire too much just before starting the speech. SA_5 A_4 U_3 D_2 SD_1

___ 20. I would be bothered by a very fast heart rate just as I started the speech. SA_5 A_4 U_3 D_2 SD_1

___ 21. I would experience considerable anxiety at the speech site (room, auditorium, etc.) just before my speech was to start. SA_5 A_4 U_3 D_2 SD_1

___ 22. Certain parts of my body would feel very tense and rigid during the speech. SA_5 A_4 U_3 D_2 SD_1

___ 23. Realizing that only a little time remained in the speech would make me very tense and anxious. SA_5 A_4 U_3 D_2 SD_1

___ 24. While giving the speech I would know that I could control my feelings of tension and stress. SA_1 A_2 U_3 D_4 SD_5

___ 25. I would breathe too fast just before starting the speech. SA_5 A_4 U_3 D_2 SD_1

___ 26. I would feel comfortable and relaxed in the hour or so just before giving the speech. SA_1 A_2 U_3 D_4 SD_5

___ 27. I would do poorly on the speech because I would be anxious. SA_5 A_4 U_3 D_2 SD_1

___ 28. I would feel uncomfortably anxious when first scheduling the date of the speaking assignment. SA_5 A_4 U_3 D_2 SD_1

___ 29. If I were to make a mistake while giving the speech, I would find it hard to concentrate on the parts that followed. SA_5 A_4 U_3 D_2 SD_1

___ 30. During the speech I would experience a feeling of helplessness building up inside me. SA_5 A_4 U_3 D_2 SD_1

___ 31. I would have trouble falling asleep the night before the speech. SA_5 A_4 U_3 D_2 SD_1

Figure 2.2

A Gauge of Communication Anxiety (Continued)

___ 32. My heart would beat too fast while I was presenting the speech. SA_5 A_4 U_3 D_2 SD_1

___ 33. I would feel uncomfortably anxious while waiting to give my speech. SA_5 A_4 U_3 D_2 SD_1

___ 34. While giving the speech I would get so nervous that I would forget facts I really knew. SA_5 A_4 U_3 D_2 SD_1

To determine your score:
1. Fill in the blank next to each item with the NUMBER accompanying the response you circled. BE CAREFUL to enter the CORRECT NUMBER. NOTICE that the numbers printed with the responses are not consistent for every question.
2. Add up the numbers you recorded for the 34 questions. The sum is your public speaking apprehension score.

Interpretation:

34–84	low
85–92	moderately low
93–110	moderate
111–119	moderately high
120 +	high

Source: Adapted from "Personal Report of Public Speaking Anxiety" by James C. McCroskey. Appeared in "Measures of Communication Bound Anxiety," *Speech Monographs* 37, (1970), p. 276. Used by permission of National Communication Association.

The greatest anxiety about public speaking generally takes place before you ever stand to speak. Your worries may begin when you register for the course, when a speech is assigned, or while you are preparing your presentation. In outside-the-classroom situations, you may begin to get nervous when you know you will be called upon to say a few words, when you have a report to make to a work group, or when you feel impelled to speak up before others on a cause you really care about. The nervousness that comes before you make a presentation is called **anticipatory anxiety**.[7]

Because you usually know well in advance that you will be giving a speech, there is a lot of time to build up fears. Understanding the causes of this anxiety can help you cope with it. Some of the sources of such anxiety are external or inherent in the situation. Other sources are internal or originate within the person.

External Factors

Let's begin with two rational reasons that people are not comfortable speaking before a group: the unfamiliarity of the situation and the importance of the occasion.

anticipatory anxiety   The fear of public speaking that occurs before the actual presentation of a speech.

InterConnections.
LearnMore 2.1

Coping With Fear

Communication Anxiety

http://chattanoogastate.edu/cde/anxiety

An online resource for working through communication anxiety; prepared as a class project under the direction of Debra Jones, Chattanooga State Community College.

Stage Fright

www.selfgrowth.com/articles/zimmer5.html

A self-help article, "Transforming Stage Fright into Magnetic Presence," prepared by Sandra Zimmer, consultant and director of the Self-Expression Center, University of Houston.

Unfamiliarity. For most of us, speaking to a large number of people face to face is not an everyday activity. Almost all of us tend to be somewhat ill at ease in unfamiliar situations. Fortunately, familiarity with a situation tends to reduce anxiety. Practice your speech before a group of friends. Enlist your roommates, friends, or family to be an audience. Practicing before someone gives you increased familiarity with the speaking situation. Although practicing may not "make it go away" as you might wish, it can help reduce your anxiety to a more manageable level. When speaking to a group outside the classroom, especially a group of people you don't know, try to arrive early and meet some audience members. By doing so, you will have a familiar face to look for in the audience as you speak.

Importance. Anxiety can also be increased by realizing that you usually have to speak in public only when a lot depends on how well you express yourself. When things matter to us, we tend to worry in anticipation of them. This anticipatory anxiety is often worse than the anxiety you may experience during the presentation of your speech. It can cause sleeplessness and irritability. To counter this problem, prepare your speech well in advance of your scheduled presentation. If you put off preparing your speech until the night before it is due, you will simply magnify your anxiety level. Try to find something relaxing to do the night before you are scheduled to speak. Watch a silly television show or go to the movies, take a long walk with a friend, or listen to someone else's problems and think about how you might help him or her.

Internal Factors

How nervous you actually feel about giving a speech also may be related to your personality. This nervousness is not always rational, but it can become a problem if you let it. You may believe you don't have a great deal of control over these factors, that it is simply the way you are, but understanding them may help you cope with them.

Anxiety Sensitivity. You may be the type of person who labels even the weakest of the symptoms we discussed earlier as signs of fear. If so, you can blow your nervousness all out of proportion. Psychologists call this tendency **anxiety sensitivity**.[8] It is a fear of fear itself. You think that you are afraid; therefore you become more afraid. Fear feeds on itself, so try not to get too uptight about your normal anxiety.

anxiety sensitivity The tendency to label weak symptoms of anxiety as fear and then to over-respond to them.

Speaker's Notes 2.1

Common Causes of Communication Anxiety

Your communication anxiety may stem from any or all of the following causes:

1. Unfamiliarity with the situation
2. Importance of the occasion
3. Anxiety sensitivity—the fear of fear itself
4. Perfectionism—the dread of making a mistake
5. Audience misperceptions
6. Expectation of dire consequences

Remember, the physical symptoms you may experience before or during speaking are also associated with other reactions that we do not usually call fear. For example, do you remember ever being so excited before a big event you looked forward to that you couldn't sleep? How did you feel when you heard the first strains of the processional for your high school graduation? Did you call these feelings "fear" or "excitement"?

Perfectionism.   Another personal factor that contributes to communication apprehension is **perfectionism**. As a beginning speaker, you may believe that your speech has to be perfect for it to be effective. No presentation is ever perfect. Even former president Ronald Reagan, who was known as "the great communicator," bumbled some lines and repeated himself in his presentations. It's all right if you make a few mistakes, and besides, your listeners probably won't even notice unless you call attention to them.

Audience Misconceptions.   You may picture your listeners as predators lying in wait, ready to pounce on any little mistake you might make. In reality, most audiences, especially college classroom audiences, want speakers to succeed. If you look out in the audience and see someone frowning, that person is probably worried about some personal problem, not preparing to pounce on you.

You also may worry that everyone in the audience will know how nervous you are. Actually, most listeners won't know this unless you tell them. They are not clairvoyant! Communication consultant H. Dennis Beaver brings this point home to his clients by having them think back to a time when they felt especially nervous speaking to a group. Then he asks:

> Did a single audience member come up to you and comment on how loud your heart was beating? Or how sweaty your hands appeared? Or how dry your voice sounded? Or what an interesting sound your knocking knees made?[9]

You may feel that the audience is just waiting for you to make a mistake, but in truth, most audiences want you to succeed.

perfectionism   Believing that you must be perfect to be effective.

One time when we were taping student speeches for a teaching video, a student began her speech with an excellent interest-arousing introduction. About a minute and a half into her speech she stopped, looked at us, and said, "I can't do this! I'm too nervous." We have used the tape of this speech in many classes. We show the speech up until right before the student stops. Then we ask the class to estimate how anxious they think this speaker is. Typically, they say, "She's not at all nervous" or "She's very poised." Then we start the tape back up and show the segment where she quits. The class is usually quite surprised, but the lesson is clear.

Dire Consequences. You may believe that as soon as you stand up to speak, something dreadful is going to happen to you—you'll throw up or pass out. This seldom happens, even with the most anxious students. In our many years of teaching, we've never seen a student throw up or pass out in a public speaking class.

Specific Fears That Bother Speakers

Two recent surveys of both the general population and college students identified some *specific* fears that people have regarding public speaking.[10] The fears cited by the general public are listed in Figure 2.3. The students surveyed also mentioned negative consequences (e.g., bad grades) as a major concern. Let's examine these fears and see how troublesome they can be.

Trembling or Shaking. Trembling or shaking was the most common specific fear mentioned in the surveys, and it may be the most common physical reaction.[11] Indeed, as you make your first presentations, your hands may tremble a bit or your leg muscles may begin to twitch. Is this really all that bad? Chances are you will be more aware of the trembling than anyone in your audience. And, if listeners do notice it, what will they think? That you're a failure? That you're incompetent? Or, that you—*like them*—are somewhat uncomfortable in front of a group?

Actually, some slight trembling may have a positive effect on how the audience reacts to you. Psychologists call this the "pratfall" effect. When people in a position of power or authority (as you are when you give a speech) make a minor mistake, they appear more human and make it more likely that people will respond positively to them. Trembling probably won't affect how competent people think you are, but it may make you seem more likeable.

Is there anything you can do to control your trembling? Probably not as much as you would like. The best thing you can do is focus on your message and not your body. Also, plan some purposeful physical activity, like gesturing or moving from behind the lectern to channel your energy. Similarly, pointing out the features of a presentation aid gives your body a positive way to work off some physical tension and, at least momentarily, distracts your attention from your anxiety.

Mind Going Blank. The second-most common specific fear people reported was that they were afraid their minds would go blank: that they would not remember how

Figure 2.3

Specific Public Speaking Fears

Type of Fear	Percent Reporting
Trembling or shaking	80%
Mind going blank	74%
Doing or saying something embarrassing	64%
Unable to continue talking	63%
Not making sense	59%
Sounding foolish	59%

they had planned to say something or what they intended to say next. Back in high school, you might have had to memorize a passage to recite in class—the Gettysburg Address, a scene from Shakespeare, or a poem—and you may have drawn a blank during your performance. It was probably traumatic standing in front of a class full of adolescents who just couldn't wait to tease you about it. Your college classroom audience will be more forgiving, but having your mind go blank is one of the major pitfalls of memorized presentations. It is one of the reasons that we do not recommend memorizing your speeches (see modes of presentation in Chapter 13).

An effective speech is presented extemporaneously—prepared and practiced but not written out and memorized. If you practice your speech using a key-word outline and keep the outline handy as you present your speech, drawing a blank should not be a major problem for you. If after all this, you do experience one of those rare moments when you simply can't remember what to say next, rephrase what you have just said. Audiences expect summaries in speeches, and going back over your material should help get you back on track.

Even if you don't say exactly what you had planned to say exactly as you had planned to say it, the audience won't know it unless you tell them.

Embarrassing Yourself.   Whenever you speak before a group, you are putting yourself in the spotlight. The spotlight is bright and all eyes are on you. One of our students brought home the meaning of being in the spotlight to us. She was a cheerleader at Indiana University. One day she came into our office to ask for advice on controlling her communication anxiety. "You're nervous about speaking to twenty students!" we exclaimed. "Why, every weekend you're out there in front of sixty thousand people in the stadium!" "That's different," she replied. "Out there, I'm not really in the spotlight. Those sixty thousand fans are focused on the game. In this class, the twenty students are focused on me."

What can you possibly do during a speech that would be all that embarrassing? Tremble in front of people?—we've already discussed that. Forget how you planned to say something?—no big deal. Mispronounce big words or technical terms?—look them up ahead of time. Flub a word?—everyone misuses or mispronounces a word from time to time. Save being embarrassed for the truly ludicrous things that might happen in your life, and keep in mind that you will survive even those.

The first class one of your authors ever taught in college was a large lecture class held in a large auditorium. During the first exam, a student asked her to cut off the air conditioners that were making a racket. She shut off the air conditioner on one side of the stage and was walking across to the other side, not looking where she was going, and tripped over the base of the free-standing chalkboard, falling flat on her face in front of 250 students.

Now, that's embarrassing, especially for a first-time teaching assistant. She was praying there'd be a trap door she could fall through, but of course there wasn't. To her amazement, however, no one was laughing. The expressions on the faces she could see were ones of concern. She picked herself up, brushed the dirt off her clothes, and muttered something like, "Grace is my middle name!" The students' looks changed from concern to relief when they realized she wasn't hurt. To her everlasting surprise, the sun rose as usual the next morning. And regardless of how embarrassed she had felt, she had to show up for the next class.

Chances are, nothing like this will happen to you in your public speaking class, but if it does, you will survive it, and you may be even stronger because of it.

Unable to Continue Talking.

Although almost two-thirds of the people in the general population survey mentioned the inability to continue talking as a specific concern, it very rarely happens even to the most anxious of students.

On very, very rare occasions, a student may experience a panic attack. You're going along presenting your speech, everything is going well, when you suddenly feel overwhelmed with fear for no apparent reason. Not only are you afraid, but you also realize that the fear is irrational, and you think perhaps you're "losing it." You really want to drop your notes and bolt for the door.

Don't do it! Decide to weather the storm. Mark Twain once said, "Courage is resistance to fear, mastery of fear, not absence of fear." A panic attack is usually short. It may last only a few seconds (although it may feel as though it's going on forever). Keep talking. Look for the friendliest face in the audience and direct your words to that person. Accept your fear for what it is, a temporary aberration. It will probably never happen again, but if you are worried about it, schedule an appointment with your instructor to discuss it.

Making No Sense and Sounding Foolish.

Most speakers who don't make sense and who sound foolish do so because they have not adequately prepared for their presentations. The remainder of this book is devoted to helping you prepare and present speeches that do make sense and sound intelligent. You will learn how to analyze your listeners and how to adapt your messages to their needs and interests. You will learn how to gain responsible knowledge through research and how to use this material to support your ideas. You will learn how to structure and organize your messages clearly and how to use oral language effectively. All of this information will help ensure that you make sense and don't sound foolish.

On the other hand, if you take your assignments lightly, don't adequately prepare, and don't practice for your presentations, you've earned the right to be anxious and to suffer the consequences.

Negative Consequences.

Anticipating negative results was an important concern of the students who were surveyed but not with the general population group. For students, the negative consequences were typically related to the grade they might receive on the speaking assignment (yet students who insist that they are most concerned about their grade are typically just as anxious when making ungraded presentations). Although grades may seem like a rational cause for concern, worrying about them diverts your focus from what should be your main concern.

If you prepare your speeches solely for the purpose of making a good grade, you are not going to be a very successful speaker. *Your main purpose for speaking must be to communicate something to your audience*—to provide them with new, interesting, or useful information or to convince them to change their ways of thinking or behaving.

Presentation Anxiety

Presentation anxiety is the discomfort you may feel while actually giving a speech. How much anxiety you experience as you present your speech is related to how much anticipatory anxiety you build up ahead of time. If you can keep your pre-speech anxiety under control, you will feel better as you give your speech.

presentation anxiety The fear reactions that occur during the presentation of a speech.

You will probably be most nervous when you first start to speak.[12] Then, as you get used to the situation, you should gain confidence. Research shows that as you get into the presentation of your speech, your nervousness diminishes. Prepare your introduction carefully, and practice it until it flows easily. Keep your focus on what you want to communicate to your audience.

Controlling Communication Anxiety

You've probably heard a lot of advice about how to control your communication apprehension. For example, picture the audience sitting there naked. (Try this and you might be really distracted!) Another pearl of wisdom is to take a really deep breath each time you feel yourself getting anxious. (Do this and you'll hyperventilate.) Or—and this is probably the worst advice we've heard—cut back on your preparation because "in general, the more you prepare, the worse you will do."[13] The people who offer such wisdom mean well, but such quick-fix techniques don't work.

You also may have been told that taking a public speaking class will cure you of your communication apprehension. One of the biggest myths about a public speaking class is that it can or should rid you of your natural fears. *There is no cure for communication anxiety, but there are strategies that can help you keep it under control.*

Research shows that the techniques we discuss in this chapter do help and that they work best when used in combination.[14] Start with one technique and move on to another until you find what works best for you. The techniques that we consider are selective relaxation, attitude adjustment, visualization, and skills training.

Selective Relaxation

A good starting point in learning how to handle your anxiety is to master the art of **selective relaxation**. Begin practicing this technique well before your first speech. Practice relaxing several times a day until it becomes second nature. Follow the sequence outlined here:

1. Find a quiet place where you can be by yourself. Sit in a comfortable chair or lie down, close your eyes, and breathe deeply in through your nose and out through your mouth. You should feel yourself beginning to relax.

2. Once you feel yourself relaxing, begin slowly repeating a selected word, such as *one*, each time you exhale. Let your mind drift freely. You should soon feel quite relaxed.

3. While you are relaxed and breathing deeply, selectively tense and relax different muscle groups. Begin by tensing your feet and legs: curl your toes, tense your arch, tighten your calves, lock your knees, contract your thigh muscles. Hold this tension for several seconds and think about how it feels. Not very comfortable, is it? Even with the tension in the lower part of your body, it's not easy to continue deep breathing.

4. Concentrate on breathing deeply again, repeating your selected word as you exhale and let your muscles relax.

5. Now, repeat steps 1 through 4, moving the focus of tensing and relaxing up your body: first move it to your abdominal muscles, then your hand and arm muscles, and finally your neck and head muscles. After you have done this a number of times, simply repeating your selected word should trigger a relaxation response.

selective relaxation The technique of tightening and relaxing muscles on command, used to help reduce communication anxiety.

InterConnections.
LearnMore 2.2

Top Ten Strategies for Wildly Effective Stress Management
http://cws.unc.edu/content/view/80/0/
> *Counseling and Wellness Web site at the University of North Carolina. Provides excellent suggestions for coping with the stress and strain of college life.*

Perfectionism
www.potsdam.edu/content.php?contentID=7EB90335A0127D15A1DFEF824DE4E2CC
> *Online brochure prepared by the SUNY Potsdam Counseling Center. Discusses the self-defeating nature of excessively high and unrealistic goals.*

Perfectionism: The Double-Edged Sword
http://usfweb2.usf.edu/counsel/b_psy/pdf/Perfectionsim.pdf
> *Developed by the Counseling Center for Human Development at the University of South Florida. Defines perfectionism as a compulsive striving toward unrealistic goals motivated by a fear of failure.*

One good thing about this exercise is that once you have mastered the technique, you can practice it unobtrusively in many situations. While you are sitting in class waiting to speak, tense your feet and leg muscles; then relax them. If you find yourself getting nervous while you are speaking, say your selected word to yourself. The word alone may be enough to help you relax and return your concentration to your message. If this technique doesn't work as well as you would like, try tensing and relaxing a hand as you speak. (Just be sure it's down at your side where it can't be seen.)

Attitude Adjustments

Throughout this chapter, we have stressed the importance of thinking of public speaking as an interactive communication act and not as a performance. Such a change in thinking may require some attitude adjustments.

Communication Orientation. When you adopt a **communication orientation** to public speaking, you concentrate on your message and your audience, not on yourself. Select a topic that is exciting and interesting and that brings new information or a new perspective to the audience, and then concentrate on communicating it effectively to them.

> One of the most communication-apprehensive students we ever taught actually left the room in the middle of her first speech to get a drink of water and try to compose herself. While she was in the hall, we discussed with the class how we as an audience might help her. When she came to our office after the speech, we tried to work with her on focusing on her message and her audience. Her second effort was a little better. She stopped during her presentation to try to "pull herself together," but she managed to finish without leaving the room. Her third speech (persuasive) was a totally different story.
>
> The student worked during the day as a dispatcher for a major interstate trucking firm. She presented a speech urging her classmates to lobby their congressional representatives to vote for a truck safety bill that was pending in

communication orientation Looking at public speaking as an interactive communication event rather than as a performance.

Speaker's Notes 2.2

Techniques for Handling Communication Anxiety

Communication scholars have suggested the following techniques for handling communication apprehension:

1. **Selective relaxation** helps reduce anticipatory anxiety.

2. **A communication orientation** helps you focus on your message.

3. **Cognitive restructuring** changes negative self-messages into positive ones.

4. **Visualization** implants a positive picture of success in your mind.

5. **Skills training** makes you more competent and more confident as a speaker.

Congress. The topic was very important to her. Her speech was filled with interesting examples of near catastrophes that this legislation would make less likely. She knew her topic. She knew it was important. She really cared about it. Consequently, she got so caught up with what she was saying that she forgot to be anxious. The audience was spellbound. When she finished, there was a moment of silence while it all sank in, then spontaneous applause— applause for a speech well given and applause for a speaker who had conquered her personal demons.

Cognitive Restructuring.   Another attitude adjustment involves changing the messages you send to yourself about your public speaking experiences. Psychologists call this **cognitive restructuring**. All of us send messages to ourselves about our behavior. If these messages are positive, they can act as self-fulfilling prophecies that help us function better. Positive messages can boost your self-confidence. When you have faith in yourself, you are better able to withstand criticism from others. Early in her career, Rosie O'Donnell appeared in a talent show. The producer told the other contestants, "She'll never be famous. She's too tough. She's too New York. And, she's too heavy." Rosie's reaction? "He's gonna feel like a jerk when I'm famous!"[15]

On the other hand, if the messages you send yourself are negative, they may invite failure. To practice cognitive restructuring, you must identify the irrational negative messages that you are sending yourself about public speaking and replace them with positive, constructive messages. For example, instead of telling yourself, "I'm going to sound stupid," say, "I've researched this topic and I know what I'm talking about." Replace "Everyone else is more confident than I am" with "I am as confident as anyone in this class." For "I really don't want to give this speech," try "This is my chance to present my ideas."

Right before you speak, summarize these positive messages into a final encouraging pep talk to yourself: "I've worked hard for this moment. I've got a good message, and I'm well prepared to present it. Now it's time to put it across, and I can do it."

Visualization

The Women's World Cup Soccer championship game was tied at the end of play. China and the United States each had five penalty kicks to determine

Star athletes often use visualization as a means of preparing for success.

cognitive restructuring The process of replacing negative thoughts with positive, constructive ones.

the winner. Before one of China's kicks, the camera zoomed in on Briana Scurry, the American goalkeeper. She had a look of intense concentration on her face. The announcer commented, "She's visualizing blocking this next kick."

Professional athletes have long used this technique to improve their performances. You can also control communication anxiety with **visualization**, in which you systematically imagine yourself succeeding as a speaker, and then practice your presentation with that image in mind.[16] To make visualization work best, you must develop a script in which you picture a day of success from the moment you get up through the moment when you enjoy the congratulations of your classmates and instructor for your excellent speech. A sample script is provided in Figure 2.4. Work from this script, changing it to fit your own needs and personality.

Figure 2.4

Sample Visualization Script*

I wake up full of energy and confidence. I look forward to the challenge of doing my best. I put on the right clothes. Dressing well makes me look good and feel good about myself. On the way to give my speech, I remind myself of how much hard work has gone into my preparation. This makes me feel even more confident. Others notice my confidence and comment positively on my appearance and poise. I feel ready to give my speech.

Now I'm in the room where I will present my speech. I chat comfortably with my classmates. They are warm and friendly to me, as always. I feel absolutely sure of my ability to present my speech in a forceful, convincing, and positive manner.

I walk to the front of the room. I feel very good about how this presentation will go. I start my speech. I am really on top of it. I sound like a polished speaker. My classmates nod their heads in agreement. They smile at me. Their feedback tells me I am on target.

My introduction goes the way I planned it. In fact, it works better than I had expected. As I move into the body of my speech, my first main point is really impressive. My evidence supporting it is relevant and striking. The audience understands what I am saying. All my main points are well received. As I near the end of my speech, my concluding remarks put a memorable stamp on what I have said.

When I finish, I know that my speech could not have been better. My introduction worked well, my main points were clear, my evidence was strong, and my conclusion ended the speech with style and flair. In addition, my voice added interest, my pauses punctuated important ideas, and my gestures were purposeful. I answer questions with confidence. I am receiving compliments from my classmates. I feel really pleased with my speech and good about myself. Way to go!

* Adapted from Joe Ayers and Theodore S. Hopf, "Visualization: Is It More Than Extra Attention?" *Communication Education* 38 (1989): 2–3.

visualization   The process of systematically picturing oneself succeeding as a speaker and practicing a speech with that image in mind.

Speaker's Notes 2.3

Ten Ways to Control Communication Apprehension

Apply the following strategies to help control your communication apprehension.

1. Prepare a well-researched and carefully organized message.

2. Practice your presentation until it flows smoothly.

3. Focus on communicating with your audience.

4. Practice selective relaxation.

5. Replace negative, self-defeating statements with positive ones.

6. Visualize yourself being successful.

7. Select a topic that excites you.

8. Master your topic so that you can speak with authority.

9. Act confident even if you don't feel that way initially.

10. Take advantage of other opportunities to speak in public.

To use visualization effectively, start with relaxation exercises and then run your script for success through your mind. Do this several times as you practice your speech, and then again immediately before you present your speech in class.

Skills Training

Think back to a time in your childhood when you acquired a new skill. It might have been learning to swim or to use a computer. The more you learned and the more you practiced, the more confident you became. The more confident you became, the less afraid you were. Before too long, you were jumping into the deep end of the pool without hesitation or finding materials online without asking anyone for help.

The same type of learning relationship exists between knowledge, practice, confidence, and public speaking. When you know how to prepare a speech and have adequately practiced your presentation, you will feel more confident and have less communication anxiety.

Although learning the fundamentals of public speaking through **skills training** is important, it is also important to have responsible knowledge of your subject matter to speak confidently on it. Select a topic you already know something about, and then conduct research to supplement that basic information. Go to the library, use the Internet, and interview a local expert. Then you will be prepared to speak with authority and confidence. (Read more about researching in Chapter 7.)

Keep in mind that practicing is an important part of your preparation. Highly anxious students often spend a lot of time researching and organizing their speeches, but then they don't spend enough time actually practicing their presentations.[17] So practice, and then practice some more. The more you master the presentation of your message, the more confident you will be.

A final word of advice: When you rise to speak, *act confident* even if you don't feel that way. Walk briskly to the front of the room, look at your audience, and establish eye contact. If appropriate to your topic and purpose, smile. Whatever happens during your speech, remember that your listeners cannot see or hear what's happening inside you. They only know what you show and tell them. Show them a controlled speaker presenting a well-researched and well-rehearsed speech. Never start

skills training   Developing speaking abilities that help speakers control communication apprehension.

your speech by telling the audience how frightened you are. When you come to the end of your message, maintain eye contact for a short time, and then walk confidently back to your seat. Even though you may feel relieved that your speech is over, don't say "Whew!" or "I made it!" And never show disappointment with your presentation. You probably did better than you thought.

Do these techniques really work, and is such advice helpful? Research related to communication anxiety has established the following conclusions: (1) *Such techniques do work*, and (2) *they work best in combination*.[18] Controlling anxiety takes time. As you become more experienced at giving speeches and at using the suggestions in Speaker's Notes 2.3, you will find your fears lessening, and you will be able to convert more of your communication anxiety into positive, constructive energy.[19]

In Summary

Communication anxiety bothers many public speakers. It can be especially debilitating to students who think that everyone in the class is more confident than they are. We use the term communication anxiety rather than stage fright because public speaking should be an interactive communication act, not a performance.

Understanding Communication Anxiety.   The symptoms of communication anxiety are more obvious to the person suffering from them than to observers. There is a positive side to communication anxiety: it can energize your presentation. Public speaking can be frightening because it is not an everyday activity and because you usually speak in public only on important occasions. If you suffer from anxiety sensitivity, your fear of fear itself may make the situation worse. If you are a perfectionist, you may put too much pressure on yourself. You may see the audience as predators waiting to make fun of you, but most college student audiences want speakers to be successful. Although you may think everyone can tell

how nervous you are, they usually cannot. You may fear that something dreadful will happen to you, but it rarely happens.

Some of the major fears that make up communication anxiety include worrying about trembling or shaking, having your mind go blank, embarrassing yourself, being unable to continue, not making sense, and sounding foolish. Many of these fears are irrational.

Ways to Control Communication Anxiety.   There are several ways you can reduce the discomfort of communication anxiety. You can practice selective relaxation to reduce bodily tension. You should adopt a communication orientation, keeping your focus on your message. Practice cognitive restructuring to replace negative messages to yourself with positive ones. Develop a visualization script that pictures you succeeding as a speaker. Learn and practice speaking skills so that you develop greater confidence. These techniques usually help, and they work best in combination.

Explore and Apply the Ideas in This Chapter

1. Write down three negative messages you often send yourself, such as "I'm going to forget what I want to say." Restate these messages in more positive ways. For example, the message just quoted could be restated as "My key-word outline will help me keep my place." Share these messages with a small group of your classmates. Were there any similarities among the negative messages? Could your classmates offer you, or could you offer them, any suggestions for improving these restatements?

2. Make a list of all the questionable things you may have tried to control your communication anxiety, such as avoiding eye contact or reading your speech (or even delaying taking the class). In what ways were these efforts self-defeating? Which of the positive techniques we have discussed (selective relaxation, communication orientation, cognitive restructuring, visualization) do you think might work best for you? Why? Share these insights with your classmates.

3. List the three major reasons that you are afraid of making a speech. Try to be precise as you complete the expressions "I'm afraid that . . ." or "I'm afraid because . . ." Go over your list and classify each of these fears as rational or irrational. Now develop a plan to counter them. Try to use selective relaxation, cognitive restructuring, visualization, and speech practice techniques. Which of these techniques proves most and least useful in controlling your fears?

4. Write out your own script for success for the presentation of your first speech in this class. Provide your instructor with a copy, and then use it as you prepare for your presentation.

3

Your First Speech: An Overview of Speech Preparation

This chapter will help you

- prepare and present your first speech
- manage the first impressions you make on others
- develop a speech in which you introduce yourself or a classmate

Without speech there would be no community. . . . Language, taken as a whole, becomes the gateway to a new world.

—*Ernst Cassirer*

Sabrina Karic worried about her first speech. Her instructor had assigned a speech of self-introduction, but Sabrina wondered how she might reach out to her University of Nevada–Las Vegas student audience. Her world and theirs seemed so far apart. She decided finally that she would share her experiences as a six-year-old child who had somehow survived ethnic cleansing in Bosnia and Herzegovina. She described having "to endure endless nights sleeping under the trees while rain poured down on us and mice crawled over our bodies. . . . Nothing," she concluded, "etches itself more in young memory than the pain of hunger." Sabrina ended her speech with a plea for "all the six year olds who experience prejudice and hatred and violence they can't understand." Her warmly received speech appears at the end of this chapter.

Many of you may share Sabrina's concerns when faced with your first speech. You may not think you have anything interesting to say, and you may not feel prepared to speak effectively. Consequently, you may be pleasantly surprised when you not only survive your first speech but actually do some things quite well.

The first speeches in a class can help build a communication climate that nurtures effective speaking and listening. No matter what the exact nature of your assignment, your first speech can serve three useful purposes.

- It gets you speaking early in the course so that you don't build up an unhealthy level of communication apprehension.

- It introduces you to the basic skills needed to develop a speech and present it effectively.

- It can establish you as a credible speaker. In this chapter, we show you how to get off on the right foot by managing the important first impressions you make as a speaker.

Before the opening round of speeches, you and your classmates are usually strangers. These first speeches are often called *icebreakers* because they offer a chance to get acquainted. You may discover that your classmates are interesting human beings. What you learn about them will help you prepare later speeches and give you insights into their knowledge, interests, attitudes, and motivations. Because it is easier to communicate with people you know, you should feel more comfortable about speaking before them.

Much of the information in this chapter is explored in greater detail later in the text. But the basics we cover here are necessary before you present your first speech. You need to know how to

- Find a subject that is right for you.

- Focus your topic so that your speech will serve listeners well.

- Use supporting materials to add interest and substance to your speech.

- Design and outline your speech.

- Develop and practice presentation skills.

This chapter provides an overview of these skills so that you can achieve initial success and then build upon it as you learn more and present other speeches.

Planning Your First Speech

Whatever your first speech assignment may be, the planning, thought, creativity, and excitement of that presentation are all up to you. Right now, standing before the class and saying something sensible may seem like a remote possibility. The challenge may seem large—and the more you think about it, the larger it becomes. Take comfort, however. This challenge can be brought down to size if you take the right steps to reach it. Eventually, you will be standing before your classmates, prepared to present an interesting speech. The stairway to speech success appears in Figure 3.1 and provides a guide to the steps you must take.

To climb this stairway requires some time. You can't delay speech preparation until the night before you must speak. Take the first step well in advance of that day. Schedule your preparation so that you have enough time to climb without skipping or hurrying any of the steps. It is better to devote an hour each day to speech preparation over five days than to cram in five hours of desperate preparation the night before you speak. A speech needs time to jell, and you need time to reflect on it. Your wise investment of time now will pay big dividends later.[1]

Figure 3.1

Stairway to Speech Success

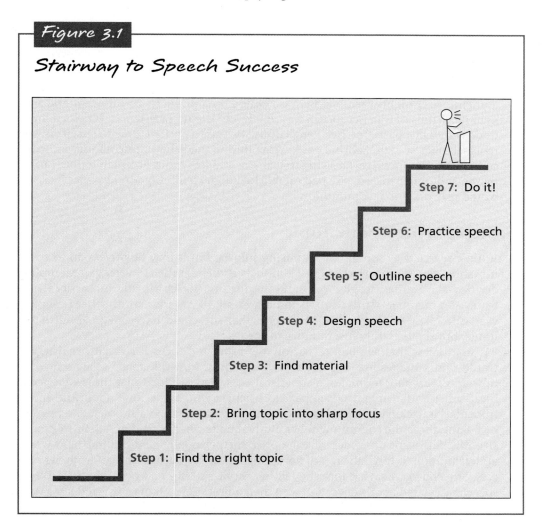

Step 7: Do it!

Step 6: Practice speech

Step 5: Outline speech

Step 4: Design speech

Step 3: Find material

Step 2: Bring topic into sharp focus

Step 1: Find the right topic

Step 1: Find the Right Topic

The nature of the first speech assignment will narrow your search for an appropriate topic. For example, if your teacher asks you to introduce yourself or a classmate, the topic area is predetermined: your personal experience or that of the other person. Or, the assignment may have some other slant that limits the topic possibilities.

Nevertheless, within that narrowed scope of selection, you still have to make important choices. The exact topic you select should be appropriate to you and your listeners. To find this topic, ask yourself

- What am I most interested in?
- What would I hope to accomplish by speaking on this subject?
- Do I know enough or could I learn enough to speak responsibly on this topic?
- Can I make the topic interesting and useful to my audience?
- Can I share ideas or experiences that might enrich my audience's lives?
- Will I be able to present this speech in the time allowed?
- Might this speech help me give future speeches?

Sabrina Karic's first speech, "A Little Chocolate," grew directly out of her experiences as a child living through a terrible conflict. Therefore, her speech seemed authentic and highly credible. Because children continue to be innocent and vulnerable victims of war, her speech was timely and useful for listeners. It helped them understand the basis for her convictions. Because she had timed herself as she rehearsed her speech, Sabrina could relax during the actual presentation and concentrate on her message, knowing that she would be within acceptable time limits. By the end of her speech, she had established high credibility for later speeches she would give on global communication.

Step 2: Focus Your Topic

A topic search may produce a promising subject, but it may be too broad to cover in a short classroom speech. Beth Tidmore, a student at the University of Memphis, decided she wanted to give her self-introductory speech on the university's rifle team. As a member of this team, Beth became an All-American during her freshman year. She knew so much about her sport that she could have talked about it for hours, but she had only five minutes to speak.

Beth knew that she had to narrow her topic and focus it so that her listeners would find it interesting. She might have explained how rifle matches are scored or how an expert shooter makes a successful shot. Beth decided that these were technical subjects that might not appeal to listeners who knew little about the sport. Instead, she decided to talk about how and why she became a shooter. She opened by talking about the commitment her mother made when she bought Beth an expensive rifle. She went on to describe the price she personally paid in time, hard work, and dedication to reach the top of her sport and the satisfaction she got from her success. She ended by saying that she felt her mother's faith had been vindicated. Her speech fascinated her listeners and won their admiration. All of us cheered her as she won the Junior Olympics competition that spring.

Beth's speech illustrates two important principles of focusing a topic:

- *You must have a clear idea of what you want to accomplish given the time available.* Beth wanted to tell us how and why rifle competition had become a central passion in her life.

- *You should be able to state the message of your speech in a single, simple sentence.* Beth's message was that faith and commitment can be justified by hard, determined, and dedicated work.

When you have properly focused your topic, you will be ready to take the next step toward speech success.

Step 3: Find Material for Your Speech

Once you have a topic and a clear idea of what you want to accomplish, you can start gathering material

Your personal experiences can provide examples and narratives for your speech.

to support your ideas and make them come to life. The four basic forms of supporting materials are narratives, examples, testimony, and facts and statistics.

Narratives.   Narratives are stories that illustrate the ideas of a speech. For your first speeches—especially introductory and self-introductory speeches—narratives are very important. They help develop a feeling of closeness between the audience and the speaker. Through the stories they tell, speakers can create desirable impressions of themselves or the classmates they introduce. Stories can make speakers seem more human. They involve the audience in the action, making it a shared adventure.

Beth Tidmore's speech, reprinted in Appendix B, offers an example. Beth opened her speech, "Lady with a Gun," by describing her mother's commitment to her:

I'm sure everybody has had an April Fool's joke played on them. My father's favorite one was to wake me up on April 1st and tell me, "School's been canceled for the day; you don't have to go," and then get all excited and say "April Fool!" . . . Well, on April 1st, 2000, my mother said three words that I was sure weren't an April Fool's joke. She said, "We'll take it." The "it" she was referring to was a brand-new Anschutz 2002 Air Rifle. Now, this is $2,000 worth of equipment for a sport that I'd been in for maybe three months—not long. That was a big deal! It meant that I would be going from a junior-level to an Olympic-grade rifle.

Somebody outside of the sport might think, "Eh, minor upgrade. A gun is a gun, right?" No. Imagine a fifteen-year-old who has been driving a used Toyota and who suddenly gets a brand new Mercedes for her sixteenth birthday. That's how I felt. And as she was writing the check, I completely panicked. I thought, "What if I'm not good enough to justify this rifle? What if I decide to quit and we have to sell it, or we can't sell it? What if I let my parents down and I waste their money?" So later in the car, I said, "Momma, what if I'm not good enough?" She said, "Don't worry about it—it's my money."

Beth's story illustrates excellent narrative technique. Her use of **dialogue**, the actual words exchanged between characters, brings listeners close to the event. They become eavesdroppers to the conversation. Notice that she uses *internal dialogue*, her conversation with herself, as well as *external dialogue*, her conversation with her mother. Beth's narrative also illustrates superb use of analogy as she invites listeners to compare her feelings with those of someone who has just received a Mercedes. The analogy highlights the significance of the gift to her. Finally, notice how well Beth builds suspense: was she able to justify the purchase of such an expensive gift? Her narrative aroused curiosity for the rest of the speech.

Stories should be short and to the point, moving naturally from the beginning to the end. The language of stories should be colorful, concrete, and active. The presentation should be lively and interesting.

After mentioning her successes in national and international competitions, Beth concluded by describing another scene that balanced her opening:

So not long ago, I asked my mother, "How did you know?" She said, "Ah, I just knew." I said, "No, Mom—*really*. How did you know that you weren't going to waste your money?" She got very serious and she took me by the shoulders and she squared me up. She looked me right in the eye and she said, "When you picked up that gun, you just looked like you belonged together. I knew there was a sparkle in your eye, and I knew that you were meant to do great things with that rifle."

Beth Tidmore's narratives helped listeners relate to her topic.

Examples. Examples illustrate points, clarify uncertainty, and make events seem authentic. When listeners ask, "Can you give me an example?" they seek clarification and reassurance. An example says, in effect, "This really happened." It takes an idea out of the abstract and places it firmly in the concrete. To illustrate her abstract argument that it is good business to serve the needs of disabled people, Karen Lovelace described a group called Opening Doors, which encourages companies to improve travel for the disabled:

One hotel chain that has used this program is Embassy Suites. Their staff is taught by Opening Doors to problem-solve based on guests' needs. And you'd better believe that the word gets around to disabled travelers!

This example made her claim seem well-grounded.

dialogue Having the characters in a narrative speak for themselves, rather than paraphrasing what they say.

To demonstrate how much she loved reading, student Erin Evans introduced a number of brief examples: "In high school, the classics came into my life. I loved *The Great Gatsby, Medea,* and then my senior year I met a real challenge—Dostoyevsky. It took me more than two months to get through *Crime and Punishment*—a long but rewarding journey!"

Whether you are piling up a number of brief examples or developing one example in detail, remember their function: *they help listeners grasp your point.* As with stories, you should use colorful, concrete, and active language in your examples.

Testimony.   Testimony offered by experts or other respected people can add authority to your speech. When you quote the words of others, you call those whom you have quoted as *witnesses* to support a point. As she developed her speech supporting better service for the disabled, Karen Lovelace cited Sandy Blondino, director of sales at Embassy Suites Hotels, who confirmed that the hospitality industry is now more receptive to disabled travelers. She concluded with Ms. Blondino's exact words: "But that's just hospitality, right?" She followed up this *expert testimony* with *prestige testimony* by quoting former President Clinton: "When I injured my knee and used a wheelchair for a short time, I understood even more deeply that the ADA isn't just a good law, it's the right thing to do."

When you quote expert testimony, be sure to mention the expert's credentials, including when and where she or he made the statement you are quoting.

Facts and Statistics.   Facts and statistics help turn assertions into well-documented arguments. To support her idea that American business has a legal as well as a moral obligation to reach out to disabled persons, Karen Lovelace offered factual information from the Americans with Disabilities Act:

> The ADA said that "privately owned businesses that serve the public such as restaurants, hotels, retail stores, taxicabs, theaters, concert halls, and sports facilities are prohibited from discriminating against individuals with disabilities." The ADA went on to say that "companies have an ongoing responsibility to remove barriers to access for peoples with disabilities."

Prestige testimony can be very effective when the speaker has personal experiences to relate.

Karen strengthened her call for reform by adding statistical support showing the percentage of American businesses that remain out of compliance with the act and demonstrating how that percentage has changed very little over the past decade.

Similarly, to support her point that Native Americans are victims of social injustice, Ashley Roberson used an array of statistical comparisons:

> Did you know that Indians have one of the lowest life expectancies of any population living in this hemisphere, second only to those living in Haiti? And did you know that the suicide rate among American Indians is seventy percent higher than that of the general U.S. population? Or, did you know that in 1999, Indians suffered

124 violent crimes for every 100,000 people—two and a half times the national average?

The effective use of facts and statistics helps convince listeners that you know what you are talking about and that you didn't just make something up. To find such supporting materials, you will have to invest some time in the library or make careful use of the Internet.

As you do this research, be sure to record *who* said something, *where* it was said, and *when* it was said. In your speech, use this material to support your claims. For example, Ashley's facts and statistics would have been more effective if she had introduced them with the following statement: "According to a Princeton research survey reported in the *Washington Post* of March 15, 2004, Native Americans are our most abused Americans."

Taken as a whole, stories, examples, testimony, and facts and statistics provide the substance that makes listeners take a speech seriously.

Step 4: Design Your Speech

Your speech should have a design or plan that arranges your material in an orderly fashion. Your ideas should fit together in a way that is easy for your listeners to follow and understand. Three designs often used in first speeches are categorical, cause-effect, and narrative.

Categorical Design.   The categorical design develops a subject according to its natural or customary divisions. Martha Larson introduced herself by explaining how she was shaped by the neighborhood where she grew up. She began with the *setting*, a description of a street scene in which she captured sights, sounds, and smells: "I can always tell a Swedish neighborhood by the smell of *lutefisk* on Friday afternoons." Next she described the *people*, focusing on a certain neighbor who influenced her. This man, the local grocer, "loved America with a passion, helped those in need, and always voted stubbornly for the Socialist Party." Finally, she talked about the *street games* she played as a child and what they taught her about people and herself. These "setting-people-games" categories structured her speech in an orderly manner.

Martha's speech also demonstrates how the introduction, body, and conclusion of a speech should work together. Her introduction, in which she aroused interest and set the mood for what would follow, was the opening street scene. In the body

Speaker's Notes 3.1

How to Develop Your First Speech

Consider the following ways to develop your first speech:

1. Tell stories that carry your message.

2. Give examples that clarify your points.

3. Cite experts or highly respected people who support your point of view.

4. Present facts and statistics that make your ideas credible.

of her speech, she elaborated her points by describing the people of her neighborhood and the childhood games that exemplified the lessons of sharing. Her conclusion clarified her message:

> I hope you have enjoyed this "tour" of my neighborhood, this "tour" of my past. If you drove down this street tomorrow, you might think it was just another crowded, gray, urban neighborhood. But for me it is filled with memories of colorful people who cared for each other and who dreamed great dreams of a better tomorrow. That street runs right down the center of my life.

Cause-Effect Design.   Should you decide to tell about something that had a great impact on you, a cause-effect design might be most appropriate. This design helps you explain how something came about. Maria One Feather, a Native American student speaker, used such a design in her speech "Growing Up Red—and Feeling Blue—in White America." She treated the condition of her background as the cause and its impact on her life as the effect.

Narrative Design.   The narrative design structures your speech by developing a story from beginning to end. It focuses on a sequence of scenes in which characters interact. The introduction, body, and conclusion all become part of the story.

Beth Tidmore's dramatic story of her rise as a competitive shooter began with the story of her mother's commitment to her, described her personal pursuit of excellence, developed a sketch of her success in rifle competitions, and concluded with a tribute to her mother's faith. The message of her speech emerged with the developing story as Beth celebrated the values of commitment, dedication, discipline, achievement, and family love.

These and other designs to develop your speeches are discussed in detail in Chapters 9, 14, 16, and 17.

More on Introductions, Bodies, and Conclusions.   In addition to arousing interest and preparing listeners for the rest of the speech, your introduction should build a good relationship between you and your audience. The best introductions are framed *after* the body of the speech has been planned—after all, it is difficult to draw a map if you don't yet know where you are going.

 **Speaker's Notes** 3.2

Ways to Structure Your First Speech

As you design your first speech, keep in mind the following options:

1. Use a categorical design that divides a subject into natural or traditional parts.

2. Use a cause-effect design that pictures a subject either as the cause of an effect or as the effect of a cause.

3. Use a narrative design that moves from scene to scene as it tells a story.

4. Be sure that you have an effective introduction, body, and conclusion.

The body of the speech is where you satisfy the curiosity aroused in your introduction. The body includes the main points, the most important ideas in your message. In a cause-effect design, the body consists of two main points: the explanation of a cause of some condition and the elaboration of its effect. In a categorical design, the body develops two or three major divisions of the subject. You won't have time to cover more than that. In our earlier example of a Swedish neighborhood, the division into setting, people, and games establishes the main points of the speech. In a narrative design, the body develops the major scenes necessary to carry the story.

The conclusion summarizes your main points and ends with reflections on the meaning of the speech. Good conclusions are easily remembered—even eloquent. Sometimes they quote well-known people who state the point very well. They may tie back to the introduction, completing a symbolic circle in a way that the audience finds satisfying. You will find more on developing introductions, bodies, and conclusions in Chapter 9.

Transitions. As you design your speech, you should also be planning **transitions**. Transitions help you move from one point to another. They are bridging devices, such as "having explained the cause, I will now discuss the effect," or "let's now consider another part of this problem," or "let me tell you what happened after I warned him." Transitions also may be used to remind listeners of the point you have just made or to preview what is going to happen next in the speech. Oral connectives like *first, second,* and *finally* can also work as transitions.

Transitions can sometimes be quite artful. To connect the major section of her speech, "Family Gifts" (see Appendix B), Marie D'Aniello focused on certain key words. *Strength* cues her to the fortitude represented by her mother. *Glory* begins her narrative concerning her brother's athletic accomplishments. *Pride* cues her discussion of her father's character and determination. These key words link the themes of her speech together.

Step 5: Outline Your Speech

Preparing an outline allows you to put your design down on paper so that you can see more clearly how it will work. The outline should contain your introduction; the message you want to get across; the body of your speech, including your main ideas and their subpoints; and your conclusion.

Full outlines help you during speech preparation, but you should not use them during presentation. During your presentation, the outline should be imprinted not on paper but—for the most part—in your mind. We cover more about outlining in Chapter 10.

In the following outline for a self-introductory speech, several critical parts—the introduction, message, and conclusion—are written out word for word. The introduction, message, and conclusion set up the meaning of your presentation and make your entrance into and exit from the speech smooth and graceful. Therefore, it is important to plan these parts of your presentation carefully, even

transitions   Connecting elements used in speeches.

though you may need to make changes while speaking to adjust to the immediate situation. To encourage spontaneity, do not try to write the body of the speech word-for-word.

"Free at Last"

Rod Nishikawa

Introduction

Attention-Arousing and Orienting Material: Three years ago I presented the valedictory speech at my high school graduation. As I concluded, I borrowed a line from Dr. Martin Luther King's "I Have a Dream" speech: "Free at last, free at last, thank God almighty we're free at last!" The words had a joyful, humorous place in that speech, but for me personally, they were a lie.

Message: I was not yet free and would not be free until I had conquered an ancient enemy, both outside me and within me—that enemy was racial prejudice.

Rod's three main points are each supported with facts, examples, or narratives. The outline uses Roman numerals to indicate main points, capital letters to indicate subpoints, and Arabic numbers to indicate sub-subpoints. These numerals and letters are indented appropriately to show their relative importance in the structure of the speech.

Body

I. When I was eight years old I was exposed to anti-Japanese prejudice.

    A. I was a "Jap" who didn't belong in America.

    B. The bully's words burned into my soul.

       1. I was ashamed of my heritage.

       2. I hated having to live in this country.

[Transition: So I obviously needed some help.]

II. My parents helped me put this experience in perspective.

    A. They survived terrible prejudice in their youth during World War II.

    B. They taught me to accept the reality of prejudice.

    C. They taught me the meaning of *gaman:* how to bear the burden within and not show anger.

[Transition: Now, how has *gaman* helped me?]

III. Practicing *gaman* has helped me develop inner strength.

    A. I rarely experience fear or anger.

    B. I have learned to accept myself.

    C. I have learned to be proud of my heritage.

Conclusion

Summary Statement: Practicing *gaman*, a gift from my Japanese roots, has helped me conquer prejudice.

Concluding Remarks: Although my Japanese ancestors might not have spoken as boldly as I have today, I am basically an American, which makes me a little outspoken. Therefore, I can talk to you about racial prejudice and of what it has meant to my life. And because I can talk about it, and share it with you, I am finally, truly "free at last."

Step 6: Practice Your Presentation

You are almost there. After you have developed and outlined your first speech, you are ready to practice your presentation. *An effective presentation spotlights the ideas, not the speaker. It should sound as though you are talking with the audience, not reading to them or reciting from memory.*

Spotlight the Ideas.   The presentation of a speech is the climax of planning and preparation—the time you have earned to stand in the spotlight. Although presentation is important, it should not overshadow the substance of the speech. Have you ever heard this kind of exchange?

> "She's a wonderful speaker—what a beautiful voice, what eloquent diction, what a smooth delivery!"
> "What did she say?"
> "I don't remember, but she sure sounded good!"

As you practice speaking from your outline, and when you present your speech, concentrate on the ideas you have to offer. *You should have a vivid realization of these ideas during your actual presentation.*[2] Your thoughts should come alive as you speak.

Speak Naturally.   An effective presentation, we noted in Chapter 1, preserves many of the best qualities of conversation. It sounds natural and spontaneous yet has a depth, coherence, and quality not normally found in conversation. The best way to approach the ideal of improved conversation is to present your speech extemporaneously. An **extemporaneous presentation** is carefully prepared and practiced but not written out or memorized. If you write out your speech, you will be tempted either to memorize it or read it to your audience. Reading or memorizing almost always results in a stilted presentation. DO NOT READ YOUR SPEECH! Always keep in mind that *audience contact is more important than exact wording.* The only parts of a speech that might be memorized are the introduction, message, conclusion, plus a few other critical phrases, such as the wording of main points or the punch lines of humorous stories.

Prepare a Key-Word Outline.   If you think you might need a cue-sheet during your presentation, use a **key-word outline**, an abbreviated version of your full-sentence outline. You should use the key-word outline as you practice your speech. Using the key-word outline will help you sound more conversational and spontaneous. *Never use your full outline as you present your speech.* You will lapse into reading if you do.

As its name suggests, the key-word outline contains only words that will prompt your memory. It can also contain presentation cues, such as *pause* or *talk slowly.* Although the full outline may require a page or more to complete, the key-word outline should fit on a single sheet of paper or on one or two index cards. To prepare it, go through your full-sentence outline and highlight the key-words in each section. Transfer them to a sheet of paper or index cards to use as prompts as you speak. The following key-word outline is based on the outline presented earlier.

---

extemporaneous presentation   A form of presentation in which a speech, although carefully prepared and practiced, is not written out or memorized.

key-word outline   An abbreviated version of a formal outline that may be used in presenting a speech.

"Free at Last"

Introduction

"Free at last"—high school valedictory speech

Not free—enemy outside and within was racial prejudice

Body

I. Encounter with bully

    A. "Jap," didn't belong [*Mime bully*]

    B. Words burned in soul

        1. Ashamed of heritage

        2. Hated living in America [*Pause, smile*]

II. Parents help

    A. Survived much worse

    B. Taught me to accept reality

    C. Taught me *GAMAN* [*Pause and write word on board*]

III. *Gaman*—inner strength

    A. No fear or anger [*Stress*]

    B. Accepted self

    C. Proud of heritage [*Pause*]

Conclusion

Gaman from my Japanese roots helps conquer prejudice. Also an American. Can talk about it: therefore, "free at last"

Note that Rod's key-word out-line reminds him not only of the flow of ideas but also of his presentation plan. It is the "game plan" of his speech.

Rehearse Your Speech.   Speech classrooms often have a speaker's lectern mounted on a table at the front of the room. Lecterns can seem very formal and can create a barrier between you and listeners. If you are short, you might almost disappear behind a lectern. If your gestures are hidden from view, your message may lose much of the power that body language adds to a speech. For these reasons, you may wish to speak either to the side or in front of the lectern.

If you plan to use the lectern, place your key-word outline high on its slanted surface so that you can see your notes easily without having to lower your head. This will help you maintain eye contact with your listeners. Print your key-word outline in large letters. If you decide to hold your outline and note cards, don't try to hide them or look embarrassed if you need to refer to them. Most listeners probably won't even notice when you use them. Remember, your audience is far more interested in what you are saying than in any awkwardness you may feel.

Imagine your audience in front of you as you practice. Start with your full outline; then move to your key-word outline as the ideas become imprinted in your mind. Maintain eye contact with your imaginary listeners, just as you will during the actual presentation. Look around the room so that everyone feels included in your message. Be enthusiastic! Let your voice suggest confidence. Avoid speaking in a monotone, which never changes pace or pitch; instead, strive for variety and color

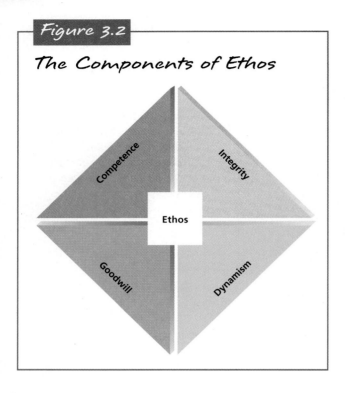

Figure 3.2

The Components of Ethos

in your vocal presentation. Pause to let important ideas sink in. Let your face, body, and voice respond to your ideas as you speak them.

Step 7: Step Up and Do It!

It's your moment to speak. You've earned it. Now enjoy it with your listeners.

Managing the Impressions You Make

As you step to the lectern to speak, your listeners begin to form impressions of you that will influence how they respond to your speeches. Aristotle called these impressions **ethos**. A person with high ethos will be listened to with respect; therefore, ethos also is a key ingredient in leadership. You can build your ethos by helping listeners form favorable impressions of your competence, integrity, goodwill, and dynamism. In this section, we explore each of these components, including ways you can encourage favorable impressions.

Competence

Competent speakers seem informed, intelligent, and well prepared. You can build a perception of **competence** by selecting topics that you already know something about and by doing the research necessary to qualify yourself as a responsible speaker. You can further enhance your competence by quoting experts and citing authorities who support your position. For example, if you are speaking on the link between nutrition and heart disease, you might quote a prominent medical specialist or a publication of the American Heart Association. One student introduced testimony into her speech in this way: "Dr. Milas Peterson heads the Heart Institute at Harvard University. During his visit to our campus last week, I spoke with him about this idea. He told me...." Note the competence-related elements in this example:

- The speaker specifies the qualifications of the expert.
- The testimony is recent.
- The connection between the expert and the speaker is direct.
- The speaker shows that she has prepared carefully for the speech.

When you cite authorities in this way, you are "borrowing" their ethos to enhance your own. Such borrowed ethos enhances but does not replace your own. Personal experience in the form of stories or examples also helps a speech seem authentic, brings it to life, and makes you appear more competent. "Been there, done that" can be a very effective strategy. Your competence is further enhanced if your speech is well organized, if you use language correctly, and if you make a polished presentation.

---

ethos   Those characteristics that make a speaker appear honest, credible, powerful, and appealing.

Competence   The perception of a speaker as being informed, intelligent, and well prepared.

Integrity

A speaker with **integrity** comes across as ethical and dependable. Listeners are more receptive when speakers are straightforward and concerned about the consequences of their words. You can encourage perceptions of integrity by presenting all sides of an issue and then explaining why you have chosen your position. You should also show that you are willing to follow your own advice. For example, in a speech that calls for commitment to action, it should be clear that you are not asking more of listeners than you would of yourself. The more you ask of the audience, the more important your integrity becomes.

How can you build a reputation for integrity? One of our students, Mona Goldberg, was preparing a speech on welfare reform. The more she learned about the subject, the more convinced she became that budget cuts for welfare programs were unwise. In her speech, Mona showed that she took her assignment seriously by citing many authorities and statistics. She reviewed arguments both for and against cutting the budget and then showed her audience why she was against reducing aid to such programs. Finally, Mona revealed that her own family had had to live on unemployment benefits at one time. "I know the hurt, the loss of pride, the sense of growing frustration. I didn't have to see them on the evening news." Her openness showed that she was willing to trust her listeners to react fairly to this sensitive information. The audience responded in kind by trusting her and what she had to say. She had built an impression of herself as a person of integrity.

Goodwill

People of **goodwill** seem to have our interests at heart. They are not self-centered; rather, they think and act in terms of what is good for the group or community to which they belong. We like such people and enjoy their company, perhaps because we feel that they like and enjoy us.

Audiences are more willing to accept ideas and suggestions from speakers who radiate goodwill.[6] A smile and direct eye contact can signal listeners that you want to communicate. Sharing your feelings as well as your thoughts conveys the same message. Speakers with goodwill also enjoy laughter at appropriate moments, especially laughter directed at themselves. Being able to talk openly and engagingly about your mistakes can make you seem more human and appealing as well as more confident.

The more speakers seem to be people of goodwill, the more audiences want to identify with them.[7] **Identification** is the feeling of sharing or closeness that can develop between speakers and listeners. It typically occurs when you believe someone is like you—that you have the same outlook on life or that you share similar backgrounds or values. Identification is more difficult to establish when the speaker and listener have different cultural backgrounds. In such situations, speakers can invite identification by telling stories or by using examples that help listeners focus on the experiences or

The character and personality of a speaker can influence how well a message is received. Likeableness is an important component of speaker ethos.

---

integrity   The quality of being ethical, honest, and dependable.

goodwill   The dimension of ethos by which listeners perceive a speaker as having their best interests at heart.

identification   The feeling of sharing or closeness that can develop between speakers and listeners.

Ethics *Alert! 3.1*

The Ethics of Ethos

Speakers can create false impressions of themselves to further their ends. When these deceptions are discovered, the speakers lose the trust of listeners. To build your ethos in ethical ways, follow these guidelines:

1. Do enough research to speak responsibly.

2. Be sensitive to the impact of your words on others.

3. Present all sides of an issue fairly before explaining your position.

4. Be honest about where you stand on your topic.

5. Acknowledge differences between your own beliefs, values, and attitudes and those that some of your listeners may hold.

6. Show how these differences might be bridged.

7. Demonstrate that you are willing to follow your own advice.

8. Trust your listeners if you would have them trust you.

beliefs that they share. Even though she was speaking before a class that included students from all sections of the United States, Marie D'Aniello encouraged identification in her self-introductory speech by developing a theme everyone could share—family pride. At one moment in her speech, Marie pointed out how she had drawn inspiration from her brother's athletic accomplishments:

You should dress nicely when you present your speech as a sign of respect for your listeners and your assignment.

> When I think of glory, I think of my brother Chris. I'll never forget his championship basketball game. It's the typical buzzer beater story: five seconds to go, down by one, Chris gets the ball and he drives down the court, he shoots, he scores! . . . I'll never forget the headline, "D'Aniello saves the game!" D'Aniello, hey wait, that's me. I'm a D'Aniello. I could do this too. Maybe I can't play basketball like Chris, but I can do other things well.

After this speech, which appears in Appendix B, it was hard not to like Marie. This aura of goodwill, combined with other favorable impressions of her competence, integrity, and dynamism, created respect for her point of view.

Goodwill and identification can also be enhanced by moments of shared laughter. For example, Marcos White, a point guard for the University of New Mexico basketball team, endeared himself to listeners during his first speech. Marcos introduced himself as the son of an African American father and a Mexican mother: "I guess," he said, "that makes me a Blaxican."

Audiences often identify with speakers who talk or dress the way they do. They prefer speakers who use gestures, language, and facial expressions that are natural and unaffected. However, you should speak a little more formally than you might in everyday conversation. Similarly, you should dress nicely but not extravagantly for your speech.

Dynamism

James Norton, who introduced his classmate Rosamond Wolford, confessed that he was nervous before he gave his speech. He was not sure how it would be received, and he worried that he might make a mistake. But when James stood to speak, he seemed confident, decisive, and enthusiastic. In short, he exhibited **dynamism**—the perception that a person is energetic, enthusiastic, and in control of the situation. Whatever he might have secretly felt, his audience responded only to what they saw—his commanding presence.

At first you may not feel confident about public speaking, but you should act as though you are. If you appear self-assured, listeners will respond as though you are, and you may find yourself becoming what you seem to be. In other words, you can trick yourself into developing a very desirable trait! When you appear to be in control, you also put listeners at ease. This feeling comes back to you as positive feedback and further reinforces your confidence.

One of our students, John Scipio, was at first intimidated by the public speaking situation, but John was blessed with two natural virtues: he was a large, imposing person and he had a powerful voice. And then he found a subject he truly believed in. When John presented his classroom tribute to the final speech of Dr. Martin Luther King, Jr., he radiated dynamism, in addition to competence, goodwill, and integrity:

> When I asked him during a telephone interview why he thought Dr. King was such an effective leader, Ralph Abernathy said, "He possessed a power never before seen in a man of color." What was this power that he spoke of? It was the power to persuade audiences and change opinions with his words. It was the power of speech. In his speech, Dr. King had to give his people hope and motivate them to go on. He spoke to all of us, but especially to those of us in the Black community, when he said, "Only when it is dark enough can you see the stars." And when he talked of standing up to the fire hoses in Birmingham, he said, "There's a certain kind of fire that no water can put out."
>
> And on the last night of his life, with less than twenty-four hours to live, he was still thinking—not of himself, but of our nation: "Let us move on," he said, "in these powerful days, these days of challenge, to make America what it ought to be."

To appear dynamic, you must also be decisive. In persuasive speeches, you should cover the important options available to your audience, but by the end of the speech there should be no doubt as to where you stand and why. Your commitment to your position must be strong.

Finally, you gain dynamism from the enthusiasm you bring to your speech. Your face, voice, and gestures should indicate that you care about your subject and about the audience. Your enthusiasm endorses your message. We discuss more specific ways of projecting confidence, decisiveness, and enthusiasm in Chapter 13.

dynamism The perception of a speaker as confident, decisive, and enthusiastic.

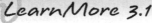

InterConnections.
LearnMore 3.1

Ethos

Ethos (Ethical Proofs)
www.lcc.gatech.edu/gallery/rhetoric/terms/ethos.html

Highly readable discussion of ethos as one of the three major sources of persuasion, prepared by Yasmin Hussain of the Georgia Institute of Technology.

Online Lesson: Ethos (Credibility)
http://jan.ucc.nau.edu/;sc315-c/class/sales/ethos/lesson3-1-2.html

Interactive lecture on ethos in sales persuasion, prepared by Kurt Billmeyer of Northern Arizona University.

Establishing Ethos Online
http://lor.trincoll.edu/;writcent/warriner.html

An interesting article, "Email Debate and the Importance of Ethos," on developing ethos in online interactions, prepared by Professor Allison Warriner, Department of English, California State University, Hayward, as part of the Electronic Democracy Project.

Introducing Yourself or a Classmate: An Application

One frequently used first speech assignment is to introduce yourself or a classmate. The speech of introduction helps warm the classroom atmosphere, creates a sense of community, and provides an opportunity for the speaker to build ethos.

The self-introductory assignment also has practical applications beyond the classroom. In later life, you may be called on to introduce yourself or an organization to which you belong. Typically, this introduction will be part of a longer speech. When he spoke to the Democratic National Convention in 2004, Barack Obama, then candidate for the U.S. Senate from Illinois, introduced himself as "a skinny kid with a funny name who believes that America has a place for him, too."[5] In the process, he established his potential for future national leadership. When the commandant of the Coast Guard spoke before the National Press Club, he introduced that branch of the military in order "to raise the visibility of . . . current and future Coast Guard service to America."[6]

A classroom speech of introduction is usually short. Since there is no way to tell an entire life story in a brief speech, you have to be selective. However, you should avoid simply reciting a few superficial facts, such as where you went to high school or what your major is. Such information reveals little about a person and is usually not very interesting. One tried-and-true way to introduce yourself or others is to answer this question: *What is the one thing that best describes me or the other person as a unique individual?* You can then develop around the answer an effective speech that builds positive ethos.

To help stimulate your creativity, conduct a **self-awareness inventory** in which you consider the following possibilities:

1. *Is your cultural background the most important thing about you?* How has it shaped you? How can you explain this influence to others? In her self-introductory speech, reprinted in Appendix B, Sandra Baltz described herself as a unique product of three cultures. She felt that this rich cultural background had widened her

self-awareness inventory   A series of questions that a speaker can ask to develop an approach to a speech of introduction.

horizons. Note how she focused on food to represent the convergence of these different ways of life:

> In all, I must say that being exposed to three very different cultures—Latin, Arabic, American—has been rewarding for me and has made a difference even in the music I enjoy and the food I eat. It is not unusual in my house to sit down to a meal made up of stuffed grape leaves and refried beans and all topped off with apple pie for dessert.

2. *Is the most important thing about you the environment in which you grew up?* How were you shaped by it? What stories or examples illustrate this influence? How do you feel about its effect on your life? Are you pleased by it, or do you feel that it limited you? If the latter, what new horizons would you like to explore? In his self-introductory speech, "My Life as a River Rat," Jimmy Green concluded by saying:

> To share my world, come up to the Tennessee River some fall afternoon. We'll take a boat ride north to New Johnsonville, where Civil War gunboats still lie on the bottom of the river, and you will see how the sun makes the water sparkle. You will see the green hills sloping down to the river, and the rocky walls, and I will tell you some Indian legends about them. Then, we'll "bump the bottom" fishing for catfish, just drifting with the current. And if we're lucky, we might see a doe and her fawn along the shoreline, or perhaps some great blue herons or an eagle overhead.

Jimmy's words conveyed his feelings about his childhood home without his having to tell us about them.

3. *Was there some particular person—a friend, relative, or childhood hero—who had a major impact on your life?* Why do you think this person had such influence? Often you will find that some particular person was a great inspiration to you. Here is a chance to share that inspiration, honor that person, and in the process, tell us much about you. In his speech before the Democratic Convention, Barack Obama paid tribute to his unique family and to their faith in American values:

> Tonight is a particular honor for me because, let's face it, my presence on this stage is pretty unlikely. My father was a foreign student, born and raised in a small village in Kenya. He grew up herding goats, went to school in a tin-roof shack. His father, my grandfather, was a cook, a domestic servant.
>
> But my grandfather had larger dreams for his son. Through hard work and perseverance my father got a scholarship to study in a magical place, America, which stood as a beacon of freedom and opportunity to so many who had come before. While studying here, my father met my mother. She was born in a town on the other side of the world, in Kansas. Her father worked on oil rigs and farms through most of the Depression. The day after Pearl Harbor he signed up for duty, joined Patton's army and marched across Europe. Back home, my grandmother raised their baby and went to work on a bomber assembly line. . . .
>
> And they, too, had big dreams for their daughter, a common dream, born of two continents. My parents shared not only an improbable love; they shared an abiding faith in the possibilities of this nation. They would give me an African name, Barack, or "blessed," believing that in a tolerant America your name is no barrier to success. . . . They are both passed away now. Yet, I know that, on this night, they look down on me with pride.

I stand here today, grateful for the diversity of my heritage. . . . I stand here knowing that my story is part of the larger American story, that I owe a debt to all of those who came before me, and that, in no other country on earth, is my story even possible.[7]

4. *Have you been marked by some unusual experience?* What was it? Why was it important? How did it affect you? What does this experience tell us about you as a person? The speech at the end of this chapter emphasizes the power of personal experience in shaping lives. Sabrina Karic tells how she survived the brutal ordeal of ethnic cleansing as a child. Her experiences have made her appreciate the small things in life that many of us may take for granted—things like a chocolate bar.

Ashley Smith, whose speech appears in Appendix B, decided to speak on her experiences as an exchange student in Costa Rica and Botswana. After she told stories to illustrate how peoples' lives were controlled and limited in those countries, Ashley confided that her travel experiences had made her want to return as an educator:

I want to teach people to succeed on their merits despite the social and economic inequalities that they're faced with. And I want to learn from them as well. I want to teach the boy who never mastered welding that he could own the factory. And I want him to teach me how to use a rice cooker. I want to teach the girl who is exhausted each afternoon after walking to the river with a jar on her head to gather water that she could design an irrigation system. But I also want her to teach me how to weave a thatched roof. I want to travel and teach and learn.

5. *Are you best characterized by an activity that brings meaning to your life?* Remember, what is important is not the activity itself but how and why it affects you. The person being introduced must remain the focus of the speech. When you finish, the audience should have an interesting picture of you. When she conducted her self-awareness inventory, Laura Haskins realized that her entire life was best described as one frenetic activity. As she considered what it took to meet the demands of her family, home, work, and her university classes, she discovered a very apt image that became the central theme of her self-introductory speech:

Come one, come all, see the great juggler! See her juggle family, home, work, college, whatever comes her way. I wasn't always this good. My juggling act began when I enrolled in nursing school. My children were preschoolers then, and I had to learn fast. . . .

Experience has taught me to plan, prioritize, adapt, and pass off to my assistant, my husband, without missing a beat. Right now the International Jugglers Association is reviewing my application for membership. I'm a shoo-in, because I'm a magnificent juggler.

6. *Is the work you do a major factor in making you who you are?* If you select this approach, focus on how your job has shaped you rather than simply describing what you do. What have you learned from your work that has changed you or made you feel differently about others? Richard Bushart was quite a spectacle as he stood to present his self-introductory speech, wearing a big red nose, a coat with a floppy bow tie, and a yellow wig that spiked in all directions. Actually, it was his work outfit—Richard was a clown! But those who were expecting a trivial or lighthearted speech were in for a surprise: Richard wanted to talk about how being a clown had admitted him into the wise and wonderful world of children.

An adult will think I'm foolish, weird, or just insane. But to a child I'm funny, caring, and a friend. Children have taught me so much. . . . They have inspired me to dream again and be creative. A child playing in the backyard can take a broom and turn it one way and it's a horse waiting to ride. Turn it another way, and it's a hockey stick. Turn it still another, and it becomes a telescope that can see the universe.

Richard's work had taught him "never to lose that childlike heart no matter how old I get."

7. *Are you best characterized by your goals or purpose in life?* Listeners are usually fascinated by those whose lives are dedicated to some purpose. If you choose to describe some personal goal, be sure to emphasize why you have it and how it affects you. Tom McDonald had returned to school after dropping out for eleven years. In his self-introductory speech, he described his goal:

Finishing college means a lot to me now. The first time I enrolled, right out of high school, I "blew it." All I cared about was sports, girls, and partying. Even though I have a responsible job that pays well, I feel bad about not having a degree. My wife's diploma hangs on our den wall. All I have hanging there is a stuffed duck!

As he spoke, many of the younger students began to identify with Tom; they saw a similarity between what caused him to drop out of school and their own feelings at times. Although he wasn't "preachy," Tom's description of the rigors of working forty hours a week and carrying nine hours a semester in night school carried a clear message.

8. *Are you best described by a value that you hold dear?* How did it come to have such meaning for you? Why is it important to you? Values are abstract, so you must rely on concrete applications to make them meaningful to others. As she described her commitment to the value of justice, Valessa Johnson also established her goal, to become an attorney, and paid tribute to her personal role model:

If you go down to 201 Poplar at nine o'clock in the morning on any weekday, you will find yourself faced with hundreds of individuals and their quest for justice. Many of these will be convicted, and rightly so. Unfortunately, while they're incarcerated, the illiterate and unlearned will remain so, as will the unskilled and the uncrafted. Who's going to stand for these so that they have an alternative to standing in the revolving doors of the criminal justice complex? Or better yet, how about those who are truly innocent? Oh yes, that's right, not everyone in the court system, not everyone institutionalized, is guilty. Who is going to stand for these? I will.

You know, we were once blessed with a true advocate for justice, attorney Barbara Jordan. She fought a long, hard battle to ensure that we all abided by the constitutional creed "All men are created equal" and "justice for all." Someone has to continue to beat the path of justice for all men. That includes black men, white men, yellow men, brown men, and *women*. Someone has got to continue to fight the good fight. And I submit to you that I am that someone.

When Valessa concluded, no one questioned the sincerity of her commitment to justice and to her chosen career.

As you explore your own background or that of a classmate, we suggest that you ask all the probe questions within the self-awareness inventory. Don't be satisfied with the first idea that comes to you. You should find this thorough examination of

Speaker's Notes 3.3

Self-Awareness Inventory

As you probe the possibilities for your speech of introduction, explore the following self-awareness inventory:

1. Was your *cultural background* important in shaping you?

2. Was your *environment* a major influence?

3. Did some *person* have an impact on you?

4. Were you shaped by an unusual *experience?*

5. Is there an *activity* that motivates you?

6. Has your *work* had a major impact on who you are?

7. Does some special *goal* or *purpose* guide the way you live?

8. Does a *value* have great meaning for you?

---

yourself and others to be quite rewarding. Just remember: You are not on a tabloid talk show. You don't want to embarrass listeners with personal disclosures they would just as soon not hear. If you are uncertain about whether to include personal material, discuss it with your instructor. The general rule to follow is, *When in doubt, leave it out!*

In Summary

Many of us underrate our public speaking potential. As you prepare your first speech, you can develop basic skills in selecting and polishing speech topics, structuring and outlining your speech, and practicing for presentation. You can communicate favorable impressions of yourself, useful for later speeches. You can contribute to the transformation of the class into a learning community.

Preparing Your First Speech. Effective preparation requires that you take a number of steps toward speech success. First, select a topic that is appropriate to you, your listeners, the assignment, and the time limits assigned for your speech. Second, narrow and focus your topic until you have a clear idea of your message and of what you want to accomplish. Third, seek narratives, examples, testimony, and facts and statistics that will make your points interesting and credible. Fourth, design your speech so that your ideas fit together in a cohesive pattern. Often-used patterns for the first speech are the categorical design, the cause-effect design, and the narrative design. Develop an introduction, body, and conclusion so that your speech forms a satisfying whole. Provides transitions that link the various parts of your speech. Fifth, outline your speech so that you can check on the soundness of your design. Sixth, practice your presentation. Develop an extempo-

raneous presentation that avoids the faults of reading and memorization. Keep the spotlight on your ideas, and strive for a conversational presentation. Seventh, step up and do it!

Managing the Impressions You Make. Listeners acquire positive impressions of you on the basis of your ability to convey competence, integrity, goodwill, and dynamism. These qualities make up the ancient concept of ethos. You can build your perceived competence by citing examples from your own experience, by quoting authorities, and by organizing and presenting your message effectively. You can earn an image of integrity by being accurate and complete in your presentation of information. You can promote goodwill by being a warm and likeable person who invites identification from listeners. Dynamism arises from listeners' perceptions of you as a confident, enthusiastic, and decisive speaker.

Introducing Yourself or a Classmate. A speech of introduction helps establish you or the person you introduce as a unique person. Prompted by your self-awareness inventory, it may focus on cultural background, environmental influences, a person who inspired you, an experience that affected you, an activity that reveals your character, the work you do, your purpose in life, or some value you cherish.

Explore and Apply the Ideas in This Chapter

1. Although we have defined ethos in terms of public speakers, other communicators also seek to create favorable impressions of competence, integrity, goodwill, and dynamism. Advertisers always try to create favorable ethos for their products. Bring to class print advertisements to demonstrate each of the four dimensions of ethos we have discussed. Explain how each ad uses ethos.

2. Select a prominent public speaker and analyze his or her ethos. On which dimensions is this speaker especially strong or weak? How do these dimensions affect the person's leadership ability? Present your analysis for class discussion.

3. Political advertisements often do the work of introducing candidates to the public and disparaging their opponents. Study the television or print advertisements in connection with a recent political campaign. Bring to class answers to the following questions:

   a. What kinds of positive and negative identities do the advertisements establish?

   b. Which of the forms of supporting material (narratives, examples, testimony, facts and statistics) do they emphasize?

   c. Which of these advertisements are most and least effective in creating the desired ethos? Why?

   d. Which of the self-awareness inventory questions discussed in this chapter might explain how the candidates are introduced?

4. As the introductory speeches are presented in your class, build a collection of "word portraits" of your classmates as they reveal themselves in their speeches. At the end of the assignment, analyze each of these "autobios" to see what you have learned about the class as a whole. What kinds of topics might your classmates prefer? Do you detect any strong political or social attitudes to which you might have to adjust? Submit a report of your analysis to your instructor, and keep a copy for your own use in preparing later speeches.

5. Summarize your own adventure of preparing for your first speech. Which of the steps identified in this chapter were most difficult for you? Why? What have you learned about speech preparation that might be useful for your next speech? Submit your report and analysis to your instructor.

A Little Chocolate

Sabrina Karic

In her prologue Sabrina orients listeners and builds identification with them.

Sabrina Karic gave this self-introductory speech to her class at the University of Nevada-Las Vegas. Her speech is built round a master narrative that features personal experience as the shaping force in her life. She tells about surviving the ethnic cleansing that took place in Bosnia and Herzegovina during the early 1990s when she was a child. As she described this situation, her listeners were spellbound by her power and passion.

[To start her speech, Sabrina plays a sound effect of an explosion.]

I want you to remember yourselves as you were when you were six years old. And now I want you to imagine yourselves living in a time, a place, a country, where you constantly hear the noise I have just played, all around you. I come from a small, incredibly durable, unspeakably tragic country named Bosnia and Herzegovina. In 1992, while many of you were playing with your toys or learning how to ride a bike, I was living through a nightmare. Yes, I was six years old, not quite ready to experience war. But on the day of May 28, I heard the first gun shots and my happy childhood ended. Almost overnight, my family, which had been rich and privileged, plunged into homelessness and poverty.

In the first major scene of her story, as her family begins to starve in Gorazde, Sabrina uses concrete detail to help her listeners visualize and share the horror of her experience. In the second major scene, waiting for the return of her parents, Sabrina describes her growing despair. This dark feeling sets up the happiness she feels over their safe return. She uses an analogy to Christmas to help her listeners appreciate her joy. In this scene chocolate begins to develop its larger symbolic meaning.

After the Serbs forced us out of our home, we had to endure endless nights sleeping under trees while rain poured down on us and mice crawled over our bodies. We finally made our way to Gorazde, a city that was surrounded by the Serbians and held under siege for months. The local authorities kept us all barely alive by distributing food among the families. Typically we would receive each week thirty pounds of flour, three pounds of beans, one pound of sugar, and two liters of oil. Each day, my mom made bread that was one inch thick. She divided it in half; one half for breakfast and the other for dinner. Then each half was divided in five even pieces, one piece for me, my mom, my dad, my sister, and my cousin, who at that time lived with us.

It was incredibly hard for us. We often ran out of food before the next week's food distribution. Sometimes the supplies were delayed or even not available. I can tell you that nothing etches itself more in young memory than the pain of hunger. During those days, I never dreamed of having a big house, a pool, or a doll I could play with. I simply prayed to God for chocolate.

On January 31st of 1993, my parents decided to leave for Grebak, where the Bosnian army was situated. They would have to sneak through the enemy lines to reach the army barracks. If they survived, the army would give them food to bring back to us. If they didn't make it—well, we didn't talk about that. If they didn't try, we were all going to starve anyway. When my parents departed, they had to leave my sister and me on our own. Luckily, we had cousins who lived in Gorazde long before the war began. They took us in, and I can tell you that if it hadn't been for them, we would have starved to death. Days passed, and each day we waited for our parents. And our despair began to grow. We heard rumors that they had run into mine fields and been killed. We felt so profoundly alone.

Then on February 7th, a miracle happened. The door opened, and there were our parents! I remember all the crying and hugging and kissing, and I remember hope flooding back into our hearts. Our parents explained that many people had in fact died, but that God had spared them.

That day I learned the meaning of gratitude, as well as sorrow for all of those whose parents would not return. But then our thoughts turned to food. My parents had brought so much of it to us. For those of you who celebrate Christmas, I'm sure I can compare my happiness on that one day to all of your holidays, added together. My parents had brought us one unforgettable treasure: Can you guess what it was?

Yes, it was chocolate, a small chocolate bar, broken into pieces during the trip. But my sister and I treasured each tiny piece, and ate it very slowly.

After the joy of that reunion, we returned to the reality of life around us. It seemed that every day, the explosions were getting closer, louder, more frequent. I remember one particular day when I was playing with my friends outside our building. Suddenly we heard a nearby explosion, and all of us dashed for the building. We knew that we had only a few seconds at best. I got inside the door and managed to close it, when a grenade exploded right where we had been playing. I fell to the floor and put my hands over my ears, waiting for the ringing to go away. After few minutes, I peeked outside to see if any of my friends had been hurt. Thank God, all of us had been spared.

In the third scene of her plot, Sabrina jerks listeners back into the daily horror of her situation. The image of a hand grenade interrupting the play of children is especially graphic and memorable.

I can't remember how this nightmare eventually ended, but somehow it did. It's clear that the whole experience has left a huge scar on my heart. To this day, I vividly remember everything, and the experience has made me the person I am today. Now, I appreciate small things in life. I find satisfaction just taking a walk in the park, thanking God I survived. The experience also made me a fighter, and gave me strength and a will to live that has carried me through life, and brought me here to share my story with you.

And even today, my experience makes me weep for all the children everywhere, Muslim, Jewish, and Christian, in Africa, the Middle East, and elsewhere—all the six year olds who experience prejudice and hatred and violence they can't understand. I weep for the loss of their innocence, for the loss of their lives. Can't we reach out to them, and make their world at least a little more livable? Can't we bring them a little chocolate?

In her epilogue Sabrina reflects on the meaning of her ordeal and invites listeners to look for ways to counter such inhumanity. Note how she applies her experience in global, contemporary ways. At this final point in the speech, chocolate has become a universal symbol for hope.

Becoming a Better Listener

Easy listening exists only on the radio.

—David Barkan

You walk to the front of the room, ready to make your first presentation. You pause to make eye contact with your audience. This is what you see:

In a far corner of the room, a student is frantically trying to finish his Spanish homework. A tablet is on his desk, a textbook is open on his lap. His eyes move from the book to the tablet. He never stops writing, and he never looks up.

In the other far corner, a student is nodding off. Her eyes are closed. Occasionally her chin drops to her chest, and she jerks herself up and tries to look alert, but within twenty seconds she has dropped off again.

Finally, you spot an attentive face—someone who actually looks as though he's ready to listen. His desk is empty except for a notebook. He is sitting alert, a pencil in his hand. His eyes are on you. He looks interested in what you have to say.

A good listener can be hard to find! Legend has it that President Franklin Delano Roosevelt was bemused by the poor listening behavior of people who visited the White House. To test his notion that people didn't really listen, he once greeted guests in a receiving line by murmuring, "I murdered my grandmother this morning." Typical responses ran along the lines of "Thank you," "How good of you," and other platitudes of polite approval. Finally he met someone who had actually listened and who responded, "I'm sure she had it coming to her."[1]

Poor listening can exact a large price, both globally and personally. Leaders may make up their minds about the intentions of other nations and then refuse to listen to information that does not support their conclusions. People in groups, swayed by the power of one member's personality, may make poor decisions. Juries may not render fair verdicts because they have not used critical listening skills. If you are not listening effectively in a classroom, you may find it hard to do well in a course.

Fortunately, effective listening can be learned.[2] In this chapter we consider why you should want to become a better listener, and we describe the process of listening. We then discuss the main causes of poor listening and suggest ways to overcome them. Next, we look at the development of critical and constructive listening and tie these skills into the evaluation of speeches. Finally, we consider your responsibilities as an ethical listener.

The Benefits of Effective Listening

Why should you want to become a better listener? In the workplace, classroom, group and community meetings, as well as in interpersonal relationships, effective listening will make a difference in how effective you are as a communicator.

Listening in the Workplace

John was a truck driver hauling a load of lettuce. He called his dispatcher early in the morning. "Where do you want me to take the load?"

"Jackson," she answered, and gave him the street address.

Around lunchtime, John called her back, "Well, I'm in Jackson, and I can't find the address."

"I've got it here, just as clear as can be. It says, get off I-40 at exit 82 and . . . ."

"Wait a minute," John interrupts. "I came down on I-55."

"I-55? In Jackson, Tennessee?"

"Hold it. You didn't tell me that. I'm in Jackson, Mississippi."

"Well, why didn't you ask me?" she countered. And while they argued over who was more to blame, the poor speaker or the poor listener, a load of lettuce wilted under the Mississippi sun.

Variations of this story are played out in different forms every day. Who can say how much time and money are lost because of poor listening? This is one reason companies assign importance to listening ability in their hiring (and firing) decisions. Many studies have identified effective listening as one of the major skills that help graduates find and retain jobs.[3] Effective listening skills are valued across jobs and across cultures.[4] This may be because ineffective listening leads to ineffective performance. If you listen effectively on the job, you will improve your chances for advancement.

The ability to listen effectively can help you in your other classes.

Listening in the Classroom

It is a warm spring day. Marie's body is sitting in her management class, but her mind is wandering somewhere else as she thinks about the past weekend and her plans for a spring break trip. The instructor's voice drones on, but the words don't register until he says: "Now, I know that Marie has worked in this kind of environment. Marie, will you tell us what it was like?"

If you have ever lived through this kind of nightmare, we won't have a hard time convincing you that listening is important in the classroom. Effective listeners read assignments ahead of time to familiarize themselves with new words and to build a basis for understanding. Students who listen effectively earn better grades because they learn to concentrate and identify what is important in a lecture.[5]

Listening is a highly-valued skill in many Native American cultures.

Effective listening is particularly important in the public speaking class. By listening carefully to speeches, you can learn which speaking techniques work best and under what circumstances. Good listeners can provide feedback that helps speakers adjust their messages. A good audience can help ease a speaker's anxiety by creating a supportive environment. As a listener, you can show support by being pleasant and responsive rather than dour and inattentive. Give speakers your undivided attention, and show respect for them as people, even if you disagree with their ideas.

Although we spend most of our communication time listening, we receive less formal training in listening than we do in speaking, writing, or reading.[6] Perhaps educators assume that we naturally know how to listen well despite a good deal

of evidence to the contrary. Also, listening may be undervalued in our culture because we associate it with following, not with leading. Or, in an action-oriented culture, we may see speaking as active and listening as passive behaviors.

Other cultures place a higher premium on listening. Some Native American tribes, for example, have a far better appreciation of its importance. The council system of the Ojai Foundation has three main rules for conducting business: "Speak honestly, be brief, and listen from the heart."[7] For the Blackfeet tribe, listening is a way of opening themselves to the sacredness of their surroundings.[8] The Lakota also recognize the value of listening:

> Conversation was never begun at once, nor in a hurried manner. No one was quick with a question, no matter how important, and no one was pressed for an answer. A pause giving time for thought was the truly courteous way of beginning and conducting a conversation. Silence was meaningful with the Lakota, and his granting a space of silence to the speech-maker and his own moment of silence before talking was done in the practice of true politeness and regard for the rule that, "thought comes before speech."[9]

The Process of Listening

You can think of the various phases of the listening process as the rungs of a ladder. The Ladder of Listening shown in Figure 4.1 illustrates the sequence of steps you must master to become an effective listener.

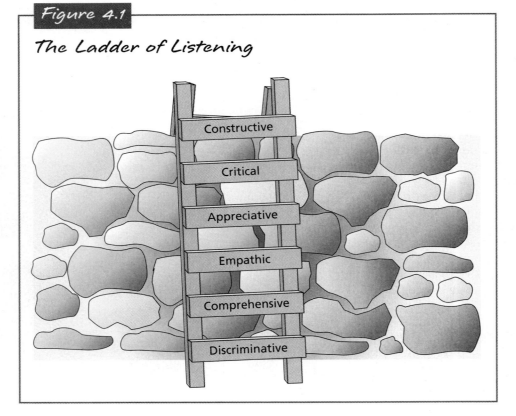

Figure 4.1

The Ladder of Listening

- Constructive
- Critical
- Appreciative
- Empathic
- Comprehensive
- Discriminative

Discriminative Listening

Before you can listen, you must be able to hear. **Hearing** is an automatic, involuntary process in which sound waves stimulate nerve impulses to the brain. It is the basis of **discriminative listening**. Normally, discriminative listening is not a problem unless you are trying to listen in a noisy environment or have a severe hearing impairment. The fact that some people can become superb listeners even though they can't hear very well is a monument to the human spirit. The life of Helen Keller, who overcame deafness to acquire speech and to become a great citizen of the world, is a story of such heroism.

hearing An automatic, involuntary process in which sound waves stimulate nerve impulses to the brain.

discriminative listening Phase of listening in which we detect sounds of spoken communication.

Comprehensive Listening

Comprehensive listening involves finding meaning in the sounds you hear. To reach this level, you must focus on the message, understand the speaker's verbal and nonverbal language, and interpret the message in terms of your own knowledge and experience. Comprehensive listening is voluntary, because you can choose whether to listen this way. In our story of Marie, discriminative listening did not become comprehensive listening until she heard her name called. At that point it was too late!

Empathic Listening

The Chinese symbol for the verb *listen* has four basic elements: attention, ears, eyes, and heart.[10] The heart in this symbol represents **empathic listening**. Empathic listening is most frequent in informal, interpersonal interactions, but it is also important in public speaking. When you listen empathically, you try to see things from the speakers' perspective. Empathic listening suspends judgment and allows others to be heard.[11] It creates a receptive environment in the classroom, and it is especially important early in the term when beginning speakers are trying to cope with communication anxiety.

Appreciative Listening

Appreciative listening is the aesthetic phase of the listening process. It involves responding to the intrinsic beauty of a message. For example, we may enjoy the simplicity and balance of a speech or the interesting examples and narratives used as supporting material. Although appreciative listening can add to the enjoyment of any speech, it is especially relevant to ceremonial speaking, when speakers often try to inspire listeners with eloquent language.

InterConnections.
Learn More 4.1

Listening

International Listening Association
www.listen.org
The official Web site of the International Listening Association, dedicated to improving listening skills, with links to exercises and resources, including ILA's quarterly publication, Listening Post.

Improving Your Listening
www.scs.tamu.edu/selfhelp/elibrary/listening_skills.asp
Techniques and principles from the Student Counseling Service, Texas A&M University.

Effective Listening Skills
www.elmhurst.edu/library/learningcenter/Listening/effective_listening_skills.htm
An interactive site with links to questionnaires on classroom listening behaviors. Developed by the Elmhurst College Learning Center, Dr. Janice Fodor, Director.

---

comprehensive listening   Phase of listening in which we focus on, understand, and interpret spoken messages.

empathic listening   Phase of listening in which we suspend judgment, allow speakers to be heard, and try to see things from their points of view.

appreciative listening   Phase of listening in which we enjoy the beauty of messages, responding to such factors as the simplicity, balance, and the eloquence of language.

The Chinese symbol for listening suggests the complexity of the process.

Critical Listening

Critical listening is the "mind" in the Chinese symbol for listening. Critical listeners analyze and evaluate the content of a message. They inspect the reasoning process, weigh the value of supporting material, and determine whether a message is successful. Critical listeners are not easily influenced by the speaker's title, reputation, or charisma, and they are resistant to emotional appeals. They are skeptical listeners who accept nothing at face value. Cultivating a critical listening orientation is a major goal of the public speaking class.

Constructive Listening

Constructive listening involves an active search for the value that messages may have for your life. It is motivated listening that presumes all messages have some value. Although alert to the possible defects of a message and wary of hidden agendas, constructive listeners go beyond critical listening. They ask themselves how they might use even a flawed message. Constructive listeners participate fully in the construction of meaning.

For example, after listening to a speech urging the importance of mathematics education in the public schools, constructive listeners in a recent class we taught asked questions about its importance in developing logical thinking and whether math education should be adapted to meet the needs and goals of local students. This discussion created a dialogue in which the ultimate meaning of the message developed out of the interaction of the participants.[12]

Overcoming Barriers to Effective Listening

What keeps us from reaching the top of the ladder of listening? And how can we overcome these barriers? Some barriers arise from problems in the speaking situation or with speakers. But the most troublesome barriers to effective listening are grounded in listeners themselves. Figure 4.2 will help you identify your own possible listening problems. Look through the list and place a check next to items that describe your listening attitudes and behaviors.

Listening Barriers Based on Situations and Speakers

Listening barriers based on the actual circumstances of speaking or on speaker problems include physical noise, flawed messages, and presentation problems.

Physical Noise.   You are working very hard listening to your English professor describe the contrasting rhyme schemes in English and Italian sonnets. Suddenly his words are lost in the noise of grounds workers mowing outside the building. "Oh,

---

critical listening Listening with careful analysis and evaluation of message content.

constructive listening Search for the value that messages may have for your life, despite their defects.

Figure 4.2

Listening Problems Checklist

- [ ] *1.* I believe listening is automatic, not learned behavior.
- [ ] *2.* I stop listening when a speech is uninteresting.
- [ ] *3.* I find it hard to listen to ideas about which I have strong feelings.
- [ ] *4.* I react emotionally to certain words.
- [ ] *5.* I am easily distracted by noises when someone is speaking.
- [ ] *6.* I don't like to listen to speakers who are not experts.
- [ ] *7.* I find some people too objectionable to listen to.
- [ ] *8.* I nod off when someone talks in a monotone.
- [ ] *9.* I can be so dazzled by a glib presentation that I don't listen critically.
- [ ] *10.* I don't like to listen to messages that go against my values.
- [ ] *11.* I think up counterarguments when I disagree with a speaker.
- [ ] *12.* I know so much on some topics that I don't need to hear more.
- [ ] *13.* I believe a speaker—not the listener—is responsible for effective communication.
- [ ] *14.* I find it hard to listen when I have a lot on my mind.
- [ ] *15.* I stop listening when a subject is difficult.
- [ ] *16.* I can look like I'm listening when I am not.
- [ ] *17.* I listen for facts and ignore the rest of a message.
- [ ] *18.* I try to write down everything a lecturer says.
- [ ] *19.* I let a speaker's appearance determine how well I listen.
- [ ] *20.* I jump to conclusions before I have heard all of a message.

no," you think, "I can't hear with all this racket!" And while you are fuming about that and the professor talks on, you lose track of his message entirely and abandon the attempt to listen.

What we have described is a crisis of discriminative listening. *If you can't hear, you can't listen.* It's as simple as that. Speakers and listeners must work together to solve such noise problems. The speaker should talk louder in order to be heard. Listeners can provide feedback to let the speaker know there is a problem. Cup your hand by your ear or lean forward, obviously straining to hear. If you still can't hear, move to a seat closer to the front of the room. If the noise comes from outside, get up and close the window or door.

Message Problems.   Before the lawnmower mercifully intervened, your instructor had just enlightened you with this blockbuster: "The Petrarchan octave and sestet are replaced by the three Shakespearean quatrains and a rhyming couplet." "Yeah, sure," you think.

Messages that are full of unfamiliar words or that are poorly organized get in the way of comprehensive listening. When speakers are insensitive to this problem, listeners must make a special effort to compensate. If you know that there may be unfamiliar words in a class lecture, read on the subject ahead of time. If a message is poorly organized, taking notes can help. Try to pick out the main points. See if you can identify key-words, and look for a pattern among them. Differentiate these points

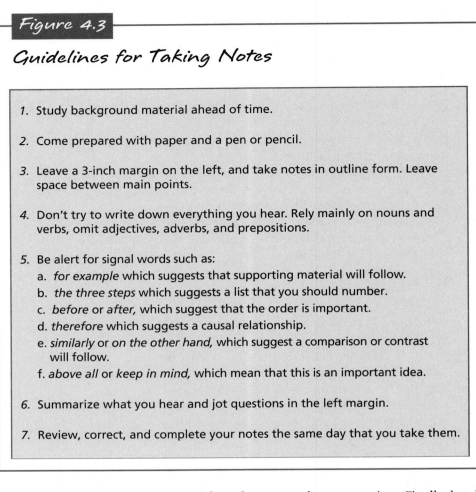

Figure 4.3

Guidelines for Taking Notes

1. Study background material ahead of time.

2. Come prepared with paper and a pen or pencil.

3. Leave a 3-inch margin on the left, and take notes in outline form. Leave space between main points.

4. Don't try to write down everything you hear. Rely mainly on nouns and verbs, omit adjectives, adverbs, and prepositions.

5. Be alert for signal words such as:
   a. *for example* which suggests that supporting material will follow.
   b. *the three steps* which suggests a list that you should number.
   c. *before* or *after*, which suggest that the order is important.
   d. *therefore* which suggests a causal relationship.
   e. *similarly* or *on the other hand*, which suggest a comparison or contrast will follow.
   f. *above all* or *keep in mind*, which mean that this is an important idea.

6. Summarize what you hear and jot questions in the left margin.

7. Review, correct, and complete your notes the same day that you take them.

and words from supporting materials such as examples or narratives. Finally, by all means, ask questions! Figure 4.3 provides some helpful suggestions for taking notes.[13]

Presentation Problems.   Speakers who talk too fast may be difficult to follow, and speakers who talk too slowly or too softly may lull you to sleep. Speakers also may have distracting mannerisms, such as swaying to and fro or fiddling with their hair. You may even encounter speakers whose dress or hair color is so unusual that you find yourself concentrating more on how they look than on what they say.

Simply realizing you are responding to irrelevant cues may help you listen more attentively. If you find yourself drifting away because of such problems, remind yourself that what speakers say is what is most important.

Listening Barriers Based in Listeners Themselves

By far, the greatest barriers to listening arise within listeners themselves. Chief among these barriers are inattention, limitations based on listening styles, bad listening habits, listener apprehension, attitudes, and reactions to words. Figure 4.4 shows how good and poor listeners respond differently to such problems.

Figure 4.4

Differences between Good and Poor Listeners

Good Listeners	Poor Listeners
1. Focus on the message	1. Let their minds wander
2. Control emotional reactions	2. Respond emotionally
3. Set aside personal problems	3. Get sidetracked by personal problems
4. Listen despite distractions	4. Succumb to distractions
5. Ignore speaker's mannerisms	5. Get distracted by speaker's mannerisms
6. Listen for things they can use	6. Tune out dry material
7. Reserve judgment	7. Jump to conclusions
8. Consider ideas and feelings	8. Listen only for facts
9. Hold biases in check	9. Allow biases to interfere
10. Realize listening is hard work	10. Confuse listening with hearing

---

Inattentiveness. One of the most common barriers affecting listening is simply not paying attention. How many times have you found yourself daydreaming when you knew you should have been listening? One cause of this problem is that our minds can process information faster than people speak. Most people talk at about 125 words per minute in public, but they can process information at about 500 words per minute.[14] This "communication gap" provides an opportunity for listeners to drift away to more interesting concerns or personal problems.

Chance associations with words are a second cause of inattention. For example, a speaker mentions the word *desk*—which reminds you that you need a better place to study in your room—which reminds you that you have to buy a new lamp—which starts you thinking about going shopping—which gets you thinking about the fried mushrooms at the restaurant in the mall—which reminds you that you didn't eat breakfast and you're hungry. By the time your attention drifts back to the speaker, it's too late.

Personal concerns are a third cause of inattention. When you are tired, hungry, angry, worried, or pressed for time, you may find it difficult to concentrate. Your personal problems may take precedence over listening to a speaker. Or, you simply may have "listening burnout" from too much concentrated exposure to oral material.[15] If you've ever attended three lecture classes in a row, you will know what this is.

Overcoming inattention requires some work. Bridge the speaking–listening gap by paraphrasing to yourself what the speaker has just said. Come to class well rested and well fed. Consciously decide to do your worrying later. Sit near the front of the room, and clear your mind of other concerns and your desk of everything except paper on which to take notes. Establish eye contact with the speaker, and consciously commit to listening.

Listening Style Preference.

Although we all may *hear* the same words in a speech, we often react to them differently according to our basic listening style. Larry Barker and Kittie Watson, contemporary communication scholars, describe four different listening styles: people-oriented, content-oriented, action-oriented, and time-oriented.[16] Your style may be based on your personality or life experiences or on the demands of the specific listening situation.

People-oriented listeners are compassionate and respond to emotional appeals. They may find it difficult to listen critically and constructively to messages. Content-oriented listeners look for strong, objective evidence and solid arguments but may ignore the human factors, including how people are reacting emotionally. Action-oriented listeners look for plans of action but may not pay enough attention to the human factors or rational justifications in a message. Time-oriented listeners become impatient with messages that are not brief and to the point and may not tune into human factors or look for adequate support or logical reasoning.

If your habitual listening style fits any of these categories, you may have to adapt to become a better listener. If you are a people-oriented listener, remind yourself to look for objective support and rational arguments. If you are more prone to listen in one of the other styles, remind yourself that the human dimensions of any subject also merit consideration.

Bad Habits.

It is easy to acquire bad listening habits. You may have learned how to feign attention while tuning out a speaker. Your experiences as a student may have conditioned you to listen just for facts. Too much television viewing may lead you into the "entertainment syndrome" in which you want speakers to be lively, funny, and engaging. Unfortunately, not all subjects lend themselves to such treatment.

Overcoming bad habits requires effort. When you find yourself feigning attention, remember that honest feedback helps speakers but that inappropriate feedback deceives them. Don't try to remember everything or write down all that you hear. Instead, listen for the main ideas and identify supporting materials. Try to get an overall idea of the meaning of the message. Pay attention to nonverbal cues. Does the speaker's tone of voice change the meaning of the words? Are the gestures and facial expressions consistent with the words? If not, what does this tell you? Remember, not all important messages will be entertaining. Focus on what you can get out of a speech beyond enjoyment.

To become effective listeners, we may have to work to overcome boredom and fatigue.

Listening Apprehension.

Receiver apprehension is "the fear of misinterpreting, inadequately processing, or not being able to adjust psychologically to messages sent by others."[17] It is related to a fear of failure and to message complexity.[18] You may experience listener apprehension when you believe a

---

receiver apprehension   Fear of misinterpreting, inadequately processing and/or not being able to adjust psychologically to messages sent by others.

message is important, when you think you may be judged on how well you respond to it, when it challenges your ability to understand the message, or when it threatens your values or beliefs.

The fear of failure may cause you to avoid listening to difficult material. If you are asked questions later, you can always say, "I wasn't really listening," instead of "I didn't understand." Additionally, wanting to have things simplified so that they are easy to understand makes all of us susceptible to snake-oil hucksters with slick solutions for problems.

Listener apprehension also can distract us and even cause us to distort what we hear.[19] To control this problem, try the techniques that work for speaker anxiety. Practice deep muscle relaxation, reword negative self-messages, and visualize successful outcomes.[20] Instead of telling yourself, "All these details are confusing," say, "I can see the overall meaning." Visualize yourself giving a critique of a message that helps both speaker and other listeners see the strong points as well as possible problems in the message.

Emotional Reactions to Words.   As you listen to a message, you react to more than just the objective meanings of words. Some words may set off such powerful emotional reactions that they derail your understanding and forestall critical listening. We call these **trigger words**. Trigger words can evoke either positive or negative reactions. Positive trigger words generally relate to values and traditions that we hold dear. Negative trigger words often relate to racial, ethnic, sexist, or religious slurs.

Positive trigger words can blind us to flawed or dangerous messages. Our reactions to them are usually subtle, and we may not realize that we are being influenced. How many times have people been deceived by such trigger words as *freedom*, *democracy*, or *progress* to justify certain courses of action?[21]

Negative trigger words invoke extreme emotional reactions in us. Often they are prejudicial forms of language that reflect the darker impulses of our culture. While they may well deserve condemnation, people should control words and not the other way around. If a speaker uses trigger words, you may lower your estimation of her or his ethos, but you should give the content of the message fair consideration. Do not let trigger words prevent you from hearing and evaluating an entire message.

How can you lessen the power of trigger words? To gain control over them, Professor Richard Halley of Weber State University suggests that you observe your own behavior over a period of time and make a list of words that cause you to react emotionally.[22] Then ask yourself the following questions:

- Do I let these words affect the way I respond to messages?

- Might speakers be using these words to test or manipulate me?

- What can I do to control my reactions?

Train yourself to listen to the entire message before allowing yourself to react. By listening before reacting, you can avoid jumping to conclusions that may not be grounded in the reality of the situation.

Attitudes.   All of us have biases of one kind or another. Listening problems arise when we let our biases prevent us from receiving messages accurately. Some of the ways in which bias can distort messages are through filtering, assimilation, and contrast effects.

trigger words   Words that arouse such powerful feelings that they interfere with the ability to listen critically and constructively.

Speaker's Notes 4.1

Improving Your Listening Skills

Use these suggestions to help improve your listening skills.

1. Identify your listening problems so that you can correct them.

2. Look for something of value in every speech.

3. Put problems and biases aside when listening.

4. Control reactions to trigger words and other distractions.

5. Delay judgments until you have heard a speech through to its conclusion.

6. Don't try to write down everything a speaker says.

7. Listen for the main ideas.

Filtering means that you don't process all incoming information. You hear what you want to hear. You unconsciously screen the speaker's words so that only some of them reach your brain. Listeners who filter hear only one side of "good news, bad news" speeches: the side that confirms their preconceived beliefs.

Assimilation means that you see positions similar to your own as being closer to it than they actually are. Assimilation occurs when listeners have a strong positive attitude toward a speaker or topic. For example, if you believe a person can do no wrong, you may assimilate everything she says so that it seems consistent with your beliefs.

A **contrast effect** occurs when you see positions different from yours as being more distant than they actually are. For example, if you are a staunch liberal, you may think anything conservatives say will differ from what you believe, even if that is not true. Biases can make you put words in a speaker's mouth, take them away, or distort them.

Attitudes are not easy to control. The first step in overcoming a bias is to admit you have it. Next, decide that you will listen as objectively as you can and that you will delay judgment until you have heard the entire message. Being objective does not mean that you must agree with a message: it only means that you believe a speech deserves to be heard on its own terms. What you hear may help you see clearly the faults or the virtues of an opposing position. As a result, you may feel confirmed in what you already believe, or you may decide to reevaluate your position. Finally, decide that you will find something valuable in what you hear. Even if you are not interested in a topic, look for something that you can use.

Developing Critical Listening Skills

Critical listening involves developing a questioning orientation to what you hear. It can protect you from manipulative messages, yet it requires you to bend over backward to give a fair hearing to ideas that go against your attitudes. Critical listening is not something that comes naturally to most people, but it is a skill that can be acquired. It consists of learning to evaluate evidence and information, assessing the credibility of sources, analyzing language usage, and examining rhetorical strategies.

filtering Listening to only part of a message, the part the listener wants to hear.

assimilation The tendency of listeners to interpret the positions of a speaker with whom they agree as closer to their own views than they actually are.

contrast effect Seeing positions different than yours as being more distant than they actually are.

Evaluating Evidence and Information

Ideas should be supported with facts and figures, testimony, examples, or narratives. Whenever speakers claim, "This is beyond dispute!" it is probably time to start a dispute. Listen also for what is *not* said as well as for what *is* said. *No evidence equals no proof. No proof should equal no acceptance.* Don't hesitate to ask speakers challenging questions.

When evaluating evidence, remember the four R's: evidence should be *relevant, representative, recent,* and *reliable.* Relevant evidence relates directly to the issue in question. The speaker who shouts, "Television is destroying family values!" and then offers statistics that demonstrate a rising national divorce rate has not established the connection between television and family values. The evidence is not relevant to the claim.

Evidence also should be representative of the situation rather than an exception to the rule. The speaker who claims, "Young people have lost their sense of values," on the basis of a study of juvenile delinquents in London, has violated this particular "R."

Facts and figures should be the most recent ones available. This is particularly important when knowledge about a topic is changing rapidly. Before the Iraqi war, the U.S. government often referred to a report from British intelligence to support its claim that Saddam Hussein possessed weapons of mass destruction. It turned out that part of the British evidence was over ten years old.[23]

Evidence should also be reliable—we must be able to depend on it. The more significant and controversial the claim, the more reliable should be the evidence. It turned out that the same report from British intelligence had been drawn not from professional sources of intelligence but from magazines and academic journals, including one article authored by a postgraduate student in California. These sources would not satisfy those who insist on a high standard of reliability in justifying decisions to go to war.

When you apply the standard of reliability, require

- that claims be confirmed by more than one source,
- that these sources be independent of each other, and
- that the sources possess expert credentials.

Even information that seems to meet these tests of evidence should be evaluated in terms of how well it fits with what you already know. Information that is inconsistent with what you know or believe should set off an alarm in your mind. You should always evaluate such material very carefully before you accept it.

When presenting evidence, speakers should make a clear distinction among facts, inferences, and opinions. **Facts** are verifiable units of information that can be confirmed by independent observation. **Inferences** are assumptions or projections based on incomplete data. **Opinions** add personal judgments to facts and inferences: they tell us what someone thinks about a subject. For example, "Mary was late for class today" is a fact. "Mary will probably be late for class again tomorrow" is an inference. "Mary is an irresponsible student" is an opinion. It may sound easy to make these distinctions among facts, inferences, and opinions, but often it is not. You must be alert to confusions among them as you listen to messages.

Just because an assertion or opinion is continually repeated in the media doesn't make it a fact. Kathleen Hall Jamieson, dean of the Annenberg School of

---

facts Information that can be verified by observation or expert testimony.

inferences Assumptions based on incomplete information.

opinions Expressions of personal attitude or belief offered without supporting material.

Critical Listening Red Flags

These red flags should alert you to potential problems in a message. When they appear, you should be extra careful in evaluating the message.

No objective evidence provided

Sources of information not identified

Questionable sources of information

Information inconsistent with what you know

Claims of exclusivity

Opinions or inferences passed off as facts

Vague or incomprehensible language

Blatant emotional appeals

Outlandish promises or guarantees

Communication, calls this the "echo-chamber" effect. The echo-chamber works this way: an unconfirmed rumor is initially published or aired by a news source, and then it is repeated by others as though it had been substantiated.[24] After a rumor has been repeated many times, people tend to accept it as fact without any verification.

It is not only the mainstream media that can get caught up in the echo-effect. For example, immediately after the April 2007 shootings at Virginia Tech, a rumor circulated on Internet social networking sites naming as a suspect a student who had pictures of himself with a gun collection posted on Facebook. This rumor was picked up by national television outlets with one network showing photos of the student and noting that he could be a suspect. The "misinformation" continued even after the police announced that the perpetrator had shot himself during the massacre. The student "target," who was never a suspect in the case, received death threats.[25]

Assessing the Credibility of Sources

Evidence and supporting material should come from sources that are trustworthy and competent in the subject area. Ethical speakers cite their sources of information. It is also wise to specify the credentials of sources unless they are widely known. If credentials are left out or described in vague terms, the testimony may be questionable. We recently found an advertisement for a health food product that contained "statements by doctors." A quick check of the current directory of the American Medical Association (AMA) revealed that only one of the six "doctors" cited was a member of AMA and that his credentials were misrepresented. Always ask yourself, *Where does this information come from?* and *Are these sources qualified to speak on the topic?*

Analyzing Language Use

When speakers want to hide something, they often use incomprehensible or vague language. Introducing people who are not physicians as "doctors" to enhance their testimony on health subjects is one form of vagueness. Another ruse is using pseudoscientific jargon, such as "This supplement contains a gonadotropic hormone similar to pituitary extract in terms of its complex B vitamin methionine ratio." If it sounds impressive but you don't know what it means, be careful.

Examining Rhetorical Strategies

It is also important to look at the *way* a speaker uses evidence and supporting material. Vivid examples and compelling stories demonstrate a speaker's passion for a subject and invite the listener to share these feelings. An ethical speaker will also include sound information and good reasons to justify such feelings.

In politics, speakers who rely heavily on emotional appeals to promote their agendas, without regard to the accuracy or adequacy of their claims, are called **demagogues**. We should always ask, *What are these speakers asking us to ignore?* Early during the Iraq war, some Republican speakers argued that it had been justified because Saddam Hussein was an evil man who had been in cahoots with terrorists. Not to be outdone, some Democrats responded that Republicans were ready to exchange American blood for Iraqi oil. Both sides were guilty of considerable demagoguery on this issue.

Critical listeners give close attention to the evidence and reasoning in a speech.

Although we have just cautioned you to be wary of speakers who rely primarily on emotional appeals, you also should be wary of speakers who ignore the emotional aspects of a situation. You cannot fully understand an issue until you understand how it affects others, how it makes them feel, how it colors the way they view the world. Suppose you were listening to a speech on global warming that contained the following statement:

> The United States has 5 percent of the world's population but produces 25 percent of the world's carbon dioxide emissions.

Although these numbers are impressive, what do they tell you about the human problems of global warming? Consider how much more meaningful this material might be if accompanied by the stories of what this can mean for our coastal cities.

The reasoning used in a speech should also make good sense. Conclusions should follow from the points and evidence that precede them. The basic assumptions that support arguments should be those that most rational, unbiased people would accept. Whenever reasoning doesn't seem plausible, question the speaker or consult with independent authorities before you commit yourself.

Speakers who wish to rush you into accepting their position or sell you something you don't need often use exaggeration. If an offer sounds too good to be true, it probably is. The health food advertisement previously described contained the following claims:

> The healing, rejuvenating and disease-fighting effects of this total nutrient are hard to believe, yet are fully documented. Aging, digestive upsets, prostrate [sic] diseases, sore throats, acne, fatigue, sexual problems, allergies, and a host of other problems have been successfully treated . . . . [It] is the only super perfect food on this earth. This statement has been proven so many times in

demagogues Political speakers who try to inflame feelings without regard to the accuracy or adequacy of their claims in order to promote their own agendas.

InterConnections.
Learn More 4.2
Critical Thinking and Listening

The Critical Thinking Community
www.criticalthinking.org

The official Web site of the Critical Thinking Community, an organization dedicated to promoting change in education and society through critical thinking. Affiliated with Sonoma State University, California. Contains numerous links to additional resources.

Cyber Listening Lab
www.esl-lab.com/index.htm

Listening exercises for English as Second Language Students, sorted by difficulty level. The materials may also be useful for other students who experience listening problems not related to their native language. Developed and maintained by Randall Davis, an ESL specialist.

Critical Thinking: What It Is and Why It Counts
www.insightassessment.com/pdf_files/what&why2007.pdf

An interesting and enlightening essay on the importance of critical thinking, prepared by Professor Peter A. Facione, Senior Associate with Stratus-Heery, a higher education consulting firm and former director of Critical Thinking Assessment and Consulting Services, California Academic Press.

the laboratories around the world by a chemical analyst that it is not subject to debate nor [sic] challenge.

Maybe the product is also useful as a paint remover and gasoline additive. As you develop effective listening skills, you develop resistance to persuasive scams from charlatans who try to mask a lack of substance or faulty reasoning with a glib presentation and irrelevant emotional appeals.[26]

You should also consider whether a speaker acknowledges alternative perspectives on issues. Ask yourself, *How might people from a different cultural background see the problem? How might someone of the other gender see it? Might these people see it differently from the speaker? Would their solutions or suggestions be different?* Whenever a message addresses a serious topic, try to consider the issue from various points of view. New and better ideas often emerge when we look at the world through a new lens.

Evaluating Speeches

Constructive listening invites you to become a creative, active listener who contributes to the meaning and value of messages. It also means helping speakers become more effective through the feedback you provide both during and after speeches. In this section we concentrate on the oral feedback provided by constructive listeners in the form of questions, appreciation of effective techniques, or suggestions for improvement.

To be able to provide such feedback, you must understand that there is an important difference between criticizing a speaker and offering a **critique** of a speech. *Criticism* suggests focusing on what someone did that was wrong. A *critique* is helpful and supportive, emphasizing strengths as well as weaknesses, showing consideration for the speaker's feelings, and focusing on how a speaker might improve.

critique   An evaluation of a speech that emphasizes strengths as well as weaknesses and that focuses on how a speaker might improve.

Speaker's Notes 4.3

Guidelines for Oral Critiques

Follow these guidelines to give feedback to speakers.

1. Be constructive and supportive.

2. Begin with a positive statement.

3. Be specific; don't just say, "I liked (or didn't like) that speech."

4. Don't criticize the speaker; analyze the speech.

5. If you point out a problem, offer suggestions for improvement.

6. Word criticisms tactfully, such as, "Did you consider doing ...?"

7. End with a positive statement.

To provide constructive feedback, you need a set of standards to help you answer the question, *What makes a good speech?* The application of standards may vary with the assignment; for example, the critique of an informative speech might focus on the adequacy of statistics and examples, and that of a persuasive speech might emphasize evidence and reasoning. Nevertheless, there are four general areas of concern for evaluating all speeches: overall considerations, substance, structure, and presentation.

Overall Considerations

Overall considerations include issues that apply to the speech as a whole: commitment, adaptation, purpose, freshness, and ethics.

Commitment.   Commitment means caring. You must sense that the speaker truly cares about the subject and about listeners. Committed speakers invest the time and effort needed to gain responsible knowledge of their subject. Commitment also shows up in how well a speech is organized and whether it has been carefully rehearsed. Finally, commitment reveals itself in the energy, enthusiasm, and sincerity the speaker projects. Commitment is the spark in the speaker that can touch off fire in the audience.

Adaptation.   For a speech to be effective, it must meet the requirements of the assignment and be adapted to its particular audience. An informative speech should extend our understanding of a topic, a persuasive speech should influence attitudes or actions, and a ceremonial speech should celebrate shared values on special occasions. The speech should also conform to the specified time limits, have at least the minimum number of references required to satisfy judicious listeners, and be presented in the style required for that assignment (such as using a presentation aid or making an extemporaneous delivery).

Effective speakers weigh each technique in terms of its appropriateness for the audience. Will this example interest listeners? Is this information important for them to know? How can I best involve my listeners? One way to involve an audience is to ask questions such as, "Have you ever thought what it would be like *not* to have electricity?" Also, the use of the pronoun *we* may draw an audience and a speaker together around a subject.

Purpose. Speeches should have a clear purpose, such as increasing listeners' knowledge of the causes of the greenhouse effect. The purpose of a speech should be evident by the time the speaker finishes the introduction and must be unmistakably clear before the speaker begins the conclusion.

A speech that lacks a clear purpose will drift and wander like a boat without a rudder, blown this way and that by whatever thoughts occur to the speaker. Developing a clear purpose begins with a consideration of audience needs. Speakers must determine exactly what they want to accomplish: what they want listeners to learn, think, or do as a result of their speeches.

Freshness. Any speech worth listening to brings something new to listeners. The topic should be fresh. A speech on an overused topic must be handled innovatively to sustain attention. One frequently overused topic for persuasive speeches is drinking and driving. When speakers choose such a topic, they can't simply reiterate the common advice "If you drink, don't drive" and expect to be effective. The audience will have heard that hundreds of times. To get through to listeners on such a subject, speakers must find a new way to present the material. One of our students gave a speech on "responsible drinking and driving" that stressed the importance of understanding the effects of alcohol and of knowing one's tolerance limits. Her fresh approach and important information provided a new perspective on an old problem.

Ethics. Perhaps the most important measure of a speech is whether it is good or bad for listeners. As we noted in Chapter 1, *an ethical speech demonstrates respect for listeners, responsible knowledge, and concern for the consequences of exposure to the message.*

Respect for the listeners means that speakers are sensitive to the cultural diversity of their audience and accept that well-meaning people may hold varying positions on an issue. Ethical speakers are considerate even as they refute the arguments of others. Ethical speakers ground their messages in responsible knowledge. They evaluate their sources of information and watch for potential bias. They acknowledge their own prejudices and strive to be objective in their presentation of information. Ethical speakers do not pass off opinions and inferences as facts, nor do they fabricate data or present the ideas or words of others without acknowledging their contributions.

Finally, ethical speakers are aware that words have consequences. Inflammatory language can arouse strong feelings that discourage critical listening. Ethical speakers think through the potential effects of their messages before they present them. The greater the possible consequences, the more carefully speakers must support what they say with credible evidence and temper their conclusions in keeping with listener sensitivities. Ethics Alert 4.1 lists these ideas.

Evaluating Substance

A speech has substance when it has a worthwhile message supported by facts and figures, testimony, examples, and/or narratives. The starting point for a substantive presentation is a topic that interests both speaker and listeners. When speakers already know something about the topics they select, their knowledge serves as the foundation for further research that enables them to speak responsibly. Although personal experience gives a good start to speech preparation, speakers should always expand such experience with research.

Skillful speakers combine different types of supporting material to demonstrate their points. Combining statistics with an example will make ideas clearer. For instance, a speaker might say, "The base of the Great Pyramid at Giza measures 756

Ethics *Alert! 4.1*

Evaluating the Ethical Dimensions of a Speech

Public speeches can give rise to a host of ethical problems. To test a speech for the presence of these problems, apply the following questions:

1. Does the speaker have responsible knowledge of the topic?

2. Does the speaker show respect for the audience?

3. Does the speaker show concern about the impact of the speech on listeners?

4. Does the speaker document sources of the information?

5. Does the speaker avoid inflammatory language that might impede critical listening?

feet on each side." Although precise, this information may be difficult for listeners to visualize. But by adding, "More than eleven football fields could fit in its base," the speaker has made the material more understandable by providing an illustration that most listeners might relate to.

Evaluating Structure

A good speech carries listeners through an orderly progression of ideas that makes it easy to follow. Without a clear design, a speech may seem to be a random collection of thoughts, and the message can get lost in the confusion.

The introduction may begin with an example, a quotation, or a challenging question that draws listeners into the topic: "So you think there's no need in Idaho to worry about climate changes? After all, you're not subject to hurricanes like those that hit the Gulf Coast. But what about forest fires? And what about the overall impact of global warming on our world?" Once speakers gain attention, they can prepare listeners for what will come by previewing the main points.

The way the body of a speech is organized will vary with its subject and purpose. A speech that tells you how to do something—like how to plan a budget—should follow the order of the steps in the process it describes. If the subject breaks naturally into parts, such as the three major types of wine (red, white, and blended), speakers might use a categorical design.

The conclusion of a speech should summarize the points that have been made and offer a final statement that helps listeners remember the essence of the message.

Effective speeches also contain transitions that link together the various parts. Transitions bridge ideas and aid understanding. During the speech, they signal listeners when one thought is ending and a new one is beginning. "Having shown you this, I will now show you that" is a common formula for transitions. They help the speech flow better and help listeners focus on the major points. Transitions are especially vital between the introduction and body of a speech, between the body and conclusion, and among main points within the body.

Evaluating Presentation Skills

No speech can be effective unless it is presented well. Both the actual words speakers use and the way they convey these words are important factors in presentation.

The Language of Speaking.   The oral language of speeches must be instantly intelligible. This means that speakers' sentences should be simple and direct. Compare the following examples:

> Working for a temporary employment service is a good way to put yourself through school because there are always jobs to be found and the places you get to work are interesting—besides, the people you work for treat you well, and you don't have to do the same thing day after day—plus, you can tailor the hours to fit your free time.

> or

> Working for a temporary employment service is a good way to put yourself through school. Jobs are readily available. You can schedule your work to fit in with your classes. You don't stay at any one place long enough to get bored. And, you meet a lot of interesting people who are glad to have your services.

Which is easier to follow? The first example rambles, with the speaker pausing only to catch a breath. The second example uses short sentences, inviting the use of pauses to separate ideas. As a result, the meaning is clearer.

Concrete words are generally preferable to abstract ones because they create vivid pictures for listeners and clarify meaning. Consider the following levels of abstraction:

most abstract	my pet
	my dog
	my puppy
	my eight-week-old puppy
	my eight-week-old black puppy
most concrete	my eight-week-old black Labrador puppy

As the language becomes more concrete, it is easier to visualize what is being said and there is less chance of misunderstanding.

Presentation.   An effective presentation sounds natural and enthusiastic and is free from distracting mannerisms. Most class assignments call for an extemporaneous presentation in which the speech is carefully prepared and practiced but *not* written out or memorized. Extemporaneous speakers do not read from a script. If listeners look confused, speakers can rephrase what they have just said or provide an example. A speech that flows smoothly indicates that the speaker has practiced well.

Speakers should talk loud enough to be heard easily in the back of the room. Their posture should be relaxed but not sloppy. Movements should seem natural and spontaneous as speakers gesture in response to their own ideas and to emphasize the points they are making.

Figure 4.5 summarizes these guidelines for evaluating speeches. You may use it as a checklist for critiquing the speeches that you hear in class and in everyday life.

Ethical Responsibilities of a Listener

The concept of constructive listening is incomplete without considering the importance of listening ethics. Constructive listeners must meet high ethical standards. Ethical listeners do not prejudge a speech but keep an open mind. John Milton, a great seventeenth-century English intellectual, observed that listening to our opponents can be beneficial. We may learn from them, thus gain-

Figure 4.5

Guidelines for Evaluating Speeches

Overall Considerations

Was the speaker committed to the topic?
Did the speech meet the requirements of the assignment?
Was the speech adapted to the audience?
Did the speech promote identification among topic, audience, and speaker?
Was the purpose of the speech clear?
Was the topic handled with imagination and freshness?
Did the speech meet high ethical standards?

Substance

Was the topic worthwhile?
Had the speaker done sufficient research?
Were main ideas supported with information?
Was testimony used appropriately?
Were the sources documented adequately?
Were examples or narratives used effectively?
Was the reasoning clear and correct?

Structure

Did the introduction arouse interest?
Did the introduction preview the message?
Was the speech easy to follow?
Were the main points of the speech evident?
Were transitions used to tie the speech together?
Did the conclusion summarize the message?
Did the conclusion help you remember the speech?

Presentation

Was the language clear, simple, and direct?
Was the language colorful?
Were grammar and pronunciations correct?
Was the speech presented extemporaneously?
Were notes used unobtrusively?
Was the speaker appropriately enthusiastic?
Did the speaker maintain good eye contact?
Did body language complement ideas?
Was the speaker expressive?
Were the rate and loudness appropriate?
Did the speaker use pauses?
Did presentation aids enhance the message?
Were presentation aids integrated into the speech?
Was the presentation free from distracting mannerisms?

ing a new perspective on an issue. Or, as we argue with them, we may discover *why* we believe as we do.

Just as we should be open to ideas, we should also be open to speakers who represent different lifestyles or cultural backgrounds. We should not deprive ourselves of the chance to explore other worlds. In comparing and contrasting our ways with those of others, we learn more about ourselves.

Finally, keep in mind the impact of your listening on others. Good listeners help develop good speakers. Good listeners are also concerned about the ethical impact of messages on others who may not be present. In the sense that they represent all who might be affected by the message, they are the **universal listener**. Such listeners practice their own version of the Golden Rule: "Listen to others as you would have them listen to you." All sides benefit when speakers and listeners take their ethical roles seriously.

Ethics *Alert! 4.2*

Guidelines for Ethical Listening

The ethical behavior of listeners is often overlooked. If you would be an ethical listener, follow these guidelines:

1. Give the speaker your undivided attention.

2. Open your mind to new ideas.

3. Park your biases outside the door.

4. Provide honest feedback to the speaker.

5. Look for what is good or useful in the message.

6. Consider how the speech might affect others.

7. Listen to others as you would have them listen to you.

In Summary

The Benefits of Listening.   Effective listening benefits both listeners and speakers. Improved listening skills can enhance both your academic performance and your career success. Effective listeners are less vulnerable to unethical advertising or to dishonest public communication. Despite this obvious importance, education in listening is often neglected.

The Process of Listening.   Listening is a process that extends from mere awareness through the most sophisticated forms of reception. In the discriminative phase of listening, we must be able to hear a message. In the comprehensive phase, we must understand and interpret what we hear. In the empathic phase, we begin to see things from the speaker's point of view, and in the appreciative phase, we enjoy the speaker's ability to structure messages skillfully and to word ideas attractively. Critical listening requires that we test messages for the soundness of their content, and constructive listening challenges us to be active participants in the process of communication.

Overcoming Listening Problems.   Some listening problems arise from the speaking situation or from speakers. These problems may include noisy surroundings, flawed messages, or poor presentations.

The most serious listening problems are grounded in listeners themselves. These problems include inattention, chance associations with words, or personal concerns. Bad habits, such as feigning attention or listening only for facts, are another cause of problems. Receiver apprehension can also block effective listening.

Still another problem occurs when trigger words set off strong positive or negative emotions in listeners. Biased attitudes can distort messages through filtering, assimilation, or contrast effects.

universal listener   Listening as though you represent all who might be affected by a message.

To overcome listening problems, concentrate on the main ideas and the overall meaning of a speech. Strive to be as objective as you can, and withhold judgment until you are certain you understand the message.

Developing Critical Listening Skills. Critical listening helps protect you from messages that wear a "halo" and ensures that you give a fair hearing to ideas that go against your beliefs. Critical listeners question what they hear, require support for assertions and claims, and evaluate the credentials of sources. They differentiate among facts, inferences, and opinions. They become wary of vague or incomprehensible language, or when inflammatory speech replaces reasoning, or when a message promises too much. When what they hear does not fit with what they know, critical listeners start asking tough questions.

Evaluating Speeches. Critiquing a speech involves positive and constructive efforts to help speakers improve.

Criteria for speech evaluation include overall considerations, substance, structure, and presentation skills. Overall considerations include the speaker's commitment, adaptation to the audience and occasion, clearness of purpose, freshness of perspective, and ethical standards. Substance involves the value of the topic, the sufficiency of research, the adequacy of supporting material, and the speaker's ability to reason. Structural criteria include the use of an effective introduction, a well-organized body with main points and supporting material, and a conclusion that provides closure. Presentation questions consider how well speakers use words and their ability to convey messages through voice and gesture.

Ethical Responsibilities of Listeners. Ethical listeners do not prejudge a speech but are open to new ideas and different perspectives. They are receptive to speakers representing different lifestyles and cultural backgrounds. Ethical listeners are also sensitive to the impact of ideas on others.

Explore and Apply the Ideas in This Chapter

1. Complete the listening problems checklist on page 77. Working in small groups, discuss your listening problems with the other members. Develop a listening improvement plan for the three most common listening problems in your group. Report this plan to the rest of the class.

2. List three positive and three negative trigger words that provoke a strong emotional reaction when you hear them. Group the words into categories, such as sexist or ethnic slurs, political terms, ideals, and so on. Discuss in class why these words have such a strong impact and how listeners might control their reactions to them.

3. Identify a speaker (outside your class) you find difficult to listen to attentively. Explore the sources of interference in yourself that make it hard for you to listen. Design a plan to overcome this problem.

4. Review your class notes from one of your lecture courses. Were you able to identify the main points, or did you try to write down everything that was said?

5. Read the following paragraph carefully:

   Dirty Dick has been killed. The police have rounded up six suspects, all of whom are known criminals. All of them were near the scene of the crime at the approximate time that the murder took place. All had good motives for wanting Dirty Dick killed. However, Larcenous Lenny has been completely cleared of guilt.

   Now determine whether each of the following statements is true (T), False (F), or an inference (?).

   1. Larcenous Lenny is known to have been near the scene of the crime.

   2. All of the rounded-up criminals were at the scene of the murder.

   3. Only Larcenous Lenny has been cleared of guilt.

   4. The police do not know who killed Dirty Dick.

   5. Dirty Dick's murderer did not confess of his own free will.

   6. It is known that the six suspects were in the vicinity of the cold-blooded assassination.

   7. Larcenous Lenny did not kill Dirty Dick.

   8. Dirty Dick is dead.

   You can find the answers in the chapter notes at the end of this book[27]. Were you able to distinguish between inferences and facts?

5 Adapting to Your Audience and Situation

This chapter will help you

- understand audience dynamics
- adapt your message to fit your audience
- meet the challenges of audience diversity
- adjust your message to the speaking situation

Orators have to learn the differences of human souls.

—*Plato*

Your just started a job in the public relations department of the local utility company. Next week you are scheduled to speak about energy conservation to three different groups. Early Monday afternoon you will talk to a hundred boys at a scout camp who would much rather be swimming or canoeing. Wednesday evening you will meet with a group of about fifty low-income homeowners at a branch library who are angry over high utility bills. Friday morning you will address a breakfast meeting of a dozen area executives who are worried about brown-outs interfering with manufacturing and production in their companies.

The general topic of your speeches will not change, but the different audiences and situations will require different approaches. Your listeners must be at the center of your thinking as you plan and develop your speeches. For example, with the scouts, you might want to stress how energy use affects the environment and suggest little things they can do to help in the conservation effort. With the homeowners, you might talk about the free energy audits offered by the utility company and how minor changes they initiate can make a difference in their bills. With the executives, your focus might be on the utility company's customized plans to lessen the impact of brown-outs on businesses.

The focus of your speech is not the only thing you might want to adjust with respect to your audience. As you consider the size of the audience and the settings for your speeches, you might decide to change the way you present them. Your manner of presentation, as well as the language you choose, may vary from the campground to the library meeting room to the restaurant.

Why Audience Analysis Is Important

The more you know about your listeners, the more effective your speech will be. A good audience analysis helps you find answers to three important questions:

1. What does my audience know about my topic?
2. How does my audience feel about my topic?
3. How can I best reach my listeners?

You gain insight into the first question through a demographic analysis of your audience as you consider such factors as age, education, occupation, and group memberships. Understanding audience dynamics, such as the attitudes of your listeners and the factors that motivate them, helps you answer the second and third questions. An effective audience analysis can also help you focus your topic and select the most effective supporting materials.

Is it ethical to adapt a message to fit a particular audience? You have probably heard about political speakers who "waffled"—taking one position with one audience and a different position with another. Such maneuvering is clearly unethical. But it is possible and ethical to adapt a message without surrendering your convictions. You can vary the language you use, the examples you provide, the stories you tell, the authorities you cite, and your manner of presentation without compromising the integrity of your message.

To help you better understand your audience, we first consider *demographic factors*, such as age, political and religious preferences, and gender. Then, we cover *audience dynamics*, the motivations, attitudes, and values of listeners. Next, we discuss some of the major challenges speakers face when addressing a *diverse audience*. Finally, we cover some aspects of the *communication situation* that may call for adaptations in your presentation.

Understanding Audience Demographics

What people know about a topic can often be determined by considering their age, gender, education, group affiliations, and sociocultural background. Such factors are called **audience demographics**. With your classroom audience, demographic information is fairly obvious. Start by looking around. How old are your classmates? What obvious kinds of diversity are represented? Listen carefully to the first round of speeches to identify topics listeners find interesting. Keep an ear tuned for the political and social concerns of your classmates. If you are speaking outside the classroom, the person who invites you may be able to supply such information.

Your demographic analysis of your audience can also provide insights into their attitudes, beliefs, and values. Much demographic and attitude information is available on public opinion Web sites sponsored by such groups as the Gallup Organization (www.gallup.com), the National Opinion Research Center (www.norc.uchicago.edu), and the Roper Center for Public Opinion Research (www.ropercenter.uconn.edu).

You should exercise caution when interpreting demographic data from such sources. First, much of this information is gathered through self-reports. In such surveys, people tend to give "socially appropriate" responses to questions. This doesn't mean that they lie, but it can mean that they report "what they think they ought to say" or "how they think they ought to feel." Be especially cautious with information from "polls" that local television stations or Internet sites conduct. Such material is rarely produced by a random sample of respondents: It may simply reflect the feelings of those prompted to reply or the agenda of those who have an axe to grind.

Finally, generic sources produce generic data. *Don't assume that what is true in general about a population will automatically be true of the particular people who will be listening to your speeches.* Demographic analyses can supply you with a list of tendencies, but you must confirm whether this list applies to your listeners. We turn now to the various elements of audience demographics: age, gender, educational level, group affiliation, and sociocultural background.

Age

Age has been used to predict audience reactions since the time of Aristotle, who suggested that young listeners are pleasure loving, optimistic, impulsive, trusting, idealistic, and easily persuaded. Older people, he said, are more set in their ways, more skeptical, cynical, and concerned with maintaining a comfortable existence. Those in the prime of life, Aristotle argued, present a balance between youth and age, being confident yet cautious, judging cases by the facts, and taking all things in moderation.[1]

Contemporary communication research supports the relationship between age and persuasibility that Aristotle identified. Maximum susceptibility to persuasion occurs during childhood and declines as people grow older. Most research also suggests that younger people are more flexible and open to new ideas and that older people tend to be more conservative and less receptive to change.[2] You can change the minds of older adults, but you'll have to work harder to do it.

audience demographics   Observable characteristics of listeners, including age, gender, educational level, group affiliations, and sociocultural backgrounds.

Age can be an important factor in the selection of speech topics. For example, an audience consisting mainly of eighteen- and nineteen-year-olds might be interested in a speech on campus social activities. To an older audience, this topic could seem trivial or uninteresting. Age can also be important in terms of the language you use and the people, places, things, or events you refer to in your speeches.

The typical college student audience falls into what has been called Generation Next. For a detailed account of this age group, see the 2007 report of the Pew Research Center, "How Young People View Their Lives, Futures, and Politics," available online at http://people-press.org/reports/pdf/300.pdf. You might also wish to access the annual report of the Higher Education Research Institute at UCLA on first-year college students, available online at www.gseis.ucla.edu/heri/heri.html. As you read this material, keep in mind that the national norms may not fit your particular classroom audience. Interpret the results in light of other information you have gathered about your classmates.

Gender

In the 1950s, *Life* magazine interviewed five male psychiatrists, who suggested that women's ambitions were the "root of mental illness in wives, emotional upset in husbands, and homosexuality in boys."[3] Needless to say, we have come a long way from that era!

In our time, ideas about gender differences continue to change rapidly. The changes are especially marked in the areas of "gender appropriate" roles and interests, where the lines are becoming blurred.[4] Some of the greatest changes in gender roles have come in the areas of education and work. In 1950, only 24 percent of all college degrees went to women; in 2005, women earned 57 percent of all degrees awarded.[5] In 1960, 38 percent of females between the ages of twenty-five and fifty-four were in the labor force; by 1996, this number had risen to about 60 percent, and the level has been consistent through the present time.[6] Thirty-seven percent of women in the labor force work in management, professional, or similar occupations, while 31 percent of the male labor force occupies such positions.[7]

From this data, we can safely conclude that the importance of women in the work force—and the importance of their occupations—has risen dramatically over the past fifty years. Therefore, we suggest caution in making adjustments based on the gender of your listeners. Be certain that any assumptions you make are based on the most current data available, because the differences are often a matter of "now you see them, now you don't." Differences that seem true as we write may be only illusions by the time you read this text. Finally, be especially careful to avoid sexism and gender stereotyping. These two topics are covered in detail later in this chapter.

The more you know about your audience, the better you can adapt your message to meet their needs and expectations.

Educational Level

You can better estimate your listeners' knowledge of and interest in a topic from their educational level than from their age or gender. The more educated your audience, the more you can assume they know about general topics and current affairs, and the broader their range of interests is apt to be. Research suggests that better-educated audiences are more interested in social, consumer, political, and environmental issues. They are more curious, and they enjoy learning about new ideas, new things, and new places. If your speech presents a fresh perspective on a problem, they should be avid listeners. Finally, better-educated audiences tend to be more open-minded. They are more accepting of social and technological changes and more supportive of women's rights and alternative lifestyles than are less educated listeners.[8]

Educational differences can also affect the strategies you use in a speech. For example, if there are several positions on an issue, you should assume that a better-educated audience will be aware of them. Therefore, you should be especially careful to acknowledge other viewpoints and to explain why you have selected your position.[9] Although you should always speak from responsible knowledge, knowing that your listeners are highly educated places even more pressure on you to prepare carefully. A well-educated audience will require that you supply evidence and examples that can stand up under close scrutiny. If you are not well prepared, such listeners will question your credibility.

Group Affiliations

The groups people belong to reflect their interests, attitudes, and values. Knowing the occupations, political preferences, religious affiliations, and social group memberships of an audience can provide useful information. This knowledge can help you design a speech that better fits the interests and needs of your listeners. It can make your message more relevant and can help promote identification between listeners and your ideas.

Occupational Groups.   Knowing your listeners' occupational affiliations or career aspirations can provide insight into how much your listeners know about a topic, the vocabulary you should use, and which aspects of a topic should be most interesting to them. For example, speeches on tax-saving techniques given to professional writers and then to certified public accountants (CPAs) should not have the same focus or use the same language. With the writers, you might stress record keeping and business deductions and avoid using technical jargon. With the CPAs, you might concentrate on factors that invite audits by the IRS, and you would not have to be so concerned about translating technical terms into lay language. Knowledge of listeners' occupations also suggests the kinds of examples you may wish to provide and the authorities listeners will find most credible. If many of your classmates are business majors, for instance, they may find information from the *Wall Street Journal* more convincing than information from *USA Today*.

Political Groups.   Members of organized political groups tend to be interested in problems of public life. Knowing how interested in politics your listeners are and their political party preferences can be useful in planning and preparing your speech.[10]

As she planned her speech attacking the U.S.-sponsored School of the Americas as a hotbed of ultra-right subversion in the Western hemisphere, Amanda Miller faced a considerable problem. Her audience analysis revealed that many of her listeners described themselves as conservative Republicans. If they sensed that she was a leftist critic, they might dismiss her arguments as exaggerated and unwarranted. Therefore, Amanda decided on the following opening to her speech:

> **"If any government sponsors the outlaws and killers of innocents, they have become outlaws and murderers themselves, and they will take that lonely path at their own peril."** President Bush spoke these words to the world shortly after the attacks on the World Trade Towers.

By citing a person who was esteemed by many of her listeners, Amanda invited them to look into an ironic mirror: Once they knew what many graduates of the School of the Americas had actually done, they could only conclude that the United States was the kind of rogue government the president had described. Her speech had a powerful impact that day because of the way she adapted it to the political leanings of her audience.

People with strong political ties usually make their feelings known. Look for indications in discussions in class. Some of your classmates may be active members of the Young Democrats or Young Republicans. Your college may conduct mock elections or take straw votes on issues of political interest, reporting the results in the campus newspaper. Be on the alert for such information.

Religious Groups. Knowing the religious affiliations of listeners can provide useful information, because religious training often underlies many of our social and cultural attitudes and values. Members of fundamentalist religious groups are likely to have conservative social and political attitudes. Baptists tend to be more conservative than Episcopalians, who in turn are often more conservative than Unitarians. In addition, a denomination may advocate specific beliefs that many of its members accept as a part of their religious heritage. Since religious affiliation may be a strong indicator of values, it is wise not to ignore its potential importance.

A word of caution must be added here. You can't always assume that because an individual is a member of a particular religious group he or she will embrace all of the teachings of that group. One thing you can count on, however, is that audiences are usually sensitive about topics related to their religious convictions. As a speaker, you should be aware of this sensitivity and be attuned to the religious makeup of your audience. Appealing to "Christian" values before an audience that includes members of other religious groups may offend listeners and diminish the effectiveness of your message.

Social Groups. Typically, we are born into a religious group, raised in a certain political environment, and end up in an occupation as much by chance as by design. But we choose our social groups on the basis of our interests. Membership in social groups can be as important to people as any other kind of affiliation. Photographers may join the Film Club, businesspeople may become involved with the Chamber of Commerce, and environmentalists may be members of the Sierra Club.

Knowing which social groups are represented in your audience and what they stand for is important for effective

Knowing the group affiliations of your listeners could help you adapt your message to their interests, concerns, and needs.

audience adaptation. A speech favoring pollution control measures might take a different focus, depending on whether it is presented to the Chamber of Commerce or to the Audubon Society. With the Chamber of Commerce, you might stress the importance of a clean environment in persuading businesses to relocate in your community; with the Audubon Society, you might emphasize the effects of pollution on wildlife. People tend to make their important group memberships known to others around them. Be alert to such information from your classmates, and consider it in planning and preparing your speeches.

Sociocultural Background.   People often are grouped by sociocultural background, a broad category that can include everything from the section of the country in which they live to their racial or ethnic identity to their economic status. Demographic Web sites provide access to a wide array of information relevant to a variety of sociocultural groups. Although such material may be fascinating, it is *your* audience for *your* speech that is important.

People from different sociocultural backgrounds often have different experiences, interests, and viewpoints. Consider, for example, the different perspectives that urban and rural audiences may have on gun control. Urban audiences may associate guns with crime and violence in the streets, and rural audiences may associate guns with hunting and recreation. A white, middle-class audience might have difficulty understanding what it means to grow up as a member of a minority. Midwesterners and Southerners may have misconceptions about each other.

With diverse audiences, your appeals and examples should relate to those experiences, feelings, values, and motivations that people hold in common. It also

InterConnections.
LearnMore 5.1

Demographics on the Web

In addition to the public opinion Web sites mentioned earlier in this chapter, you might also check out those listed here for interesting demographic insights into your audience.

VALS
www.sric-bi.com/VALS/
> *A marketing research site that combines demographic and values data to classify people into clusters or types. Take the online survey and get immediate feedback on where you fit into the VALS typology.*

Pew Research Center
www.people-press.org
> *A reputable political ideology research group that is often cited during political campaigns. Current poll results and commentary are available online.*

American Demographics
http://adage.com/americandemographics
> *The online edition of a major marketing magazine containing a variety of articles and other interesting information useful to marketers and speechmakers.*

The Polling Report
www.pollingreport.com
> *This online service provides copies of polling reports from a variety of American public opinion polls.*

may be helpful to envision smaller audiences within the larger group. You may even want to direct specific remarks to these smaller groups. You might say, for example, "Those of you majoring in the liberal arts will find computer skills just as important in your work as they are for business majors," or "Those of you majoring in business may discover that large corporations are looking for employees with the breadth of perspective that comes from a liberal arts education." Direct references to specific subgroups within the audience can keep your speech from seeming too general.

Understanding Audience Dynamics

*O*nce you have assessed the demographic characteristics of your audience, you are ready to consider the final two questions: *How does my audience feel about my topic?* and *How can I best reach my listeners?* To discover the answers to these questions, you must understand the psychological forces at work in listeners. While you may never attain a complete understanding of these factors, the more you know about how your audience feels and what moves them, the better your speech will be. In short, you must tune into audience dynamics.

Audience dynamics are the attitudes, beliefs, values, and motivations that affect how listeners receive a message. An understanding of how these dynamics work is vital for adapting your message. The more you understand what makes people tick, the better you can tailor your message so that it serves their interests and needs.

Attitudes, Beliefs, and Values

Attitudes typically refer to our *feelings* about things—whether we like or dislike, approve or disapprove of people, places, events, or ideas. Our **beliefs** express what we *know* or *think we know* about subjects. Our important social attitudes are anchored by our **values**, the moral *principles* we live by that suggest how we should behave or what we see as an ideal state of being. To be an effective speaker, you must consider your listeners' attitudes, beliefs, and values as you plan and prepare your speeches.

Attitudes. Your audience's feelings toward your topic can affect the way it receives your message. For example, suppose you are preparing a speech favoring amnesty for illegal immigrants. You know that many members of your audience strongly oppose this policy. An audience that disagrees with you may distort your message, discredit you, or even refuse to listen to you.

Knowing how listeners feel about your topic allows you to plan your strategies to minimize the impact of negative attitudes. It can suggest what sources you might use to support your ideas, the types of examples you might choose, or even what your specific purpose might be. For example, with a reluctant audience, you should work hard to establish identification early in your speech, perhaps pointing out the values that you and your audience share. You might also want to avoid emotional appeals and limit what you want to accomplish. These and other techniques for persuading a reluctant audience are covered in more detail in Chapter 16.

Beliefs. Beliefs are acquired through experience and education. Some beliefs may be learned through direct contact: "The waiters at that restaurant are very attentive

---

audience dynamics   The motivations, attitudes, beliefs, and values that influence the behavior of listeners.

attitudes   Feelings we have developed toward specific kinds of subjects.

beliefs   What we know or think we know about subjects.

values   The moral principles that suggest how we should behave or what we see as an ideal state of being.

and helpful." Other beliefs may be acquired indirectly from family, friends, and authority figures as we grow up: "My Uncle Jake says the Republican Party favors the wealthy." "Well, my Aunt Leslie says that the Democrats always want to raise taxes."

Many beliefs are based on verifiable facts, such as, "The price of personal computers has dropped dramatically over the past five years." Other beliefs are based more on faith or even legend: "You should always buy a Ford truck" or "Southerners make better soldiers." At their worst, beliefs express demeaning stereotypes about races, religions, or cultures. Information about your listeners' beliefs can suggest what additional information you need to provide or what misinformation you may need to correct.

Values. Values may include such ideals as honesty, equality, peace, freedom, and salvation. Our personal, social, religious, and political values guide much of our thinking and behavior. They are the foundation for our most important beliefs and attitudes, providing us with standards for evaluation.

Values are at the core of our identity. As principles that govern our behavior and our way of seeing the world, they are highly resistant to change. Information that clashes with a listener's values is likely to be rejected without much thought. Speakers don't normally try to change values. Rather, they try to show how values relate to a topic in order to justify certain interpretations and recommendations. References to shared values, however, can increase identification between a speaker and the audience and strengthen the persuasive impact of a speech.

Insight into the attitudes, beliefs, and values of your audience can help you plan your messages. It can aim you in the proper direction so that you select the most effective appeals, decide what authorities to cite, and determine what examples and stories might work best in your speeches.

Gathering Information about Attitudes

How can you find out about attitudes toward your topic? In the classroom, this is not difficult because people reveal this kind of information readily as they take part in class discussions. Outside the classroom, you might question the person who invites you to speak about those aspects of the audience's attitude that are related to your topic.

To understand more fully how your listeners' attitudes may relate to your topic, you can conduct a survey to explore what your listeners know about your topic, how they feel about it, and how they might respond to different sources of information. Figure 5.1 shows a sample audience survey questionnaire on the subject of capital punishment that may be used as a guide to developing a questionnaire on your subject.

When preparing an attitude survey questionnaire, you should use the following guidelines:

- Use simple sentences with a single idea.
- Use clear, concrete language.
- Keep questions short.
- Avoid words such as *all, always, none,* and *never.*
- Keep your own biases out of the questions.
- Keep the questionnaire short.
- Provide room for comments.

Figure 5.1

Sample Attitude Questionnaire

For each question, please circle the number that most clearly represents your position.

1. How interested are you in the topic of capital punishment?

Very Interested			Unconcerned			Not Interested
7	6	5	4	3	2	1

2. How important do you think the issue of capital punishment is?

Very Important			No Opinion			Very Unimportant
7	6	5	4	3	2	1

3. How much do you know about capital punishment?

Very Little			Average Amount			Very Much
7	6	5	4	3	2	1

4. How would you describe your attitude toward capital punishment?

Total Opposition			"On the Fence"			Total Support
7	6	5	4	3	2	1

5. Please place a check beside the sources of information on capital punishment that you would find the most acceptable.

    _____ Attorney general's office
    _____ FBI
    _____ Local police department
    _____ Criminal justice department of the university
    _____ American Civil Liberties Union
    _____ Local religious leaders
    _____ Conference of Christians and Jews
    _____ NAACP
    _____ Other (please specify)_____

Comments:

Finally, keep in mind that any questionnaire results you get, either from one you conduct yourself or from one that is professionally administered, provide only a general snapshot of where your audience stands on a topic. Compare what you learn from a questionnaire with what you hear as you listen to others talking about the issue in question.

Motivation

To answer the question, *How can I best reach my audience?*, you must explore what motivates your listeners. Motivation is the psychological force that moves people to action and directs their behavior toward certain goals. Motivation helps explain *why* people behave as they do.

Therefore, while motivation is important in all speaking, it is especially vital to informative and persuasive speeches. People will listen, learn, and remember a message only if it relates to their needs, wants, or wishes. Moreover, people will change their attitudes or behavior only if they are motivated to do so. Understanding motivation can also help a speaker appeal to the common humanity in listeners that crosses cultural boundaries.

Motives can vary in importance according to the person, situation, and culture. *People are motivated by what they don't have that they need or want.* If you have recently moved to a new town, your need to make friends may attract you to places where you can meet others. Even when needs are satisfied, people still respond to wants. Suppose you have just eaten a very filling meal. You're not hungry, but if someone enters the room with a tray of freshly baked brownies, the sight and smell can make your mouth water.

Psychologists have been studying human motivation since the early twentieth century. Social scientists first concentrated on identifying different types of human motivation. In a pioneering study published during the 1930s, Henry A. Murray and his associates at Harvard identified more than twenty-five human needs.[12] The late psychologist Abraham Maslow arranged needs in a five-tiered hierarchy of potency with the lower level needs (physiological and safety/security) having to be satisfied before the higher level needs (belonging, esteem, and self-actualization) come into play.[13]

What is most important to you as a speaker is that appealing to needs and motivations helps you reach your audience. Consider how you might frame appeals for use in your speeches based on the following types of motivation.

Comfort. The need for comfort involves such things as having enough to eat and drink, keeping warm when it's cold and cool when it's hot, and being free from pain. Most middle-class Americans take comfort for granted, so speeches appealing to this need level must awaken an awareness of potential problems. One student speaker caught the attention of his classmates as he

InterConnections. *LearnMore 5.2*

Audience Dynamics

Motivation

http://psychclassics.yorku.ca/Maslow/motivation.htm

A reprint of Maslow's original article, "A Theory of Human Motivation," setting forth his theory of motivation. The essay was originally published in Psychology Review *in 1943.*

Values

www.zetterberg.org/Papers/ppr1997b.htm

"The Study of Values," an article that covers a variety of approaches to the study of human values, by Professor Hans L. Zetterberg, sociologist and director of the Social Research Consulting Group in Stockholm, Sweden.

Attitudes

http://jonathan.mueller.faculty.noctrl.edu/crow/topicattitudes.htm

A variety of links to Web sites on attitudes and behaviors sponsored by Course Resources on the Web and the Associated Colleges of Illinois. Provides links to general resources defining the attitude–behavior relationship and survey/polling data on specific attitudes. Developed and maintained by Jon Mueller, Professor of Psychology at North Central College.

Speeches that discuss ways to promote physical and psychological well being are interesting to most audiences.

appealed to this need in the introduction of his speech on the benefits of yoga:

> No pain, no gain! Right? No, wrong. If workout routines leave you heading for the medicine cabinet, look for another way to get your body and heart in shape. An exercise program that combines yoga and power walking improves both your body tone and your cardiovascular system.

Other speech topics that focus on comfort might include "Meals in Your Room: Alternatives to Cafeteria Food" and "Who Turned Down the Thermostat? Keeping Warm in the Dorm."

Safety.   We all need to feel free from threats. Crimes on campus, natural disasters such as hurricanes, contaminated food or water, and accidents are major sources of concern. Appeals to the need for safety are usually based on arousing a sense of fear. You should be cautious when using fear appeals in speeches. If fear appeals are too obvious, your listeners may feel manipulated. They may resent you and reject your message. Should you decide to use appeals to safety in your speech, be sure to provide clear instructions on how the dangers can be averted or avoided. Some topics that would relate to this need include "Setting Up a Campus-Wide Emergency Notification System" and "What To Do When the Sirens Go Off: Tornado Preparedness."

Belonging.   People need other people who provide acceptance, affection, companionship, approval, and support. Our friends and families help define who we are and make the world a less lonely place. Our need to belong explains our desire to join groups and take pride in our membership. The need to belong may be the most prevalent motivational appeal in contemporary American advertising. How many advertisements have you seen that suggest that if you don't use the "right" deodorant or drive the "right" car, you risk losing friends? Some speech topics based on this need might include "Love Makes the World Go 'Round: A Look at Computer Dating Services" and "Overcoming Loneliness: Volunteers Help Themselves While Helping Others."

Independence.   Although we need other people, we also need independence. The desire to feel that "I can do it myself" is strongly embedded in the American culture. This need is especially strong in young adults who are in the process of finding themselves. The quest for independence allows young people to develop into fully functioning adults, to make decisions on their own, and to take responsibility for their own lives. Consequently, college audiences may be especially responsive to speeches that stress the need for freedom from arbitrary constraints on their ideas, actions, or lifestyles. Speeches that teach listeners how to "do it yourself" rather than pay someone to do it for you appeal to this need.

Nurturance.   It makes people feel good to be able to care for, protect, and comfort others. Appeals to this need can be especially strong when speakers discuss children who have problems. Beth Tidmore used this appeal when she described the benefits disabled children receive from the Special Olympics:

> They experience courage and victory—and, yes, they also experience defeat. They get to interact with others with disabilities and with people without disabilities. And their mental disability is not a problem. It's not weird. Their biggest achievements aren't recognized with a medal. Their biggest achievements take place over time in the growth they make through being a part of the Special Olympics.

Fairness.   The need for fairness envisions a moral balance in the world. We like to feel that we deserve what happens to us, both the good and the bad. For idealistic college audiences, fairness can be a strong source of motivation. Speeches that express outrage over human rights abuses, racism in the workplace, or the past and present treatment of Native Americans draw heavily on this need. In a speech urging equal pay for equal work, Kayla Roberts reported:

> A recent study reported by Reuters News shows that even though women academically outperform males in college, regardless of their majors, within one year of graduation, women working full time earn only 80 percent of what men earn. After ten years have passed, women earn only 69 percent as much as men. Shocking, isn't it? A problem? It is if you're a woman! Equal work should be equally rewarded and corporate America needs to address this issue.

Tradition.   People place a premium on things that give them a sense of roots. There are some things we don't want to change. For example, Thanksgiving dinner means turkey and dressing, sweet potato casserole, cranberries, and pumpkin pie. People often rely on traditions to anchor their beliefs and sustain them in times of trouble. Showing listeners that you share their traditions and values can help create identification in speeches. In a speech explaining the similarities and differences between holidays in the United States and Mexico, Stephanie Herrera shared the following:

> Christmas in Mexico is not really a gift-giving holiday like it is in the United States. It's more of a religious observance. People walk through the neighborhood in a *posada.* This means "where they stop." The stops along the way are beautifully decorated homes where the walkers sing carols and are given gifts of food—like cookies and candies. The *posada* is a parade to honor Niño Dios, which means "baby God" in English.

Variety.   Too much of anything, even a good thing, can be dull. The need for variety can include a longing for adventure, a desire to do something different and exciting, or a yen to travel to exotic places or to meet new and interesting people. Brandon Rader presented a speech on gender bending, public dress and behavior that appears more appropriate to the opposite sex, that captured the attention of his listeners. He argued that gender is a social construct that has been subject to great variation over time and across cultures, and that our expectations for how men and women are supposed to behave are not engraved somewhere in stone. The effect of his speech was to create more space for gender benders to explore the potential of their lives without earning social disdain. Speeches that focus on fresh topics or that offer a vicarious adventure tap into this appeal.

Understanding.   People are by nature curious. They want to know, What is it? How does it work?, and Why is this happening? When we satisfy curiosity, we increase our understanding. The quest for understanding has never been more important than in today's workplace, which demands that we adapt to rapid changes in knowledge.[14] Speech topics that are unusual, such as foreign customs or

Figure 5.2

Motivational Appeals for Use in Speeches

Consider these motivational appeals as you plan your speeches	
Comfort	Having enough to eat and drink, maintaining a comfortable temperature, being free from pain
Safety	Feeling physically safe and psychologically secure, having a sense of stability and order in your life
Belonging	Having warm relationships with others, being a member of a group, being accepted by others, having someone to love and be loved by
Independence	Being self-sufficient, making your own decisions, being your own person
Nurturance	Taking care of others, providing comfort and aid, giving to charities, volunteering service, promoting the well-being of others
Fairness	Trying to establish or restore moral balance in the world so that people get the treatment they deserve
Tradition	Having a sense of roots, doing things as they have always been done, honoring ancestors, appreciating your history
Variety	Longing for change and adventure, trying different things, exploring different majors, meeting new people
Understanding	Investigating the world around you, learning more about yourself, understanding others, questioning why things happen
Achievement	Accomplishing something of significance, overcoming obstacles in pursuit of goals, doing better than expected
Recognition	Being treated as valuable and important, being praised for accomplishments, receiving awards, being the center of attention
Enjoyment	Having fun, taking a vacation, pampering yourself, pursuing a hobby

exotic locales, also arouse curiosity. Similarly, speeches that explain medical advances or useful technical innovations can help expand understanding.

Achievement.   The need for achievement, accomplishment, and success is one of the most thoroughly studied human motives. Although winning may not be everything, most of us feel that losing does not have much to recommend it. You can tap this need for achievement when you present speeches that show listeners how they can improve themselves and increase their chances for success.

Recognition.   Most people like to be treated as valuable and important. They like others to acknowledge their existence and accomplishments. Advertisements that associate products with visible symbols of success and recognition, such as elegant homes or expensive cars, appeal to this need. Speakers tap into the need for recognition when they find ways to compliment the audience in their introductory remarks. Sincere compliments put listeners in a positive frame of mind, making them more attentive and more receptive to the speaker's message.

Enjoyment.   People need to have some fun in their lives, especially college students who often find themselves overwhelmed with assignments, tests, speeches to give, and papers to write, not to mention full- or part-time work. Speeches that introduce listeners to new activities or places can fill this need. Here are some sample topics: "Fifteen-Minute Time Outs: Life's Short Pleasures" and "Weekend Break-Aways: The Alternative to Long Vacations."

All of these motivational appeals can be useful in speeches. They are summarized in Figure 5.2.

Meeting the Challenges of Audience Diversity

*D*iversity in the American classroom is an important factor in audience analysis. More and more, we are a coat of many colors, a quilt of many patches, a song sung by many singers.[15] Learning to communicate with others from different backgrounds and cultures can be one of the most rewarding experiences of your public speaking class. You can learn a great deal from others and expand your horizons. At the same time, diversity offers a challenge to the speaker, who must adapt a message so that it crosses the cultural boundaries represented in the typical classroom audience.[16] This cultural diversity is deeply rooted in different experiences: different attitudes, different loyalties, different goals, different religions, different fears, and what may seem to be different values. These differences can become barriers to communication. You can overcome these barriers by calling on universal values, making strategic uses of speaking resources, and avoiding rhetorical land mines that could destroy the effectiveness of your efforts.

Apply Universal Values

The Institute for Global Ethics has identified a number of universal values that you can use in your speeches to help build common ground (see Figure 5.3).[17] These values transcend cultural differences.

The first thing you may notice is how closely this list parallels the motivational appeals we discussed earlier. At times, the parallels are exact (tradition, achievement,

Figure 5.3

Universal Values

Power	Social power, authority, recognition from others, wealth
Achievement	Success, ambition, influence
Tradition	Acceptance of one's fate, devoutness, humility, respect for cultural heritage
Enjoyment	Pleasure
Self-Direction	Freedom, independence, choice of own goals, self-respect, curiosity, creativity
Security	National security, social order, family security, sense of belonging, personal health, reciprocity in personal relationships
Unity	Unity with nature, protecting the environment, inner harmony, social justice, equality, tolerance, a world at peace
Benevolence	Honesty, helpfulness, forgiveness, loyalty, responsibility, friendship, love, spiritual life, meaning in life
Conformity	Politeness, obedience, self-discipline, honoring parents and elders
Stimulation	Variety, excitement, daring

enjoyment). At other times, they are almost identical (independence/self-direction, safety/security, nurturance/benevolence). This is good news for the speaker, because it suggests that at the same time you are developing general appeals, you can also be reaching across the cultural divide.

How can you ground your speech in universal values? Consider how effectively Anna Aley used them in her speech asking for reform in the housing laws that governed rental properties in Manhattan, Kansas (see her speech at the end of Chapter 16). First, Anna found a subject that concerned practically all of her listeners, however diverse their backgrounds. They either rented such properties themselves or had friends who rented them. Anna had found a *unity* that joined them in a shared problem.

By depicting the dangers of this situation, Anna framed an appeal to *safety-security*—in this case, the lack of it. She asked them to come together to protest (appeal to *power*) and to take control of their lives (appeal to *independence/self-direction*). Implicitly, she appealed to their sense of adventure (taking on the slumlords would provide excitement in their lives). And she envisioned their success (*achievement*). Is there little wonder that Anna was able to find common ground among her listeners or that she delivered such an effective persuasive speech?

InterConnections.
LearnMore 5.3

Seeking Common Ground

National Conference for Community and Justice

www.nccj.org

> *Formerly known as the National Conference of Christians and Jews, this organization promotes understanding among all races, religions, and cultures.*

Stop the Hate

www.stop-the-hate.org

> *An antiviolence Web site aimed at creating an awareness of intercultural hate problems with links to a variety of antihate resources.*

Institute for Cultural Partnerships

www.culturalpartnerships.org.

> *The Web site of a nonprofit organization dedicated to bringing people and communities together so that individuals may successfully live, learn, and work in our increasingly diverse society.*

Use Speaking Resources Skillfully

A second way that speakers can rise to the challenge of cultural diversity is to make strategic use of communication resources, such as supporting materials and language.

Supporting Materials.   Supporting materials, discussed in detail in Chapter 7, provide the substance of all speeches. Their skillful use is essential when speaking to diverse audiences. The individuals who make up such audiences may have different susceptibilities when it comes to what they expect or prefer as support for ideas or suggestions. Some may be fact-oriented, priding themselves on their respect for reality. Others may rely more on authority, depending on the advice of elders, religious leaders, or respected others. Still others may see themselves as participants in ongoing stories that give meaning to their lives.

This diversity of propensities may suggest different strategies for the use of the facts, examples, testimony, and narratives in a speech. The first strategy is to *provide variety*. Present facts and expert testimony from unbiased sources for those who think of themselves as reality-minded. Offer quotations from respected leaders who support your point of view to reach those most influenced by authority. Avoid citing people who might set off extreme negative reactions. Develop stories for those attracted to narratives. Match the diversity of your audience with the variety of your supporting material.

The second special strategy for the use of supporting materials is to *emphasize the use of narratives*. Nothing can bring diverse people together more effectively than stories that help them discover their common humanity. Al Gore suggests that storytelling can even help old enemies make peace. On one occasion, when he was vice president, he met with Palestinian, Israeli, Jordanian, and Syrian leaders to discuss a peace treaty. Gore saw the negotiations faltering. The situation looked hopeless. But then a "miracle" happened. In Gore's words, "The breakthroughs came when they told stories about their families. I have seen time and time again how storytelling brings people together."[18] Stories can give meaning and life to universal values.

Avoid Language Pitfalls

The language you use can stand in the way of communication with diverse audiences (see Chapter 12). When audience members are unfamiliar with your topic, you should use lay language and define any terms that might be misunderstood. Consider using presentation aids to make your ideas clearer.

If your audience contains listeners for whom English is a second language, don't use slang terms that may confuse them. Our colloquial language uses many idioms drawn from sports, such as "he left it all out on the floor" and "she hit the wall." These and similar expressions can bring utter confusion to those who are new to our language or who do not share the speaker's enthusiasm for sports.

Another problem arises from cross-cultural language blunders. In the spring of 2007, a presidential candidate presented a speech that he hoped would win the support of the Cuban expatriate community in Florida. As he concluded, he shouted: *"Patria o muerte, venceremos!"* ("Fatherland or death, we shall overcome"). He did not understand the cold reaction to his words until someone explained that they were the trademark signoff of Fidel Castro. The lesson to you? Treat words like explosives: Don't play with them when you're not sure what you're doing!

Avoid Rhetorical Land Mines

The discussion of cross-cultural language blunders is similar to the third major consideration for reaching diverse audiences: Avoid stepping on land mines that can explode your efforts to communicate. These land mines include stereotypes and the three troublesome *-isms*: ethnocentrism, sexism, and racism.

Stereotypes.   All of us use our past experiences to make sense of new information and to guide our interactions with others. To use our experiences efficiently, we react in terms of categories.[19] For example, having heard about poisonous reptiles, we may be leery of all snakes. Problems arise, however, when we start putting people into categories. The categories can easily harden into **stereotypes**, rigid sets of beliefs and expectations about people in a certain group that reflect our attitudes or biases toward the group. When stereotypes dominate our thinking, we react more to them than to the people they represent. For example, we may stereotype the elderly as frail and impoverished or athletes as unintelligent and insensitive.

Stereotypes also may be related to ethnicity, religion, occupation, or place of residence. We may form stereotypes from direct experiences with a few individuals who we assume are representative of a group. Most stereotypes, however, are learned indirectly from our families and friends, schools and churches, or media exposure. For example, our stereotype of Native Americans may come from exposure to Western movies, or our stereotype of Italian Americans may have been shaped by TV shows like *The Sopranos*.

Whatever their origin, stereotypes can have a powerful influence on our thinking. We may judge people on the basis of stereotypes rather than on their merits as individuals. Stereotypes are also persistent: We are reluctant to give them up, especially when they agree with the stereotypes held by our friends and families. When we encounter people who do not fit our stereotypes, we may simply discount them as "exceptions to the rule."

Remember, your audience is a conglomerate of individuals, most of whom will not conform to any stereotyped beliefs you may have concerning the groups into which they might fit. Examine your thinking for stereotypes and consciously resolve not to let them surface in your message. If critical listeners detect stereotypes in your

stereotypes   Generalized pictures of a race, gender, or group that supposedly represent its essential characteristics.

thinking, they may reject both you and your speech. And it may take you some time to overcome the negative impressions you created.

Troublesome *-isms*. The three troublesome *-isms* that impede effective communication—especially with a diverse audience—are ethnocentrism, sexism, and racism.

Ethnocentrism. Ethnocentrism is the belief that our way of life is the "right" and superior way. In its milder form, ethnocentrism reveals itself as patriotism or national pride. But ethnocentrism has a darker side. When ethnocentrism goes beyond pride in one's own group to include the rejection or derogation of others, it becomes a real problem in human relations and a barrier to communication.

The first step in controlling ethnocentrism is to recognize any tendencies you may have to overestimate your own and underestimate other cultures. For example, most Americans believe that over half of the world's population speak English, when actually only about 20 percent do.[20] To avoid the impression of ethnocentrism in your speeches, *your language must show respect for the humanity of all people and recognize that this humanity transcends race and culture.*

Common values and interests can help bring groups together despite differences of age, gender, race or ethnicity.

Sexism. Sexism occurs when we allow gender stereotypes to control our interactions with members of the opposite sex. **Gender stereotyping** involves making broad generalizations about men or women based on outmoded assumptions, such as "men don't know how to take care of children" or "women don't understand finances." Gender stereotyping is especially problematic when it implies that the differences between men and women justify discrimination.

As you plan and prepare your message, be aware of any gender stereotyped ideas you have that could interfere with effective communication. Be careful not to portray gender roles in ways suggesting superiority or inferiority. For instance, when you use examples or stories to illustrate a point, don't make all your authority figures male.

Gender stereotyping often reveals itself in the use of **sexist language**, which involves making gender references in situations in which the gender is unknown or irrelevant, such as talking about a male nurse or a female police officer. It also can involve the generic use of masculine nouns or pronouns, such as referring to "man's advances in science" or using *he* when the intended reference is to both sexes. You can avoid this problem simply by saying "she or he" or by using the plural *they*.

Racism. Just as stereotyping and sexist language can block communication, so also can racism. Although blatant racism and discrimination are no longer socially acceptable in most circles, a subtle form of such prejudice can still infect our thinking. Although we may pay lip service to the principles of racial equality, we may still engage in **symbolic racism**, which is expressed subtly or covertly. For example, if we

---

ethnocentrism The tendency of any nation, race, religion, or group to believe that its way of looking at and doing things is right and that other perspectives have less value.

sexism Allowing gender stereotypes to control interactions with members of the opposite sex.

gender stereotyping Generalizations based on oversimplified or outmoded assumptions about gender roles.

Ethics *Alert!* 5.1

The Ethical Adaptation of Messages

Ask yourself, Will I have any special ethical problems in adapting my message to my audience? *To counter possible problems, keep in mind the following guidelines:*

1. Change your strategies, not your convictions.

2. Appeal to shared needs, values, and beliefs to help bridge cultural differences.

3. Respect individual differences among listeners.

4. Resist stereotypes that lead you to misjudge or derogate others.

5. Avoid using slang terms to refer to racial, gender, ethnic, or religious groups.

6. Suppress any impulse toward ethnocentrism.

---

say, "In *our* neighborhood, *we* believe in family values," the unspoken message may be, "*You* don't, and therefore *we* are superior." Or we might say, "We believe in hard work and earning *our* way," when we really mean, "Why don't *you* get off welfare?" Thus we may excuse the vestiges of racial stereotypes by appeals to values like family stability or the work ethic. In such cases, our underlying message may be, "*We* honor such values, and *you* don't."

As you take the factor of race into consideration in your audience analysis, examine your thinking for any lurking bias. Such biases may inadvertently break through in unexpected ways even though you don't intend them to. Stay away from examples that cast members of a particular ethnic group into stereotypical roles that imply inferiority. And of course, avoid racist humor.

Adjusting to the Communication Situation

inally, we come to the setting for your speech. You must consider the time, place, occasion, size of the audience, and overall context of recent topic-related events as you make final adjustments to your presentation.

Speaker's Notes 5.1

Avoiding Racist and Sexist Language

To avoid racist and sexist innuendos in your speeches, keep these rules in mind:

1. Do not use slang terms to refer to racial, ethnic, religious, or gender groups.

2. Avoid using the generic *he* and gender-specific titles such as *chairman.*

3. Avoid stereotypic references that imply inferiority or superiority.

4. Do not use sexist, racist, ethnic, or religious humor.

---

sexist language Making gender references in situations in which the gender is unknown or irrelevant, or using masculine nouns or pronouns when the intended reference is to both sexes.

symbolic racism An indirect form of racism that employs code words and subtle, unspoken contrast to suggest that one race is superior to another.

Time

The time of day, day of the week, time of the year, and—of course!—amount of time allotted for speaking can all affect your plans. If you are speaking early in the morning, you may need to be more forceful to awaken listeners. The energy in your voice must underscore the importance of your message. Since we tend to grow drowsy after we eat, after-dinner speeches (discussed in Chapter 17) need lively examples and humor. Speeches presented in the evening also present a problem. Most listeners will have completed a day's work and will have left the comforts of home to hear you. You must justify their attendance with good ideas well presented.

If your speech is scheduled for a Monday, when people have not yet adjusted to the weekend's being over, or a Friday, when they are thinking of the weekend ahead, you may need especially interesting material to hold attention. Similarly, gloomy winter days or balmy spring weather can put people in a different frame of mind, and their mood can color how they receive your speech. Your materials and presentation style will have to be bright and engaging to overcome the blahs or to ward off daydreaming.

The amount of time allotted for your presentation is also critical. *A short speech does not necessarily mean shorter preparation time.* Actually, shorter speeches often require longer preparation. Short speeches require you to focus and streamline your topic so that it can be handled in the time allotted. You must limit the number of main points and use supporting materials selectively. Choose the most relevant and impressive facts, statistics, and testimony, the most striking examples and stories. Plan your speech so that you begin with a burst and end with a bang.

Place

The place where you will be speaking can also be a factor. When speaking outside, you may have to cope with unpredictable distractions. When speaking inside, you need to know the size and layout of the room and whether a lectern or any needed electronic equipment will be available.

Even in the classroom, speakers must learn to cope with distractions—noise may filter in from outside, or people in the hall may be loud and inconsiderate. How can you handle such problems? If the noise is temporary, you should pause and wait until it stops, then repeat your last words and go on with your message. If the noise is constant, you may have to speak louder to be heard. You may even have to pause and close a window or door. The important thing is to take such problems in stride and not let them distract you or your audience from your message.

 **Speaker's Notes 5.2**

Checklist for Analyzing the Communication Situation

Use this checklist to determine whether and how you will need to adapt to situational factors in the presentation of your speech.

1. Will the time or timing of my speech present any challenges?

2. Will room arrangements be adequate?

3. Will I have the equipment I need to use presentation aids?

4. Is there any late-breaking news on my topic that I should acknowledge in my speech?

5. Will I possibly have to adjust to previous speakers?

6. How large will my audience be?

Speaking before a large audience requires adjustments in presentation style.

Occasion

As you plan your message, you must take into account *why* people have gathered to listen. When an audience is required to attend a presentation, such as a mandatory employee meeting, you may have to work hard to arouse interest and sustain attention. When audience members voluntarily attend a presentation, they usually are more motivated to listen. Understanding why your audience is present is especially important for speeches given outside the classroom setting. If your topic has been publicized and you have factored in audience dynamics and demographics, you should have a good idea of why listeners are present and the needs they expect you to meet. When a speaker does not offer the kind of message listeners expect, they may be annoyed. For example, if they are expecting an informative presentation on investment strategies and instead get a sales pitch for a particular mutual fund, they may feel exploited, which could result more in irritation than in persuasion.

Size of Audience

The size of your audience can affect how you speak. A small audience provides feedback and an opportunity for interaction. Generally, a small group of listeners invites a more casual presentation. A formal oratorical style, too loud a voice, or exaggerated gestures could easily overwhelm them.

On the other hand, large audiences offer less feedback. Because you cannot make or sustain eye contact with everyone, you should choose representative listeners in various sections of the audience and change your visual focus from time to time. Establishing eye contact with listeners in all sections of the room helps more people feel included. With large audiences you should also speak more deliberately and distinctly. Your gestures should be more emphatic so that everyone can see them, and any presentation aids used must be large enough for those in the back of the audience to see without strain.

Context

Anything that happens near the time of your presentation becomes part of the context of your speech. Both recent speeches and recent events can influence how the audience responds to you.

Recent Speeches.   Any speeches presented immediately before yours create an atmosphere in which you must work. This atmosphere has a **preliminary tuning effect** on listeners, preparing them to respond in certain ways to you and your message. At political rallies, patriotic music and introductions prepare the audience for the appearance of the featured speaker. At concerts, warm-up groups put listeners in the mood for the star.

Preliminary tuning may also influence classroom presentations, either positively or negatively. Earlier speeches may affect the mood of the audience. For example, if the

preliminary tuning effect   The effect of previous speeches or other situational factors in predisposing an audience to respond positively or negatively to a speech.

speech right before yours aroused strong emotions, you may need to ease the tension in the introduction to your speech. You can make such an impromptu adjustment by acknowledging listeners' feelings and using them as a springboard into your own speech:

> Obviously, many of us feel very strongly about the legalization of same-sex marriages. What I'm going to talk about is also very important—but it is something I think we can all agree on—the challenge of finding a way to stop children from killing other children in our community.

Figure 5.4

Audience Analysis Worksheet

Topic: _____

Audience: _____

	Factor Description	**Adaptations Needed**
Audience Dynamics	Audience Attitude: _____ _____	_____ _____
	Relevant Values: _____	_____ _____
	Motivational Appeals: _____ _____	_____ _____
Audience Demographics	Age: _____	_____
	Gender: _____	_____
	Education: _____	_____
	Group Affiliations: _____ _____	_____
	Sociocultural Background: _____ _____	_____ _____
	Interest in Topic: _____ _____	_____ _____
	Knowledge of Topic: _____ _____	_____ _____
Speaking Situation	Time: _____	_____
	Place: _____	_____
	Occasion: _____	_____
	Audience Size: _____	_____
	Context: _____	_____

Another technique might be to begin with a story that involves listeners and refocuses their attention. At times, humor can help relieve tension, but people who are upset may be in no mood for laughter. Your decision on whether to use humor must be based on your reading of the situation: the mood of listeners, the subject under discussion, and your own ability to use the technique effectively.

In addition to dealing with the mood created by earlier speeches, you may also have to adapt to their content. Suppose you have spent the past week preparing a speech on the *importance* of extending endangered species legislation. Then the speaker before you makes a convincing presentation on the *problems* of extending endangered species legislation. What can you do? Try to turn this to your advantage. Point out that the earlier speech established the importance of the topic but that—as good as that effort was—it did not give the total picture: "Now you will hear the *other* side of the story."

Recent Events. When listeners enter the room the day of your speech, they bring with them information about recent events. They will use this knowledge to evaluate what you say. If you are not up on the latest news concerning your topic, your credibility can suffer. A student in one of our classes once presented an interesting and well-documented speech comparing public housing in Germany with that in the United States. Unfortunately, she was unaware of a local scandal involving public housing. For three days before her presentation, the story had made the front page of the local newspaper and had been the lead story in area newscasts. Everyone expected her to mention it. Her failure to discuss this important local problem weakened her credibility.

Figure 5.4 provides an Audience Analysis Worksheet that will help you consider all the factors we have discussed in this chapter as you plan for the audience and situation of your speech. When you have sized up the situation, adding this knowledge to your analysis of audience dynamics and demographics, you will be ready for your next challenge—choosing a suitable topic for speaking.

In Summary

Both the audience you anticipate and the setting of your speech are critical to your planning. Successful audience adaptation requires that you have relevant information concerning audience demographics, understand audience dynamics, be sensitive to the challenges of audience diversity, and be able to adjust to situational factors.

Adjusting to Audience Demographics. Audience demographics include information about the specific characteristics of your listeners, such as their age, gender, educational level, group membership, and sociocultural makeup (race, social class, and so forth). The more you know about such factors, the better you can tailor your speech so that it serves your listeners' interests and needs.

Adapting to Audience Dynamics. Your audience's attitudes, beliefs, and values affect the way they receive and interpret your message. If your listeners are initially negative toward your topic, you must adjust your presentation to receive a fair hearing. Motivation explains why people behave as they do. People will listen, learn, and retain your message only if you can relate it to their needs, wants, or wishes. Some motives you may call on involve understanding, control, health and safety, nurturance and altruism, friends and family, self-actualization, and the desire for fairness.

Meeting the Challenges of Audience Diversity. We live in a world of many diverse groups, and often the audiences for our speeches reflect that diversity.

Learning to understand and adapt to diversity will help you prepare more effective messages. Build your speeches on the common ground made possible by universal human values. Match the diversity of your audience with the variety of your supporting materials. Avoid language barriers that might block communication. Finally, avoid rhetorical land mines that might destroy your efforts at communication: stereotypes that inflexibly categorize people and the three notoriousisms: ethnocentrism, sexism, and racism.

Adjusting to the Communication Situation.   You must be flexible enough to adjust to particular features of the speaking situation. The time when you speak, the place of your speech, the constraints of the occasion, and the size of your audience can all pose challenges. In addition, you will be speaking in a context of other speeches and recent events: These can have a preliminary tuning effect to which you must adjust as you make your presentation.

Explore and Apply the Ideas in This Chapter

1. How might the following situations affect a speech you are about to give, and how would you adapt to them?

   a. You are the last speaker during the last class period before spring break.

   b. The speaker right before you gives an incredibly successful speech that brings spontaneous applause from the class and high praise from the instructor.

   c. The speaker right before you bombs badly. The speech is poorly prepared, and the speaker is very nervous and simply stops in the middle and sits down, visibly upset.

   d. (It rarely happens, but . . .) the speaker right before you gives a speech on the same topic, taking the same general approach.

2. Rank the ten universal values in Figure 5.3 in terms of their importance to you. Discuss how the three values you ranked highest might make you susceptible to certain speech topics and approaches.

3. Explain how you would tailor a speech on the general topic of global warming for an audience composed of

   a. middle-school Girl Scouts

   b. the local Chamber of Commerce

   c. your classmates

   d. the local women's garden club

4. If you were to speak on the general topic of global warming, what kinds of examples might you develop to appeal to the following audience needs:

   a. safety

   b. nurturance

   c. comfort

   d. recognition

5. Write a one page commentary on the ethical ramifications of the situation described in the following example.

   > A Boston couple decided to spend their vacation in Memphis, where they had grown up and had families. On their way, they stopped at the Shiloh Civil War Battleground, where the guide extolled the virtues of the Northern forces in that battle. When their tour was finished, they thanked the guide and told her they wanted to get back home to Memphis before dark. She looked surprised and said, "From your license, plate I assumed you were Yankees. I should have given you the 'Southern Tour.'"

6

Finding Your Topic

The life of our city is rich in poetic and marvelous subjects . . . but we do not notice it.

—Baudelaire

I n Chapter 3 we described seven steps to making a successful speech. Sounds simple enough, but when you are standing at the bottom of those steps, looking up, and when you have never climbed them before, they can seem to reach as high as a mountain.

Preparing to speak before an audience can seem somewhat overwhelming, and simply getting started may be the most difficult part of all. If the task before you seems formidable, take it in small steps, advises Robert J. Kriegel, a performance psychologist who has counseled many professional athletes. Kriegel looks at the mountain we have mentioned from a different point of view. While working as a ski instructor, Kriegel found that beginners would look all the way to the bottom of a slope. The hill would seem too steep and the challenge too difficult, and the skiers would back away. However, if he told them to think only of making the first turn, their focus would change to something they knew they could do.[1]

On the "first turn" in speech preparation, you will decide on a topic that is right for you and your listeners and that fits the assignment and the time you have to speak. Surprisingly, you will find that five minutes goes by quickly when you are talking about something that really interests you. Fortunately, there are some good ways to help you find the right topic for your speech. On the "second turn," you will focus your topic and develop a clear sense of purpose for your speech. On the "third turn," you will expand your knowledge so that you can make a responsible presentation. This chapter helps you negotiate the first two of these turns. Chapter 7 shows you how to research your topic efficiently and effectively.

What Is a Good Topic?

A good topic is one that involves you and that you care about. It allows you to express convictions that are important to you or to explore something you find fascinating. In fact, a good topic involves you so much that you may forget to be frightened as you speak. It should also enrich the lives of your listeners. Finally, a good topic is one that you can speak about responsibly, given the time allotted for the preparation and presentation of your speech.

A Good Topic Involves You

Imagine yourself speaking successfully:

> You're enthusiastic about what you're saying. Your face shows your involvement in your topic. Your voice expresses your feelings. Your gestures reinforce

your meaning. Everything about you says, "This is important!" "This is interesting!" or "This will make a difference in your lives!"

Once you can identify a subject that makes you feel this way, you know you have found your topic. The enthusiasm you generate when you speak on it will be infectious. It will spread to your listeners.

Your topic does not have to be on an earth-shaking issue, but it should be something your listeners ought to know more about. Trivial topics such as "how to twirl a baton" or "how to kick a football" waste the time of both speakers and listeners. Overworked topics such as "don't drink and drive" also waste time unless they offer listeners a new slant.

A passion for sports can prompt ideas for speech topics.

Above all, your topic should be important to you personally. It takes time to think through your ideas, research them, organize what you discover, and practice your presentation. If your topic is not important to you, you will find it hard to invest the time and effort required to speak responsibly.

A Good Topic Involves Your Listeners

Picture an audience of ideal listeners:

> Their faces are alive with interest. They lean forward in their seats, intent on what you are saying. They nod or smile appropriately. At the end of your speech, they break out in applause. They want to ask you questions about your ideas or voice their reactions. They really don't want you to stop speaking!

What topic will help you create this kind of audience response? By now, you probably have heard the first speeches in your class, and you know something about your listeners. Ask yourself, *What are my audience's interests? What do they care about? What do they need to know more about?*

Before you finish this chapter, you should have an extensive list of potential speech topics.

A Good Topic Is One You Can Manage

The final test of a good topic is whether you can acquire the knowledge you will need to speak responsibly. The time you have for the preparation and presentation of your speech is limited. Consequently, you should select a topic area you already know something about and then develop a *manageable part* of it for your presentation. Instead of trying to cover the entire subject of preventing terrorism, it would be better to focus on your community's antiterrorism plan. The more limited topic should also lend itself better to your audience's interests and should encourage more responsible preparation.

The Process of Finding a Good Topic

Now that you understand what makes a good topic, the larger question rises: *How do you find one?* Think of your search for the right topic as a process that goes through phases of discovery, exploration, and refinement.

- In the **discovery phase**, you uncover promising topic areas.

- In the **exploration phase**, you focus on specific speech topics within these areas.

- In the **refinement phase**, you identify the general and specific purposes of speeches you might give on these topics and write out your thesis statements.

It is important to realize that *this process takes time.* Give yourself at least a week to select your topic, do your research, outline your speech, and practice your presentation. You will find that this time is well invested. Nothing comforts you more on the eve of a presentation than knowing you are well prepared.

Discovering Your Topic

You may be wondering, "What can I talk about? I don't know anything. I'm not even interested in very much. Am I hopeless?" If you are harboring such misgivings, we have reassuring news. There are three techniques that can help you discover promising speech topics: brainstorming, interest charts, and media prompts.

Brainstorming

Brainstorming is a technique that encourages free associations. Ask yourself, If I had to pick one topic area to explore for my next speech, what would it be? At the top of a legal pad, write down the first idea that occurs to you. Below this idea, write down at least six more ideas that spontaneously occur to you in association with this topic. Do not try to think critically about these ideas until you have a sizeable list. Let your mind wander. You may discover, as did a student of ours, that such "daydreaming" can be productive and creative.

Zachary came to our office one day early in the term with a serious case of topic anxiety. After we convinced him that his symptoms were not terminal, he accepted our invitation to participate in brainstorming. Zachary wrote down "Wyoming" at

---

discovery phase   Phase of the process of finding speech topics that identifies large topic areas.

exploration phase   Phase of the process of finding speech topics that involves the close examination of large topic areas to identify more precise topics that might be developed.

refinement phase   Identifying the general and specific purposes of a speech topic and framing its thesis statement.

the top of his legal pad. He then wrote down the following associations: trout, Yellowstone, fire, drought, George Anderson (a well-known fly fisherman), catch and release, and wolves. He paused for a moment and studied this list closely. "You know," he said, "I could speak on 'Fire and Water in Yellowstone: Too Much of One, Too Little of the Other.'" And eventually he did.

Interest Charts

The classical writers on rhetoric were the first to discover that the mind follows certain habitual paths that are productive in creative thinking. They called these paths *topoi*: You already used topoi when you developed the Self-Awareness Inventory in Chapter 3. The productive paths you explored in that chapter can be easily adapted and enlarged here into **topoi of topic discovery**. They appear in the form of questions that guide the mind:

1. What *places* do you find interesting?

2. What *people* do you find fascinating?

3. What *activities* do you enjoy?

4. What *things* do you find interesting?

5. What *events* stand out in your mind?

6. Which *ideas* do you find intriguing?

7. What *values* are important to you?

8. What *problems* concern you most?

9. What *campus concerns* do you have?

You can use the topoi of topic discovery to develop an **interest chart** that projects a comprehensive visual display of your interests. To create such a chart, write out brief responses to the probe questions. Try to come up with at least five responses for each question. Your interest chart might then look like that in Figure 6.1.

Once you have completed your personal interest chart, make a similar chart of audience interests as revealed by class discussion and your audience analysis. What places, people, events, activities, objects, ideas, values, problems, and campus concerns seem to spark discussions in class? Study the two charts together, looking for shared interests. To do this systematically, make a three-column **topic area inventory chart**. In the first column (your interests), list the subjects you find most appealing. In the second column (audience interests), list the subjects that seem most interesting to your listeners. In the third column, match columns 1 and 2 to find the most promising areas of speech topics. Figure 6.2 shows a sample topic area inventory chart.

In this example, your interests in travel and hiking coincide with the audience's interest in unusual places and suggest a possible topic area: "Weekend Adventures Close to Campus." Similarly, your concern for physical fitness pairs with the audience's interest in deceptive advertising to generate another possibility: "Exercise Spa Rip-offs." Your interest in Cuba intersects with audience interests in foreign policy to lead to "Continue Cuban Trade Embargo?" Finally, your concern over preemptive war resonates with audience fear of terrorism to suggest a provocative topic area: "Is Preemptive War the Answer to Terrorism?"

---

brainstorming Technique that encourages the free play of the mind.

topoi of topic discovery Probe questions used to stimulate the mind during topic exploration, centering on places, people, activities, things, events, ideas, values, problems, and campus concerns.

interest chart Visual display of a speaker's interests, as prompted by certain probe questions.

Figure 6.1

Your Interest Chart

Places	People	Activities
The Four Corners	Osama Bin Laden	hiking
Cuba	Peyton Manning	doing crossword puzzles
New Orleans	Wilma Mankiller	watching basketball
Route 66	Charles Lindbergh	cooking
New York City	Sojourner Truth	traveling

Objects	Events	Ideas
Kachinas	Olympics	objectivity in journalism
movie posters	World Trade Center	religious tolerance
old cars	canoeing the Colorado	anarchy
political cartoons	Mardi Gras	freedom of expression
graffiti	Cody Rodeo	creation myths

Values	Problems	Campus Concerns
close family ties	air and water pollution	race relations
tolerance	pre-emptive war	off-campus housing
physical fitness	substance abuse	date rape
respect	Internet censorship	campus security
world peace	coping with terrorism	escalating tuition costs

Figure 6.2

Topic Area Inventory Chart

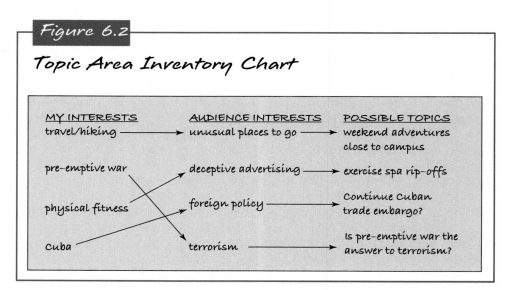

MY INTERESTS	AUDIENCE INTERESTS	POSSIBLE TOPICS
travel/hiking	unusual places to go	weekend adventures close to campus
pre-emptive war	deceptive advertising	exercise spa rip-offs
physical fitness	foreign policy	Continue Cuban trade embargo?
Cuba	terrorism	Is pre-emptive war the answer to terrorism?

topic area inventory chart A means of determining possible speech topics by listing topics you find interesting and subjects your audience finds interesting, and then matching them.

InterConnections.
LearnMore 6.1

Speech Topics on Public Policy Issues
www.libraries.psu.edu/socialsciences/cas/speechtopics/pick.htm
Topic areas inviting persuasive policy speeches, prepared by librarians at Pennsylvania State University.

Sample Topics for Informative, Expository, and Demonstrative Speeches
www.angelfire.com/ca3/phsspeech/topics.html
List of topic prompts for informative speeches. Caution: Many of these might lead to trivial speeches.

"Comprehensive Topic Selection" Helper
www.hawaii.edu/mauispeech/html/public_speaking.html
Excellent guide prepared by Ron St. John of the University of Hawaii's Maui Community College Speech Department.

Topics Dealing with the Environment
www.libraries.psu.edu/socialsciences/cas/speechtopics/air.htm
Topic areas specializing in environmental problems.

Media Prompts

If brainstorming and interest charts don't produce enough promising topic discoveries (an unlikely possibility), there's still another excellent source. When using **media prompts**, you jump-start the creative process by scanning newspapers, magazines, and the electronic media for ideas. Go through the Sunday paper, scan *Time* and *Newsweek* or quality periodicals such as *The Atlantic* or *Smithsonian*, or read the daily headlines of the *New York Times* online. Also, if you type in the words *Speech Topics* on a search engine, you may find a few gems among the garbage. See InterConnections.LearnMore 6.1 for Web sites containing lists of possible speech topics.

As you scan the media, consider the headlines, advertisements, and pictures. What catches your attention? The headline "Travel Money Tips Offered" might inspire you to speak on "Champagne Travel on a Beer Budget." Or the personals section in the classified ads might prompt a speech on "The Dangers of Computer Dating Services."

The media-prompts technique has one great advantage: The topics it generates are timely. But be careful not to misuse this technique. The media can suggest ideas for speeches, but you can't simply summarize an article and use it as a speech. The article should be only a starting point for your thinking. *Your* speech must be *your* message, designed to appeal to *your* specific audience. You should always bring something new to your topic—a fresh insight or a special application for your listeners.

Exploring Your Topic Area

What you typically discover as you brainstorm, develop interest charts, and employ media prompts are not actual topics for speeches but topic *areas*. Topic areas are promising but broad subjects that often cover too much ground for typical classroom speeches. You must explore topic areas carefully and narrow and focus them until they become specific enough to handle in the limited

media prompts Sources such as newspapers, magazines, and the electronic media that can suggest ideas for speech topics.

time allotted for your speech. As Winston Churchill once noted, "A speech is like a spotlight; the more focused it is, the more intense the light."[2] The two primary techniques available to you as you explore promising topic areas are the nondirective technique of mind mapping and the directive technique of topic analysis.

Mind Mapping

Mind mapping changes customary patterns of thinking in order to free our minds for creative exploration.[3] These habitual patterns can produce what communication theorist Kenneth Burke once called a "trained incapacity" to think fully and freely about subjects. Mind mappers start with a sheet of paper, which they turn on its side to emphasize width rather than length. Instead of starting at the top of the page, they start at the center. Instead of flowing down the page, thinking radiates out from this center so that it forms a coherent system.

Mind mapping taps into the creative power of metaphorical thinking. It starts with a concept of our minds as uncharted territories waiting to be explored. We may think of this uncharted territory as intellectual space.[4] The central concept in this spacescape functions like a star, and the major ideas that circle it are its associated satellites. These satellites can be circled by even more particular associations that belong to them. Figure 6.3 illustrates this way of thinking.

Let us assume that you have carefully completed the interest charts. You have discovered your strongest interest is in American popular music. You think this interest will be shared by many of your listeners. This convergence of interests has produced a promising topic area, the innovative music that flowed out of Sun Studio in Memphis, Tennessee, during the last half century. You have already begun to read about this

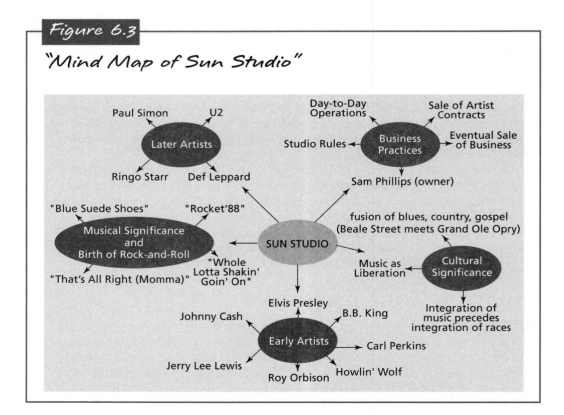

Figure 6.3

"Mind Map of Sun Studio"

---

subject, and have started to accumulate information. To explore this topic area using mind mapping, place it at the center of your page, as indicated in Figure 6.3.

As your mind roams freely around this central idea, you come up with five major satellite ideas: "Early Artists," "Later Artists," "Business Practices," "Musical Significance: Birth of Rock-and-Roll," and "Cultural Significance." As you reflect on each of these satellite ideas, you develop even more specific associations that radiate from each.

Looking at these ideas in space, you can see any number of speech topic possibilities. One of these might connect three of the major satellite ideas. You could focus on the early artists who performed the first significant rock-and-roll hits and show how they blended elements of blues, country, and gospel music into rock-and-roll. You might title this speech "Sun Studio: Birthplace of an American Musical Form." You could develop presentation aids using photographs and excerpts from the music to make the speech truly colorful, enjoyable, and informative.

Mind mapping is a technique that can result in interesting discoveries. But because it is nondirective, there is no assurance that it will produce useful results. If you are convinced that mind mapping is not helping you explore a topic area, you should try the more disciplined technique of topic analysis.

Topic Analysis

The beginning college course in journalism introduces fledgling reporters to the topoi of their craft: *what? why? when? how? where?* and *who?* Rudyard Kipling once described these prompt questions as follows:

> I keep six honest serving-men
> (They taught me all I knew):
> Their names are What and Why and When
> And How and Where and Who.[5]

The idea is that if reporters ask these questions as they explore a story, the odds increase that they will do a competent job of reporting the news.

The respected literary scholar Wayne Booth has advised fledgling academic researchers to deploy the same system of questions as they seek promising topics: "Decide which questions stop you for a moment, challenge you, spark some special interest."[6] These same "honest serving-men" can also work for the public speaker who is exploring the possibilities of a topic area. They make possible the technique we call **topic analysis**. Let's take global warming as a topic area and see how these questions might prompt inquiry:

- *What* is global warming? What are the major causes of it? What are the contributing causes in our community? What part can individuals play in reducing it? What can government do to control it? What is the role of international organizations?

- *Why* do we have global warming? Why are some companies reluctant to stop greenhouse emissions? Why are some states moving more aggressively than the national government in combating global warming? Why does our government refuse to participate in the Kyoto protocol?

- *When* did global warming first become an issue? When was the first important book about global warming published? When were the first U. S. laws relating to global warming passed?

topic analysis Using questions often employed by journalists to explore topic possibilities for speeches (who, what, why, when, where, and how).

- *How* can global warming be controlled? How can companies be encouraged to cooperate in the anti-warming campaign? How can individuals help the cause?

- *Where* is global warming of most concern? Where are endangered species most susceptible? Where are human health problems most acute? Where have cities or states done the most to control global warming?

- *Who* suffers most from global warming? Who is responsible for enforcing emission controls? Who brought global warming most forcefully to public awareness?

As you consider the six prompts, write down as many specific ideas about your topic area as you can. You may notice in our example that certain clusters of ideas emerge: Some entries center on the impact of global warming on people and the environment, while others concern individual and governmental responsibility, the role of companies and industries, and political leadership at state, national, and international levels.

What would be the best topic for your speech on global warming? That depends a great deal on your audience and locale. If you live in an area with an obvious emissions problem, a speech describing that situation might have specific local appeal. Your listeners might also be interested in the history of relevant legislation in your city or state. On the other hand, if you live in an area where the impact of global warming is not immediate or apparent, you may have to work hard to convince listeners that they should be concerned about it.

The preceding topic analysis was geared to exploring what are primarily informative speech topics but can easily be adapted to the analysis of persuasive topics. Because persuasion addresses problems, you simply change the focus of the questions and add a few that are specific to persuasive situations:

Who is affected by this problem?
What are the most important issues?
Why did the problem arise?
Where is this problem happening?
When did the problem begin?
How is this problem like or unlike previous problems?
How extensive is the problem?
What options are available for dealing with the problem?

Selecting Your Topic

After you have discovered topic areas and explored their potential, one or several topics should emerge as promising possibilities for your speech. Now you should ask yourself:

- Does this topic fit the assignment?

- Could I give a speech on this topic in the time available?

- Why would I want to speak on this topic?

- Could I interest my listeners in this topic?

- Would a speech on this topic be good and useful for listeners to hear?

- Can I learn enough about this topic to give a responsible speech?

As you consider your options in light of these questions, you should be able to make a final choice.

Refining Your Topic

*H*aving discovered and explored promising topic areas, you have finally decided on a topic. Now you move to the final phase of topic selection: refining and focusing your topic in preparation for speaking. To complete this phase, you must

- consider the general purpose of your speech.
- determine your specific purpose.
- prepare a clearly worded thesis statement.

General Purpose

Invitations to speak outside class will usually specify the **general purpose** of your speech. An invitation might include, "Could you help us understand changes in the tax code?" or "Would you tell us why you are opposed to changes in the tax code?" or "Will you help us thank the senator for her leadership in changing the tax code?" Speeches that would address such questions seek understanding, encourage taking a position on a controversial issue, or invite participation in a ritual of appreciation.

In class, the general purpose of your speech is usually assigned. For example, the three questions on the tax code correspond to the general purposes of *informing, persuading,* and *celebrating.*

- *The general purpose of a speech to inform is to share knowledge with listeners.*

- *If your general purpose is to persuade, you will advise listeners how to believe or act and give them sound reasons to accept your position.*

- *A speech of celebration emphasizes the importance of an occasion, event, or person, often with the intention of amusing or inspiring listeners.* Speeches of celebration include eulogies, toasts, after-dinner speeches, and tributes.

Although it is easy to separate these purposes on paper, they often overlap in practice. For example, Marge Anderson, chief executive of the Mille Lacs Band of the Ojibwe, informed her mainstream Minnesota audience of her people's contributions to the larger community, celebrated the values of her culture, and urged listeners to begin a dialogue of learning, understanding, and appreciation—all in the same speech (reprinted in Appendix B).

A speech about hiking in Shenandoah National Park presents a clearer focus than a speech about the park itself.

general purpose The speaker's overall intention to inform or persuade listeners, or to celebrate some person or occasion.

Specific Purpose

Determining your **specific purpose** helps you narrow your topic until it comes into sharp focus. It states precisely what you want your listeners to understand, believe, feel, or do. Having your specific purpose clearly in mind helps direct your research so that you don't waste valuable time wandering around the library or surfing the Internet for irrelevant material. You should be able to state your specific purpose clearly in a single phrase. Let's look at how a specific purpose statement can give focus to a speech:

> Topic: Exploring Shenandoah National Park
> General purpose: To inform

The topic as stated in this example is too general for a five- to six-minute speech. If you tried to cover the entire range of ideas about the topic in the time allotted, you would be stretched too thin. As you attempted to discuss driving the Skyline Drive, hiking the Appalachian Trail, and horseback riding—to name just a few of the possible subtopics—you would find yourself in an impossible bind. You would not have time to produce any concrete examples or fascinating stories. All you might do would be to provide a vague sketch of possibilities that would leave your listeners disappointed or (even worse) bored. So after confirming the general purpose of your speech (to inform), you need to come up with a specific purpose that will narrow the focus of your speech so that it points in a precise direction (hiking trails):

> Specific purpose: To inform my audience about exciting hiking trails in Shenandoah National Park

You have just made a major move in refining your topic. Now you can test and improve this specific purpose statement.

Testing Your Specific Purpose Statement.
Developing a successful specific purpose statement is one of the most important steps in topic refinement. But how do you know when you have done this successfully? The following tests will help you determine whether you have succeeded.

   1. *Does the specific purpose promise new information or fresh advice?* You may be greeted with yawns if you propose "to inform listeners that drunk driving is dangerous." You will have tied yourself to a tired topic. When you tell listeners something they have already heard many times, you simply waste their time.

   2. *Can you satisfy your specific purpose statement in the allotted time?* If you propose "to persuade listeners that clean air standards in the United States are too lax," you may have bitten off more than you can chew. Remember, in a five-minute speech you have only about seven hundred words to get your message across. You may need to focus your remarks on air quality in your community so that you can meet your time restrictions. That strategy also would address the specific interests of your listeners.

   3. *Have you avoided the double-focus trap?* It is sometimes difficult to make that final decision to narrow your topic to a single focal point. It may be tempting to fall into the trap of double focus: "to inform my listeners of hiking opportunities and environmental problems in Shenandoah National Park." If you attempt to

specific purpose   The speaker's particular goal or the response that the speaker wishes to evoke.

address both these subjects in any meaningful way, you may go beyond your time limits. The "and" in such statements is a red flag that you may have a double-focus problem.

   4. *Have you avoided the triviality trap?* When you speak to twenty-four people for five minutes, you will be taking up two hours of their collective time. What are you offering them in return? If you promise to inform them about "how to mix a martini" or "how to punt a football," you may well leave your listeners feeling short-changed. They may react with a blunt "So what?" You must convince listeners that you have a specific purpose that promises them important information, insights, or advice so that by the end of the speech they feel they have invested their time wisely.

   5. *Have you avoided the technicality trap?* Sometimes speakers forget that their listeners may not share the technical vocabulary of a subject. They feel hurt when listeners respond with dazed, bewildered looks and the question, "Huh?" Speakers who promise "to inform listeners of the principles of thermonuclear energy" or "to inform my audience concerning the intellectual evolution of Kant's meta-ethics" are stepping directly into this trap. They have not factored audience background into their topic selection. This failure becomes evident when they write out their specific purpose statements.

Improving Your Specific Purpose Statement.

Let's look at an example of a flawed specific purpose statement and see how it might be improved:

Flawed: To persuade my audience that driving while distracted is dangerous

Improved: To persuade my audience not to talk on a cell phone while driving

The flawed specific purpose is vague, and it tells the audience nothing new. Who would argue that driving while distracted is not dangerous? The improved version focuses more precisely on a contemporary problem.

Thesis Statement

Writing your **thesis statement** is the final refinement in preparing a topic for a speech. Sometimes called the central idea, the thesis statement summarizes in a single sentence the message of your speech. For example, your thesis statement might read, "*Terrorism* has acquired many meanings in the speeches of our leaders" (informative speech) or "We need to define *terrorism* more precisely to avoid damaging the Constitution" (persuasive speech). Such a sentence, notes Booth, "states a potential claim" that the speech itself must demonstrate or prove.[7] It is usually worked into your introduction so that listeners will know your intentions from the outset.

   Most of the time, your specific purpose will be revealed in your thesis statement, but the two are not identical. The specific purpose expresses what you want to accomplish; the thesis statement summarizes what you intend to say. A recent student speech developed a relationship between the specific purpose and thesis statement as follows:

Specific purpose: To persuade listeners that date rape is a serious problem on our campus

Thesis statement: Today I want to discuss a major problem on campus—date rape—and what we can do about it.

thesis statement   Sometimes called the "central idea," it summarizes in a single sentence the message of your speech.

Ethics *Alert! 6.1*

The Ethics of Topic Selection

Ethical problems can infiltrate the process of topic selection for speeches. To avoid many of these problems, follow these guidelines:

1. Do not select a topic that could be hurtful, such as "How to Make a Pipe Bomb."

2. Do not select a topic that invites illegal activity, such as "How to Get Forbidden Objects through Airline Security Checks."

3. Do not select a topic on which you cannot obtain responsible knowledge.

4. Do not purposely obscure your thesis statement in order to hide your specific purpose.

In ethical speaking, the thesis statement will usually reveal the speaker's specific purpose; at the very least, it will not disguise it. *But let the listener beware!* Not all speakers are totally candid. Although a telemarketer's specific purpose may be to sell trips to vacation destinations, the thesis statement may suggest a different intention altogether:

> The government of [fill in the country] wants to advertise and create international goodwill by offering you a free vacation trip to [whatever dream destination applies]. Your only obligation is to let us use a photo of you in our future advertising.

Only toward the end of the pitch does the real purpose come out: "And of course we ask that you prepay the necessary taxes and custom duties on the trip before you embark."

Such disguised intentions may seem fairly trivial (unless you find yourself responsible for paying an enormous "tax" bill!). But, if you consider the hidden motives of cult leaders or even leaders of nations, you can see how serious this problem can become. *The greater the distance between the hidden specific purpose and the thesis statement, the larger the ethical problem.*

At times, ethical speakers may omit the thesis statement from their presentations, leaving it to be constructed by listeners from cues within the speech. Cecile Larson left the thesis statement implicit in her speech "The 'Monument' at Wounded Knee," which appears in Appendix B. Her intent was to create a dramatic effect as listeners discovered her thesis statement for themselves. But this technique also entails considerable risk. Listeners may miss the point! In most cases, speakers should integrate the thesis statement into the introduction of their speeches.

The thesis statement should adapt your specific purpose to listeners in a way calculated to gain their attention. Note how the language grows more direct and personal as one moves from specific purpose to thesis statement in the following example:

Specific purpose: To persuade listeners to lobby state representatives to support the bill limiting cell phone use by drivers

Thesis statement: Using a cell phone while driving a car should be illegal: That's the message we need to bring—right now—to our legislators.

Important Qualities of Thesis Statements. Because preparing the thesis statement is the climax of the process of topic selection, it is critical that the statement should possess two qualities that the preceding example illustrates:

1. *A sharp, clear focus.* The speech that lacks a sharp, clear thesis statement is likely to ramble about in a disorganized way and leave no lasting impression on listeners. Speeches are structured to develop an idea. When that idea is obscure, there is no central focus to hold the structure of thoughts together. When listeners ask, "What exactly are you trying to say?" or "What would you like us to do?" you know the thesis statement has not been carefully stated.

2. *Colorful, engaging language.* The language of thesis statements should be colorful and concrete. Such language evokes pictures in listeners' minds and encourages constructive listening. Famous speeches like Martin Luther King's "I Have a Dream" and Franklin Delano Roosevelt's "First Inaugural Address" ("We have nothing to fear but fear itself") illustrate how effective language can make thesis statements both eloquent and memorable. On the other hand, vacuous expressions like "I want to show you that camping in the Rockies is really awesome" discourage constructive listening.

An Overview of the Topic Selection Process

*L*et us now look at the entire process of moving from general topic area to thesis statement to see how these steps evolve in speech preparation:

Topic area:	Vacations in the United States
Topic:	Camping in the Rockies
General function:	To inform
Specific purpose:	To inform my audience that there are beautiful, uncrowded places to camp in the Rockies
Thesis statement:	Three beautiful yet uncrowded camping areas in the Rockies are Bridger-Teton National Forest in Wyoming, St. Charles Canyon in Idaho, and Dinosaur National Monument in Utah.

It becomes clear that the refinement phase of topic selection is similar to looking at a topic through the lenses of a microscope. First, you see the topic as it emerges in rough form from the processes of discovery and exploration. Then, you view the topic through the general-purpose lens to test its appropriateness for the assignment. Next, you view the topic through the much finer lens of the specific purpose as it converges with your interests and intentions. Finally, you view the topic as it might actually appear in the thesis statement. From the initial phase of discovery through the final phase of refinement, the process of topic selection is an intellectual adventure that is critical to successful speaking.

As our metaphor of the microscope suggests, when you identify the general purpose, specific purpose, and thesis statement of a speech topic, you bring the topic into sharper and sharper focus. The structure of your speech comes into view, and you can see how the speech might develop. You also get a clearer idea of the kind of research you will need to acquire responsible knowledge of your topic. How to conduct such research is covered in the next chapter.

Testing Your Topic Selection: An Application

*I*n business settings, managers often make short presentations called briefings. Briefings may include both reports on ongoing projects and proposals for approval. They can be both informative and persuasive, especially when they present a plan of action. The persuasive briefing, often called a *prospectus*, is an occasion for both testing and "selling" an idea before a group of decision makers.

A similar speaking or writing assignment on topic selection is called a **topic briefing**. *The topic briefing is a prospectus for a speech or series of speeches you propose to give.* In it, you explain why you want to speak on a particular topic and why others should want to listen. You anticipate problems you might encounter and reassure listeners that you can deal with them. In short, you report the results of the discovery and exploration phases of topic selection. You also anticipate the refinement process by suggesting how one or more later speech topics might develop out of the topic area. The object of the assignment—and the special advantage of giving it orally—is to get feedback from the audience that will either encourage or discourage you from proceeding further. The audience can also make specific suggestions on how you might develop your speeches.

For example, when one of our students made a topic briefing proposing a set of speeches on mathematics education, she received a great deal of helpful feedback. First, the sheer volume of such feedback (at least six members of the audience made comments, asked questions, or offered suggestions) indicated that she had touched on an area rich with potential interest. But one of the questions ("What are your speeches going to be on?") indicated that she had a great deal of work to do in focusing and refining her topic. Another classmate challenged her to "show how this applies to me," indicating that the speaker would have to give more attention to adapting her speech to her audience. Still another asked, "Why do American high school students often perform poorly on math tests when compared to students from other nations?"—an invitation for her to consider a comparative-cultures approach. She emerged from her presentation both encouraged by this intense interest and aware that she had a great deal of work to do.

Topic briefings offer other advantages. They help you avoid the traps of trivial, overly technical, double-focused, or tired topics. If you propose a trivial topic, look for signs of audience contempt and lack of interest. If you offer an overly technical subject, expect to find confusion reflected on the faces of your listeners. If you drift into a double-focus as you identify specific speech topics, expect someone to ask: "How are you going to do all that in six minutes?" If you present a topic area that is simply stale from overuse, expect signs of boredom. The topic briefing assignment offers a way to monitor the results of your topic selection process to ensure that it is free of such problems. It encourages you to think less about personal anxieties and more about the strategies of topic refinement. Finally, it encourages the research necessary for you to strengthen and justify your speeches with responsible knowledge.

Developing the Topic Briefing

First, as in any speech, *you have to gain the attention and interest of your listeners*. David Zaborowski began his briefing by making a statement that aroused curiosity: "Children

---

topic briefing   Prospectus for a speech or series of speeches you propose to give.

are not hamburgers." Of course not, we thought. Whoever would say that they were? What could they possibly mean if they made such an assertion? We were primed to listen intently to the rest of his topic briefing proposing speeches on educational reform.

Second, *you should explain why you are drawn to the topic area.* Erin Bourg opened her speech on medical malpractice by telling the story of how her mother had been the victim of a doctor's bad diagnosis. When you establish a personal connection with a topic, you become an *authentic* voice. You suggest that you can bring personal knowledge and experience to bear.

Third, and even more important, *you must show your listeners what they have to gain from hearing a speech on your topic.* Erin Evans proposed speeches that would inform her listeners about the abuse of prescription and over-the-counter drugs. On a humorous note, Erin asked. "Did you know that birth control pills can be canceled by antibiotics? My cousin confirmed that—her daughter is now two years old." On a more somber note, Erin quoted a recent story in the campus newspaper about a student who had died by accidently mixing an antidepressant with other prescription drugs. Erin's conclusion seemed self-evident: "Don't you think we should learn a little bit more about what we're putting in our bodies?"

Fourth, *you should point out how you might develop specific speech topics out of your topic area.* In her topic briefing, Leslie Eason proposed to explore racial identity in American life on the basis of her personal experience with and resentment over what she felt was an overemphasis on race. This was such an all-consuming passion for her that she planned to devote all her speeches to this topic. In her informative speech, she would examine the extent of the problem and explain its consequences for society. For her persuasive speech, she would advocate specific changes in government policies and practices. For her ceremonial speech, she would offer tribute to a public figure who had resisted being placed in a racial box. Her tribute to golfer Tiger Woods appears at the end of Chapter 17.

Fifth, *you should be able to assure listeners that sufficient resources are available to develop "responsible knowledge" for your speeches.* Erin Evans was able to offer such assurance to her listeners—not only that the resources existed but that she was aware of them:

> The National Institutes of Health, the Food and Drug Administration, and the Substance Abuse and Mental Health Administration conduct ongoing research on drug usage and side effects. They are all wonderful resources. There is also useful information on WebMD—a commercial Web site that gathers articles from medical publications and makes them readily available. They want to make us more aware of symptoms and side effects.

Sixth, *you should identify any special problems you think you might have, and explain how you intend to cope with them.* Leslie Eason was convinced that many in her audience might think that her topic had been overused or exaggerated, that she might be "beating a dead horse." To overcome this possible objection, she presented powerful personal evidence suggesting

Following a topic briefing, a speaker must respond to questions from the audience.

How to Develop a Topic Briefing

As you develop a topic briefing, there are a number of steps you should take:

1. Arouse audience interest on a subject.

2. Explain your attraction to the topic area.

3. Convince listeners they need to learn more about the subject.

4. Show how specific topics can be drawn out of the topic area.

5. Assure listeners that you can build responsible knowledge for your speech(es).

6. Anticipate problems and show how you will handle them.

7. Conclude by reinforcing the importance of the subject.

that the problem had simply been neglected rather than solved and that it remained serious. The imaginative development of her briefing indicated that she would bring a fresh, insightful point of view to the problem of racial identity. Therefore, her creativity became an implicit argument against the objection that there was little to be learned about the topic area.

Seventh, *you should conclude by reminding listeners of the importance of your topic both to you and to them.* Ashley Roberson ended her proposal to develop speeches on Native American themes in the following way:

> Through my mission trip experiences with the Navajos, I have learned a lot about Native American culture. Through these experiences, I have gained a love and respect for the Native American people. I hope through my upcoming speeches about the Navajo code talkers and about social injustices on the Reservation that you too will share my feeling for them.

Listening Constructively to Topic Briefings

Topic briefings place a great burden of responsibility on the listener. You can help the speaker focus later speeches or even change directions before it is too late. Indeed, much of the assignment's value comes after the briefing itself, when you have a chance to help speakers pursue promising opportunities or avoid pitfalls. If the briefing is not very interesting, you should find a tactful way to let the speaker know this. Reporting your honest reactions may encourage the speaker to explore other, better options. To provide helpful feedback, audiences should keep these questions in mind:

- Would you like to hear more about this topic? Why or why not?

- What suggestions do you have for developing the topic?

- Are you convinced this topic could generate successful speeches?

- Do you have any reservations about the topic? What might the speaker do to avoid or minimize them?

In Summary

To give a successful speech, you must discover promising topic areas, explore the specific topics they might offer, and refine the topic you select into sharply focused statements of purpose and theme. A good topic is one that involves and interests both you and your audience. It will be focused so that you can research it adequately and develop a speech that will fit within the allotted time.

Discovering Topic Areas. Three techniques can help you discover promising topic areas. The first, brainstorming, is a nondirective technique that encourages the free play of the mind in quest of topics. The second, the interest chart, is a directive technique that uses probe questions to guide the mind in a systematic discovery process. As you record your interests and those of your listeners in a topic area inventory chart, you can often find points where these interests converge. These points often suggest promising topic areas. When you use the third technique, media prompts, you scan newspapers, magazines, electronic media, and the Internet to generate ideas.

Exploring Topic Areas. Two techniques help you explore topic areas to determine specific topic possibilities. The first, mind mapping, imagines a topic area at the center of a system of ideas. You are encouraged to explore the ideas that surround and associate with the topic area. The second, topic analysis, uses a set of specific questions. Asking this list of questions can prompt a productive exploration of a topic area.

Refining Your Topic. As you seek to refine and focus your topic, you need to work through three phases. The first phase confirms the general purpose of the speech: whether it is to inform, to persuade, or to celebrate. Speeches that inform share knowledge with listeners. Speeches that persuade advise listeners how to believe or act. Speeches that celebrate emphasize the importance of some occasion, event, or person, often with the intention of entertaining or inspiring listeners.

The second phase of refinement pinpoints the specific purpose of the speech. The specific purpose states precisely what you want your listeners to understand, believe, feel, or do. It should avoid the traps of double focus, triviality, and technicality.

The third phase of refinement, the thesis statement, summarizes in a single sentence the meaning or message of the speech. The distance between the unstated specific purpose and the stated thesis statement is often a measure of the ethics of a speech. Qualities important to the thesis statement include clarity, focus, color, and concreteness.

Testing Your Topic. A speech or written exercise in which you "sell" your listeners on the importance of a topic you propose to develop is called the topic briefing. To develop a successful topic briefing, you must gain your listeners' attention, establish the importance of your topic both to you and to them, assure listeners that sufficient resources are available to develop responsible knowledge, and identify any reservations you must counter to speak successfully.

Explore and Apply the Ideas in This Chapter

1. Make a list of trivial or tired topics. What makes them trivial? Is there any way you might make them nontrivial? Can you think of a way to put new life in tired topics?

2. Use brainstorming, interest charts, and media prompts to discover a minimum of three promising topic areas on which you might speak. Now rank these in order of preference. Explain in class or in a brief paper how you discovered these areas and why you have ranked them in this order.

3. Use mind mapping and topic analysis to explore the preferred topic area identified in the previous exercise. List in order of preference three promising speech topics that emerge from this exploration. Explain in class or in a brief paper how and why

these topics emerged and why you ranked them in the order selected.

4. Refine the preferred topic possibility discovered in exercise 3 until you have determined the general purpose, specific purpose, and thesis statement. Report on this process either in class or in a brief paper. Point out the strengths and possible limitations of the speech you might give on the basis of this work. Be sure to consider the assignment, your time limits, and audience needs and interests, as well as the intrinsic value of the topic.

5. Prepare a list of at least three topics you believe it would be unethical to develop for classroom speeches. Explain why these topics seem unethical.

Fast Food Nation

Hannah Johnston

Hannah's topic briefing followed David Zaborowski's on "Children Are Not Hamburgers." She connected her speech to David's in her opening, and then she gained attention by asking a startling question. She then defines the problem area she wishes to deal with.

Speaking of hamburgers and McDonald's, what would you say if I asked you if you've ever eaten spinal cord? You'd probably think I was crazy, wouldn't you? But what if I asked you, "Have you ever eaten a fast-food hamburger?" What's really crazy is the fact that those two questions may be interchangeable.

There's been a lot of controversy lately on what can really be defined as *meat*, and technically, now that's anything that can be separated from the skeleton by AMR—or Advanced Meat Recovery systems. The problem with this is most AMR meat samples contain either bits of spinal cord, brain, and/or nervous tissues. And aside from being really gross, there are serious health risks involved in this; one of the most obvious and most dangerous would be mad cow disease.

What led to the outbreaks of mad cow disease? It began in the eighties when the British were looking for a cheap bone and meat supplement to fatten their cattle. And they made the supplement from, among other things, road-kill, dead pets from animal shelters, and slaughterhouse waste. This is what they were feeding their cows. Some of those animals became diseased, contracting BSE—bovine spongiform encephalopathy, or mad cow disease.

BSE can be transmitted to humans when they ingest the beef from such cattle. The tissues that most easily transmit this disease are the brain and spinal cord tissue—the same tissues which were being labeled as *meat* and put inside our hamburgers.

As Hannah moves into her discussion of resources, she reassures listeners that good information exists. She indicates that the real issue is whether the problem remains timely.

People began to die from this in Britain, which prompted investigations and inspections of the slaughterhouses. And this led in turn to several sensational books—exposés of what was really going on behind the slaughterhouse scenes.

These books were in the tradition of Upton Sinclair's *The Jungle*—which, when he wrote it in 1906, led to a revolution in the meat packing industry and opened people's eyes. One in particular—a book called *Fast Food Nation: The Dark Side of the All-American Meal*—began to turn heads and stomachs nationwide as Americans became aware of what they'd really been consuming.

This topic can easily be developed into an informative speech. I found so much information from newspapers of documented cases of food poisoning, mad cow disease, that sort of thing, to online journals and books like the one I mentioned that describe all the gory details of what's really being put in our food.

I don't know yet whether I'm going to carry it into a persuasive speech. I will have to do some more research before I decide one way or another, because most of the outbreaks of mad cow and things like that in people were in the mid- to late nineties. So, I need to confirm where we stand now: whether there have been any real changes in how we retrieve meat, whether there have been new laws reforming the safety procedures—things like that.

The only major problems I've encountered in researching this problem are following supposedly legitimate links to Web sites that turn out to be just anti-meat sites by crazy vegetarians and that sort of thing. But there's enough real information from journals and books and offshoots of the U.S.D.A. food inspection Web site that I've got a lot to investigate.

So you can look forward to a real queaser of a speech. Sorry for ruining lunch!

◀ *Hannah ends rather abruptly. She might have developed the lunch idea further by mentioning fast-food houses near campus and suggesting alternative eating plans.*

7 Researching Your Topic

- acquire responsible knowledge
- evaluate research materials
- conduct a strategic search in the library and on the Internet
- plan interviews to acquire special information
- develop a system for recording research

Learn, compare, collect the facts! Always have the courage to say to yourself, "I am ignorant."

—*Ivan Petrovich Pavlov*

I found this really neat-looking ring offered at a super price on this e-mail I received. I wanted it for my mother's Christmas present, so I ordered it. The deal was, I had to send a money order for half of what it cost to this post office box, and when I got the ring, I would send them the rest. So I sent the money, and that's the last I ever heard from them. No ring, and I lost my money. Boy, did I feel like a chump! That's the story I want to tell in my speech to inform."

"That's a good topic and interesting story," agreed Beth's instructor, "but if you want to give a speech on that topic, you're going to have to do some more research. Your personal experience just isn't enough."

"Why?" asked Beth. "I know what I'm talking
about. Why do I have to do research?"

This chapter answers Beth's question and points you toward the path to responsible knowledge for your speeches. Even though personal experience adds authenticity, it is seldom adequate as the basis for public speaking. And although we covered selecting your topic before research, you may well have to explore your topic before you can focus it and determine your main points. Once you read what others have to say, you may feel the need to rethink your specific purpose.

One of the major goals of an education is to help students become information literate. At a time when information seems to grow exponentially, you need a way to break through the "data smog" that occurs when too much information comes at you too fast.[1] **Information literacy** provides you with the skills you need to locate information efficiently and to evaluate what you learn. A word of caution as we begin this chapter: Information resources are changing rapidly. What we write about libraries and the Internet may change before this book goes to press. What we hope to teach you is the ability to wade through the morass and become a lifetime learner who can investigate ideas from a variety of perspectives by locating, evaluating, and using sound sources of information.

Acquiring Responsible Knowledge

Responsible knowledge is the most comprehensive understanding of your topic that you can develop in the time available for preparation. It includes information on

- the main issues of your topic.
- what respected authorities say about it.
- the latest developments relevant to it.
- related local applications of special interest to your audience.

To develop responsible knowledge, you should begin work on your speech well before the time you are scheduled to present it. Otherwise, you will be tempted to rush through your research, which means you may miss valuable information. You should also conduct your research with an open mind. Even if you are convinced that one side is correct on a controversial topic, try to discover why others might feel differently. Doing so will help you develop speeches that reach out to more people.

Having responsible knowledge earns you the right to speak. It allows you to enrich the lives of listeners with good information or advice. Whenever you speak, you put your mind and character on display. If you haven't made an effort to acquire responsible knowledge, you are saying, in effect, "I don't have much to offer, and I really don't care." On the other hand, having responsible knowledge may enhance your ethos in terms of both competence and character.

Although you cannot become an authority on most topics with ten hours or even ten days of research, you can certainly learn enough to speak responsibly.

---

information literacy   The skills one needs to locate information efficiently and to evaluate what one learns.

responsible knowledge   An understanding of the major features, issues, information, latest developments, and local applications relevant to a topic.

Because your research time will be limited, you should develop a three-step strategic research plan:

1. Assess your personal knowledge and experience to determine what additional information you need to obtain.

2. Retrieve this material using library and Internet resources and interviewing people for information and opinions.

3. Take careful notes for use in preparing your speech.

As you pursue your quest for responsible knowledge, the checklist below, "Checklist for Acquiring Responsible Knowledge," offers an overview of possible resources. Keep in mind that not every source will be appropriate for every topic, and some sources will be more appropriate than others for a particular speech. By checking off the items one by one as they apply in your situation, you can be sure you have conducted your research thoroughly and systematically.

Drawing on Personal Knowledge and Experience

Personal knowledge and experience add credibility, authenticity, and interest to a speech. You may not be an acknowledged authority on a subject, but personal stories or examples suggest that you have unique insights. They also make it easier for an audience to identify with you and the topic.

If you lack direct experience with a topic, you can arrange to acquire some. Suppose you are planning a speech on how local television stations prepare newscasts. You have gathered information from books and periodicals, but it seems rather dry and lifeless. How can you make this information interesting? Call a local television station and ask the news director if you might spend an afternoon in the newsroom so that you can get a feel for what goes on during that hectic time right before a newscast. Take in the noise, the action, and the excitement before and

---

Speaker's Notes 7.1

Checklist for Acquiring Responsible Knowledge

Use this checklist to assure that you have covered all the bases in your research.

1. _____ I have explored my personal knowledge of the topic.

2. _____ I have consulted general and/or specialized dictionaries or encyclopedias.

3. _____ I have checked newspaper indexes and recent newsmagazines to ensure that my information is up to date.

4. _____ I have used library and Internet search services to identify books and articles on my topic.

5. _____ I have looked for materials in periodicals to enrich my speech.

6. _____ I have considered the usefulness of the following sources:

_____ atlases
_____ biographical resources
_____ books of quotations
_____ almanacs
_____ government documents

7. _____ I have looked for local materials relevant to my topic.

8. _____ I have interviewed experts about my topic.

Figure 7.1

Personal Knowledge Summary

Topic: Eating Right on Campus

What I Know (or Think I Know)	Where/How I Learned It	What I Need to Find Out
College students don't eat right	Gained 15 lbs on junk food Note what friends & I eat	Average frosh gain Average college diet
Lack time and opportunity	Always rushed so choose fast foods	What sells best in student center
Cafeteria food unhealthy	Choices limited, I eat there	What is offered each day
Fresh fruit & veggies good	High school life skills class Mom's wisdom	Nutritional recommendations for balanced diet

Examples/Narratives I Might Use in Speech:

Today I grabbed a slice of pizza, a can of cola, and a chocolate bar for lunch. Not really nutritious, but it was all I had time for. I had just 25 minutes to get from my work-study job in Roslyn Hall to this class. At least the student center is on the way! But that's not enough time to sit down and eat a good meal. And even if I had the time, choices are limited. Yesterday the main options were sliced pizza, hamburgers, spaghetti and meat balls, and macaroni and cheese. Heavy on the starches and fats. No wonder the average freshman here gains 10 pounds.

during a show. This experience can help enrich your speech. You might also schedule an interview with the news director while you are at the station.

As valuable as it is, personal experience is seldom sufficient to provide all the information, facts and figures, and testimony that you will need for your speech. Your personal knowledge may be limited, the sources from which you learned may have been biased, or your experiences may not have been typical. Even people who are acknowledged authorities on a subject look to other experts to give added authority to their messages. Use your personal knowledge and experience as a starting point and expand it through research.

Prepare a personal knowledge summary sheet similar to the one shown in Figure 7.1. Include on your summary sheet what you know (or think you know) about the topic, where or how you learned it, and what additional information you might need to find. Also, jot down any examples or narratives from personal experience so that you can remember them as you develop your speech. Use your summary sheet to direct your research.

Doing Research in the Library

Although knowledge obtained from the library may lack the excitement and immediacy of personal experience, it has definite advantages. Library research can give you a broad perspective and a sound basis for speaking responsibly. It can extend, correct, and enrich your experience by acquainting you with the experience and knowledge of others.

Because college and university libraries vary widely in the resources they offer and the means of accessing those resources, we strongly suggest that you take the guided tour usually offered at the beginning of each term by your campus library. Even if you took the tour last year, take it again. You may have missed some important information the first time through, or your library may have changed. If a hands-on tour is not available, access your library's Web site to see if there is an online tutorial that will help you use the resources most effectively.

As a general rule, most college and large municipal libraries have the following major research resources:

Library materials are an excellent source of information for speeches.

- **Reference or research librarian:** The most valuable resource in the library, this person can steer you to the most helpful materials in the library.

- **Online catalog:** The catalog lists the books and periodicals available in the library and also tells you whether an item has been checked out, placed on reserve, or is available.

- **Online and hard copy general periodical databases:** These databases search a variety of periodicals and may provide abstracts or direct access to the full text of articles. Examples include FirstSearch, LexisNexis Academic, Reader's Guide Full Text, and ProQuest.

- **Online and hard copy special area databases:** These databases include such resources as Bus Management (business management), ERIC (Educational Resources Information Center), and Humanities Abstracts (humanities). Most provide abstracts, and some provide full texts of articles.

- **Online and hard copy news resources:** These resources include indexes to local and state newspapers plus computerized databases that access many news sources, such as Newsbank Infoweb, World News Connection, and Ethnic Newswatch.

- **Reference area:** This special section of the library contains encyclopedias, yearbooks, dictionaries, almanacs, atlases, and print indexes to periodicals.

- **Government documents area:** This area is a repository for federal, state, and local government publications.

- **Nonprint media archives:** Collections of films, videos, CDs, recordings, and microfilms can be found in the nonprint media archives.

- **Special collections area:** Clippings and other materials that can help you adapt your topic to local needs and interests are maintained in the special collections area.

Doing Research on the Internet

The Internet offers a wealth of information. It is an excellent source of breaking news, contemporary speech texts, and other time-sensitive material. It is also a helpful source of local news, offering area newspaper and television station Web sites that are automatically refreshed as information becomes available. Finally, the Internet is available 24/7, so when your library is not open, you can still find material for your speeches or update them at the last minute. This section helps you become an efficient and critical Internet user.

As you read through this material, keep in mind that the Internet is constantly changing. If a URL provided in this chapter doesn't open for you, try running the name of that Web site through a general search engine to see if it has moved, or simply wait a while and try the site again.

The first step in learning to do Internet research is determining which search engine to use. You have probably used one of the more popular search engines, such as Google or Yahoo!, but you may not know that there are different, more sophisticated types of search engines available. The major types useful for research include general search engines, metasearch engines, subject directories, and gateways to the "invisible web."

General Search Engines. A **general search engine** allows you to enter a key-word or phrase, then search the World Wide Web for sites containing that word or phrase. The searches are conducted by computer robots. The results may be organized in terms of relevance, popularity, or date of placement on the Web. The references cited are not screened for quality, so you may find links to everything from scholarly reports to Bubba's Home page. You should be aware that many general search engines start their lists of sites with "sponsored" links, links to Web sites that pay the search engine for optimal placement. Although the results from general search engines may contain a lot of useless links, they can be a good starting point for your research. Three of the more useful general search engines are Google (www.google.com), Yahoo! (www.yahoo.com), and Alltheweb (www.alltheweb.com).

Metasearch Engines. A **metasearch engine** engages several general search engines at the same time, so it expands the scope of your research. Metasearch

InterConnections.
LearnMore 7.1
Conducting Internet Research

Research-Quality Web Research
www.lib.berkeley.edu/TeachingLib/Guides/Internet/About.html#New
> *This online tutorial, developed by the University of California–Berkeley Library, provides a detailed, step-by-step, guided approach to Internet research.*

Internet Research Skills
www.virtualchase.com/researchskills/
> *This online seminar was developed as part of the Drexel University Continuing Professional Education Program. The site contains much interesting information not found in other online tutorials.*

Guide to Effective Searching of the Internet
www.brightplanet.com/resources/details/searching.html
> *This online tutorial provides detailed instruction on searching the Web. It was developed by BrightPlanet, a provider of business solutions for researching, monitoring, and indexing both surface and deep Web content. This same group also sponsors the CompletePlanet search tool mentioned in this chapter.*

general search engine An Internet search engine that allows you to enter a key-word and find related Web sites.

metasearch engine A search engine that combines the results from several general search engines.

engines work in much the same manner as general search engines, but they provide a broader base of information. Many of the metasearch engines cluster their results into subareas of the topic searched. Some offer suggestions for refining your search to get more topic-specific results. Three of the more useful metasearch engines are Clusty (http://clusty.com), Ixquick (www.ixquick.com), and Dogpile (www.dogpile.com).

Subject Directories.   A **subject directory** organizes links on topic-specific materials. For example, a subject directory may contain links to categories such as humanities, education, entertainment, and sports as some of their options. Many of the subject directories contain subdirectories within their major groupings. Education, for example, may be broken down into K–12 resources, bilingual education, and the like. The subject directories are compiled by humans, the Web pages are handpicked, and the entries tend to be well annotated. Three of the more useful subject directories are Infomine (http://infomine.ucr.edu/main.html), Librarians' Index to the Internet (www.lii.org), and About.com (www.about.com).

Invisible Web Gateways.   The **invisible web**, or deep web, as it is sometimes called, is a multitude of databases on the Internet that are not included in the searches of the more popular general search or metasearch engines. The invisible web contains much high-quality information from reputable sources and scholarly periodicals. Search tools to uncover resources in the invisible web often provide subject directories with links to these otherwise difficult-to-find databases. Three major gateways to the invisible web are Google Scholar (http://scholar.google.com), Direct Search (www.freepint.com/gary/direct.htm), and Complete Planet (www.completeplanet.com). The main Google Scholar page is shown in Figure 7.2.

Additional Suggestions.   As you may have guessed from this information, there is often little overlap among the various search engines, metasearch engines, directories, and invisible web gateways. Therefore, *you should always try at least three search engines to get the best results.* Most search tools also contain an "advanced search" option that instructs you how to limit or expand your inquiry. Running a **Boolean search** can also help you limit or expand your research.

When you access an article on the Internet, take careful notes on the specific information needed to document the source before you save the information on your computer. Note the author's name and credentials if stated, the sponsoring source, the date of publication, the date you accessed the material, and the URL (Universal Resource Locator) or Web address, which may be lost when you download the material

Figure 7.2

Invisible Web gateway

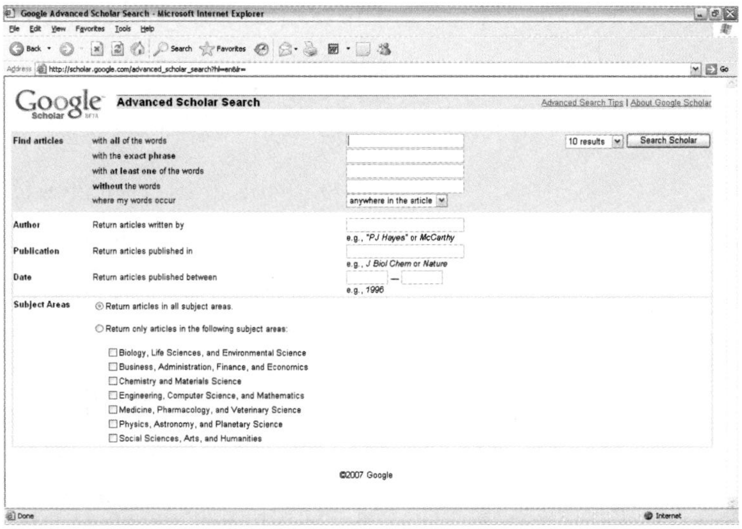

subject directory   An organized list of links to Web sites on specific topics.

invisible web   High-quality databases generally not included in the searches conducted by general or metasearch engines.

Boolean search   Techniques that can help one limit or expand research on the Internet.

Tips for Conducting a Boolean Search

Running a Boolean search can help you limit or expand your research:

1. Use AND or a plus sign to focus your search: mammogram AND ultrasound or mammogram+ultrasound.

2. Use OR or a slash mark to broaden your search: mammogram OR ultrasound or mammogram/ultrasound.

3. Use NOT to restrict or narrow your search: Lions NOT NFL.

4. Use NEAR when words should be close to each other in the document: moon NEAR river.

5. Use quotation marks to be more specific in your search: Baltimore Preparatory School gives 2,765 hits. "Baltimore Preparatory School" gives 275 hits.

6. When all else fails, read the instructions under "Advanced Search Tips" on the search engine home page.

to your desktop. Better still, save the link with your "Favorites" or "Bookmark" command so that you can easily return to the site.

Remember, you must be careful when you cut and paste material from Internet documents to your research notes. Unless you specify the source of the material and indicate in some way that a passage is a direct quotation, you could find yourself inadvertently committing plagiarism. It may be helpful to highlight direct quotes in yellow so that you don't confuse them with your personal summaries or reactions.

One final caution: Be careful when typing in the Web address of an Internet site you wish to reach. Once, when trying to access a popular computer magazine online, one of your authors inadvertently typed in *.net* rather than *.com*, and she ended up at a porn site. To see what such a seemingly minor difference in a URL can mean, access and compare the www.whitehouse Web sites from the following domains: .gov, .org, .net, and .com.

Evaluating Research Materials

hen you find material that you think might be usable in your speeches, you must test it carefully. As you research your topic, ask yourself the following questions:

- Does this article contain relevant and useful information?

- Does this article cite experts that I can quote in my speech?

- Are there interesting examples that make my ideas clearer?

- Are there stories that can bring my topic to life?

Beyond these simple questions, it is important that the material you use in your speech meets the basic criteria we suggested for critical listening and critical thinking: It must be relevant, representative, recent, and reliable. As we noted in Chapter 4:

- Relevant material applies directly to your topic and specific purpose.

- Representative material depicts a situation as it typically exists.

- Recent material contains the latest knowledge.

- Reliable material comes from credible sources and is confirmed by other authorities.

We cover the application of these criteria to each type of supporting material in Chapter 8.

Evaluating Material from Library Resources

As you do research in the library, be alert to two potential problems. First, you must consider the credibility of your sources in terms of the ethos of both the author and the publication. Second, you must remember that the timeliness of information is critical for some topics, so you must seek out the most up-to-date information available.

As you assess the credibility of an author, ask yourself, *Is this author an expert on my topic?* If the author is not well known or not associated with a prestigious organization or institution, check out his or her credentials in one of the biographical indexes. Some of the material you find may be written by professional journalists. In such cases, you should evaluate the credibility of the "experts" cited in the articles.

You must also consider the ethos of the publication in which the material appears. Professional journals are generally seen as more credible than popular periodicals such as magazines and newspapers. In turn, popular periodicals themselves vary in terms of their credibility. For most audiences, mainline newspapers are considered more credible than tabloids, and upscale magazines such as *Atlantic Monthly* are seen as more credible than *Reader's Digest*. Popular periodicals may also reflect political or social biases. For example, the *New Republic* offers a liberal perspective on contemporary issues, and the *National Review* presents a conservative outlook. Consequently, as you select authors and publications to cite in your speeches, you should consider how their reputations might affect the way your listeners receive your message.

The more sensitive or controversial your topic, the more important the credibility of your sources. For example, let us assume that you wish to present a speech supporting a ban on semiautomatic weapons. From previous class discussions, you suspect that many in your audience may not be friendly to that point of view. For these listeners, citing information or opinions that support your case from more conservative sources such as the American Medical Association might surprise them and get them to listen more sympathetically.

Evaluating Material from the Internet

You must be especially careful while evaluating information you find on the Internet. Remember, anyone can put anything on the Internet. Internet material is subject to few—if any—legal, financial, or editorial constraints. How can you determine whether the information you find there satisfies the requirements of responsible knowledge?

First, you must determine the kind of Web site you have accessed. Then, you must apply an especially rigorous set of standards as you evaluate what you find. The basic types of Web sites you will encounter on the Internet are advocacy sites, information sites, and personal sites.

Advocacy Web Sites.

The purpose of an **advocacy Web site** is to change attitudes or behaviors. An advocacy site might ask for contributions, try to influence voting, or simply strive to promote a cause. The URL of a nonprofit advocacy site often ends with .org. Some examples of advocacy sites include the Sierra Club

---

advocacy Web site   A Web site whose major purpose is to change attitudes or behaviors.

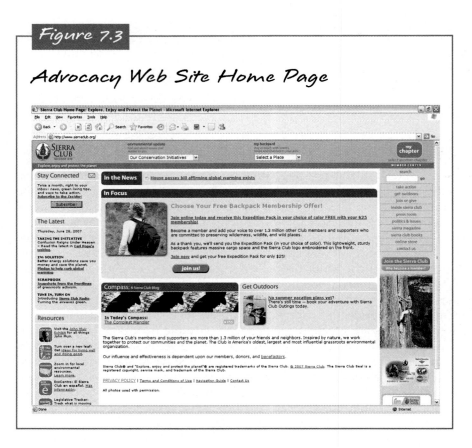

Figure 7.3

Advocacy Web Site Home Page

(www.sierraclub.org), the National Rifle Association (www.nra.org), the Children's Defense Fund (www.childrensdefense.org), and People for the Ethical Treatment of Animals (www.peta.org).

The Sierra Club home page shown in Figure 7.3 illustrates many of the features that should alert you that this is an advocacy Web site. For example, in the menu on the right is a button to click to make a donation or join the group. At the left of the page is a frame containing links to the various projects the group is involved in. Another frame near the top provides a "Stay Connected" link that signs you up for the organization's newsletter.

Most nonprofit advocacy group Web sites contain credible information, although they typically present only one side of an issue. Knowing that the group has an agenda it wants to promote, you should evaluate the material on advocacy sites very carefully. Additionally, when you access a Web site that champions one side of an issue, try to find another Web site that represents the other side. For example, if you look up information on the National Association for Biomedical research (favors animal testing) Web site (www.nabr.org), also check out the National Anti-Vivisection Society (opposes animal testing) Web site (www.navs.org).

Information Web Sites.   The purpose of an **information Web site** is to provide factual information on a specific topic. Information Web sites may include research reports; current world, national, or local news; government statistics; or simply general information such as you might find in an encyclopedia or almanac. The URLs of information Web sites may have a variety of suffixes, such as .edu, .gov, or .com. For example, both the Mayo Clinic Web site (www.mayoclinic.com) and the

information Web site   A Web site designed to provide factual information on a subject.

MEDLINEplus Web site (www.medlineplus .gov) are excellent sources of information about health issues. The material on the Mayo Clinic Web site has been prepared by physicians and scientists affiliated with the clinic; the material on the MEDLINEplus Web site comes from the government-sponsored National Library of Medicine.

Figure 7.4 shows the Mayo Clinic home page. Even though this Web site is registered in the commercial domain (.com), the only thing it seems to be selling is good health practices. Note some of the differences between this information home page and the advocacy home page shown in Figure 7.3. You are not asked for a donation, and the only thing you can sign up for is a free electronic newsletter on health information.

It is not always so easy to differentiate between advocacy Web sites and information Web sites. Some advocacy Web sites may deliberately downplay their true role so that they appear to be presenting straightforward information that is unbiased and free from persuasive intent. Caution should be the rule that guides you through such Web sites. A reputable information Web site will typically designate the author of the information and specify that person's credentials. It may also include the date that information was posted and provide links to other related sources of information. When an information Web site includes advertising, it will separate such entries clearly so that there is little chance for confusion.

Figure 7.4

Information Web Site Home Page

Personal Web Sites.   The purposes of a **personal Web site** are many and varied. They represent the work or opinion of a single individual who may or may not be affiliated with an official organization. They can contain anything from a list of a person's favorite restaurants in Boston to a professor's supplemental course material to incoherent ramblings about conspiracy theories.[2]

Because there are absolutely no controls over what can be published on personal home pages, you should be very careful about evaluating and using material from them.

Criteria for Internet Evaluation

Janet E. Alexander and Marsha Ann Tate, information specialists at the Wolfgram Memorial Library of Widener University, suggest five criteria for evaluating Internet research:[3]

- authority
- accuracy
- objectivity
- currency
- coverage

personal Web site   A Web site designed and maintained by an individual; contains whatever that person wishes to place on it.

InterConnections.

LearnMore 7.2

Evaluating Internet Resources

FactCheckEd.Org
www.factchecked.org
> *Developed and maintained by the Annenberg Public Policy Center, this Web site provides tools for uncovering deceptive information found on the Internet or in print materials.*

Evaluating Web Resources
www2.widener.edu/Wolfgram-Memorial-Library/webevaluation/webeval.htm
> *One of the first and best Web sites offering information on evaluating Internet resources, with checklists for evaluating advocacy, information, and personal Web sites, this site was prepared by Jan Alexander and Marsha Ann Tate and sponsored by the Widener University Library.*

The Virtual Chase
www.virtualchase.com/quality/index/html
> *This online guide for evaluating Internet resources is part of a public service Web site sponsored by Ballard, Spahr, Andrews, & Ingersoll, LLP. Also included are articles about conducting Internet research. The materials are prepared and maintained by Genie Tyburski, author of a law office computing column on electronic research strategies, and Greg Kaplan, Internet services librarian from Drexel University.*

These criteria are also useful for evaluating material from any source.

Authority.   To determine the **authority** of information you find on the Internet, you must evaluate the credentials of both the source and the sponsor of the information. Most reputable Web sites provide information regarding the source or author of the material and the sponsoring agency. If no one takes credit for what is on the site, don't trust it.

It is always wise to investigate the author's credentials regardless of the information about him or her provided on the Web site. Is there contact information that would allow you to reach the author? Is a URL or e-mail address provided? Is a postal address included? You might contact the person via e-mail, or if a mailing address is provided, you might look for a phone number in an online telephone directory (www.switchboard.com) and call the author. If authors seem defensive when you contact them, you might want to think twice about using their material.

You can often verify an author's credentials by running an Internet search with the person's name enclosed in quotation marks. If the author claims an academic affiliation, go to that institution's Web site and look in the faculty directory. Many colleges and universities include faculty résumés and links to faculty members' home pages on their Web sites. If the

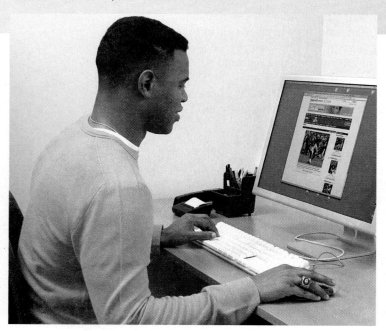

To ensure responsible knowledge in your speeches, carefully evaluate materials you find on the Internet.

authority   Criterion for evaluating the credentials of the author.

author claims a medical affiliation, run the name through the Medline Index on the National Institutes of Health Web site (www.nlm.nih.gov) and see what comes up. If the author claims a hospital or clinic affiliation, check that source as well. If the author reports having written books on the subject, check the Library of Congress catalog (www.loc.gov) or access Amazon.com (www.amazon.com) for a listing of books by that person and for biographical data that is often provided on the site.

You should also evaluate the sponsorship of a Web site. Most reputable Web sites have an "About Us" or "About This Web Site" link on the home page. Check out this information before doing anything else. If the sponsor is not immediately obvious, you can determine who it is by deleting parts of the URL, starting at the right and moving toward the left. A tilde (~) suggests a personal home page. The information immediately to the left of the domain (right before .com, .gov, etc.) suggests the sponsoring organization. For example, a URL with "nih.gov" indicates that the National Institutes of Health is the sponsoring agency. Run a search with the name of the organization or association enclosed in quotation marks for additional information and news about the sponsor. You can also check out an organization or association using the Scholarly Societies Project Web site (www.lib.uwaterloo.ca/society/overview.html).

Be especially careful if the sponsor may have a vested interest in the outcome of research. For example, in 2007, a pro-private-enterprise think tank and a major oil company both offered scientists rewards of up to $10,000 to encourage "research" that would discredit the findings of a study on global warming conducted by the United Nations' Intergovernmental Panel on Climate Change. Such "sponsored" research is ethically questionable.[4]

Once you have verified the credentials of the author and sponsoring agency, ask yourself if the person's or group's expertise is appropriate to the material in question. For example, a lawyer could provide credible information on legal issues, but she might not be considered an expert on medical questions. Also consider how your audience might evaluate controversial sources of information. If listeners would not accept them as authorities because of their reputation, it will not help you to cite them in your speech.

Accuracy.   One way to evaluate the **accuracy** of information is to look for links to other Web sites or citations to print documents that relate to the topic. Check these sources out to confirm the correctness of the information. Material that is accurate and reliable should be verifiable through other sources. If the site claims that this is "exclusive" information that is so "new" or "revolutionary" that no one else has access to it, beware!

The sources of statistical information should be identified, and the originating reports should be available either online or as print materials accessible in libraries. The results of proprietary research that has been done exclusively for an organization or company for compensation may not be available to the general public. This does not mean that such information is not reliable, only that it should be subject to intense critical scrutiny, since there is no way for other experts to check it out. If you cannot ascertain the accuracy and reliability of the information you find, don't use it in your speeches.

Be especially wary of Internet materials containing spelling or grammatical errors. These problems could indicate incompetence, a lack of quality control, and/or carelessness on the part of those posting the material. At the very least, such problems raise significant questions concerning the accuracy and reliability of the material offered.

Finally, you should evaluate what you find in terms of how accessible the information would be to an average, educated consumer. Most reputable information

accuracy   Criterion for evaluating the correctness of information by checking it against other information.

Web sites present material in a way that is understandable to a lay audience. If the writing seems purposely obscure, exercise caution when using it. One excellent Web site guide for evaluating the overall accuracy of online materials may be found at Virtual Chase (www.virtualchase.com/quality/index.html), a Web site devoted to teaching legal professionals and legal librarians how to do quality research online.

To find information that is accurate, stick with major, well-established sources of basic information, such as the *Encyclopedia Britannica* (www.britannica.com) or the *Columbia Encyclopedia* (www.bartleby.com/65/). Be very careful about using sources such as Wikipedia or Conservapedia, which allow almost anyone to contribute and/or edit entries and do not rely on formal peer reviews by topic area experts to verify information. Such material may contain misinformation or biased perspectives that are passed off as "true."[5]

Objectivity.   The **objectivity** of information on a Web site concerns its freedom from bias or personal feelings. It goes without saying that advocacy Web sites and many commercial Web sites contain elements of bias. Advocacy Web sites try to sell you a particular point of view; most commercial Web sites try to sell you a product line. Many advocacy and commercial Web sites are upfront with their intentions. This does not necessarily mean that you cannot find reliable or accurate information on their sites. In fact, these Web pages may use "unimpeachable data to influence readers."[6] However, knowing that a source of information is not objective should be a cue to look for additional information from differing perspectives.

The biased Web sites that try to hide their objectives are the ones you really must be wary of. The lack of an "About Us" or "Mission Statement" link should be a clear indication that the site may be peddling something other than what seems evident. Disreputable Web sites may provide misleading medical information or dispense hatred while seeming benign.[7] For example, a search for Web sites on alternative medicine led the authors to the Bamboo Delight Company, which offers links to anti-Semitic and racist Web sites along with information on "Chinese herbal medicine." Also be wary of sites that dazzle you with stunning graphics or special effects, where the sizzle may cover up either a lack of substance or malicious intent. Verify any information from such sites from other well-established sources.

Currency.   The **currency** of information on the Internet relates to the date of posting or revising material. Currency is particularly important on time-sensitive topics such as medical research and foreign relations. The most timely materials on the Internet may be found on newspaper Web sites. The NewsDirectory.com Web site (www.ecola.com) contains links to daily and weekly newspapers, television stations, magazines, and other media outlets throughout the world. Many of the online newspapers, such as the *New York Times* (www.nytimes.com), have searchable archives of past issues, allowing you to trace the evolution of news on a specific topic up to the present.

Coverage.   The **coverage** of material concerns the breadth and depth of information provided. No single article can provide all the information you need on a topic. Reputable Web sites will contain links to additional information or research that should be useful. When you are visiting an advocacy site, you should realize that other opposed positions may not even be mentioned there. You should seek additional perspectives on the topic. In general, you should assume that any single source offers only a partial view. Check other sites to ensure that you are getting a more complete and less distorted picture.

---

objectivity   Criterion for evaluating whether or not a source is free from bias.

currency   Criterion for evaluating whether or not the information on a Web site is up-to-date.

coverage   Criterion for evaluating the breadth of information on a topic.

Guide to Evaluating Internet Materials

If you are using the Internet to do research, you should use the following guide to evaluate the information you find.

1. What type of a Web site have I accessed? Advocacy? Information? Personal?

2. Is the author or sponsoring agency identified?

3. Does the author or sponsoring agency have appropriate credentials to address the issue?

4. Does the material contain links to other information on the subject or citations of available print resources?

5. Is the material objective, or does it seem biased?

6. Do other authorities confirm the information on the Web site?

7. Is the material up to date on time-sensitive topics?

8. Is the material covered with enough breadth and depth?

For example, if you researched teaching evolution, you would encounter advocacy sites as diametrically opposed as the National Center for Science Education (www.natcenscied.org), which advocates teaching evolution as part of a student's science curriculum, and Intelligent Design Network Seeking Objectivity in Origins Science (www.intelligentdesignnetwork.org), which opposes teaching evolution in public schools.

You would have to read these opposed perspectives carefully to understand the background of the dispute, the major issues in conflict, what each side had to gain or lose, what each proposed or opposed, and the major arguments each offered. Only then could you meet the standard of responsible knowledge needed to develop informative or persuasive speeches on the topic.

The depth of information needed to acquire responsible knowledge varies with the topic you are researching and the audience for whom the material is intended. For example, the more important a topic is to the well-being of your audience, the greater the depth of information you need. It may be acceptable to cite a public periodical such as the *Reader's Digest* on a topic that has benign consequences for your audience, such as cell phone etiquette. However, if the topic is a more important one, such as the effects of air pollution on the health of listeners, you should search for material from sources that are more scientifically oriented. To find this deeper information, run your topic through a search engine that accesses the invisible web.

Conducting Strategic Research

*B*egin your research by developing a strategic plan. The Research Strategy Worksheet, shown in Figure 7.5, should help you conduct this work efficiently. Fill in this form and accumulate research notes until you are satisfied that you have acquired responsible knowledge. As you move from top to bottom of the form, you will be following these steps:

1. Developing an overview of your subject

2. Building a bibliography on your topic

3. Acquiring in-depth knowledge from reputable sources

Figure 7.5

Research Strategy Worksheet

Topic: _____

Specific Purpose: _____

General Information Sources: (List sources of general information applicable to your topic) _____

Key Terms and Access to Information Sources: (List the key terms you will use and 2 sources of access to information you will use to identify specific and/or in-depth references)

Key Terms   *1.* _____   *2.* _____

             3. _____   *4.* _____

Access   *1.* _____   *2.* _____

Specific and/or In-Depth Information References: (List 3 or 4 references to specific and/or in-depth information applicable to your topic, of which at least 2 must be from periodicals or books)

1. _____

_____

2. _____

_____

3. _____

_____

4. _____

_____

Current Information References: (List 1 or 2 sources of current information if applicable to your topic)

1. _____

_____

2. _____

_____

Local Applications Sources: (List 1 or 2 sources for local applications material if applicable to your topic)

1. _____

_____

2. _____

_____

4. Checking to see that your information is up to date

5. Discovering local applications for your topic

We discuss each step in the following sections.

Develop an Overview

You should begin developing a comprehensive picture of your subject by consulting sources of background information about it. Even if you have extensive personal experience, you may find that your knowledge is incomplete, or you may discover areas of the topic that you had overlooked. The reviews also can help you focus your speech by pointing out the most important ideas concerning your topic.

Review articles are found mainly in encyclopedias and specialized dictionaries, housed in the reference section of the library. On the Internet, go to the Library Spot (www.libraryspot.com) for links to most of the major encyclopedias online. General encyclopedias contain background information, specify key-words to use in your search for in-depth information, and often list references for additional research. The articles are brief and written in lay language.

Specialized encyclopedias, such as the *International Encyclopedia of the Social and Behavioral Sciences*, cover specific topics in greater detail. Specialized dictionaries, available on diverse subjects ranging from American slang to zoology, provide more than definitions and pronunciations. For example, the *Oxford English Dictionary* presents the origin, meaning, and history of English words. A directory of dictionaries on the Internet is located at the Open Directory Project (http://dmoz.org/reference/dictionaries).

Once you have found sources of general information that are relevant to your topic, read the background material, take notes on what you find, and identify at least four key-terms you can use to access in-depth information.

Build a Bibliography

Because your preparation time for speeches is limited, you must know how to access information quickly. The major sources of access to information in the library include periodical indexes, newspaper indexes, and the card or online catalog. Some of the periodical indexes, such as the *Reader's Guide to Periodical Literature*, cover publications of general interest. Others, such as the *Business Periodicals Index*, are specific to a subject area. Many indexes are now available on computers in the library, which saves research time. To access information from an index, you must enter the key-terms you have identified for your topic.

On the Internet, the major sources of access to information are the search engines discussed in detail earlier in this chapter. Use all these materials to build a bibliography on your topic. From your bibliography, identify those articles or books that seem most relevant to your specific purpose.

Acquire In-Depth Knowledge

Most of the facts and figures, testimony, examples, ideas for narratives, and materials for presentation aids will come from in-depth sources of information, such as periodicals and books. As you research your speech, try to use a variety of sources representing different perspectives on your topic. As we mentioned earlier, periodicals have a reputation of their own. Some periodicals, such as *Scientific American*, are

Current periodicals can provide up-to-date information and opinions.

perceived as highly credible and objective, whereas others may be less acceptable to critical listeners. As you read articles in periodicals, you may discover that one book is frequently mentioned. Read it, and check the *Book Review Index* for summaries of reviews of it.

When you need facts and figures, consult an almanac, yearbook, or atlas. Almanacs and yearbooks provide accurate, up-to-date compilations of information on a wide range of topics. Such materials go beyond simple lists, often including short articles and graphics that you can adapt for presentation aids. Atlases are useful when your topic calls for geographic information. They include data on such things as population density or industrial production and are a good source of materials for presentation aids. Biographical resources can provide information about the qualifications of experts you might cite in a speech. Books of quotations can offer material for the introductions and conclusions of speeches. Most such books are indexed by topic and author, making it easy for you to find what others have had to say about your subject. Most of these resources are available on the Internet as well as in the library.

A word of caution: *The articles you find do not provide you with a speech*; rather, they provide ideas, information, opinions, examples, and narratives for use in the speech that *you* prepare for *your* particular audience. If you simply summarize an article and present it as though it were your own, you are committing plagiarism. Although we discussed plagiarism in Chapter 1, these guidelines for avoiding plagiarism bear repeating:

■ Introduce authors of quotations.

■ Identify sources of information.

■ Give credit to the originators of important ideas.

Ethics *Alert! 7.1*

Guidelines for Ethical Research

To be sure your research meets the ethical standard of respect for the integrity of ideas, apply the following guidelines:

1. Allow sufficient research time.

2. Investigate differing perspectives on your topic.

3. Access credible sources of information.

4. Never fabricate or distort information.

5. Take careful notes on what you read.

6. Cite your sources in your presentation.

Be Sure Your Information Is Up to Date

As we noted earlier, the timeliness of information is important for topics that change rapidly, such as medical research and computer technology. In addition, if you are not aware of current happenings related to your topic, your credibility will suffer. The best source of timely information is the Internet. By logging on to local newspapers and television stations throughout the world, you can keep abreast of what is happening during crisis situations. One of the best library sources for current information is *Facts on File*, a weekly publication that reports on current events by topics. Additional sources of current information include the most recent issues of weekly newsmagazines and newspapers.

Include Local Applications

An effective way to involve listeners with your subject is to show them how it relates to them and their community. For example, if you were discussing methods of disposing hazardous waste, it would be especially effective to talk about how that problem affects the local area. Your library may index local newspapers and may subscribe to regional magazines. Local newspapers may have archives that you can search online.

Many libraries maintain a vertical file that contains newspaper clippings, pamphlets, and other materials about important local people or issues. These materials may contain names of people you could interview to hear the kind of personal stories and inside information that might really make your speech come to life.

Interviewing for Information

Personal interviews can be an excellent source of information and opinions that add credibility to your speech. Citing material from an interview demonstrates your commitment to creating a speech with value for your audience. If you can say, "Sherlyn LaCosta, the director of research and development at New Age Electronics, told me . . . ," your audience will sit up and listen. Interviews often yield stories and inside information that make speeches come to life.

As valuable as they are, interviews also pose some challenges. Finding the right person to interview can be difficult. Once you find the person and are granted an interview, you may feel so grateful that you simply accept what the person says without critically evaluating the information. If you don't know a great deal about the subject, it may be hard for you to judge what you hear. However, the potential benefits of a good interview far outweigh any possible shortcomings. To minimize problems, use these strategies:

- Make interviews the final phase of your research preparation.

- Check your library's local clipping service or local newspaper archives to help you identify nearby prospects for interviews.

- Through your initial research, identify widely recognized experts for possible telephone or e-mail interviews.

- Although it is generally preferable to conduct an interview face to face, e-mail and telephone interviews can be used to verify information, acquire a brief quotation, or discover a person's opinion.

- Don't overlook the possibilities on your own campus. Every college and university has faculty members with expertise on a wide array of topics, and they are often willing to grant interviews to students.

Once you have identified prospects for interviews, you must establish contact, prepare for the interview, conduct the interview, and record what you learn so that it is readily accessible for speech preparation.

Establish Contact

The best way to initiate contact with interviewing prospects is to write them a letter in which you explain why you would like to interview them. You might even include a list of the questions you would like to ask. Such a letter helps the prospects evaluate your motives, builds your credibility, and sets the agenda for the interview. It also gives the experts, who probably are busy people, some idea of how much time you will need.

In your letter, express your sincere interest in the subject, and explain the significance of your request: You are preparing a public speech on a topic that is important to both them and you. Follow up the letter with a telephone call to schedule the interview. If time is short, initiate contact directly through a telephone call or e-mail. Don't be shy. A request for an interview is a compliment because it suggests that you value the person's information.

Consider whether to record your interview. A recorder can free you from having to take notes to get down the exact wording of answers. However, many people do not like being recorded, so always get your expert's permission. A good time to ask is during your initial contact. If the expert seems reluctant, don't press the issue.

Prepare for the Interview

Complete most of your library and Internet research before you conduct the interview so that you know what questions to ask and can talk intelligently on the subject. Also learn as much as you can about the person you will interview. This knowledge helps you establish rapport with your expert. Write out interview questions that are relevant to your specific purpose.

Plan open questions that invite discussion, not yes-or-no answers. Never supply the answer you want in your question, as in "Don't you think that global warming is a crisis that demands our attention?" Arrange your questions in a sequence so that the answers form a coherent line of thought:

What are the causes of air pollution in New Bedford?
What is the impact of air pollution on the citizens of our area?
Is there a serious effort under way to minimize air pollution?
What can students do to help the effort?

Plan your wording so that your questions don't sound abrasive. Save any controversial questions for late in the interview, after you have established rapport. Ask such questions tactfully: "Some people say that experts like you need to 'dirty their hands more' in the day-by-day effort to improve the environment. How do you respond to such criticism?" If asked with sincerity rather than hostility, this type of question can produce the most interesting part of your interview.

Conduct the Interview

Dress appropriately to show that you take the interview seriously, and arrive on time. Take time for a little small talk before you get into your prepared questions.

probes Questions that ask someone being interviewed to elaborate on a response.

Talk about things you may have in common. This might include such things as where the person lived, where he or she went to school, or simply your mutual interest in the topic.

Let the expert do most of the talking while you do the listening. Allow the person you are interviewing to complete the answer to one question before you ask another. Don't interrupt and jump in with another question every time your expert pauses. Your expert may go from one point to another and may even answer a question before you ask it. You should adapt to the flow of conversation.

Be alert for opportunities to follow up on answers by using probes, mirror questions, verifiers, or reinforcers. **Probes** are questions that ask a person to elaborate on a response: "Could you tell me more about the part played by auto emissions?" **Mirror questions** reflect part of a response to encourage additional discussion. The sequence might go as follows:

"So I told Anthony, 'If we want people to change their attitudes, we're going to have to start marching in the front of the movement.'"

"You felt you were moving toward a leadership role?"

A **verifier** confirms the meaning of something that has been said, such as "If I understand you correctly, you're saying, . . ." A **reinforcer** provides encouragement for the person to communicate further. Smiles, nods, or comments such as "I see" are reinforcers that can keep the interview moving.

If you feel the interview beginning to drift off course, you can often steer it back with a transition. As your expert pauses, you can say, "I believe I understand now the causes of air pollution. But can you tell me more about how this level of pollution affects our lives?"

Do not overstay your welcome. As the interview draws to a close, summarize the main points you have heard and how you think they may be useful in your speech. A summary allows you to verify what you have heard and reassures the expert that you intend to use the information fairly and accurately. Thank your expert for his or her time, and follow up with a telephone call or thank-you note in which you report the successful results of your speech.[8]

Material from face-to-face interviews can add much to a speech.

Record What You Learn

If you plan to take notes during an interview, tell your expert you want to be sure to quote him or her correctly in your speech. If you are not certain you wrote down an answer correctly, read it back for confirmation. As we noted earlier, do not plan to tape-record an interview without prior consent of your expert.

Follow Up on What You Learn

After you have completed the interview, find a quiet place to go over your notes and write out the answers to important questions while your expert's wording is still fresh in your mind. Also, follow up with a "thank you" note in which you report the successful results of your speech.

---

mirror questions Questions that repeat part of a previous response to encourage further discussion.

verifier A statement by an interviewer confirming the meaning of what has just been said by the person being interviewed.

reinforcer A comment or action that encourages further communication from someone being interviewed.

Speaker's Notes 7.4

Interviewing for Information

To conduct an effective information interview, complete the following steps:

1. Locate and contact an expert on your topic.

2. Research your topic before the interview.

3. Plan a series of questions that relate to your specific purpose.

4. Be on time.

5. Be courteous and tactful.

6. Don't ask leading questions.

7. Let your expert do most of the talking.

8. Summarize what you hear so your expert can verify it.

Taking Notes on Your Research

The best research in the world will not do you any good unless you take notes to help you prepare your speech. Take notes on anything you read or hear that might be usable in your speech. It is better to have too much material to work with than to know you read something important about a point but can't remember where.

Preparing Source and Information Cards

You may find it is useful to prepare research cards because they are easy to handle and sort by categories. The 4 × 6 index cards often work best because they provide adequate space for any information you want to record.

Preparing research cards also may help you avoid cut-and-paste plagiarism. You should prepare both source and information cards for each article or book you might use.

A **source card** should contain standard bibliographical information (see Figure 7.6). You also may wish to include a short summary of the material, information

Figure 7.6

Source Card

Source Card

Kennedy Warne, "Organization Man," *Smithsonian* (May 2007) 105–111.

Describe the work of Carl Linnaeus, an 18th century scientist, who classified and named more than 4,000 animals and 8,000 plants long before Darwin.

Author was the founding editor of *New Zealand Geographic*, and frequent contributor to National Geographic.

source cards   Records kept of the author, title, place and date of publication, and page references for each research source.

Figure 7.7

Information Card

> **Information Card**
>
> Warne, "Organization Man," p. 109
>
> "Many of his ideas now seem ludicrous. He believed epilepsy could be caused by washing one's hair, and leprosy caught by eating herring worms."
>
> direct quote!

---

about the author's credentials, and any of your own comments or reactions to the material. Use an **information card** to record facts and figures, examples, or quotations (see Figure 7.7). Include only one idea on each information card to make it easier to sort cards later. Label the top of each card with a heading that includes an abbreviated identification of the source.

Taking Notes on Your Computer

An alternative to using index cards is taking notes on your computer. For each paragraph in your notes, include a heading and an identification of its source, just as you would for an index card. You can rearrange these paragraphs in the same way that you sort index cards. It is usually wise to download and print Internet materials as you access them to be certain you have the correct URL. Make a backup copy of your notes to store on a CD or other device so that you don't accidentally lose them.

Know What Information to Record

The following checklists indicate the type of information you need to record about each source you consult:

For each book, record the

_____ Author

_____ Editor (if listed)

_____ Edition number (if listed)

_____ Full title, including subtitle

_____ Name and location of publisher

_____ Copyright date

_____ Page numbers for passages that you quote, summarize, or paraphrase

For each article, record the

_____ Author

_____ Full title, including subtitle

---

information cards Research notes on facts and ideas obtained from an article or book.

_____ Title of periodical

_____ Volume number

_____ Issue number

_____ Issue date

_____ Page numbers for passages that you quote, summarize, or paraphrase

For each computer-based source, record the

_____ Author

_____ Full title of the page or article, including subtitle

_____ Sponsor of the site

_____ Dates the document was posted and/or revised

_____ Date you accessed the source

_____ URL for Web pages (Web site address)

_____ Volume, issue number, and date for online journals

For each interview, record the

_____ Name of the person you interviewed

_____ Professional title of the person you interviewed

_____ Contact information: mailing address, phone number, e-mail address

_____ Date of the interview[9]

In Summary

Acquiring Responsible Knowledge. Information-literate students know how to access and evaluate information and cut through the data fog in our communication environment. To give a successful speech, you must acquire responsible knowledge that gives you a good grasp of the main issues on a topic, what experts say about it, the most recent developments, and how it applies specifically to your listeners. You can acquire responsible knowledge from personal experience, Internet and library research, and interviews.

Personal knowledge and experience add credibility, authenticity, and interest to a speech, but they should be supplemented with library and/or Internet research. In the library, use the online catalogs of books and periodicals to locate materials. Start with the general periodicals databases, and then move on to specialized databases as needed. The Internet offers a wealth of information, including late-breaking news. It can be searched using a general search engine, a metasearch engine, or subject directories. Invisible web search engines allow you to find scholarly materials. Since there is little overlap in the materials covered, search for information on the Internet using at least three different search engines.

Evaluating Research Materials. It is important to evaluate articles and information from both the library and the Internet. When using the Internet for research, differentiate between advocacy Web sites, information Web sites, and personal Web sites. Evaluate all material you plan to use in terms of its authority, accuracy, objectivity, currency, and breadth and depth of coverage.

Conducting Strategic Research. Develop a research plan that steers you systematically through developing an overview of your topic, building a bibliography, acquiring in-depth knowledge, checking to see that information is current, and developing local applications. Interviewing for information can add freshness, vitality, and local relevance to your speeches.

Taking Notes on Research. Take careful notes so that you can incorporate what you learn into your speeches. Prepare source cards with publication information for each article, book, or Internet entry. Prepare information cards to preserve quotations or precise bits of information. You can also take notes on your computer.

Explore and Apply the Ideas in This Chapter

1. Use the World Advocacy Web site (www.worldadvocacy.com) to identify and access an advocacy Web site on a controversial issue such as gun control, abortion, or smokers' rights. Select an article from the Web site and analyze it in terms of its authority, accuracy, objectivity, currency, and coverage.

2. Access an information Web site on the same issue used for Exercise 1. Select an article from the site and analyze it in terms of the same criteria of authority, accuracy, objectivity, currency, and coverage. Compare the results of this analysis with those of your advocacy Web site analysis.

3. Search a topic you are considering for your informative speech in the library using an online periodical index. Print out the results of this search. Using the same topic, run a search on an Internet general search engine. Print out the results of this search. Compare the results of the two searches and share them with your classmates, discussing the pros and cons of both types of research tools.

4. Take a walking tour of your library and locate the various resources described in this chapter. While you are there, try to find the answers to the following questions. Do not ask the librarian for assistance. Keep track of how long it takes you to find the information, and record the source of each answer.

   a. What was the population of the city in which you were born in the year of your birth?
   b. What television show had the highest Nielsen rating when you were six years old?
   c. Select the contemporary figure that you admire most. When was he or she born? What awards has he or she received?
   d. Who won the Pulitzer Prize for literature in the year your most admired public figure was born? For what work was this awarded? For what other works is the author noted?
   e. What actress won the Academy Award for best supporting actress in the year of your birth? What movie was she in?
   f. What noteworthy event took place during the month and year of your birth? When and where did this happen?

5. In the questions above, substitute your mother for yourself. Then use the Internet to locate the answers to these questions. Keep track of how long it takes you to find the information, and record the source of each answer. Compare the results obtained from the Internet with those you found in the library.

8

Supporting Your Ideas

Outline

This chapter will help you

- use facts and statistics to substantiate ideas
- use expert, lay, and prestige testimony to make your speech credible
- use examples to bring your speech to life
- use narratives to involve your audience
- select the most appropriate supporting material for your speech

The universe is made up of stories, not of atoms.

—*Muriel Rukeyser*

Even if you haven't seen one in person, you've probably seen a railroad trestle in an old western movie. These magnificent examples of architectural and engineering excellence must carry many times their own weight as they span deep canyons and cross fast-flowing rivers. To bear such a burden, they need strong supports that are braced and cross-braced. Not only do the supports and braces add strength, but they also add beauty to the structure. Throughout the next several chapters, picture yourself as an architect—a builder of ideas. Think of your speeches as thought-structures built on solid pillars of supporting materials. To be a good architect or builder, you must know your materials and what they can support. You need to know how to select and use them wisely. Just as a train trestle is built to carry heavy weights and withstand storms and high winds, your speech must withstand doubt and controversy. When you rise to speak, you must be confident of its structural integrity.

Facts and statistics, testimony, examples, and narratives are the major forms of **supporting materials** used in building speeches. Facts and statistics are the most basic type of supporting material and should underpin almost every informative or persuasive speech. They ground a message in reality and are especially important when you need to verify controversial statements or claims. Testimony, examples, and narratives add credibility and human interest to speeches. They help create and sustain interest, explain the meaning of ideas, make interpretations more credible, and underscore the importance of ideas.

Your personal experience, Internet and library research, and interviews with experts (described in Chapter 7) should have provided you with a good supply of supporting materials for your speeches. In this chapter, we discuss each type of supporting material, explain when it is most useful, and describe how to put it to work in your speeches.

Facts and Statistics

Facts and statistics are the most objective forms of supporting material, so they are indispensable to responsible speaking. **Facts** are statements that can be verified by independent observers. **Statistics** are numerical facts. Neither facts nor statistics depend on the experience of a single person or group; rather, they are confirmed repeatedly by people from all walks of life. They therefore add credibility to your ideas. If "the facts are in your favor," it creates a presumption that what you are saying is true. Therefore, facts and statistics are especially important when your topic is unfamiliar or your ideas are controversial.

Facts

The more personally important an issue is, the more any speech addressing that issue must be grounded in reality. Richard Weaver, a noted communication critic writing in the 1950s, suggested that Americans honor facts and numbers as the highest form of knowledge, much as some other societies respect divine revelations.[1] This is especially true when the facts are based on science. In a more recent Gallup survey, 86 percent of those polled agreed that "references to scientific research in a story increased its credibility."[2]

---

supporting materials The facts and figures, testimony, examples, and narratives that are the building blocks of successful speeches.

facts Information that can be verified by observation or expert testimony.

statistics Numerical information.

The following statements are factual because they can be shown to be either true or false:

> Ford Explorer is an American-made sports utility vehicle.
>
> Most students at our college work while attending school.
>
> Television advertisements often rely on emotional appeals.

Facts appear to be a quite dependable form of knowledge, but actually they can sometimes be unstable.

Their Objectivity Can Be Compromised.

Although factual statements can stand by themselves, speakers seldom use them without interpreting them. What do the facts mean? How should we understand them? Interpretations also often contain value terms that can transform the factual statements into judgments, claims, or opinions:

> Ford Explorer is a *superior* American-made sports utility vehicle.
>
> Most *industrious* students at our college work while attending school.
>
> Television advertisements often rely on *unethical* emotional appeals.

There is nothing inherently wrong with making interpretations or voicing opinions. We often present factual information that reflects our point of view. The problem comes when facts and opinions are confused. Factual statements normally require only minimal support. But the addition of such words as *superior, industrious,* or *unethical* requires additional support. Speakers must now provide more facts or statistics, examples, expert testimony, or stories to prove that their claims are justified— that they are more than just expressions of personal feeling.

To Verify Facts, We Must Often Depend on the Word of Others.

We usually cannot personally demonstrate the factual accuracy of our statements. Consequently, we must look for support from independent experts who have no vested personal or financial interest in what they report. For example, we might say, "According to the latest issue of *Consumer Reports,* which did extensive tests on many SUVs, the Ford Explorer is superior." This type of support is called expert testimony, which we discuss later in this chapter.

Such sources of verification have their own ethos, just as speakers do. For example, *Consumer Reports* is known for its objective testing of products. On social or political issues, the ideological position of the source may be important. If you cited the *National Review* in support of a claim, skeptical listeners might respond, "Well, that's a conservative magazine. Of course they will support this right-wing claim!" On the other hand, if you also cite the *New Republic,* a more liberal publication, then skeptical listeners might think, "Well, if both left and right agree, then perhaps what she's saying is true."

Even seemingly neutral sources present "factual" information that is colored by its cultural environment. Compare the following excerpts from the same encyclopedia in its 1960 hard copy and 2007 online editions:

> **1960:** Kiowa Indians hunted buffalo on the southwestern plains of the United States. The Kiowa and their allies, the Comanche, raided many Texas ranches. They probably killed more whites than any other Indian tribe. . . . By [a] treaty signed in 1868, the Kiowa agreed to go with the Comanche to a

reservation in Indian territory (now Oklahoma). But only the Kiowa chiefs had signed the treaty, and no chiefs could force their young men to make such a sacrifice. Many struggles and arrests occurred before the Kiowa finally went to live on the reservation. When trouble broke out in 1874, Satanta, one of the most daring Kiowa leaders, was arrested and sentenced to prison. There he committed suicide. The Kiowa then "put their hands to the plow." They now live peacefully as farmers. Several have become well-known artists.

2004: Kiowa Indians are a tribe that lives largely in Oklahoma and elsewhere in the Southwestern United States. According to the 2000 U.S. census, there are about 8,600 Kiowa. Most of them live in rural communities near Anadarko, Carnegie, and Mountain View, Oklahoma. Other tribal members live in urban areas and work in law, medicine, teaching, and other professions. . . . The tribe is governed by the Kiowa Indian Council, which consists of all members who are at least 18 years old. The Kiowa Business Committee, an elected group, manages tribal programs in such fields as business, education, and health.[3]

Both of these accounts are "factual," but the first dwells on past conflicts and portrays the Kiowas as historically warlike, while the second emphasizes their present governance and business programs.

The contrast reminds us that even relatively objective descriptions are selective and incomplete. We should always ask ourselves what any given description leaves out and whether that omission might be critical. In short, we should try to determine what is information, what is misinformation, and what is **disinformation**—or deliberately false, fragmented, irrelevant, or superficial information supplied by "authorities" with the intention of influencing policies or opinions.[4]

The 1960 encyclopedia entry stressed the warlike qualities of the Kiowa.

Statistics

Statistics are numerical facts that describe the size of something, make predictions, illustrate trends, or show relationships. Statistics are a powerful form of supporting material, especially in persuasive speeches. Note the following example from a student speech advocating a ban on smoking in public spaces:

> The American Lung Association reports that secondhand smoke causes more than 3,000 cancer deaths a year and between twenty-three and seventy thousand heart disease deaths a year in non-smokers. They also indicate that it contributes to 150,000 to 300,000 respiratory infections in babies, mainly bronchitis and pneumonia, and causes two to three thousand SIDS (sudden infant death syndrome) deaths in the United States each year. And, if that is not enough, secondhand smoke aggravates asthma symptoms in 400,000 to 1 million asthmatic children as well.

If the figures are very striking, as in the following example from a speech on medical research by Michael J. Fox, you may not need to include as much detail:

> There are 30,000 known human diseases; but we have treatments for only 10,000.[5]

disinformation Deliberately false, fragmented, irrelevant, or superficial information designed to influence policies or opinions.

Note that in these examples the speakers round off the numbers. Rounding off is typical when the central point is not really in dispute but when the magnitude of the problem is not well appreciated. The statistics in these examples create a lasting impression of the enormity of the problems.

On more controversial issues, when listeners strongly disagree, precise figures may make the statistical evidence seem more credible and difficult to dismiss. The prevalence of guns in our society, as well as how, whether, and how much to control them, is an ongoing issue that truly concerns many people. Dr. Richard Corlin, president of the American Medical Association, used exact numbers to confront his listeners with what he called the "epidemic" of gun violence in America:

> Since 1962, more than a million Americans have died in firearm suicides, homicides, and unintentional injuries. In 1998 alone, 30,708 Americans died by gunfire. . . .
>
> This is a uniquely American epidemic. In the same year that more than 30,000 people were killed by guns in America, the number in Germany was 1,164. In Canada, it was 1,034. In Australia 391. In England and Wales 211. And in Japan the number for the entire year was 83.[6]

Dr. Corlin's exact numbers suggest that his facts are authoritative. They make his comparisons among nations compelling, which in turn makes it difficult for listeners to ignore his argument. To determine which of these techniques you should use—rounded-off or exact numbers—you will have to decide what you want your statistics to accomplish. Do you want to impress listeners with the magnitude of an issue they may have ignored, or do you want to demonstrate the validity of an issue they may have doubted?

When presented orally, statistics can be overwhelming. Don't simply drown your listeners in a bath of numbers. Use presentation aids to display your data. Many of your listeners may be visual learners, and an effective presentation aid adds authority and interest values to your numbers. We describe strategies for effective presentation aids in Chapter 11.

Another way to add meaning to your statistics is to bring them alive through comparison and contrast. Note how Dr. J. Edwin Hill used contrast to add impact to his statistics in a speech on the impact of Hurricane Katrina on medical services in Louisiana:

> Katrina dislocated almost 6,000 patient-care physicians, the largest single displacement of doctors in U.S. history. More than 4,500—two-thirds of those displaced physicians—were in the three central New Orleans parishes. To put that into context, that number was more than one-quarter of the total number of new physicians who start practice in the United States each year.[7]

We discuss the uses of comparison and contrast later in this chapter.

Evaluating Facts and Statistics

For almost any speech topic, your research notes should contain a good array of facts and statistics. Before you decide which of these materials you will use in your speech, apply the critical evaluation skills we discussed in Chapter 7. The information you use should be relevant, representative, and current and should come from credible, objective sources. It should also be consistent with what other reputable sources

InterConnections.
LearnMore 8.1

Understanding Statistics

Statistics

www.unc.edu/depts/wcweb/handouts/statistics.html

This primer on understanding and using statistics in writing is also applicable to the use of statistics in speeches. Developed and maintained by The Writing Center of the University of North Carolina at Chapel Hill.

MeanDeviation

www.meandeviation.com/tutorials/stats/

This online tutorial helps students understand and interpret the meaning of statistics. Compiled and maintained by Dr. Alan Dix, professor, Computer Department, Lancaster University, United Kingdom.

Statistics Every Writer Should Know

www.robertniles.com/stats/

This Web site explains basic statistical concepts in lay language and offers guidelines for how not to get duped by numbers. Provides really interesting articles on detecting statistical scams. Compiled and maintained by Robert Niles, former financial management consultant turned journalist.

report. Finally, the information you use should be complete. It should not leave out important material that could alter its interpretation.

As you review your research notes, you may discover interesting information about your topic that does not relate directly to the purpose of your speech. No matter how fascinating it seems, if the information does not fit, don't use it. A speech that is cluttered with interesting digressions is hard for listeners to follow. You should also consider how current the information is, especially if your topic is one on which information changes rapidly. On such fast-breaking subjects, yesterday's news may be obsolete. Save yourself the embarrassment of having a listener point out that your ideas are wrong because of what happened this morning!

Test even "factual" material for potential bias, distortions, or omissions. Don't be taken in by scientific-sounding names, especially if the information contradicts common sense. To guard against deceptive information, do not rely too heavily on any one source. Compare what different expert sources have to say. Tell listeners how you have evaluated your information, especially if the facts contradict what listeners believe. As you consider facts and statistics, be careful not to read into them what you want to find or to exaggerate the results. Guard against distorting information by the way you word it. Don't ignore information that contradicts your claims by simply rejecting it as atypical or irrelevant.

Be especially careful when using statistics. Keep in mind that statistical predictions are based on probability, not certainty. You should also be certain that any statistics you cite are relevant to your locale. If you talk about the "crisis of unemployment" in your area, basing your claim on a national average of 7 percent, you could have a problem if someone points out that the local rate is only 4 percent.

Figure 8.1

Checklist for Evaluating Facts and Statistics

____ Is this information relevant to my purpose?

____ Is this information the most recently available?

____ Is this information truly representative of the subject?

____ Is this information from a credible source?

____ Is this information consistent with what other reputable sources report?

____ Is this information free from bias?

____ Is this information complete?

Using Facts and Statistics

Obviously, you can't just stand up and rattle off facts and numbers and expect your speech to be effective. You must artfully integrate this material into your message. Three effective techniques for presenting facts and statistics in a speech are definitions, explanations, and descriptions.

Definitions.   A **definition** translates unfamiliar or technical terms into words your listeners can understand. Definitions help ensure that the speaker and listeners will be talking and thinking about the same things. As a general rule, you should provide definitions for unfamiliar terms the first time you use them. In her informative speech on genetic testing, Ashlie McMillan first offered a technical definition: "According to 'The Genetic Revolution,' an article in *Scientific* magazine, genetic testing 'is co-relating the inheritance of a distinctive segment of DNA, a marker localizing the mutant gene on a DNA strand which composes our chromosomes.'" Noting the puzzled looks on her listeners' faces, Ashlie then said, "I found that a little confusing too, so I tried to put it in my own words: Genetic testing looks at people's DNA to see if they have a genetic condition or disease, or are likely to get the disease. That's basically what it is."

Explanations.   Longer and more detailed than a definition, an **explanation** helps clarify a topic or demonstrates how it works. John F. Smith Jr., former chairman of the board of General Motors Corporation, used an explanation to both define and clarify the OnStar system:

> Basically, the OnStar system combines the Global Positioning System (GPS) satellite network with wireless technology to link the driver and vehicle to the OnStar Center. There are currently two centers, in Michigan and North Carolina. Each is staffed by real human beings, 24 hours a day, 7 days a week, 365 days a year. . . . They are there to offer immediate, real-time, personalized help to any query.
>
> OnStar has been used to assist subscribers in everything from emergency services to tracking stolen vehicles; getting the doors opened when the keys are accidentally locked inside; finding the nearest ATM machine; guiding the driver to the local zoo or gasoline station; and arranging dinner reservations and theater ticket purchases. If an OnStar-equipped vehicle is in a crash that deploys an airbag, the car itself automatically "calls" the Center and an advisor immediately calls the vehicle to see what kind of assistance is needed.[8]

 *Speaker's Notes 8.1*

Using Facts and Statistics

Follow these guidelines for using facts and figures in your speeches.

1. Check several sources to verify important information.
2. Use information from sources with no vested interest in what they report.
3. Do not distort the meaning of information.
4. Use the latest facts and figures.
5. Make statistics more understandable with examples or presentation aids.

---

definition   A translation of an unfamiliar word into understandable terms.

explanation   Discussion that helps clarify a topic or demonstrates how a process works.

The verbal description of this monument at Wounded Knee helps establish a mood for the rest of the speech.

It is important to offer such explanations early in your speech to help listeners understand your message.

Descriptions.   A **description** is a "word picture" that helps listeners visualize what you are talking about. The best descriptions evoke vivid images in the minds of the audience. The great Roman rhetorician Longinus once said that images occur when, "carried away by enthusiasm and passion, you think you see what you describe, and you place it before the eyes of your hearers."[9] Images not only increase understanding, they also color information with the speaker's feelings and establish a mood that affects how listeners perceive a subject. Note how the following description of the monument at Wounded Knee, which commemorates the massacre of hundreds of Sioux men, women, and children, both paints a picture and establishes a mood:

> Two red brick columns topped with a wrought iron arch and a small metal cross form the entrance to the grave site. The column to the right is in bad shape: Cinder blocks from the base are missing; the brickwork near the top has deteriorated and tumbled to the ground; graffiti on the columns proclaim an attitude we found repeatedly expressed about the Bureau of Indian Affairs: "The BIA sucks!" Crumbling concrete steps lead you to the mass grave. The top of the grave is covered with gravel, interrupted by unruly patches of chickweed and crabgrass.

This description works well because it is *understated*. As you provide descriptions, be careful about injecting too much emotionality into them. If that "grave site" was that "lonely grave site," or if that "mass grave" was that "abandoned mass grave," the description would have been less effective. Let listeners provide the adjectives in their minds. That way, they participate in creating images and feel engaged rather than manipulated by the speech.

Testimony

Testimony, which involves citing the words or ideas of others, can help reinforce the facts and figures in your message. Testimony provides witnesses in support of your message, adds authenticity to it, or blesses your speech with eloquent words. Three types of testimony are useful as supporting material. Expert testimony comes from sources who are authorities on the topic. Lay testimony comes from ordinary citizens who may have firsthand experience with the topic or strong feelings about it. Prestige testimony comes from people who are highly regarded but not necessarily experts on the specific topic.

descriptions   Word pictures that help listeners visualize what you are talking about.

testimony   Citing the opinions or conclusions of other people or institutions to clarify, support, and strengthen a point.

Expert Testimony

Expert testimony comes from people who are qualified by training or experience to speak as authorities on a subject. Using expert testimony allows you to borrow credibility and provides validity for your ideas. Expert testimony is especially important when a topic is innovative, unfamiliar, highly technical, or controversial.

When you use expert testimony, remember that competence is area-specific: Your experts can speak as authorities only within their area of expertise. As you introduce such testimony, establish that your source is an authority on the specific topic of your speech. If the testimony is recent, mention that as well. If the testimony appears in a prestigious journal, book, or newspaper, let listeners know where you found it. Note how the speaker in the following example weaves these various considerations together as he presents the credentials of his expert:

> Dr. Frances Gonzales, chair of our Criminal Justice Department and former member of the Presidential Task Force on Inner-City Violence, said last week in the *Washington Post* that a law requiring the licensing of handguns would. . . .

Be on guard for bias as you select expert testimony. Sources who are passionately involved in a topic may not be objective. There is, however, one situation in which bias enhances the usefulness of a source. This occurs in the case of **reluctant testimony**, in which people speak *against* their apparent self-interest. Listeners give high marks for character and honesty to those who feel compelled to tell the truth *despite* their own agendas.[10] Therefore, reluctant testimony is useful in persuasive speeches. In his speech on the epidemic of gun violence, Dr. Richard Corlin cites the words of a respected conservative chief justice of the Supreme Court, the late Warren Burger:

> "The Second Amendment has been the subject of one of the greatest pieces of fraud, I repeat the word fraud, on the American people by special interest groups that I have ever seen in my lifetime. The very language of the Second Amendment refutes any argument that it was intended to guarantee every citizen an unfettered right to any kind of weapon. Surely the Second Amendment does not remotely guarantee every person the constitutional right to have a Saturday night special or a machine gun."[11]

Burger's words carry more weight because of his reputation for supporting conservative positions.

Lay Testimony

Lay testimony represents the wisdom of ordinary people. It is highly regarded in democracies in which elections are the source of political power. In these societies, "the people" often become a mythical symbol invoked to justify policy.[12] Lay testimony may come from people who have firsthand experience with a topic or who have strong feelings about it. It is useful for providing an understanding of the real-life consequences of issues and adds authenticity and compassion to ideas. It is not appropriate, however, to use lay testimony to establish the objective validity of ideas.

As he addressed the annual meeting of the Public Broadcasting System, Bill Moyers used lay testimony to emphasize the value of public radio and television:

> There was a cabbie [in New York City] named Youssef Jada. He came here from Morocco six years ago. . . . Youssef kept his car radio tuned to

---

expert testimony Offers judgments from those who are qualified by training or experience to speak as authorities on a subject.

reluctant testimony Highly credible form of supporting material in which sources speak against their apparent self-interest.

lay testimony Citing the views of ordinary people on a subject.

National Public Radio all day and his television set at home on Channel Thirteen. He said—and this is a direct quote—"I am blessed by these stations." He pointed me to a picture on the dashboard of his thirteen-month-old son, and he said: "My son was born in this country. I will let him watch Channel Thirteen so he can learn how to be an American."

Think about that. . . . Why shouldn't public television be the core curriculum of the American experience?[13]

This lay testimony illustrates what a powerful influence public broadcasting can be to the "common people."

There are many sources of lay testimony to use in a speech. You can find out how people feel about an issue from public opinion polls such as Gallup International's "The Voice of the People" (www.voice-of-the-people.net). You can also tune into this "voice" in the "Letters to the Editor" section of newspapers. When popular periodicals publish articles on issues, they almost invariably include stories from people who are involved in the issue. Should you choose to use lay testimony in your speeches, keep in mind that such material may represent a point of view that may be quite narrow and even inaccurate. When you are citing a single person, as in the example from Moyer's speech, remember that this is a very limited perspective, regardless of how well you personally feel it applies to the issue at hand.

When Lance Armstrong speaks in support of cancer research, he provides lay, prestige, and expert testimony.

Prestige Testimony

Prestige testimony associates your message with the words of a respected public figure. While this person may not necessarily be an expert on your particular topic, she or he has nevertheless voiced some important opinion or timeless truth that supports, illuminates, or elevates your ideas. Citing such testimony can add distinction to your speech. It allows you to connect your message with the ethos of the esteemed person. Because of these qualities, prestige testimony is often used as a source of inspiration in ceremonial speaking.

In a speech at the cemetery at Normandy, France, commemorating the sixtieth anniversary of the Allied invasion of Europe, President George W. Bush cited former President Dwight D. Eisenhower, who also had been the commander of the Allied forces during that invasion:

Twenty years after D–Day, former President Eisenhower returned to this place and walked through these rows. He spoke of his joy of being a grandfather, and then he said, "When I look at all these graves, I think of the parents back in the states whose only son is buried here. Because of their sacrifice, they don't have the pleasure of grandchildren. Because of their sacrifice, my grandchildren are growing up in freedom.[14]

In this example, Bush used Eisenhower's exact words so that he would not lose the elegance and force of the language. If

prestige testimony Citing the views of someone who is highly regarded, but not necessarily an expert on a topic.

you must paraphrase a lengthy passage, be sure that you reflect fairly the spirit and meaning of the words you summarize.

Evaluating Testimony

As with any form of supporting material, consider the relevance of testimony. Also be sure you are accurately quoting or paraphrasing what was said. Beyond these basic considerations, the questions you should ask will vary with the type of testimony involved.

If you are using expert testimony, evaluate the credentials of your source; check them out using the Web sites suggested in Chapter 7. Determine if the source is an expert in the area of your topic, and consider the possibility of bias. You should also compare the testimony from this source with that of other authorities and check the date to be sure it is recent.

If you are using lay testimony, you should consider whether it will help listeners understand the human aspects of your message. Also determine how this testimony might increase identification among the speaker, the topic, and the audience. The source of lay testimony should be someone the audience will find likeable and attractive. If your lay testimony comes from survey data, check to be sure that it is from a reputable polling organization and is up to date. Finally, be sure you are using lay testimony appropriately. Remember, lay testimony cannot be used to verify facts.

Figure 8.2

Checklist for Evaluating Testimony

General
- ____ Is this testimony relevant to my purpose?
- ____ Am I quoting or paraphrasing accurately?
- ____ Am I using the appropriate type of testimony for my purpose?

Expert Testimony
- ____ Have I verified the credentials of my source?
- ____ Are my expert's credentials appropriate for my topic?
- ____ Will this expert be acceptable to my listeners?
- ____ Is my expert free from vested interest?
- ____ Is this testimony consistent with that of other authorities?
- ____ Does this testimony reflect the latest knowledge on my topic?

Lay Testimony
- ____ Does this testimony demonstrate the human applications of my topic?
- ____ Does this testimony enhance identification with my topic?
- ____ Are the people cited likeable and attractive?
- ____ Is polling data from a reputable organization?
- ____ Is polling data recent?

Prestige Testimony
- ____ Do my listeners believe this person is prestigious?
- ____ Does this testimony add grace and dignity to my speech?
- ____ Does associating with this person enhance my credibility as a speaker?
- ____ Does associating with this person enhance the credibility of my speech?

If you are using prestige testimony, think about how your listeners might feel about the person you are citing. You should also consider if associating with this person will increase your credibility as a speaker and the credibility of your message. You don't have to worry about the recency of prestige testimony: In contrast with expert or lay testimony, where "latest is best," the rule for prestige testimony is often "the older the better." Wisdom ages well. Finally, be sure you are using this type of testimony appropriately. Like lay testimony, prestige testimony cannot be used to verify facts.

Be aware that in some cases, these types of testimony may overlap. For example, if you were citing Lance Armstrong in support of cancer research, you would be providing lay testimony because he is a cancer survivor, prestige testimony because he is the seven-time Tour de France champion, and expert testimony because he established and directs LIVESTRONG, a cancer support and research foundation.

Using Testimony

When you repeat the exact words of others, you are using a **direct quotation**. Direct quotations are useful when the material is brief, the exact wording is important, or the language is especially eloquent. When ideas are controversial, a direct quotation can seem especially authoritative and conclusive. You also may **paraphrase**, or restate in your own words, what others have said, especially when repeating the exact words would be too long for your speech. When you paraphrase testimony, cite the source, identifying who said it, his or her credentials, and when it was said.

As you use testimony, be sure that the quotation you select reflects the overall meaning and intent of its author. Never twist the meaning of testimony to make it fit your purposes—this unethical practice is called **quoting out of context**. Because political candidates try to put a positive spin on their image, political advertising is often rife with this abuse. For example, during a political campaign in Illinois, one state representative sent out a fundraising letter that claimed he'd been singled out for "special recognition" by *Chicago* magazine—and, indeed, he had. He had been cited as "one of the state's ten worst legislators."[15]

Write out quotations on note cards so that you can read them and get the exact wording as you present your speech. A transition, such as "According to . . . " or "In the words of . . . ," leads gracefully into such material. Finally, don't simply accept what experts say uncritically. Experts have been known to be wrong. In 1903, the president of the Michigan Savings Bank advised Henry Ford's lawyer not to

Speaker's Notes 8.2

Using Testimony

Keep these guidelines in mind as you plan the use of testimony in your speeches.

1. Select sources your audience will respect.

2. Quote or paraphrase material accurately.

3. Point out the qualifications of sources as you cite them.

4. Use expert testimony to validate information.

5. Use lay testimony to build identification and add authenticity.

6. Use prestige testimony to enhance the general credibility of your message.

---

direct quotation   Repeating the exact words of another to support a point.

paraphrase   Summarizing in your own words something said or written.

quoting out of context   An unethical use of a quotation that changes or distorts the original speaker's meaning or intent by not including parts of the quote.

invest in the Ford Motor Company, saying, "The horse is here to stay, but the automobile is only a novelty—a fad." In 1943, Thomas Watson, chair of IBM, reached the following brilliant conclusion: "I think there is a world market for maybe five computers." And in 1968, a respected business periodical suggested, "With over fifty foreign cars already on sale here, the Japanese auto industry isn't likely to carve out a big slice of the U.S. market for itself."

Examples

*E*xamples bring a speech to life. Just as pictures serve as graphic illustrations for a printed text, **examples** serve as verbal illustrations for an oral message. In fact, some scholars prefer the term *illustration* to *example*. This term derives from the Latin *illustrare*, which means "to shed light" or "to make bright." Good examples illuminate the message of your speech, making it clearer and more vivid for your audience. In addition to clarifying ideas, examples also attract attention and sustain interest. They demonstrate that what you have said either has happened or could happen. Examples may also be used to personalize your topic, especially when you draw them from your own experience. Speakers acknowledge the importance of examples when they say, "Let me give you an example." Examples about people give the audience someone with whom they can identify, thus involving them in the speech. Shared personal examples help the audience to *experience* your ideas, not simply to understand them.

Examples that point out common experiences, beliefs, or values also help to bridge gaps in cultural understanding. In her self-introductory speech defining herself in terms of the pictures that hang on her wall, Ashley Smith provided three major examples about youngsters from different cultures that helped increase intercultural understanding. She provided examples about the students her age with whom she had interacted as an exchange student in Costa Rica, on a mission trip to Botswana, and in her suburban high school in Florida. These examples increased identification between the speaker, her listeners, and the message of her speech. (The text of this speech can be read in Appendix B.)

Examples also provide emphasis. When you make a statement and follow it with an example, you are pointing out that what you have just said is *important*. Examples amplify your ideas. They say to the audience, "This bears repeating." Examples are especially helpful when you introduce new, complex, or abstract material. Not only can they make such information clearer, but they also allow time for the audience to process what you have said before you move on to your next point.

Types of Examples

Examples take different forms, and these forms have different functions. An example may be brief or extended and may be based either on an actual event or on something that might have happened.

Brief Examples. A **brief example** mentions a specific instance to demonstrate a more general statement. Brief examples are concise and to the point. Often, a series of brief examples are used to bring home a point. In a speech to the National Prayer Breakfast, the rock star and social activist Bono urged American leaders to tithe 1 percent of the federal budget to the poor. He provided a series of brief examples about what this 1 percent could do:

---

examples Verbal illustrations of the speaker's points.

brief example Using a concise instance or allusion to illustrate or develop a point.

One percent is not merely a number on a balance sheet. One percent is the girl in Africa who gets to go to school, thanks to you. One percent is the AIDS patient who gets her medicine, thanks to you. One percent is the African entrepreneur who can start a small family business, thanks to you. One percent is not redecorating presidential palaces or money flowing down a rat hole. This one percent is digging waterholes to provide clean water.[16]

Extended Examples.   An **extended example** contains more detail and allows you to dwell more fully on an illustration. Jane Goodall, the noted naturalist and U.N. Messenger of Peace, made good use of the technique to explain how she maintained her optimism following 9/11:

A lot of people have said to me, "But, Dr. Jane, surely after 9/11 that damaged your optimism for the future." I was in New York when the World Trade Towers were destroyed, and I felt with everyone in New York the shock, the numbness, the terrible grief, the mounting anger of the city as it struggled in the aftermath of 9/11. That one day, I think we saw the sort of ultimate in human evil, using innocent people to kill innocent people.

But we also saw this amazing heroism, the people who risked and lost their lives to rescue those trapped in the rubble. . . . And there was this outpouring of generosity; people gave whatever they had to give. . . . They opened their homes, they gave clothes, they gave blood, they gave what they could. And for a while people questioned their values: Were we spending too much time searching for more and more wealth and not enough time with our families? And even today . . . there are still people who tell me that they have much more contact with their families than they did before.[17]

Extended examples give us more details. They allow speakers to develop the message of their speeches as they develop the examples.

Factual Examples.   A **factual example** is based on an actual event or the experiences of a real person. Factual examples provide strong support for your ideas because they actually did happen: They authenticate the point you are trying to make. University of Memphis student Michele Brooks Gwinn used the following factual example in a speech on capital punishment:

Let me tell you about Earl Washington. Earl was easy pickings for the police when they could not solve a difficult rape and murder case. Agreeable and eager to please, with the mental age of a young child, Washington was quick to confess. It didn't seem to matter to the police or prosecutors that Earl did not have the basic facts straight. Earl said the victim was black—she was white. He said she was stabbed two or three times—she had been stabbed thirty-eight times. He said he kicked in a door—the door was found intact. The police were willing to overlook all of this to solve their case. Earl Washington was convicted and sentenced to death. He spent eighteen years behind bars before he was cleared through DNA evidence.

Hypothetical Examples.   Examples need not be real to be effective. A **hypothetical example** is a composite of actual people, situations, or events. Although created by the speaker, a hypothetical example claims to represent reality and therefore must be plausible. The following hypothetical example was used by a student speaker to illustrate the growing problem of childhood obesity:

---

extended example A detailed illustration that allows a speaker to build impressions.

factual example An illustration based on something that actually happened or that really exists.

hypothetical example A representation of reality, usually a synthesis of actual people, situations, or events.

Let me introduce you to Madison Cartwright. Madison is twelve years old. She's four feet eleven inches tall. She weighs 145 pounds. Her body mass index is over twenty-nine. This means that Madison is one of the more than nine million children and teenagers who can be classified as obese.

How does this affect her? Not only is she a prime candidate for health problems such as childhood diabetes, but she also has other problems. She loves softball but has difficulty playing because she gets short of breath. So she sits in the bleachers and watches her classmates. Madison is very smart, but she hates school. She is often the butt of "fat" jokes and teasing by her classmates. Instead of playing outside or socializing with friends after school, Madison goes home and watches TV by herself. Her self-esteem is very low.

Is Madison a real person? Well, yes and no. You may not find someone with her name at the middle school you attended, but you will find many Madisons in the seventh grade there. Childhood obesity in the United States has reached epidemic proportions.

You should use hypothetical examples when the factual examples you find don't adequately represent the truth of a situation or when a factual example might embarrass the person involved. Be careful that your hypothetical examples are representative of an issue. Don't distort the truth just to make your point. Always alert your listeners to the hypothetical nature of your example. You can do this as you begin presenting your example with introductory phrases such as "Imagine yourself . . . " or "Picture the following . . . " Or, as in the example above, you can let listeners know near the end.

Evaluating Examples

You should evaluate examples in terms of their relevance. If an example does not fit your specific purpose, leave it out. Be sure that your examples help clarify the point you want to illustrate. If they don't make your message more understandable or more memorable, don't use them. Your examples should accurately represent a situation as it exists. Avoid examples based on exceptions to the rule. Moreover, your examples should be believable. If they are too far-fetched, your listeners will sense this, and it could damage your credibility.

Figure 8.3

Checklist for Evaluating Examples

____ Is this example relevant to my topic and purpose?
____ Does this example fairly represent the reality of a situation?
____ Will this example make my ideas more understandable?
____ Will this example make my point more memorable?
____ Will my listeners find this example believable?
____ Is this example appropriate for this audience?
____ Is this example in good taste?
____ Is this example interesting?

Keep in mind that what works well with one audience may seem out of place with another. Ask yourself if this example will be a good match with the motives, attitudes, or values of your listeners. Examples should promote the mood of the occasion and must meet the tests of good taste and propriety. You should risk offending listeners only when they must be shocked into attention before they can be informed or persuaded. Last, but not least, be sure any example you use is interesting. Dull examples never help a speech.

Using Examples

Examples often make the difference between a speech that is just so-so and one that is outstanding. Be selective in your use of examples. Develop them to support your main points, gain attention, and clarify key ideas. Don't make your speech a running series of examples. This can confuse listeners as they wonder what point you are trying to make.

Keep examples brief and to the point, even when you are using extended examples. Cut out all unimportant details: One of the great lessons Ernest Hemingway learned as a developing writer was that the more selective he was in describing scenes, the more effective they were. When you keep examples brief and striking, listeners are stimulated to provide details on their own, and their imaginations are engaged more closely with your message. This doesn't mean that you should avoid concrete details. Name the people, times, places, and groups in your examples. Listeners will relate more to Luis Francesco with the United Postal Service than they will to some unnamed delivery person. Finally, use transitions to move smoothly from statement to example and from example to statement. Phrases such as "For instance . . . " or "As you can see . . . " work nicely.

Narratives

A narrative is a story that illustrates an idea. Narratives are effective in speeches because people enjoy listening to stories. Humans have been storytellers from the dawn of time. Most children are brought up on narratives—stories that entertain, fables that warn of dangers, and parables that teach virtues. Narratives involve listeners in creating meaning, so that the message becomes *their* discovery, *their* truth. Narratives help us recall the past and envision the future. They allow us to express emotions vicariously, and they set a mood for the speech. Narratives illustrate our ideals and transmit our cultural traditions. Thus, they help define who we are and what we are about.

narrative   A story used to illustrate some important truth.

Narratives also do important practical work in a speech. They serve many of the same functions as examples. Narratives can

- add interest to a message.

- attract and sustain attention.

- draw listeners into a message.

- provide models of good and poor behavior.

- bridge cultural differences that separate people.

- be remembered after facts and statistics have been forgotten.

People organize their experiences and memories in terms of the stories they tell. Moreover, when information seems odd (for example, a Harvard-educated plumber), people look for stories that will explain the phenomenon and satisfy their curiosity. The power of narratives, however, goes beyond simply explaining unusual phenomena. The author Norman Mailer has noted:

> We tell stories in order to make sense of life. Narrative is reassuring. There are days when life is so absurd, it's crippling—nothing makes sense, but stories bring order to the absurdity. Relief is provided by the narrative's beginning, middle, and end.[18]

Perhaps for all these reasons, Walter R. Fisher, who introduced the importance of narrative to communication studies, actually defines humans as storytelling animals *(homo narrans)*.[19]

Because they can be so effective at involving the audience, narratives are often used in the introductions of speeches. Heather Rouston Ettinger, an executive with Roulston & Company, told a story to illustrate the emerging status of women:

Maya Angelou often uses narrative to illustrate ideas in her speech.

> **Last summer, Buffalo Bills quarterback Doug Flutie was watching the final game of the Women's World Cup soccer match on TV with his 12-year-old soccer-playing daughter, Alexa. During the soccer match between the USA and China teams, the hugely successful advertisement for Gatorade featuring Michael Jordan and Mia Hamm came on. As most of you well know, Michael Jordan, formerly of NBA fame, is the most influential athlete of the last century. Mia Hamm was the star forward of the USA national team. You might remember the theme to this was "Anything you can do I can do better." As Doug Flutie tells the story, when the ad came on, Alexa asked, "Dad, who's the guy with Mia?"[20]**

Such an example we call an **embedded narrative**, because it is a part of the overall structure of a speech.

Speakers who want to maximize the involvement of the audience often use a **vicarious experience narrative**. Such a narrative invites listeners into the action so that they seem to participate in the story. A vicarious narrative often begins

embedded narrative Stories inserted within speeches that illustrate the speaker's point.

vicarious experience narrative Speech strategy in which the speaker invites listeners to imagine themselves enacting a story.

with a statement such as "Come along with me . . . " or "Picture yourself. . . . " Dan Rader used this type of a narrative in the introduction to his persuasive speech urging University of Memphis students to protest proposed cuts in higher education spending in Tennessee:

> Imagine that instead of being here in this nice facility, in a class of twenty students, you are sitting in a large lecture hall with 250 students around you. And instead of paying $2,100 per semester in tuition, imagine you are paying $2,500. So for the privilege of getting less personal attention, and a subsequently worse education, you get to pay about four hundred dollars more per semester. Sounds like a pretty raw deal, doesn't it? I tell you this story because it's a very real possibility. Today I'd like to tell you what Tennessee's government has proposed and why it's a bad idea.

Still another form of narrative, the **master narrative**, occurs when the entire speech is told in the form of a story. It does not support the speech—it is the speech. We say more about this form and narrative design in Chapter 17.

Embedded narratives can perform a variety of roles as supporting materials. In addition to introducing a speech, narratives can develop humor. Humorous narratives help put the audience at ease and promote identification through the laughter people share. Marvin Olasky, professor of journalism at the University of Texas, opened a speech about the role of the media in promoting victim assistance following Hurricane Katrina:

> I'll be noting today some ways that government officials failed during Katrina and at other times, so let me begin with a Texas story about how officials do offer help.

> It starts with a mom on a farm looking out the window. She sees the family cow munching on grass and her daughter talking to a strange man. The mom furiously yells out the window, "Didn't I tell you not to talk to strangers? You come in this house right now."

> The girl offers a protest, "But Mama, this man says he's a United States senator." The wise mother replies, "In that case, come in this house right now, and bring the cow with you!"[21]

Finally, concluding narratives leave the audience with something to remember and extend the impact of a message. They can establish a mood that will last long after the closing words have been spoken. In a speech presented to the Economic Club in Chicago, Newton Minow, former chair of the Federal Communications Commission, concluded his plea for campaign finance reform with the following:

> I leave you with a story President Kennedy told a week before he was killed. The story was about French Marshal Louis Lyautey, who walked one morning through his garden with his gardener. He stopped at a certain point and asked the gardener to plant a tree there the next morning. The gardener said, "But the tree will not bloom for one hundred years!" The Marshal looked at the gardener and replied, "In that case, you had better plant it this afternoon."[22]

Avoid stories that are funny at the expense of others. If you poke fun at anyone, let it be yourself. Speakers who tell amusing stories about themselves sometimes rise in the esteem of listeners. When this technique is effective, the stories that seem to put the speakers down are actually building them up. Note how former President

master narrative Form of speaking in which the entire speech becomes a story that reveals some important truth.

Jimmy Carter used this type of humor as he acknowledged his introduction as a commencement speaker at Rice University:

> For those who have been in politics and who are introduced, you never know what to expect. There was a time when I was introduced very simply, "Ladies and gentlemen, the President of the United States," period. But when I left office I was quite often invited by lowly Democrats who were in charge of a program at an event. Then when I got there with two or three TV cameras, the leaders of the organization—almost invariably Republicans—would take over the introduction of me, and quite often the introduction would be a very negative one derived primarily from President Reagan's campaign notes. I had to do something to heal my relationship with the audience before I could speak so I always would tell them after that, "Ladies and gentlemen, of all the introductions I've ever had in my life, that is the most recent."[23]

Evaluating Narratives

As with all other forms of supporting materials, narratives must be relevant to your message. Speakers sometimes "borrow" a story from an anthology and then strain to connect it with their topic. This is not good. Narratives should never be used simply to amuse listeners—they should also help you make your point.

Narratives should illustrate a situation as it actually exists. They should help listeners better understand your message and create identification among the speaker, topic, and audience. Narratives must also meet the test of propriety. Audiences can be turned off by stories that foster negative stereotypes or that contain offensive language. Ask yourself if the narrative is fresh and original. If listeners have already heard your story, they may decide you have nothing new to say in the rest of your speech.

Finally, you should evaluate narratives in terms of what Professor Fisher calls their "narrative coherence" and "narrative fidelity." **Narrative coherence** means that the story fits together well. Events must seem to flow within the proper order from beginning to end, and the characters must seem to fit the actions they perform. **Narrative fidelity** means that the story resonates with what you already know about the world. It rings true and makes sense.[24]

Using Narratives

You may think that storytelling is an easy skill to acquire, but that is not always true. We recently had a student who "teased" his listeners with vague promises of stories that never materialized in his speech. He would say, "That was really funny," and then ramble on without telling us the story. At best, he would simply paraphrase the story or present a punch line without any preparation. Listening to him was frustrating.

It takes time to tell a story. Beyond having a beginning, middle, and end, a story must have a scene, characters, and plot. Remember how the fairy tales of your youth started—"Once upon a

InterConnections.
LearnMore 8.3

Storytelling

International Storytelling Center
www.storytellingfoundation.com
Organization dedicated to enriching the human experience through the power of storytelling; sponsors the annual National Storytelling Festival in Jonesborough, Tennessee. Provides links to information on activities and articles on storytelling.

Storytelling Resources
www.timsheppard.co.uk/story/index.html
A comprehensive collection of links for storytellers with a focus on skill development. Also contains links to full texts of stories. Compiled and maintained by Tim Sheppard, founder of Wordweavers, an innovative storytelling group in England.

Effective Storytelling
www.eldrbarry.net/roos/eest.htm
A short, well-written, engaging manual on the art of storytelling. Developed by Barry McWilliams, pastor, stimulating speaker, and gifted storyteller.

---

narrative coherence   Whether a narrative or story flows well and fits together smoothly.

narrative fidelity   Whether a narrative seems true and makes sense.

Figure 8.4

Evaluating Narratives

____ Is the narrative relevant to my topic and purpose?
____ Does the narrative fairly represent the situation?
____ Will the story help listeners make sense of things?
____ Will the narrative draw listeners into the action?
____ Is the narrative appropriate for this audience?
____ Will the story provide appropriate role models?
____ Will the story enhance identification among listeners, topic, and speaker?
____ Will the narrative make my speech more memorable?
____ Does the story set an appropriate mood for my message?
____ Is the narrative fresh and interesting?
____ Does the story flow well?
____ Is the narrative believable?
____ Is the narrative in good taste?

time . . . "—and built up from there. Similarly, narratives in a speech must build up to a climax or punch line. The characters in your narratives must come alive. You must let listeners see things by using colorful language rich in imagery.

As you tell a story, let yourself get caught up in it. Enjoy yourself! If telling the story is fun for you, your listeners will probably enjoy it too. Set the narrative off from the rest of your speech by pausing before you begin and after you end the story. Pauses help an audience reflect on what they have heard. Use voice and dialect changes to signal that a "character" is speaking.

Since storytelling is an intimate form of communication, reduce the distance between yourself and your listeners and move closer to your audience. You can also be less formal than in the rest of your speech. If your story evokes laughter, wait for it to die down before going on. Practice telling your story so that you get the wording and timing just right. Polish and memorize the punch line: The story exists for it. It is the gem at the center, the capstone at the top.

Use dialogue in a narrative rather than paraphrasing what someone says. Paraphrasing can save time, but it robs a story of power. Let people speak for themselves! The late senator Sam Ervin of North Carolina was a master storyteller. Note how he used dialogue in the following narrative, which opened a speech on the Constitution and our judicial system:

> Jim's administrator was suing the railroad for his wrongful death. The first witness he called to the stand testified as follows: "I saw Jim walking up the track. A fast train passed, going up the track. After it passed, I didn't see Jim. I walked up the track a little way and discovered Jim's severed head lying on one side of the track, and the rest of his body on the other." The witness was asked how he reacted to his gruesome discovery. He responded: "I said to myself, 'Something serious must have happened to Jim. '"
>
> Something serious has been happening to constitutional government in America. I want to talk to you about it.[25]

Had "Mr. Sam" paraphrased the punch line by saying, "The witness reported that he knew instantly that the victim had had a serious accident," he would have destroyed its effect. Dialogue makes a narrative come alive by bringing listeners close to the action. Paraphrase distances the audience.

A well-told narrative can add much to a speech, but too many stories can turn a speech into a rambling string of tales without a clear focus. Save narratives for special occasions. Use them to arouse or sustain attention, to create a special mood for your message, or to demonstrate some important truth.

Three Techniques for Using Supporting Materials

*T*he effectiveness of supporting materials for speeches depends on the skill of speechmakers. Much of the art of using supporting materials rests on the skillful application of three techniques: comparison, contrast, and analogy.

Comparison

A **comparison** helps an audience understand a subject by pointing out its similarities to something else. These similarities provide a context in which the subject can be understood. A comparison can make an unfamiliar or controversial idea seem clearer or more acceptable by connecting it with something the audience already understands or agrees with. Comparisons can also help the audience see the significance of supporting materials. Consider how Maurice Johnson used comparison in a classroom speech to point up the meaning of a statistic:

> Let's suppose that you have a job offer in Oklahoma City that pays $45,000 per year. You're not really sure you want to live in Oklahoma City, and you know salaries are higher in other cities. But how do these salaries really compare? Will that higher salary in Chicago, or Boston, or Los Angeles actually be higher than what you could earn in Oklahoma City? About.com's Web site has a "Career Comparator" that lets you see how the salaries stack up. For example, in 2007, to equal the purchasing power of the Oklahoma City $45,000 salary, you'd have to make $56,000 in Chicago; in Boston, you'd have to make $66,000; and, in Los Angeles you'd have to make a whopping $79,000.

comparison   Using supporting material to point out the similarities of an unfamiliar or controversial issue to something the audience already knows or accepts.

Figure 8.5

Uses of Supporting Material in Speeches

Type	Uses
Facts	To substantiate ideas with information, to ground ideas in reality
Statistics	To illustrate size, to make predictions, to demonstrate trends, to show relationships
Definitions	To clarify unfamiliar or technical terms, to reflect your way of seeing something
Explanations	To clarify an idea or process, to explain how something works
Descriptions	To present word pictures, to evoke vivid images
Expert Testimony	To further substantiate ideas, to verify information, to support a controversial position
Lay Testimony	To humanize a topic, to present how people feel about something
Prestige Testimony	To eloquently express support for your ideas, to provide distinction for your speech
Examples	To arouse and sustain attention, to clarify concepts, to emphasize what is important, to aid understanding, to make a speech interesting
Narratives	To involve listeners with your topic, to enhance identification among topic, speaker, and listener, to make a speech interesting, to clarify abstract ideas
Comparisons	To point out similarities between ideas, to make unfamiliar ideas clearer
Contrasts	To point out differences between things, to make your points stand out
Analogy	To point out similarities between things that are essentially dissimilar, to establish a frame of thinking

Here the comparisons make the meaning of the hypothetical salary offer stand out in bold relief. Before you decide to use a comparison, ask yourself these questions:

- Are there enough similarities to justify the comparison?
- Are the similarities significant to the idea you wish to support?
- Are there important differences that might invalidate the comparison?

Contrast

A **contrast** emphasizes the differences between or among things. Just as a red cross stands out more vividly against a white background than against an orange one, contrasts make facts and statistics, examples, testimony, and narratives stand out. In

contrast   Arranging supporting materials to highlight differences or gaining attention by using abrupt changes in presentation, dwelling upon opposites, or framing the pros and cons of a situation.

his speech comparing the differences between government responses to disasters and the responses of church groups and private companies, Marvin Olasky presented a striking comparison coupled with expert testimony:

> Sheriff Harry Lee talked about conditions in his Jefferson Parish, just outside of New Orleans, "FEMA executives were there, but they didn't do anything. They weren't up and running for four or five days. If the federal government would have responded as quickly as Wal-Mart, we could have saved more lives." Lee said FEMA made things worse rather than better. When Wal-Mart sent three trailer trucks with water to a FEMA compound, FEMA officials said they needed written authorization to accept such supplies and didn't have any. Wal-Mart ended up distributing the water directly.[26]

Here are some questions to ask as you consider whether to use a contrast:

- Is the contrast dramatic enough to help my case?
- Is the contrast relevant to the point I wish to make?
- Are there other points of contrast that might invalidate the point?

Analogy

An **analogy** combines the principles of both comparison and contrast by pointing out similarities between things or concepts that are essentially dissimilar. Analogies come in two forms. The first, **literal analogy**, is much the same as comparison in that it ties together subjects from the same realm of experience, such as football and soccer, to reinforce a point. The second form, **figurative analogy**, combines subjects from different realms of experience. Our opening to this chapter uses a figurative analogy between building railroad trestles and building speeches.

Successful analogies make ideas that are remote or abstract seem more immediate and comprehensible. They are especially useful near the beginnings of speeches, where they establish a frame of thinking in which the speech can develop. They make possible the sharing of personal feeling. An analogy can also present a persuasive challenge, as in this excerpt from a speech by former vice president and environmental activist Al Gore:

> I do not believe that the climate crisis should be a partisan political issue. I just returned from the United Kingdom, where last week the two major parties put forward their climate change platforms. The Tory and Labour parties are in vigorous competition with one another—competing to put forward the best solution to the climate crisis. I look forward to the day when we return to this way of thinking here in the U.S.[27]

As you consider using an analogy, ask yourself the following:

- Will the analogy help listeners better understand my ideas?
- Might the analogy distract my listeners?
- Does the analogy establish a beneficial association for my subject?

---

analogy   A connection established between two otherwise dissimilar ideas or things.

literal analogy   A comparison made between subjects within the same field.

figurative analogy   A comparison made between things that belong to different fields.

Ethics *Alert! 8.1*

The Ethical Use of Supporting Material

To be certain that you are using supporting materials in ethical ways, follow these guidelines.

1. Provide the date, source, and context of information cited in your speech.

2. Don't present a claim or opinion as though it were a fact.

3. Remember that statistics are open to differing interpretations.

4. Protect your listeners from biased information.

5. Don't "quote out of context" to misrepresent a person's position.

6. Be sure examples reflect reality.

7. Don't present hypothetical examples as though they were factual.

Deciding What Support Material You Should Use

*E*very main point in your speech should be supported with a variety of materials. Select your supporting materials to meet the challenges of your speaking situation.

1. If your ideas are *controversial*, rely primarily on facts, statistics, factual examples, or expert testimony from sources the audience will respect and accept.

2. If your ideas or concepts are *abstract*, bring them to life with examples and narratives.

3. If a point is highly *technical*, supplement facts and statistics with expert testimony.

4. If you need to *excite emotions*, use lay or prestige testimony, examples, or narratives.

5. If you need to *defuse emotions*, emphasize facts, statistics, and expert testimony.

6. If your topic is *distant* from the lives of listeners, use examples and narratives.

7. If your ideas are *novel*, use comparisons, contrasts, or analogies to help your listeners better understand them.

Although the need for particular types of supporting material may vary with different topics and audiences, *you should always support each main point with the most important and relevant facts and statistics available.* For additional clarity, use testimony, definitions, explanations, and descriptions. *Also support each main point with at least one interesting example or narrative.*

Above all else, as you decide which supporting materials to use, place your audience at the center of your thinking and ask yourself these critical questions:

■ Which of these materials will make the biggest impression on my listeners?

■ Which of these materials will listeners be most likely to remember?

■ Which of these materials will listeners find most credible?

■ Which materials will be most likely to make listeners want to act?

A design format for integrating supporting materials into your speech is provided in Chapter 9.

In Summary

Facts and statistics, testimony, examples, and narratives are the major forms of supporting materials. They provide the substance, strength, credibility, and appeal a speech must have before listeners will place their faith in it.

Facts and Statistics.   Information in the form of facts and statistics is the most objective type of supporting material and is especially useful for unfamiliar or controversial topics. Facts are verifiable by independent observers. Statistics are numerical facts that describe the size of something, make predictions, illustrate trends, or show relationships. Use definitions, explanations, and descriptions to augment facts and statistics. A definition states the meaning of a term in words the audience can understand. An explanation expands on what something is or how it works. A descriptions is a word picture that helps the audience visualize what you are talking about.

Testimony.   Testimony cites the ideas or words of others. When you repeat the exact words of others, you use a direct quotation. When you summarize what others say, you paraphrase them. Expert testimony comes from recognized authorities. Lay testimony represents "the voice of the people." Prestige testimony connects your message with the words of some esteemed figure. Be sure that the sources you cite are free from bias. Present their credentials as you introduce their testimony, and never quote them out of context.

Examples.   Examples serve as verbal illustrations. They add interest, clarify ideas, hold attention, personalize a topic, provide emphasis, show how ideas can be applied, and aid retention of a message. Brief examples mention specific instances. Extended examples contain more detail. Factual examples are based on actual events and persons. Hypothetical examples are invented by the speaker to represent reality.

Narratives.   A narrative tells a story that draws listeners into the action and helps establish a mood for the speech. Narratives should be told in colorful, concrete language using dialogue instead of paraphrasing. A lively and informal style of presentation can enhance narration.

Three Techniques for Using Supporting Materials.   Comparison, contrast, and analogy can be used to make the most of supporting materials. Comparison points out the similarities of something unfamiliar to something the audience already understands. Contrast emphasizes the differences among things to support an important point. Analogy combines the principles of comparison and contrast to heighten awareness.

Explore and Apply the Ideas in This Chapter

1. Find the text of a recent speech in *Vital Speeches of the Day* that contains statistical information. Were the statistics convincing? Were examples used to make the numbers more meaningful? Was the source of the statistics clearly identified? How did the use of statistics affect your perception of the credibility of the speech?

2. Look in newspapers or magazines for statements by public officials that claim to be factual but that may actually contain distortions. What tips you off to the distortion? In your judgment, would most readers be likely to detect this bias?

3. Think back to your childhood and remember your favorite story. Prepare a brief (less than three minutes) presentation of this story. Practice presenting it as if you were telling it to a group of first-graders. Working in small groups, share your story with other group members. Listen to theirs.

What storytelling techniques seemed most effective? What made some of the stories less effective?

4. Develop a hypothetical example or narrative to illustrate one of the following abstract concepts: love, compassion, charity, peace, justice.

5. Determine which types of supporting material might best support the following claims:

   a. Native Americans don't get a square deal in the United States.

   b. Campus security measures are inadequate.

   c. America should lift (or not lift) the embargo on Cuba.

   d. Asian American children are outperforming Anglo-American children in our public schools.

Explain and defend your choices.

Structuring Your Speech

This chapter will help you

- develop a simple, balanced, and orderly speech design
- select and arrange your main points
- plan transitions to make your speech flow smoothly
- prepare effective introductions and conclusions for your speeches

Every discourse ought to be a living creature; having a body of its own and head and feet; there should be a middle, beginning, and end, adapted to one another and to the whole.

—Plato

Suppose you must take a course in physics next semester, and you get the following evaluations from RateMyProfessors.com of the two instructors scheduled to teach the course:

JOHNSON, DENNIS: Professor Johnson is really cool. He tells a lot of funny stories and his lectures are always entertaining. But he doesn't explain difficult material in any systematic fashion, so it's hard to take notes. When it's time for departmental examinations, you often don't know how or what to study.

MARTINEZ, MARIA: Professor Martinez is very businesslike when explaining her expectations for class assignments. She starts each lecture by reviewing the material covered in the last session and asks if anyone has questions. Her lectures are easy to follow. She points out what is most important for students to know and uses clear examples that make difficult ideas easier to understand and apply.

Which instructor would you choose? If you care about your education, chances are you'd choose Professor Martinez. Everyone likes to be entertained, but most people prefer well-organized speakers when the message is important. Indeed, studies suggest that students learn more from instructors who are well focused and businesslike, and they generally dislike instructors who persistently go off on tangents, jump from one idea to another, ramble, or are generally disorganized.[1]

This preference highlights the importance of structure and organization for effective public speaking. Presenting well-organized speeches helps listeners to follow, understand, and remember your message. Being well organized also enhances audience perceptions of your credibility and helps you cope with communication apprehension. The better prepared you are, the less anxious you will feel.

In this chapter, we discuss some principles and offer advice to help you structure speeches that will be readily understood, compelling, and easily remembered. We begin with the basic principles underlying "good form." Then we offer some practical advice concerning how to develop the body of your speech, how to add transitions to make your speech flow smoothly, and how to prepare effective introductions and conclusions.

Principles of Good Form

The principles of good form for effective speech organization reflect the way that people, either by nature or custom, tend to arrange and make sense of ideas and information. To develop good form, you should keep your presentations simple, balance the parts of your speeches, and arrange your main points so that they develop in a meaningful pattern. In short, good form depends on simplicity, balance, and order.

Simplicity

A simple design makes it easy for listeners to follow, understand, and remember your message.[2] To achieve **simplicity** in your speeches, you should limit the number of your main ideas, repeat them for emphasis, and keep your wording direct and to the point.

Number of Main Points. The fewer main points in a speech, the better, because each main point must be developed with supporting material. It takes time to present information, examples, narratives, and testimony effectively. Short speeches like those you will present in class should rarely have more than three main points. Consider what happens when a speech becomes overburdened with main points:

Thesis statement:	Our approach to welfare does not work.
Main points:	I. There are too many programs.
	II. The programs often duplicate coverage.
	III. Some people who need help are left out.
	IV. The programs are poorly funded.
	V. The programs waste money.
	VI. Recipients have no input into what is needed.
	VII. The programs create dependence.
	VIII. The programs stifle initiative.
	IX. The programs rob the poor of self-respect.

Each of these points may be important, but presented this way, they could be confusing. It would be hard for listeners to remember them because they are not organized in a meaningful way. Let's see how these ideas might be clustered into a simpler structural pattern:

Thesis statement:	Our approach to welfare does not work.
Main point:	I. Our approach does not work because it is inadequate.
Subpoints:	A. We don't fund it sufficiently.
	B. Some people who need help get left out.
Main point:	II. Our approach does not work because it is inefficient.
Subpoints:	A. There are too many programs.
	B. There is too much duplication.
	C. There is too much waste of money.
Main point:	III. Our approach does not work because it is insensitive.
Subpoints:	A. It creates dependence.
	B. It stifles initiative.
	C. It robs people of self-respect.

This simple structure makes the speech easier to follow. The thesis statement offers an overview of the message. Each main point elaborates and develops the thesis statement. The subpoints organize and focus the secondary ideas so that they support the major ideas. Overlapping ideas have been combined, and unnecessary ideas have been omitted. The new structure answers the questions raised in the minds of

simplicity Suggests that a speech has a limited number of main points and that they are short and direct.

A well-organized speech is easy to follow.

thoughtful listeners in response to the thesis statement: *Why isn't our approach to welfare working?* The overall result is a design that satisfies such listeners and helps them remember what they have heard.

Repeating Key Points for Emphasis.   Repeating key ideas and information is a time-honored strategy of simplifying the structure of a speech. Consider the revised example. The central message that "our approach to welfare does not work" is reinforced by repeating that point while discussing each of the system's shortcomings. Strategic repetition is such a powerful tool for simplifying speeches that it has been built into the standard speaking format in which speakers preview their messages in the introduction, develop them in the body of the speech, and then review them in the conclusion. Strategic repetition is summed up in the following adage:

- Tell them what you're going to tell them.

- Tell them.

- Tell them what you told them.

Phrasing Main Points.   You should state your main points as simply as possible for easy understanding and retention. The ability to state your major ideas and present information in simple, direct statements is crucial to developing your communication skills. Again, consider our revised example. Not only has the wording been simplified, but the use of the same word pattern to introduce each main point makes for a message that is easy to understand. The repeated phrase "Our approach does not work because it is" suggests that these are the main points and makes them easy to remember. It further helps the differences to stand out as the speaker refers to the "Three I's" of welfare (inadequacy, inefficiency, and insensitivity). We further discuss the use of the parallel construction of main points in Chapter 10.

Balance

Balance means that the major parts of your speech—the introduction, the body, and the conclusion—receive appropriate development. Instructors generally specify time limits for speeches, so keep these in mind as you plan your message. It can be very upsetting to finish the first main point of your speech and find that you have only one minute left and two more main points plus your conclusion to present. Time yourself as you practice your speech to be sure it fits within the time limits. The following suggestions will help you plan a balanced presentation:

1. *The body should be the longest part of your speech.* It contains your major ideas. If you spend three minutes on your introduction, a minute and a half on the body, and thirty seconds on the conclusion, your speech will be out of balance.

2. *Balance the development of each main point.* If your main points seem equally important, you should give each point *equal emphasis.* This strategy might be appropriate for the speech on the Three I's of welfare policy, in which each point merits equal attention. If your main points differ in importance, you might start

balance   Suggests that the introduction, body, and conclusion receive their proper share of the time allotted for the speech.

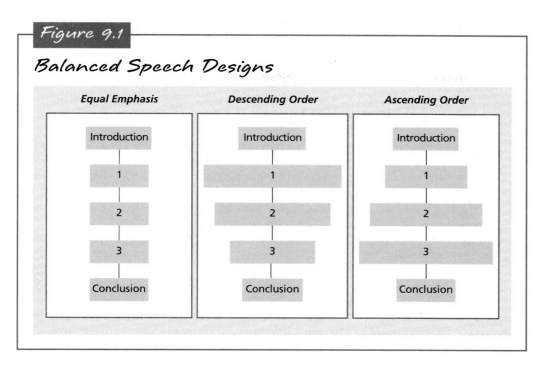

Figure 9.1

Balanced Speech Designs

Equal Emphasis	Descending Order	Ascending Order

with the most important point, spending the most time on it, and then present the other points with a *descending* emphasis, according to their importance. For example, in a speech that follows the problem–solution design, you may need to convince listeners first that there actually is a problem. Thus, you should devote most of your time to establishing this first point. Alternatively, you might wish to develop your main points with an *ascending* emphasis. If listeners agree there is a problem but don't know what to do about it, then you should devote most of your time to your solution, the second main point. Figure 9.1 illustrates these variations of emphasis.

3. *The introduction and conclusion should be approximately equal in length.* Your introduction may be slightly longer than your conclusion, but the total amount of time spent on your introduction and conclusion should be less than the amount spent on the body of your speech. As a general rule, in a five-minute presentation, the combined length of the introduction and conclusion should last about a minute. This leaves four minutes to develop the main points of the message.

Order

Order in a speech requires a consistent pattern of development from beginning to end. A well-ordered speech starts by introducing its subject and purpose, continues by developing the main ideas in the body of the speech, and ends by summarizing and reflecting on the meaning of what has been said. To build an orderly speech, you should follow the advice implied by Plato in our chapter-opening epigram: Design the body of the speech first, because that is where you will do the work of presenting, illustrating, and proving your message. Once you have structured the body of your speech, you can prepare an introduction and a conclusion that are custom-tailored for your message.

order   A consistent pattern used to develop a speech.

Structuring the Body of Your Speech

 he body of your speech should highlight your main points and develop them effectively. The process of structuring the body of your speech includes selecting, arranging, and supporting your main points.

Selecting Your Main Points

The **main points** are the most important ideas of your message, the points that fulfill your specific purpose. As you research your topic, you should discover some repeated themes. These are the most important issues connected with your topic. Consider how they relate to your specific purpose, your thesis statement, and the needs and interests of your listeners. Your main points will come from these repeated themes and your analysis of their relevance.

Let's look at how you might select the main points for a speech on global warming. Begin by preparing a **research overview**, listing your main sources of information and a summary of the major ideas from each. Figure 9.2 presents a sample research overview based on four sources of information: a *Time* magazine special issue, summary reports from the Intergovernmental Panel on Climate Change, an article from *U.S. News & World Report*, and research reports from the Environment News Service. Scanning the overview, you might come up with the following repeated themes:

- Increased temperatures are evidence of global warming.

- Human activities cause global warming.

- Global warming will cause climate changes.

- Global warming will cause health, environmental, and economic problems.

Once you have identified the main themes from the research, you should determine how they relate to your specific purpose and your audience. In this example, let us assume that your specific purpose is "to inform my audience about the problem of global warming." You anticipate that the audience's knowledge of the subject may be limited and possibly even confused. Therefore, you decide that your first major challenge is to define global warming in terms these listeners can understand,

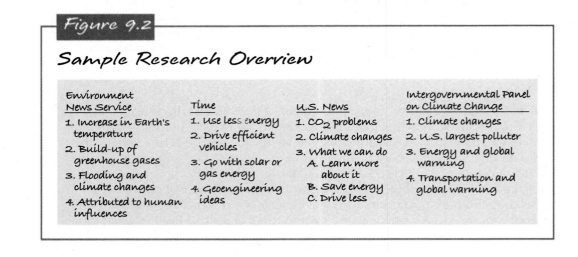

Figure 9.2

Sample Research Overview

Environment News Service	Time	U.S. News	Intergovernmental Panel on Climate Change
1. Increase in Earth's temperature	1. Use less energy	1. CO_2 problems	1. Climate changes
2. Build-up of greenhouse gases	2. Drive efficient vehicles	2. Climate changes	2. U.S. largest polluter
3. Flooding and climate changes	3. Go with solar or gas energy	3. What we can do A. Learn more about it B. Save energy C. Drive less	3. Energy and global warming
4. Attributed to human influences	4. Geoengineering ideas		4. Transportation and global warming

main points   The most prominent ideas of the speaker's message.

research overview   A listing of the main sources of information that could be used in a speech and of the major ideas from each source.

using simple language, everyday comparisons, and clear explanations. After that, you want to increase your audience's understanding of the causes and potential effects of global warming. In light of the repeated themes you identified in your research overview, you might come up with the following main points:

1. Global warming is a gradual warming of the earth's surface.

2. Humans are contributing to global warming through industrial emissions, environmental destruction, and personal energy use.

3. Global warming may cause severe climate changes and health problems.

Arranging Your Main Points

Once you have decided on your main points, you should arrange them using a design that is appropriate for your audience, fits your material, and serves your specific purpose. As noted earlier in this chapter, people organize ideas and information into patterns that are easy to comprehend and remember. These patterns serve as templates through which we perceive and experience the world. They set up expectations for processing incoming information. The way you arrange material in your speeches should be in harmony with these expectations. The major designs for organizing brief presentations are categorical, comparative, spatial, sequential, chronological, causation, problem–solution, refutative, and narrative.

Categorical.   A categorical design arranges the main ideas of a speech in terms of natural or customary divisions. For instance, speakers addressing the "three causes of global warming" or "three strategies to avoid paying excessive taxes" would probably arrange their main ideas in a categorical design. Categories are useful for arranging large amounts of information, and they reflect our basic tendency to group bits of information on the basis of their perceived similarity.

Comparative.   A comparative design begins with determining the similarities or differences between things, events, and ideas. For instance, an informative speaker might compare the San Andreas and New Madrid fault zones in terms of the frequency and severity of major earthquakes. Similarly, persuasive speakers might compare the Republican Party and Democratic Party positions on important issues. Speakers often try to explain the meaning of current events by comparing them with similar events in the past. For example, opponents of our military involvement in Iraq often invoke comparisons to the conflict in Vietnam. Comparative speeches are especially useful for topics that are new or difficult for audience members to understand.

Spatial.   A spatial design arranges the main points as they occur in physical space, often taking listeners on an orderly, imaginary tour. For example, if you were asked to give a group of incoming freshmen a tour of your school library, you might use a floor plan as a presentation aid as you lead them through a guided tour of the different departments of the library where they can access reference materials, periodicals, local applications, and so on. An effective spatial design provides your audience with a verbal map.

Sequential.   A sequential design explains the steps of a process in the order in which they should be taken. Most how-to speeches use a sequential design scheme. For instance, if you were to give a speech on how to calibrate a piece of high-tech equipment, or how to make origami cranes, you would probably use a sequential

Speeches that use sequential design follow a step-by-step pattern of development.

design. Sequential designs are most effective when speakers offer a stepwise procedure that makes it easy for audience members to follow.

Chronological.   A chronological design explains events or historic developments in the order in which they occurred. Chronological designs often survey the pattern of events that led up to a present-day situation. For example, speakers favoring the privatization of social security sometimes trace the financial history of the program to suggest that it simply will not be there for future generations. Chronological presentations are effective when speakers keep their presentation of events simple, in the order in which they occurred, and related to the message of the speech. Never present a history lesson for its own sake. Use history to illuminate your specific purpose.

Causation.   A causation design addresses the causes and/or consequences of a given situation or event. This design proceeds logically from cause to effect or from effect to cause. Causation designs are often used for forecasting future events. For instance, you might give a speech explaining the causes of a budget shortfall on your campus and close by predicting larger class sizes, cuts in student services, and tuition increases. By providing explanations for current events and developments, causation designs satisfy our need for understanding a predictable, if not always controllable, world.

Problem–Solution.   The problem–solution design focuses attention on a problem and then provides the audience with potential solutions for resolving it. A popular extension of the problem–solution design, the motivated sequence design follows five steps: (1) calling attention to a situation, (2) demonstrating a need to change it, (3) explaining how that need might be satisfied, (4) visualizing the results of following or not following the speaker's advice, and (5) issuing a call for action. Problem–solution speeches are most effective when they convince audience members that a given problem exists, that the proposed solutions will make a difference, and that these solutions are practical. Effective problem–solution speeches empower listeners by offering ways to change problematic situations.

Refutative.   The refutative design is used to speak for or against an issue by repudiating opposing arguments and positions. For example, if you were to give a speech favoring affirmative action on your campus, or opposing a specific type of immigration reform, you might well use a refutative design. This design would include stating opposing views and identifying weaknesses in the reasoning and evidence of opponents. If you suspect that listeners are sympathetic to opposing views, you should concentrate on developing powerful evidence and reasoning that support your position.

Narrative.   In contrast to speech designs that follow a linear, logical pattern of development, a narrative design follows a dramatic pattern that proceeds from prologue to plot to epilogue. The **prologue** introduces the story by setting the scene for action. It foreshadows the meaning of the story and introduces the main characters. The **plot** is the body of the narrative. In it, the action of the story unfolds through a

---

prologue   An opening that establishes the context and setting of a narrative, foreshadows the meaning, and introduces major characters.

plot   The body of a speech that follows narrative design; unfolds in sequence of scenes designed to build suspense.

Figure 9.3

Speech Designs

Categorical	Arranges points in terms of their natural or customary divisions. Useful for organizing large amounts of material. (Chapter 14)
Comparative	Juxtaposes two different ideas so that their similarities and differences are obvious. Useful when a topic is new to listeners or difficult to understand. (Chapter 14)
Spatial	Arranges points as they occur in physical space taking listeners on an orderly tour. (Chapter 14)
Sequential	Arranges points in their order of occurrence. Useful for explaining the steps in a process. (Chapter 14)
Chronological	Arranges points in terms of their development in time. Useful for providing a historical perspective. (Chapter 14)
Causation	Presents the causes and/or effects of a problem. Useful when you want to account for a present situation or forecast future events. (Chapter 14)
Problem-Solution	Discusses a problem and then offers a solution. Useful when your topic involves a situation that needs to be corrected. (Chapter 16)
Refutative	Persuades listeners by repudiating arguments against your position. Useful when you must discredit the opposition. (Chapter 16)
Narrative	Follows the form of a story with a prologue, plot and epilogue. Useful as an indirect form of providing information or persuading listeners. (Chapter 17)

scene or series of scenes that build to a climax. The **epilogue** reflects on the meaning of the story by drawing a lesson from it that audience members can apply to some situation.

While commonly used in introductory and ceremonial speeches, a narrative design can also be incorporated into informative and persuasive presentations to help illustrate and add human interest to the speech.

Whatever design you choose should fit your purpose for speaking, accommodate the main ideas that emerge from your research, and be appropriate for the needs of your audience. For an overview of your design options, see Figure 9.3. More detailed explanations and examples of speech designs are provided as appropriate for informative, persuasive, and ceremonial speaking in Chapter 14, 16, and 17.

Supporting Your Main Points

Once you have selected and arranged your main points, you should work on subpoints and supporting material. Your subpoints should develop the ideas and information necessary for listeners to accept your main points. For example, assume

epilogue   The final part of a narrative that reflects upon its meaning.

you are presenting a speech on the topic "New Developments in the War on Cancer." As you design your speech, you come up with the following main point: "Scientists have transformed medical approaches to researching and treating cancer." To develop this main point, you realize that you must establish two subpoints: "Scientists have largely abandoned the search for a *final cure*" and "Scientists have made tremendous advances in *controlling and living with* cancer."

You strengthen both main points and subpoints by providing supporting materials. As Chapter 8 demonstrated, *facts, figures*, and *expert testimony* help support ideas that are disputed, complicated, or new to your audience. *Examples* and *narratives* engage listeners by showing how these ideas apply in specific situations. As powerful as these forms of information may be in isolation, they are more effective when used in combination. An *ideal model of support* includes the most relevant facts and statistics, the most authoritative testimony, and at least one story or example that clarifies your idea and brings it to life. Figure 9.4 provides an outline format for supporting a point.

Consider, for example, how we might support the second subpoint, "Scientists have made tremendous advances in controlling and living with cancer." We would

---

Figure 9.4

Format for Supporting a Point

Statement:_____

_____

Transition into facts or statistics: _____

    1. Factual information or statistics that support statement: _____

_____

_____

Transition into testimony: _____

    2. Testimony that supports statement:_____

_____

_____

Transition into example or narrative: _____

    3. Example or narrative that supports statement:_____

_____

_____

_____

Transition into restatement: _____
Restatement of original assertion: _____

_____

Speaker's Notes **9.1**

Determining, Arranging, and Supporting Your Main Points

Follow these steps to determine, organize, and develop your main points.

1. Prepare a research overview to identify repeated ideas.

2. Create main points that fit your purpose and the needs of your audience.

3. Limit your main points to three or fewer for a short speech.

4. Arrange your main ideas using a coherent design.

5. Develop your main ideas with subpoints and supporting material.

want to present factual information concerning latest treatments, drugs, and improved rates of detecting and controlling various forms of cancer that were until recently considered a death sentence. Expert opinions about latest developments in the war on cancer and promising future directions would also help. But our speech would be much more effective and moving if illustrated with the real-life examples and success stories of figures such as Pennsylvania Senator Arlen Specter or seven-time Tour de France winner Lance Armstrong.

Also note how our example illustrates two of the powerful techniques for presenting information that are discussed in Chapter 8. The first is *contrast*, drawn here between past and present research programs, between the dream of a cure and the reality of increasing control over the disease. These contrasts should interest listeners and help them to see your point clearly.

The second technique is *analogy*, especially the figurative analogy between scientific research and war (often seen in such forms as "new weapons," "war on cancer," the researcher as heroic "warrior," etc.). This technique heightens the drama of related narratives and can aid understanding, especially when subjects are complex and abstract. Note how Dr. Leonard Saltz, a colon cancer specialist at Memorial Sloan-Kettering, used another figurative analogy to illustrate the significance of the contrast in research approaches: "I don't think we're going to hit home runs, but if we can get a series of line-drive singles going and put enough singles back to back, we can score runs."[3]

Using Transitions

O nce you have determined, arranged, and supported the main points of your speech, you must develop transitions for moving smoothly from point to point. By **transitions**, we mean verbal and nonverbal cues that let your audience know you are finished making one point and are moving on to the next. Effectively planned transitions connect your main points and tie the body of your speech to its introduction and its conclusion. They serve as signposts that help your audience see and follow the overall structure and direction of your speeches.

Some transitions are quite subtle. A brief pause coupled with a change in vocal inflection can cue your audience that you are moving on to the next point or part of your speech. Short, simple phrases such as "For my next point . . ." and "Having said that, I'd like you to consider this . . ." can help your audience see the connection between your ideas. Phrases such as *until now* and *just last week* point out

transitions Connecting elements used in speeches.

Figure 9.5

Common Transitions

To Indicate	Use
Time Changes	until, now, since, previously, later, earlier, in the past, in the future, meanwhile, five years ago, just last month, tomorrow, following, before, at present, eventually
Additions	moreover, in addition, furthermore, besides
Comparison	compared with, both are, likewise, in comparison, similarly, of equal importance, another type of, like, alike, just as
Contrast	but, yet, however, on the other hand, conversely, still, otherwise, in contrast, unfortunately, despite, rather than, on the contrary
Cause-Effect	therefore, consequently, thus, accordingly, so, as a result, hence, since, because of, due to, for this reason
Numerical Order	first, second, third, in the first place, to begin with, initially, next, eventually, finally
Spatial Relations	to the north, alongside, to the left, above, moving eastward, in front of, in back of, behind, next to, below, nearby, in the distance
Explanation	to illustrate, for example, for instance, case in point, in other words, to simplify, to clarify
Importance	most importantly, above all, keep this in mind, remember, listen carefully, take note of, indeed
The Speech Is Ending	in short, finally, in conclusion, to summarize

time changes. Transitions such as *in addition* show that you are expanding on what you have already said. The use of the word *similarly* indicates that a comparison follows. Phrases such as *on the other hand* cue listeners to a contrast. Cause-and-effect relationships can be suggested with *as a result, consequently,* and similar phrases. Introductory phrases such as *traveling north* can indicate spatial relationships. Phrases or words such as *in short, finally,* or *in conclusion* signal that the speech is coming to an end. Figure 9.5 contains a list of some commonly used transitions.

Preview and summary statements may also be used as effective transitions to connect the major parts of a speech. We discuss these special transitions in the next two sections of this chapter on introducing and concluding your speeches. Sometimes—especially with longer, complicated presentations—an **internal summary** within the body of a speech can help remind listeners of the points you have already covered before moving to your next point. Internal summaries are especially useful in causation and problem–solution speeches, where they signal that you have finished your discussion of the causes or problem and are now going to describe the

internal summary   A transition that reminds listeners of major points already presented in a speech before proceeding to new ideas.

effects or solution. By condensing and repeating your ideas, an internal summary can help listeners remember your message. Consider the following example:

> So now we see what the problem is. We know the cost in human suffering, the terrible political consequences, and the enormous economic burden. The question is, what are we going to do about it? Let me tell you about a plan that experts agree may turn things around.

Preview and summary statements should be brief and to the point so that they highlight only the major ideas in your message.

Speakers sometimes use parallel structure by beginning successive points with similar wording. This pattern itself can signal listeners when you move from one point to another.

Whatever transitional techniques you use, you should plan your transitions carefully. Otherwise, you may ramble awkwardly or over-rely on vocalized pauses such as "uh" and "you know." If you have trouble developing effective transitions, rethink the structure of your message. Outline your thoughts to be sure that they move in a clear direction and in an orderly sequence. We cover outlining in Chapter 10.

Once you have organized the body of your speech—identified and arranged your main points, decided how to develop them with supporting materials, and planned how to connect them with transitions—you should prepare an introduction and conclusion to begin and end your speech effectively. Introductions and conclusions are important because listeners tend to be most affected by what they hear at the beginning and end of a message. The introduction allows you to make a good first impression and to set the stage for how your audience will respond. The conclusion gives you a final opportunity to make a lasting impression.

The introduction of your speech must immediately engage your audience. If you don't get their attention within the first minute of speaking, they may be lost to you forever.

Introducing Your Message

When you first begin to speak, the audience will have three basic questions in mind: *Why should I listen to this speech? Why should I listen to this speaker?* and *What should I understand?* To answer these basic questions, an introduction should capture your audience's attention and involve them with your topic, establish your ethos as a credible speaker, and preview your message to make it easier for the audience to follow.

Capturing Attention

All too often, speakers open their presentations with something like "Good morning. My speech today is on . . . ," and then jump right into their message. Needless to say, this is not a good way to begin a speech because it does not make the audience want to listen. The opening of a speech should arouse attention and involve listeners with the speaker's message. This is especially important when your topic might seem distant from your audience in terms of time, space, and relevance.

There are several ways to attract, build, and hold the interest of your audience as you open your speeches. You might acknowledge the audience, location, or occasion; invoke shared interests and values; solicit audience participation; open with a narrative; use humor; develop suspense; begin with a quotation; or startle your audience.

Acknowledge the Audience, Location, or Occasion. When you speak outside a classroom, it is customary to make some brief opening remarks that acknowledge your audience, the location, or the purpose or meaning of the occasion. People like to hear good things about themselves and their community. Note how Jerry Daniels, president of Boeing Military Aircraft and Missile Systems, opened a speech before the Dayton, Ohio, Chamber of Commerce:

> It's a pleasure to be here at the cradle of aviation—two years and two weeks before the 100th anniversary of the "Miracle at Kitty Hawk." In paying tribute to Orville and Wilbur, historian Darrel Collins noted: "Before the Wright brothers, no one in aviation did anything fundamentally right. Since the Wright brothers, no one has done anything fundamentally wrong."[4]

These introductory remarks can be very brief, but they should also contain a touch of eloquence, as illustrated by the opening words of President John F. Kennedy in a speech given at a White House dinner honoring Nobel Prize winners:

> I think this is the most extraordinary collection of talent, of human knowledge, that has ever been gathered together at the White House, with the possible exception of when Thomas Jefferson dined alone.[5]

With this elegant tribute, Kennedy was able to honor his guests without embarrassing them or going overboard with praise. His reference to the genius of Thomas Jefferson also paid tribute to the past, as did Daniels's reference to the Wright brothers.

Invoking Shared Interests and Values. Invoking shared interests and values is another strategy for capturing audience attention and involving listeners with a topic. Appeals to your listeners' needs for material and financial security can work well in this respect. For example, most young people say they would someday like to marry and have children. Given that assumption about your audience, you might effectively introduce a speech on "new" investment possibilities by citing experts on how expensive it will be to put their future children through college when they reach that age.

Speakers on controversial social or political issues often open by associating the purpose of their speech with moral goals or commitments. Consider the following passage from the introduction to Martin Luther King Jr.'s "I Have a Dream," delivered at the height of the Civil Rights Movement in late summer of 1963:

> Five score years ago, a great American, in whose symbolic shadow we stand today, signed the Emancipation Proclamation. This momentous decree came as a great beacon of light and hope to millions of Negro slaves, who had been seared in the flames of withering injustice. It came as a joyous daybreak to end the long night of their captivity.
>
> But one hundred years later, the Negro is still not free. . . .[6]

Soliciting Audience Participation.   Another opening technique is to solicit the actual participation of audience members. A well-worded series of questions or a simple show of hands can help to promote audience involvement and strengthen audience commitment to your message. Consider the introduction to Beth Tidmore's student speech encouraging audience members to volunteer to work with the Special Olympics:

> Please repeat after me: "Let me win, but if I cannot win, let me be brave in the attempt." [Audience repeats the words.] This is the Special Olympics oath, and this is something that the Special Olympians take every year before they are allowed to compete.
>
> Now, a lot of you have heard what I have to say about Special Olympics. You know the philosophy, you know the history. But what you might not know is what it's like to be a volunteer. . . .

Not all strategies for soliciting audience participation require a direct response. The simple use of inclusive pronouns such as "we" and "our" can help promote identification and involvement with a message. Another technique for promoting the tacit participation of audiences is to use rhetorical questions. **Rhetorical questions** such as "Have you ever thought about what your life would be like if you were a different color?" arouse curiosity and start listeners thinking about the topic. Erin Bourne opened her classroom speech with the following rhetorical question:

> How would you feel if you were a perfect driver—never had a car wreck, never had a speeding ticket—and you got your car insurance bill one day, and it had gone up so high that you could no longer afford to drive? So, you call your insurance company, thinking that there must be some mistake, and they tell you that they had to raise your rates to compensate for all of the not-so-good drivers out there on the road and the claims that they had to pay out for those.
>
> This is analogous to a healthcare problem that is widespread in the United States right now. A few bad doctors are driving malpractice insurance rates up so high in some areas that good doctors are having to either quit practicing medicine or move out of their states.

By posing this rhetorical question and framing the analogy between automobile insurance and medical insurance, Erin gained the attention of her listeners for a topic that otherwise might have seemed distant from them.

Opening with a Narrative.   We humans began our love affair with stories around the campfires of ancient times. Stories help us remember the past and envision the future. They entertain and educate us by framing abstract concerns and challenges in the concrete form of a narrative. They help us "see" a subject in human terms. Stories may be imaginary or based on real-life experiences and historic events. Depending or your purpose for speaking, they may be lighthearted and humorous, or somber and serious. In either case, storytelling is a good way to promote identification and involvement with your message. Introductory narratives should be kept brief. They often rely on vivid language to establish an appropriate mood.

Consider the opening narrative to Ashlie McMillan's introductory speech on scuba diving:

> Imagine you're sitting aboard a dive boat. It's rocking back and forth, you can feel the sun beating down on you. You can feel the wind blowing on you. You

---

rhetorical questions   Questions that have a self-evident answer, or that provoke curiosity that the speech then proceeds to satisfy.

> smell the ocean, the salt water. You can hear the waves crashing up against the boat. You put on your dive pack with your heavy oxygen tank and you walk unsteadily across the deck of the rocking boat. And all of a sudden you plunge into a completely different environment. All around you is vast blueness and infinite space, a world completely different from the one you left above. But all you have to do is turn on your back and look above you and you see the sunlight streaming in through the top of the water. And you can see the world that you left behind.

Ashlie's skillful use of action words—such as *rocking, blowing, crashing*—and her vivid appeal to the senses made this scene come alive for her listeners and placed them in the middle of it.

An opening narrative may also be based on a historical event. Sandra Baltz, a premed major, opened a speech on setting priorities for organ transplants with the following narrative:

> On a cold and stormy night in 1841, the ship *William Brown* struck an iceberg in the North Atlantic. Passengers and crew members frantically scrambled into the lifeboats. To make a bad disaster even worse, one of the lifeboats began to sink because it was overcrowded. Fourteen men were thrown overboard that horrible night. After the survivors were rescued, a crew member was tried for the murders of those thrown overboard.

> Fortunately, situations like this have been few in history, but today we face a similar problem in the medical establishment: deciding who will live as we allocate scarce medical resources for transplants. Someday, your fate—or the fate of someone you love—could depend on how we resolve this dilemma.

In this example, the story sets a somber mood for the serious message that follows. Stories can also be used to establish a lighter mood through the use of humor.

Appropriate Humor.   Humor can put your audience in a receptive mood for your message. But humor is also one of the most misused techniques for introducing speeches. Because someone once told them that starting with a joke will ensure success, beginning speakers often search through anthologies of "canned humor" to find something that will make people laugh. If you choose to open your speech with humor, keep it fresh and relevant to the situation or your topic. It also should be appropriate for your audience and the occasion, and brief so that it doesn't upstage your message.

Humor can be grossly inappropriate for some topics and occasions. Keep in mind that what you might get away with saying in an informal conversation may be inappropriate, if not offensive, to the same people in a more formal setting. Finally, do not let a humorous introduction trivialize the rest of your speech. We once heard a student open a speech with a rather risqué quotation from Mae West, "Is that a gun in your pocket, or are you happy to see me?" It drew an initial gasp followed by some hearty laughter. Unfortunately, as the speech continued, one student would chuckle over the remembered joke, and then the audience would start laughing all over again even when nothing funny had been said. After the speaker finished, we questioned the audience about their "inappropriate" responses. They said, "We kept remembering that Mae West line. We just couldn't help it." And to this day, none of your authors can remember the topic of the speech, either!

Finally, discover what works for you. Be cautious about using planned humor if you are still coping with communication anxiety. A joke that works can put both a speaker and audience at ease, but one that falls flat can have just the opposite effect. Remember that humor is not a prerequisite for a good speech; there are other ways to come across as likeable and capture audience attention. Play to your strengths.

Develop Suspense.   You can attract and hold your listeners' attention by arousing their curiosity and then making them wait before you satisfy it. The following introduction creates curiosity and anticipation:

> Getting knocked down is no disgrace. Champions are made by getting up just one more time than the opponent! The results are a matter of record about a man who suffered many defeats: Lost his job in 1832, defeated for legislature in 1832, failed in business in 1833, sweetheart died in 1835, had nervous breakdown in 1836, defeated for nomination for Congress in 1843, elected to Congress in 1846, lost renomination in 1848, rejected for land officer in 1849, defeated for Senate in 1854, defeated for nomination for vice president in 1856, defeated for Senate in 1858. In 1860 Abraham Lincoln was elected President of the United States. . . . The greatest failures . . . are those who fail by not doing anything.[7]

The use of humor in an introduction can help set the stage for acceptance of a message.

Reciting the list of failures aroused the audience's curiosity: Who was this loser? Many were surprised when they discovered his identity. This effective introduction set the stage for the speaker's message that perseverance is the key to success.

Begin with a Quotation.   Starting your speech with a striking quotation or paraphrase from a highly respected text or historical figure can both arouse interest and dignify your speech. References to revered political texts such as the Declaration of Independence can command attention. Well-known authors are often gold mines

Speaker's Notes   9.2

Using Humor

Keep the following in mind when considering the use of humor in your speeches.

1. Don't use humor just to be funny. Keep it relevant to your topic.

2. Use humor to put the audience at ease and make them receptive to your ideas.

3. Avoid religious, ethnic, racist, or sexist humor that speaks poorly of you.

4. If you must poke fun at someone, let it be yourself.

5. Don't use humor that might trivialize a serious topic.

6. Avoid planned humor if you are really anxious about speaking.

of eloquence and wisdom. Student speaker David Rasmussen found this nugget among George Orwell's essays: "Every generation imagines itself to be more intelligent than the one that went before it, and wiser than the one that comes after it." David suggested that such arrogance explains the difficulty of passing knowledge from one generation to another. It makes it really hard to talk across time barriers when one generation thinks it is wiser and smarter.

Most effective opening quotations are short and to the point, and they need not come from such elevated sources. Ashlie McMillan used a brief quote from folklore as a lead-in to her informative speech on cystic fibrosis:

> "Woe to the child who when kissed on the forehead tastes salty. He is bewitched and he soon will die." This northern European folk adage is a reference to the genetic disorder cystic fibrosis. Well, we know today that children with cystic fibrosis aren't bewitched. And we have a lot better ways to test for cystic fibrosis than to kiss them on the forehead.

Most books of quotations are indexed by key-words and subjects as well as by authors. Collections of quotations are also available on the Internet. They are an excellent source of statements you might use to introduce your topic. InterConnections.LearnMore 9.1 will guide you to some of these sources.

InterConnections.
LearnMore 9.1
Online Sources of Quotations

Quoteland.com
www.quoteland.com
   A compilation of quotations from literature, accessible by topic or author.

Bartleby.com
www.bartleby.com/quotations/
   A collection of quotations from contemporary and classic sources with a search tool. Provides links to other well-known compendiums of quotations.

Dictionary of Scientific Quotations
www.naturalscience.com/dsqhome.html
   A short collection of interesting quotations from scientists.

Creative Quotations
http://creativequotations. com
   An excellent source of quotes from over 3,000 famous people. Also contains biographical information on the sources of the quotes. Searchable by key-words and such unique categories as creative women, creative wit, and quotational poetry.

Good Quotations by Famous People
www.cs.virginia.edu/~robins/quotes.html
   A compilation of pithy epigrams, such as "Not everything that can be counted counts, and not everything that counts can be counted" (Albert Einstein). Much material that might be useful in introductions and conclusions of speeches. Not categorized by topic or author, but well worth reading through for that special gem you might find! Compiled and maintained by Professor Gabriel Robins, University of Virginia.

Startle the Audience. Anything out of the ordinary draws attention to itself and arouses curiosity. This "startle factor" can come in the form of a powerful piece of information or a truly unusual approach to introducing your speech. For instance, opening with a startling statistic such as "One in six American women will be victims of sexual assault—half of them children!" can help to shock and involve your audience. One of our more creative students used the following technique to open his speech:

> [Sound of cell phone ringing: speaker takes phone from pocket and speaks into it.]
>
> "Hey!" (pause)
>
> "Nah, that's okay. What's up?"
>
> "Cool!" (short pause, light laugh)
>
> "Yeah! Well, hey, uh—Can I call you back after a while? I'm in my speech class right now—getting ready to give my speech." (pause)
>
> "Okay—just a minute."
>
> [Speaker leaves podium, goes to classmate in front row.]
>
> "Can I borrow your pen? I've got to write down her cell phone number."
>
> [Speaker returns to podium, writes something on speaking outline.]
>
> "Gotta go. Catch you later."
>
> [Speaker pushes phone button, puts cell phone in pocket; long pause, speaker looks around at audience.]
>
> "Sorry 'bout that. Was that rude of me?" (long pause)
>
> Today I want to talk with you about cell phone etiquette, about what annoys other people, and about the polite way to use your phone.

This unusual introduction was so artfully handled that the students thought the student actually had received a call during class. Fortunately, the instructor had been prepped on what to expect, so she didn't stop the speaker before he got started.

The startle technique must always be used with care. You don't want your introduction to arouse more interest than the body of your speech can satisfy. If your

Capturing Attention

Try the following strategies to gain attention in the introduction of your speech.

1. Acknowledge the audience, location, or occasion.

2. Invoke shared interests and values.

3. Solicit audience involvement and participation.

4. Open with a narrative that relates to your topic.

5. Engage your listeners with appropriate humor.

6. Begin with a striking quotation.

7. Develop a suspenseful introduction.

8. Startle your audience with powerful information or a novel approach.

opening is too sensational, it will upstage the rest of your speech. Similarly, be careful not to go beyond the bounds of propriety. You want to startle your listeners, not offend them.

Establishing Your Credibility

The second major function of an effective introduction is to establish your ethos as a credible speaker. People tend to form first impressions of speakers that color their later perceptions. In Chapter 3, we discussed the importance of developing your ethos in terms of competence, integrity, goodwill, and dynamism. You enter a speaking situation with some initial ethos based on audience members' knowledge of and previous experience with you—what they have learned about you from previous presentations and class discussions.

You can enhance perceptions of your competence by being well organized, using language effectively and correctly, and demonstrating that you know what you are talking about. You will seem more competent if you select a topic you already know something about and have done sufficient research to speak responsibly on it.

Citing relevant training and personal experience at the beginning of your speech can be extremely effective. Michael J. Fox is not a medical scientist, but he has used his own personal struggle with Parkinson's disease to become a credible advocate for stem cell research. Similarly, Lance Armstrong has, through his personal experience and self-education, qualified himself to speak in favor of cancer research. Speakers without such expertise and personal experience can help to establish the competence dimensions of their ethos by citing respected sources of information early in their speeches. The opening of this student speech on consumer culture and advertising follows this guideline:

Calling on personal experience at the beginning of a speech can gain attention and create credibility for the speaker.

I was amazed to learn in my psychology classes that research does not support a strong link between exposure to persuasive communications and behavior. This discovery led me to do more reading on the relationship between advertising and consumer activity. What I found was even more surprising, especially when you consider that, according to *American Demographics*, advertisers routinely paid over $550,000 for a half minute of air time on *ER*.

To strengthen impressions of integrity, you should try to come across as straightforward, sincere, and genuinely concerned about the consequences of your words. You can accomplish this by demonstrating respect for those who hold different opinions while still maintaining your personal commitment to your topic and position. It should also be clear to your audience that you will not ask more of them than you will ask of yourself. If you demonstrate consideration, understanding, tolerance, and respect, the audience should gain a positive impression of your integrity as a speaker.

You should also present yourself as a likeable and confident speaker, someone who is pleasant and tactful. Likeable speakers treat listeners as friends, inspiring affection in return. They share their feelings and are able to laugh at themselves.

To come across as a confident speaker, you must appear in control of the situation from the outset. Your introduction should reflect your enthusiasm for your message. A smile and eye contact signal listeners that you want to communicate. These qualities build an overall impression of dynamism that should make you more effective.

When you establish favorable ethos in the introduction of your speech, you also lay the foundation for one of the most powerful effects of communication: identification between yourself and listeners. As discussed in Chapter 1, identification helps people overcome the personal and cultural differences that separate them and share thoughts and feelings as though they were one.[8] When you seem likeable, sincere, competent, and dynamic, your listeners want to identify with you, and your effectiveness as a speaker is magnified.

Previewing Your Message

The final function of an introduction is to preview the body of your speech. The **preview** indicates the main points you will cover and offers your listeners an overview of the speech to come. Previews are very useful for speeches on unfamiliar, complicated, or technical subjects. They help listeners follow what you are saying.

Hannah Johnston provided a preview in the introduction to her speech on the perils of fast food:

> I'm sure most of you saw the famous old movie *Soylent Green*. Or, you've heard about the ending, where Charlton Heston finds out what he's really been eating for so long and screams, "Soylent Green is people!"

> Well, I'm not saying we need to run around shouting, "McDonald's is feeding us spinal cords," or anything of the sort, but we do need to be aware of a few important things.

> First, exactly what ends up in our fast food that shouldn't be there? Second, what conditions in slaughterhouses can lead to mistakes in food preparation? And finally, what are the global health consequences of increased fast-food consumption?

By informing her listeners of her intentions and letting them know how her speech would develop, Hannah helped her audience listen intelligently to her message. Previews are most essential for informative and persuasive speeches. In ceremonial speeches that tell a story rather than develop a topic by logical design, the preview may take the form of a prologue using a **foreshadowing** technique: "I never expected that my life would be forever changed by what would happen that day." When speakers foreshadow their stories, they don't tell their listeners exactly what will happen, but they do alert them that something important will happen. Thus, they prepare them to listen intently to the story.

Selecting and Using Introductory Techniques

A successful introduction can help you as well as your listeners. A smooth presentation of your introduction can ease communication anxiety and carry over into the rest of your speech. Prepare your introduction carefully, and practice it aloud until you are confident and comfortable in your ability to carry it off. Establish eye contact as soon as you rise to speak. Do not read your introduction!

There are no hard and fast rules for determining exactly how you should open a speech. As you review your research notes, look for material that would make an

preview The part of the introduction that identifies the main points to be developed in the body of the speech and presents an overview of the speech to follow.

foreshadowing Hints to the meaning of the story that will follow.

effective introduction. The following guidelines may help you make a wise selection:

- Consider your audience. Use your introduction to tie your topic to their needs, interests, or well-being.

- Determine the mood you want to establish. Some topics call for a light touch. Others may require you to be more serious.

- Keep it brief. If you are to speak for seven minutes, you can't use a five-minute introduction.

- Do what you do best. Some people are effective storytellers, and others are better at using striking statistics or quotations. Go with your strength!

Developing an Effective Conclusion

Beginning speakers often end their presentations awkwardly. The conclusion of your speech should not be that point at which you just got tired of talking or ran out of time. "That's it, I guess" or "Well, I'm done," and then giving a sigh of relief, suggests that you have not planned your speech carefully. The final words of your speech should stay with listeners, remind them of your message, and when appropriate, move them to action.

Summarizing Your Message

Your conclusion should usually include a summary and final remarks. The more complicated your topic, the more important a summary becomes. A brief **summary** of your main points can serve as a transition between the body of your speech and your final remarks. It signals the audience that you are about to finish.

A summary should not be a simple repetition of the main points of your speech. In his informative speech on the causes of global warming, Josh Logan identified three main sources of the problem: the loss of woodlands around the globe, agricultural and industrial emissions, and personal energy consumption involving especially the use of fossil fuels. Instead of summarizing his speech in a paint-by-numbers manner— "Today I've shown you three causes of the greenhouse effect"—this is what Josh said:

> In conclusion, if you want to understand why global warming has become one of the great crises of our time, you've simply got to step outside into the greenhouse. Listen for the falling trees, watch the industrial smokestacks darkening the sky, and smell that rich bouquet of exhaust fumes that we are constantly pumping into the atmosphere.

By using such colorful language, Josh summarized his main points in a way that listeners would remember.

Concluding Remarks

Although a summary statement can offer listeners a sense of closure, to seal that effect, you need to provide some concluding remarks that stay with your listeners. Many of the techniques that create effective introductions can also be used to develop memorable conclusions.

summary   The speaker's reinterpretation of the speech's main ideas at the end of a presentation.

Echo Your Introduction. Sometimes called a "book-end," a conclusion that applies the same technique used in the introduction can help to provide a nice sense of closure. For example, if you begin your speech with a story, you might end with a different story that reinforces the meaning. You might also finish a story that you started in the introduction. Referring back to the introduction can be an effective means of letting listeners know you are bringing your message full circle. For example, the student speaker who told the story of Earl Washington's wrongful conviction for murder in the introduction of her speech echoed this story as she concluded: "The Earl Washingtons out there are counting on you!"

Many persuasive speeches end with a call for action.

Restate the Relevance to Audience. At the beginning of a speech, you should involve the audience by showing them how your message relates directly to their lives. At the conclusion of your speech, you should remind them of what they personally have at stake. In Josh Logan's informative speech on global warming, the summary statement was followed immediately by remarks that brought the message close to the lives of listeners:

> Global warming is a monster of our making. If we don't stop it now, we, our children, and our children's children will have to pay the price: sky-high temperatures, rising seas, violent storms, and a host of dangerous health problems that will make future generations wonder why we sacrificed the quality of their lives. They will ask of us, "How did you let this happen?"

Call for Action. In persuasive speeches, concluding remarks often urge listeners to take the first step to confirm their commitment to action and change. This call for action should make it easy for listeners to comply. Note how Beth Tidmore used the technique to conclude her speech urging her classmates to volunteer for Special Olympics:

> Becoming a volunteer is the best way that you can help. If you can't give a weekend, give a couple of hours. If you can't become a leader, just become a cheerleader. Show up. Be a happy, smiling face. It's the best way to give to charity, because you can see the results right in front of you. You can see the shiny medals, the triumphant finishes, the happy faces, the screaming fans. And you know that you're helping someone else and giving of yourself to them. The benefits are truly rewarding, even if the only thing you get out of it is the satisfaction of knowing you've made a difference.
>
> Can drives need cans. Blood drives need blood. And, the Special Olympics need volunteers. They need warm hearts and open minds. In Special Olympics, everyone is a winner—especially the volunteers.

At the end of her speech, Beth distributed sign-up forms that helped her listeners make their commitment.

Ask Rhetorical Questions. When used in an introduction, rhetorical questions help arouse attention and curiosity. When used in a conclusion, they give your audience something to think about after you have finished.

Elinor Fraser opened a speech attacking the use of cell phones while driving in the following way: "How many of you were chatting on your cell phones while driving to class this morning?" After a speech that established the danger of such behavior in graphic terms, her final words were:

> "So, now that you know the risk you are running, are you going to use your cell phones again while you're on the way home? If so, let me know so I can drive in a different direction."

End with a Story.   Stories are remembered long after facts and figures are forgotten. A concluding narrative can help your audience *experience* the meaning of your message. To end her speech on dangerous off-campus housing conditions, Anna Aley told the following story about her neighbor:

> I got out of my apartment with little more than bad memories. My upstairs neighbor was not so lucky. The main problem with his apartment was that the electrical wiring was done improperly; there were too many outlets for too few circuits, so the fuses were always blowing.
>
> One day last November, Jack was at home when a fuse blew—as usual. And, as usual, he went to the fuse box to flip the switch back on. When he touched the switch, it delivered such a shock that it literally threw this guy the size of a football player backwards and down a flight of stairs. He lay there at the bottom, unable to move, for a full hour before his roommate came home and called an ambulance. Jack was lucky, His back was not broken. But he did rip many of the muscles in his back. Now he has to go to physical therapy, and he is not expected to fully recover.

If time constraints are a consideration, a shorter story may work almost as well. As he concluded his lengthy speech on the New Madrid earthquake zone, Stephen Huff told the following story:

> I now know what I should do if an earthquake hits, but I'm not really sure how I would react. Even the experts don't always react "appropriately." When an earthquake hit the Los Angeles area at about six o'clock one morning, Charles Richter, the seismologist who developed the Richter Scale to measure earthquakes, was in bed at the time. According to his wife, "He jumped up screaming and scared the cat!"

Close with a Quotation.   Brief quotations that capture the essence of your message can make for effective conclusions. For example, if one historic quotation opens a speech, another on the same theme or from the same person can provide an elegant sense of closure. Be sure to quote someone the audience respects. In a speech urging students to encourage young children to become volunteers for worthy causes, Rebecca Levinson used the following "classic" quotation:

> Making a difference in the life of a child is a noble thing indeed. When we encourage them to raise money or give of their time to help others, we are helping them prepare to be contributing citizens as adults. In the words of Aristotle, "The habits we form in childhood make no small difference. Rather, they make all the difference."

Chapter 9 Structuring Your Speech   219

End with a Metaphor. A memorable metaphor can end your speech effectively.[9] As we discuss in more detail in Chapter 12, **metaphors** combine things that are apparently unalike so that we see unexpected relationships. In the conclusion of a speech, an effective metaphor may reveal hidden truths about the speaker's subject in a memorable way. Melodie Lancaster, president of Lancaster Resources, used such a metaphor as she concluded a speech to the Houston Council of the American Business Women's Association:

> We recall the story of the three stonemasons who were asked what they were doing. The first said, "I am laying brick." The second replied, "I am making a foundation." And the third said: "I am building a cathedral." Let's you and I set our sights that high. Let's build cathedrals of success today, tomorrow, and the day after tomorrow.[10]

Consider the different meanings this example might evoke in the minds of listeners. First, it suggests that listeners must work hard. Second, it suggests they must work with specific goals in mind. Third, it suggests they must have a vision that gives significance to their work. All these meanings are packed into the metaphor, "building cathedrals of success."

Use Strategic Repetition. Repetition helps implant ideas in the minds of your listeners. When repetition is combined with parallel construction, in which certain phrases are repeated in close succession for added emphasis, the results can be both elegant and dramatic. Note how Bob Dinneen, president of the Renewable Fuels Association, used this technique to conclude a speech on the use of ethanol to reduce greenhouse gases:

> Who is prepared to stand and take these new steps for change?
> Who is willing to stand up to the skeptics, firm in the conviction that our farmers can produce enough corn to meet the needs of both food and fuel?
> Who is willing to stand and join the effort to reduce greenhouse gases by expanding and improving ethanol technology?
> Who is willing to stand and say, "I'll be the first to commercialize cellulosic ethanal production!"?[11]

Speaker's Notes 9.4

Techniques for Ending Your Speech

Select from the following techniques to develop an effective conclusion for your speech.

1. Echo your introduction to provide a sense of closure.

2. Point out the relevance of your message to listeners.

3. Issue a call for action to get listeners to confirm their commitment.

4. Ask rhetorical questions that give listeners something to consider after your speech.

5. End with a memorable story that helps listeners experience your message.

6. Close with a quotation that captures the essence of your ideas.

7. End with a metaphor that implants your message in listeners' minds.

8. Use strategic repetition to reinforce your ideas.

metaphor Brief, concentrated form of comparison that is implied and often surprising. It connects elements of experience that are not usually related in order to create a new perspective.

Selecting and Using Concluding Techniques

Whatever closing technique you choose, be certain that it satisfies your audience that what was promised in the beginning has now been delivered. Plan your summary statement and concluding remarks carefully, just as you did with your introduction. Practice them until you are confident you will end your speech impressively. After your final words, pause a moment to let them sink in, then take your seat.

As with introductions, there are no absolute criteria for deciding what concluding techniques you should use. Here we provide some general guidelines for their selection as we did with selecting introductory techniques:

■ Think about what will work best for your audience.

■ Consider the message you want your listeners to take with them.

■ Use your conclusion to reinforce feelings about your topic.

■ Remember time constraints and be brief. Make every word count.

■ Play to your strengths as a presenter. Do what you do best.

In Summary

A carefully structured speech helps the audience understand the message and enhances the speaker's ethos.

Good Form. A well-structured speech has good form: It is simple, balanced, and orderly. Simplicity occurs when you limit the number of main points; repeat them for emphasis; and use clear, direct language. A speech has balance when the major parts receive proper emphasis and work together. An orderly speech follows a consistent pattern of development.

Structuring the Body of Your Speech. You should structure the body of your speech first so that you can fashion an introduction and a conclusion that fit your message. To develop the body, determine your main points, decide how to arrange them, and then select effective supporting materials. To identify your main points, prepare a research overview of the information you have collected. This summary can help you spot major themes that can develop into main points.

Arrange your main points so that they fit into a design that is appropriate to the material and that reflects the way people tend to arrange things in their minds. These include categorical, comparative, spatial, sequential, chronological, causation, problem–solution, refutative, and narrative designs.

Supporting materials fill out the speech and buttress ideas. In an ideal arrangement, you should support each point with information, testimony, and an example or story that emphasizes its human aspects.

Using Transitions. Effective transitions point up the relationships among ideas in your speech and tie the speech together. Internal summaries remind listeners of the points you have made in one part of your speech before you move on to another.

Preparing an Effective Introduction. The introduction to a speech should arouse your listeners' interest, establish your credibility, and focus and preview your message. Some useful ways to introduce a speech include acknowledging the audience, location, or occasion; invoking shared interests and values; soliciting audience participation; opening with a narrative; using appropriate humor; beginning with a quotation; developing suspense; and startling the audience. As you build credibility, you also make possible identification between yourself and the audience. When you preview your message, you give your readers the blueprints of the speech that will follow.

Developing an Effective Conclusion. An effective conclusion should review the meaning of your speech in a summary statement, provide a sense of closure, leave the audience with final reflections on the significance of the speech, and if appropriate, motivate listeners to act. Techniques that are useful for conclusions include echoing the introduction, calling for action, reemphasizing relevance to audience, asking rhetorical questions, closing with a quotation, telling a story, ending with a metaphor, and using strategic repetition. Your speech will seem more symmetrical and satisfying if your conclusion ties into your introduction.

Explore and Apply the Ideas in This Chapter

1. Working in small groups, share your research overviews for your next speeches. What major themes emerge, and how might these develop into main points in light of your specific purpose and your listeners' needs? Encourage input from group members to help you select the main points for your speech.

2. Share the organizational plan for your next speech with a classmate so that you become consultants for each other. Help each other come up with alternative patterns for your main points. After the speeches are presented, each consulting team should explain the options it considered and why it chose the particular structure used for each speech.

3. Select a speech from Appendix B and write a thorough critique of its structure. Consider the following questions:

   a. Did this speech satisfy the requirements of "good form"? Did it meet the needs of simplicity, balance, and order?

   b. What design for the main ideas did the speech use?

   c. Did transitions keep the message in focus for listeners?

4. For the same speech critiqued in exercise 3, write an alternative introduction and conclusion, using a different technique. Compare the effectiveness of the new introduction and conclusion with the ones actually used by the speaker. Which work better and why?

5. What type of introductory and concluding techniques might be most effective for speeches based on the following specific purpose statements?

   a. To inform my audience of the steps to follow to get financial assistance.

   b. To persuade my audience that it is better to marry than to live together.

   c. To inform my audience of the signs of child abuse.

   d. To persuade my audience to begin recycling.

10 Outlining Your Speech

This chapter will help you

- appreciate the value of outlining
- develop a working outline
- prepare a formal outline
- prepare a key-word outline to use as you speak

*Our plans miscarry because they have
no aim. When a man does not know
what harbor he is making for, no wind
is the right wind.*

—*Seneca*

As we planned our home on the Tennessee River, we often met with the builders to consider our options. We knew what materials we had to work with, and we had a general sense of what we wanted. But before construction could begin, we would have to make and then remake several important decisions. To help us sort through our choices, our builders developed a series of rough sketches that allowed us to see the relative size, layout, and features of each room in relation to the house as a whole. A later set of blueprints provided the final detailed plans of the home that would rise on the hilltop above the river.

Like a home, a good speech requires careful systematic planning. In Chapter 9, we discussed the process of structuring speeches that are coherent, substantive, and easily remembered. *Outlining is a disciplined process that provides for the final polishing of well-organized speeches.* As with the blueprints to our home, a well-prepared outline helps you see the structure of your presentations as they develop—how your main ideas and supporting materials fit together as they give form to your speech. Outlining assists you in this process in five important ways:

- It objectifies your thinking: It takes ideas out of your head, where they can get all tangled up, and puts them down on paper, where you can see them and work with them.

- It is both a creative and a corrective process. As you think about the relationships among your points, you may come up with new ideas. You can see where you may need more research, whether a point is really relevant, and whether the overall structure is well balanced. You may need to add something here, subtract something there.

- It helps you find and correct problems before they become mistakes.

- It points out where you need transitions.

- It helps you see whether your planned introduction and conclusion actually fit your speech.

In this chapter, we provide sample outline formats that can be adapted for general use. In Chapter 14, we provide abbreviated sample outlines for specific designs that are especially useful in informative speeches: spatial, sequential, chronological, categorical, comparative, and causation. In Chapter 16, we provide abbreviated outlines for the major persuasive speech designs: problem–solution, motivated sequence, and refutative. In Chapter 17, we provide a brief sample outline for the narrative design, which is especially useful in ceremonial speaking.

As you prepare your speech, you may well develop several working outlines, a formal outline, and a key-word outline or note cards to use as a prompt during presentation.

Developing a Working Outline

A working outline helps you to develop a *tentative* plan for your speech. It displays the relationships among your main ideas and allows you to identify potential gaps and trouble spots in your thinking. Assume that you plan to present an informative speech on the greenhouse effect. You have done some research, but you are not completely sure how your speech should develop. Your working outline can help reduce your uncertainty by systematically organizing your thoughts and materials. Outlining forces you to think clearly about the design of your speech. Figure 10.1 provides a format for developing a working outline.

In this early stage of developing your speech, don't worry about the formalities of outlining. Your working outline is simply a tool to help you arrange your thoughts. You should not think of this format as a final structure. Adapt it so that it works for you. You will probably prepare and discard several working outlines before you find the right approach.

A good starting point for your working outline is to write out your specific purpose and thesis statement. As discussed in Chapter 6, your thesis statement should

working outline A tentative plan showing the pattern of a speech's major parts, their relative importance, and the way they fit together.

Figure 10.1

Format for a Working Outline

Topic: _____
Specific purpose: _____
Thesis statement: _____

INTRODUCTION

Attention material: _____
Thesis statement: _____
Preview: _____

(Transition to body of speech)

BODY

First main point: _____
    Subpoint: _____
      Sub-subpoint: _____
      Sub-subpoint: _____
    Subpoint: _____

(Transition to second main point)

Second main point: _____
    Subpoint: _____
    Subpoint: _____
      Sub-subpoint: _____
      Sub-subpoint: _____

(Transition to third main point)

Third main point: _____
    Subpoint: _____
    Subpoint: _____

(Transition to conclusion)

CONCLUSION

Summary statement: _____
Concluding remarks: _____

---

present the central idea of your speech as a short declarative statement. Your specific purpose statement should specify exactly what you want your audience to understand, agree with, do, or appreciate as a result of hearing your speech. Having your specific purpose and thesis statements clearly defined and written out will help you see how well your main points advance them.

Specific purpose: My audience should understand how the greenhouse effect contributes to global warming.

Thesis statement: We must understand the greenhouse effect before we can hope to counter global warming.

Developing Your Main Points

The second step in preparing a working outline is to sketch the body of your speech. Start by selecting and arranging your main points. As you determine these principal

InterConnections.
LearnMore 10.1

Outlining Aids

Basic Outlining
www.lib.jjay.cuny.edu/research/outlining.html

> *A brief online guide to outlining with suggestions for further reading. Developed and maintained by the Lloyd Sealy Library, John Jay College of Criminal Justice.*

Outlining
www.ceap.wcu.edu/Houghton/EDELCompEduc/Themes/Outlining/outlining.html

> *An excellent guide to outlining on your computer. Developed and maintained by Professor Robert S. Houghton, College of Education and Allied Professions, Western Carolina University.*

Organizing Information
www.ipl.org/div/aplus/linksorganizing.htm

> *An online directory of links to Internet sites on outlining and organizing information by cubing, mapping, and more. Developed and maintained by Kathryn L. Schwartz, School of Information, University of Michigan.*

points of focus for your speech, be sure to consider the main themes developed in the research overview described in Chapter 9. Factor in your audience's needs and interests, the specific purpose and thematic statement of your speech, and the amount of time you will have to speak. In our ongoing example of preparing a speech on the greenhouse effect, the *first* working outline contained the following main points:

First main point: Harmful agricultural and industrial emissions accelerate the greenhouse effect.

Second main point: Personal energy consumption magnifies the greenhouse effect.

Third main point: The loss of woodlands adds to the greenhouse effect.

Once you have the main points written out, ask yourself the following questions:

- Will these points make my message clear to my audience?
- Is this the right order in which to develop them?
- Have I left out anything important?

As you consider these questions, you realize that you have left out something important. While you address some prominent *causes* of the greenhouse effect, you do not really explain what it is or why your audience should care. What's more, there is no clear, logical order in your arrangement of main points. However, if you opened by explaining what the greenhouse effect is and why we should care about it, and then proceeded to explain its principle human causes, your speech would more likely involve and inform your listeners. So you revise your first working outline as follows:

First main point: The greenhouse effect is a process by which certain gases in the atmosphere retain the heat of the sun.

Second main point: The loss of woodlands adds to the greenhouse effect.

Third main point: Agricultural and industrial emissions accelerate the greenhouse effect.

Fourth main point: Personal energy consumption magnifies the greenhouse effect.

Developing Subpoints

Once you have determined and arranged your main points, you should develop and support them as discussed in Chapter 9. These more specific statements are the **subpoint** level of your outline. Each main point will be buttressed by two or more subpoints that make it more understandable, believable, or compelling.

To identify the subpoints for each of your main points, imagine a critical listener in front of you. When you state the main point, this listener will want to know:

■ What do you mean?

■ Why should I care?

■ How do I know this is true?

The subpoints for each main point should answer these questions. If the main points are columns built on the foundation of your purpose and thesis statement, the subpoints reinforce these columns so that they will stand up under critical scrutiny. For example, as you develop your working outline, you might list the following subpoints for your first main point:

First main point: The greenhouse effect is a process by which certain gases in the atmosphere retain the heat of the sun.

Subpoints: A. The major greenhouse gases are carbon dioxide and methane.
   B. They form a window that holds the heat.
   C. This natural process has been unbalanced by human activities.
   D. Too many gases are holding in too much heat.
   E. Heat waves are breaking temperature records.
   F. This situation is causing a climate and health crisis.

You notice that you have listed six subpoints. Recalling the principles of good form learned in Chapter 9, you conclude rightly that you have *too many* subpoints for your speech to be simple, balanced, and orderly.

At this point, you should examine how your subpoints relate to one another. Can you combine any of them? Do you need to break down your subpoints into more specific **sub-subpoints**? For example, you might develop the first main point in this working outline as follows:

First main point: The greenhouse effect is a process by which certain gases in the atmosphere retain the heat of the sun.

Subpoint A: This natural process makes the earth livable.

Subpoint B: Process now unbalanced by human activities.

Sub-subpoints: 1. High concentrations of carbon dioxide and methane in the atmosphere.
   2. Heat waves are breaking temperature records.
   3. This threatens many living things.

Follow this same procedure as you develop each main point. When you finish, review the working outline of the body of your speech and ask yourself:

■ Will a speech based on this outline satisfy my specific purpose and thesis statement?

■ Will it seem relevant to the interests and concerns of my listeners?

■ Will I be able to accomplish this in the time available?

---

subpoints The major divisions of a speech's main points.

sub-subpoints Divisions of subpoints within a speech.

Speaker's Notes 10.1

Checklist for a Working Outline

You can trust your working outline if the following statements accurately describe it:

1. My topic, specific purpose, and thesis statement are clearly stated.

2. My introduction contains attention-getting material, establishes my credibility, and focuses and previews my message.

3. My main points represent the most important ideas on my topic.

4. I have an appropriate number of main points for the time allotted.

5. Each subpoint supports its main point with more specific detail.

6. My conclusion contains a summary statement and concluding remarks that reinforce and reflect on the meaning of my speech.

7. I have planned transitions to use between the introduction and body, between each of my main points, and between the body and conclusion of my speech.

Be honest with yourself. It's better to be frustrated now than disappointed after your presentation. In addition, be sure your ideas are arranged in an orderly manner that is easy to follow. Make certain that each subpoint relates directly to the main point above it and that you have enough supporting material to build a strong, responsible structure of ideas. If you are lacking in any of these respects, now is the time to discover and correct the problem.

Completing Your Working Outline

To complete your working outline, prepare an introduction that gains attention, enhances your credibility, and focuses and previews your speech, as we discussed in Chapter 9. Next, develop a conclusion that includes a summary and concluding remarks. Finally, add transitions to tie your speech together. Transitions should connect the introduction to the body, tie each point to the next point as you develop the body, and move the speech from the body to the conclusion.

Now, take a final look at your working outline. (Figure 10.2 is a sample working outline for a speech on global warming.)

Review your outline using the Checklist for a Working Outline in Speaker's Notes 10.1. Go over the outline with someone whose judgment you respect. Another person sometimes can see problems you might miss because you are too close to the material.

As you review your working outline, keep the audience at the center of your thinking. Remember the advice given to beginning journalists: *Never overestimate your audience's information, and never underestimate their intelligence!* Ask yourself the following questions:

■ Are my main points arranged so they are easy to follow?

■ Do I have sufficient supporting material for each main point?

■ Do I have a variety of supporting materials for each main point?

Speech preparation proceeds in fits and starts, periods of frustration followed by moments of inspiration and revision. You may find yourself making and revising several working outlines before you are satisfied.

Figure 10.2

Sample Working Outline

Topic:	The Greenhouse Effect
Specific purpose:	To inform my audience of the significance of the greenhouse effect.
Thesis statement:	We must understand the greenhouse effect before we can hope to counter global warming.

INTRODUCTION

Attention material:	Antarctic icebergs breaking loose: ominous signs of global warming. Nero fiddled while Rome burned: we're fiddling while the Earth burns.
Thesis statement:	We must understand the greenhouse effect before we can hope to counter global warming.
Preview:	We need to be concerned especially about the loss of woodlands, harmful agricultural and industrial emissions, and our own energy consumption.

(**Transition** to body of speech: "Let's begin by understanding the greenhouse effect.")

BODY

First main point:	The greenhouse effect is a process by which certain gases in the atmosphere retain the heat of the sun.
Subpoint A:	This natural process makes the Earth livable.
Subpoint B:	Process now unbalanced by human activities.
Sub-subpoints:	1. High concentrations of carbon dioxide and methane in the atmosphere.
	2. Artificial heat wave is breaking all temperature records.
	3. This threatens Earth's climate and many living things.

(**Transition** to second main point: "Let's examine the causes, one by one.")

Second main point:	The loss of woodlands adds to the greenhouse effect.
Subpoint A:	Loss from cutting.
Subpoint B:	Loss from clearing.
Subpoint C:	Loss from burning.

(**Transition** to third main point: "An even greater cause is harmful agricultural and industrial emissions.")

Third main point:	Agricultural and industrial emissions accelerate the greenhouse effect.
Subpoint A:	Farming an important part of problem.
Sub-subpoints:	1. Frequent tilling and massive CO_2.
	2. Rice farms and methane.
	3. Cattle ranches and more methane.
Subpoint B:	Industrial emissions from burning fossil fuels another big source of problem.

Begin by writing down your topic, specific purpose, and thesis statement so that you have them clearly in mind.

Sketch your introduction, including attention-getting materials. Notice that this first draft omits any direct effort to build credibility. Establishing your credibility on a topic can sometimes be an important strategy early in the speech.

Labeling the body of the speech points out its importance. Be sure to develop the body of the speech first.

Include transitions to remind yourself to tie material together and make it flow smoothly.

The purpose of the working outline is to allow you to organize ideas and see how they fit together. It does not necessarily follow the numbering and lettering of a formal outline.

Figure 10.2

Sample Working Outline (Continued)

The working outline serves as a guide and provides a check on the structure of the speech.

(**Transition** to fourth main point: "Finally, let's consider the most important cause of the runaway greenhouse effect—ourselves.")

Fourth main point: Our personal energy consumption magnifies the greenhouse effect

    Subpoint A: Both population and prosperity fuel the problem.

       Sub-subpoints: 1. More people = more energy consumption.

             2. Improved living standards add to the problem.

    Subpoint B: Personal energy consumption single largest cause of greenhouse effect.

       Sub-subpoints: 1. Fossil fuels account for 90% of U.S. personal energy consumption.

             2. Personal cars tripled since 1950.

(**Transition:** "In conclusion . . .")

CONCLUSION

Like the introduction, the conclusion is sketched in the working outline. Specific techniques are worked out as outlining proceeds.

Summary statement: The greenhouse effect is the key to understanding global warming. Major causes are loss of woodlands, agricultural and industrial emissions, and increased personal consumption.

Concluding remarks: Future generations will ask why we did this to the quality of their lives.

Developing a Formal Outline

Once you are satisfied with your working outline, you can prepare your formal outline. Developing a **formal outline** is the final stage of planning and structuring your speeches. It imposes a discipline on your preparation and demonstrates to your instructor that the research and planning phase of your work is completed. The formal outline for a speech typically follows basic conventions of outlining. Figure 10.3 shows a formal speech outline format illustrating these conventions:

1. Identification of speech topic, specific purpose, and thesis statement

2. Separation of speech parts: introduction, body, and conclusion

3. Use of numbering and lettering to display coordination and subordination

4. Wording of main points and subpoints as simple declarative sentences

5. A title

6. A list of major sources consulted

formal outline The final outline in a process leading from the first rough ideas for a speech to the finished product.

Figure 10.3

Format for a Formal Outline

TITLE

Topic: _____
Specific purpose: _____
Thesis statement: _____

INTRODUCTION

Attention material: _____
_____

Thesis statement: _____
_____

Preview: _____
_____

(**Transition** into body of speech)

BODY

I. **First main point:** _____
   A. Subpoint or supporting material:_____
   B. Subpoint or supporting material: _____
      1. Sub-subpoint or supporting material: _____
      2. Sub-subpoint or supporting material: _____

(**Transition** into next main point)

II. **Second main point:** _____
   A. Subpoint or supporting material: _____
      1. Sub-subpoint or supporting material: _____
      2. Sub-subpoint or supporting material: _____
   B. Subpoint or supporting material:_____

(**Transition** into next main point)

III. **Third main point:** _____
   A. Subpoint or supporting material: _____
   B. Subpoint or supporting material: _____
      1. Sub-subpoint or supporting material: _____
      2. Sub-subpoint or supporting material: _____
         a. Sub-sub-subpoint or supporting material: _____
         b. Sub-sub-subpoint or supporting material: _____

(**Transition** into conclusion)

CONCLUSION

Summary statement: _____
_____

Concluding remarks: _____
_____

WORKS CONSULTED

Topic, Specific Purpose, and Thesis Statement

Some student speakers recite their topic, specific purpose, and thesis statement at the beginnings of each speech as though they had been programmed: "My topic is. . . . My specific purpose is. . . . My thesis statement is. . . ." This is not a good way to begin a speech! Nevertheless, you should write these headings out at the top of your outline because they help you focus your message. Just don't read the headings to your audience.

Separation of Speech Parts

As you did in the working outline, separate the introduction, body, and conclusion of the speech so that you give each section the careful attention it requires.

Note from the formal outline format shown in Figure 10.3 that only the body of the speech follows an outlining format. In contrast, the introduction and conclusion should be written out as you plan to speak them. As we suggested in Chapter 3, it is better to write out and commit your introduction and conclusion to memory. Doing so helps you get into and out of your speech gracefully and effectively. Although there may be times when you must adapt and change your introduction in light of the situation (we discussed these moments in relation to context in Chapter 5), as a general rule, a carefully worded beginning works best. Knowing *exactly* what you want to say and how you want to say it gets you off to a good start and helps build your confidence. At the end of your speech, the exact wording of your conclusion can influence whether you make a lasting impression.

Numbering and Lettering Your Outline

Figure 10.3 shows you how to use letters, numbers, and indentation to set up a formal outline that follows the principles of coordination and subordination. The actual number of main points and levels of subpoints may vary, but the basic format remains the same. Roman numerals (I, II, III) identify the main points of your speech. Capital letters (A, B, C) identify the subpoints under each main point. Arabic numbers (1, 2, 3) identify the sub-subpoints under any subpoint.

The principle of **coordination** suggests that all statements at a given level (your *I*'s and *II*'s, *A*'s and *B*'s, and so forth) should be of similar importance and receive similar development. In the sample formal outline shown later in this chapter, the main points include an explanation of the greenhouse effect and its three major causes arranged in ascending order of importance (see Figure 9.1 in the previous chapter). Think how strange it would seem if a fifth main point, "The greenhouse effect will decrease our recreational opportunities," were added to this outline. This statement would not be coordinate in importance with the other

Your outline transfers your ideas for your speech from your head onto a piece of paper.

coordination The requirement that statements equal in importance be placed on the same level in an outline.

main points. Nor would it fit within the pattern of relationships. Adding such a main point would violate the principle of coordination.

The principle of **subordination** requires that material descend in importance from the general and abstract main points to the concrete and specific subpoints and sub-subpoints related to them as shown below:

More important   I. Main point   more general

         A. Subpoint

           1. Sub-subpoint

Less important   a. Sub-sub-subpoint more specific

The more important a statement is, the farther to the left it is positioned. If you rotate an outline clockwise so that it rests on its right margin, the "peaks" will represent the main points, the most important ideas in your speech, with the height of the other points representing their relative significance.

The easiest way to demonstrate the importance of coordination and subordination is to look at an abbreviated sample outline that violates these principles. The following "outlines" a speech of demonstration on how to mat a picture to decorate your dorm room or living quarters:

 I. Decide what color mat to use.
   A. Determine the size of your mat.
   B. Select the proper equipment.

 II. You must choose how to back the picture.
   A. How you cut the mat offers options.
   B. Matting the picture requires a decision.

 III. Decide between a straight and bevel cut.
   A. Draw lines before you cut.
   B. Plan the project before taking action.

This collection of ideas may look like an outline, but it isn't. It violates the principles of coordination and subordination. The points at each level are not equal in importance, nor are they related to one another. The most basic problems are that the main points—the major steps in the process—have not been clearly identified and their proper order has not been determined. The main points should focus on planning the project, gathering equipment, cutting the mat, and matting the picture. Once you have the main points clearly in place and entered at the Roman numeral level of the outline, you can arrange the subpoints where they fit:

 I. Planning the project should be your first step.
   A. You must decide on the color of your mat.
   B. You must determine its size.
   C. You must select a type of cut.

 II. You should gather the equipment you will need.
   A. You will need drawing equipment.
   B. You will need cutting equipment.
   C. You will need matting materials.

 III. You can now cut the mat.
   A. Draw the lines for cutting.
   B. Make the cut.

subordination The requirement that material in an outline descend in importance from main points to subpoints to sub-subpoints to sub-sub-subpoints.

    IV. Matting the picture is the final step.
        A. Attach the picture to the mat.
        B. Back the picture.

Even the improved version hardly qualifies as a completed outline. The outline would have to proceed to the sub-subpoint level, offering further details, for example, on equipment options, choices among matting materials, and different strategies for cutting. But at least it would be headed *in the direction* of a useful outline, thanks to observing the principles of coordination and subordination.

Wording Your Outline

Each main point and subpoint in your outline should be worded as a simple declarative sentence containing only one idea. It should not be weighted down with qualifying, dependent clauses. For example, the following does not make a good main point sentence:

"Bad eating habits endanger health and lower feelings of self-worth, reducing life span and causing personal anguish." The sentence works better in an outline if it is simplified in the following way:

    I.   Bad eating habits are a threat to our well-being.
        A. Bad eating habits endanger health.
            1. They can result in increased heart disease.
            2. They can shorten the life span.
        B. Bad eating habits can damage self-image.
            1. Obese people sometimes dislike themselves.
            2. They can feel that they have nothing to offer others.

Breaking the complex sentence down into outline form helps you to focus what you are going to say. It simplifies and clarifies both the structure and the logic of your speech.

Try to use **parallel construction** when wording the main points of your speech. In parallel construction, *successive sentences or phrases follow the same pattern of wording to emphasize an idea.* If you were developing a speech on the need for reforms in political campaign financing, you might word your main points as follows:

    I. We need reform at the national level.
    II. We need reform at the state level.
    III. We need reform at the local level.
    IV. But first, we need to reform ourselves.

If you used these words in the introduction of your speech, the parallel construction would give listeners a guide to the structure of your speech. You could also repeat the parallel pattern as you summarize your speech, further imprinting its message on the minds of your listeners.

Parallel construction has many advantages. Because each sentence has the same basic structure, it can serve as a transition between main ideas. And because any variations tend to stand out sharply, such variation helps to emphasize important points. In this example, the parallel structure helps the speech narrow its focus like a zoom lens as it moves from a national to an individual perspective.

Using parallel construction for your main points can also help you develop internal summaries: "We have looked at reform at the national, state, and local levels, so

parallel construction Wording points in a similar fashion to emphasize their importance and to help the audience remember them.

now we come to the most important part of the problem—ourselves." Since it involves repetition, it makes your message easy to remember. It satisfies the principles of good form, as discussed in Chapter 9.

Supporting Your Main Points

Your formal outline should show how supporting materials fit into your speech. As we noted in Chapter 8, supporting materials strengthen the points you make. For example, a subpoint that states, "Global warming is causing climate changes" might need a factual example and expert testimony to substantiate that claim: "According to statistics from the National Atmospheric and Oceanic Association, the summer of 2006 was the hottest on record." In particular, be sure that each main point receives the type and amount of supporting material it needs to be effective. In Chapter 8, we offered guidelines for deciding what supporting materials you should use if your ideas are controversial, abstract, technical, or distant from the lives of your listeners. In Chapter 9, we described how to work supporting materials into your speech. You should go back and review this material as you prepare your outline.

Title

For speeches given outside the classroom, a title may help attract listeners to a presentation. A good title arouses curiosity. It makes people want to hear the message. You may wish to mention your title in your introduction and then refer to it throughout the speech as a reminder of your thesis statement. However, you don't want to begin your speech by simply stating your title. Rather, find some artful way to weave the title into your introduction in order to focus attention. The following provides a model:

> As I think about the meaning of my speech, I am drawn to my title, "Life in the Greenhouse." How is "Life in the Greenhouse"? I can tell you in one word, "Warm." Warm and getting warmer. Warmer and going global.

You should wait until you have outlined your speech before you select a title. Your title should not promise too much or deceive the audience. Titles that promise everything from eternal peace of mind to the end of taxation often disappoint listeners. Overblown titles also can damage your ethos.

Changing Your Working Outline to a Formal Outline

How can you change your working outline to a formal outline? In the working example provided in Figure 10.2, the third main point appears as follows:

Third main point: Agricultural and industrial emissions accelerate the greenhouse effect.
Subpoint A: Farming an important part of problem.
Sub-subpoints: 1. Frequent tilling and massive CO_2.
2. Rice farms add methane.
3. Cattle ranches add more methane.
Subpoint B: Industrial emissions from burning fossil fuels are another big source of the problem.

To transform this into a formal outline, first, you must use numbering and lettering to indicate coordination and subordination among your points. Second, you should write your points in complete sentences and finish any incomplete structuring, such as we see in subpoint B (it has no sub-subpoints). In the formal outline shown in Figure 10.4, the third main point would take the following form:

III. Farming and industrial practices add more heat to the greenhouse effect (Kluger, "Tipping Point").

 A. Farming is no small part of the problem.
  1. Frequent tilling releases massive CO_2.
  2. Rice farms add methane.
  3. Cattle ranches add still more methane.

 B. Industrial emissions from fossil fuels are a major part of the problem.
  1. Smokestacks strain to produce more energy.
  2. Fleets of trucks crowd the nation's highways.
  3. Flocks of airplanes crisscross the skies.

The final step is to add source citations. Notice that the major source of supporting material (Kluger, "Tipping Point") is indicated in parentheses at the end of the statement of the main point. This brief **source citation** is a cue to the full citation in the list of **works cited** or **works consulted** at the end of the formal outline. Placement of the citation at the end of the main point means that this source supports all claims in the subpoints and sub-subpoints below it. If the citation were placed at the end of a subpoint or sub-subpoint, the citation would apply only to that subpoint or sub-subpoint.

Putting abbreviated source citations in your outline reminds you of the importance of documenting points as you speak. These citations tell your instructor that you have integrated your research into your speech and have met the challenge of acquiring responsible knowledge. Follow these simple guidelines for making brief citations within the outline:

- List the last name of the author plus the page number when more than one page is cited: (Kluger 34).

- List the author's last name with an abbreviated title if you are citing more than one work by the same author: (Kluger, "What now?").

- If the "author" is a group or institution, list the name: (*Science & Space*); if the sponsoring group is not provided, list the first words of the title ("God's Green Soldiers").

Remember: Documenting your sources in your outline does not satisfy the need for oral documentation as you present your speech. Your listeners are not privy to the written citations in your formal outline. Listeners do not really want or need to know every detail offered in these citations. Rather, oral documentation is selective, focusing on the source, source's credentials, the publication, and date as these become more or less relevant to making a point authoritatively and impressively. In other words, you hit the highpoints of your written citations, but you avoid the pedantic repetition of every detail.

Oral documentation in your presentation allows you to give credit where credit is due and to enjoy credit for your own careful research. Citing expert sources as you speak also enhances your ethos and helps forestall any suspicion of plagiarism.

---

source citation References in a speech to sources used.

works cited A form of bibliography in an outline that lists those sources of supporting material actually used in the speech.

works consulted A form of bibliography that lists all sources of research considered in the preparation of the speech.

Figure 10.4

Sample Formal Outline

Title:	Life in the Greenhouse
Topic:	Major Causes of the Greenhouse Effect
Specific Purpose:	To inform listeners of the major causes of the greenhouse effect
Thesis Statement:	Before we can control global warming. we must understand the nature and causes of the greenhouse effect.

INTRODUCTION

Attention Materials:	Seas rising along our coastlines. Temperatures setting new records almost every year. Wildfires raging out of control in the West and South. The number and ferocity of hurricanes and tornadoes doubling over the past 30 years. These are the symptoms of global warming, the great environmental disease of our time. But global warming happens because of a phenomenon called "the greenhouse effect."
Thesis Statement:	Before we can control global warming, we must understand the nature and causes of the greenhouse effect.
Preview:	We need to understand first, the loss of woodlands, second, harmful agricultural and industrial practices, and third, our own personal energy consumption.

(Transition: "Let's begin by defining the greenhouse effect.")

BODY

I. The greenhouse effect is a process by which certain gases in the atmosphere retain the heat of the sun (*Science & Space*).
    A. This natural process makes the earth livable.
    B. Process is now unbalanced by human activities.
        1. High concentrations of carbon dioxide have collected in the atmosphere.
        2. Artificial heat wave is breaking all temperature records: 2006 hottest year of the millennium.
    C. This threatens earth's climate and many living things—including us!
(Transition: "Let's examine the causes.")

II. Loss of forests adds to the greenhouse effect. (Kluger, "What now?")

    A. Cutting the woods and rain forests for timber is major global problem.
    B. Deliberate burning to create land for farming is even worse.
    C. Wildfires in our country are still another symptom of earth's sickness.
(Transition: "Agricultural and industrial emissions are even greater causes of the greenhouse effect.")

III. Farming and industrial practices add more heat to the greenhouse effect (Kluger, "The Tipping Point").

Stating your specific purpose and thesis statement helps you keep them in mind as you outline your speech.

Labeling the introduction shows that it is an important part of the speech.

Examples help gain attention. Citing numerous sources early in the speech enhances credibility.

Previewing the speech helps listeners follow the message.

The use of transitions helps listeners track the progress of the speech.

The first main point defines the greenhouse effect and provides reasons to listen.

Placing the citation at the end of the first point indicates that it is important.

This transition signals a change of focus from explanation to causes.

The causes of the greenhouse effect are arranged in order of increasing importance. Since the loss of woodlands contributes less than the other causes discussed, it receives less attention.

Figure 10.4

Sample Formal Outline (Continued)

The third main point is more developed than the second. The presentation will be more interesting if examples are used.

A. Farming is no small part of the problem.
　　1. Frequent tiling releases massive CO_2.
　　2. Rice farms add methane.
　　3. Cattle ranches add still more methane.
B. Industrial emissions from fossil fuels are a major part of the problem.
　　1. Smokestacks strain to produce more energy.
　　2. Fleets of trucks crowd the nation's highways.
　　3. Flocks of airplanes crisscross the skies.

This transition signals a change of focus.

(Transition: "Finally, let's consider the most important cause of the greenhouse effect—ourselves.")

IV. Our personal energy consumption magnifies the greenhouse effect (*Science & Space*).
　　A. Both population and prosperity fuel the problem.
　　　　1. More people means more energy consumption.
　　　　2. The quest for better global living standards compounds the problem.
　　B. We—the Americans—are the world's greatest energy hogs!
　　　　1. Fossil fuels account for 90% of our personal energy consumption.
　　　　2. Number of personal cars has tripled since 1950.

CONCLUSION

The conclusion creates a startling image as it summarizes the message. It uses rhetorical questions arranged in parallel construction for concluding remarks.

Summary statement:　Step outside into the greenhouse. Listen for the falling trees, watch the smokestacks darkening the sky, smell the rich bouquet of fumes.

Concluding remarks:　Future generations will ask: Why did we carelessly, willfully, ignorantly allow this to happen to their world? Why did we poison planet Earth?"

The references in the works consulted follow the MLA format.

WORKS CONSULTED

"Global Warming Is Rapidly Raising Sea Levels, Studies Warn," *National Geographic News*, 23 March 2006, http://news.nationalgeographic.com/news/2006/03/0323_060323_global _warming.html.
"God's Green Soldiers," *Newsweek*, 13 Feb, 2006: 49.
"GOP Ex-EPA Chiefs Bash Bush Policies," CNN:com, 18 Jan. 2006, www.cnn.com/2006/POLITICS/01/18/global.warming.ap/index.html, 19 Jan. 2006.
Kluger, Jeffrey, "What now? Our Feverish Planet Badly Needs a Cure," *Time*, 9 Apr. 2007: 51–60.
Kluger, Jeffrey, "The Tipping Point," *Time*, 3 Apr. 2006: 28–42.
"Report: Humans 'Very Likely' Cause Global Warming," *Science & Space*, 2 Feb. 2007, www.cnn.com/2007/TECH/science/02/02/climate.change.report/index.html, 2 Feb 2007.

Speaker's Notes *10.2*

Guidelines for Oral Documentation

To develop effective oral documentation, follow these guidelines:

1. Identify the publication in which the material appears.

2. Identify the time frame of the publication.

3. Offer "highlight" credentials for the experts you cite.

4. Select direct quotations that are brief and that will have an impact.

5. Avoid presenting every detail of the written citation.

6. Controversial and time-sensitive material requires fuller oral documentation.

Listing Your References

A list of your major sources of information should appear at the end of your formal outline as "Works Cited" or "Works Consulted." The former lists just those sources you actually cite in your speech; the latter lists all works you consulted during research preparation. Ask your instructor which of these procedures she or he prefers.

The references indicate the range of your research. They are evidence that you have searched for responsible knowledge of your subject. If any of your sources are challenged, the list provides information to validate what you have said. When citing

InterConnections.
LearnMore 10.2

Online Guides to Citation Style

Citing Sources and Avoiding Plagiarism: Documentation Guides

www.lib.duke.edu/libguide/citing.htm

A comprehensive resource that can help you find examples of all types of citations rendered side by side in APA, Chicago, MLA, and Turabian formats. Developed and maintained by Kelley A. Lawton and Laura Cousineau, Duke University Libraries, and Van E. Hillard, The University Writing Program, Duke University.

Columbia Guide to Online Style

www.columbia.edu/cu/cup/cgos2006/basic.html

This well-developed site includes material excerpted from Columbia University Press's hard-copy style guide covering the elements of citation and the preparation of bibliographic material. Contains abundant examples. Developed and maintained by Columbia University Press.

Citing Electronic Documentation: APA, Chicago, and MLA Styles

www.rhetoric.umn.edu/Student/Graduate/%7Emstewart/citations

An up-to-date guide for citing electronic resources using three major style manuals. Contains separate links for the guidelines of each style. Developed and maintained by Professor Mark D. Stewart, Department of Rhetoric, University of Minnesota.

Electronic References

www.apastyle.org/elecref.html

This Web site contains material excerpted from the Publication Manual of the American Psychological Association. You can sign up for automatic e-mail updates and hints issued weekly.

Figure 10.5

MLA and APA Citation Styles

Book: Single Author
MLA   Mann, Thomas. <u>The Oxford Guide to Library Research</u>. New York:
            Oxford UP, 1998.
APA   Mann, T. (1998) <u>The Oxford Guide to Library Research</u>. New York:
            Oxford University Press.

Book: Two or More Authors
MLA   Alexander, Janet E., and Marsha Anne Tate. <u>Web Wisdom: How to</u>
            <u>Evaluate and Create Information Quality on the Web</u>. Mahwah, NJ:
            Lawrence Erlbaum, 1999.
APA   Alexander, J. E., & Tate, M. A. (1999) <u>Web Wisdom: How to</u>
            <u>Evaluate and Create Information Quality on the Web</u>. Mahwah, NJ:
            Lawrence Erlbaum.

Book: Second or Later Edition
MLA   Schlein, Alan M. <u>Find It Online: The Complete Guide to Online Research</u>.
            3rd ed. Tempe, AZ: Facts on Demand Press, 2003.
APA   Schlein, A. M. (2003). <u>Find It Online: The Complete Guide to Online</u>
            <u>Research</u> (3rd ed.). Tempe, AZ: Facts on Demand Press.

Book: Corporate Authors
MLA   American Association of Cereal Chemists. <u>Sweeteners</u>. St. Paul, MN:
            American Association of Cereal Chemists, 1998.
APA   American Association of Cereal Chemists. (1998). <u>Sweeteners</u>. St. Paul,
            MN: American Association of Cereal Chemists.

Signed Article in Reference Work
MLA   Richardson, Brenda L. "Heart Health." <u>Everywoman's Encyclopedia</u>.
            New York: Wellness Press, 2003.
APA   Richardson, B. L. (2003) Heart health. In <u>Everywoman's Encyclopedia</u>
            (pp. 202-206). New York: Wellness Press.

Unsigned Article in Reference Work
MLA   "Musik, Melody." <u>Who's Who in the South, 2003-2004</u>. Mentone, AL:
            Southern Who's Who, 2004.
APA   Musik, Melody (2004). In <u>Who's who in the south, 2003-2004</u> (p. 146).
            Mentone, AL: Southern Who's Who.

Signed Magazine Article
MLA   Stix, Gary. "Ultimate Self-Improvement." <u>Scientific American</u> Sept.
            2003: 44-45.
APA   Stix, G. (2003 September) Ultimate Self-Improvement. <u>Scientific</u>
            <u>American</u>, pp. 44-45.

Unsigned Magazine Article
MLA   "Primary Sources." <u>Atlantic Monthly</u> Nov. 2003: 54-55.
APA   Primary Sources (2003 October). <u>Atlantic Monthly</u>, pp. 54-55.

Figure 10.5

MLA and APA Citation Styles (Continued)

Journal Article
MLA   Barge, J. Kevin. "Hope, Communication, and Community Building."
          Southern Communication Journal 69 (2003): 63-81.
APA   Barge, J. K. (2003). Hope, Communication, and Community Building.
          Southern Communication Journal, 69, 63-81.

Signed Newspaper Article
MLA   Beifuss, John. "Who's Hoping for an Oscar?" Memphis Register 14 Feb.
          2004: E6.
APA   Beifuss, J. (2004, Feb. 14). Who's hoping for an Oscar? Memphis
          Register, p. E6.

Unsigned Newspaper Article
MLA   "It's Gut-check Time," Louisville Chronicle, 23 February 2004: C1.
APA   It's gut-check time. (2004, Feb. 23). Louisville Chronicle, p. C1.

Government Publication
MLA   United States. Environmental Protection Agency. New Motor Vehicles
          and New Motor Vehicle Engines Air Pollution Control: Voluntary
          Standards for Light-Duty Vehicles. Washington, D.C. : Government
          Printing Office, 1998.
APA   U.S. Environmental Protection Agency. (1998). New Motor Vehicles
          and New Motor Vehicle Engines Air Pollution Control: Voluntary
          Standards for Light-Duty Vehicles. Washington, D.C. : Government
          Printing Office.

Personal Interview
MLA   Hogan, Michael. Personal interview. 19 Feb. 2004.
APA   Hogan, M. (2004, February 19). [Personal interview].

Letter or E-Mail Communication
MLA   McGee, Michael Calvin. E-mail to the author. 9 July 2002.
APA   McGee, M. C. (mmcgee@dreammail.net). (2002, July 9). Reply to
          Questions for Book. E-mail to S. Osborn (sso@mailmyth.net).

Speech or Lecture
MLA   Vidulic, Robert. Lecture on dogmatism. Psychology 4231: Social
          Psychology. University of Memphis, 15 March 2004.
APA   Vidulic, R. (2004, March 15). Dogmatism [Lecture]. In Psychology
          4231: Social Psychology. University of Memphis.

World Wide Web Document
MLA   Today: Health. "Can You Spot a Liar?" 29 Jan. 2004.
          <http://www.msnbc.msn.com/id/4072816/> 29 Jan. 2004.
APA   Today: Health. (2004, January 29). Can you spot a liar? [Online].
          Available: http://www.msnbc.msn.com/id/4072816/. [2004, 29
          January].

Checklist for a Formal Outline

To test the completeness of your formal outline, see if it passes the following tests:

1. My topic and specific purpose are clearly stated.

2. My thesis statement is written as a declarative sentence.

3. My introduction contains material to create attention, establish my credibility, and preview my message.

4. My main points represent the most important ideas on my topic.

5. My main points are similar in importance.

6. My main points are stated as declarative sentences.

7. Each main point is supported by facts, statistics, testimony, examples, or narratives.

8. My subpoints are divisions of the main points they follow and are written as simple sentences.

9. My subpoints are more specific than the main points they follow.

10. My conclusion contains a summary statement and concluding remarks that reflect on the meaning of the speech.

11. I have provided transitions where they are needed to make my speech flow smoothly.

12. I have compiled a list of works cited or consulted in the preparation of my speech.

Internet sources, be sure to provide full citations that include dates accessed so that your instructor can verify your research. The Modern Language Association (MLA) and the American Psychological Association (APA) have published guidelines for constructing such lists. Other protocols include the *Chicago Manual of Style* and the *Turabian Manual for Writers of Term Papers, Theses, and Dissertations*. Ask your instructor which style you should use. For your convenience, Figure 10.5 provides an abridged compilation of the MLA and APA citation formats for the kinds of sources most frequently used in speeches.

After you have completed your formal outline, review it using the Checklist for a Formal Outline in Speaker's Notes 10.3.

Developing a Key-Word Outline

Your formal outline is a blueprint of your speech but not the speech itself. *Do not use your formal outline as you present your speech.* If you do, you will be tempted to read it, which in turn will prevent effective eye contact and authentic interaction with your audience. Instead, you should prepare and speak from a **key-word outline**, usually recorded on index cards, that reduce the main and supporting points of your formal outline to essential words or phrases that will jog your memory and keep you on track during your presentation.

To develop such an outline, simply identify one to three "key" terms in each main point, subpoint, and sub-subpoint and record them on index cards so that they provide an essential overview of the speech. Depending on the length of your speech, you may wish to prepare separate cards for the introduction, the conclusion, and each main point. Include prompts that will remind you to document points. Write out quotations in full on separate cards so that you can quote them with accuracy. You may find it helpful to put your key-word outline on white cards and use colored cards for quotations or material you want to read. Number your cards so you can keep them in order as you speak. Remember that the more cards you carry

key-word outline An abbreviated version of a formal outline that may be used in presenting a speech.

to the lectern, the greater the possibility of confusion. Do not write on both the front and back of note cards.

Keep your note cards as uncluttered as possible so you can refer to them at a glance. *As a general rule, the more your speech is outlined in your head rather than on paper, the better.*

When writing your key-word outline, print in large letters and keep a generous amount of space between points so they stand out clearly. As you practice, add presentation cues to the cards, such as "pause here" or "slow down." Above all, *do not write a mini manuscript of your speech on twenty note cards!* As with trying to speak from a formal "full-sentence" outline, it simply won't work.

Let's return to the third main point of the formal outline on the greenhouse speech to see how it might be turned into a key-word outline format:

III. Agricultural and industrial **emissions** accelerate the greenhouse effect (Kluger, Turning Point)
    A. **Farming** is an important part of problem.
        1. Frequent **tilling** releases massive CO_2.
        2. **Rice farms** add methane.
        3. **Cattle** ranches add more methane.
    B. **Industrial** emissions from fossil fuels are a major part of problem.
        1. **Smokestacks** strain to produce more energy.
        2. Fleets of **trucks** crowd the nation's highways.
        3. Flocks of **airplanes** crisscross the skies.

In this example, we bold-faced the key-words for the main point, each subpoint, and each sub-subpoint. They then convert into the following key-word format:

III. Cause 2: Emissions (Kluger, TP, Card 3)
    A. Farming
        1. Tilling
        2. Rice farms
        3. Cattle
    B. Industrial
        1. Smokestacks
        2. Trucks
        3. Airplanes (pause for emphasis)

Your key-word outline should fit onto a single sheet of paper or a few note cards.

Once you have reduced your speech to a key-word outline, practice using it several times. Speak up, work in your gestures, and force yourself not to look constantly at your cards. Your audience, however, will not notice nor care if you glance occasionally at them, so do not try to hide them. If you are right handed, hold them in your left hand so that you leave the other hand free to gesture. Shuffle your cards from front to back as you move from point to point during your presentation.

When you feel confident that you know your speech, put your notes aside and rest a while before practicing again. If the key-words still jog your memory and keep you on track, you should be ready for your presentation. See Chapter 13 for an extended discussion of rehearsing your speech.

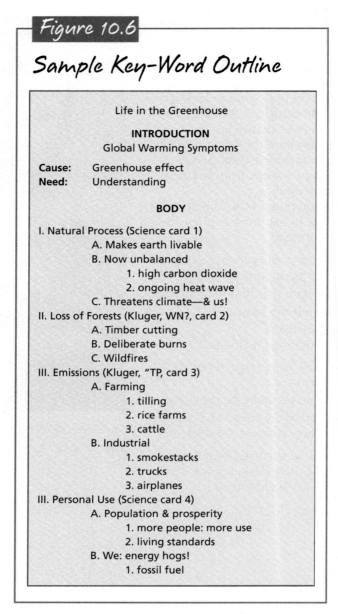

Figure 10.6

Sample Key-Word Outline

Life in the Greenhouse

INTRODUCTION
Global Warming Symptoms

Cause: Greenhouse effect
Need: Understanding

BODY

I. Natural Process (Science card 1)
     A. Makes earth livable
     B. Now unbalanced
         1. high carbon dioxide
         2. ongoing heat wave
     C. Threatens climate—& us!
II. Loss of Forests (Kluger, WN?, card 2)
     A. Timber cutting
     B. Deliberate burns
     C. Wildfires
III. Emissions (Kluger, "TP, card 3)
     A. Farming
         1. tilling
         2. rice farms
         3. cattle
     B. Industrial
         1. smokestacks
         2. trucks
         3. airplanes
III. Personal Use (Science card 4)
     A. Population & prosperity
         1. more people: more use
         2. living standards
     B. We: energy hogs!
         1. fossil fuel

The speaker has added prompts for presentation.

This key-word outline follows the same format used in the formal outline. It contains just enough information to keep the speaker focused on the sequence of points and subpoints. The single words and short phrases prevent the speaker from reading the speech.

In Summary

An outline provides an overview of what you want to say and how you want to say it. It can sharpen and improve the structure of your speech.

Your working outline is a tentative plan of your speech that helps you clarify the relationships among your ideas, shows the relative importance of your points, and depicts how they fit together. By developing working outlines, you can judge the effectiveness of your research and determine if you need additional material.

The formal outline follows the conventions of coordination and subordination. Coordination requires that statements that are alike in type and importance be at the same level in the outline. Subordination requires that statements descend in importance from main points through subpoints and sub-subpoints. As you descend through these points, they become more specific and concrete.

The main points in a formal outline should be worded as simple declarative sentences containing only one idea. Parallel construction helps listeners remember your message. Source citations provide documentation. Do not forget to provide oral documentation for major evidence and ideas as you present your speech.

A formal outline concludes with a list of works cited or works consulted. The most frequently used formats for such lists are those issued by the Modern Language Association and the American Psychological Association.

A key-word outline reduces the formal outline to a few essential words or phrases that remind you of the content and design of your speech. Notes on the key-word outline can also remind you of presentation strategies. Put quotations on index cards to use during presentation.

Explore and Apply the Ideas in This Chapter

1. Working in small groups, share a working outline for your next speech. Explain your strategy for structure, and show how your outline satisfies the principles of coordination and subordination. Demonstrate that you have adequate supporting materials for each main point in your speech. Revise your outline as appropriate in light of the group discussion that follows.

2. Select one of the speeches from Appendix B and prepare a formal outline of it. Does this outline clarify the structure of the speech? Does it reveal any structural flaws? Can you see any different ways the speaker might have developed the speech? Present your thoughts on these questions in class discussion.

3. Thinking back to the last round of speeches you heard in your class, come up with titles for three of them that could be used in advance advertising to attract an audience.

4. See if you can "unjumble" the following outline of the body of a speech using the principles of coordination and subordination. What title would you suggest for this speech?

Thesis statement: Deer hunting with a camera can be an exciting sport.

    I.   There is a profound quiet, a sense of mystery.
       A. The woods in late fall are enchanting.
          1. The film-hunter becomes part of a beautiful scene.
          2. Dawn is especially lovely.
       B. Time that a big doe walked under my tree stand.
          1. When they appear, deer always surprise you.
          2. How a big buck surprised me after a long stalk.

   II. Hunting from a stand can be a good way to capture a deer on film.
       A. The stalk method on the ground is another way to hunt with a camera.
          1. Learn to recognize deer tracks and droppings.
             a. Learn to recognize deer signs
             b. Learn to recognize rubs and scrapes.
          2. Hunt into the wind and move slowly.
       B. There are two main ways to hunt with a camera.
          1. Stands offer elevation above the deer's line of sight.
          2. Portable stands are also available.
          3. Locating and building your permanent stand.

  III. The right camera can be no more expensive than a rifle.
       A. Selecting the right camera for film-hunting is important.
       B. Certain features, such as a zoom lens, are necessary.

  IV. Display slide of doe.
       A. You can collect "trophies" you can enjoy forever.
       B. Display slide of buck.
       C. You can also use a camcorder.
       D. Not all hunters are killers.
       E. The film-hunter celebrates life, not death.

11

Presentation Aids

*Seeing . . . most of all the senses, makes
us know and brings to light many
differences between things.*

—*Aristotle*

And, the winner of the 2007 Academy Award for the best documentary film is—*An Inconvenient Truth*! This film is a state-of-the-art multimedia presentation. According to its director, Davis Guggenheim, the producers came to him and said: "Gore's got a slide show on Global Warming. We want to make a movie. I thought it was a terrible idea—a film about a slide show, starring a former politician! They insisted I see Gore give the slide show. It blew my mind, I was shaken to my core."[1]

The presentation aids you learn to develop and use in this class will not be as elaborate or as sophisticated as those in the award-winning film, but the principle remains the same: *Presentation aids can really make a difference in the effectiveness of your speeches.* You should learn how to produce simple presentation aids and how to integrate them into your speeches.

With the advent of computer technologies, the types and uses of presentation aids are multiplying rapidly. In this chapter, we describe both the traditional and newer kinds of presentation aids, identify the ways they can be used in speeches, offer suggestions for preparing them, and present guidelines for their use.

You should use presentation aids only when they increase the clarity and effectiveness of your speech. As you read this chapter, you will notice that certain suggestions are repeated time and again: Keep things simple and be consistent! These considerations are primary to whatever type of presentation aid you use.

The Advantages and Disadvantages of Presentation Aids

 resentation aids give your audience direct sensory contact with your message. When properly prepared and used, they can help speeches in many different ways. But if they are used improperly, they can become a liability.

Advantages of Presentation Aids

Presentation aids complement the weakness of words as communication tools. As powerful as words can be, they are essentially abstract. They represent objects and ideas, but they are not the objects and ideas they represent. Thus, words can create a barrier of abstraction between listeners and reality. Imagine how hard it would be through words alone to describe the carburetor system of a car. Even with models or charts, such a speech would still be difficult for many of us to understand. It can require both words and presentation aids, used skillfully together, to explain some topics to some audiences. The concreteness of presentation aids gives them some specific advantages:

- **Presentation aids increase understanding.** Words are abstractions that listeners transform into mental images. A real problem arises when different listeners conjure up different mental images for the same words. Some of these images in the minds of listeners may not be consistent with what you intend. As a speaker, you have more control over these images when you present both words and visuals to augment them. It is easier to give directions to someone when there is a map that both of you can see. Similarly, it is easier to explain the steps in a process when listeners are shown the numbered steps on a list.

- **Good presentation aids make your speech more memorable.** Recent research suggests that audiences recall an informative presentation better when visuals are used and that recall is even better when the visuals are in high-quality color.[2] Other research suggests that we typically remember only 20 percent of what we hear, but if we *both hear and see* something, we remember more than 50 percent.[3] Presentation aids are easier to remember than words because they are concrete. A photograph of a hungry child may linger in your memory, thus increasing the influence of a speech urging you to contribute to a cause.

presentation aids Visual and auditory illustrations intended to enhance the clarity and effectiveness of a presentation.

■ **Presentation aids help establish the authenticity of your words.** When you show listeners what you are talking about, you demonstrate that it actually exists. This type of evidence is important in both informative and persuasive messages. If your audience can actually see the differences between videotapes and DVDs, they are more likely to be convinced that one is better than the other.

■ **Neat, well-designed presentation aids enhance your credibility.** They tell listeners that you put extra effort into preparing your speech. Speakers who use presentation aids are judged to be more professional, better prepared, more credible, more interesting, more concrete, and more persuasive than speakers who do not use such aids.[4] In some organizational settings, audiences expect speakers to use presentation aids, such as PowerPoint slides. If you don't have them, the audience may be disappointed, and your credibility may suffer.

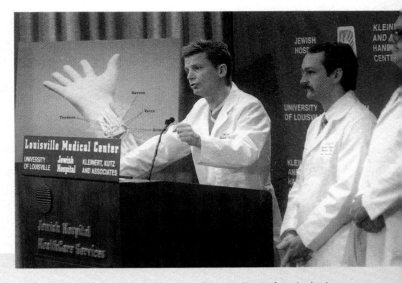

Presentation aids help increase understanding of technical concepts.

■ **Presentation aids can help improve your delivery skills.** Using a presentation aid encourages movement as you display your aid. Movement energizes a speech. It gets you away from the "stand behind the lectern/talking head" mode of delivery that many audiences find boring. If you have problems with communication apprehension, purposeful movement—such as pointing to something on an aid you are displaying—provides a constructive outlet for nervous energy. It directs your attention away from yourself and away from your problem.

■ **Presentation aids add variety and interest to a speech.** Too much of a good thing, even a well-fashioned fabric of words, can seem tedious. Just as pictures and boxed materials may be used to break up long stretches of text in a book, presentation aids can be used to break up long stretches of words in a speech. Variety creates interest and helps sustain or recapture attention.

Disadvantages of Presentation Aids

Occasionally, presentation aids can do your speech more harm than good. It is important to be aware of these potential problems so that you can plan to lessen their impact.

■ **Presentation aids may distract listeners.** They can draw attention away from your message if they are not used properly. For example, if an aid is difficult for listeners to read, they may strain to see it and not listen to what you are saying. You may also create a distraction if you pass around objects or pictures during a speech or if you distribute handouts before speaking. Listeners may become so engrossed in your presentation aids that they ignore your real message.

An unusual presentation aid can upstage a speaker completely. We once had a student who was a volunteer with the local rescue squad. He gave a persuasive speech urging his classmates to volunteer. After his introduction, he announced, "Now we are all going outside." When we got outside, there was

---

Figure 11.1

Major Advantages and Disadvantages of Presentation Aids

Advantages	Disadvantages
1. Increased understanding	1. Can distract listeners
2. Makes message memorable	2. Can distract speaker
3. Adds authenticity	3. Reduced eye contact
4. Improved speaker credibility	4. Damaged credibility if sloppy
5. Improves delivery	5. Takes time to prepare
6. Adds variety and interest	6. Depends on equipment availability

---

an emergency vehicle. While the speaker tried to tell listeners about the equipment, they were climbing in and out of the vehicle. He lost their attention completely and was never able to complete his speech. Don't make this type of mistake. Keep the focus on your words, not your presentation aid.

■ **Presentation aids can distract speakers.** If you haven't practiced your speech using your presentation aid, you may worry so much about how you are going to use it that you lose track of what you are saying. If you are not confident in your ability to use electronic equipment, this uneasiness may show up in your presentation. If something goes awry with the equipment, it might throw you completely off course.

■ **Presentation aids can reduce eye contact between the speaker and the audience.** Remember, eye contact is very important to an effective presentation. If you talk to your charts, graphs, or pictures rather than to your listeners, you will lose effectiveness.

■ **A poor presentation aid can damage your credibility.** If your aid is sloppy or inaccurate, your credibility will suffer. Listeners may think you did not care enough about your presentation to invest the time and effort needed to prepare an effective presentation aid. Worse still, they may think you are incapable of preparing one. So allow enough time to do a good job preparing your presentation aids. And don't forget to practice using your aids so you can integrate them smoothly into your presentation. If you are artistically challenged, use all the tools available to put together an effective presentation aid.

■ **Presentation aids put you at the mercy of the equipment.** If the speech site is not equipped to handle computerized presentation aids, then you must use other forms. Be sure you know in advance what kind of equipment is available. Also be sure you know how to operate the equipment and have a plan to fall back on in case anything goes wrong.

InterConnections.
LearnMore 11.1
Presentation Aids

Think Outside the Slide

www.thinkoutsidetheslide.com

Contains a variety of how-to articles for technology-enhanced presentations. Presents good, practical advice for beginning or advanced speakers who wish to improve their presentations. Developed and maintained by Dave Paradi, communicating with technology specialist.

Designing Effective Visuals

www.kumc.edu/SAH/OTEd/jradel/Effective_visuals/VisStrt.html

An online tutorial designed to help medical personnel make better oral presentations. Contains guidelines for deciding which presentation aids to use and how to maximize their visual impact. Designed and maintained by Jeff Radel, professor in the Department of Occupational Therapy Education, University of Kansas Medical Center.

Types of Presentation Aids

The number and types of presentation aids you might use are limited only by your imagination. In this section, we discuss some of the more frequently used kinds of presentation aids: people, objects, models, graphics, and pictures.

People

You are always a presentation aid (for good or for bad) for your speeches. Your body, grooming, actions, gestures, voice, facial expressions, and demeanor are important considerations. What you wear for a presentation can influence how your speech is received. If you will be speaking on camping and wilderness adventures, blue jeans and a flannel shirt might be appropriate. If you are a nurse discussing a medical topic, your uniform might enhance your credibility. If you are talking about how to dress for an employment interview, your own attire should illustrate your recommendations. We discuss the importance of personal appearance in more detail in Chapter 13.

You can also use other people as presentation aids. John Kache was a freshman in college when he contracted meningococcal meningitis, a life-threatening disease for which immunizations are available. John survived his illness, but he lost his right leg and all of the fingers on his hands. After his recovery, he often spoke to high school students, urging them to get their shots before they went off to college. Typically, he would use a volunteer from the audience to demonstrate what life without fingers was like for him. As he put it, "I'd wrap up one of the student's hands in an Ace bandage, then throw him a bag of candy and tell him to open it and pass the candies around."[5] This demonstration dramatically illustrated the seriousness of this disease and the importance of being immunized.

Your use of people as a presentation aid does not need to be this dramatic to be effective. One of our students, Neomal Abyskera, used two of his classmates to illustrate the lineup positions in the game of rugger, as played in his native Sri Lanka. At the appropriate moment, Neomal said, "Pete and Jeff will show you how the opposing players line up." While his classmates demonstrated the shoulder grip position, Neomal explained when and why the position was assumed. The demonstration was more understandable than if he had simply tried to describe the positioning verbally or had used stick-figure drawings.

The people you ask to function as a presentation aid should be willing to do so. They should understand that their role is to illustrate your message, *not draw attention away from it,* and should agree to meet with you to rehearse the presentation. During the presentation, they should sit in the front row so that they can come forward when you need them.

Objects and Models

Displaying the actual objects you are discussing can gain attention, increase understanding, and add authenticity to your speech. If using actual objects is a problem, models can be used.

Objects.   An object for a presentation aid should be portable and easy for listeners to see without straining. You should also be able to keep the object out of sight when you are not talking about it. If you display the object throughout your speech, listeners may pay more attention to it than to your message. If you will be using more than one object, display them one at a time, and then conceal them when you have finished. One student speaker brought in six different objects to illustrate her talk. She lined them up across the front of the desk before beginning to speak. A classmate in the front row was so fascinated with them that he scooted his chair closer to the desk and picked up one to examine. The speaker had to stop and ask him to put it back. If she had concealed the objects until she was ready to use them, this problem would have been avoided.

Inanimate objects work better than living things, which you can't always control. One of our students brought a small puppy to use in a speech on caring for young animals. At the beginning of her speech, she spread out some newspapers on the table and placed the puppy on them. We are sure you can imagine what happened. The first thing the puppy did was wet on the papers (including her note cards, which she had put on the table while trying to control the puppy). The first thing the audience did was giggle. From there it was all downhill. The puppy squirmed, yipped, and tried to jump on the speaker the whole time she was talking. She was totally upstaged by her presentation aid.

Presentation aids meant to shock the audience into attention can cause serious problems. *Objects that are dangerous, illegal, or potentially offensive, such as guns, drugs, or pornography, must not be used in classroom speeches.* Even replicas of such materials can cause problems. One of our students brandished a very realistic-looking "toy" semiautomatic weapon that he pulled from beneath the lectern during the introduction of a speech on gun control. Several audience members became so upset that they could not concentrate on his message.

Another student was more successful at shocking the audience into attention with a presentation aid. During a speech describing her adventures with her roommate while dieting to lose her "freshman fat," she noted that her roommate complained about dieting for a month and losing only five pounds. At that point, she pulled a white wrapped package from under the lectern. When she opened it, there lay five pounds of fat she had bought at the grocery store. "This," she said, "is what five pounds of fat looks like." Although the spectacle was rather gross, it did grab our attention and reinforced the meaning of her message.

Most how-to speeches require objects as presentation aids to demonstrate procedures. In a classroom speech on how to carve a jack-o'-lantern, the speaker showed listeners how to draw the face on a pumpkin with a felt marker and then how to make a beveled cut around the stem so that the top wouldn't fall in. As she showed her listeners how to do these things, she told stories of the ancient myths surrounding jack-o'-lanterns. Her presentation aid and her words helped each other: The demonstration enlivened her speech, and the stories gave the demonstration depth and meaning. When she came to her closing remarks, she reached under the lectern and produced a finished jack-o'-lantern complete with a lighted candle. The effect was memorable.

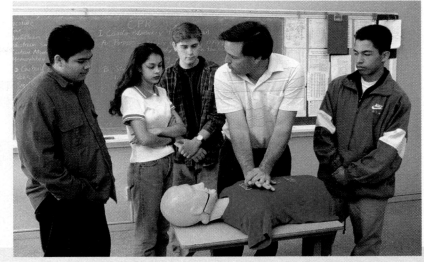

Models are useful as presentation aids when the real object would be difficult to exhibit.

Models. When an object is too large to carry, too small to be easily seen, very rare, expensive, fragile, or simply unavailable, a replica of the object can work well as a presentation aid. George Stacey brought a slightly smaller-than-life-sized model of a person to demonstrate cardiopulmonary resuscitation (CPR). The model folded into a suitcase so that it could be kept out of sight when not in use. When using a model as a presentation aid, it should be constructed to scale and large enough for all listeners to see. Any presentation aid that the audience must strain to see will be more of a distraction than a help.

Graphics

Graphics are visual representations of information, such as sketches, maps, graphs, charts, and textual materials. Because graphics will be displayed for only a short time during your speech, they must be instantly clear. Each graphic should focus on one idea. Because they will be viewed from a distance, the colors should be intense and should contrast sharply with the background. We cover such considerations more fully under "Preparing Presentation Aids" later in this chapter. Graphics may be prepared on poster board or on computers for use as projections.

Sketches. Sketches are simplified representations of what you are talking about. If you don't draw well, search children's coloring books for drawings that you can trace or look for clip art on your computer. If you are drawing a sketch, make it first on paper; then enlarge it or transfer it onto a transparency on a copier. One student speaker used a sketch transferred to a transparency to illustrate the measurements one should take before buying a bicycle. While talking about making bar-to-pedal and seat-to-handlebar measurements, he pointed to them as he said, "Let me show you how to take some basic measurements."

Maps. Commercially prepared maps contain too much detail to use as presentation aids. The best maps are those that you make specifically for your speech so

graphics Visual representations of information, such as sketches, maps, graphs, charts, and textual materials.

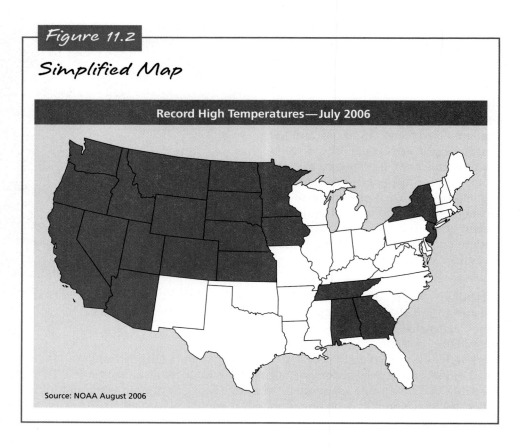

Figure 11.2

Simplified Map

Record High Temperatures—July 2006

Source: NOAA August 2006

that they are simple, relevant to your purpose, and uncluttered. Maps can be used to put problems into perspective and show listeners where things are happening, as in Figure 11.2. Another student speaker used a simplified map to help his listeners see where a series of earthquakes occurred along the New Madrid fault and understand how a recurrence of such earthquakes might endanger his mid-South classmates.

Maps are also useful for illustrating speeches based on spatial relationships. It is hard to give people instructions on how to get somewhere with words alone. In a speech on the major attractions in Yellowstone Park, Tiffany Brock used an outline map of the park showing the route from the South Visitor's Center to Old Faithful, Mammoth Hot Springs, and the Grand Canyon of the Yellowstone River. Seeing the map helped listeners put the locations and distances into perspective.

Whether a map works well as a presentation aid depends on how effectively you integrate it into your presentation. Elizabeth Walling used a map of the wilderness canoe area in northern Minnesota to familiarize her Memphis audience with that area. She made a double-sided poster that she kept hidden behind the speaker's table until she was ready to use it. On one side, she highlighted the wilderness canoe area on an outline map of northern Minnesota, pointing out various places of interest. To illustrate how large the area is, Elizabeth said, "Let me put this in a more familiar context for you." She turned the poster over, revealing an outline map of western Tennessee on which she had superimposed the wilderness area. At a glance, we could see that the area would extend from Memphis to beyond Jackson, Tennessee, some eighty miles away. Elizabeth's artful use of the two maps created a striking visual comparison. The same type of effect can be obtained by overlaying transparencies.

Graphs.   Mrs. Robert A. Taft, wife of a prominent former senator and lioness of Washington society, once commented, "I always find that statistics are hard to swallow and impossible to digest. The only one I can ever remember is that if all the people who go to sleep in church were laid end to end, they would be a lot more comfortable."[6] Many people share Mrs. Taft's feelings about statistics. As we noted in Chapter 8, masses of numbers presented orally can be overwhelming. But a well-designed graph can make statistical information easier for listeners to understand.

A **pie graph** shows the size of a subject's parts in relation to one another and to the whole. The "pie" represents the whole, and the "slices" represent the parts. The segments or slices are percentages of the whole and must add up to 100 percent. The most effective pie graphs for use as presentation aids have six or fewer segments. Too many segments make a graph difficult to read. The pie graph in Figure 11.3 shows Internet users' perceptions of the reliability of information from Internet Web sites.

A **bar graph** shows comparisons and contrasts between two or more items or groups. Bar graphs are easy to understand because each item can be readily compared with every other item on the graph. Bar graphs can also have a dramatic visual impact. Figure 11.4 is a bar graph that illustrates the number of major wildfires per decade from 1950 to 2000.

Some bar graphs make use of pictographs, or stylized drawings, in place of linear bars. If you plan to use pictographs in place of bars, be sure they do not distract from the impact of your material.[7]

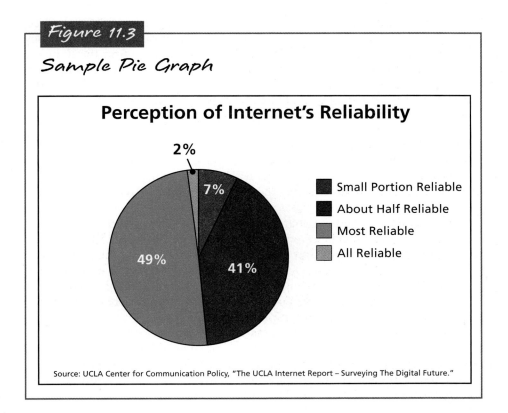

Figure 11.3

Sample Pie Graph

Perception of Internet's Reliability

- Small Portion Reliable
- About Half Reliable
- Most Reliable
- All Reliable

2%
7%
49%
41%

Source: UCLA Center for Communication Policy, "The UCLA Internet Report – Surveying The Digital Future."

pie graph   A circle graph that shows the size of a subject's parts in relation to each other and to the whole.

bar graph   A graph that shows comparisons and contrasts between two or more items or groups.

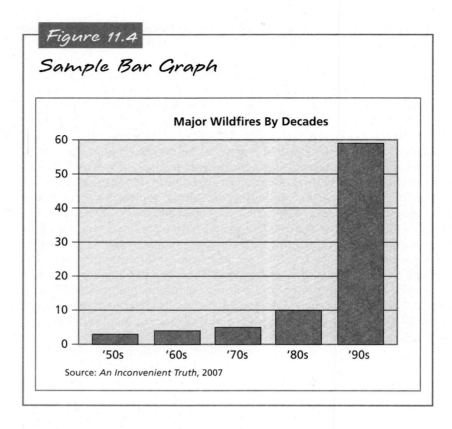

Figure 11.4

Sample Bar Graph

A **line graph** demonstrates changes across time, and it is useful for showing trends in growth or decline. Figure 11.5 shows the number of college graduates by gender from 1950 through 2000. The upward-sloping lines confirm the dramatic increases in the numbers of both male and female graduates across this time span. When you plot more than one line on a graph, use different colors. To avoid confusing listeners, never try to plot more than three lines on a graph.

Charts.   Charts provide visual summaries of relationships that are not in themselves visible. In print communications, charts can be quite complex: The challenge to the speaker is to simplify them without distorting their meaning. The listener must be able to understand them instantly and to read them from a distance.

One frequently used type of chart is a flow chart. A **flow chart** can show the steps in a process, the hierarchy and accountability in an organization, or the genealogy of a family tree. In a flow chart that explains a process, the levels, lines, and arrows indicate what steps occur simultaneously and what steps occur sequentially. Figure 11.6 (page 258) is a flow chart that illustrates the major steps in the preparation of a speech. Notice the double-ended arrows in this chart, which suggest that a speaker works back and forth between the steps.

A problem that often arises with charts used in speeches is that they get overloaded with too much information. Cluttered presentation aids distract listeners. They compete with the speaker for attention. One way around this problem is to use a series of charts, presented in succession. It is much better to have several clean, clear charts than one that tries to do too much.

---

line graph A visual representation of changes across time; especially useful for indicating trends of growth or decline.

flow chart A visual method of representing power and responsibility relationships, or describing the steps in a process.

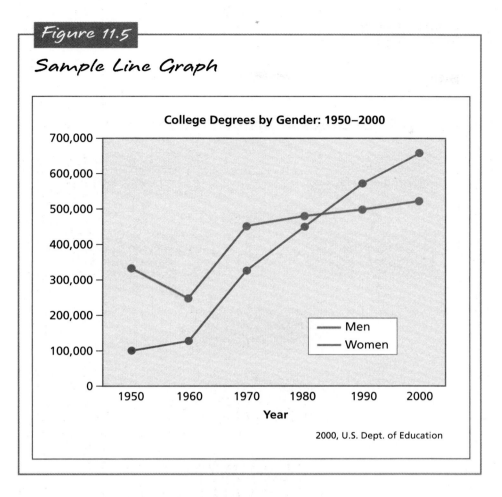

Figure 11.5

Sample Line Graph

College Degrees by Gender: 1950–2000

2000, U.S. Dept. of Education

Textual Graphics. **Textual graphics** are visuals that contain words, phrases, or numbers. Unfamiliar material is clearer and easier for listeners to remember when they can both hear and see the message. Presenting the key-words in a message visually can help an audience follow complicated ideas more easily. For example, in an informative speech that describes a process, you might use a series of posters or slides numbering the steps in the process and containing a key-word or phrase for each step.

The most frequently used textual graphics contain **bulleted lists** of information such as that shown in the computer-generated slide in Figure 11.7 on page 259. When you make a bulleted list, begin with a title, and then place the material under it. Keep the graphic simple. Use intense colors with good contrast. In a bulleted list, have no more than six lines of information and no more than six words to a line.

Another frequently used type of textual graphic presents an **acronym** composed of the initial letters of words to help your audience remember your message. The transparency in Figure 11.8 (page 259) used the acronym EMILY (adapted from Emily's List, a woman's political network) in a persuasive speech urging students to start saving early for retirement. When preparing such a graphic, use the acronym as a title; then list the words under it. Use size and/or color to make the first letters of the words stand out.

Keep textual graphics simple. Limit the columns and rows in any chart. Use colors to make ideas stand out. Textual graphics designed for handouts can contain more information but not so much that they compete with your words for attention.

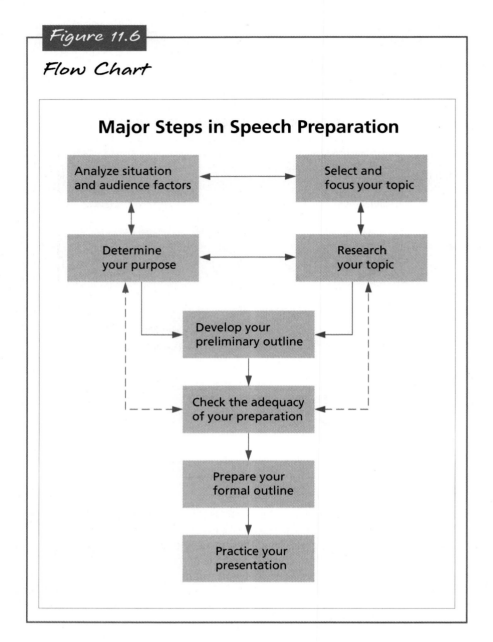

Figure 11.6

Flow Chart

Major Steps in Speech Preparation

Analyze situation and audience factors ⟷ Select and focus your topic

Determine your purpose ⟷ Research your topic

Develop your preliminary outline

Check the adequacy of your preparation

Prepare your formal outline

Practice your presentation

Pictures

Although a picture may be "worth a thousand words," pictures and photographs are difficult to use in speeches. Small photographs cannot be seen by anyone beyond the first row, and passing them around during a presentation is distracting. Another problem with using pictures as presentation aids arises when speakers rely too heavily on the pictures, forgetting that the focus should be on their words. Moreover, pictures with disturbing content can be distracting. One student who was a paramedic showed pictures of child abuse victims taken in a local emergency room. Some members of the audience became so upset that they were not able to concentrate on her message.

Despite these problems, pictures and photographs projected onto a screen or enlarged enough to be easily seen can be striking presentation aids. A good photograph can authenticate a point in a way that words cannot. It can make a situation seem more vivid and realistic. For instance, if a speaker talking about climate changes said, "The snows of Kilimanjaro that Ernest Hemingway loved have almost disappeared," the statement might evoke a modest response from the audience. Suppose, however, the speaker also projected the photographs in Figure 11.9 on a screen in the front of the room as she said these words. Which strategy—with or without pictures—do you think would have the greater impact?

Pictures should be selected for their relevance to your speech. As a general rule, they should be shown only as you discuss a point and should then be put out of sight. Although running slides of pictures while you are speaking can be a distraction, one student used this technique very effectively as a backdrop for a speech on capital punishment.[8] The slides were a series of photos of children and adults with the simple caption "Murder Victim" across the bottom. In his speech, the student did not directly refer to the photos as he presented his substantive arguments. They simply served to provide an aura of pathos that framed his message and demonstrated the authenticity of the problem.

Color copiers can make inexpensive eleven-by-seventeen-inch enlargements from snapshots. This is the minimally acceptable size for use in most classroom settings. Mount pictures on poster board for ease of presentation. Digital photographs can be used as PowerPoint projections or be made into transparencies on most computer printers.

Presentation Media

There are many different types of presentation media. Traditional media include flip charts, posters, handouts, chalk or marker boards, transparencies, videotapes, and audiotapes. Newer presentation media use computer programs, such as PowerPoint, that can incorporate slides, films, DVDs, and sound. These newer media are rapidly becoming the standard for presentations in organizational and educational settings.

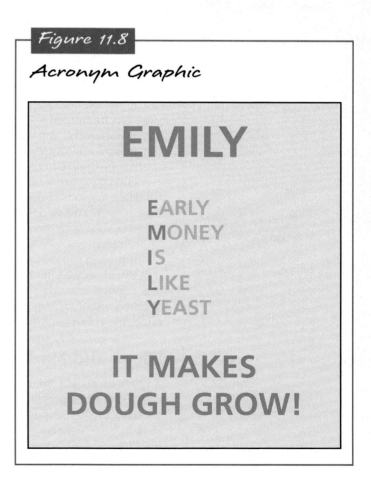

Figure 11.7

Sample Bulleted List

Using Presentation Aids

- Helps you seem better prepared
- Helps you seem more professional
- Makes your message more persuasive
- Helps listeners understand complex material

Presentations/3M, 2000.

Figure 11.8

Acronym Graphic

EMILY

EARLY
MONEY
IS
LIKE
YEAST

IT MAKES DOUGH GROW!

Figure 11.9

These two photos illustrate the dramatic reduction in the size of the ice cap on Mt. Kilimanjaro between 1970 and 2005.

Flip Charts

A **flip chart** is a large, unlined tablet. Most flip charts are newsprint pads that measure about two feet wide by three feet high. They are placed on an easel so that each page can be flipped over the top when you are done with it. Flip charts are convenient, inexpensive, and adaptable to many settings. Business meetings, decision-making groups, and organizational training sessions often use flip charts in addition to more sophisticated types of presentation tools.

Flip charts are meant to be used spontaneously. This makes them especially useful when subjects come up in a meeting that should be written out so that they can be analyzed and understood. When using flip charts, keep each page as simple as possible. Use wide-point felt markers in strong colors, and print or write legibly in large letters.

Although flip charts can be effective in some group communication settings, they don't work as well in classroom speeches. Their use suggests that the speaker did not care enough to prepare a polished presentation aid. Writing on a flip chart also forces speakers either to stop speaking while they write or to speak with their backs to the audience. This loss of direct audience contact can offset any gain from using the charts.

Chalk and Marker Boards

A chalk or marker board is a presentation medium that is available in almost every classroom or corporate conference room. Like flip charts, these boards are best used spontaneously. Despite careful speech preparation, there may be times when you look at your listeners and realize that some of them have not understood what you have just said. One way you can respond to such feedback is by writing a few words on the board or by drawing a simple diagram to help reduce audience confusion.

flip chart A large, unlined tablet, usually a newsprint pad, that is placed on an easel so that each page can be flipped over the top when it's full.

When you write on a board, use large letters so that people in the back of the room can read them without straining. Write or print legibly. Clear the board before you begin, and, as a courtesy to later speakers, erase the board when you are finished. Because you inevitably lose eye contact with listeners while writing on a board, do not use this medium for anything that will take more than a few seconds to write or draw. Never use chalk or marker boards simply because you did not want to take the time to prepare a polished presentation aid.

Computerized slide presentations and flip charts are frequently used as presentation aids in business meetings.

Posters

Posters can be used to display pictures, sketches, maps, charts, graphs, or textual graphics. In an average-size room with a small audience, posters about fourteen by seventeen inches may work best. They are easier to handle than larger posters. You can place them face down on the lectern or table and display them as you refer to them. You can also use the back of a poster as a "cheat sheet" that cues you to the next point in your presentation.

When using a series of posters, be sure to number them on the back so they don't get out of order. Keep posters simple and neat. Use large letters in strong colors that are easy to read. Keep a lot of white space. Rehearse your speech using the posters so you can integrate them smoothly into your presentation.

Handouts

Handouts are useful when your subject is complex or your message contains a lot of statistical information. Pass these handouts out *after* your speech so listeners have something to remind them of what you said. Handouts can also extend the impact of your speech and validate the information you have presented. If you distribute a handout before you speak, it will compete with your words for attention. The audience may read the handout rather than listen to you. Therefore, you should distribute handouts before your speech *only* when it is necessary for listeners to refer to them during your presentation. Never distribute handouts during your speech. This is a sure-fire way to disrupt your presentation and confuse or lose listeners. Multipaged handouts are multidistracting.

Transparencies and Slides

Transparencies and slides allow audiences to see graphics or photographs more easily, especially when audiences are large or spread out in a large room. Business speakers often prefer them to posters or flip charts because they look more professional.

Transparencies are easier to use than slides because you don't have to darken the room when you show them. They are simple to make and inexpensive. You can write on a transparency while it is being shown, adding spontaneity to your presentation. You can also use a pencil as a pointer to direct listeners' attention to features you want to emphasize.

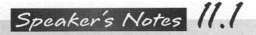

Speaker's Notes 11.1

Deciding What Presentation Media to Use

Let the following suggestions guide your selection of presentation media.

1. Use flip charts and chalk or marker boards to adapt to audience feedback.

2. Use posters to display maps, charts, graphs, or textual graphics.

3. Use handouts to present complex information or statistical data.

4. Use transparencies or slides to display graphics or photos to a large audience.

5. Use audios (tapes, CDs, MP3s) and videos (tapes or DVDs) to authenticate a point.

6. Use computerized materials to make your presentation appear more professional.

When you show slides with a carousel projector, the room usually has to be darkened. Unfortunately, this means that, instead of you, the illuminated screen becomes the center of attention. One major disadvantage of using either transparencies or slides is that often you must speak from where your equipment is located. You may have to stand behind listeners or in the middle of the audience to run the projector. This means you will be talking to someone's back. If remote-controlled equipment is not available, your best solution may be to have a classmate change the projections or slides on cue. You will need to practice with your assistant to coordinate the slides with your words.

Most transparencies and slides are now prepared on personal computers. You can purchase transparency sheets for use with most printers. You also can draw or print your material onto plain paper and convert it to a transparency on a copying machine. If you have access to only a black-and-white copier or printer, you can add color with opaque markers.

To prepare materials for use as transparencies, follow the general guidelines presented earlier for the use of graphics. You should frame your transparencies to avoid glare from light showing around the outside edges of the projection. Frames can be purchased at most copy shops or made from construction paper.

When you arrange slides in a carousel, be sure they are in the proper order and that none of them are upside down. Today, most personal computers are packaged with software that allows you to prepare and present slides without a carousel projector. We discuss this in greater detail in our section on computer-assisted presentations.

If you decide to use transparencies or slides, check the equipment ahead of time and become familiar with its operation. You may need a long extension cord to position the equipment where you want it. Practice using the equipment as you rehearse your speech. One final caution: Don't use too many slides or transparencies in a short speech. A presentation aid should do just that—*aid* your speech, not compete with it or replace it.

Videotapes, DVDs, Audiotapes, and MP3s

Videotapes, DVDs, audiotapes, and MP3 recordings can add variety to your presentation. Be sure in advance that the place where you will be making your presentation has the proper equipment to work with your materials.

Videos and DVDs are useful for transporting the audience to distant, dangerous, or otherwise unavailable locations. Although you could verbally describe the beauty of the Montana Rockies, your word-pictures might come to life if reinforced with actual scenes projected electronically.

Using videos on tape or DVDs pose some special problems for speakers. Moving images attract more attention than the spoken word, so they can easily upstage you. Moreover, a videotape segment must be edited so that splices blend without annoying static. Such editing takes special skill and equipment. Transferring this material onto CDs is simpler, easier to handle, and can be done on most personal computers with a DVD/CD burner. Finally, such clips can be difficult to work into a short speech without taking up all of your time. In a short speech, a clip should be no more than thirty seconds long.

For certain topics, however, carefully prepared videos can be more effective than any other type of presentation aid. One student at Northwest Mississippi Community College, who was a firefighter, used videotape in an informative speech on fire hazards in the home. By customizing the video to fit the precise needs of his speech, he was able to show long shots of a room and then zoom in on various hazards.[9] He prepared the video without sound so that his speech provided the commentary needed to interpret and explain the pictures. Using this technique, he made his subject much more meaningful for listeners.

Audiotapes, audio on CDs, or MP3 files may also be useful as presentation aids. If you wanted to describe the alarm cries of various animals or the songs of different birds, an audiotape could be essential. When in doubt about the wisdom or practicality of using such aids, consult your instructor.

Computer-Assisted Presentations

Personal computers can generate a variety of presentation aids, including sketches, maps, graphs, charts, and textual graphics for handouts, slides, and transparencies. The materials produced on computers are neater and more accurate than most drawn by hand. Presentation software programs, such as PowerPoint, are readily available. Your campus computer lab may have training programs to help you learn how to prepare these materials. You may also use the basic PowerPoint tutorial that follows this chapter.

Computer-assisted presentations can bring together text, numbers, pictures, music, video clips, and artwork made into slides, videos, animations, and audio materials. Materials such as graphs and charts generated with the computer can be changed at any time, even during a presentation. The programs come with a variety of templates to assist you in designing your presentation aids. The templates can be adapted to suit your particular needs.

When using a computer for developing presentation aids, be careful not to get so caught up with the glitz and glitter that you lose sight of the fact that *your speech is what is most important*. In cautioning against the misuse or overuse of such technology, Rebecca Ganzel in *Presentations* magazine pictured the following scenario:

> It's that nightmare again—the one in which you're trapped in the Electronic Presentation from Hell. The familiar darkness presses in, periodically sliced in half by a fiendish light. Bullet points, about 18 to a slide, careen in all directions. You cringe, but the slides keep coming, too fast to read, each with a new template you half-remember seeing a hundred times before: Dad's Tie! Sixties Swirls! Infinite Double-Helixes! A typewriter clatters; brakes squeal. Somewhere in the shadows, a voice drones on. Strange stick people shake hands and dance around a flowchart. Typefaces morph into Word Art.
>
> But the worst is yet to come. As though you're watching a train wreck in slow motion, you look down at your hand—and *you're holding the remote*.[10]

computer–assisted presentation The use of commercial presentation software to join audio, visual, textual, graphic, and animated components.

InterConnections.
LearnMore 11.2

PowerPoint Presentations

Microsoft PowerPoint

http://office.microsoft.com/en-us/powerpoint/default.aspx

Microsoft PowerPoint home page; contains links to tips, tricks, how-to articles, and other online course materials.

PowerPoint in the Classroom

www.actden.com/pp/

A simple online tutorial that walks you through the basics of preparing a PowerPoint presentation, incorporating all the bells and whistles. A good resource for the technophobic student.

Internet4Classrooms

www.internet4classrooms.com/on-line_powerpoint.htm

A directory of links to many PowerPoint resources. Developed primarily for teachers but useful to anyone interested in improving their ability to create PowerPoint slides. Includes basic and advanced tutorials. Developed and maintained by Susan Brooks and Bill Byles.

Using technology in your presentation does not excuse you from the usual requirements for speaking. In fact, if your presentation aids attract more attention than your ideas, they may be a hindrance instead of a help. Be careful not to get caught up with swirling backgrounds and flashy transitions. *Remember, it is better to be subtle than sensational.* Follow the general guidelines for developing and using presentation aids described in this chapter.

PowerPoint Presentations. More than 90 percent of all computerized presentations in the United States are created using the PowerPoint program, which is distributed as part of the Microsoft Office software.[11] Why is PowerPoint so popular? For starters, it is the most widely available software of its type and is prepackaged on many computers sold to businesses and educational institutions. PowerPoint is also fairly easy to use. The software contains templates and comes with a step-by-step online tutorial. If you need to change a presentation aid during your speech, you can insert new material as you are talking.

PowerPoint may also be the most frequently misused type of presentation aid. We probably have all been subject to poor PowerPoint presentations. Their ease of use is a double-edged sword. It is too easy to put together a bad PowerPoint presentation that actually annoys an audience and does little to enhance the understanding of a message or the credibility of the presenter. A survey conducted by technology specialist Dave Paradi identified the most annoying elements of PowerPoint presentations:

1. Reading slides to the audience.

2. Using text too small to be easily read.

3. Writing full sentences instead of bulleted points.

4. Making poor color choices that make slides hard to see.

5. Using moving or flying text or graphics.

6. Interjecting annoying sounds.

7. Projecting complex diagrams or charts.[12]

Fortunately, these are things a speaker can control. Avoid these problems by following a few simple directives:

- Never substitute a PowerPoint slide show for a speech.

- Do not put your outline on PowerPoint slides and then read it to the audience.

- Be sure your slides are easy to read. Use a large, plain font and select colors that provide good contrast, such as light on dark or dark on light. Avoid shaded backgrounds that might make some of the words unreadable.

- Keep slides simple by limiting the amount of information on each one.

- Use bulleted points instead of full sentences.

- Don't try to project complex charts or graphs; simplify them or distribute them as handouts.

- Avoid overly dramatic techniques such as flying text and startling sound effects.

Figure 11.10 contains examples of a good and a poor PowerPoint slide.

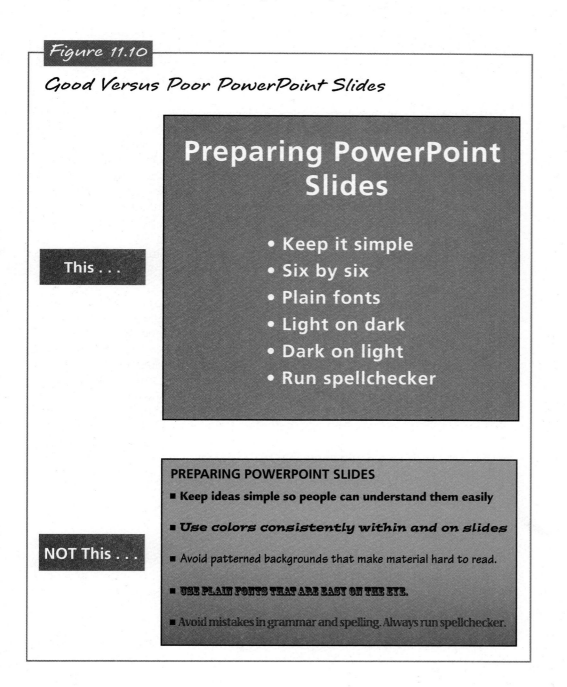

Figure 11.10

Good Versus Poor PowerPoint Slides

Preparing Presentation Aids

*P*resentation aids should be carefully thought out and planned to fit your message. Regardless of the type of media you use, they should be created following basic principles of design and color. Always practice using your presentation aids so that you don't end up fumbling around when you are making your presentation.

Principles of Design

A good presentation aid is simple, easy to see, focuses on what is important, and is well balanced. Consider the basic principles of simplicity, visibility, emphasis, and balance as you plan and prepare your materials. Look at your aids from the perspective of an audience member and see if they meet these criteria.

Simplicity. Many speakers, novices and professionals alike, try to cram too much information into a single presentation aid. Too much information on a presentation aid distracts listeners who have to figure out what everything is and what it means. We had one student divide a standard two-by-three-foot poster into twelve segments, glue samples of medicinal herbs in each box, and then print its name and use under each sample. Needless to say, only listeners in the front row could actually read any of the print, and the aid created more confusion than illumination. He would have been better served had he used a series of smaller posters, each featuring one herb and the simple facts about it.

Each aid should focus on a single idea that you want to illustrate. Apply the KISS principle (Keep It Simple, Stupid!) as you design your presentation aids.

Visibility. The size of any presentation aid must be appropriate to the setting in which it is used. A very large aid will be cumbersome to handle and can overwhelm listeners in a small room. Similarly, a small aid will not be effective in a large room. Listeners in the back of the room must be able to see your presentation aid without straining. In classrooms that hold up to forty students, poster boards work fairly well. In a larger room with a larger audience, you should use projection equipment.

When preparing a poster board presentation aid for the standard classroom, follow these minimum size guidelines: Your titles should be about three inches high and other text at least an inch and a half high. If you generate slides or transparencies on a computer, use a large font. Computer print is typically sized in terms of points (pt). Such presentation aids should use the following sizes of letters:

	Transparencies	Slides	Handouts
Title	36 pt	24 pt	18 pt
Subtitles	24 pt	18 pt	14 pt
Other text	18 pt	14 pt	12 pt

Use a plain font that is easy to read. The following fonts work best on presentation aids: **Arial Rounded Bold**, **Franklin Gothic**, `Courier`, Times New Roman, **Impact**, and **Microsoft Sans Serif Bold**. Avoid script and decorative fonts such as ALGERIAN, *Brush Script*, Curlz, Old English, and **Snap**.

Emphasis. Your presentation aids should emphasize what your speech emphasizes. Your listeners' eyes should be drawn immediately to what you want to illustrate.

On the acronym chart (see Figure 11.8), the first letters of each word stand out. The map of Yellowstone Park mentioned earlier contained only the attractions the speaker planned to talk about and the route between them. Had she added pictures of bears to indicate grizzly habitats, drawings of fish to show trout streams, and mountains, the presentation aid would have seemed cluttered and distracting. Avoid cuteness! Graphics prepared for handouts may be more detailed than those used for posters, slides, or transparencies, but they should not contain extraneous material. When in doubt, leave the details out. Let your words provide the elaboration.

Balance. Presentation aids that are balanced are pleasing to the eye. You achieve balance when you position textual materials so that they form a consistent pattern. Don't try to use every square inch of a poster board or overload a slide. White space is important! You should have a margin of at least two inches at the top and bottom of a poster board. Side margins should be about one and a half inches wide. On computer-generated slides, you should leave blank space at both the top and bottom and have equal side margins. In the computer-generated slides in Figure 11.10, the first slide illustrates a balanced design. The second is unbalanced and cluttered and violates all of the principles of design.

Principles of Color

As many of the illustrations in this chapter show, color adds impact to presentation aids. Most color presentation aids attract and hold attention better than black-and-white ones. Color also can convey or enhance meaning. For example, a speech about crop damage from a drought might use an enlarged outline map showing the least affected areas in green, moderately damaged areas in orange, and severely affected areas in brown. The natural colors would reinforce the message.

Color can also be used to create moods and impressions. Figure 11.11 shows some of the reactions that various groups might have toward colors. For most Americans, blue suggests power, authority, and stability (blue chip, blue ribbon, royal blue). Using blue in your graphics can evoke these associations. Red signals excitement or crisis (in the red, red ink, "I saw red"). Line graphs tracing a rise in campus crimes could be drawn in red to convey the urgency of the problem. You should avoid using red when presenting financial data unless you want to focus on debts or losses. In our American culture, green is associated with both money (greenbacks) and environmental concerns (Greenpeace). The green in Figure 11.8 echoes the green of U.S. currency. When selecting colors, you should also be aware of cultural differences. For example, in the United States, white is associated with weddings, baptisms, confirmations, and other joyous rituals. In Japan, white is a funeral color, associated with sadness.

The way you use colors in combination can convey subtle nuances of meaning. An **analogous color scheme** uses colors that are adjacent in the color spectrum, such as green, blue-green, and blue. At the same time this

Figure 11.11

Meanings of Colors

	Movie-goers	Financiers	Doctors
Blue	Tender emotions	Reliable	Cold
Green	Playful	Profitable	Infection
Yellow	Happy	Highlighted/important	Jaundice
Red	Exciting	Unprofitable	Hot/radioactive

Source: *How to Lie with Charts*, 2000

analogous color scheme Colors adjacent on the color wheel; used in a presentation aid to suggest both differences and close relationships among the components.

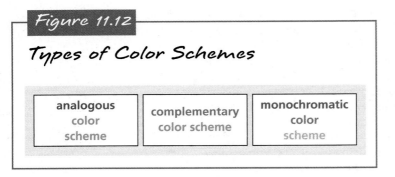

Figure 11.12

Types of Color Schemes

| analogous color scheme | complementary color scheme | monochromatic color scheme |

type of color scheme shows the differences among elements, it also suggests their close connection and compatibility. For example, a pie graph could use analogous colors to represent the students, faculty, and administration of a university. The different colors suggest that although these parts are separate, they belong together. In this subtle way, the presentation aid implies that these components of a university should work together.

A **complementary color scheme** uses colors that are opposites on the color wheel, such as red and green. Complementary color schemes suggest tension and opposition among elements in a speech. Because they heighten the sense of drama, they may enliven informative speaking and encourage change in persuasive speaking.

A **monochromatic color scheme** uses variations of a single color. The acronym graphic (Figure 11.8) uses a monochromatic color scheme. These schemes suggest variety within unity. A monochromatic color scheme would be inappropriate for bar graphs or line graphs, because they require more contrast to be effective. Figure 11.12 illustrates these three types of color schemes.

The colors you use for text in a presentation aid should contrast with the background. Patterned or shaded backgrounds can make words difficult to read. With poster board, it is best to use a white- or cream-colored board and strong primary colors such as red, blue, and green for contrast. However, don't use red letters against a light background on slides or transparencies. Red tends to bleed, making the words blurry and difficult to read, and a light background can create glare. Therefore, you might want to use a strong primary color for the background and have the text or other graphic elements printed in white.

Color contrast is especially important for computer-generated slides and transparencies, because the colors will appear less distinct when projected than they do when seen on a computer monitor. Colors like pastel pink, light blue, and pale yellow, or those with a grayish tinge, may not be strong enough for good graphic emphasis in any type of presentation aid.

A final word of caution concerning color: When you prepare presentation aids on a computer, the colors on your monitor will differ from the final colors when they are printed on a transparency or slide. For example, the rich burgundy background

Speaker's Notes 11.2

Checklist for Preparing Presentation Aids

Your presentation aid should meet these criteria:

1. My presentation aid is as simple as I can make it.

2. I have limited myself to one major idea per aid.

3. I have ample margins at the top, bottom, and sides of my aid.

4. My print is large enough to be read from the back of the room.

5. My aid emphasizes what I want to emphasize.

6. I have good color contrast on my aid.

7. I use colors and lettering consistently.

8. I have checked for spelling errors.

---

complementary color scheme Colors opposite one another on the color wheel; used in a presentation aid to suggest tension and opposition.

monochromatic color scheme Use of variations of a single color in a presentation aid to convey the idea of variety within unity.

you would like to use for your slides might look more like muddy water once it is projected. Run a sample and project it to see how the final colors will actually look to an audience. If the results are not what you expected, try other colors until you are satisfied.

Making Presentation Aids

To make handmade charts, graphs, or other poster aids, start with a rough draft that allows you to see how your aid will look when it is finished. If you are making a poster, prepare your draft on newsprint or butcher paper of the same size. With a light pencil, mark off the margins to frame your aid. Divide your planning sheet into four equal sections to help you balance the placement of material. Use a wide-tipped felt marker to sketch in your design and words.

Now step back and inspect your presentation aid from about the same distance as the back row of your audience. Can you read it without straining? Is everything spelled correctly? Is your eye drawn to what is most important? Have you positioned your material so that it looks good? Does the poster look balanced?

Remember, keep your presentation aid simple! Be sure your margins and borders are large enough to provide ample white space. See if there is anything you can cut. If your draft looks "busy," make a series of presentation aids instead of just one. Once you have completed a rough draft of the aid, construct the final product. If you are artistically challenged, use stencils or stick-on letters and numbers.

If you use a computer to produce slides, transparencies, or handouts, experiment with several different designs. Limit the amount of information on slides and transparencies to a maximum of six lines per slide and six words per line. Limit the number of slides or transparencies you use in a speech. You should probably have *no more than four aids for a six-minute presentation and no more than six aids for a ten-minute presentation.* If you use more than this, your speech may become just a voice-over for a slide show. At the end of this chapter, we provide step-by-step instructions for preparing simple PowerPoint slides.

Using Presentation Aids

As we discussed each type of presentation aid, we made suggestions on how to use it in a speech. Here, we bring these suggestions together and extract some general guidelines.

Try out your presentation aids as you practice your speech. Plan transitions such as "As you can see on this chart . . ." to integrate the material into your message. Well before your speaking time, check out the site to determine where you will place your aid both before and after you use it and how you will display it. Be sure it can be seen well from all points in the room. Also decide what you will need to display your presentation aid. Is there an easel you can use for a poster board or flip chart? Should you bring masking tape or push pins to display your aid? Will you need to bring something to conceal it until you are ready to use it?

Check out any electronic equipment you will use (slide projector, overhead projector, VCR, computer, etc.) in advance of your presentation. Be certain that you can operate it and that it is working properly. If you are using computerized materials on a CD, be sure that they are compatible with the equipment in the room.

Do not display your presentation aid until you are ready to use it; otherwise, it will distract your audience. When you have finished using the aid, cover or conceal

Figure 11.13

The Dos and Don'ts of Using Presentation Aids

Do	Don't
1. Practice using your aids.	1. Try to "wing it" using your aids.
2. Display aids only when referring to them.	2. Leave aids in view throughout speech.
3. Stand to the side of aid as you speak.	3. Stand in front of aid as you speak.
4. Point to what is important on aid.	4. Make listeners search for what's important.
5. Maintain eye contact with listeners.	5. Deliver your speech to your aid.
6. Distribute handouts after your speech.	6. Distribute handouts during speech.
7. Limit the number of aids in your speech.	7. Become a voice-over for a slide show.

it. Never stand directly in front of your presentation aid; rather, stand to the side of it and maintain eye contact with listeners. You want them to see both you and your presentation aid. As you refer to something on the presentation aid, point to what you are talking about: Don't leave your audience searching for what you are describing. Never deliver your speech to your presentation aid; instead, maintain eye contact with your listeners.

Do not distribute materials during your speech. If you have prepared handouts, the best time to distribute them usually comes after you speak. Don't pass around pictures or objects for listeners to examine. You want them to focus on your message, not on your presentation aid.

Finally, do not use too many presentation aids in one speech. Remember, they should strengthen your speech, not replace it.

Ethical Considerations for Using Presentation Aids

Presentation aids can enlighten a message, but they can also mislead listeners. The way you use presentation aids can raise challenging ethical questions. Graphs and charts, for example, can be rigged so that they misrepresent reality.[13] Figure 11.14 shows how a recent decade's growth in the percentage of women partners in major accounting firms might be misrepresented in bar graph A to make a small gain look like a large gain. Bar graph B in the same figure puts these slight gains into the proper perspective.[14] Be careful to prepare graphs so that they honestly represent a situation.

You must also remember to credit your sources on your presentation aids. Be sure to include this information in smaller (but still visible) letters at the bottom of any material you plan to display (see how this is done in Figure 11.7). Citing your source on your presentation aid verifies the information presented and reminds you to mention the source in your oral presentation.

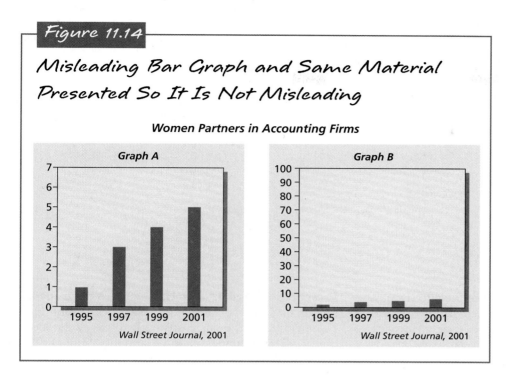

Figure 11.14

Misleading Bar Graph and Same Material Presented So It Is Not Misleading

Women Partners in Accounting Firms

Graph A — *Wall Street Journal, 2001*

Graph B — *Wall Street Journal, 2001*

Some of the most interesting ethical questions involve the use of film and tape materials. For example, the most famous photographer of the Civil War, Matthew Brady, rearranged bodies on the battlefield to enhance the impact of his pictures. Eighty years later, another American war photographer carefully staged the now celebrated photograph of marines planting the flag at Iwo Jima.[15] Fifty years after that, *Time* magazine electronically manipulated a cover photograph of O. J. Simpson (at the time of his murder trial) to "darken it and achieve a brooding, menacing quality."[16] On one hand, these famous images are fabrications: They pretend to be what they are not. On the other hand, they bring home reality more forcefully. In other words, the form of the photos may be a lie, but the lie may reveal a deeper truth. So are these photographs unethical, or are they simply artistic?

With today's technology, the potential for abuse looms ever larger. Video and audio editing easily produces illusions of reality. Consider how moviemakers depicted Forrest Gump shaking hands with Presidents Kennedy, Johnson, and Nixon. Notice how televised political commercials often use a shot from a video that catches an opponent with eyes half-shut or mouth gaping open. In movies and ads, such distortions can be easily discerned and therefore don't do much damage. In real life, however, they can be dangerous. When doctored images are passed off as actual objects or events, as when television networks or newspapers "stage" crashes to make their stories more dramatic, they can be quite deceptive.[17] We have been conditioned by experience and taught by tradition to trust the "reality" revealed by our eyes and ears. Adherence to the adage that "seeing is believing" can make us prey for unscrupulous manipulators.

To be an ethical communicator, you should alert your listeners to an illusion whenever you manipulate images so that they reveal your message more forcefully. You should also be able to defend your "creation" as a "better representation" of the truth. As a listener, you should develop a skeptical attitude about images and seek additional evidence if there is any question concerning their validity.

Ethics *Alert!* 11.1

The Ethical Use of Presentation Aids

Follow these guidelines to avoid unethical use of presentation aids:

1. Be certain charts or graphs do not distort information.

2. Never manipulate visual images to deceive your audience.

3. If you alter an image to reveal some deeper truth, let the audience know.

4. Cite the source of your information on a presentation aid.

5. As a listener, be on guard against the power of presentation aids to trick you.

In Summary

Presentation aids are tools to enhance the effectiveness of speeches. They can increase comprehension, improve retention, authenticate a point, add variety, increase your credibility, and help your speech have lasting impact.

Kinds of Presentation Aids. Every speech has at least one presentation aid: the speaker. Your appearance, clothing, and body language should be in concert with your message. Objects should be large enough to be seen, small enough to be portable, and easy to control. If they are not all of the preceding, use a model or sketch instead. Maps should contain only the material you wish to emphasize. Graphs can help make complex numerical data more understandable to an audience. Pie graphs illustrate the relationships between parts and a whole. Bar graphs highlight comparisons and contrasts. Line graphs show changes over time. Flow charts may be used to outline the steps in a process or to show power and authority relationships within an organization. Textual graphics are lists of phrases, words, or numbers. They are often presented as bulleted lists or acronyms Photographs and pictures should be enlarged so that everyone in the audience can see them.

Presentation Media. Flip charts and chalk or marker boards may be used as spontaneous presentation aids. These aids should be used sparingly to clarify questions that arise during a presentation. Handouts should be distributed either before or after a speech. Transparencies and slides are popular options because they are easy to make and inexpensive. Videos and audiotapes add variety to a message. Most computers can produce effective, professional-looking presentation aids.

Preparing Presentation Aids. Follow the basic principles of design and color in preparing presentation aids. They should be easy for listeners to see, emphasize what the speech emphasizes, and exclude extraneous material. Aids should be balanced and pleasing to the eye. Use strong colors with good contrast and lots of white space. Do not try to put too much on any single aid.

Using Presentation Aids. Practice using your presentation aids. Maintain eye contact with listeners, and do not talk to your presentation aid. Keep aids out of sight when they are not in use. Be sensitive to the potential ethical impact of your presentation aids. Be certain that they represent their subjects without distortion.

Explore and Apply the Ideas in This Chapter

1. Recall classes in which your instructors used presentation aids. Which of the following functions discussed in this chapter did these aids serve?

   a. Did they aid your understanding of the material?

   b. Did they authenticate a point in the lecture?

   c. Did they enhance your instructor's presentation skills?

   d. Did they enhance your instructor's credibility?

e. Did they add variety or make the lecture more interesting?

f. Did they make the material easier to remember? Why or why not?

2. Describe a situation you witnessed (outside of this class) in which a speaker was or was not an effective presentation aid for his or her own speech? How did the speaker's appearance enhance or detract from the speech?

3. Look through a recent magazine and analyze the advertisements according to the principles of design discussed in this chapter. Do the presentation aspects of the ads work in concert with the words to emphasize the message? Which of the ads seem most balanced and pleasing to the eye? Do any of the ads violate the rules of simplicity and ease of understanding? Which ads used color most and least effectively? Bring copies of the most interesting ads to class and discuss your findings.

4. Select a speech from Appendix B and prepare the rough draft of a presentation aid that might have been used with it. Would the aid have helped the speech? What other options did you consider?

5. What kinds of presentation aids might be most useful for the following speech topics?

a. Nuclear waste disposal sites in the United States

b. Surviving a hurricane

c. The evolution of cell phone technology over the past decade

d. How your school's budget is divided into major categories

e. Administering your college: Who has the power to do what to whom?

f. How we got laptop computers: the growth of an invention

g. The sounds of navigation and what they mean

*T*his tutorial will help you prepare a simple slide or series of slides for use in your speeches using Microsoft's software for PowerPoint 2000 or PowerPoint 2002. Because of the planned obsolescence of software programs, the materials that follow may not be exactly the same as what you will see on your computer screen. But while programs change from version to version, the general directions remain similar.

We begin with a series of cautions. First, don't develop your slide(s) until after you have prepared your speech. Second, include information and material on your slide(s) only when it adds to your oral message. Third, don't simply copy your speech outline onto slides and then read them to the audience.

Begin preparing your slide(s) by opening the PowerPoint program on your computer. You can access this by using the "Start" button in the bottom left corner of the screen, then opening Programs, and clicking on PowerPoint. The first screen that will be displayed contains three options for creating a PowerPoint presentation: an AutoContent Wizard, a Design Template format, and a Blank Presentation option.

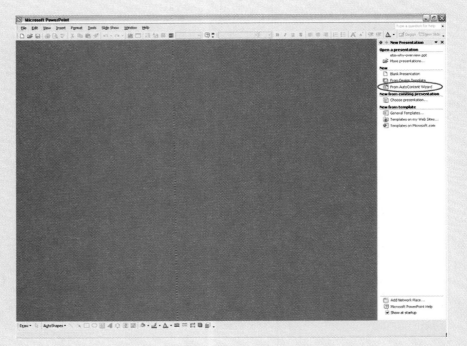

Screenshot(s) reprinted by permission of Microsoft® Corporation.

The AutoContent Wizard provides a fixed set of templates and formats. It guides you through the process by asking questions about the type of presentation you plan to make. Although this may sound like an easy way to develop your slide(s), it is probably not the best approach for learning the basics of preparing such materials. Most of the presentation options in the AutoContent Wizard do not match the typical public speaking class assignments. They are designed to prepare "slide shows"—often with sound and animated graphics—not to prepare presentation aids for speeches.

The Design Template format provides a large selection of slide backgrounds on which you can type your text. Each template can be viewed on the right of your screen by clicking the button next to the template name. Many of these backgrounds are attractive, but some of them are "busy." Busy backgrounds can distract listeners. Slides with shaded backgrounds often make some of the text difficult to read.

The Blank Presentation option allows you to control everything that goes on your slide(s). Consequently, you should prepare your slide(s) using either a very simple background from the Design Template format or build them from scratch using the Blank Presentation option. Our instructions will take you through working with the Blank Presentation option, but they are applicable to the Design Template format as well.

No matter which option you choose, the Office Assistant will appear as an icon (usually an animated paper clip) on your screen. If you get confused or can't remember how to do something, simply click on the icon and a box will appear.

Type a question in the space provided, click the "Search" command, and the Office Assistant will provide an answer.

When you choose the Blank Presentation option, the next screen that comes up on your monitor will provide slide layout options.

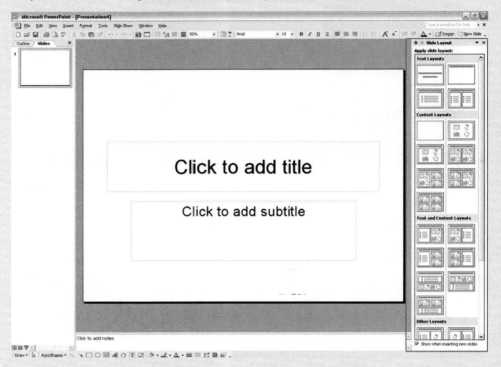

On this screen, you can choose from a title page, a bulleted list, and a variety of chart, graph, and clip art options. Select the bulleted list by clicking on the icon showing a bulleted list. Now the working box on your screen will show a slide with the appropriate layout.

Decide what background color you want for your slides. Remember, if you choose a light background, you must use dark text to provide the contrast necessary for your slide(s) to be easily read. Also keep in mind that white backgrounds are prone to glare. If you want a light background for your slide(s), choose a pale cream or ivory. If you choose a dark background, you will need to use a light text color for clear definition. To add background color to your slide, pull down the Format menu from your top toolbar, and click on Background.

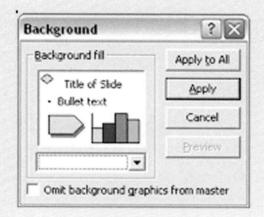

To find the color you want to use as the background for your slide(s), click the arrow for the blank pull-down box at the bottom of the menu. Select the "More Colors" command, which will display the entire color spectrum available.

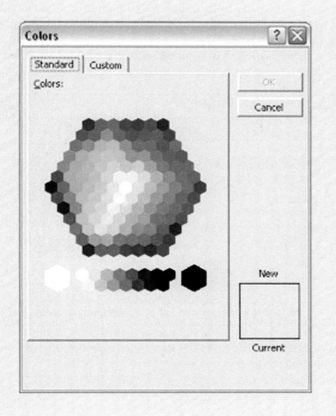

Choose your background color, then click "Apply to All." Each slide you prepare for this presentation will have the same background. We have selected a rich royal blue as a background color.

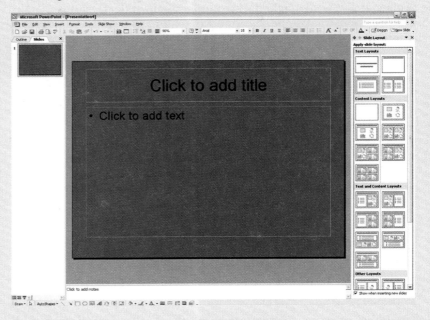

Before you begin typing material onto your slide, you must select the font style and color for the text on your slide. Return to the Format menu on your top tool-bar. Open this and click Font. Choose a simple, easy-to-read font. Some good choices include Arial, Century Gothic, Courier, and Times New Roman. Avoid any font that has the word *narrow* in its name: it will be hard to read when projected in a slide. Don't use script or decorative fonts such as Dauphin and GoudyHandtooled, which are also difficult to read.

Next, select a font color that contrast with the background of your slide. We have chosen white text for use on the blue background.

Now you can begin adding text to your slide. Type the title of your slide in the title box and the text in the text box.

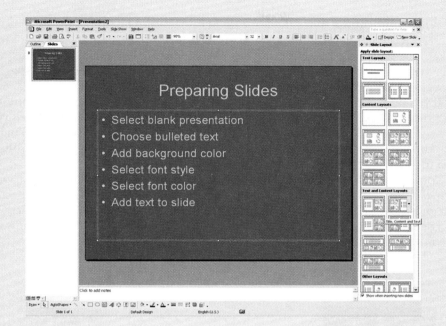

Don't try to cram too much material into a slide. For a bulleted list, you should have no more than six lines or bullets, and no more than six words to a line. Do not write out your bulleted points as full sentences. They will be too long and will draw attention away from your spoken words as listeners read them. If you have too much material to meet the six-by-six guidelines, consider making a series of slides.

To make additional slides for your presentation, go to the "New Slide" command on the top toolbar on your screen. The "Layout Options" box will open, and you can then choose the layout you want for this slide.

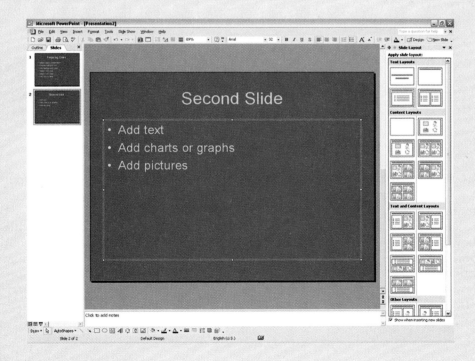

When you will use more than one slide in your presentation, be sure that the slides are visually consistent with one another. Each slide should have the same background and the same color scheme. The slides should use the same fonts, the same type of bullets for multiple bulleted lists, and the same type of spacing between words and lines.

If you prepare a slide and decide you want a different layout, open the Common Tasks menu, click on Slide Layout, and then select the layout you want. When you have completed all of your slides, save them in a folder on your desktop and make a backup copy on a disk. Once you have prepared the slides, you can open them from this folder and edit them by changing colors or text.

You can preview your complete presentation by using the Slide Sorter view from the View menu on the toolbar. This screen shows you all the slides in your presentation. Use the slide sorter to rearrange the order of your slides. To change the order of your slides, click on the slide, then drag it to where you want it positioned.

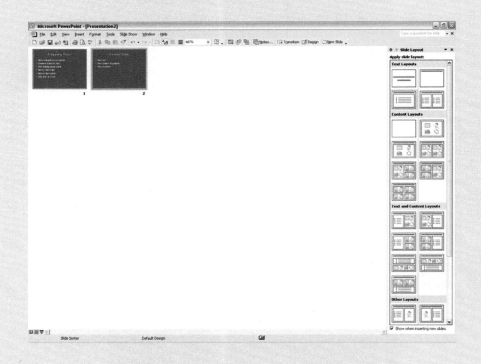

With Microsoft's Excel program, you can prepare charts and graphs on your computer and import them into your PowerPoint slides. You can also import clip art and pictures to add variety to your presentation.

Once you have prepared all of your materials, your next step is to open the Slide Show menu on your toolbar. This allows you to view your presentation on your computer monitor. For a speech before an audience, select the Manual Timing option so that you can control the appearance of slides by left-clicking your mouse. Show a slide only when you refer to it in a speech. You can make the screen go black between slides by hitting the "b" on your computer keyboard.

If you need immediate help while preparing and previewing your PowerPoint presentation, click on the Office Assistant. For additional information and instructions for more advanced presentations with clip art, transitions, and animation, consult one of the online resources listed in InterConnections 11.1, "PowerPoint Presentations."

12 Using Language Effectively

This chapter will help you

- understand the power of language
- apply standards to use language effectively
- learn how to magnify the power of language

Give me the right word and the right accent, and I will move the world.

—Joseph Conrad

A legislator was asked how he felt about whiskey. He replied, "If, when you say whiskey, you mean the Devil's brew, the poison scourge, the bloody monster that defiles innocence, dethrones reason, creates misery and poverty—yes, literally takes the bread from the mouths of little children; if you mean the drink that topples Christian man and woman from the pinnacle of righteous, gracious living into the bottomless pit of degradation, despair, shame and helplessness, then certainly I am against it with all my power.

"But if, when you say whiskey, you mean the oil of conversation, the philosophic wine, the ale that is consumed when good fellows get together, that puts a song in their hearts and the warm glow of contentment in their eyes; if you mean Christmas cheer; if you mean the stimulating drink that puts the spring in an old gentleman's step on a frosty morning; if you mean that drink, the sale of which pours into our treasury untold millions of dollars which are used to provide tender care for our crippled children, our blind, our deaf, our dumb, pitiful, aged and infirm, to build highways, hospitals, and schools, then certainly I am in favor of it.

"That is my stand, and I will not compromise."[1]

The "Whiskey Speech," a legend in southern politics, was originally presented some years ago by N. S. Sweat Jr. during a heated campaign to legalize the sale of liquor-by-the-drink in Mississippi. Because about half of his constituents favored the question and the other half were vehemently opposed, Representative "Soggy" Sweat decided to handle the issue with humor. In the process, he provided an illustration of the magical power of words.

In this chapter, we discuss this power and explain six standards you must satisfy to make language work ethically and effectively in your speeches. We conclude by exploring some special techniques you can use to magnify the power of words.

The Power of the Spoken Word

he ability to use language effectively is one of the most important skills you will ever acquire. There are three important reasons this is so.

1. *Most of us think in words, and the words of our language shape the way we think.* For example, in most parts of the United States, we have just one word for and one conception of snow. However, in the land of the Eskimos, where snow is a constant phenomenon, there are many words to describe it and many ways to think about it.

2. *Language is the basis of all our social interactions.* Our choice of words can determine the success or failure of these interactions.

3. *Words are the essence of our being, of what and how we think about ourselves.* Our language is an integral part of our cultural identity. This becomes especially

important when a language faces the possibility of extinction. D. Y. Begay, a prominent Navajo weaver and art curator, noted, "My father says when you stop speaking the language is when you stop being Navajo."[2]

What Makes the Spoken Word Special

To understand the special powers of the spoken word, we must contrast it with writing.

- **The spoken word is more spontaneous and less formal than the written word.** A journalist might write, "Eight thousand, three hundred twenty-three cases of measles have been reported in Shelby County." But a speaker, communicating the same information, would more likely say, "More than eight thousand cases of measles have been reported in Shelby County!" It's not really important that listeners remember the exact number of cases. What's important is that they see the magnitude of the problem. Rounding off numbers helps listeners focus on the large picture.

- **The spoken word is more colorful and intense than the written word.** These qualities are vital to the effectiveness of communication, as numerous studies of language intensity have demonstrated.[3] Sentence fragments and slang expressions can add to these qualities and are more acceptable in speeches than in essays.

- **Oral language is more interactive, engaging listeners in the feelings and thoughts of the speech as they develop.** Such language depends on audience involvement for its effectiveness. Consider the following excerpt from a speech:

> You want to know what we're going to do? Well, let me tell you what we're not going to do. We're not going to play along! This is a rule that deserves to be broken. Yes, broken! And we're going to do the breaking.

This brief example illustrates the spontaneous, informal, intense, fragmentary, and interactive qualities of oral language. The speaker is keenly aware of her audience. Her words illustrate the conversational character of effective speeches that we discussed in Chapter 1. Moreover, as we discuss in detail in Chapter 13, oral language uses pauses, vocal emphasis, and pitch variations to clarify and reinforce meaning. Such resources are not available in written communication.

- **The spoken word offers special constraints as well as opportunities.** The speaker must remain sensitive to the limitations of live audiences. Communication consultant Jerry Tarver reminds us that listeners cannot "reread" words that are spoken: Oral language must be simpler, and speakers often must repeat themselves to be understood. Speakers may need to amplify ideas with examples to ensure that listeners get the point.[4]

But speakers can arrange the order of words to achieve special impact. Tarver's example is excellent:

> I recently read in a newspaper column a spirited defense of a public figure. The last line of the column was, "For that he should be congratulated, not chastised." Well and good. The reader gobbles up the line in an instant and digests the contrast between congratulations and chastisement. But when

Winston Churchill's radio messages comforted the British people during WWII.

we speak the line we feed it to a listener morsel by morsel. And the last two words prove to be rather bland. We need to hear "For that he should not be chastised, he should be congratulated." More words; but more important, a different order. . . . In the slower pace of speech, individual words stand out more, and thus time accords a special emphasis to the last idea, the climactic idea in the sentence.

As a rule, then, the stronger, more impressive idea should be saved for the end. And it will often be the case that the punch comes from a positive rather than a negative thought.[5]

Tarver's advice to *build up* to your most important point within a sentence repeats a structural principle discussed in Chapter 9—that the main points of a speech often work best when arranged in an order of ascending importance.

Tarver also advises us to take full advantage of the rhythm of oral speech. Spoken language can play on the senses like a drum. The beat of the words can embed them in memory and charge them with emotion. At a low point during World War II, when a German invasion of Great Britain seemed imminent, Prime Minister Winston Churchill spoke on radio to the British people in words that seemed to march in military formation. Read the following language aloud to savor its full oral power:

> We shall not flag nor fail. We shall go on to the end. We shall fight in France and on the seas and oceans; we shall fight with growing confidence and growing strength in the air. We shall defend our island whatever the cost may be; we shall fight on beaches, landing grounds, in fields, in streets and on the hills. We shall never surrender. . . .[6]

■ **When used skillfully, the spoken word has special power to influence listeners.**

1. It can influence how listeners see subjects.

2. It can influence how listeners feel about those subjects.

3. It can influence how listeners identify with one another.

4. It can influence how listeners act.[7]

Understanding this special power—and how it can be abused as well as used—is essential for both speaker and listener.

The Power to Make Listeners See

Speakers and listeners often see subjects in different ways. The artful use of language, however, can close the gap that separates them. Consider, for example, the problem

Speaker's Notes 12.1

Features of the Spoken Word

Consider these features of the spoken word compared to the written word:

1. The spoken word is more spontaneous and less formal.

2. It can be more colorful and intense.

3. It is more interactive and personal.

4. It is simpler, more repetitive, and may need amplification.

5. It arranges the order of language for maximum impact.

6. It takes advantage of rhythm to engage listeners.

7. It can influence how listeners see their world, how they feel about it, how they identify with each other, and how they act.

that confronted one of our students, Scott Champlin. Scott wanted to share an experience he had had while serving in the military. One option was to describe the experience matter-of-factly:

> While I was parachuting into Panama as part of Operation "Just Cause," I was wounded by a tracer bullet.

InterConnections.
LearnMore:

The Spoken Word

Verbivore: for Lovers of Language

http://verbivore.com

> *Site devoted to "verbivores," who "feast on the English language." Written and maintained by Richard Lederer, author of* Anguished English: An Anthology of Accidental Assaults upon Our Language *(Dell, 1989), it explores the uses and misuses of language; see especially its "Language Links on the Net," a comprehensive guide to classic sites focusing on style, grammar, and the ways of words.*

Power of Words

http://prisonsucks.com/scans/instead_of_prisons/index.shtml

> *Fascinating study of the power of words in the criminal justice system, especially as language functions as a semantic prison in support of the literal penal system; authors are activists who wish to abolish prisons.*

Language as the Tool of Thought

www.bartleby.com/64/

> The American Heritage Book of English Usage *offers a practical guide to contemporary English. See especially the sections on style and diction.*

Avoiding Common Errors in English

www.wsu.edu/~brians/errors/index.html

> *A useful Web site designed to help students keep from sounding unintelligent or ignorant; concentrates mainly on errors of usage in American English; developed and maintained by Professor Paul Brians, Department of English, Washington State University.*

But that option seemed less than adequate. How could he use words to convey the *true sense* of that experience? The depiction he developed allowed listeners to share his leap into danger:

> The darkness of two o'clock in the morning was penetrated by streaks of red light marking the paths of tracer rounds as they cut their way through the night. Suddenly, I felt something hit me in the right leg with a force that spun me around like a twisted yo-yo at the end of a string.

Here the use of contrast—between "darkness" and "streaks of red light"—paints a vivid word picture. Action verbs such as *penetrated, cut,* and *spun* enliven the picture. The simile—"like a twisted yo-yo at the end of a string"—brings the picture into sharp focus. Through his artful word choice, Scott was able to share the meaning of his experience.

The power to influence how listeners see things is particularly important when a topic is unfamiliar or unusual. In such cases, your words can become windows that reveal the subject with startling clarity. There can, however, be a negative side to this power of depiction. When listeners don't have a picture of their own to compare with the one revealed by the speaker's words, they are susceptible to deception. Over four hundred years ago, the Renaissance scholar Francis Bacon suggested that the glass in the windows of depiction can be "enchanted": That is, the perspective may be distorted. Words can color or alter things, thus disguising or obscuring reality. The power to make listeners see can also be a power that blinds them.

The Power to Awaken Feelings

Language also can awaken powerful feelings. It can touch listeners and change their attitudes. Nowhere have we seen this power described more eloquently than by twelve-year-old Katherine Stout of Goodlettsville, Tennessee. In her entry in a junior-high school "Letters About Literature" competition sponsored by Humanities Tennessee, Katie wrote: "Words cannot break bones, but they can break hearts."[8] This power of words is used ethically when it *supplements* sound reasoning and credible evidence. It is abused if speakers *substitute* appeals to feelings for evidence or reasoning.

To arouse emotions, language must overcome the barriers of time, distance, and apathy.

Overcoming Time.   Listeners live in the present. This makes it difficult for speakers to awaken feelings about events that lie in the remote past or the distant future. To overcome this obstacle, speakers can use language to make the past and future come alive. Stories that recapture feelings from the past are often told at company meetings to re-create the human dimension of the business and to reestablish corporate heritage and culture. In the following story, the speaker reminds listeners of the legend of Federal Express, a pioneer in overnight delivery:

> You know, we take a lot for granted. It's hard to remember that Federal Express was once just a fly-by-night dream, a crazy idea in which a few people had invested—not just their time and their money but their lives and futures. I remember one time early on when things weren't going so well. We were really up against it. Couldn't even make the payroll that week. It looked like we were going to crash. Fred [Smith, founder of the company] was in a deep funk. Never saw him quite like that before or since. "What the hell," he said, and flew off to Las Vegas. The next day he flew back and his face was

shining. "We're going to make it," he said. He had won $27,000 at the black-jack table! And we made it. We met the payroll. And then things began to turn around, and Federal Express grew into the giant it is today.[9]

This story enlivens the past by emphasizing the contrast of emotions—the "deep funk" versus the "shining" face. The use of lively, colloquial dialogue—"What the hell," and "We're going to make it!"—re-creates the excitement and brings those feelings into the present. It would not have been as effective had the speaker simply said, "Fred was depressed, but after he got back from Las Vegas he was confident." Such a bare summary would have distanced the listener and diminished the emotional power of the scene.

Language can also bring the future close to listeners. Because words can cross the barrier of time, both tradition and a vision of tomorrow can guide us through the present.

Overcoming Distance. The closer anything is to us, the easier it is to develop feelings about it. But what if speakers must discuss faraway people, places, and objects? Words can telescope such subjects and bring them close to hand. Beth Tidmore, our student who won the U.S. Junior Olympics air rifle event at Colorado Springs, demonstrated a special gift for overcoming distance between herself and her listeners.

When she wanted to share her feelings about her shooting experiences, she concentrated on sensory details of touch and smell. "My friends," she said, "don't know what it's like to feel the cold, smooth wood of the cheekpiece against your face. And they don't know the rich smell of Hoppe's No. 9 [oil] when you're cleaning your rifle." Through such sensory descriptions, she was able to communicate with listeners who themselves were far removed from such experiences.

Beth was even more effective when she appealed to her listeners to become involved in Special Olympics events. To move their feelings, Beth used a technique that—when successful—collapses the distance between listeners and subjects. This technique, the vicarious experience narrative, described earlier in Chapter 8, *invites listeners to imagine themselves participating in the action advocated by the speaker.*

> I've had so many great experiences, but these are hard to describe without overworking words like "fulfilling" and "rewarding." So I'm going to let you experience it for yourself. I want everybody to pack your bags—we're going to the Special Olympics summer games in Georgia!

Beth then became a tour guide for her listeners, walking them through the moments that would move them in such dramatic ways. Again, she had effectively bridged the distance between her subject and her audience.

Overcoming Apathy. We live in an age of communication overkill. Modern audiences are beset with an endless barrage of information, persuasion, and entertainment. As a result, many of us become jaded—we may even develop a *resistance* to communication and turn away from appeals to our feelings and commitment.

Sally Duncan found an especially poignant way to overcome such apathy. Interestingly, it worked because of incompetent language usage. Sally began her informative speech by projecting a picture of her grandmother on the screen behind the lectern. She described her as a cultured, elegant woman who had a masters degree, taught English, and took Sally to art museums and the theater. "Now," she said, "let me read my last letter from Nanny:"

> Dear Sally. I am finally around to answer your last. You have to look over me. Ha. I am so sorry to when you called Sunday why didn't you remind me. Steph had us all so upset leaving and not telling no she was going back but we have a good snow ha and Kathy can't drive on ice so I never get a pretty card but they have a thing to see through an envelope. I haven't got any in the bank until I get my homestead check so I'm just sending this. Ha. When you was talking on the phone Cathy had Ben and got my groceries and I had to unlock the door. I forgot to say hold and I don't have Claudette's number so forgive me for being so silly. Ha. Nara said to tell you she isn't doing no good well one is doing pretty good and my eyes. Love, Nanny.

Sally paused for a long moment, and then said, "My Nanny has Alzheimer's." We were riveted as she went on to describe the disease and its effects, and all of us were ready to support any effort to overcome it.

The role of language in arousing feeling is also underscored by the contrast between denotative and connotative forms of meaning. The **denotative meaning** of a word is its dictionary definition or generally agreed-on objective usage. For example, the denotative definition of *alcohol* is "a colorless, volatile, flammable liquid, obtained by the fermentation of sugars or starches, which is widely used as a solvent, drug base, explosive, or intoxicating beverage."[10] How different this definition is from the two connotative definitions offered in this chapter's opening example! **Connotative meaning** invests a subject with the speaker's personal connections and emotions. Thus, the "intoxicating beverage" is no longer just a chemical substance but rather is "the poison scourge" or "the oil of conversation." Connotative language intensifies feelings: Denotative language encourages detachment.

The Power to Bring Listeners Together

In many situations, individual action is not enough. It may take people working together to get things done, and language can bring them together. Words can also bring people together in times of grief. On April 16, 2007, a lone gunman killed 32 innocent victims at Virginia Tech University before turning his gun on himself. At a memorial ceremony the next day, the faculty and student body met to find what comfort they could during those tragic days. The honor of closing the ceremony fell to Nikki Giovanni, an acclaimed poet who was also a University Distinguished Professor. In her remarks, Giovanni combined the power of poetry and prose to express feelings appropriate to the moment:

Poet and professor Nikki Giovanni's eloquent language brought listeners together during a memorial service at Virginia Tech University.

> We are Virginia Tech.
> We are strong enough to stand tall
>   tearlessly;
> We are brave enough to bend to cry
> And sad enough to know we must laugh
>   again.
> We are Virginia Tech.

---

denotative meaning The dictionary definition or objective meaning of a word.

connotative meaning The emotional, subjective, personal meaning that certain words can evoke in listeners.

. . . We will continue to invent the future through our blood and tears, through all this sadness . . . . We will prevail![11]

Note the emphasis on "We," the great pronoun of inclusion. Note also how Giovanni combines opposites to create a sense of unity: sadness and laughter, "standing tall tearlessly" and "bending to cry," proposing that a promising future will grow out of the tragic past—that the past and future will come together just as her listeners are brought together by her words.

Although words can unite people, they can also drive them apart. Name calling, exclusionary language, and unsupported accusations can be notorious dividers.

The Power to Encourage Action

Even if your listeners share an identity, they still may not be ready to act. What might stand in their way? For one thing, they may not be convinced of the soundness of your proposal. They may not trust you, or they may not think they can do anything about a problem. Finally, they may not be ready to invest the energy or take the risk that action demands.

Your language must convince listeners that action is necessary, that your ideas are sound, and that success is possible. In her speech urging students to act to improve off-campus housing conditions (see Chapter 16), Anna Aley painted vivid word-pictures of deplorable off-campus housing. She supported these descriptions with both factual examples and her personal experiences. She also reminded listeners that if they acted together, they could bring about change:

> What can one student do to change the practices of numerous Manhattan landlords? Nothing, if that student is alone. But just think of what we could accomplish if we got all 13,600 off-campus students involved in this issue! Think what we could accomplish if we got even a fraction of those students involved!

Anna then proposed specific actions that did not call for great effort or risk. In short, she made commitment as easy as possible. She concluded with an appeal to action:

> Kansas State students have been putting up with substandard living conditions for too long. It's time we finally got together to do something about this problem. Join the Off-Campus Association. Sign my petition. Let's send a message to these slumlords that we're not going to put up with this any more. We don't have to live in slums.

Anna's words expressed both her indignation and the urgency of the problem. Her references to time—"too long" and "it's time"—called for immediate action. Her final appeals to join the association and sign the petition were expressed in short sentences that packed a lot of punch. Her repetition of "slumlords" and "slums" motivated her listeners to transform their indignation into action.

Anna also illustrated another language strategy that is important when you want to move people to action: the ability to depict dramas showing what is at stake and what roles listeners should take.[12] Such scenarios draw clear lines between right and wrong. Be careful, however, not to go overboard with such techniques. Ethical communication requires that you maintain respect for all involved in conflict. As both

Uniting a Divided Group

Use the following strategies to unite a divided group:

1. Bring to life images of common heroes and enemies.

2. Describe group traditions they may have forgotten.

3. Depict the deeper values they share.

4. Picture common problems.

5. Illustrate goals they share.

6. Spell out the first step they can take together, and urge them to take it.

7. Speak the language of inclusion, such as using family or team metaphors.

speaker and listener, be wary of melodramas that offer stark contrasts between good and evil. Such depictions often distort reality.

The Six C's of Language Use

o harness the power of language in your speeches, your words must meet certain standards: clarity, color, concreteness, correctness, conciseness, and cultural sensitivity. We call these the six C's of oral language.

Clarity

Clarity is the first standard, because if your words are not clear, listeners cannot understand your meaning. This may seem obvious, but it is often ignored! To be clear, you must yourself understand what you want to say. Next, you must find words that convey your ideas as precisely and as simply as possible. Your voice, face, and gestures should help to reinforce the idea as you present it, a process we discuss in Chapter 13. Your listeners must be capable of interpreting your words and nonverbal cues, so they must be able to see and hear you unimpeded by lecterns or by competing noise. The standard of clarity is met when something closely approximating the idea you intend is reproduced in the minds of these listeners.

One factor that impairs clarity is the use of **jargon**, the technical language that is specific to a profession. Such language is often referred to with an *-ese* at the end, as in "speaking computerese." If you use jargon before an audience that doesn't share that technical vocabulary, you will not be understood. For example, "We expect a positive vorticity advective" may be perfectly understandable to a group of meteorologists, but for most audiences, simply saying, "It's going to rain" would be much clearer. Speakers who fall into the jargon trap are so used to using technical language that they forget that others may not grasp it. It does not occur to them that they must translate the jargon into lay language to be understood by general audiences. Adapting technical language so that nonspecialists can understand it can be challenging, but an example in Chapter 8 (page 175), explaining how the OnStar system works in cars, shows how this can be done effectively.

A similar problem is using words that are needlessly overblown and pretentious. A notorious example occurred when signmakers wanted to tell tourists how to leave the Barnum museum. Rather than drawing an arrow with the word Exit above it, they wrote "To the Egress." There's no telling how many visitors left the museum by

jargon Technical language related to a specific field that may be incomprehensible to a general audience.

mistake, thinking that they were going to see that rare creature—a living, breathing "Egress."

Sometimes speakers may deliberately avoid clarity—because the truth may hurt. At moments, these efforts may be rather lighthearted, as when a sports commentator, speaking of the quarterback on a football team, said, "He has ball security issues." The issue he was trying to soften was that the quarterback fumbled a lot. Such efforts to evade and obscure the truth are called **euphemisms**. At other moments, such efforts may seem less innocent. When questioned in 2007 over whether government efforts to find Osama bin Laden should be described as a "failure," a homeland security official responded: "It's a success that hasn't occurred yet."[13]

Even more unethical is the use of words to deliberately befuddle listeners and hide unpleasant truths. One term for such language is **doublespeak**, in which words can point in the direction opposite from the reality they should be describing. (See Figure 12.1.) The *New York Times* charged that the Bush administration developed what they call *ecospeak* (an apparent variation of *doublespeak*) to disguise pro-business and anti-environmental initiatives:

> Mr. Bush . . . may fairly be said to have become the master of the ostensibly ecofriendly sound bite. . . . "Healthy Forests," for instance, describes an initiative aimed mainly at benefiting the timber industry rather than the communities threatened by fire. "Freedom Car" (to be powered by "Freedom Fuel") describes a program to develop a hydrogen-fueled car that, while beguiling in the long term, absolves automakers from making the near-term improvements in fuel economy necessary to reduce oil dependence and the threat of global warming . . . . [In another case] Mr. Bush's purpose was to defend his controversial decision in August to rewrite the Clean Air Act in ways that spared power companies the expense of making investments in pollution controls. . . . His basic argument was that the rules thwarted modernization and economic growth . . . and that his own initiative—dubbed "Clear Skies," in the come-hither nomenclature favored by the White House—would achieve equal results at lower cost.[14]

Figure 12.1

Doublespeak

When they say:	What they often mean is:
Marital discord	Spouse beating
Department of human biodynamics	Department of physical education
Downsizing	Firing
Making a salary adjustment	Cutting your pay
Failed to fulfill wellness potential	Died
Chronologically experienced citizen	Old codger
Initial and pass on	Let's spread the blame
Friendly fire	We killed our own people
Collateral damage	We killed innocent people

---

euphemism Sometimes humorous use of words to soften or evade the truth of a situation.

doublespeak Using words that point in the direction opposite from the reality they should be describing.

Fearing the reactions of listeners who might actually understand their meaning, such speakers hide behind a cloud of technobabble.

How can you avoid such violations of the clarity standard? One way is through **amplification**, which extends the time listeners have for contemplating an idea and helps them bring it into sharper focus. You amplify an idea by defining it, repeating it, rephrasing it, offering examples of it, and contrasting it with more familiar and concrete subjects. In effect, you tell listeners something and then expand what you have just said. Bill Gates used amplification effectively in his speech on reforming high school education. The following statement from the speech illustrates how definition and contrast especially can clarify an idea:

> America's high schools are obsolete. By obsolete, I don't just mean that our high schools are broken, flawed, and underfunded—though a case could be made for every one of those points.
>
> By obsolete, I mean that our high schools—even when they're working exactly as designed—cannot teach our kids what they need to know today.
>
> Training the workforce of tomorrow with the high schools of today is like trying to teach kids about today's computers on a 50-year-old mainframe. It's the wrong tool for the times.[15]

Color

Color refers to the emotional intensity or vividness of language. Colorful words are memorable because they stand out in our minds. Speakers who use them also are remembered.

In political campaigns, colorful language often gives one candidate an edge over others. During the 1996 presidential primaries, Pat Buchanan became a leading contender, at least partially because of his skill with words. Early in the campaign, another candidate had gained a great deal of attention by proposing tax reform. A third contender, Senator Phil Gramm, criticized this proposal as follows:

> I reject the idea that income derived from labor should be taxed and that income derived from capital should not.[16]

Nice contrast, but about as flat as the tax he was talking about. Now look at how Buchanan expressed the same idea:

> Under Forbes's plan, lounge lizards in Palm Beach would pay a lower tax rate than steelworkers in Youngstown.

Whereas Gramm's words were abstract, Buchanan's were colorful. "Lounge lizards" is striking. So is the use of contrast, setting the "lounge lizards" against steelworkers, Palm Beach against Youngstown. It's sloth and privilege against character and virtue, and we know which side Buchanan is on.

Colorful language paints striking pictures for listeners. Notice how student Leslie Eason made Tiger Woods come alive in her speech of tribute:

> Mothers with daughters of a certain age (mine included) describe him as the son-in-law they'd like to have. Six foot two, a hundred fifty-five pounds, smart—Stanford, remember. Clean cut in his creased khakis, curly hair, gorgeous teeth. Skin the color of what they used to call "suntan" in the Crayola box. And rich. Very rich.

amplification The art of developing ideas by finding ways to restate them in a speech.

He's the very opposite of the gangsta boys in the hood. Boys who wear their pants hanging below their belt as though they were already in the penitentiary. Next to them he's prep school and Pepsodent.

Colorful language is also the key to humor. Note how country humorist "Cotton" Ivy used simple and colorful language to describe his adventures with dieting:

> The doctor told me to watch my weight and I got it out there so I can watch it. Anyway, I figured he'd put me on a diet 'cause I can take a shower and my knees not get wet. So Doc said I had to cut back on bread. I said, "Doc, if I don't have bread, what on earth will I use to sop gravy with?" . . . I always thought a balanced diet was a fried pie in each hand.[17]

One very special type of colorful language is **slang**. You've probably been told most of your life not to use slang, that it is a mark of illiteracy and coarseness, that it is vulgar, that it epitomizes "bad" English. But according to general semanticist S. I. Hayakawa, slang can also be "the poetry of everyday life." Or, as the poet Carl Sandburg noted, slang is "language that rolls up its sleeves, spits on its hands, and goes to work."

Slang has its use in speeches: It can add vigor to your message and be a source of identification between you and listeners. But use it with caution. Slang is inappropriate on formal occasions when a high level of decorum is called for. Moreover, you must be certain that your audience will understand your slang. If you have to stop and define your words, they will lose their punch. In such cases, slang will distance you from your listeners, not create identification. You must also be careful about using ethnic slang or other words that your audience might find offensive. Finally, slang should be used sparingly—to emphasize a point or add a dash of humor and color. It should supplement Standard English usage in your speech, not replace it.

Using colorful language makes a speech interesting. It can enhance your ethos by increasing your attractiveness. For these reasons, color is an important standard for the effective use of language.

Concreteness

It is almost impossible to discuss any significant topic without using some abstract words. However, if you use language that is overly abstract, your audience may lose interest. Moreover, because abstract language is more ambiguous than concrete language, a speech full of abstractions invites misunderstanding. Consider this continuum of terms describing a cat.

Speaker's Notes 12.3

The Six C's of Effective Language Use

Make certain your language meets these criteria for effective language use.

1. Clarity makes speeches understandable.

2. Color adds punch to your message.

3. Concreteness reduces misunderstandings.

4. Correctness enhances your credibility.

5. Conciseness keeps you from wasting your audience's time.

6. Cultural sensitivity is an ethical imperative.

slang The language of the street.

Mehitabel is a/an

| creature | animal | mammal | cat | Persian cat | gray Persian cat |

abstract ————————————————————————————▶ concrete

A similar continuum can be applied to active verbs. If we wanted to describe how a person moves, we could use any of the following terms:

Jennifer

| moves | walks | strides |

abstract ————————————————————————————▶ concrete

The more concrete your language, the more pictorial and precise the information you convey. Concrete words are also easier for listeners to remember. Your language should be as concrete as the subject permits.

Correctness

Nothing can damage your credibility more than the misuse of language. Glaring mistakes in grammar can make you seem uneducated and even ignorant. While touting his education plan, one prominent politician told listeners that the most important consideration should be, "Is your children learning?" Other common grammatical errors that make listeners cringe are listed in Figure 12.2.

Mistakes in word selection can be as damaging as mistakes in grammar. Occasionally, beginning speakers, wanting to impress people with the size of their vocabulary, get caught up in the "thesaurus syndrome." They will look up a simple word to find a synonym that sounds more impressive or sophisticated. What they may not realize is that the words shown as synonyms often have slightly different meanings. For example, the words *disorganize* and *derange* are sometimes listed as synonyms. But if you refer to a disorganized person as "deranged," the person's reaction could be interesting.

People often err when using words that sound similar. Such confusions are called **malapropisms**, after Mrs. Malaprop, a character in an eighteenth-century play by Richard Sheridan. She would say, "He is the very *pineapple* of politeness," when she meant *pinnacle*. A prominent baseball player, trying to explain why he had forgotten an appointment for an interview, said, "I must have had *ambrosia*" (which probably caused his *amnesia*, which is what he apparently meant). Archie Bunker, in the classic TV show *All in the Family*, was prone to malapropisms, such as "Don't let your imagination run *rancid*" when he meant *rampant*. William J. Crocker of Armidale College in New South Wales, Australia, collected the following malapropisms from his students:

A speaker can add interest to his talk with an *antidote*. [anecdote]

Disagreements can arise from an unintended *conception*. [Indeed they can! Inference would work better]

The speaker hopes to arouse *apathy* in his audience. [sympathy? empathy?]

Good language can be reinforced by good *gestation*. [gestures]

The speaker can use either an inductive or a *seductive* approach. [deductive][18]

Students, ballplayers, and fictional characters are not the only ones who make such blunders. Elected officials are also not above an occasional malapropism. One former United States senator declared that he would oppose to his last ounce of energy any effort to build a "nuclear waste *suppository*" [repository] in his state. A

malapropisms Language errors that occur when a word is confused with another word that sounds like it.

Figure 12.2

Grammatical Errors

1. Using the wrong tense or verb form:
   Wrong: He *done* us a big favor.
   Right: He *did* us a big favor.

2. Lack of agreement between subject and verb:
   Wrong: *Is* your students giving speeches?
   Right: *Are* your students giving speeches?

3. Using the wrong word
   Wrong: *Caricature* is the most important factor in choosing a mate.
   Right: *Character* is the most important factor in choosing a mate.

4. Lack of agreement between a pronoun and its antecedent:
   Wrong: A hyperactive *person* will work *themselves* to death.
   Right: Hyperactive *people* will work *themselves* to death.
   or
   A hyperactive *woman* will work *herself* to death.

5. Improper type of pronoun used as subject:
   Wrong: *Him* and *me* decided to go to the library.
   Right: *He* and *I* decided to go to the library.

6. Improper type of pronoun used as object:
   Wrong: The speaker's lack of information dismayed my students and *I*.
   Right: The speaker's lack of information dismayed my students and *me*.

7. Double negative:
   Wrong: I *don't never* get good grades on my speeches.
   Right: I *never* get good grades on my speeches.

long gone but not forgotten Chicago mayor once commented that he did not believe "in casting *asparagus* [aspersions] on his opponents." And the Speaker of the Texas legislature once acknowledged an award by saying, "I am filled with *humidity*" (perhaps he meant moist hot air as well as humility).

The lesson is clear. To avoid being unintentionally humorous, use a current dictionary to check the meaning of any word you feel uncertain about.

Conciseness

In discussing clarity, we talked about the importance of amplification in speeches. Although it may seem contradictory, you must also be concise, even while you are amplifying your ideas. You must make your points quickly and efficiently.

Simplicity and directness help you be concise. Thomas Jefferson once said, "The most valuable of all talents is that of never using two words when one will do."

Abraham Lincoln was similarly concise as he criticized the verbosity of another speaker: "He can compress the most words into the smallest idea of any man I know." As you work for conciseness, use the active voice rather than the passive in your verbs: "We want action!" is more concise—and more direct, colorful, and clear—than "Action is wanted by us."

You can also achieve conciseness by using **maxims**, those compact sayings that encapsulate beliefs. During the Chinese freedom demonstrations of 1989, a sign carried by students in Tiananmen Square adapted the maxim of Patrick Henry: "Give Me Democracy or Give Me Death." Sadly, the Chinese authorities took them at their word. To reinforce his point that we need to actively (and audibly) confront the problems of racism, sexism, and homophobia, Haven Cockerham, vice president of human resources for Detroit Edison, invented this striking maxim: "Sometimes silence isn't golden—just yellow."[19]

Beyond their conciseness, maxims often evoke cultural memories and invite identification. When the Chinese students adapted the Patrick Henry maxim, they were in effect both declaring that they shared American values and appealing for our assistance in their struggle. When their cause was crushed, many Americans felt the injustice in a personal way, and the resulting tension between the Chinese government and our own lingers to this day.

Maxims have the potential to attract mass-media attention during demonstrations. When printed on signs, they can be picked up as signature statements for movements or campaigns. For example, their brevity and dramatic impact make them well suited to display on television's evening news.

A caution is in order about using maxims. They should not be substituted for a carefully designed and well-supported argument. However, once you have developed a responsible and substantive speech, consider using maxims to reinforce your message.

Cultural Sensitivity

Because words can either lift and unite or wound and hurt your audience, you must exercise **cultural sensitivity** in your choice of language. Looking back into the history of human communication, you will find little about cultural sensitivity. The ancient Greeks, for example, worried only about speaking to other male Athenians who were "free men" and citizens. Today, with the increasing emphasis on empowering diverse cultures, lifestyles, and races and the pursuit of gender equity, cultural sensitivity becomes an important standard for effective language usage.

As we noted in Chapter 5, your classroom audience may represent many different cultures. As listeners, they will be sensitive to clumsy efforts by speakers to identify with folkways that aren't their own. We have already noted how one Republican presidential hopeful offended the Cuban expatriate community. While speaking in Miami, he ended his speech by shouting a political maxim that also, unfortunately, happened to be the favorite sign-off of Fidel Castro's speeches.

Democrats too have had their share of cultural blunders. Once, while speaking in Wisconsin during the 2004 presidential campaign, the democratic candidate, John Kerry, mentioned the much-beloved Green Bay Packers. In the process, however, he referred to Lambeau Field as "Lambert Field." Bad mistake! He had mispronounced the name of "the hallowed grounds on which the Packers play, the frozen tundra of Curly Lambeau Field." Jim VandeHei, writing for the *Washington Post*, pointed up the significance of this boner:

> That's akin to calling the Yankees the Yankers or the Chicago Bulls the Bells. This is a place where . . . thousands of fans wear a big chunk of yellow foam

---

maxims Brief and particularly apt sayings.   **cultural sensitivity** The respectful appreciation of diversity within an audience.

Ethics *Alert! 12.1*

The Ethical Use of Powerful Language

To use the power of words in ethical ways, follow these guidelines:

1. Avoid depictions that distort reality: Let your words illuminate the subject, not blind the listener.

2. Use words to support sound reasoning, not substitute for it.

3. Use language to empower both traditions and visions.

4. Use images to renew appreciation of shared values.

5. Use language to strengthen the ties of community, not divide people.

6. Use language to overcome inertia and inspire listeners to action.

7. Be cautious about melodramatic language that reduces complex issues and the people in disputes into good versus evil.

cheese atop their head with the pride of a new parent. "I got some advice for him," [President] Bush told Wisconsinites a few days after the Lambert gaffe. "If someone offers you a cheesehead, don't say you want some wine, just put it on your head and take a seat at *Lambeau* Field."[20]

The seemingly innocent mistake played into the Republican strategy of depicting Kerry as an elitist and a patrician who was uncomfortable with the culture of the people.

A lack of cultural sensitivity almost always has negative consequences. At best, audience members may be mildly offended; at worst, they will be irate enough to reject both you and your message. Cultural sensitivity begins with being attuned to the diversity of your audience and careful about the words you choose. Don't be like the politician who singled out some audience members in wheelchairs for special praise. After lauding their accomplishments, he said, "Now, will you all stand and be recognized?"

Although you must make some generalizations about your audience, avoid getting caught up in stereotypes that suggest that one group is inferior in any way to another. Stay away from racial, ethnic, religious, or gender-based humor, and avoid any expressions that might be interpreted as racist or sexist (see Speaker's Notes 5.1 for guidelines on avoiding racist and sexist language).

Magnifying the Power of Language

There are critical moments in a speech—at the beginning, at the ending, or as arguments reach their conclusions—when you want your words to be most effective. At these moments, you can call on special techniques that magnify the power of language.

The branch of communication study that deals with identifying and understanding these techniques is called *rhetorical style*. Over the centuries, many such techniques have been identified; they seem to be grounded in our nature and to have evolved to meet our need for effective communication. Here we discuss three broad categories of techniques that are especially useful for public speaking: various forms of *figurative language*, techniques that alter the customary *order* of words, and

Cultural sensitivity requires that you be attuned to the diversity of your audience, respectful of the differences between cultural groups, and careful about the words you choose.

techniques that exploit the *sounds* of words for special effects.

Using Figurative Language

Figurative language uses words in surprising and unusual ways. Although many kinds of such language have been identified, we focus on six forms that are especially useful: metaphors, enduring metaphors, similes, personifications, culturetypes, and ideographs.

Metaphors. As we noted in Chapter 8, drawing comparisons is a fundamental way in which our minds work to understand unfamiliar or abstract ideas. A **metaphor** offers a brief, concentrated form of comparison that is implied, unexpected, and sometimes even startling. It connects elements of experience that are not usually related. When you use a metaphor, you pull a rabbit out of a hat. Having read that, your first reaction might be, "Wait a minute, words are not rabbits and language is not a hat!" But when a metaphor works, the listener's next reaction is, "Oooh, I see what you mean!" Good metaphors reveal unexpected similarities in striking ways. They also can add color and concreteness to your message.

Metaphors may be our most useful and versatile stylistic tool. They can be especially helpful in introductions and conclusions. At the beginnings of speeches, metaphors can offer an overall frame of understanding in which a topic can develop. Note how Antoinette M. Bailey, president of the Boeing-McDonnell Foundation, used a wave metaphor to open a speech presented to the International Women in Aviation Conference:

> Suppose we have gone down to the beach on a quiet day. We are standing in the water, admiring the view. Suddenly, a speedboat zooms by at full throttle. Seconds later, we are struck by a powerful wave. This is a bow wave, and it can knock you off your feet if you aren't prepared for it. A very large and fast-moving bow wave is just now beginning to hit the aerospace industry. This morning I want to talk about what we, as an industry, and we, as women, should do to prepare for it.[21]

In a similar vein, concluding metaphors can offer a final frame of understanding that interprets the meaning of a speech for its listeners. When Martin Luther King Jr. spoke to the striking sanitation workers in Memphis the night before he was assassinated, he talked of the "spiritual journey" that his listeners had traveled. He ended his speech by saying that he had climbed the mountain ahead of them—that he had "seen the Promised Land." These metaphors of the journey and the mountain lifted his listeners and allowed them to share his vision, just as he had earlier shared his "dream" with them in his famous "I Have a Dream" oration. More than just communicating in a superficial way, such metaphors may reveal the speaker's soul.

figurative language The use of words in certain surprising and unusual ways in order to magnify the power of their meaning.

metaphor Brief, concentrated form of comparison that is implied and often surprising. It connects elements of experience that are not usually related in order to create a new perspective.

Because metaphors can be so powerful, you should select them carefully and use them with restraint. First, *the gravity of the metaphor must match the seriousness of your subject.* Just as you would not typically wear formal attire to a basketball game, you should not use certain metaphors to express certain subjects. If you used Dr. King's mountaintop image to express your overview of the can recycling industry, the effect might be more comic than persuasive.

Second, *mixing metaphors by combining images that don't fit together can confuse listeners and lower their estimation of your competence.* The politician who attacked an opponent saying, "You can't have it both ways in the political process. You can't take the high horse and then claim the low road," mixed his metaphors.

Third, *you also should avoid trite metaphors,* such as "that person [or idea or practice] is so cool" or "I was on an emotional roller coaster." Overuse has turned these metaphors into clichés that no longer affect people. Not only are they ineffective, but using them may again damage your ethos. Tired comparisons suggest a dull mind.

Enduring Metaphors. One special group of metaphors taps into shared experience that persists across time and that crosses many cultural boundaries. These **enduring metaphors** are especially popular in speeches, perhaps because they invoke experience that has great meaning and that can bring people together. They connect their particular, timebound subjects with timeless themes, such as light and darkness, storms, the sea, disease, and the family. A brief look at three of these metaphors demonstrates their potential power to magnify meaning.[22]

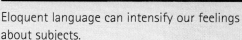
Eloquent language can intensify our feelings about subjects.

Light and Darkness. From the beginning of time, people have made negative associations with darkness. The dark is cold, unfriendly, and dangerous. On the other hand, light brings warmth and safety. It restores control. When speakers use the light–darkness metaphor, they usually equate problems or bad times with darkness and solutions or recovery with light. The speaker's proposal may offer the "dawn," a "candle to light our way," or a "beacon of hope."

Storms and the Sea. The storm metaphor is often used when describing problems. Typically, the storm occurs at sea—a dangerous place under the best of conditions. When political problems are the focus of the speech, the "captain" who "steers the ship of state" can reassure us with his programs or principles—and make them seem very attractive in the process. In his 2001 inaugural address, George W. Bush noted that "through much of the last century, America's faith in freedom and democracy was a rock in a raging sea."[23]

The Family. Family metaphors express the dream of a close, loving relationship among people through such images as "the family of humanity."[24] These metaphors can be especially useful when listeners may feel alienated from each other and from their surroundings. In such situations, family metaphors can be a powerful force to bring listeners together and to effect identification. Wade Steck demonstrated the

enduring metaphors Metaphors of unusual power and popularity that are based on experience that lasts across time and that crosses many cultural boundaries.

potential of such metaphors as he was describing his experiences at the University of Memphis Frosh Camp Program, his introduction to college life:

> As we were riding to camp, my heart was beating really fast. I guess I was kind of nervous—didn't know what I was getting into, wasn't sure I was ready to meet all these new people. But when I got to Frosh Camp, they made me feel at home. First thing they did was to break us into "families" of ten to twelve people who would share the same cabin for those few days. Each "family" had its counselors, carefully selected juniors and seniors who were really called your "mom" and "dad." Sounds corny, I guess, but it did put my mind at ease. . . . The thing I liked most were the Fireside Chats. At night under the stars, watching the logs burn and listening to the crickets chirp, people would just relax and talk about what was in their hearts. I found out those in my family shared my concerns and anxieties. Once we got those out in the open and talked about them, we were ready to go on to college and to start our new lives.

Similarly, the *disease* metaphor pictures our problems as illness and offers solutions in the form of cures.[25] Metaphors of *war and peace* can frame conflict situations and our quest for their resolution.[26] The *building* metaphor, as when we talk about "laying the foundation" for the future, emphasizes our ancient impulse to shape and control the conditions of our lives. And *spatial* metaphors often reflect striving upward and moving forward toward goals.[27]

Perhaps the reason such metaphors are so powerful is that they express the motives we discussed in Chapter 5. Light and darkness, for example, may connect with safety needs (representing our fears as darkness) or esteem and self-actualization needs (representing our successes and growth in terms of light).

Similes.   A **simile** is a variation of metaphor that tips its hand by warning listeners that a comparison is coming. Words such as *like* or *as* function as signals that soften the impact of the expression. The result is to offer a more controlled form of figuration in which the speaker guides the comparison in order to create certain planned effects. One such effect is to help listeners imagine things that are far removed from their experience. Remember Scott Champlin's words, "a force that spun me around *like* a twisted yo-yo at the end of a string"? Most of us, we hope, will never be hit by a tracer bullet while parachuting, but helped by the simile, we can imagine the experience.

A second intended effect is to add interest and concrete focus to experience that may seem dull and remote from listeners' lives. Big business decisions can seem far removed from everyday experience, and not very interesting. But note how John Thorne, a critic of business practices at AT&T, used simile to bring color and interest values to his subject:

> By 1996, AT&T had latched onto a business strategy that *resembled* the actions of a balloonist desperate to clear the Alps. AT&T started heaving things overboard, its smart plays along with the bad plays, in order to stay aloft.[28] [italics added]

Similarly, another critic used simile as a lens to focus her feelings about a presidential proposal to send astronauts on an expedition to Mars: "Spending billions in outer space is *like* buying a new Lexus when the fridge is empty and the roof is leaking."[29]

simile A language tool that clarifies something abstract by comparing it with something concrete; usually introduced by "as" or "like."

A final effect of simile, as all these examples illustrate, is to dramatize a subject so that it appeals to our imagination. As he described reaction to his Oscar-winning film, *An Inconvenient Truth*, Al Gore used simile to place interest in global warming into a dramatic frame: "I've seen times in the past when there was a flurry of concern about global warming, and then, *like* a summer storm, it faded. But this time, it may be different."[30]

Although simile is related to metaphor, it is certainly not the same thing. During the 2004 Democratic primary campaign for the presidency, Howard Dean complained about certain below-the-belt tactics being used against him. When his opponents responded that he himself was guilty of using dehumanizing metaphors, Dean responded in effect that what he had actually used was a simile. Here is how the exchange went, as recorded in *Newsweek*:

> [Interviewer]: There are some people who would say that it takes a little bit of chutzpah for you to complain since at various times you've called the people inside Washington cockroaches—
> [Dean]: That actually is not true. What I said was that they'll be scurrying around in Washington just like cockroaches. That is not calling members of Congress cockroaches.[31]

Dean, at least, believed that there was a substantial difference between metaphor and simile! As the Dean example indicates, you should be careful about the words you choose. When they work well, however, similes can magnify the effect of comparison.

Personifications. One persistent form of figurative speech, **personification**, treats inanimate subjects, such as ideas or institutions, as though they had human form or feeling. The Chinese students who were demonstrating for freedom in Tiananmen Square also carried a statue they called the "Goddess of Liberty." They were borrowing a personification that has long been used in the Western world: the representation of liberty as a woman.[32] When those students then had to confront tanks, and their oppressors destroyed the symbol of liberty, it was easy for many, living thousands of miles away in another culture, to feel even more angry over their fate. Personification makes it easier to arouse feelings about people and values that might otherwise seem abstract and distant.

Culturetypes. **Culturetypes**, sometimes stated in the form of metaphor, express the values, identity, and goals of a particular group and time.[33] In 1960, John F. Kennedy dramatized his presidential campaign by inviting Americans to explore with him "new frontiers" of challenge and discovery. That metaphor worked well in American culture, but it probably would not have made much sense in other countries. For Americans, the frontier is a unique symbol that offers the promise of freedom and opportunity.

Some words that have culturetypal quality include what rhetorical critic Richard Weaver once described as "god and devil terms."[34] He suggested that *progress* has been a primary "god term" of American culture. People often seem willing to follow that word as though it were some kind of divine summons. Tell us to do something in the name of "progress," and many of us will feel obligated to respond. Other terms, such as *science*, *modern*, and *efficient*, are similarly powerful because they seem rooted in American values. If "science" tells us something, we are apt to listen respectfully. If something is "modern," many of us think it is better, probably

---

personification A figure of speech in which nonhuman or abstract subjects are given human qualities.

culturetypes Terms that express the values and goals of a group's culture.

Ethics *Alert! 12.2*

Questions for Resisting Culturetypes and Ideographs

To become more resistant to the power of certain words, we must cultivate a questioning attitude toward them. The following questions may be helpful:

1. Is the substance of the claim really what it purports to be?

2. Are there hidden motives beneath the surface of words?

3. What values are *not* represented here that ought to be considered?

4. What am I being asked to support or do? Can I defend that position or effort?

because it has benefited from "progress." If something is "efficient," many Americans will more often select it over options that are perhaps more ethical or beautiful. On the other hand, words like *terrorist* and *terrorism* are "devil terms." They can make a person, group, or action seem repulsive and threatening.

Culturetypes can change over time: In recent years, words like *natural, communication,* and *environment* have been emerging god terms; *liberalism* and *pollution,* if not devil terms, seem increasingly undesirable.

Ideographs. Communication scholar Michael Calvin McGee identified an especially potent group of culturetypes that he called **ideographs**. These words express a country's basic political values.[35] McGee suggested that words like *freedom, liberty,* and *democracy* are important because they are shorthand expressions of political identity. It is inconceivable to us that other nations might not wish to have a "democratic" form of government or that they might not prize "liberty" over every other value. Expressions such as *"freedom* fighters" and *"democracy* in action" have unusual power for us because they utilize ideographs.

As an audience, we can be especially vulnerable to such language, and it can be dangerous. After all, one person's "freedom fighter" can be another person's "terrorist." We must look behind such glittering generalities to inspect the agendas they may hide. You may recall that in Chapter 4 we discussed "trigger words," the idea that we as individuals may react unthinkingly to certain words that trigger emotional response and short-circuit reflection. Ideographs and culturetypes can function as widely shared, cultural trigger words. They are capable of honorable work: They can magnify the appeal of sound arguments, remind us of our heritage, and suggest that we must be true to our values. But the potential for abusing such words in unethical communication is considerable. You must prove that they apply correctly to your topic. As a speaker, use them sparingly, and as a listener, inspect them carefully.

To develop a healthy resistance to such words, we must learn to apply a system of critical questions whenever we encounter them:

1. *Is this really what it claims to be?* For example, does the development of increasingly more powerful weapons of mass destruction really represent "progress"? Are "freedom fighters" actually thugs?

---

ideographs Compact expressions of a group's basic political faith.

2. *Are those who make these claims legitimate speakers?* For example, are those who advance the "science" of cryonics really "scientists"? Or do they simply exploit our fears of mortality?

3. *Do these claims reflect a proper hierarchy of values?* For example, lopping off the top of a mountain to strip-mine coal may be a highly "efficient" form of mining, but should we be featuring efficiency here? Could protection of the environment be a more important value?

4. *What kinds of actions are these words urging me to endorse or undertake?* For example, should I be asked to support and even die for "democracy" in a nation whose citizens may prefer a different form of government?

Changing the Order of Words

We grow accustomed to words falling into certain patterns in sentences. Strategic changes in the order of words violate these expectations and call attention to the meaning intended. *Antithesis, inversion,* and *parallel construction* all involve changes in the way words are ordered in messages. Their primary functions are to magnify the speaker as a leader and to enhance appeals to action. Let's consider them briefly.

Antithesis.   **Antithesis** arranges different or opposing ideas in the same or adjoining sentences to create a striking contrast. Beth Tidmore used the technique well in her speech on Special Olympics: "With the proper instruction, environment, and encouragement, Special Olympians can learn not only sport skills but life skills." Antithesis also can suggest that the speaker has a clear, decisive grasp of options. It magnifies the speaker as a person of vision, leadership, and action.

President John F. Kennedy often used antithesis in his speeches. Consider these famous words from his Inaugural Address:

> Ask not what your country can do for you—ask what you can do for your country.

You may have learned this quotation in high school and, prompted with the first few words, could probably recite it verbatim today. But Kennedy said essentially the same thing during a campaign speech in September 1960:

> The new frontier is not what I promise I am going to do for you. The new frontier is what I ask you to do for your country.

Same message, different words. The first is memorable; the second is not. The difference is effective antithesis (as well as effective inversion and parallel construction).[36] In its entirety, the passage from the inaugural was as follows:

> And so, my fellow Americans: Ask not what your country can do for you—ask what you can do for your country.
>   My fellow citizens of the world: Ask not what America will do for you, but what together we can do for the freedom of man.

Inversion.   **Inversion** reverses the expected order of words in a phrase or sentence to make a statement more memorable and emphatic. Consider how the impact of Kennedy's statement would have been diminished had he used "Do not

---

antithesis A language technique that combines opposing elements in the same sentence or adjoining sentences.

inversion Changing the normal order of words to make statements memorable.

ask" instead of "Ask not." Paul El-Amin concluded his criticism of internment practices after the 9/11 disaster by adapting the same passage from the poem by John Donne: "Ask not for whom the bell tolls. It tolls for me. And it tolls for thee. For all of us who love the Bill of Rights, it tolls." The "ask not" that begins this statement and the final sentence are both inverted from their usual order. The unusual order of the words gains attention and makes the statement impressive. Moreover, the "thee" adds to the impression that this is old, even religious, wisdom. Used in student speeches, inversion works best as a beginning or ending technique, where it can gain attention, add dignity to the effort, and/or frame a memorable conclusion.

At times, inversion goes beyond reversing the expected order of words. In a baccalaureate address presented at Hamilton College, Bill Moyers commented on the many confusions of contemporary life and concluded: "Life is where you get your answers questioned."[37] Here the inversion of the conventional order of thoughts, in which answers usually follow questions rather than the other way around, makes for a witty, striking observation.

Parallel Construction. **Parallel construction** repeats the same pattern of words in a sequence of phrases or sentences for the sake of impact. We discussed the use of parallel construction for framing the main points in a speech in Chapter 10, but parallel construction can occur at any critical moment in a speech. As the Kennedy example illustrates, the repetition of the pattern of words can stamp its message into the mind and make its statement memorable. Perhaps the most famous examples in American public address are Martin Luther King's repeated phrase "I have a dream . . ." in his classic March on Washington speech and Lincoln's "of the people, by the people, and for the people . . ." near the end of the Gettysburg Address. More recently, President George W. Bush also used the technique strikingly. As he announced that military strikes against the Taliban had begun in Afghanistan, the president sounded very much like Winston Churchill as he proclaimed:

> The battle is now joined on many fronts. We will not waver; we will not tire; we will not falter; and we will not fail. Peace and freedom will prevail.[38]

In her tribute to Tiger Woods (see the complete text at the end of Chapter 17), Leslie Eason also used parallel construction in her introduction:

> You're at the Western Open, where Tiger Woods could be Elvis resurrected. People clap when he pulls out the club. They clap when he hits the ball. They clap no matter where that ball lands. They clap if he smiles. They clap because he is.

Exploiting the Sounds of Words

As they are pronounced, words have distinctive sounds. Part of the appeal of parallel construction is that it repeats these sounds. As the Bush example also illustrates, the rhyming of these sounds can add a striking, pleasing effect. At least two other techniques, alliteration and onomatopoeia, also arrange these sounds in distinctive ways. Both techniques magnify the language of feeling.

Alliteration. **Alliteration** repeats the initial sounds in a closely connected pattern of words. One student speaker who criticized the lowering of educational standards paused near the end of her speech to draw the following conclusion: "We don't need the doctrine of dumbing down." Her repetition of the *d* sound was

---

parallel construction Wording points in the same way to emphasize their importance and to help the audience remember them.

alliteration The repetition of initial consonant sounds in closely connected words.

distinctive and helped listeners remember her point. It expressed her strong feeling about practices she condemned.

Onomatopoeia. **Onomatopoeia** is the tendency of certain words to imitate the sounds of what they represent. For example, suppose you were trying to describe the scene of refugees fleeing from war and starvation. How could you bring that scene into focus for listeners who are far removed from it? One way would be to describe an old woman and her grandson as they *trudge* down a road to nowhere.

Figure 12.3

Magnifying the Power of Language

Using Figurative Language

Technique	Definition	Example
Metaphors	An unexpected figurative comparison	An iron curtain has descended across the continent.
Enduring metaphors	Metaphors that transcend time and cultural boundaries	The development of the Internet marked the dawn of a new way of learning.
Similes	Figurative comparison using *like* or *as*	The jellyfish is like a living lava lamp.
Personifications	Attributing human characteristics to things or events	Liberty raises her flame as a beacon.
Culturetypes	Words that express the values, identity, and goals of a group	This company is devoted to the ideals of modern, efficient, progressive science.
Ideographs	Words that express a country's basic political beliefs	All we ask is liberty and justice.

Manipulating the Order of Words

Technique	Definition	Example
Antithesis	Presenting contrasting ideas in parallel phrases	There is a time to sow and a time to reap.
Inversion	Changing the expected word order	This insult we did not deserve, and this result we will not accept.
Parallel construction	Repetition of words/phrases at beginning or end of sentences	It's a program that … It's a program that … It's a program that …

Exploiting the Sounds of Words

Technique	Definition	Example
Alliteration	Repetition of initial sounds in closely connected words	Beware the nattering nabobs of negativism.
Onomatopoeia	Words that imitate natural sounds	The creek gurgled and babbled down to the river.

---

onomatopoeia The use of words that sound like the subjects they signify.

The very sound of the word "trudge" suggests the weary, discouraged walk of the refugees. Hannah Johnston also used the technique when she described packing-house workers as "literally drenched in a river of blood." By its very sound, *drenched* suggests the unpleasant idea of being soaked with blood as you work. Combined with the "river of blood" metaphor, the technique draws listeners close to what the language describes. Onomatopoeia has this quality of conveying listeners into a scene by allowing them to hear its noises, smell its odors, taste its flavors, or touch its surfaces. The technique awakens sensory experience.

These various ways to magnify the power of language are summarized in Figure 12.3. As you contemplate using them, remember that your words must not seem forced or artificial. For these techniques to work, they must seem to arise naturally and spontaneously in your speaking, and they must seem to fit both you and your subject. You should use them sparingly so that they stand out from the rest of your speech. Used artfully, and in concurrence with the six standards discussed earlier, they can both increase and harness the power of language so that it works productively.

In Summary

Many of us underestimate the power of our words. The language we select can determine whether we succeed or fail as communicators.

The Power of the Spoken Word. Oral language is more spontaneous, less formal, and more interactive than written communication. The spoken word can be more colorful and expansive; it alters the structure of sentences, and it depends more on the rhythm of language as it is voiced.

Words can shape our perceptions. They invite us to see and share the world from the speaker's point of view. They can arouse intense feeling by overcoming the barriers of time, distance, and audience apathy. The spoken word can bring listeners together in a common identity. Finally, words can prompt us to action.

The Six C's of Language Use. As you speak, strive to meet the standards of clarity, color, concreteness, correctness, conciseness, and cultural sensitivity. Clear language is simple and direct: It draws its comparisons from everyday life and avoids jargon.

Color refers to the emotional intensity and vividness of language and is especially vital to the sharing of feeling. The more concrete a word, the more specific the information it conveys. Correctness is vital to ethos because grammatical errors and improper word choices can lower perceptions of your competence. Concise speakers strive for brevity, often using comparisons that reduce complex issues to the essentials. Cultural sensitivity requires that a speaker be aware of the diversity within an audience and respectful of cultural differences.

Magnifying the Power of Language. Certain techniques can magnify the power of words at critical moments in your speeches. Figurative language, techniques that alter the natural order of words, and techniques that exploit the sounds of words are all devices of magnification.

Prominent forms of figurative language are metaphors, enduring metaphors, similes, personifications, culturetypes, and ideographs. Metaphor surprises us with implied, unusual comparisons. Enduring metaphors are rooted in basic human experience and appeal across time and culture. Similes signal and soften the comparison with words such as "like" or "as." Personifications, as in "lady liberty," attribute human form and feeling to inanimate subjects. Culturetypes express the values of a particular people. Ideographs are compact expressions of political faith.

Techniques that alter the natural order of words include antithesis, inversion, and parallel construction. Antithesis arranges opposing ideas in the same or adjoining sentences to create a striking contrast. Inversion reverses the expected order of words in a phrase or sentence to make a statement distinctive. Parallel construction repeats the same pattern of words in a sequence of phrases or sentences for the sake of impact.

Alliteration and onomatopoeia are techniques that exploit the sounds of words. Alliteration repeats initial sounds in a closely connected pattern of words. Onomatopoeia is the tendency of certain words to imitate the sounds of what they represent. Both techniques magnify the language of feeling.

To be effective, all such techniques must seem natural.

Explore and Apply the Ideas in This Chapter

1. What words would you nominate as culturetypes in contemporary society? (Remember, you should be looking for "devil" as well as "god" terms.) Find examples of how these words are used in public communication. Are there any ethical problems with the way these words are used?

2. Analyze how you used the power of language in your last speech. Did you have to overcome any barriers to perception or feeling among your listeners? What techniques did you use? Could you have done better?

3. Look for examples of the use of enduring metaphor in contemporary public communication (speeches, editorials, advertising, visual, and televisual communication). Explain the power of these metaphors by connecting them to motivation as it is explained in Chapter 5.

4. Study the language used in a contemporary political speech. How is the power of language exercised? What special techniques are used to magnify this power? Evaluate the effectiveness of this usage according to the six C's discussed in this chapter: clarity, color, concreteness, correctness, conciseness, and cultural sensitivity.

5. Your instructor will assign different language techniques to members of the class and then present a subject. Your task is to make a statement about this subject, using the technique you have been assigned. Share these statements in class. What does this exercise reveal about the power of the spoken word?

13 Presenting Your Speech

There is no gesture that does not speak.
—Montaigne

The texts of Beth Tidmore's speeches on pages 209 and 217 convey her intense desire to communicate with listeners. Her words have that "oral" quality we discussed in Chapter 12.

What these texts cannot convey, however, is the energy Beth brought to her presentations, the excitement in her voice, the sincerity in her face, and the intensity of her connection with listeners. Beth believed in her subjects and wanted her audience to believe in them as well.

As she presented her speeches, Beth established eye contact, moved out from behind the lectern, and stepped toward her listeners as though inviting closeness. Her face was alive with the meaning of her words. Her entire body—gestures, movements, and posture at the lectern—amplified the meaning of her message. These missing dimensions of meaning from the printed texts suggest strongly that the written word can not convey the rich totality of a living communication event.[1]

To get a better idea of what is missing from the printed page and of what it was like to be in Beth's audience, see her speeches on MySpeechLab.

Beth exemplified what we call **integrated communication**—the coming together and interaction of body, voice, and speech content to produce a larger-than-life communication experience for all who share it.

We have spent much of our time thus far helping you develop a plan for your speech. Planning, however, can take you only so far. Now you must actually present the speech to an audience of listeners, giving it a chance to influence their thinking and giving them a chance to respond to your ideas. This is the moment of **presentation**.

In this chapter, we help you prepare for this important event by discussing two major resources, your voice and your body. We also want to help you become more versatile in using various techniques of presentation and more flexible for special communication situations. Finally, we coach you through practicing your presentation.

Developing your presentation skills should help you in other settings, such as job interviews, meetings, and even social occasions. Learning how to present yourself and your ideas tends to stay with you over the years, providing what Renaissance intellectual Francis Bacon once called "continual letters of recommendation."

The Goal of Integrated Communication

*I*ntegrated communication is both an ideal and a goal. The word *communication* stems from the Latin word *communis*, meaning "common." Integrated communication encourages speaker and audience to hold ideas and feelings in common, even when they come from different cultural backgrounds. Such a presentation combines the power of words with the nonverbal power of voice and gesture to create shared meaning. Beth Tidmore's presentations clearly illustrated the harmonious interplay of verbal and nonverbal symbols.

An ideal can also be defined by performance that falls far short of it. We remember another student speaker who described her childhood in these terms: "I was always getting into trouble." But as she said these words, she seemed listless; she slouched at the podium and avoided eye contact. Her passive manner did not reinforce her self-portrait as a boisterous child. Instead, *there was an incongruity between what she said and what she showed.* Law enforcement interviewers often refer to such moments as "discrepancies, places where words, facial expressions, and body language do not jibe."[2]

Whenever verbal and nonverbal symbols seem out of sync, listeners typically assign more importance to the nonverbal message. One interesting explanation for this tendency is

---

integrated communication An ideal, harmonious convergence of voice, body language, and speech content to produce a self-reinforcing interplay of meanings.

presentation The act of offering a speech to an audience, integrating the skills of nonverbal communication with the speech content.

that nonverbal language is older and more biologically embedded than verbal language. Psychologist Paul Ekman argues that facial expressions

> have their own evolutionary history. Smiling, for example, is probably our oldest natural expression. For humans, as for monkeys, smiling is a way to disarm and reassure those around us. . . . Some geneticists date the origin of language back as little as 50,000 years, and the richness of words actually seems to distract us from the older medium of faces.[3]

Clearly, communication is far more complex than the mere exchange of words.

Requirements of Integrated Communication

What is needed for integrated communication? Some requirements are obvious: Listeners must be able to hear you easily, and your pronunciation must not be a barrier to understanding. Nor should listening to your voice be a painful, unpleasant experience. Indeed, your nonverbal behavior should not call attention to itself or distract from your message. Thus, you should also avoid pompous pronunciations, an artificial manner, and overly dramatic gestures.

Instead, *an effective presentation should sound natural and conversational*—as though you were talking *with* listeners, not *at* them. Your goal should be an **expanded conversational style** that is direct, spontaneous, colorful, and tuned to the responses of listeners. Although a bit more formal than everyday conversation, such a style still sounds *natural*.

Beyond the surface requirements for an effective presentation are deeper requirements of *attitude*. As a speaker, you must be committed to your topic and want to share this commitment. As a listener, you should meet the speaker's commitment with respect and receptivity, the conviction that you can learn and grow by sharing the spoken word. As both speaker and listener, *you should want to communicate.*

This point may seem obvious, but we remember another student in whom this desire to communicate seemed oddly lacking. She had done well in high school speaking contests, she told us in her first speech, and thought of herself as a good speaker. And in a technical sense, she was right. Her voice was pleasant and expressive, her manner direct and competent. But there was a false note, an overtone of artificiality. As a result, her listeners gave her a rather chilly reception. It was clear that, for her, speaking was an exhibition. *She* was more important than her ideas. Listeners sensed that she had her priorities wrong.

The desire to communicate produces a sense of **immediacy**, a closeness between speaker and listeners.[4] Immediacy relates to the likeableness dimension of ethos, which we discussed in Chapter 3. It encourages listeners to open their minds to you and to be influenced by what you say.[5]

You can encourage immediacy by reducing the actual distance between yourself and listeners. If possible, move closer to them. Smile at them when appropriate, maintain eye contact, use gestures to clarify and reinforce ideas, and let your voice express your feelings. Even if your heart is pumping, your hands are a little sweaty, and your knees feel wobbly, the self you show listeners should be a person in control of the situation. Listeners admire and identify with speakers who maintain what Ernest Hemingway once called "grace under pressure."

To summarize, *an effective presentation realizes the goal of integrated communication: It makes your ideas come alive while you are speaking.* It blends nonverbal

---

expanded conversational style A presentational quality that, while more formal than everyday conversation, preserves its directness and spontaneity.

immediacy A quality of successful communication achieved when the speaker and audience experience a sense of closeness.

An effective presentation, including vocal technique, body language, self-presentation, and speech content, makes your ideas come alive while you are speaking.

with verbal symbols so that reason and emotion, heart and head, mind and body all work together to advance your message. The remainder of this chapter helps you move closer to a presentation that reaches the goal of integrated communication.

Developing Your Voice

To improve as a speaker, you must improve your voice as an instrument of communication. Consider the following simple sentences:

> I don't believe it.
> You did that.
> Give me a break.

How many different meanings can you create as you speak these words, just by changing the rhythm, pace, emphasis, pitch, or inflection of your voice?

The quality of your voice affects your ethos as well as your message. If you sound confident and comfortable with your own identity, and if listening to you is a pleasant experience, listeners are likely to raise their estimation of you. But if you sound tentative, people may think you are not very decisive, perhaps not even convinced by your own message. If you mumble, they may think you are trying to hide something. If you are overly loud or strident, they may conclude you are not very likeable.

How you talk is actually part of your identity. Someone who talks in a soft, breathy voice may be thought of as "weak"; someone who speaks in a more forceful manner may be considered "authoritative." For some speakers, a dialect is part of their ethnicity and a valued part of their personality.[6]

Although you may not want to make radical changes in your speaking voice, minor improvements can produce big dividends. As one voice specialist put it, "Though speech is a human endowment, how well we speak is an individual achievement."[7] With a little effort and practice, most of us can make positive changes. However, simple vocal exercises will not fix all physical impairments. If you have a serious vocal problem, contact a speech pathology clinic for professional help.

The first step in learning to use your voice more effectively is to evaluate how you usually talk. Tape-record yourself while speaking and reading aloud. When you hear yourself, you may say, "Is that really me?" Most tape recorders will slightly distort the way you sound because they do not exactly replicate the spectrum of sounds made by the human voice. Nevertheless, a tape recording gives you a good idea of how you may sound to others. As you listen, ask yourself:

- Does my voice convey the meaning I intend?

- Would I want to listen to me if I were in the audience?

- Does my voice present me at my best?

If your answers are negative or uncertain, you may need to work on pitch, rate, loudness, variety, articulation, enunciation, pronunciation, or dialect. Save your original tape so that you can hear yourself improve as you practice.

Pitch

Pitch is the placement of your voice on the musical scale. Vocal pitches can range from low and deep to high and squeaky. For effective speaking, find a pitch level that is comfortable and that allows maximum flexibility and variety. Each of us has a **habitual pitch**, the level at which we speak most frequently. We also have an **optimum pitch**, the level that allows us to produce our strongest voice with minimal effort and that permits variation up and down the scale. You can use the following exercise to help determine your optimum pitch:

> Sing the sound *la* down to the lowest pitch you can produce without feeling strain or having your voice break or become rough. Now count each note as you sing up the scale to the highest tone you can comfortably produce. Most people have a range of approximately sixteen notes. Your optimum pitch will be about one-fourth of the way up your range. For example, if your range extends twelve notes, your optimum pitch would be at the third note up the scale. Again, sing down to your lowest comfortable pitch, and then sing up to your optimum pitch level.[8]

Tape-record this exercise, and compare your optimum pitch to the habitual pitch revealed during your first recording. If your optimum pitch is within one or two notes of your habitual pitch, you should not experience vocal problems related to pitch level. If your habitual pitch is much higher or lower than your optimum pitch, you may not have sufficient flexibility to raise or lower the pitch of your voice to communicate changes in meaning and emphasis. You can change your habitual pitch by practicing speaking and reading at your optimum pitch.

Read the following paragraphs from N. Scott Momaday's *The Way to Rainy Mountain* at your optimum pitch level, using pitch changes to provide meaning and feeling. To make the most of your practice, tape-record yourself so you can observe both problems and progress.

> A single knoll rises out of the plain in Oklahoma, north and west of the Wichita Range. For my people, the Kiowas, it is an old landmark, and they gave it the name Rainy Mountain. The hardest weather in the world is there. Winter brings blizzards, hot tornadic winds arise in the spring, and in the summer the prairie is an anvil's edge. The grass turns brittle and brown, and it cracks beneath your feet. There are green belts along the rivers and creeks, linear groves of hickory and pecan, willow, and witch hazel. At a distance in July or August the steaming foliage seems almost to writhe in fire. . . . Loneliness is an aspect of the land. All things in the plain are isolate: There is no confusion of objects in the eye, but one hill or one tree or one man. To look upon that landscape in the early morning, with the sun at your back, is to lose the sense of proportion. Your imagination comes to life, and this, you think, is where Creation was begun.[9]

This exercise should help you explore the full range of variation around your optimum pitch and make you more conscious of the relationship between pitch and effective communication. Tape yourself reading the passage again, this time exaggerating the pitch variations as you read it. Play back both of the taped readings. If you have a problem with a narrow pitch range, you may discover that exaggerating makes you sound more effective.

---

pitch The position of a human voice on the musical scale.

habitual pitch The vocal level at which people speak most frequently.

optimum pitch The level at which people can produce their strongest voice with minimal effort and that allows variation up and down the musical scale.

When you speak before a group, don't be surprised if your pitch seems higher than usual. Pitch is sensitive to emotions and usually goes up when you are under pressure. If pitch is a serious problem for you, hum your optimum pitch softly to yourself before you begin to speak, so that you start out on the right level.

Rate

Your **rate**, or the speed at which you speak, helps set the mood of your speech. Serious material calls for a slow, deliberate rate; lighter topics need a faster pace. These variations may involve the duration of syllables, the use of pauses, and the overall speed of presentation.

The rate patterns within a speech produce its **rhythm**, an essential component of all communication.[10] With rhythmic variations, you point out what is important and make it easier for listeners to comprehend your message.

Beginners who feel intimidated by the speaking situation often speed up their presentations and run their words together. What this rapid-fire delivery communicates is the speaker's desire to get it over with and sit down! At the other extreme, some speakers become so deliberate and slow that they almost put themselves and their audiences to sleep. Neither extreme lends itself to effective communication.

As we noted in Chapter 3, the typical rate for extemporaneous speaking is approximately 125 words per minute. You can check your speed by timing your reading of the excerpt from *Rainy Mountain*. If you were reading at the average rate, you would have taken about sixty seconds to complete that material. If you allowed time for pauses between phrases, which is appropriate for such formal material, your reading may have run slightly longer. If you took less than fifty seconds, you were probably speaking too rapidly or not using pauses effectively.

Pausing before or after a word or phrase highlights its importance. Pauses also give your listeners time to contemplate what you have said. They can help build suspense and maintain interest as listeners anticipate what you will say next. Moreover, pauses can clarify the relationships among ideas, phrases, and sentences. They are oral punctuation marks, taking the place of the commas and periods, underlines, and exclamation marks that occur in written communication. Experienced speakers learn how to use pauses to maximum advantage. Humorist William Price Fox once wrote of Eugene Talmadge, a colorful Georgia governor and fabled stump-speaker, "That rascal knew how to wait. He had the longest pause in the state."[11] Be sure to use pause and vocal emphasis to state your main ideas forcefully.

Read the following passage aloud again, using pauses (where indicated by the slash marks) and rate changes (a faster pace is indicated by italic type and a slower pace by capital letters) to enhance its meaning and demonstrate mood changes. This exercise will give you an idea of how pausing and changing rate can emphasize and clarify the flow of ideas:

> A single knoll rises out of the plain in Oklahoma / north and west of the Wichita Range // For my people / the Kiowas / it is an old landmark / and they gave it the name / Rainy Mountain /// The hardest weather in the world is there // *Winter brings blizzards / hot tornadic winds arise in the spring / and in the summer the prairie is an anvil's edge // The grass turns brittle and brown / and it cracks beneath your feet //* There are green belts along the rivers and creeks / linear groves of hickory and pecan, willow, and witch hazel // At a distance / in July or August / the steaming foliage seems almost to writhe in fire /// LONELINESS IS AN ASPECT OF

rate The speed at which words are uttered.

rhythm Rate patterns of vocal presentation within a speech.

THE LAND//ALL THINGS IN THE PLAIN ARE ISOLATE /// THERE IS NO CON-
FUSION OF OBJECTS IN THE EYE//BUT ONE HILL//OR ONE TREE//OR ONE
MAN///To look upon that landscape in the early morning / with the sun at your
back / is to lose the sense of proportion//Your imagination comes to life//AND
THIS/YOU THINK/IS WHERE CREATION WAS BEGUN.

Just as pausing can work for you, the wrong use of silence within a speech can
be harmful. *There is considerable difference between a pause, which is deliberate, and a hesitation, which can signal confusion, uncertainty, and/or a lack of preparation.* Moreover,
some speakers habitually use "ers" and "ums," "wells" and "okays," or "you knows"
in the place of pauses without being aware of it. These **vocal distractions** may fill in
the silence while the speaker thinks about what to say next, or they may be signs of
nervousness. They may also be signals that speakers lack confidence in themselves or
their messages. To determine if you have such a habit, tape-record yourself speaking
extemporaneously about one of the main points for your next speech. Often, simply
becoming aware of such vocal distractions is enough to help you control them. Also,
don't use "okay," "well," or "you know" as transitions in your speech. Plan more
effective transitions (see Chapter 9). Practice your presentation until the ideas flow
smoothly. Finally, don't be afraid of the brief strategic silence that comes when you
pause. Make silence work for you.

If your natural tendency is to speak too slowly, you can practice developing a
faster rate by reading light material aloud. Try reading stories by Dr. Seuss to children. Such tales as *The Cat in the Hat* and *Green Eggs and Ham* should bring out the
ham in you! Children normally provide an appreciative audience that encourages
lively, colorful, dramatic uses of the voice.

Different cultures have different speech rhythms. In the United States, for example, northerners often speak more rapidly than southerners. These variations in the
patterns of speech can create misunderstandings. Californians, who use longer
pauses than New Yorkers, may perceive the latter as rude and aggressive. New
Yorkers may see Californians as too laid back or as not having much to say. Guard
against stereotyping individuals on the basis of what may be culturally based speech
rate variations.

Loudness

No presentation can be effective if the audience can't hear you. Nor will your presentation be successful if you overwhelm listeners with a voice that is too loud. When
you speak before a group, you usually need to speak louder than you do in general
conversation. The size of the room, the presence or absence of a microphone, and
background noise may also call for adjustments. To develop the capacity to deal
with such noise, speech teachers of ancient Greece often took their students to the
beach and had them practice over the sound of crashing waves. To adjust your loudness, take your cues from audience feedback. If you are not loud enough, you may
see listeners leaning forward, straining to hear. If you speak too loudly, they may
unconsciously lean back, pulling away from the noise.

You should also be aware that different cultures have different norms and expectations concerning appropriate loudness. For example, in some Mediterranean cultures, a loud voice signifies strength and sincerity, whereas in some Asian and
American Indian cultures, a soft voice is associated with good manners and education.[12] When members of your audience come from a variety of cultural and ethnic
groups, be especially attentive to feedback on this point.

vocal distractions Filler words, such as
"er," "um," and "you know," used in the
place of a pause.

To speak with proper loudness, you must have good breath control. If you are breathing improperly, you will not have enough force to project your voice so that you can be heard at the back of a room. Improper breathing can also cause you to run out of breath before you finish a phrase or come to an appropriate pause. To check whether you are breathing properly for speaking, do the following:

> Stand with your feet approximately eight inches apart. Place your hands on your lower rib cage, thumbs to the front, fingers to the back. Take a deep breath—in through your nose and out through slightly parted lips. If you are breathing correctly, you should feel your ribs moving up and out as you inhale.

Improper breathing affects more than just the loudness of your speech. If you breathe by raising your shoulders, the muscles in your neck and throat will become tense. This can result in a harsh, strained vocal quality. Moreover, you probably will not take in enough air to sustain your phrasing, and the release of air will be difficult to control. The air and sound will all come out with a rush when you drop your shoulders, leading to unfortunate oral punctuation marks when you don't want or need them. To see if you have a problem, try this exercise:

> Take a normal breath and see how long you can count while exhaling. If you cannot reach fifteen without losing volume or feeling the need to breathe, you need to work on extending your breath control. Begin by counting in one breath to a number comfortable for you, and then gradually increase the count over successive tries. Do not try to compensate by breathing too deeply. Deep breathing takes too much time and attracts too much attention while you are speaking. Use the longer pauses in your speech to breathe, and make note of your breathing pattern as you practice your speech.

You should vary the loudness of words and phrases in your speech, just as you vary your pitch and your rate of speaking. Changes in loudness are often used to express emotion. The more excited or angry we are, the louder we tend to become. But don't let yourself get caught in the trap of having only two options: loud and louder. Decreasing your volume, slowing your rate, pausing, or dropping your pitch can also express emotion quite effectively. Vanderbilt student speaker Leslie Eason illustrated this point dramatically as she introduced her speech on racism. As she read the concluding lines of her poem ("What if I go to Heaven, and then at me they yell, White Angels enter here, Black Angels go to Hell"), Leslie reduced her loudness, lowered her pitch, and slowed her rate. These vocal contrasts had a dramatic impact on listeners.

To acquire more variety in loudness, practice the following exercise recommended by Ralph Hillman: "First, count to five at a soft volume, as if you were speaking to one person. Then, count to five at medium volume, as if speaking to ten or fifteen people. Finally, count to five, as if speaking to thirty or more people."[13] If you tape-record this exercise, you should be able to hear the clear progression in loudness.

Variety

The importance of vocal variety shows up most in speeches that lack it. Speakers who drone on in a monotone, never varying their pitch, rate, or loudness, send a clear message: They tell us that they have little interest in their topic or their listeners or that they fear the situation they are in. Variety can make speeches come to life by adding color and interest. One of the best ways to develop variety is to read aloud materials that require it to express meaning and feeling. As you read the following selection from *the lives and times of archy and mehitabel*, strive for maximum variation of pitch, rate, and loudness. Incidentally, archy is a cockroach who aspires to be a writer. He leaves typewritten messages for his newspaper-editor mentor, but because he is a cockroach, he can't type capital letters and never uses punctuation marks. His friend mehitabel, whom he quotes in this message, is an alley cat with grandiose dreams and a dubious reputation.

> archy what in hell have i done
> to deserve all these kittens
> life seems to be just one damn litter after another
> after all archy i am an artist
> this constant parade of kittens
> interferes with my career
> its not that i am shy on mother love archy
> why my heart would bleed if anything happened to them
> and i found it out
> a tender heart is the cross i bear
> but archy the eternal struggle between life and art
> is simply wearing me out[14]

Tape-record yourself while reading this and other favorite poems or dramatic scenes aloud. Compare these practice tapes with your initial self-evaluation tape to see if you have developed variety in your presentations.

Patterns of Speaking

People often make judgments about others on the basis of their speech patterns. If you slur your words, mispronounce familiar words, or speak with a dialect that sounds unfamiliar to your audience, you may be seen as uneducated or socially inept. When you sound "odd" to your listeners, their attention will be distracted from what you are saying to the way you are saying it. In this section we cover articulation, enunciation, pronunciation, and dialect as they contribute to or detract from speaking effectiveness.

Articulation.   Articulation is the way you produce individual speech sounds. Some people have trouble making certain sounds. For example, they may substitute a *d* for a *th*, saying "dem" instead of "them." Other sounds that are often misarticulated include *s*, *l*, and *r*. Severe articulation problems can interfere with effective communication, especially if the audience cannot understand the speaker or if the variations suggest low social or educational status. Such problems are best treated by a speech pathologist, who retrains the individual to produce the sound in a more acceptable manner.

Enunciation.   Enunciation is the way you pronounce words in context. In casual conversation, it is not unusual for people to slur their words—for example, saying

---

articulation The manner in which individual speech sounds are produced.

enunciation The manner in which individual words are articulated and pronounced in context.

"gimme" for "give me." However, careless enunciation causes credibility problems for public speakers. Do you say "Swatuh thought" for "That's what I thought"? "Harya?" for "How are you?" or "Howjado?" for "How did you do?" These lazy enunciation patterns are not acceptable in public speaking. Check your enunciation patterns on the tape recordings you have made to determine if you have such a problem. If you do, concentrate on careful enunciation as you practice your speech. Be careful, however, to avoid the opposite problem of inflated, pompous, and pretentious enunciation, which can make you sound phony. You should strive to be neither sloppy nor overly precise.

Pronunciation. Pronunciation involves saying words correctly. It includes both using the correct sounds and placing the proper accent on syllables. Because written English does not always indicate the correct pronunciation, we may not be sure how to pronounce words that we first encounter in print. For instance, does the word *chiropodist* begin with a *sh*, a *ch*, or a *k* sound?

If you are not certain how to pronounce a word, consult a dictionary. An especially useful reference is the *NBC Handbook of Pronunciation*, which contains 21,000 words and proper names that sometimes cause problems.[15] When international stories and new foreign leaders first appear in the news, newspapers frequently indicate the correct pronunciation of their names. Check front-page stories in the *New York Times* for guidance with such words.

In addition to problems pronouncing unfamiliar words, you may find that there are certain words you habitually mispronounce. For example, how do you pronounce the following words?

government	library
February	picture
ask	secretary
nuclear	just
athlete	get

Unless you are careful, you may find yourself slipping into these common mispronunciations:

goverment	liberry
Febuary	pitchur
axe	sekaterry
nuculer	jist
athalete	git

Mispronunciation of such common words can damage your ethos. Be sure to verify your pronunciation of troublesome words as you practice your speech.

Dialect. A **dialect** is a speech pattern typical of a geographic region or ethnic group. Your dialect usually reflects the area of the country where you were raised or lived for any length of time or your cultural and ethnic identity.[16] In the United States, there are three commonly recognized dialects: eastern, southern, and midwestern. Additionally, there are local variations within the broader dialects. For example, in South Carolina, one finds the Gullah dialect from the islands off the coast, the low-country or Charlestonian accent, the Piedmont variation, and the Appalachian twang.[17] And then there's always "Bah-stahn"[Boston], where you can buy a "lodge budded pup con" [large, buttered popcorn] at the movies!

---

pronunciation The use of correct sounds and of proper stress on syllables when saying words.

dialect A speech pattern associated with an area of the country or with a cultural or ethnic background.

There is no such thing in nature as a superior or inferior dialect. However, there can be occasions when a distinct dialect is a definite disadvantage or advantage. Listeners prefer speech patterns that are familiar to their ears. Audiences may also have stereotyped preconceptions about people who speak with certain dialects. For example, those raised in the south often associate a northeastern dialect with brusqueness and abrasiveness, and midwesterners may associate a southern dialect with slowness of action and mind. Comedian Jeff Foxworthy has noted:

> A lot of people think everyone in the South is a redneck. . . . I went to Georgia Tech. I was an engineer at IBM. I just sound stupid. I can't help this, because where I grew up everybody else talked this way. People hear the accent and they want to deduct 100 IQ points.[18]

You may have to work to overcome such a prejudice against your dialect.

Your dialect should reflect the standard for educated people from your geographic area or ethnic group. You should be concerned about tempering it only if it creates barriers to understanding and identification between you and your audience. Then you may want to work toward softening your dialect so that you can lower these barriers for the sake of your message.

Developing Your Body Language

Communication with your audience begins before you ever open your mouth. Your facial expression, personal appearance, and air of confidence all convey a message. How do you walk to the front of the room to give your speech? Do you move with confidence and purpose, or do you stumble and shuffle? As you begin your speech, do you look listeners directly in the eye, or do you stare at the ceiling as though seeking divine inspiration?

Body language is a second great resource you must manage and develop to achieve the goal of integrated communication.[19] *Your body language must reinforce your verbal language.* If your face is expressionless as you urge your listeners to action, you are sending inconsistent messages. Be sure that your body and words both "say" the same thing. Although we discuss separate types of body language in this section, in practice they all work together and are interpreted as a totality by listeners.[20]

Facial Expression and Eye Contact

> I knew she was lying the minute she said it. There was guilt written all over her face!

> He sure is shifty! Did you see how his eyes darted back and forth? He never did look us straight in the eye!

Most of us believe we can judge people's character, determine their true feelings, and tell whether they are honest by watching their facial expressions. If there is a conflict between what we see and what we hear, we usually believe our eyes rather than our ears.

The eyes are the most important element of facial expressiveness. In mainstream American culture, frequent and sustained eye contact suggests honesty, openness, and respect. We may think of a person's eyes as windows into the self. If

body language Communication achieved using facial expressions, eye contact, movements, and gestures.

you avoid looking at your audience while you are talking, you are drawing the shades on these windows. A lack of eye contact suggests that you do not care about listeners, that you are putting something over on them, or that you are afraid of them. Other cultures may view eye contact somewhat differently. In China, Indonesia, and rural Mexico, traditional people may lower their eyes as a sign of deference. In general, people from Asian and some African countries engage in less eye contact.[21] Some Native Americans may even find direct eye contact offensive or aggressive. Therefore, with culturally diverse audiences especially, don't conclude that listeners who resist eye contact are necessarily expressing their distrust or refusal to communicate.

When you reach the podium or lectern, turn, pause, and engage the eyes of your audience. This signals that you want to communicate and prepares people to listen. During your speech, try to make eye contact with all sectors of the audience. Don't just stare at one or two people. You will make them uncomfortable, and other audience members will feel left out. First, look at people at the front of the room, then shift your focus to the middle and sides, and finally, look at those in the rear. You may find that those sitting in the back of the room are the most difficult to reach. They may have taken a rear seat because they don't want to listen or be involved. You may have to work harder to gain and hold their attention. Eye contact is one way you can reach them.

Smile as you start your speech unless a smile is inappropriate to your message. A smile signals your goodwill toward listeners and your ease in the speaking situation—qualities that should help your ethos.[22] From your very first words, your face should reflect and reinforce the meanings of your words. An expressionless face suggests that the speaker is afraid or indifferent. A frozen face may be a mask behind which the speaker hides. The solution lies in selecting a topic that excites you, concentrating on sharing your message, and having the confidence that comes from being well prepared.

You can also try the following exercise. Utter these statements using a dull monotone and keeping your face as expressionless as possible:

I am absolutely delighted by your gift.
I don't know when I've ever been this excited.
We don't need to beg for change—we need to demand change.
All this puts me in a very bad mood.

Now repeat them with *exaggerated* vocal variety and facial expression. You may find that your hands and body also want to get involved. Encourage such impulses so that you develop an integrated system of body language.

Movement and Gestures

Most actors learn—often the hard way—that if you want to steal a scene from someone, all you have to do is move around, develop a twitch, or swing a leg. Before long, all eyes will be focused on that movement. This theatrical trick shows that physical movement sometimes can attract more attention than words. All the more reason that your words and gestures should work in harmony and not at cross-purposes! This also means you should avoid random movements, such as pacing back and forth, twirling your hair, rubbing your eyes, or jingling change in your pockets. Once you are aware of such mannerisms, it is easier to control them. Videotape yourself as you practice for your next speech. Just as audiotape can reveal aspects of your voice that are surprising, so can videotape reveal unsuspected habits of movement that you must correct.

Your gestures and movement should grow out of your response to your message.[23] You may have developed a strategic awareness of body language as you practice, such as: "When I reach this moment in the speech, I've got to stop, pause, look hard at listeners, and use my gestures and voice together to really drive my point home." But body language should always *appear* natural and spontaneous, prompted by your ideas and feelings at the moment you are speaking. They should never *look* contrived or artificial. For example, you should avoid framing a gesture to fit each word or sequence of words you utter. Perhaps every speech instructor has encountered speakers like the one who stood with arms circled above him as he said, "We need to get *around* this problem." That's not good body language!

Effective gestures involve three phases: *readiness*, *execution*, and *return*. In the readiness phase, you must be prepared for movement. Your hands and body should be in a position that does not inhibit free action. For example, you cannot gesture if your hands are locked behind your back or jammed into your pockets or if you are grasping the lectern as though it were a life preserver. Instead, let your hands rest in a relaxed position, at your sides, on the lectern, or in front of you, where they can obey easily the impulse to gesture in support of a point you are making. As you execute a gesture, let yourself move naturally and fully. Don't raise your hand halfway, and then stop with your arm frozen awkwardly in space. When you have completed a gesture, let your hands return to the relaxed readiness position, where they will be free to move again when the next impulse to gesture arises.

Effective gestures seem natural and unforced.

Do not assume that there is a universal language of gesture. Rwandans, for example, learn an elaborate code of gestures that is a direct extension of their spoken language.[24] In contrast, our "gesture language" is far less complex and sophisticated. Still, it can perform important communication functions, reinforcing, amplifying, and clarifying the spoken word and signaling listeners of your feelings and intentions.

The Factor of Distance.   From **proxemics**, the study of how humans use space during communication, we can derive two additional principles that help explain the effective use of movement during speeches. The first suggests that *the actual distance between speakers and listeners affects their sense of closeness or immediacy.* Bill Clinton made effective use of this principle during the second of the televised debates of the 1992 presidential campaign. In the town meeting setting of that debate, Clinton actually rose from his seat after one question and approached the audience as he answered it. His movement toward his listeners suggested that he felt a special concern for that problem and for them. Clinton's body language also enhanced his identification with the live audience and with the larger viewing audience they represented. In contrast, his opponents, President George H. Bush and Ross Perot, were made to seem distant from these audiences.

proxemics The study of how human beings use space during communication.

distance Principle of proxemics involving the control of the space.

Reducing the physical distance between the speaker and audience can help increase identification with the speaker.

It follows also that the greater the physical distance between speaker and audience, the harder it is to achieve identification. This problem gets worse when a lectern acts as a physical barrier. Short speakers can almost disappear behind it! If this is a problem, try speaking from either beside or in front of the lectern so that your body language can work for you.

A related (but quite different) problem arises if you move so close to listeners that you make them feel uncomfortable. If they pull back involuntarily in their chairs, you know you have violated their sense of personal space. A form of this problem occurred during the Bush–Gore presidential debates of 2000. In the third and last of these debates, Gore on several occasions moved aggressively toward Bush's side of the platform as he answered questions. Some viewers felt that Gore had come too close to his opponent; this behavior, they thought, was boorish and inappropriate. For these viewers, this behavior reinforced a related bad impression Gore had made during the first debate when he constantly interrupted Bush, sighed and rolled his eyes during Bush's statements, often went overtime during his own answers, and generally seemed not to respect either his opponent or the rules of the debate. Gore's lack of sensitivity to the first law of proxemics and to debate etiquette made him look bad to many, especially when he had been expected to dominate the debates. The lesson should be clear: To increase your effectiveness, you should seek the ideal zone of physical distance—not too far and not too close—between yourself and listeners.

The Factor of Elevation. The second principle of proxemics suggests that *elevation also affects the sense of closeness between speakers and listeners.* When you speak, you often stand above your seated listeners in a "power position." Because we tend to associate *above* us with power over us, speakers may find that this arrangement discourages identification with some listeners. Often, they will sit on the edge of the desk in front of the lectern in a more relaxed and less elevated stance. If your message is informal and requires close identification, or if you are especially tall, you might try this approach.

Personal Appearance

Your clothing and grooming affect how you are perceived and how your message is received.[25] How we dress can even influence how we see ourselves and how we behave. A police officer out of uniform may not act as authoritatively as when dressed in blue. A doctor without a white jacket may behave like just another person. You may have a certain type of clothing that makes you feel comfortable and relaxed. You may even have a special "good luck" outfit that raises your confidence.

When you are scheduled to speak, dress in a way that makes you feel good about yourself and that respects the audience and the occasion. How you dress reflects how you feel about the importance of the event. Think of your speech as a *professional* situation, and dress accordingly. By dressing a little more formally than you usually

InterConnections.

LearnMore 13.1

Nonverbal Communication

Essentials of Nonverbal Communication

www3.usal.es/~nonverbal/introduction.htm

An extensive directory of materials and Web sites devoted to the study of nonverbal communication; developed and maintained by Professor Jaume Masip, Department of Social Psychology and Anthropology, University of Salamanca, Spain.

Body Language

http://digilander.iol.it/linguaggiodelcorpo/nonverb

An interesting collection of information and links available in English, Italian, and Spanish; a useful online library of resources in proxemics, gestures, facial expressions, and paralinguistics; covers a range of topics from flirting behavior to subliminal advertising; developed and maintained by Professor Marco Pacori, University of Padova, Italy, and Professor Aleksandra Kostic, University of Nis, Serbia. Note: Much, but not all, of the material linked on the home page has been translated into English.

Body Language in Business: A Tutorial

www.businessweek.com/careers/content/feb2007/ca20070207_700175.htm?campaign_id=nws _insdr_feb10&link_position=link18

Useful discussion of the importance of body language in business communications, prepared by Carmine Gallo, a corporate presentation coach. Comes with slide show, "The Silent Language of Success," illustrating the dos and don'ts of body language.

do, you emphasize both to yourself and to the audience that your message is important. As we noted in Chapter 11, your appearance can serve as a presentation aid that complements your message. Like any other aid, it should never compete with your words for attention or be distracting. Always dress in good taste for the situation you anticipate.

Developing Versatility in Presentation

To develop more competent presentation skills, you must do more than develop your natural resources of voice and body language. You must also master the four types of presentation: impromptu speaking, memorized text presentation, reading from a manuscript, and extemporaneous speaking. You may have to use all of these forms, even in the same speech. A versatile speaker is able to move easily among them as they become appropriate in different situations.

Impromptu Speaking

Impromptu speaking is speaking on the spur of the moment in response to unpredictable situations with limited time for preparation. Such speaking is sometimes called "speaking off the cuff," a phrase that suggests you could put all your notes on the cuff of your shirt. Even in a carefully prepared speech, there may be moments of impromptu presentation—times when you must make on-the-spot adjustments to audience feedback or respond to questions at the end of your speech.

Many situations call for impromptu speaking. At work, you might be asked to make a presentation "in fifteen minutes." Or in meetings, you may decide to "say

impromptu speaking A talk delivered with minimal or no preparation.

Speakers in public meetings must adapt to the situations that confront them.

a few words" about a new product. In both cases, you will make impromptu speeches. You can also use impromptu speaking skills in other classes—to answer or to comment on a point made by your professor.

When you have just a few minutes to prepare, first *determine your purpose*. What do you want the audience to know? Why is this important? Next, *decide on your main points*. Limit yourself to no more than three main points. Don't try to cover too much. If you have access to any type of writing material—a note pad, a scrap of paper—jot down a memory-jogging word for each idea, either in the order of importance or as the ideas seem to flow naturally. This skeletal outline will keep you from rambling or forgetting something that is important.

Stick to the main points, using simple transitions as you go: "My first point is. . . . Second, it is important to. . . . Finally, it is clear that. . . ." Use the **PREP formula** to develop each point: State the *p*oint, give a *r*eason or *e*xample, then restate the *p*oint. Keep your presentation short, and end with a summary of your remarks.

Point:	The proposal to allow John Clark to operate a helicopter port in the neighborhood is not sound.
Reason(s):	The noise generated by helicopters taking off and landing would destroy the tranquility of this quiet residential neighborhood.
Example(s):	It would be especially disturbing to the residents of the nursing home one block from the proposed facility.
Restatement of Point:	Therefore, this proposal is not a good idea. It ought to be rejected.

An impromptu speech often is one of several such speeches as people express their ideas in meetings. The earlier speeches create the context for your presentation. If others stood at the front of the room to speak, you should do so as well. If earlier speakers remained seated, you may wish to do the same. However, you should consider whether earlier speakers have been successful. If these speakers offended listeners while making standing presentations, you may wish to remain seated to differentiate yourself from them. If seated speakers have made trivial presentations, you may wish to stand to signal that what you are going to say is important.

Fortunately, most impromptu speaking situations are relatively casual. No one expects a polished presentation on a moment's notice. However, the ability to organize your ideas quickly and effectively and to present them confidently puts you at a great advantage. The principles of preparing speeches that you are learning in this course will help you become a more effective impromptu speaker.

Memorized Text Presentation

Memorized text presentations are written out, committed to memory, and delivered word for word. There are moments in speechmaking that may call for memorization. Because the introduction and conclusion of a speech are especially important—the introduction for gaining audience attention and the conclusion for

---

PREP formula A technique for making an impromptu speech: state a point, give a reason or example, and restate the point.

memorized text presentations Speeches that are committed to memory and delivered word for word.

leaving a lasting impression—their wording should be carefully planned and rehearsed. You might also want to memorize short congratulatory remarks, a toast, or a brief award-acceptance speech.

In general, you should avoid trying to memorize entire speeches because this method of presentation poses many problems. Beginning speakers who try to memorize their speeches can get so caught up with *remembering* that they forget about *communicating*. The result often sounds stilted or sing-songy. Speaking from memory also inhibits adapting to feedback. It can keep you from clarifying points that the audience doesn't understand or from following up on ideas that seem especially effective.

Another problem with memorized speeches is that they must be scripted word for word in advance. Many people do not write in a natural oral style. The major differences between oral and written language, covered in Chapter 12, bear repeating. Good oral style uses short, direct, conversational speech patterns. Even sentence fragments can be acceptable. Repetition, rephrasing, and amplification are more necessary in speaking than in writing. The sense of rhythm and saving the most forceful idea for the end of the sentence are more important in oral style. Imagery can be especially useful to help the audience visualize what you are talking about.

If you must memorize a speech, commit it so thoroughly to memory that you can concentrate on communicating with your audience. If you experience a "mental block," keep talking. Restate or rephrase your last point to put your mind back on track. If this doesn't work, you may find yourself forced into an extemporaneous style and discover that you can actually express your ideas better without the constraints of exact wording.

Reading from a Manuscript

When you make a **manuscript presentation**, you read to an audience from either a text or a teleprompter. Manuscript presentations have many of the same problems as memorized presentations. Because speakers must look at a script, they lose eye contact with listeners, which in turn causes a loss of immediacy and inhibits adapting to feedback. Moreover, as with memorized presentations, you may have trouble writing in an oral style.

Some problems are exclusive to manuscript presentations. Most people do not read aloud well. Their presentations lack variety. Also, when people plan to read a speech, they often do not practice enough. Unless speakers are comfortable with the material, they can end up glued to their manuscript rather than communicating with listeners, even when they are using teleprompters.

President George W. Bush sometimes had trouble with making manuscript presentations, especially early in his presidency. He was far more comfortable out on the "stump," interacting with local audiences in the rough-and-tumble of politics than on ceremonial occasions. For example, on the evening of the devastating terror attack on the World Trade Center, Bush spoke to the nation from the Oval Office in the White House, trying to bring words of comfort and reassurance. Somehow, "the president could not find the right words."[26] His language was uninspiring and flat.[27]

Later that week, however, he visited the ruins at ground zero in New York City, and there, for the first time in his presidency, he found his voice. The scene Bush encountered was like an illustration from Dante's *Inferno*. Thousands of firemen, policemen, and rescue workers were combing the scattered, smoking ruins, still looking for survivors. The president, holding a bullhorn, climbed a pile of debris above the crowd and, as he started to speak, he was interrupted:

manuscript presentation A speech read from a manuscript.

President George W. Bush was more effective at impromptu speaking than reading from a manuscript.

Audience member: Can't hear you.

The President: I can't go any louder. (Laughter) I want you all to know that America today—America today is on bended knee in prayer for the people whose lives were lost here. . . . This Nation stands with the good people of New York City and New Jersey and Connecticut as we mourn the loss of thousands of our citizens.

Audience member: I can't hear you.

The President: I can hear you. I can hear you. The rest of the world hears you. And the people who knocked these buildings down will hear all of us soon.

Audience members: U.S.A.! U.S.A! U.S.A.![28]

In retrospect, these moments were charged with symbolism. The audience member who could not hear represents all those who indeed could not "hear" the president before this crisis. Bush, obviously sensitive to the larger meaning of the moment, built on its symbolic significance—first expanding it, then giving it an ominous turn. Stephen Wayne, a presidential scholar and professor of government at Georgetown University, believes this was the first time Bush had met the "challenge of a leader," which was to have his speech "capture the needs and mood of his country."[29] Later Bush would give successful manuscript speeches, but it is interesting that he should first find his voice in the give-and-take of impromptu speaking.

Manuscript presentations are most useful when the speaker seeks accuracy or eloquence or when time constraints are severe as in media presentations that must be timed within seconds. Extemporaneous presentations may also include quotations or technical information that must be read if they are to achieve their effect. Because you will need to read material from time to time, we offer the following suggestions:

- Use large print to prepare your manuscript so you can see it without straining.
- Use light pastel rather than white paper to reduce glare from lights.
- Double- or triple-space the manuscript.
- Mark pauses with slashes.
- Highlight material you want to emphasize.
- Practice speaking from your manuscript so that you can maintain as much eye contact as possible with your audience.

Figure 13.1 shows a sample manuscript prepared for presentation. Note that two or three slashes together indicate longer pauses. The speaker highlights emphasized material by underlining it.

As you make final preparations, ask a friend to videotape your rehearsal. Review the tape and ask yourself: Do I sound as though I'm *talking with* someone, or as if I'm reading a text? Do I maintain eye contact with my imaginary audience? Do I pause effectively to emphasize the most important points? Does my

Figure 13.1

Sample Speech Script

We Americans are big on monuments. / We build monuments

in memory of our heroes. // Washington, Jefferson, and Lin-

coln live on in our nation's capital. // We erect monuments

to honor our martyrs. / The Minute Man still stands guard

at Concord. / The flag is ever raised over Iwo Jima. / Some-

times we even construct monuments to commemorate vic-

tims. // In Ashburn Park downtown there is a monument to

those who died in the yellow fever epidemics. /// However,

there are some things in our history that we don't memori-

alize // Perhaps we would just as soon forget what hap-

pened. /// Last summer I visited such a place — // the

massacre site at Wounded Knee.

body language reinforce my message? Revise and continue practicing until you are satisfied.

Extemporaneous Speaking

Extemporaneous speaking *is prepared and practiced, but not written out or memorized.* Rather than focusing on the exact wording of the speech, the speaker concentrates instead on the sequence of ideas that will develop in the speech, on its underlying message, and on the final impression the speech should leave with listeners. Extemporaneous speaking features a spontaneous and natural-sounding presentation and makes it easier to establish immediacy with an audience. The speaker is not

extemporaneous presentation A form of presentation in which a speech, although carefully prepared and practiced, is not written out or memorized.

the prisoner of a text, and each presentation will vary according to the audience, occasion, and inspiration of the moment.

Another large advantage is that extemporaneous speaking encourages interaction with an audience. A Vanderbilt student speaker who distributed photographs and then instructed listeners on how to view them, and another student who asked listeners to close their eyes and to imagine themselves living as dwarfs, were playing up these advantages. Such interaction encourages the audience to participate in constructing the message of the speech. It becomes their creation as well, which is especially important when persuading listeners.

Because it requires speakers to master the overall pattern of thought within their speeches, extemporaneous speaking emphasizes the importance of preparation and practice. At its best, such speaking combines the advantages of the other modes of speaking, the spontaneity and immediacy of impromptu speech, and the careful preparation of manuscript and memorized presentations. *It is therefore the master mode of speaking*, the best for most speaking situations, preferred by most instructors for most classroom speeches. Its special advantage is that it encourages you to adapt to audience feedback in creative and constructive ways.

Responding to Feedback from Your Audience.

As we saw in Chapter 1, **feedback** is the message listeners send back to you as you speak. Facial expressions, gestures, or sounds of agreement or disagreement let you know how you are coming across. Since most feedback is nonverbal, you should maintain eye contact with your audience so that you can respond to these signals. Use feedback to monitor whether listeners understand you, are interested, and agree with what you are saying. Negative feedback in particular can alert you that you need to make on-the-spot adjustments.

Feedback That Signals Misunderstanding. Listeners' puzzled expressions can signal that they don't understand what you are saying. You may need to define an unfamiliar word or rephrase an idea to make it simpler. You could add an example or story to make an abstract concept more concrete. It might help to compare or contrast an unfamiliar idea with something the audience already knows and understands. When you detect signs of misunderstanding, you can say, "Let me put it another way." Then provide a clearer explanation.

Feedback That Signals Loss of Interest. Bored listeners wiggle in their seats, drum their fingers, or develop a glazed look. Remind them of the importance of your topic. Provide an example or story that makes your message come to life. Involve listeners by asking a question that calls for a show of hands. Startle them with a bold statement. Keep in mind that enthusiasm is contagious: your interest can arouse theirs. Move from behind the lectern and come closer to them. Whatever happens, do not become disheartened or lose faith in your speech. In all likelihood, some people—probably more than you think—will have found the speech interesting.

Feedback That Signals Disagreement. Listeners who disagree with you may frown or shake their heads to indicate how they feel about what you are saying. A number of techniques can help you soften disagreement. If you anticipate resistance, work hard to establish your ethos in the introduction of your speech. Listeners should see you as a competent, trustworthy, strong, and likeable person who has their best interests at heart.

To be perceived as competent, you must *be* competent. Arm yourself with a surplus of information, examples, and testimony from sources your audience will

feedback Speaker's perception of how audience members react to the message both during and after its presentation.

Ethics *Alert! 13.1*

The Dos and Don'ts of Presentation

The ethics of presentation center on the following rules:

1. Don't use presentation skills to disguise faults of content.

2. Don't judge the character of others by how they sound.

3. Don't let culturally based variations in eye contact, loudness, or gesture control how you respond to speakers.

4. Don't speak unless you are convinced of the value of your message. Then let your entire body confirm that fact to listeners.

respect. Practice your presentation until it is polished. Set an example of tolerance by respecting positions different from your own.

You may find that although you differ with listeners on methods, you agree with them on goals. Stress the values that you share. Appeal to their sense of fair play and

---

Figure 13.2

Methods of Presentation

Method	Use	Advantages	Disadvantages
Impromptu	When you have no time for preparation or practice	Is spontaneous; can meet demands of the situation; is open to feedback.	Is less polished, less well-researched, less organized; allows less use of supporting material.
Memorized	When you will be making a brief remark, such as a toast or award acceptance, or when the wording of your introduction or conclusion is important	Allows planning of eloquent wording; can sound well polished.	Must be written out in advance; can make you forget to communicate; can sound sing-songy.
Manuscript	When exact wording is important, time constraints are strict, or your speech will be telecast	Allows planning of precise wording; can be timed down to seconds.	Requires practice and an ability to read well; inhibits response to feedback.
Extemporaneous	For most public speaking occasions	Is spontaneous; encourages responding to audience feedback; encourages focusing on the essence of your message.	Requires considerable preparation and practice; experience needed for excellence.

their respect for your right to speak. You should be the model of civility in the situation. Avoid angry reactions and the use of inflammatory language. Think of these listeners as offering an opportunity for your ideas to have impact.

Developing Flexibility in Special Situations

o the versatility you develop as you master and integrate the various modes of speaking, you should add flexibility in special speaking situations. We address two such situations: question-and-answer sessions and video presentations.

Handling Questions and Answers

If you are successful in arousing interest and stimulating thinking, your listeners may want to ask questions at the end of your speech. You should welcome and encourage this sign of success. The following suggestions should make handling questions easier for you.[30]

- **Prepare for questions.** Try to anticipate what you might be asked, think about how you will answer these questions, and do the research required to answer them effectively. Practice your speech before friends, and urge them to ask you tough questions.

- **Repeat or paraphrase the question.** This is especially important if the question was long or complicated and your audience is large. Paraphrasing ensures that everyone in the audience hears the question. It gives you time to plan your answer, and it helps verify that you have understood the question. Paraphrasing also enables you to steer the question to the type of answer you are prepared to give.

Answering questions gives you a chance to extend and increase the influence of your speech.

- **Maintain eye contact with the audience as you answer.** Note that we say "with the audience," not just "with the questioner." Look first at the questioner, and then make eye contact with other audience members, returning your gaze to the questioner as you finish your answer. The purpose of a question-and-answer period should be to extend the understanding of the entire audience, not to carry on a conversation with one person.

- **Defuse hostile questions.** Reword emotional questions in more objective language. For example, if you are asked, "Why do you want to throw our money away on people who are too lazy to work?" you might respond with something like, "I understand your frustration and think what you really want to know is 'Why aren't our current programs helping people break out of the chains of unemployment?'"

- **Don't be afraid to concede a point or to say, "I don't know."** Such tactics can earn you points for honesty and can also help defuse a difficult question or hostile questioner. Senator Joe Biden of Delaware, while highly regarded as a foreign policy expert, entered the 2008 presidential sweepstakes with a reputation for being a compulsive talker and for putting his foot in his mouth. At the first nationally televised debate for Democratic Party hopefuls, the moderator skewered him with an unfriendly question:

Moderator: An editorial in the *Los Angeles Times* said, "In addition to his uncontrolled verbosity, Biden is a gaffe machine."' Can you reassure voters in this country that you would have the discipline you would need on the world stage, Senator?

Sen. Biden: Yes.

(Audience laughter. Long moment of silence)

Moderator: Thank you, Senator Biden.

(More laughter)[31]

As the *New York Times* described the moment, "The audience laughed at his brevity. Mr. Biden, looking proud of himself, said nothing else, as Mr. [Brian] Williams silently if slightly uncomfortably waited for him to expand on his remarks."[32] Commentator Chris Matthews described it as "a Johnny Carson moment." Fellow commentator Margaret Carlson added, "In a debate with that many [eight] people, a one-liner stands out. And the best one-liner is a one-word one-liner."[33] Especially, she might have added, when the one-liner comes from Senator Biden! While the senator seemed on the surface to concede the assumption behind the question, the brevity of his answer really worked as a refutation to the charge that he was uncontrollably verbose. His lightheartedness also drew a lot of the poison out of the question.

Joe Biden's bright moment leads directly to the next consideration:

■ **Keep your answers short and direct.** Don't give another speech.

■ **Handle nonquestions politely.** If someone starts to give a speech rather than ask a question, wait until he or she pauses for breath and then intervene with something like, "Thank you for your comment" or "I appreciate your remarks."

Speaker's Notes **13.1**

Handling Questions and Answers

Strengthen your message during the question-and-answer time by observing the following guidelines:

1. Practice answering tough questions before an audience of friends.

2. Repeat or paraphrase the question you are asked.

3. Maintain eye contact with the audience as a whole as you answer.

4. Defuse hostile questions by rewording them in unemotional language.

5. Don't be afraid to say, "I don't know."

6. Keep answers short and to the point.

7. Handle nonquestions politely.

8. Bring the question-and-answer session to a close by reemphasizing your message.

Your question, then, is . . ." or "That's an interesting perspective. Can we have another question?" Don't get caught up in a shouting match. Stay in command of the situation.

■ **Bring the question-and-answer session to a close.** Call for a final question, and as you complete the answer, summarize your message again to refocus listeners on your central points.

Making Video Presentations

It is quite likely that at some time in your life you will make a video presentation. You may find yourself speaking on closed-circuit television, videotaping instructions or training materials at work, using community access cable channels to promote a cause, running for public office, or even appearing on commercial television. Many video presentations utilize a manuscript printed on a teleprompter. In other situations, such as in small group discussions or question-and-answer formats, you may have to utilize impromptu or extemporaneous techniques. With some minor adaptations, the skills you are developing should help you make effective video presentations.[34]

Television encourages a conversational mode of presentation. Your audience may be single individuals or small groups assembled in their homes. Imagine yourself talking with another person in an informal setting. While intimate, however, television is also remote—you can't see the faces of viewers as they respond to what you're saying. Since you have no immediate feedback to help you, your meaning must be instantly clear. Use language that is colorful and concrete so that your audience remembers your points. Use previews and internal summaries to keep viewers on track. If you would like to use visual aids, be sure to confer in advance with studio personnel to be certain your materials will work well in that setting. For example, large poster boards displayed on an easel are more difficult to handle in video presentations than smaller materials. (See related considerations in Chapter 11.)

Television magnifies all your movements and vocal changes. Slight head movements and underplayed facial expressions should be enough to reinforce your ideas. Avoid abrupt changes in loudness as a means of vocal emphasis. Rely instead on subtle changes in tempo, pitch, and inflection, and on pauses, to drive your points home.

Because television brings you close to viewers, it also magnifies every aspect of your appearance. You should dress conservatively, avoiding shiny fabrics, glittery or dangling jewelry, and flashy prints that might "swim" on the screen and distract viewers. Do not wear white or light pastels that could reflect glare. Ask in advance about the color of the studio backdrop. If you have light hair or if the backdrop will be light, wear dark clothing for contrast. If you have a dark skin tone, request a light or neutral background and consider wearing light-colored clothes.

Both men and women need makeup to achieve a natural look on television. Have powder available to reduce skin shine or to hide a five o'clock shadow. Use makeup conservatively, because the camera will intensify it. Avoid glasses with tinted lenses, which appear even darker on the screen. Even untinted lenses can reflect glare from the studio lights. Wear contact lenses if you have them. If you can see well enough to read the monitor without glasses, leave them off.

For most televised presentations, timing is crucial. Five minutes of air time means five minutes, not five minutes and ten seconds. For this reason, television favors manuscript presentations read from a teleprompter. The teleprompter controls timing and preserves a sense of direct eye contact between speakers and listeners. The rolling script appears directly below or on the lens of the camera. Practice your speech ahead of time until you *almost* have it memorized so that you can glance at the script as a whole. If you have to read it word for word, your eyes may be continually shifting (and shifty eyes do not correlate with high credibility in American culture!).

Try to rehearse your presentation in the studio with the production personnel. Develop a positive relationship with studio technicians. Your success depends in large part on how well they do their jobs. Provide them with a manuscript marked to show when you will move around or use a visual aid. Practice speaking from the teleprompter and learn how to use the microphone correctly. Remember that the microphone picks up *all* sounds, including shuffling papers and tapping on a lectern. If you use a stand or handheld microphone, position it about 10 inches below your mouth. The closer the microphone is to your mouth, the more it picks up unwanted noises like whistled *s* sounds or tongue clicks. Microphones with cords restrict your movement. If you plan to move about during your presentation, know where the cord is so you won't trip over it.

Don't be put off by distractions as you practice and present your speech. Studio technicians may need to confer with one another while you are speaking. This is a necessary part of their business; they are not being rude or inattentive. Even though they are in the room with you, they are not your audience. Keep your mind on your ideas and your eyes on the camera. The camera may seem strange at first, but think of it as a friendly face waiting to hear what you have to say. During lighting and voice checks before the actual taping begins, use the time to run through your introduction. Before you begin your speech and after you finish, always assume that any microphone or camera near you is "live." Don't say or do anything you wouldn't want your audience to hear or see.

Even though the situation may seem strange, make a conscious effort to relax. If you are sitting, lean slightly forward as though you were talking to someone in the chair next to you. The floor director will give you a countdown before the camera starts to roll. Clear your throat and be ready to start on cue. Begin with a smile, if appropriate, as you make eye contact with the camera. If several cameras are used, a red light on top will tell you which camera is on. Make smooth transitions from one camera to the other. During your presentation, the studio personnel may communicate with you using special sign language. The director will tell you what cues they will use.[35]

If you make a mistake, keep going. Sometimes "mistakes" are improvements. Do not stop unless the director says "cut." If appropriate, smile when you finish and continue looking at the camera to allow time for a fade-out.

Practicing for Presentation

I t takes a lot of practice to sound natural. Although this statement may seem contradictory, it should not be surprising. Speaking before a group is not your typical way of communicating. Even though most people seem spontaneous and relaxed when talking with a small group of friends, something happens when they walk to the front of a room and face a larger audience of less familiar faces. They often freeze or become stilted and awkward. This blocks the natural flow of communication.

The key to overcoming this problem is to practice until you can respond fully to your ideas as you present them. Don't fall into the trap of avoiding practice because it reminds you that you are not confident about your upcoming speech: That makes you a prime candidate for a self-fulfilling prophecy![36] Instead, rehearse your speech until your voice, face, and body can express your feelings as well as your thoughts. On the day of your speech, you become a model for your listeners, showing them how they should respond in turn.

To develop an effective extemporaneous style, practice until you feel the speech is part of you. During practice, you can actually hear what you have been preparing and try out the words and techniques you have been considering. What looked like a good idea in your outline may not seem to work as well when it comes to life in spoken words. It is better to discover this fact in rehearsal than before an actual audience.

You will probably want privacy the first two or three times you practice. Even then, you should try to simulate the conditions under which the speech will be given. Stand up while you practice. Imagine your listeners in front of you. Picture them responding positively to what you have to say. Address your ideas to them, and visualize your ideas having impact.

If possible, go to your classroom to practice. If this is not possible, find another empty room where the speaking arrangements are similar. Such onsite rehearsal helps you get a better feel for the situation you will face, reducing its strangeness when you make your actual presentation. Begin practicing from your formal outline. Once you feel comfortable, switch to your key-word outline, and then practice until the outline transfers from the paper to your head.

Keep material that you must read to a minimum. Type or print quotations in large letters so you can see them easily, and put each quotation on a single index card or sheet of paper. If using a lectern, position this material so that you can maintain frequent eye contact while reading. If you will speak beside or in front of the lectern, hold your cards in your hand and raise them when it is time to read. Practice reading your quotation until you can present it naturally while only glancing at your notes. If your speech includes presentation aids, practice handling them until they are smoothly integrated into your presentation. They should seem a natural extension of your verbal message.

During practice, you can serve as your own audience by recording your speech and playing it back. If videotaping equipment is available, arrange to record your

Speaker's Notes **13.2**

Practicing for Presentation

To develop proficiency during practice, follow these suggestions:

1. Practice standing up and speaking aloud, if possible in the room where you will be making your presentation.

2. Practice first from your formal outline; then switch to your key-word outline when you feel you have mastered your material.

3. Work on maintaining eye contact with an imaginary audience.

4. Practice integrating your presentation aids into your message.

5. Check the timing of your speech. Add or cut if necessary.

6. Continue practicing until you feel comfortable and confident.

7. Present your speech in a "dress rehearsal" before friends. Make final changes in light of their suggestions.

speech so that you can see as well as hear yourself. Always try to be the toughest critic you will ever have, but also be a constructive critic. Never put yourself down. Work on specific points of improvement.

As you develop confidence, you may also find it helpful to ask a friend or friends to observe your presentation and offer suggestions. Recent findings confirm that speakers who practice before audiences receive higher evaluation scores later. The researchers explain, "Realistic practice is often sought to develop skills, hence the development of flight simulators to train pilots and scrimmage games to prepare athletes for the big game."[37]

The suggestions of others may be more objective than your self-evaluation, and you will get a feel for speaking to real people rather than to an imagined audience. Seek constructive feedback from your friends by asking them specific questions. Was it easy for them to follow you? Do you have any mannerisms (such as twisting your hair or saying "you know" after every other sentence) that distracted them? Were you speaking loudly and slowly enough? Did your ideas seem clear and soundly supported?

On the day that you are assigned to speak, get to class early enough to look over your outline one last time so that it is fresh in your mind. If you have devoted sufficient time and energy to your preparation and practice, you should feel confident about communicating with your audience. Speaker's Notes 13.2 summarizes our suggestions for practicing.

Taking the Stage

As you step to the front of the room at the moment you are asked to speak, you should do so with a certain panache. You should radiate the expectation that you have something worthy and important to say that listeners should consider carefully. This confidence, this air of leadership, is what communication consultant Judith Humphrey calls "taking the stage."[38] This theatrical metaphor summarizes much of what we have said to this point about preparing for public speaking. Taking the stage, Humphrey says, implies six steps.

1. Adopt the *attitude* that every public communication situation is an opportunity to influence, inspire, and motivate others.

2. Have the *conviction* that what you bring to others will have great value.

3. Create the *character of leadership* as you speak. Humphrey says: "A leader has vision. A leader has a point of view and is not afraid to express it. A leader must also be . . . totally authentic."[39]

4. Follow a great *script*. You should have a simple, clear, positive message.

5. Use the *language* of leadership. Your words should be forceful and should avoid indirection and self-correction. Don't overuse phrases like "in my opinion" or "maybe I'm wrong but." Don't soften your point or subvert yourself.

6. Finally, *believe in your views*. As you stand at the lectern, don't shrink into yourself. Stand still and don't fidget. Establish firm eye contact and make strong gestures. Use pauses to make your points. "Taking the stage" is your invitation and opportunity to lead others.

In Summary

The goal of integrated communication is to combine the power of body language, voice, and speech content to produce a larger-than-life communication experience for all who participate in it. The moment of presentation represents the goal and climax of speech preparation. To prepare for this moment, you must develop your natural resources of voice and body, become versatile in the various modes of speaking, and become flexible in special situations.

The Goal of Integrated Communication. Integrated communication allows speaker and listeners to share a special moment of meaning. To make this moment happen, tangible, technical requirements must be met: You must be heard, and you must sound natural and conversational. Even more important are the intangibles: You must want to communicate. Immediacy describes the closeness that develops when speaker and listeners share this attitude.

Developing Your Voice. A good speaking voice conveys your meaning fully and clearly. Vocal expressiveness depends on your ability to control your pitch, rate, loudness, and variety. Your habitual pitch is the level at which you usually speak. Your optimum pitch is the level at which you can produce a clear, strong voice with minimal effort. You can control rate to your advantage by using pauses and by changing your pace to match the moods of your material. To speak loudly enough, you need proper breath control. Vocal variety adds color and interest to a speech, can make a speaker more likeable, and encourages identification between speaker and audience.

Articulation, enunciation, pronunciation, and dialect are the unique qualities that give voice to words. Articulation concerns the manner in which you produce individual sounds. Enunciation is the way you utter words in context. Proper pronunciation means that you say words correctly. Your dialect may identify your cultural or ethnic background or the area of the country in which you learned language.

Developing Your Body Language. You communicate with body language as well as with your voice. Eye contact signals listeners that you want to communicate. Your facial expressions should reinforce, not contradict, the meanings of your words. Movement attracts attention; therefore, your movements and gestures must complement your speech, not compete with it. Proxemics is the study of how humans use space during communication. Two proxemic principles, distance and elevation, can affect your identification with an audience as you speak. Be sure your grooming and dress are appropriate to the speech occasion and do not detract from your ability to communicate.

Developing Versatility in Presentation. To be a versatile speaker, you must be adept in the different modes of presentation. The four methods of speech presentation are impromptu speaking, memorized presentation, reading from a manuscript, and extemporaneous speaking. In impromptu speaking, you talk with minimal or no preparation and practice. Both memorized and manuscript presentations require that your speech be written out word for word. The usual preferred mode, extemporaneous presentation, requires careful planning, but the wording is spontaneous. Extemporaneous speaking allows you to adapt to feedback from your audience. Be especially alert for signs that your audience doesn't understand, has lost interest, or disagrees with you, and then make adjustments to your message to cope with these problems.

Developing Flexibility in Special Situations. Two special situations, question-and-answer sessions and video presentations, require that you develop specialized presentation skills. Following any presentation, you may need to answer questions about your material and ideas. Although your responses will be impromptu, you should prepare for questions in advance. Video presentations require a conversational manner in which vocal variety and facial expressions assume special importance. To cope with time constraints, video presentations often encourage manuscript speaking, using the teleprompter to create the sense of directness and immediacy.

Practicing for Presentation. You should practice your speech until you have the sequence of main points and supporting materials well established in your mind. As you prepare for the moment when you will "take the stage," it is best to practice your presentation in conditions similar to those in which you will give your speech.

Explore and Apply the Ideas in This Chapter

1. Attend a lecture or political speech. Evaluate the speech by applying the standards of integrated communication. Did the speaker read from a manuscript, make a memorized presentation, or speak extemporaneously? Was the speaker adept at moving from one mode of presentation to another? How flexible was the speaker in answering questions? Was the speaker's voice effective or ineffective? Why? How would you evaluate the speaker's body language? Report your observations in class.

2. Comedians often capture the personalities of public figures by exaggerating their verbal and gestural characteristics in comic impersonations. Be alert for such impersonations on late-night television. Which identifying characteristics do the comedians exaggerate? What might this indicate about the "real" speaker's presentation peculiarities? Contribute your observations to a class discussion.

3. Make a list of questions you think you might be asked following your next speech. Plan the answers you might make to these questions. Working in small groups, distribute your questions to group members to ask of you. Invite them to evaluate your responses.

4. Exchange your self-evaluation audiotape with a classmate and write a critique of that person's voice and articulation. Emphasize the positive, but make specific recommendations for improvement. Work on your classmate's recommendations to you, and then make a second tape to share with your partner. Do you detect signs of improvement in each other's performance?

5. As you practice your next speech, deliberately try to speak in as dull a voice as possible. Stifle all impulses to gesture. Then practice speaking with as colorful a voice as possible, giving full freedom to movement and gesture. Notice how a colorful and expressive presentation makes your ideas seem more lively and vivid.

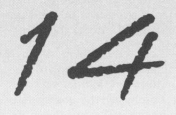

Informative Speaking

This chapter will help you

- understand the importance of informative speaking
- learn how to develop different types of informative speeches
- know how to help listeners learn
- arrange information for maximum effectiveness
- respond to the special challenge of informative speaking

The improvement of understanding is for two ends: first our own increase of knowledge; secondly, to enable us to deliver that knowledge to others.

—John Locke

I n ancient Greek mythology, Prometheus was punished by the other gods for teaching humans how to make fire. According to the myth, these jealous gods knew that people would now be able to keep warm, cook food, use the extended light, and share knowledge as they huddled around their campfires. Eventually they would build civilizations and challenge the gods themselves with the power of their new learning. These mythical gods had every right to be angry with Prometheus. He had given the first significant informative speech.

This tale of Prometheus reminds us that information is power. Because we cannot personally experience everything that may be important or interesting to us, we must rely on the knowledge of others to expand our understanding and competence. _Sharing knowledge is the essence of informative speaking._

Shared information can be important to survival. Early detection and warning systems alert us to storms, and news of medical breakthroughs tell us how to stay healthy. Beyond simply enabling us to live, information helps us to live _better_. It helps us deal with our world and the people in it. In this chapter, we look more closely at the nature and types of informative speaking, suggest ways to help your listeners learn, and identify and evaluate the basic designs in which informative speeches develop. We also describe the special challenge posed by informative speaking. Our objective is to help you bring fire to your listeners.

Informative Speaking: An Orientation

An informative speech _gives_ to listeners rather than _asks_ of them. As an informative speaker, you want listeners to pay attention and understand, but you do not try to make them change their behavior. For example, Heide Norde presented an informative speech to her class on the dangers of prolonged exposure to ultraviolet radiation, but she did not urge listeners to boycott tanning salons. What they did in response to this new knowledge was up to them. Similarly, in the speech reprinted at the end of this chapter, Marie D'Aniello deepened her audience's appreciation for the meaning of friendship, but she did not advocate that they go out and seek friends.

By sharing information, an informative speech reduces ignorance. It does not simply repeat something the audience already knows. Rather, the **informative value** of a speech is measured by _how much new and important information or understanding it provides the audience_. As you prepare your informative speech, ask yourself the following questions:

- Is my topic significant enough to merit an informative speech?

- What do my listeners already know about my topic?

Ethics _Alert! 14.1_

The Ethics of Informative Speaking

As you prepare your informative speech, keep these ethical considerations in mind.

1. Be sure you can defend the morality of your choice of topic.

2. Mention all major positions on a topic when there are differing perspectives.

3. Present all information that is vital for audience understanding.

4. Do not distort information that is necessary for audience understanding.

5. Do sufficient research to speak responsibly on your subject.

6. Do not omit relevant information because it is inconsistent with your perspective.

7. Strive to be as objective as possible.

informative value A measure of how much new and important information or understanding a speech conveys to an audience.

- What more do they need to know?

- Do I understand my topic well enough to help others understand it?

The answers to these questions should help you plan a speech with high informative value.

It is clear that informative speakers carry a large ethical burden to communicate responsible knowledge of their topics. A responsible informative speech should cover all major positions on a topic and present all vital information. Although speakers may have strong feelings on a subject, it is unethical to deliberately omit or distort information that is necessary for audience understanding. Similarly, speakers who are unaware of information because they have not done sufficient research are irresponsible. As you prepare your speech, you should seek out material from sources that offer different perspectives on your subject.

Forms of Informative Speaking

 f it's true that we live in an age of information, then the importance of informative speaking can hardly be exaggerated. Informative speaking arises out of three deep impulses within us:

1. *We seek to expand our awareness of the world around us.* Perhaps we sense that to stretch our horizons is also to grow in power. This impulse may account for the value of **speeches of description**.

2. *We seek to become more competent, to develop skills that are vital or enjoyable.* This impulse accounts for the importance of **speeches of demonstration**.

3. *We have an abiding curiosity about how things work and how they are made.* This is especially true when these things are important to our quality of life and when it becomes clear that fascinating stories are just waiting to be told. This impulse may account for the importance of **speeches of explanation**.

Speeches of Description

Often, the specific purpose of a speech is to describe what's "out there" or "in here." Such a speech might focus on an activity, event, object, person, or place in the world outside the listener. Or the speech might describe the unseen world inside the human body. Either way, a **speech of description** should give the audience a clear picture of your subject. The words must be concrete and colorful to depict the subject precisely and to convey the feeling of the message. The speech "The Monument at Wounded Knee" in Appendix B describes a *place* and an *object* by providing vivid word-pictures. Thus, the landscape is not simply desolate; it is characterized by "flat, sun-baked fields and an occasional eroded gully." Cecile Larson goes on to describe the monument:

> The monument itself rests on a concrete slab to the right of the grave. It's a typical, large, old-fashioned granite cemetery marker, a pillar about six feet high topped with an urn—the kind of gravestone you might see in any cemetery with graves from the turn of the century. The inscription tells us that it

speech of description An informative speech that creates word-pictures to help the audience understand a subject.

speech of demonstration An informative speech aimed at showing the audience how to do something or how something works.

speech of explanation Offers understanding of abstract and complex subjects.

was erected by the families of those who were killed at Wounded Knee. Weeds grow through the cracks in the concrete at its base.

Can you "see" the monument? If so, Cecile's pictorial language has done its descriptive work. While she describes a place and an object, Cecile's purpose is also to deepen historical understanding of an *event* that occurred there.

In her speech exposing conditions in the fast-food industry, student speaker Hannah Johnston used vivid language to describe an *activity*—what it's like to work in a slaughterhouse.

> Slaughterhouse work conditions have not changed much over the past fifty to one hundred years. Now the work is done mostly by underpaid migrant workers who have virtually no other job options. But who would choose to work in a place like this if they did have options? Who, for example, would choose to become a "sticker," a person who, for about eight and a half hours a day, does nothing other than stand, literally drenched in a river of blood, slitting the throats of steers that pass every ten seconds or so?

Hannah's speech expanded audience awareness of a world foreign to most of us.

As these examples make clear, the art of verbal description comes down to one basic rule: *You must create in the minds of your listeners a sharp picture of what your subject looks like.* Concrete, colorful language can obviously help. Such language relies heavily on the principles of contrast, intensity, and activity, which we discuss in more detail in the next section.

The topic, purpose, and strategy of your speech of description should suggest the appropriate design for it. The "Wounded Knee" speech follows a spatial pattern in that it develops within a verbal map of the Pine Ridge reservation. Hannah's descriptions of slaughterhouse conditions occur within a categorical design as she discusses the content of fast food, the conditions under which it is produced, and its increasingly global health consequences. We discuss these and other design options later in this chapter.

Speeches of Demonstration

The **speech of demonstration** shows its audience how to do something. Dance instructors teach us the Texas two-step. Others may tell us how to do research on the Internet, how to prepare for the law school admission test, or even how to build a fire. The tip-off to the speech of demonstration is the phrase "how to." What these examples have in common is that they demonstrate a process.

Successful speeches of demonstration empower listeners so that they can perform the process themselves. Jeffrey O'Connor showed his University of New Mexico classmates how to read a textbook efficiently. He guided them through five steps of effective reading, each step representing a main point of his speech. His presentation, outlined later in this chapter, follows a sequential design.

Suzanne Marchetti illustrated another form of the speech of demonstration when she took her classmates on a verbal tour of Yellowstone Park, showing them how to access major attractions there. Her speech, again outlined later in this chapter, employs a spatial design.

Most speeches of demonstration are helped by the use of presentation aids. The speaker can present and discuss objects that listeners must use to accomplish something, show slides that reveal the steps in a process, or actually demonstrate how to perform an activity. If you are preparing a speech of demonstration, review the materials on presentation aids in Chapter 11 to determine how you might help your audience understand. When you are demonstrating a process, "show and tell" is usually much more effective than just telling.

Speeches of Explanation

A **speech of explanation** offers information about subjects that are abstract or complicated. Because the object of such a speech is understanding, a speech of explanation should present the critical characteristics of a subject and offer abundant examples.[1] In her speech explaining Alzheimer's disease, student speaker Amanda Miller presented the critical features of her subject in the following way:

Speeches of demonstration show the audience how to do something.

1. She justified her speech by quoting a famous victim, Ronald Reagan, who asked for greater public awareness and understanding of the disease as he left public life.

2. She defined the disease.

3. She explained the significance of the disease for those afflicted with it, their families, and the nation (in terms of cost).

4. She described the process of the disease.

5. She identified the risk factors associated with it.

6. She explained how to minimize susceptibility to it.

Similarly, Marie D'Aniello, in her classroom speech "What Friends Are All About," defined the nature of friendship, explained its significance to her listeners, and traced the evolution (process) of friendship as people mature. Like Amanda, she offered examples and expert testimony at every step to clarify and authenticate her explanations.

As you present the critical features of your subject in a speech of explanation, be sure to go through the essential phases of defining your subject, explaining its significance to the lives of your listeners, and describing any processes by which it develops. Include a variety of examples and testimony.

Speeches of explanation face a considerable challenge when their information runs counter to generally accepted beliefs. Professor Katherine Rowan provides an example of how this can work in public service campaigns:

A particularly resilient obstacle to [seat] belt use is the erroneous but prevalent belief that hitting one's head on a windshield while traveling at 30 miles per hour is an experience much like doing so when a car is stationary. . . . If people understood that the experience would be much

Speaker's Notes 14.1

Rules for Effective Informative Speaking

Keep these rules in mind as you develop an informative speech.

1. Speeches of description should come alive through colorful language.

2. Speeches of demonstration should present a clear, orderly sequence of steps.

3. Speeches of demonstration are helped by presentation aids.

4. Speeches of explanation need clear definitions of important terms.

5. Speeches of explanation require good examples.

> more similar to falling from a three-story building and hitting the pavement face first, one obstacle to the wearing of seat belts would be easier to overcome.[2]

As her example indicates, dramatic analogies—such as comparing an auto accident at thirty miles per hour to falling from a building—can help break through our resistance to new ideas that defy folk wisdom. The use of such strategic comparisons and contrasts can help listeners accept new information and use it in their lives.

Helping Listeners Learn

ow many times have you had a conversation like the following?

She:	I told you that two days ago.
He:	No, you didn't. I told you yesterday that you didn't tell me that.
She:	No, you didn't tell me that yesterday.

What we have here is a perfect circle of communication frustration. Yes, she did tell him that two days ago, and yes, he did tell her yesterday that she hadn't told him. In one ear, out the other. As a matter of fact, we are exposed to countless messages during a normal day—from television, radio, friends, and loved ones—and many of these messages simply don't register. We attend selectively to messages that interest us, concern us, engage us, and even alarm us: The rest simply don't penetrate our listening barriers and filters.

What will be the fate of your informative speech? Will it register with listeners and be remembered? Or will it simply drift into instant forgetfulness? It may have impact if you make a conscious effort to help listeners learn.

Begin by considering how much listeners know initially about your topic, how interested they may be in it, what preconceptions they may have about it that might help or hinder your purpose, and how they regard you as a speaker. These basic audience considerations can help you select strategies for your presentation. Figure 14.1 charts these audience considerations and directs you to possible strategies you can use.

Figure 14.1

Audience Considerations for Informative Speeches

Audience Type	Strategies
Interested but uninformed	• Provide basic information in clear, simple language. • Avoid jargon, define technical terms. • Use examples and narratives for amplification. • When communicating complicated information, use analogies, metaphors, and/or presentation aids. • Use voice, gestures, and eye contact to reinforce meaning.
Interested and knowledgeable	• Establish your credibility early in the speech. • Acknowledge diverse perspectives on topic. • Go into depth with information and expert testimony. • Offer engaging presentation that keeps focus on content.
Uninterested	• Show listeners what's in it for them. • Keep presentation short and to the point. • Use sufficient examples and narratives to arouse and sustain interest. • Use eye-catching presentation aids and colorful language. • Make a dynamic presentation.
Unsympathetic (toward topic)	• Show respect for listeners and their point of view. • Cite sources the audience will respect. • Present information to enlarge listeners' understanding. • Develop stories and examples to arouse favorable feeling. • Make a warm, engaging presentation.
Distrustful (of speaker)	• Establish your credibility early in the speech. • Rely heavily on factual examples and expert testimony. • Cite sources of information in your presentation. • Be straightforward, business-like, and personable. • Keep good eye-contact with listeners.

To help your listeners learn and remember your message, you must motivate them by establishing its relevance to their lives, hold their attention throughout your message, and structure your speech to help listeners retain its meaning.

You should also keep in mind that there are different types of intelligence and learning styles.[3] For example, some people are *aural learners* who learn well through the spoken word alone. Others are *print learners* who learn better when they see things in writing. These people respond well when you provide charts and textual graphics to illustrate your words. A third group, *visual learners*, need something to watch as they listen; they are helped especially by demonstrations, pictures, and models. Keep these various learning styles in mind as you design your speeches. To serve such a wide population of listeners, you may have to reinforce your carefully designed fabric of words with charts and graphs, and

InterConnections.
LearnMore 14.1

Learning Styles

Index of Learning Styles

www2.ncsu.edu/unity/lockers/users/f/felder/public/ILSpage.html

Links to learning-style sites and a self-administered, computer-scored quiz that reflects four dimensions of learning: active versus reflective, sensing versus intuitive, visual versus verbal, and sequential versus global. Developed by Professor Emeritus Richard Felder of North Carolina State University.

Seven Perceptual Styles

www.learningstyles.org/menu.html

Overview of the seven ways people learn: print, aural, interactive, visual, haptic (touch), kinesthetic, and olfactory; sponsored by the Institute for Learning Styles Research.

Chart Your Learning Style

www.chaminade.org/inspire/learnstl.htm

Offers chart to help you determine your own learning style preference. Adapted from Colin Rose, Accelerated Learning (Dell, 1987).

you may have to offer demonstrations or enlarged photos that illustrate what you are saying.

Motivation

To motivate listeners, especially those who are not initially interested in your subject, you must tell them why your message is important to them. In Chapter 5, we discussed motivation as a general factor in audience analysis. Now we consider using motivation to give listeners a reason to learn. Ask yourself why listeners would want to know what you have to tell them.

- Will it help them understand and control the world around them?

- Will it satisfy their curiosity?

- Will it improve their health, safety, or general well-being?

- Will it give them a sense of making a contribution by caring for others?

- Will it help them establish better relations with family and friends?

- Will it give them a sense of accomplishment and achievement, thus enhancing their personal growth, power, and independence?

- Will it contribute to the restoration of moral balance and fairness in the world?

- Will it provide them with enjoyment?

Go back over the motivations discussed in Chapter 5 and determine which of these are most relevant to your topic and your audience. Then develop your speech so that it connects with these needs.

For example, you might relate a speech on how to interview for a job to the motivation for achievement. You could begin by talking about the problem of finding a good job in today's market-place and provide an example that illustrates how a successful interview can make the difference in who gets hired and who does not. As you preview the body of your speech, you might say, "Today, I'm going to describe four factors that can determine whether you get the job of your dreams. First, . . ." In this case you have given your audience a reason for wanting to listen to the rest of your speech. You have begun the learning process by motivating your listeners.

Hannah Johnston began her speech on the fast-food industry by appealing to health and safety motivations: "If you had a choice, I'm sure you wouldn't choose to eat some of the stuff that can end up in processed meat." Hannah ruined lunch for some of her classmates, but they could not help but listen closely. Marie D'Aniello opened her speech on the nature of friendship with a narrative that aroused curiosity: "It's nine o'clock at night. I'm curled up in the back seat of a new truck and my friends, Cammy and Joe, are in the front singing along with the radio." Hmmm, her listeners puzzled. What happened in the truck? Why were Cammy and Joe singing? They were ready to listen to the rest of her informative speech.

Listeners must be motivated to learn new information. Organizational training programs must combine motivation and information to help employees become more effective.

Attention

Once you have motivated your audience to listen, you must hold their attention throughout your speech. In Chapter 7, we discussed how to attract audience attention in the introduction of your speech. Here we focus on how to sustain that interest. You can do so by applying one or more of the six factors that affect attention: intensity, repetition, novelty, activity, contrast, and relevance.

Intensity.   You can determine the **intensity** of an object by how much it contrasts with its background. Merely printing the word "intensity" in boldface is an example of this principle at work. It signals that this term is important by making it stand out against the words that surround it. In speeches, intense language and vivid images can be used to attract and hold attention. You can further emphasize a point by using examples that magnify its importance. You can also achieve intensity through the use of presentation aids and by vocal emphasis and variety. Note how Stephen Huff held the attention of his classmates through the intensity of his descriptions of the New Madrid earthquakes that struck the south central United States in the early nineteenth century:

> The Indians tell of the night that lasted for a week and the way the "Father of Waters"—the Mississippi River—ran backward. Waterfalls were formed on

intensity Attention factor concerning how much an object contrasts with its background.

the river. Islands disappeared. Land that was once in Arkansas ended up in Tennessee. Cracks up to ten feet wide opened and closed in the earth. Geysers squirted sand high into the air. Whole forests sank into the earth as the land turned to quicksand.

Repetition.   Repeated sounds, words, or phrases attract and hold attention. Skillful speakers may use **repetition** to emphasize points, help listeners follow the flow of ideas, and embed their messages in audience memory. As we saw in Chapter 12, repetition underlies alliteration and parallel construction. Alliteration lends vividness to main ideas: "Today, I will discuss how the *M*ississippi River *m*eanders from *M*innesota to the sea." The repetition of the *m* sound catches attention and emphasizes the statement. Similarly, parallel construction establishes a pattern that sticks in the mind. Repeated questions and answers such as "What is our goal? It is to . . ." sustain attention.

Novelty.   We are attracted to anything new or unusual: thus, the importance of **novelty**. If you have a fresh way of seeing and saying things, uninterested or distrustful listeners may increase both their respect for you and their interest in your subject. A novel phrase can fascinate listeners and hold their attention. In a speech on environmental stewardship, Jim Cardoza found a novel way to describe the magnitude of pollution. After reporting that nineteen million tons of garbage are picked up each year along the nation's beaches, he concluded: "And that's just the tip of the wasteberg." His invented word, *wasteberg*, reminded listeners of *iceberg* and suggested the enormity of the problem.

Activity.   As we noted in Chapter 13, anything that moves attracts attention. Gesturing, approaching the audience to add emphasis to a point, and referring to presentation aids can all add **activity**. An exciting story or example can also bring a speech to life and attract attention. You can further create a sense of activity by using vivid words, rhythm, and vocal variety. Stephen Huff used a clever stylistic technique near the beginning of his speech on "The New Madrid Earthquake Area" to create the sense of living presence:

> How many of you can remember what you were doing around seven o'clock on the evening of October 17th? If you're a sports fan like me, you had probably set out the munchies, popped a cold one, and settled back to watch San Francisco and Oakland battle it out in the World Series. . . . You may not have been paying close attention to the TV—*until—until—until* both the sound and picture went out because of the Bay Area earthquake.

Here the repetition of "until" simulates the sense of trembling instability one experiences during an actual earthquake.

Josh Logan, on the other hand, used a graphic action picture to leave a vivid impression on his listeners as he concluded his speech, "Life in the Greenhouse." He invited his audience to sample what he had been talking about in his speech, a narrative effect we call *vicarious experience*:

> If you want to understand why global warming has become one of the great crises of our time, you've simply got to step outside into the

---

repetition Repeating sounds, words, or phrases to attract and hold attention.

novelty The quality of being new or unusual.

activity Holding audience attention by offering a vigorous presentation, telling exciting stories, and using language that creates the sense of action.

greenhouse. Listen for the falling trees, watch the industrial smokestacks darkening the sky, and smell that rich bouquet of exhaust fumes that we are constantly pumping into the air. The greenhouse effect is a monster we all are creating.

Whether you are beginning or concluding your speech, creating the sense of activity can earn favorable attention for your speech.

Contrast. The principle that *opposites attract attention* explains the importance of **contrast**. If you work in a noisy environment and it suddenly becomes quiet, the stillness can seem deafening. Similarly, abrupt changes in your pitch or rate of speaking will draw attention. Presenting the pros and cons of a situation creates a sense of conflict and drama that listeners often find arresting. You can also highlight contrasts by speaking of such opposites as life and death or the highs and lows of a situation.

In a speech dramatizing the need to learn more about AIDS, a speaker introduced two or three specific examples with the statement "Let me introduce you to *Death*." Then, as the speech moved to the promise of medical research, she said, "Now let me introduce you to *Life*." This usage combined repetition and contrast to create a dramatic effect.

Similarly, Cecile Larson used contrast between the grand monuments of American life—such as the heroes sculpted on Mount Rushmore—and the much more humble "monument" at Wounded Knee to focus audience attention on a less proud incident in the nation's history.

When contrast works, it produces a shock effect. Once people become accustomed to an established pattern, they no longer think about it. But they notice any abrupt, dramatic change from the pattern.

Relevance. Things that relate to our specific needs, interests, or concerns hold our attention. Often listeners who may be unconcerned about a subject need to be shown how it relates to their lives. Allison McIntyre created **relevance** for her speech on smoking advertisements by placing a large jar of cigarette butts on the table by the lectern.

> So you think the cigarette advertisers are losing their fight to recruit smokers at American colleges and universities? Here's what I collected myself in about 45 minutes at noon yesterday, right around the outside of this building. These are our butts. Vanderbilt student butts. Think of all the damaged lungs these represent, right here in this building.

The striking relevance of her presentation aid made it hard to ignore her speech.

Stephen Huff created relevance for his earthquake speech by relating the San Francisco earthquake to the New Madrid area in which he and his listeners lived. Then he dramatized this relevance through the use of contrast, pointing out that the energy level of the New Madrid quakes of the previous century "was over nine hundred times more powerful than the Hiroshima atomic bomb and more than thirty times more powerful than the 7.0 quake that hit San Francisco." Needless to say, Stephen had his listeners' attention as he talked about how to prepare for the next major quake in the area.

---

contrast Arranging supporting materials to highlight differences or gaining attention by using abrupt changes in presentation, dwelling upon opposites, or framing the pros and cons of a situation.

relevance Holding attention by pointing out a subject's importance or value to vital interests.

Attention Techniques

Use the following strategies to attract and sustain the attention of your listeners.

1. *Motivate* listeners by showing them how they can benefit from your message.

2. *Speak with intensity*—develop word-pictures that vividly depict your topic.

3. *Use strategic repetition* to amplify your message.

4. *Rely on novelty* by using fresh expressions and providing new examples.

5. *Use active language* that makes your subject come to life.

6. *Present contrasts* to show what your topic is not.

7. *Highlight relevance* to connect your subject directly to the experience of listeners.

Retention

Even the best information is useless unless your listeners remember and use it. Repetition, relevance, and structural factors can all be used to facilitate audience **retention**. The more frequently we hear or see anything, the more likely we are to retain it. This is why advertisers bombard us with slogans or characters such as the Geico gecko to keep their product names in our consciousness. These slogans may be repeated in all of their advertisements, regardless of the visuals or narratives presented. The repetition of key-words or phrases in a speech also helps the audience remember. In his famous civil rights speech in Washington, D.C., Martin Luther King's repetition of the phrase "I have a dream . . ." became the hallmark of the speech and is now used as its title.

Relevance is also important to retention. Our minds filter incoming information, associating it with things we already know and evaluating it for its potential usefulness. *If you want listeners to remember your message, tell them why and how it relates to their lives.*

Structural factors also affect how well a message is retained. Previews, summaries, and clear transitions can help your audience remember your message. The way you organize your material also affects retention. Suppose you were given the following list of words to memorize:

> north, man, hat, daffodil, green, tulip, coat, boy, south, red, east, shoes, gardenia, woman, purple, marigold, gloves, girl, yellow, west

It looks rather difficult, but look what happens when we rearrange the words:

> north, south, east, west
> man, boy, woman, girl
> daffodil, tulip, gardenia, marigold
> green, red, purple, yellow
> hat, coat, shoes, gloves

In the first example, you have what looks like a random list of words. In the second, the words have been organized by categories: Now you have five groups of four related words to remember. Material that is presented in a consistent and orderly fashion is much easier for your audience to retain.

retention The extent to which listeners remember and use the speaker's message.

Speech Designs

*L*et us assume at this point that you have now gone through a careful process of preparing for your informative speech. You have selected a topic that promises important new information for your listeners. You have researched carefully, gathered responsible knowledge, and jotted down some striking ideas that should interest them. You think you know how you can motivate your listeners and hold their attention.

Still, your preparation will not be complete until you find the right design for your ideas—the overall structure that will frame your speech in an effective pattern. Six design formats serve the needs of most informative speeches: spatial, sequential, chronological, categorical (topical), comparative, and causation. These designs may also be adapted for use in persuasive and ceremonial speeches.

Spatial Design

A **spatial design** is appropriate for speeches that develop their topics within a physical setting. The order of discussion is based on the nearness of things to one another. Suppose someone asked you to name the time zones in the United States. If you live in Washington, D.C., you would probably reply, "Eastern, Central, Mountain, and Pacific." If you live in Oregon, you might answer, "Pacific, Mountain, Central, and Eastern."[4] Either answer would follow a spatial pattern, taking where you are as the initial point of reference.

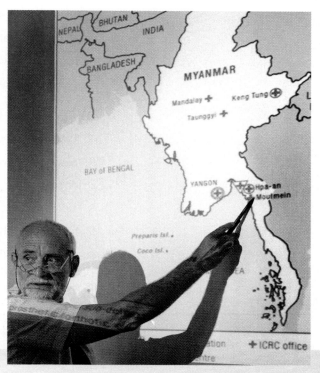

Speeches that follow a spatial design often use maps to help people visualize directions.

Most people are familiar with maps and can readily visualize directions. A speech using a spatial design provides listeners with an oral map, such as we see in Cecile Larson's "Wounded Knee" speech. Spatial designs are especially useful for speeches of description in which they help listeners visualize the physical relationships of objects to one another.

To develop a spatial design that is easy for listeners to follow, select a starting point and then take your audience on an orderly, systematic journey to a destination. Once you begin a pattern of movement, stay with it to the end of the speech. If you change directions in the middle, the audience may get lost. Be sure to complete the pattern so that you satisfy listeners' desire for closure. Suzanne Marchetti's informative speech introducing Yellowstone Park developed within a spatial design.

Preview: When you visit Yellowstone, stop first at the South Entrance Visitor's Center, then drive northwest to Old Faithful, north to Mammoth Hot Springs, and then southeast to the Grand Canyon of the Yellowstone.

I. Your first stop should be at the South Entrance Visitor's Center.

    A. Talk with a park ranger to help plan your trip.

    B. Attend a lecture or film to orient yourself.

    C. Pick up materials and maps to make your tour more meaningful.

spatial design A pattern for an informative speech that orders the main points as they occur in actual space.

II. Drive northwest through Geyser Valley to Old Faithful.

  A. Hike the boardwalks in the Upper Geyser Basin.

  B. Join the crowds waiting for Old Faithful to erupt on schedule.

  C. Have lunch at Old Faithful Inn.

III. Continue north to Mammoth Hot Springs.

  A. Plan to spend the night at the lodge or in one of the cabins.

  B. Attend the evening lectures or films on the history of the park.

IV. Drive southeast to the Grand Canyon of the Yellowstone.

  A. Take in the view from Inspiration Point.

  B. Hike down the trail for a better view of the waterfalls.

Suzanne's speech design described an approximate circular pattern that was orderly and provided her listeners with a good sense of the location of important places within the park. Each of her main points received about the same amount of attention, so her speech seemed well balanced as it traced this circle. Speakers using the spatial pattern often use a presentation aid, such as a map, to reinforce the sense of space created in their speeches.

Sequential Design

A **sequential design** moves listeners through time. Speeches built on a sequential design typically present the steps in a process. This design is especially appropriate for speeches of demonstration. You begin by identifying the necessary steps in the process and the order in which they must take place. These steps become the main points of your speech. In a short presentation, you should have no more than five steps as main points. You can assign numbers to these steps as you make your presentation. The following abbreviated outline, developed by Jeffrey O'Connor, illustrates a sequential design.

Preview: The five steps of efficient textbook reading include skimming, reading, rereading, reciting, and reviewing.

 I. First, *skim* through the chapter to get the overall picture.

  A. Identify the major ideas from the section headings.

  B. Read any summary statements.

  C. Read any boxed materials.

  D. Make a key-word outline of major topics.

II. Second, *read* the chapter a section at a time.

  A. Make notes in the margins on questions you have.

  B. Look up definitions of unfamiliar words.

  C. Go back and highlight the major ideas.

sequential design A pattern for an informative speech that presents the steps involved in the process being demonstrated.

III. Third, *reread* the chapter.

    A. Fill in your outline with more detail.

    B. Try to answer the questions you wrote in the margin.

    C. Frame questions for your instructor on anything you don't understand.

IV. Fourth, *recite* what you have read.

    A. Use your outline to make an oral presentation to yourself.

    B. Explain the material to someone else.

V. Finally, *review* the material within twenty-four hours.

    A. Review your outline.

    B. Reread the highlighted material.

Presenting the steps in this orderly, sequential way helped Jeffrey "walk" his University of New Mexico classmates through the process.

Chronological Design

The **chronological design**, which is closely related to the sequential design, follows the sequence of important events in the history of a subject. However, the sequential design works best for speeches of demonstration, and the chronological pattern is better suited to speeches of explanation. The first focuses on *how to do something*, the second on *how something happens or works*.

Using the chronological design, you may start with the beginnings of the subject and trace it up to the present through its defining moments. Or, you may start with the present and trace the subject back to its origins. To keep your listeners' attention and to meet time requirements, you must be selective. Choose landmark events as the main points in your message, and then arrange them in their natural order. D'Angelo Dartez used a chronological design for a speech on the evolution of the T-shirt.

Preview: The T-shirt began as an undergarment, developed into outerwear as a bearer of messages, and has emerged as high-fashion apparel.

  I. The T-shirt originated as an undergarment early in the twentieth century.

    A. The first undershirts with sleeves were designed for sailors, to spare sensitive people the sight of hairy armpits.

    B. They were first sold commercially in the late 1930s.

    C. During World War II, T-shirts were used as outerwear in the tropics.

 II. After World War II, civilians began using T-shirts as outerwear.

    A. They were comfortable and absorbent.

    B. They were popularized in movies like *Rebel Without a Cause*.

    C. They were easy to care for.

chronological design A pattern of speech organization that follows a sequence of important events in a historical pattern.

III. T-shirts soon became embellished with pictures and messages.

    A. Children's T-shirts had pictures of cartoon characters.

    B. Adult T-shirt designs were usually related to sports teams.

    C. T-shirts soon were used for "political" statements.

IV. Today's T-shirts are unique.

    A. You can customize a message.

    B. You can put your picture on a T-shirt.

    C. You can buy bejeweled T-shirts.

Speeches of explanation such as the T-shirt speech are generally the most complex types of informative speaking. Rather than indicating how to do things or describing objects or events, they develop ideas. Therefore, we should not be surprised to find that the designs for such speeches are also often more complex. The T-shirt speech illustrates what we might call a *combination design*. While it traces the chronology of events over time, it also discusses categories of development: in this case, steps in the evolution of undergarments into outerwear. This example provides a convenient bridge into our next pattern, categorical design.

Categorical Design

Consider using the **categorical design**—sometimes called the topical design—when you want to explain subjects that have natural or customary divisions. Natural divisions may exist within the subject itself, such as red, white, and blended wines. Customary divisions represent typical ways of thinking about a subject, such as the four food groups that are essential to a healthy diet or, as we just saw, undergarments and outerwear. *Categories are the mind's way of ordering the world by seeking patterns within it or by supplying patterns to arrange it.* Categories help us sort information so that we can make sense of it.

Each category in the design becomes a main point for development. For a short presentation, you should limit the number of categories to no more than five: Three is often better for a short speech. Remember, you must develop these points with supporting material that details, authenticates, and illustrates what you are talking about. That takes time! You don't want to go beyond the time limits set by your instructor. Nor do you want to overtax your listeners' ability to remember and their willingness to give you their attention.

In her informative speech, Nicolette Fisk described architectural answers to a dilemma posed by terrorist attacks: how to keep our greatest monuments and buildings safe but still beautiful. Here is an abbreviated outline of the categorical design of her speech.

Preview: Architects have developed three innovative answers to the question of how to both guard and beautify our greatest buildings and shrines.

    I. Retaining walls provide one such answer.

        A. Protecting the Washington Monument from explosive-laden vehicles posed a real challenge

categorical design The use of natural or customary divisions within a subject as a way of structuring an informative speech.

   1. The first answer offered was a monument all right—a monument to ugliness! (shows projection)

   2. The new look shows how this scene has been transformed. (shows projection)

   B. Overlapping stone walls provide a granite barrier to prevent terrorist vehicles from reaching the monument base.

   C. Architect Laurie Olin said, "The point is to turn this security thing into a beautiful walk."

II. Collapsible concrete is a second answer to the problem.

   A. Tiger Trap is a new type of concrete that collapses under extreme pressure.

      1. It was developed by Rogers Marvel Architects and Rock Twelve Security Architecture Company.

      2. It provides concrete strong enough for pedestrians, but collapses under the weight of large vehicles.

   B. Therefore, it both preserves open public space and creates an urban booby trap for terrorists.

   C. Tiger Trap is being used widely in New York City. (shows projection)

III. Street furniture is being added to protect pedestrians along sidewalks.

   A. Bollards, for example, were first designed for military security measures.

      1. They are designed to absorb huge vehicular impacts.

      2. Now they function as fashionable, decorative features around buildings. (shows projection)

   B. Heavy benches and boulders along the street provide seating as well as protection for strollers. (shows projection)

As we noted earlier, some speeches combine designs to accomplish their aims. Marie D'Aniello's speech on friendship at the end of this chapter uses the chronological design to arrange the main points of her speech and the categorical design to order the subpoints under them. This combination of patterns, which works perfectly well in Marie's speech, is evident in her preview:

> In this speech, I'm going to take you through the development of friendship, beginning in childhood and going up through adolescence all the way to young adulthood (*chronological*). I'm going to talk about how we define our friends, the roles that friends play in our lives, and the effect conflicts have on friendship during each stage (*categorical*).

Comparative Design

You may find a **comparative design** useful when your topic is unfamiliar, abstract, technical, or difficult to understand. This design can also help you describe dramatic changes in a subject. A comparative design should relate your topic to something the audience knows and understands. It can be especially useful in speeches of explanation. Three basic variations of the comparative design are literal analogy, figurative analogy, and comparison and contrast.

comparative design A pattern for an informative speech that relates an unfamiliar subject to something the audience already knows or understands.

In a **literal analogy**, the subjects compared are drawn from the same field of experience. One student compared the game of rugger as played in his native Sri Lanka to the American game of football. Since both rugger and football are contact sports, the comparison between them was literal.

In a **figurative analogy**, the subjects are drawn from different fields of experience. Paul Ashdown, a professor of journalism at the University of Tennessee, used an extended figurative analogy comparing the World Wide Web to America's "Wild West."[5] Another example of a figurative analogy could relate the body's struggle against infection to a military campaign. In such a design, the speaker might identify the nature of the armies, the ways they fight, and the consequences of defeat and victory. Both literal and figurative analogy designs can be insightful and imaginative, helping listeners see subjects in surprising, revealing ways. But if the comparison seems strained or farfetched, the speech will collapse and the speaker's ethos will be damaged.

A **comparison and contrast** design points out the similarities and/or differences between subjects or ideas. In this design, each similarity or difference becomes a main point. In the interest of simplicity, you should limit yourself to five or fewer points of similarity and difference in a short presentation. In the following example, Don Carson emphasized contrast as he organized the body of his speech.

Preview: Over the past forty years, the women seen in American advertising changed with respect to the products they pitched, their roles and ages, and the attitudes expressed toward them.

I. The products they advertised changed.

   A. In the 1960s, most women were pitching products in the kitchen or bathroom.

   B. By the year 2000, more women were selling high-ticket items.

II. Women began to appear in different roles.

   A. In the 1960s, most women were shown in domestic (wife/mother) roles.

   B. By the year 2000, more women were shown in professional roles.

III. The apparent ages of women changed.

   A. In the 1960s, most women in ads appeared to be under thirty.

   B. By the year 2000, older women were well represented in ads.

IV. Attitudes toward women expressed in the ads also changed.

   A. In the 1960s, most women were portrayed as dumb, dependent, and controlled.

   B. By the year 2000, more women were portrayed as intelligent, independent, and in control.

By now, we are not surprised to discover that Don's design actually blends categories and chronology with contrast to produce a complex example of combination design.

---

literal analogy A comparison made between subjects within the same field.

figurative analogy A comparison made between things that belong to different fields.

comparison and contrast An informative speech design that points out similarities and differences between subjects or ideas.

Causation Design

A **causation design**, often used in speeches of explanation, interprets a subject either as an effect of certain causes or as the cause of certain effects. The speaker usually begins by describing the subject and its importance, and then either asks how it came about or what its consequences may be. The major causes or consequences become main points in the body of the speech.

Speeches that use the causation design are subject to one serious drawback—the tendency to oversimplify. Any complex situation generally has many underlying causes, and any given set of conditions may lead to many different future effects. Be wary of overly simple explanations and overly confident predictions. Such explanations and predictions are one form of faulty reasoning (fallacy), discussed further in Chapter 15.

Patsy Lenzini announced at the outset of her informative speech that research had revealed the existence of a new wonder drug—aspirin! In her classroom speech based on causation design, Patsy discussed aspirin therapy as the cause of many possible consequences. An abbreviated form of her outline follows.

Preview: The humble aspirin can benefit your heart, prevent cancer, and help your brain avoid Alzheimer's.

I. Daily small doses can benefit your heart.

   A. Reduce risk of first heart attack by 44%.

   B. Lower chance of second heart attack by 30%.

   C. Reduce risk of death during heart attack by 23%.

II. Daily doses can also prevent certain cancers.

   A. Lower risk of colon cancer by 40–50%.

   B. Reduce risk of esophageal cancer by 80–90%.

   C. Lower ovarian cancer risks by 25%.

III. Daily doses offer other great possible benefits.

   A. Reduce risk of stroke by 25%.

   B. Help counter dementia and Alzheimer's by increasing blood flow in the brain.

IV. Daily doses may also have some drawbacks.

   A. Can cause gastrointestinal bleeding.

   B. Delay blood clotting to stop bleeding.

   C. Could encourage another kind of stroke.

   D. Ask your doctor's advice.

Any of the six design options we have discussed—either alone or in combination—can help you present information in ways that expand the knowledge and competency of your listeners and earn you their gratitude.

causation design A pattern for an informative speech that shows how one condition generates, or is generated by, another.

Figure 14.2

What Speech Design to Use When

Design	Use When
Spatial	Your topic can be discussed by how it is positioned in a physical setting or natural environment. It allows you to take your audience on an orderly "oral tour" of your topic.
Sequential	Your topic can be arranged by time. It is useful for describing a process as a series of steps or explaining a subject as a series of developments.
Chronological	Your topic can be discussed as a historical development through certain defining moments.
Categorical	Your topic has natural or customary divisions. Each category becomes a main point for development. It is useful when you need to organize large amounts of material.
Comparative	Your topic is new to your audience, abstract, technical, or simply difficult to comprehend. It helps make material more meaningful by comparing or contrasting it with something the audience already knows and understands.
Causation	Your topic is best understood in terms of its underlying causes or consequences. May be used to account for the present or predict future possibilities.

Rising to the Challenge of the Informative Speech

*I*nformative speaking can pose a special challenge for speakers. Self-introductory speaking often reveals fascinating insights into the minds and personalities of speakers. Persuasive speeches offer the drama of controversy and the excitement of watching speakers take public stands on issues. Ceremonial speeches can entertain and inspire us. In contrast, informative speeches can sometimes seem a bit dull. On the other hand, many of the informative speeches we have heard in class, including those cited here, have managed to be very interesting. What can we learn from these successful speakers to help us avoid the information doldrums?

First, these speakers selected good topics, topics that offered information inherently interesting to listeners, fascinating to the speakers themselves, and important to the lives of listeners.

Second, these speakers used their time well, finding topics well in advance of their speaking assignments and leaving plenty of time for research and to reflect on what they learned.

Third, these speakers devised artful designs for their speeches, introducing topics in ways that grabbed and held attention, establishing a clear understanding of their purposes, developing ideas so that they satisfied the expectations of listeners, and finding a conclusion that would make it hard for audiences to forget their most important themes.

Fourth, these speakers filled these designs with colorful and striking content: facts and figures that confronted listeners with a reality they had not expected, examples and stories that awakened feeling and stirred the imagination. They used language in ways that made their ideas stick in the memory.

Fifth, they put a lot of energy into their presentations. They set a varied and lively pace, using pauses for emphasis. Their voices came alive with the importance of their messages, and their gestures emphasized what they were saying. The lesson here is clear: To avoid glazed eyes and muffled yawns, focus on

- finding a good topic.
- leaving yourself plenty of time for research and preparation.
- developing an artful overall structure for your speech.
- filling that structure with lively, striking content.
- making an energetic presentation of your speech.

If you follow these guidelines, chances are that at the end of your speech you won't be singing the information blues.

Briefings: An Application

A briefing is a specialized form of informative speaking offered in an organizational setting. It may involve description and demonstration, but more generally, it emphasizes explanation. Briefings often take place during meetings, as when employees gather at the beginning of a workday to learn about plans or policy changes.[6] At such meetings, you might be asked to give a status report on a project. Briefings also take place in one-on-one situations, as when you report to your supervisor at work. They can take the form of a press briefing that follows a crisis or major event.[7] Often, a question-and-answer period follows the briefing.[8]

Although briefings occur frequently, they are not often done well. Most how-to books on communicating in organizations deplore the lack of brevity, clarity, and directness in presentations.[9] When executives in eighteen organizations were asked, "What makes a presentation poor?" they offered the following answers:

- It is badly organized.
- It is not presented well.
- It contains too much jargon.
- It is too long.
- It lacks examples or comparisons.

briefing A short informative presentation offered in an organizational setting that focuses upon plans, policies, or reports.

This situation offers you quite an opportunity. Developing the art of presenting a briefing will increase your value in an organization. The following rules should guide your preparation:

1. *A briefing should be what its name suggests: brief.* Cut out any material that is not related directly to your main points. Keep your introduction and conclusions short. Begin with a preview and end with a summary.

2. *Organize your ideas before you open your mouth.* How can you possibly be organized when you are called on without warning in a meeting to "tell us about your project"? The answer is simple: Prepare in advance (also review our guidelines for making impromptu speeches in Chapter 13). *Never go into any meeting in which there is even the slightest chance that you might be asked to report without a skeleton outline of a presentation.* Select a simple design and make a key-word outline of points you would cover. Take this to the meeting with you.

3. *Rely heavily on facts and figures, expert testimony, and short examples for supporting materials.* Don't drift off into long stories. Use comparison and contrast to make your points stand out and come alive.

4. *Adapt your language to your audience.* If you are an engineer reporting on a project to a group of managers, use the language of management, not the language of engineering. Tell them what they need to know in language they can understand. Relate the subject to what they already know.

5. *Present your message with confidence.* Be sure everyone can see and hear you. Stand up, if necessary. Look listeners in the eye. Speak firmly with an air of assurance. After all, the project is yours, and you are the expert on it.

6. *Be prepared to answer tough questions.* Respond forthrightly and honestly. No one likes bad news, but worse news will come if you don't deliver the bad news to those who need to know it *when* they need to know it. Review our suggestions for handling question-and-answer sessions in Chapter 13.

In Summary

Sharing knowledge is the essence of informative speaking. It helps us to live better and work smarter. In short, information is power. The informative value of a speech is measured by how much new and important information or understanding it provides listeners. To meet their ethical challenge, informative speakers must offer responsible knowledge to their listeners.

Forms of Informative Speeches. Informative speaking arises out of three deep human impulses: to expand our awareness, to become more competent, and to satisfy our curiosity. Accordingly, informative speeches include speeches of description, demonstration, and explanation. Speeches of description create word-pictures that help the audience visualize a subject.

Speeches of demonstration may give listeners an understanding of a process or teach them how to perform it. Speeches of explanation inform the audience about abstract and complex subjects, such as concepts or programs.

Helping Listeners Learn. You make it easier for listeners to learn by motivating them, showing how your subject fits their basic needs. To gain and maintain their attention, apply principles of intensity, repetition, novelty, activity, contrast, and relevance. The intensity of information measures the impact it makes upon listeners. Speakers use repetition to emphasize points, to help listeners follow the flow of ideas, and to embed their messages in audience memory. The novelty of information fascinates listeners, draws their attention, and raises their curiosity. Activity adds the sense of liveliness and often invites listeners to participate vicariously in the experience depicted. Contrast follows the principle that opposites attract attention. Relevance ties the subject to specific needs, interests, or concerns of the audience. Increase audience retention by organizing your message clearly and providing previews and summaries.

Speech Designs. The patterns most often used in informative speeches are spatial, sequential, chronological, categorical, comparative, and causation designs. A spatial design orders the main points according to the arrangement of a subject within a physical setting, such as the relationships among objects or places. Most speeches of demonstration use a sequential design, which follows a time pattern to present steps in a process. A chronological design follows the sequence of important events in the history of a sub-

ject. A categorical design represents natural divisions of a subject or traditional ways of thinking about it. A comparative design is especially effective when your topic is new to the audience, when it has undergone dramatic changes, or when you wish to establish right and wrong procedures. This design is often based on literal or figurative analogies, depending on whether the compared subjects are drawn from the same or from different fields of experience. A causation design explains how one condition generates or is generated by others. Sometimes you may decide to combine several designs within the same speech.

Rising to the Challenge of the Informative Speech. Informative speakers must work hard to create and maintain attention and interest. Finding the right topic, taking the time to prepare, designing speeches artfully, developing striking and colorful content, and making an energetic presentation can ensure success.

Explore and Apply the Ideas in This Chapter

1. The status of "information" concerning the presence of WMDs (weapons of mass destruction) in Iraq, a major rationale for our 2003 preemptive war on that country, has been subject to a great deal of debate. A number of positions have been argued:

   a. The information was faulty. Blame it on the CIA.

   b. The information was faulty, but the president was responsible for verifying it, especially when he used it to justify war. Blame it on him.

   c. The information was accurate, but it was used selectively to justify an *a priori* decision to invade Iraq. The information was manipulated to influence public opinion.

   d. Whether the information was or was not accurate is irrelevant. Either way, we made the right choice: to take Saddam out. The ends justified the means.

   Research this issue and decide which of these or other possible arguments you favor. Be prepared to defend your position in classroom discussion.

What does this situation teach you about the ethics of using information in speeches?

2. You can probably recall one or several outstanding teachers who have helped you learn. How did they encourage learning? Using them as models of excellence, what can you learn about communicating information?

3. As you submit the outline for your informative speech, include a "strategy plan" as well. In your strategy plan, identify the following:

   a. The kind of informative speech you will present

   b. How you will apply principles of motivation, attention, and retention to help your listeners learn

   c. How you will use attention factors (intensity, repetition, novelty, activity, contrast, relevance) to make your speech more effective

   d. Why you chose a specific design option to structure your speech

   e. How you will meet the challenge of presenting an interesting informative speech

4. Informative speeches presented within a context of controversy are often distorted and misunderstood because of the fears, suspicions, and prejudices that abound in many audiences. As we write, for example, a controversy rages in many quarters concerning the legality and morality of gay marriage. If you wished to present an informative speech summarizing the arguments on both sides of this issue, what strategies might you employ to minimize such distortion before most audiences?

SAMPLE INFORMATIVE SPEECH

What Friends Are All About
Marie D'Aniello

It's nine o'clock at night. I'm curled up in the back seat of a new truck and my friends, Cammy and Joe, are in the front singing along with the radio. As I listen to them sing, and I'm lying there, I start to think about my life and all the changes that have occurred in the past year. A year ago I didn't even know who Cammy and Joe were. And now they're two of my best friends. It makes me wonder about friendship and its meaning.

According to Webster's dictionary, to be a friend means that you're someone who someone else feels comfortable with and is fond of. But friendship is so much more than that. According to Plato, true friendship rises out of basic human needs and desires, such as striving for goodness, reaching out to others, and seeking self-understanding. And loving and being loved. Friendship should benefit all who are involved in it and should occur between people who value each other's good qualities. As human beings we need friends in order to survive and grow.

Through our friends, we learn who we are and what we like and don't like. We learn about strengths we never knew we had, weaknesses that maybe we can overcome. Think about your friendships. I'll bet you've learned a great deal and grown a great deal because of them.

If you're like me, you probably have one or two really close friends and a lot of great acquaintances. But that's what you need. According to Dr. John Litwac of the University of Massachusetts medical center, people in modern society require a variety of friends to meet their needs. And the variety of friends we need varies over time. In his book *Adult Friendship*, Dr. Litwac says that the friendships we enjoy when we are young differ from those we experience as we grow older. As we develop, so do the complexity and intimacy of our relationships.

In this speech I'm going to take you through the development of friendship, beginning in childhood and going up through adolescence all the way to young adulthood. I'm going to talk about how we define our friends, the roles that friends play in our lives, and the effect conflicts have on friendship during each stage.

The saga of friendship begins when we are quite young. And the concepts we have of friendship change dramatically over the first decade of life. Psychologists classify childhood as the stage occurring between the ages of 4 and 10. During childhood, our friends are those whom we have the most contact with, the children we play with. In childhood that's what friendship is all about. According to Dr. William Rawlings, friendships exist while children are playing together. For example, when I was in kindergarten, I was friends with Michelle when we were playing tag. But the next day I would go and play with others and make friends with them. The friendship vanished until the next time we played together. It had little to do with who Michelle really was. She was simply there and I could play with her.

But when we play as children, we're not only having fun, we're also learning how to assimilate into society and how to develop more lasting friendships. We learn to inhibit our actions, to deal with other people's emotions, and to follow rules. Because we're just starting out and just trying to figure out how everything works, we may run into a lot of conflicts with our friendships during childhood. We may get into silly fights about whose toy is this and whose toy is that, but the fights don't usually last very long and can be resolved fairly easily. Behavior is based on the moment, and the moment turns on what things appear to be.

During childhood, friendship often depends on looks. Maybe that's why some children are so popular and others are ignored. In fact, a study conducted

Marie opens her speech of explanation with a narrative that gains attention by arousing curiosity. Quickly she shifts that attention to the focus of her speech.

Throughout her opening, Marie leaves listeners waiting for a direct statement of her purpose. It soon becomes clear that she wants to share ideas and deepen audience understanding. She sold this speech by her warm, vital manner of presentation. She stood in front of the lectern near listeners to encourage identification.

In her preview, Marie promises to follow a chronological design that will trace "the saga of friendship" to the point of young adulthood. At the subpoint level of her speech, Marie follows a categorical pattern, discussing the definitions, roles, and conflict resolution during each phase of development.

She has researched her speech diligently, but needs to establish the credentials of her experts and to document her evidence more carefully.

by Dr. William Lipit concluded that children between the ages of 4 to 9 base their descriptions of their friends completely on their looks. That may be sad, but it's just the way it is. Think of this as a phase in the process of growing up.

At the end of childhood, friends become more than just playmates. They're people who share our interests—they're the ones we share our feelings with. Play becomes less, talk becomes more important. Friendship evolves steadily to a new level, called adolescence.

I'm sure you remember adolescence. It usually occurs between the ages of 11 and 17. As we live through it, friendship involves revealing and discussing one's personal thoughts and feelings. Just talking can be more important than anything, especially for girls. Boys, male friendships, still involve a good deal of activity, as in organized sports, but even here there is more verbal communication than before. The critical task of adolescence is to develop one's identity, and friends are crucial in that respect. Dr. Graham Allen observes in the book *Friendship* that people in adolescence, more than at any other time in their lives, need to share strong, often confusing emotions. Did you have a best friend in junior high school? A very special friend you would sit and talk with on the phone for hours on end? Well if you did, that's good, that's normal. According to Dr. Allen, that's what you needed.

Marie relies on examples for her supporting material. In her first main point, she draws on personal experience. In the second main point, she invites listeners to supply examples from their own experience. She uses rhetorical questions to stimulate reflection. She also uses the contrast between play and talk to underscore the difference between the childhood and adolescent phases of friendship.

Think back. Think back to friendship pins, and side ponytails and matching outfits, and sleep-over parties. Think of your first best friend. That person probably knew more about you than anyone in the whole world. She or he was probably your age, in your class, lived near you, and shared your social status. In adolescence we seek out those who are like us because they make us feel more normal. Because the level of intimacy is so much greater in adolescence, the potential for conflict and jealousy also increases. There's so much emotion at stake that an argument in adolescence can easily ruin a friendship. The way we learn to deal with such problems in adolescence prepares us for young adulthood.

Now young adulthood is classified as the stage between 18 and 24, the stage we're all in now. Here at Vanderbilt and I suppose elsewhere, a "friend" can mean many things. Friends can be playmates, confidants, lovers, listeners. Rosemary Adams, writing in the book *Adult Friendship*, tells us that during the college years friends can provide crucial input regarding self-conceptions, career options, and recreational activities. Patterns of friendship vary a lot, and we have many different types of friends. We have party friends. We have classroom friends. And then we have our good, good friends. But you need all of those kinds of friends as you grow older because you are becoming a more complex individual.

In her final main point, Marie continues to engage listeners directly by asking rhetorical questions and by inviting them to consider their own friendships.

Why do you like your good friends? Do you like them because of what they can do for you? Or do you like them because you can relate to them and share a bond with them? Our friends prevent us from being lonely. In fact, 40 percent of college freshmen who reported they felt homesick also reported not having made new friends in college.

Why do some people make friends easily while others struggle to? Researchers speculate that how open and honest you are with others and how much you are willing to give of yourself can affect your forming friendships. Talking and sharing is important because it creates a sense of intimacy. Friendship also depends a great deal on attraction. Whatever attracts you to people is why you like them. Maybe you like people who smile a lot, or maybe you like those who are serious. Maybe you like people who are the complete opposite of you and who possess qualities you wish you had. Or maybe you like people who are just like you, whom you feel you know inside and out.

When we're younger, friendships are based on what people appear to be. As we grow older, friendships are based more on what people really are. If you got in a fight with your best friend, would you tell him to hit the road? Chances are you'd probably try to work it out. As we get older, it's easier for us to accept differences in others. Serious betrayals could end friendships. But the researchers I read concluded that the older you get and the older the friendship is, the harder you will work to preserve it because it is all the more precious to you.

Friendship is hard to define, and I think that's probably because it involves your heart and your soul. But out of all the research I've done and all the people I've talked to, no one said that they thought friendship was a bad thing. Of course there are downsides like peer pressure and conflict and sometimes stress, but 91 percent of the college freshmen studied by Dr. Adams felt that the benefits of friendship far outweigh the disadvantages. All I know is that from the day we're born until the day we die, other people affect the way we live. If we're lucky, maybe we'll come to know some of them as friends.

The dynamics of friendship change rapidly throughout our lives. During childhood, friendship is based on play, while in adolescence it turns more on emotion. In young adulthood, I think friendship is based on a combination of acceptance, respect, and trust. I am reminded of the words of William Butler Yeats, who said, "Think where man's glory most begins and ends. And say my glory was to have such friends."

◀ *At this point, Marie reflects on the meaning of her subject, signaling that she is moving into her conclusion. By citing Plato at the beginning of her speech and concluding with a quotation from Yeats, she dignifies her subject and emphasizes its importance in listeners' lives.*

15 Persuasion and Argument

newspaper, which followed it up with investigative reports and a supportive editorial. Brought to the attention of the mayor and city commission, Anna's speech helped promote reforms in the city's rental housing policies. Her words are still reverberating in Manhattan, Kansas.

Perhaps your classroom speech will not have that kind of impact, but you never know who or what may be changed by it. In this chapter, we explore the nature of persuasive speaking in contrast with informative speaking. Then we turn to using evidence and reasoning to build powerful arguments that provide the substance of ethical and enduring persuasion.

The Nature of Persuasive Speaking

*P*ersuasive speaking differs from informative speaking in eight basic ways:

First, informative speeches reveal options: Persuasive speeches urge a choice among options. Informative speakers expand our awareness. For example, an informative speaker might say: "There are three different ways we can deal with the budget deficit. Let me explain them." In contrast, a persuasive speaker would evaluate these options and urge support for one of them: "Of the three different ways to deal with the budget deficit, we should choose the following course of action."

Second, informative speakers act as teachers: Persuaders act as advocates. The difference is often one of passion and engagement. Persuasive speakers are more vitally committed to a cause. This does not necessarily mean that persuaders are loud; the most passionate and intense moments of a speech can be very quiet.

Third, informative speeches offer supporting material to illustrate points: Persuasive speeches use supporting material as evidence that justifies advice. An ethical persuader interweaves facts and statistics, testimony, examples, and narratives into a compelling case based on responsible knowledge and sensitivity to the best interests of listeners.

Fourth, the role of the audience changes dramatically from information to persuasion. Informed listeners expand their knowledge, but persuaded listeners become *agents of change.* Their new attitudes, beliefs, and actions will affect themselves and others.

Fifth, persuasive speeches ask for more audience commitment than do informative speeches. Although there is some risk in being exposed to new ideas, more is at stake when listening to a persuasive message. What if a persuasive speaker is mistaken or even dishonest? What if her proposed plan of action is defective? Doing always involves a greater risk than knowing. Your commitment could cost you—and those who may be influenced by your actions—dearly.

Sixth, leadership is even more important in persuasive than in informative speeches. Because persuasive speeches involve risk, listeners weigh the character and competence of speakers closely. Do they really know what they are talking about? Do they have their listeners' interests at heart? As a persuasive speaker, your ethos will be on public display and will be scrutinized carefully.

Seventh, appeals to feelings are more useful in persuasive than in informative speeches. Because of the risk involved, listeners may balk at accepting recommendations, even when those recommendations are supported by good reasons. To overcome such inertia, persuaders must sometimes appeal to feelings,[1] which is why they often use emotional appeals to open their speeches. For example, the informative statement "A 10 percent rise in tuition will reduce the student population by about 5 percent next term" might take the following form in a persuasive speech:

Persuasive speeches can help raise support for worthy causes. Here actor Danny Glover speaks out on behalf of the National Kidney Foundation.

The people pushing for the tuition increase don't think a few hundred dollars more each semester will have that much effect. They think we can handle it.

Let me tell you about my friend Tricia. She's on the Dean's List in chemistry, the pride and hope of her family. Tricia will get a great job when she graduates—if she graduates! But if this increase goes through, Tricia won't be back next term. Her dreams of success will be delayed, if not denied!

Perhaps you're in the same boat as Tricia— paddling like mad against the current. We all need to work together to defeat this tuition increase.

Emotional and graphic language, developed through examples or narratives, can help people see the human dimension of problems and move these listeners to the right action.

Eighth, the ethical obligation for persuasive speeches is even greater than that for informative speeches. As Isocrates said (see Chapter 16's opening quotation), persuasion can be a great blessing to humankind. This great educator of the Golden Age of Greece knew that at their best, persuasive speakers make us confront our obligation to believe and act in socially and morally responsible ways. By describing how they themselves became persuaded, they model how we should deliberate in difficult situations. By making intelligence and morality effective in public affairs, they can help the world evolve in more enlightened ways.

The major differences between informative and persuasive speaking are summarized in Figure 15.1.

Figure 15.1

Informative Versus Persuasive Speaking

Informative Speaking	Persuasive Speaking
1. Reveals options.	1. Urges a choice among options.
2. Speaker acts as teacher.	2. Speaker acts as advocate.
3. Uses supporting material to enlighten listeners.	3. Uses supporting material to justify advice.
4. Audience expands knowledge.	4. Audience becomes agent of change.
5. Asks for little audience commitment.	5. Asks for strong audience commitment.
6. Speaker's credibility is important.	6. Speaker's credibility more important.
7. Fewer appeals to feelings.	7. More appeals to feelings.
8. High ethical obligation.	8. Higher ethical obligation.

Argumentative Persuasion

As he finished his speech, "Cooling the World's Fever," Josh Logan knew that he had been effective. Listeners seemed concerned and attentive as he presented his *evidence*. They nodded in agreement as he developed convincing *proofs* to support his points. At the end of the speech, many listeners seemed ready to accept his *argument* that global warming would require far-reaching changes both at the government level and in the ways people lived.

Some persuasive efforts lift and inspire us, while others seem degrading. What is the critical difference? There is a kind of persuasion—**manipulative persuasion**—that has become part and parcel of life in media America. Such persuasion works by suggestion, colorful images, appealing music, and attractive spokespersons. It reveals itself in thirty-second television commercials that sell us everything from deodorant to political candidates. In his recent book, *The Assault on Reason*, Al Gore argues that contemporary politics especially attracts the manipulator and compromises the quality of persuasive discourse:

> Voters are often viewed mainly as targets for easy manipulation by those seeking their "consent" to exercise power. By using focus groups and elaborate polling techniques, those who design these messages are able to derive the only information they're interested in receiving *from* citizens—feedback useful in fine-tuning their efforts at manipulation.[2]

Such persuasion is not *always* unethical, because it often supports good and useful causes and might even be justified if challenged. But it is not inherently ethical either, because it sidesteps a careful consideration of supporting evidence and arguments. *It avoids the ethical burden of justification.*

There is another kind of persuasion that is part of the Western tradition reaching back over several thousand years to the speeches of Pericles and Demosthenes in ancient Greece. **Argumentative persuasion**, as we shall call it, builds arguments out of evidence and reasoning. It displays patterns of reasoning for critical inspection and asks for agreement and action. It is not *always* ethical, because evil speakers can sometimes twist evidence and disguise bad reasoning, deceiving even careful listeners. But it is inherently ethical, because it assumes the burden of justification, addresses our judgment rather than our impulses, and honors the intellectual behaviors that make us human.

Argumentative persuasion is the business of this chapter. We consider ways *to build powerful arguments that deserve respectful attention from thoughtful listeners.* We show how to develop evidence and proofs, build patterns of effective reasoning, and avoid defects of evidence, proof, and reasoning.

Developing Evidence

In Chapter 8, we explored the use of supporting materials. In persuasive speaking, these materials function as **evidence**, the foundation of ethical argument.

- **Facts and figures are often the ultimate justification for asking us to believe or act in different ways.**[3] As we shall see, they can be especially important during the awareness phase of the persuasive process when they reveal a reality that calls for action. Recent research has confirmed the importance of statistical evidence in persuading others: Such evidence can be highly credible in our no-nonsense society.[4] Statistical knowledge becomes

---

manipulative persuasion Persuasion that works through suggestion, colorful images, music, and attractive spokespersons more than through evidence and reasoning. It avoids the ethical burden of justification.

argumentative persuasion Persuasion built on evidence and reasoning.

evidence Supporting materials used in persuasive speeches, including facts and figures, examples, narratives, and testimony.

embedded in our thinking and helps persuasion endure beyond the moment. This is why the corruption of such evidence, revealed recently in efforts to bribe scientists into reporting certain conclusions about global warming, threatens the integrity of public understanding and the communication based on it.[5]

■ **Examples can awaken feelings that make listeners want to act and can help bring factual situations into sharp focus.** One of the most memorable moments of the 2004 Democratic convention occurred when Ron Reagan, son of the late Republican president, urged the delegates to support embryonic stem cell research. To arouse sympathy for this cause, he developed an extended example:

> I know a child—well, she must be 13 now—I'd better call her a young woman. . . . She has memories. She has hopes. And she has juvenile diabetes.
>
> Like so many kids with this disease, she has adjusted amazingly well. The insulin pump she wears—she's decorated hers with rhinestones. She can insert her own catheter needle. She has learned to sleep through the blood drawings in the wee hours of the morning. She's very brave. She is also quite bright and understands full well the progress of her disease and what that might ultimately mean: blindness, amputation, diabetic coma. Every day, she fights to have a future.
>
> What excuse will we offer this young woman should we fail her now? What might we tell . . . the millions of others who suffer? That when given an opportunity to help, we turned away? That facing political opposition, we lost our nerve? That even though we knew better, we did nothing?[6]

This powerful example helped prepare Reagan's listeners emotionally for his final appeal.

The other great function of examples is to empower factual evidence by bringing situations into sharp, living focus for listeners. Whenever listeners ask, "Can you give me an example?" they are asking for this kind of clarification and authentication. Philanthropist Bill Gates, as he argued for reform in American high school education, used three key examples as evidence to prove his point that raised expectations can improve student performance. As he pointed to dramatic successes in Kansas, Rhode Island, and California, Gates built a compelling case in support of his argument.[7]

■ **Narratives can carry listeners to the scene of a problem and make them witnesses to a living drama.** Student speaker Kirsten Lientz illustrated this function when she opened a speech with the following narrative:

> It's a cold, icy December afternoon. You hear a distant crash, then screams, and finally the unending moan of a car horn fills the silence. You rush the short distance to the scene of the crash, where you find an SUV overturned with a young woman and two small boys inside. The woman and one of the boys climb from the wreckage unhurt; the other boy, however, is pinned between the dashboard and the roof of the car, unconscious and not breathing.
>
> Would you know what to do? Or would you stand there wishing you did? These events are real. Bob Flath saved this child with the skills he acquired at his company's first aid workshop.

After this dramatic narrative introduction, Kirsten's listeners were ready to listen to her speech urging them to take the first aid course offered at her university.

Recent research confirms that narratives can be a powerful form of evidence, perhaps because they are so vivid.[8] Moreover, when they are effective, examples and stories enjoy a special advantage in persuasion because listeners find them hard to argue with.[9] We can dispute the meaning of facts and figures, and even debate them. But a good example or story is hard to deny and lingers in memory.

■ **When you use testimony in a persuasive speech, you call on experts as witnesses to support your position.** Expert testimony is most effective when (1) the audience knows little about the issue because it is new or complicated; (2) listeners don't feel that the issue affects them directly; and/or (3) listeners lack the ability or motivation to analyze the situation independently.[10]

Introduce your witnesses carefully, pointing out their credentials. To support her call for air safety improvements, one of our students, Juli Pardell, cited eight authoritative sources of information. In his plea for organ donors, Paul Fowler, another student, cited four reputable books. It was not just Juli or Paul speaking—it was *all* these sources of testimony together, supporting the speaker's voice.

Witnesses who testify *against* their apparent self-interest are called **reluctant witnesses**. They provide some of the most powerful evidence available in persuasion. Democratic critics of President Clinton's personal behavior or Republican critics of President George W. Bush's foreign policies often had more impact because they appeared to be speaking against their political affiliations.

In ethical persuasive speaking, you should rely mainly on expert testimony. Use prestige or lay testimony as secondary sources of evidence. You can use prestige testimony to stress values you want listeners to embrace. You can use lay testimony to relate an issue to the lives of listeners. Keep in mind that when you quote others, you are associating yourself with them. Be careful with whom you associate!

As you search for evidence, keep an open mind. Consider different points of view, so that you don't simply present one perspective without being aware of others.

Ethics *Alert! 15.1*

Guidelines for the Ethical Use of Evidence

To earn a reputation for the ethical use of evidence, follow these rules:

1. Provide evidence from credible sources.

2. Identify your sources of evidence.

3. Use evidence that can be verified by experts.

4. Be sure such evidence has not been corrupted by outside interests.

5. Acknowledge disagreements among experts.

6. Do not withhold important evidence.

7. Use expert testimony to establish facts, prestige testimony to enhance credibility, and lay testimony to create identification.

8. Quote or paraphrase testimony accurately.

reluctant witnesses Witnesses who testify against their apparent self-interest.

Personal experience with a situation can qualify a speaker's testimony as was the case when former New York City mayor Rudy Giuliani testified before the 9/11 commission.

Gather more evidence than you think you will need so that you have a wide range from which to choose. Be sure you have facts, figures, or expert testimony for each of the major points you want to make. Use multiple sources and types of evidence to strengthen your case.

Developing Proofs

To build strong arguments, persuaders must develop powerful proofs. **Proofs** may be based on evidence, may tap into our emotional reactions, may be based on our social heritage, or may call on the personal leadership qualities of speakers in an effort to influence us.

The nature of proof has been studied since the Golden Age of Greece. In his *Rhetoric*, Aristotle identified three forms of proof. The first, **logos**, recognizes that we respond to reason. *At least we like to think that we are reasonable creatures*. When speeches make good sense to us, when they are grounded in strong evidence and move logically to the conclusions they want us to accept, we find them hard to resist.

The second, **pathos**, affirms that we can be touched by appeals to personal feelings such as fear, pity, and anger. Examples and narratives often provide the evidence this kind of proof emphasizes, just as Ron Reagan aroused both sympathy and indignation with his story of a 13-year-old girl fighting for her future against juvenile diabetes.

The third form, **ethos**, recognizes that we respond to our perceptions of a speaker's competence, character, goodwill, and dynamism. When these qualities seem positive, we *want* to agree with speakers. When these qualities seem negative or are lacking, speakers will have a hard time winning us over. We are also affected by the credibility of the evidence cited in a speech. If we respect the people you quote in your speech, we will listen respectfully to their testimony. If we are not impressed by them, you have created a problem for yourself.

In our time, the work of many scholars has confirmed the presence of a fourth dimension of proof, **mythos**, which suggests that we respond to appeals to the traditions and values of our culture and to the legends and folktales that embody them.[11] We are social beings who build much of our identity on our membership in groups, ranging from churches and universities to cities, states, and nations. If you can make a connection between your proposal and this social and cultural identity, listeners will give your ideas a careful hearing.

A persuasive speech rarely relies on a single kind of proof. Each type of proof brings its own coloration and strength to the fabric of persuasion. For this reason, perhaps, the traditional forms of proof are often discussed as though they were of equal importance to persuasion. But in manipulative persuasion, ethos, pathos, and mythos may be used more frequently than logos. Fast-food and automobile commercials rarely treat us as reasoning creatures.

On the other hand, argumentative persuasion stresses logos and assigns supporting roles to ethos, pathos, and mythos. Even if these latter forms of proof are vital in adding energy, color, and human interest to persuasion, they supplement the basic appeal to our rational nature. These priorities among the forms of proof are shown in Figure 15.2.

proof An interpretation of evidence that provides a good reason for listeners to agree with the speaker.

logos A form of proof that makes rational appeals based on facts and figures and expert testimony.

pathos Proof relying on appeals to emotions.

ethos A form of proof that relies on the audience's perceptions of a speaker's competence, character, good will, and dynamism.

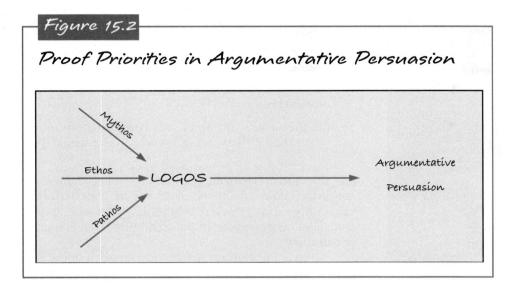

Figure 15.2

Proof Priorities in Argumentative Persuasion

In the section that follows, we discuss ethos, pathos, and mythos as we build up to the consideration of logos. We discuss the strengths and qualities of these proofs so that you may weave them effectively into your own persuasive speech.

Proof by Ethos. When you speak, listeners must sense that you are a person of strong conviction and that you know what you are talking about. Your sincerity and personal commitment must be beyond question. Listeners must feel that they can trust you—that you will not distort the truth for personal advantage. Ideally, they will also conclude that you are a likeable person who in turn likes them—that you are a person of goodwill.[12]

Clearly, listeners are strongly influenced by the credibility of speakers. Social scientists have discovered that credibility is a dynamic, not a stable quality: It can change during a speech.[13] As you stand to speak, listeners may already have some impressions of your character, ability, goodwill, and confidence. This is your **initial credibility** that you bring to a speech.

As you are actually speaking, your **emerging credibility** begins to build. We recall a student who, as a result of some very unpleasant speaking experiences before taking our class, suffered from acute communication apprehension. His nervousness caused him to read his first two speeches, speaking in a monotone and avoiding eye contact. It was hard to tell whether his speeches had good content because they were presented so poorly. We worked with him outside class, trying to build up his confidence. Finally, one day he broke through the wall he had built between himself and listeners. The process of his emerging credibility, as we experienced it that day, can be reconstructed in the following sequence of moments:

1. *Initial credibility* (as he rises to speak): We are smiling encouragement, but thinking to ourselves, "This is going to be painful."

2. "Well, he looks more comfortable. He is actually making eye contact! He is even smiling, and what a nice smile! Lights up the room."

3. "He clearly cares a lot about arts education. Didn't know he was capable of such feeling."

---

mythos A form of proof that connects a subject to the culture and tradition of a group of narratives.

initial credibility The audience's assessment of your ethos before you begin your speech.

emerging credibility The changes in the audience's assessment of ethos that occur as you present your speech.

Trustworthiness is an important dimension of proof by ethos. Former President Carter instills confidence when he speaks on humanitarian issues.

4. "Wow, he really knows his stuff. That's effective testimony, and impressive facts and statistics. Moving example too. The way he just used language—very good."

5. "That makes good sense. I'll go along with those recommendations."

6. (As the speech concluded in a congratulatory round of applause): "Well, we've got ourselves a speaker!"

The speaker's emerging credibility either changes or confirms initial credibility, resulting in your **terminal credibility**. Your terminal credibility when one speech concludes becomes your initial credibility when you present another.

As the example illustrates, the gap between initial and terminal credibility can be dramatic. The interesting thing is that more than the audience changed their assessment of credibility that day. The speaker had risen in his own estimation as well.

If you enjoy high ethos in the eyes of listeners, all your other proofs will be more effective as well. Your examples and stories will have more impact, and your facts and figures will be more believable. Even the words you use can be more intense and colorful, and such language itself can assure greater persuasive effects.[14] In sum, your personal ethos can be the key to whether you succeed or fail as a persuasive speaker.

The sources of information you cite in your speech provide another type of proof by ethos. Listeners also evaluate these sources in terms of their competence, character, goodwill, and power. If the evaluation of these sources is positive, audiences are more inclined to accept your position. Let's look at how student speaker Heide Nord used the ethos of her sources to help persuade her listeners to change their attitudes about suntanning. To support the claim "We should avoid prolonged exposure to the sun," Heide emphasized expert testimony backed up by lay testimony:

> The most recent *Consumer Report* of the Food and Drug Administration tells us, "Prolonged exposure to sunlight without protection is responsible for about 90 percent of skin cancer." The article describes the case of Wendell Scarberry, a skin cancer patient who has had over a hundred surgeries. Wendell talks about the seriousness of the disease and urges us to be careful about sun exposure. "You can't cure skin cancer," he says, "by just having the doc whack it off." Finally, the American Cancer Society, in its pamphlet *Fry Now Pay Later*, says that skin cancer most often occurs among people who spend a lot of time in the sun, especially if they have been overexposed during their teens or twenties. Well, that's where most of us are right now. The FDA, the American Cancer Society, and Mr. Scarberry speak loudly together, and we ought to listen to them.

Heidi's obvious commitment, together with the combination of expert and lay testimony, made her speech highly credible.

terminal credibility The audience's assessment of your ethos after you have made a presentation.

Proof based on the testimony of reliable, competent, and trustworthy sources is extremely important in persuasive speaking. *Identify your sources and point out why they are qualified to speak on the subject.* It is also helpful if you can say that the testimony is recent. For maximum effect, quote experts directly rather than paraphrasing them.

Proof by Pathos.   People usually respond strongly when they feel angry, afraid, guilty, excited, or compassionate toward others. If used ethically in a context of argumentative persuasion, appeals to personal feelings can change bad attitudes or move people to act for good causes.[15]

When speakers tell personal stories, emotional appeals can be especially effective. Personal narratives blend the power of feeling with strong credibility. During a congressional debate on handgun control legislation, James Brady, the presidential press secretary who was shot during the assassination attempt on President Reagan, testified before the U.S. Senate Judiciary Subcommittee. Speaking from his wheelchair, he said:

> There was a day when I walked the halls of this Senate and worked closely with many of you and your staffs. There was a wonderful day when I was fortunate enough to serve the President of the United States in a capacity I had dreamed of all my life. And for a time, I felt that people looked up to me. Today, I can tell you how hard it is to have people speaking down to me. But nothing has been harder than losing the independence and control we all so value in life. I need help getting out of bed, help taking a shower, and help getting dressed.
>
> There are some who oppose a simple seven-day waiting period for handgun purchases because it would inconvenience gun buyers. Well, I guess I am paying for their convenience. And I am one of the lucky ones. I survived being shot through the head. Other shooting victims are not as fortunate.[16]

Often, appeals to emotions are the only way to convince people of the human dimensions of a problem or the need for immediate action. So how can you use proof by pathos effectively? Consider again the section on motivation in Chapter 5. Motives, you may recall, drive our behavior. We tend to become emotional when our motives are frustrated. Therefore, effective appeals to pathos often connect the speaker's points in personal ways with this underlying pattern of motives. Figure 15.3 illustrates how such connections might be made to relevant motives.

Figure 15.3

Connecting Pathos with Motives

Motives	Personal Emotions	Possible Connection
Health/Safety	Fear/Security	Does my subject affect the personal well-being and safety of listeners?
Nurturance/ Altruism	Sympathy/Caring for others	Does my subject invite feelings of sympathy and benevolence for the fate of others?
Family/Significant Others	Love	Might my subject ignite feelings for loved ones?

The Western frontier is a major source of mythos in American speeches. *American Progress*, a painting by American artist John Gast, portrays many icons and ideographs. Which ones can you identify?

As powerful as emotional proof may be, it should be used with caution. If an appeal to feeling is too obvious, audiences may suspect you are trying to manipulate them. Appeals to negative emotions such as fear or guilt are especially tricky because they can boomerang, causing listeners to discredit both you and your speech. When you use appeals to feeling, justify them with solid evidence. In your presentation, let your voice and body language understate rather than overstate the emotional appeal. Don't engage in theatrics.

Proof by Mythos.   Appeals to the values, faith, and feelings that make up our social identity can be a powerful source of proof. Such appeals, often expressed in traditional stories, sayings, and symbols, assume that audiences value their membership in a culture and share its heritage. Communication scholar Martha Solomon Watson has noted, "Rhetoric which incorporates mythical elements taps into rich cultural reservoirs."[17]

Appeals to cultural identity often call on patriotism and remind us of our heroes or enemies. They may gain power from political narratives, such as the story of George Washington's harsh winter at Valley Forge. Or they may be embedded in folk sayings, as when speakers remind us that ours is "the land of opportunity."[18] Appeals to mythos also may be grounded in economic legends, such as American stories of success through hard work and thrift that celebrate the rise to power from humble beginnings. Such stories justify economic power in our society while assuring the powerless that they too can make it if only they have "the right stuff."

Appeals to cultural identity may also draw on religious narratives. Sacred documents, such as the Bible, provide a rich storehouse of parables, used not only in sermons but also in political speeches.[19] For example, references to the Good Samaritan are often used to justify government efforts to help those who are in need.

Stories need not be retold in their entirety each time they are invoked. Because they are so familiar, allusions to them may be sufficient. The culturetypes discussed in Chapter 12 are often called into service, because they compress myths into a few provocative words. Words like *progress, science,* and *education* have positive mythic overtones, and *terrorist, pollution,* and *weapons of mass destruction* are negatively charged. In his speech accepting the Democratic presidential nomination in 1960, John F. Kennedy called on the myth of the American frontier to move Americans to action:

> The New Frontier of which I speak is not a set of promises—it is a set of challenges. It sums up not what I intend to offer the American people, but what I intend to ask of them.[20]

This appeal to cultural identity emerged as a central theme of Kennedy's presidency. He didn't need to refer directly to the legends of Daniel Boone and Davy Crockett or to the tales of the Oregon Trail to meet the challenges that lay ahead—he was able to conjure up those thoughts with the phrase "the New Frontier."

How can you use proof by mythos in a classroom speech? Once again, we return to the earlier discussion of motivation in Chapter 5. The social motives discussed there, which tend to engage group emotions, may also suggest guides to the development of proof by mythos. Figure 15.4 shows how connections might be made between mythos and motives.

Let's see how Robert Owens used such appeals to urge stronger action against drug traffic in urban slums. Robert wanted to establish that "we must win the battle against drugs on the streets of America." He supported this statement by creating a sense of outrage in listeners over the betrayal of the American dream in urban America:

> Read the latest issue of *Time* magazine, and you'll meet an America you never sang about in the songs you learned in school. It's an America in which hope, faith, and dreams are nothing but a bitter memory.
>
> They call America a land of hope, but it's hard to hope when your mother is a cocaine addict on Susquehanna Avenue in North Philadelphia.
>
> They call America a land of faith, but what faith can you cling to when even God seems to have abandoned the street corners to the junkies and the dealers!
>
> They call America a land of dreams, but what kind of dreams can you have when all you hear at night as you lie in bed are the curses and ranting of buyers and dealers.
>
> We might be able to redeem the hope, the faith, and the dreams Americans like to talk about. But we have to do more than just declare war on drugs. We've got to *go* to war, and we've got to win! If we don't, the crack in the Liberty Bell may only symbolize a deadly drug that is destroying the American spirit all over this land.

These appeals to a betrayed mythos justified Robert's concluding plea for a broad-based, aggressive campaign to rid America of its drug culture. *The unique function of appeals to cultural identity is to help listeners understand how the speaker's*

Figure 15.4

Connecting Mythos with Motives

Motives	Group Emotion	Possible Connection
Maintain Control/ Stability	Respect for/love of tradition	Does my proposal reaffirm traditions that my listeners want to protect?
Honor Affiliations	Feelings of group pride/patriotism	Does my subject connect with audience feelings of loyalty to a group and pride in membership?
Preserve Group Identity	Respect for heroes/great deeds	Does my speech connect with models of heroism and memories of great events? Does my speech call upon values that are vital to group identity?

When and How to Use Proof

As you decide how to align your proofs for maximum effectiveness, follow these guidelines:

1. To increase awareness and understanding, use rational appeals based on facts, statistics, and expert testimony *(logos)*.

2. To communicate the human dimensions of a problem, stir listeners with moving examples and stories *(pathos)*.

3. To reassure listeners that you are a credible speaker, convince them that you know what you are talking about,

   that you are fair and honest, and that you have audience interests at heart *(ethos)*.

4. To connect a problem with group culture, show how it relates to popular traditions, legends, and symbols *(mythos)*.

recommendations fit into the total belief and value patterns of their group. An appeal that accomplishes this goal gives such proof a special role in the persuasive process we discuss in Chapter 16. It can help integrate new attitudes and action into the group's culture.

Like appeals to personal feeling, appeals to cultural identity can be a great good or a considerable evil. At their best, such appeals heighten our appreciation of who we are *as a people* and promote consistency between cultural values and public policy. However, when misused, these appeals can make it seem that there is only *one legitimate culture.* Some of those who argued for introducing democratic government to Iraq and the Middle East seemed to base their arguments on the United States model. To the extent they implied that our system is superior to all other options, no matter what the circumstances, they may have been guilty of abusing the appeal to mythos. Also, certain appeals to cultural identity can abuse those who choose not to conform to the dominant values or those who belong to marginalized cultural and religious groups, such as Latinos or Muslims. Such appeals can tear apart the social fabric of our society, and even of our world.

Patterns of Reasoning

A persuasive speech that is effective may activate the power of ethos, pathos, and mythos. Yet these proofs are all secondary to the central focus of ethical persuasion: proof by logos. Thoughtful listeners must be convinced by the patterns of reasoning you develop in your speech. Such listeners will apply the following critical tests:

- Have central issues and terms been clearly and fairly defined?
- Does the speech reason from sound principles?
- Is the speech firmly anchored in reality?
- Does the speech reason acceptably from similar or parallel cases?

In the sections that follow, we consider each of these tests, explain its meaning, and indicate how you might pass it successfully.

Definitions of Central Concepts

The Greek philosopher Socrates was one of the first to insist that ethical persuasion begins with a clear understanding of the meanings of important terms. Have you ever had a heated discussion with someone, only to discover later that the two of you were not even talking about the same thing? If speakers and listeners don't share such understanding from the outset, it is difficult to communicate. When the speaker and audience come from different backgrounds, careful definitions are even more important. Opening his speech on "gender bending," Brandon Rader was careful to offer the following definition: "If you are a gender bender, you dress or act or think or talk like people in your community assume someone of the opposite sex would do or act or talk or dress." Having shared this understanding, Brandon went on to argue that most assumptions about gender benders are quite wrong. Definitions like Brandon's take a term that may be unfamiliar to many audience members and translate it into simpler, more familiar language.

Not all definitions involve translating technical language into familiar terms. Some of the most interesting definitions offered by speakers are efforts to change listeners' perspectives so that they will be more sympathetic to the arguments that will follow. Should alcohol be defined as a drug? Should a fetus be defined as a human being? Definitions that affirm or deny such questions can prepare the way for elaborate arguments advocating different kinds of public policy.

In the 1968 Memphis sanitation strike that led to the assassination of Dr. Martin Luther King Jr., the workers marched carrying signs that read, "I Am a Man." This simple definitional statement was actually the tip of a complex underlying moral argument. The strikers were claiming they had *not* been treated like men in social, political, and economic terms.

An especially interesting effort to redefine perspectives occurred in a speech by Richard Corlin, president of the American Medical Association, at the 2001 AMA annual meeting (see his speech at the end of this chapter). Alarmed over the rise in gun-related fatalities, Dr. Corlin wanted to redefine gun violence in America as a "public health crisis." Here is the section near the beginning of his speech in which he introduces this attempted change of perspectives:

Dr. Richard Corlin, former president of the American Medical Association, used many types of evidence in his speech on gun violence. His use of analogy was especially striking.

> With the preponderance of weapons these days, it comes as no surprise that gun violence—both self-inflicted and against others—is now a serious public health crisis. No one can avoid its brutal and ugly presence. No one. Not physicians. Not the public. And most certainly—not the politicians—no matter how much they might want to.[21]

Having introduced a perspective that was no doubt novel for many members of his audience, Dr. Corlin went on build extensive arguments to support it. By the end of his speech, the "public health crisis" he had identified near the opening of his speech had evolved into a "uniquely American epidemic." As these examples make clear, definitions can be *the fundamental issues at the heart of controversies.* If you attempt to redefine your audience's perspective on a subject, you may have to defend your effort with all the evidence, proof, and credibility you can muster.

Reasoning from Principle

As we absorb the folkways of our culture, we acquire principles that guide the way we think and live. For example "freedom of speech" is written into the Constitution of the United States as a principle of government.

When we **reason from principle**, we use such guides to justify our value judgments and calls to action. Such reasoning is sometimes called **deductive**, because it deduces from some general principle a conclusion about a particular relevant case. Consider a hypothetical example. A speaker begins by reminding listeners of a principle she believes they all accept: "We all believe in freedom of speech." In logical terms, such a principle is known as the **major premise**. Next, the speaker relates a specific issue to that principle, creating what is called the **minor premise**: "Melvin would like to speak." Finally, the speaker reaches her **conclusion**: "We should let Melvin speak." Because of their respect for the principle expressed in the major premise, many listeners would nod assent, even though they might not particularly like Melvin.

When this pattern of major premise/minor premise/conclusion occurred in persuasion about public issues, Aristotle called it the **enthymeme**. He described enthymemes as vital in the persuasion of everyday life. Indeed, he said, they are the most important rhetorical resource. In his 2003 State of the Union address, President Bush developed a major premise that justified conclusions ranging from a massive program to relieve AIDS in Africa to a threat to invade Iraq. Here is what he said:

> The American flag stands for more than our power and our interests. Our founders dedicated this country to the cause of human dignity, the rights of every person and the possibilities of every life. This conviction leads us into the world to help the afflicted, and defend the peace, and confound the designs of evil men.[22]

Because it begins by reminding listeners of shared values, reasoning from principle is useful for establishing common ground with reluctant audiences. Such reasoning can also point out inconsistencies between beliefs and behaviors—the gap between what we practice and what we preach. For example, if you can show that the censorship of song lyrics is inconsistent with freedom of speech, then you will have presented a good reason for people to condemn such censorship. *We are more likely to change a practice that is inconsistent with cherished principles or values than we are to change the principles or values.* Because people like to be consistent and maintain the integrity of their values, reasoning from principle becomes a powerful way to achieve harmony among attitudes, beliefs, and values.

Occasionally, the pattern of reasoning in an enthymeme is not entirely visible in a speech. For example, the major premise may not be stated: Speakers may simply assume that the principle it expresses is already accepted by listeners. When offered appropriate cues, listeners will think of these principles and complete the

---

reasoning from principle Argumentative reasoning that is based upon shared principles, values, and rules, sometimes called deductive reasoning.

deductive reasoning Arguing from a general principle to a specific case.
major premise The statement of a general principle on which an argument is based.

minor premise The statement of a specific instance that relates to the general principle on which an argument is based.

speaker's line of thought on their own. As she spoke of the problems of Native Americans, Ashley Roberson spent much of her time demonstrating the reality of "social injustice on reservations," which functioned as the minor premise in her enthymeme. She did not think it necessary to state the implied major premise, "Social injustice in the United States should not be tolerated." Instead, she felt justified in concluding, "We must eradicate social injustice on reservations." As she indicted the School of the Americas, Amanda Miller concentrated on demonstrating that the school had been training terrorists. She did not think it necessary to state the major premise, "The United States should try to end terrorism, not perpetuate it." Instead, she felt justified in drawing her conclusion, "We ought to close the School of the Americas now."

We should realize, however, that not all members of the audience might accept principles that seem to us beyond question. For example, some researchers have discovered that if you read the Bill of Rights to people without telling them it is part of the United States Constitution, an alarming percentage will describe it as "radical" or "communistic." Therefore, you should not take such principles for granted. You may have to explain and defend them to reinforce your listeners' belief in them. You may need to reawaken faith in the principles by telling stories or offering examples that demonstrate their value.

Another point critical to such reasoning comes when a speaker tries to show that a condition or situation—the minor premise—actually exists. People may not argue passionately about the *principle* of environmental protection, but assertions about a specific case of pollution can generate a good deal of heat. Your persuasive efforts may have to focus on that issue, emphasizing the kind of reasoning we discuss in the next section.

As you develop a principled pattern of reasoning for your speech, keep these cautions in mind:

- **Be certain your audience will accept the major premises on which your arguments are based.** Remind listeners why they believe as they do. Cite prestige sources who testify to the importance of such faith. Use appeals to feeling and to cultural identity to reinforce the principles. Use rational appeals to show their practical importance.

- **Demonstrate the existence of relevant conditions.** This, as we shall see in the next section, is where empirical reasoning joins with principled reasoning to build convincing arguments.

- **Explain the relationship between principles and conditions (the major and minor premises).** Don't expect your audience to get the point automatically. Listeners may not see the connection between their responsibility to maintain the natural beauty of their country and specific environmental conditions that need reform. Help them by drawing the point explicitly.

- **Be certain your reasoning is free from flaws and fallacies.** We discuss such problems of argument in the final section of this chapter.

- **Be sure your conclusion offers a clear direction for listeners.** Don't leave them foundering without a clear idea as to what you want them to do.

Reasoning from Reality

Persuasive speakers must have an accurate grasp of the situation they are discussing. **Reasoning from reality** depends either on the speaker's personal experience or on

---

conclusion The ending of the speech, which summarizes the message and leaves listeners with something to remember. Also, the final statement of

the relationship between the major and minor premises of an argument.

enthymeme Pattern of deductive reasoning as it occurs in persuasion about public issues.

reasoning from reality Emphasis on factual evidence in guiding one's general conclusions and decisions.

Speaker's Notes 15.2

Reasoning from Principle

Let your reasoning from principle follow these procedures:

1. If there is any doubt, remind listeners why they honor the principles from which you reason.

2. Demonstrate that the conditions relevant to the principle you invoke actually exist.

3. Show how these conditions and principles are related and why that relationship requires action.

4. Check for flaws in your reasoning.

5. Make it easy for listeners to enact what you advance.

knowledge provided by experts. This knowledge is reflected in the facts, statistics, examples, and testimony used in the speech. Reasoning from reality is sometimes called **inductive** because it draws general conclusions from particular instances. Inductive reasoning is the classic method of scientific investigation, and science remains a "god term" for many listeners in our culture:[23] if you can show that "science supports my argument," you will have strengthened your case for most audiences. Again, for this reason, the abuse of scientific evidence, attempted when so-called "think tanks" offer financial inducements to scientists to reach certain predetermined conclusions, is an ominous practice in a society that depends on the integrity of public deliberation.[24]

Dr. Richard Corlin, in his presidential address before the American Medical Association on gun violence, was uniquely positioned to speak both from direct personal experience and as a careful observer of the work of other experts. In the section that follows, we can see how he reasons from reality, citing statistic after statistic and example after example, using contrast to highlight the force of his evidence. Note also how he speaks *as a scientist addressing other scientists:*

> In 1993 and 1994, we resolved that the AMA would, among other actions, "support scientific research and objective discussion aimed at identifying causes of and solutions to the crime and violence problem." Scientific research and objective discussion because we as physicians are—first and foremost—scientists. We need to look at the science of the subject, the data, and—if you will—the micro-data, before we make a diagnosis. Not until then can we agree upon the prognosis or decide upon a course of treatment.
>
> First, let's go straight to the science that we do know. How does this disease present itself? Since 1962, more than a million Americans have died in firearm suicides, homicides, and unintentional injuries. In 1998 alone, 30,708 Americans died by gunfire:
>
> - 17,424 in firearm suicides
> - 12,102 in firearm homicides
> - 866 in unintentional shootings
>
> Also in 1998, more than 64,000 people were treated in emergency rooms for nonfatal firearm injuries.

inductive reasoning Reasoning from specific factual instances to reach a general conclusion.

This is a uniquely American epidemic. In the same year that more than 30,000 people were killed by guns in America, the number in Germany was 1,164; in Canada, it was 1,034; in Australia, 391; in England and Wales, 211; and in Japan, the number for the entire year was 83.[25]

Although reasoning from principle and reasoning from reality may seem quite different, they actually work together. Reasoning from reality can reinforce principles so that they don't appear to be simply items of blind faith. For example, if we can demonstrate empirically that "free and open discussion actually results in better public decisions," then we bring both morality and practicality to the support of freedom of speech.

Reasoning from reality is critical for demonstrating the truth of the minor premise in an enthymeme. Is the censorship of song lyrics an actual threat, or is it merely some bogeyman in the minds of liberals? Again, testimony from those who wish to censor and who have the power to censor would authenticate the threat. Similarly, Ashley Roberson had to prove with facts, statistics, and examples that the problems existing on Native American reservations were of such magnitude that they constituted "social injustice." Clearly, reasoning from reality can empower reasoning from principle in persuasive speeches, and the two forms are often found woven together.

Reasoning from reality also implies an understanding of cause–effect relationships. In his speech on gun violence, once Dr. Corlin had described the magnitude of the problem, he went on to explore its causes. One such cause pinpointed the culture of violence accessible to young children through video games. As he put it:

> The spread of gun-related injuries and death is especially tragic when it involves our children. Like young lungs and tar and nicotine—young minds are especially responsive to the deadliness of gun violence.
>
> Lieutenant Colonel Dave Grossman, a West Point professor of psychology and military science, has documented how video games act as killing simulators, teaching our children not just to shoot—but to kill. Grossman, who calls himself an expert in "killology," cites as evidence the marksmanship of the two children, aged 11 and 13, in the Jonesboro, Arkansas, shootings in 1998. Both shooters were avid video game players. And just like in a video game—they fired off 27 shots—and hit 15 people. Killing four of their fellow students—and a teacher. Such deadly accuracy is rare and hard to achieve—even by well-trained police and military marksmen.[26]

As you incorporate reasoning from reality into your arguments, keep in mind these basic requirements:

- You must be objective enough to see the situation clearly. Do not let your biases warp your perceptions. Look at an issue from as many perspectives as possible.

- You must compile a sufficient number of observations. One or two isolated incidents cannot justify reality claims.

- Since situations surrounding relevant issues are constantly changing, you must be sure your observations are up to date.

- Your observations must be truly representative of the situation. The exception does not prove the rule.

Speaker's Notes 15.3

Reasoning from Reality

To ground your reasoning in reality, satisfy the following tests:

1. Are your observations objective?

2. Have you observed enough?

3. Are your observations recent?

4. Are your observations representative of the situation?

5. Do your observations adequately justify your conclusion?

6. Have you read widely enough to see if experts agree?

7. If experts disagree, will you acknowledge their disagreement and explain and defend your preferences among them?

8. Have you verified your experts' credentials so you can present them in your speech?

■ Your observations must actually justify your conclusion. They must be relevant to the claim you wish to demonstrate.

■ If your inductive exposure comes from library or Internet research, don't just accept the testimony of the first expert you encounter. Read more widely to see whether experts agree with each other, and if they disagree, decide which of them are most credible. Be prepared to justify and defend your evaluation of evidence in your speech.

■ As you present facts, statistics, examples, and testimony, be sure to introduce the experts who are the sources of the evidence. Establish their credentials to reassure thoughtful listeners. Beginning speakers often neglect this important requirement of successful persuasion.

Reasoning from Parallel Cases

When we deal with a problem by considering a similar situation and drawing lessons from it, we are **reasoning from parallel cases**. Such **analogical reasoning**, as it is sometimes called, can be useful to frame an unfamiliar, abstract, or difficult problem in terms of something that is more familiar, more concrete, or more easily understood. It also can be used to dramatize the speaker's claim: "If we don't deal with global warming, our children will inherit a degraded environment. Just like the tiger and the elephant, our habitat is in crisis."

Dr. Corlin used a vivid analogy to underscore the importance of video games in acclimating susceptible young minds into America's culture of gun violence. Reasoning from parallel cases helped him both magnify the problem and bring it into the understanding of listeners:

> I want you to imagine with me a computer game called "Puppy Shoot." In this game, puppies run across the screen. Using a joystick, the game player aims a gun that shoots the puppies. The player is awarded one point for a flesh wound, three points for a body shot, and ten points for a head shot. Blood spurts out each time a puppy is hit—and brain tissue splatters all over whenever there's a head shot. The dead puppies pile up at the bottom of the screen. When the shooter gets to 1,000 points, he gets to exchange his pistol for an Uzi, and the point values go up.

reasoning from parallel cases Presenting a similar situation and how it was handled as the basis of an argument. Often called analogical reasoning.

analogical reasoning Creating a strategic perspective on a subject by relating it to something similar about which the audience has strong feelings.

> If a game as disgusting as that were to be developed, every animal rights group in the country, along with a lot of other organizations, would protest, and there would be all sorts of attempts made to get the game taken off the market. Yet, if you just change puppies to people in the game I described, there are dozens of them already on the market—sold under such names as "Blood Bath," "Psycho Toxic," "Redneck Rampage," and "Soldier of Fortune."[27]

As useful as analogical reasoning can be in dramatizing arguments, it can be even more useful in persuading listeners to accept solutions. For example, in the continuing debate over our nation's drug policy, those who favor legalizing "recreational" drugs frequently base their arguments on an analogy to Prohibition.[28] They claim that the Prohibition amendment caused more problems than it solved because it made drinking an adventure and led to the rise of a criminal empire. They then claim that our efforts to outlaw recreational drugs have had the same result. The reason, they say, is that it is impossible to ban a human desire—that to try to do so simply encourages contempt for the law. Moreover, they assert that legalizing drugs would help put the international drug dealers out of business, just as the repeal of Prohibition helped bring about the downfall of the gangsters of the 1930s. Finally, they argue, if drug sales were legal, it would be easier to control the quality of drugs, thus reducing the danger to users (parallel to the health problems associated with bootleg whiskey during Prohibition).

As this example shows, analogical reasoning emphasizes strategic points of comparison between similar situations. People on both sides of an issue will focus on these points, using evidence and proofs to defend or attack them. Opponents to legalizing drugs claim that there are many important differences between drugs and alcohol.[29] They say that alcohol is not as addictive for casual users as heroin or cocaine. They contend that legalization would multiply the drug problem, not reduce it, because it would make drugs more accessible and make them seem acceptable. They further suggest that since many drug abusers are prone to violence, the cost to society would increase. Thus, the public debate rages on over these crucial points of comparison.

What makes analogical reasoning work? It is similar to empirical reasoning from reality in that it seeks insight through careful observation. Analogy, however, concentrates *on one similar situation* rather than ranging across many. This means that although analogical reasoning may seem more concrete and interesting than some forms of inductive reasoning (such as that based often on statistical evidence), it can also be less reliable. Before you decide to develop an analogy as part of your argument, be sure that the important similarities outweigh the dissimilarities. If you must strain to make an analogy fit, rely on other forms of reasoning.

Speaker's Notes 15.4

Developing Powerful Arguments

To build arguments that will influence thoughtful listeners, follow these guidelines:

1. Provide clear definitions of basic terms.

2. Justify arguments by reasoning from accepted principles.

3. Remind listeners of why they honor these principles.

4. Convince listeners that your arguments are based in reality.

5. Create a vivid sense of problems.

6. Use a similar situation as a model from which to draw comparisons that illustrate and favor your position.

7. Build arguments to answer questions reasonable listeners might ask.

The Interplay of Reasoning

Patterns of reasoning often interact in persuasive speeches. One model that displays this interaction was developed by Stephen Toulmin, a British logician.[30] The Toulmin model (see Figure 15.5) includes six elements: data, claim, warrant, backing, reservations, and qualifier.

Data.   Facts, statistics, examples, and expert testimony constitute **data** in the Toulmin model. By featuring the importance of data, the model emphasizes the role of inductive reasoning. Dr. Richard Corlin established a rich array of data in his speech, "The Secrets of Gun Violence in America." Similarly, Josh Logan's speech, "Global Burning," reprinted in Appendix B, presented a range of data to justify his arguments.

Claim.   The **claim** is the conclusion the speaker draws from the data. Dr. Corlin wanted his audience of physicians to accept his claim that gun violence in America is an epidemic that demands a search for cures. Josh wanted us to accept his claim that controlling global warming is a personal, national, and international imperative.

Warrant.   The **warrant** supplies the principle that justifies the movement from data to claim. It functions like a major premise and represents the role of deductive reasoning in the model. Dr. Corlin's speech began by establishing a critical definition: *Gun violence is an epidemic and therefore a medical emergency.* His warrant, which he leaves audience members to draw on their own, might be reconstructed: *Whenever an epidemic exists, physicians—by the nature of their calling—must seek remedies and cures.* Those who accepted this warrant might feel compelled to accept the claim: *The AMA should initiate an aggressive campaign to find cures for gun violence in America.*

Similarly, in Josh's speech concerning the legitimacy of global warming, the warrant might be reconstructed as follows: *Whenever hundreds of scientists, working independently in countries around the globe, come to the same or similar conclusions, we can rely on the results.* Listeners who affirmed this warrant should also then accept the claim: *We must accept the reality of global warming.*

Toulmin's model can also supply a warrant for the use of analogical reasoning in argument. That warrant might be stated as follows: *Whenever a parallel case*

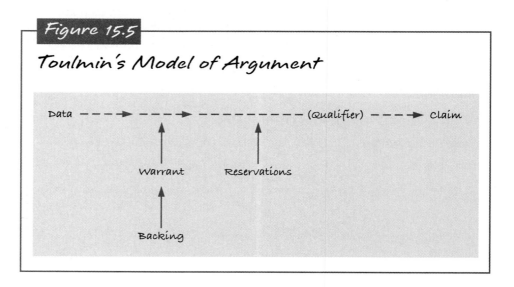

Figure 15.5

Toulmin's Model of Argument

Data ----> ----> ---------- (Qualifier) ----> Claim

Warrant   Reservations

Backing

---

data The factual evidence in an argument as featured in the Toulmin model.

claim The conclusion the speaker draws based on the data in an argument. Also, conclusions that go beyond factual statements to make judgments about their subjects.

warrant The principle that justifies moving from data to claim in an argument.

presents a set of compelling similarities to the subject we are discussing, and no significant dissimilarities exist, we can draw a relevant claim about our subject. We have seen how Dr. Corlin used a hypothetical analogy—the game he called "Puppy Shoot"—to dramatize the danger of the culture of violence encouraged by computer games.

Backing.   Occasionally, critical listeners or opponents may question the warrant. At such moments, you can defend the warrant by introducing support for it, called *backing*. Dr. Corlin anticipated that critics might question the activism in his implied warrant, so he introduced backing into his speech:

> We, as physicians, and as the American Medical Association, have an ethical and moral responsibility to do this—as our mission statement says—"to promote the science and art of medicine and the betterment of public health." If removing the scourge of gun violence isn't bettering the public health—what is?[31]

Thus, he defends his warrant in advance of attacks by citing the AMA mission statement as backing. Similarly, had anyone questioned Joshua's warrant, he could have pointed to past international research efforts on dread diseases to back his principle that when scientists agree on a global scale, one can rely on their conclusions.

Reservations.   Reservations acknowledge conditions under which the claim may not follow. Ethical persuaders have an obligation to inform listeners of such conditions, and thoughtful listeners will appreciate their candor. Not acknowledging legitimate reservations risks real damage to one's ethos should a critical listener point them out.

When conditions do create an element of uncertainty, reservations are signaled by the word *unless*. Josh might have introduced a reservation had he added, "Unless anyone can show that all these scientists were somehow mistaken, or in some sort of conspiracy, we must accept the ominous reality of global warming." Josh felt no need to acknowledge any such reservation.

Ethics *Alert! 15.2*

Building Ethical Arguments

To earn your reputation as an ethical persuader, observe the following guidelines:

1. Emphasize logical reasoning built on facts, statistics, and expert testimony.

2. Always supplement proof by pathos with hard evidence.

3. Never allow proof by mythos to become a mask for intolerance or an excuse to attack the rights of individuals who resist group values and culture.

4. Test the ethics of any persuasive strategy by considering how it will be judged by a thoughtful listener.

5. Strive to maintain consistency among attitudes, beliefs, values, and actions.

6. Acknowledge conditions that might disprove your argument.

7. As you research a problem, keep an open mind so that you can understand the various sides in a dispute.

Qualifiers.   Qualifiers are terms that address the force of the claim, taking into account possible reservations. Qualifiers often appear in such terms as *probably*, *almost certainly*, and *in all likelihood*. Dr. Corlin acknowledged no reservations in his speech, so he does not qualify the strength of his claim. Likewise, Josh was confident of the power of his data and the certainty of his claim concerning global warming, so he also did not use qualifiers.

You can use Toulmin's model of argument either as a critical template to help you become a more thoughtful listener or to gain an overview of your own reasoning processes in a speech you are designing. In the latter case, you may be able to identify any weak points during preparation and correct them before you make your presentation.

Avoiding Defective Persuasion

*I*t takes a lot of work to prepare a persuasive speech—analyzing your audience, researching your topic, planning your strategy, and developing powerful arguments that will convince judicious listeners. Do not ruin all your hard work by committing **fallacies**, or errors of reasoning. Fallacies may crop up in the evidence you use, the proofs you develop, or the reasoning in your arguments. There are also fallacies particular to some speech designs. In this section, we identify some of these major errors so that you can guard against them, both as speaker and as listener.

Defective Evidence

Evidence is defective if the speaker misuses facts, statistics, or testimony, or uses evidence inappropriately.

The evidence used in a persuasive speech must be representative of the situation.

Misuse of Facts.   The **slippery slope fallacy** assumes that once something happens, it will establish an irreversible trend leading to disaster. The slippery slope fallacy often involves oversimplification and outlandish hyperbole. For example, a prominent religious leader once suggested that feminism was "a socialist, antifamily political movement that encourages women to leave their husbands, kill their children, practice witchcraft, destroy capitalism, and become lesbians."[32] In the slippery slope fallacy, it is not logic but rather our darkest fears that drive the prediction of events.

A second misuse of facts involves the **confusion of fact and opinion**. A factual statement is objective and verifiable, such as "Most Republican governors support the lowering of taxes." An opinion is a personal interpretation of information: a statement of belief, feeling, attitude, or value. Normally, factual and opinion statements stay in their proper places. The problem comes when speakers make impassioned claims based on opinions, such as "The Republicans have done it now! They're violating our Constitution. They're tossing children out into the cold. They're depriving retired people

---

fallacies   Errors in reasoning that make persuasion unreliable.

slippery slope fallacy   The assumption that once something happens, an inevitable trend is established that will lead to disastrous results.

confusion of fact and opinion   A misuse of evidence in which personal opinions are offered as though they were facts, or facts are dismissed as though they were opinion.

of their right to a secure old age. These are the *facts* of what they're doing." Opinions can be useful in persuasive speeches when they represent careful interpretations that are supported by evidence. However, treating an opinion as a fact, or a fact as an opinion, is the source of many problems. It can make you seem to claim too much or too little and can raise questions about your competence and ethics.

At one time, hunters used to distract their dogs from a trail by dragging a smoked herring across it. In our time, the **red herring fallacy** occurs when persuaders try to draw attention away from the real issues in a dispute, perhaps because they feel vulnerable on those issues or because they see a chance to vilify the opposition. Often, the "red herring" they use is some sensational allegation. In the ongoing abortion controversy, some pro-choice advocates tried to discredit their opponents by associating them with terrorists, assassins, and bombers. In return, some pro-life advocates tried to smear their opposition by suggesting that abortion clinics were underwritten by "mafia money." Such charges from both sides divert attention from the central issues of the controversy.

Statistical Fallacies. Audiences are often intimidated by numbers. We've all been taught that "figures don't lie" without being reminded that "liars figure." Speakers can exploit this tendency by creating statistical deceptions. For example, consider the **myth of the mean**. If you've ever vacationed in the mountains, you know that a stream may have an "average depth" of six inches, yet a person could drown in one of its deep pools. A speaker could tell you not to worry about poverty in Plattsville because the average income is well above the poverty level. Yet this average could be skewed by the fact that a few families are very wealthy, creating an illusion of well-being that is not true for most people. Averages are useful to summarize statistical information, but be sure they do not mask the reality of a situation.

Another statistical fallacy occurs when we offer **flawed statistical comparisons** that start from unequal bases. Suppose you have two salespersons, George and John, working for you. George has just opened a new account, giving him a total of two sales. John has opened three new accounts for a total of thirteen. George comes to you and asks for a promotion, arguing, "My success rate this year rose by 100 percent, while John's rose only 30 percent." George would be guilty of fallacious reasoning, if not bad salesmanship.

Defective Testimony. Testimony can be misused in many different ways. Speakers may omit *when* a statement was made to hide the fact that the testimony is dated. They may leave out important facts about their experts, intimidating us with titles in statements such as "*Dr.* Michael Jones reported that smoking does not harm health." What the speaker *didn't* reveal was that Dr. Jones was a marketing professor who was writing public relations material for the Tobacco Growers Association. Speakers also abuse testimony when they cite words out of context that are not representative of a person's actual position. This can happen when a qualifier is presented as though it represented a concession, misquoting a statement such as "unless the growers are no longer using herbicides" as "Ah hah! He admits—and I quote him—'growers are no longer using herbicides.'" As we noted in Chapter 8, prestige and lay testimony can be misused if they replace expert opinion when facts must be established. Finally, the "voice of the people" can be easily misrepresented, depending on *which* people you choose to quote.

---

red herring fallacy The use of irrelevant material to divert attention.

myth of the mean The deceptive use of statistical averages in speeches.

flawed statistical comparisons Statistical reasoning that offers fallacious conclusions by comparing unequal or unlike situations.

InterConnections.

LearnMore 15.2

Fallacies

Fallacy Files

http://fallacyfiles.org

> An interactive site containing an extensive collection of fallacies and bad argument, with definitions and examples; well organized and entertaining as well as educational (see especially "Stalking the Wild Fallacy"); developed by Gary N. Curtis.

Watch Out for these Common Fallacies

www.coping.org/write/percept/fallacies/content.htm

> Offers good discussion and often striking examples of fallacies in everyday reasoning; developed by James J. Messina and Constance M. Messina.

Soyouwanna Avoid Common Logical Errors?

www.soyouwanna.com/site/syws/logic/logic.html

> Discusses the logical rules that govern the making and evaluation of arguments from a philosophical perspective.

Fallacies Drawn from Aristotle's *Rhetoric*

www.cc.utah.edu/~sms5/wrtg3700/bgtexts/fallacies.htm#Appeals

> A discussion of common fallacies as they are developed in Aristotle's Rhetoric, one of the first books on public communication and perhaps the greatest.

Inappropriate Evidence.   Other abuses occur when speakers deliberately use one form of evidence when they should be using another. For example, you might use facts and figures when examples would bring us closer to the human truth of a situation. Welfare statistics are sometimes misused in this way. When a speaker talks about poverty in terms of abstract numbers only, it distances listeners from the human reality of the problem. George Orwell once complained that such language "falls upon the [truth] like soft snow, blurring the outlines and covering up all the details."[33] On the other hand, speakers may use examples to arouse emotions when what is needed is the dispassionate picture provided by facts and figures. Testimony is abused when it is used to compensate for inadequate facts. Narratives that create mythos may also be used inappropriately. Calling someone a "Robin Hood who steals from the rich and gives to the poor" has been used to justify more than one crime.

Defective Proof

Any element of proof can be defective. We have already pointed out the danger when appeals to feelings overwhelm judgment and cloud the issue. Speakers might also misuse appeals to cultural identity to promote intolerance, such as "When are Native Americans going to start being *good* Americans?"

Similarly, speakers may abuse appeals to credibility by attacking the person instead of the problem. This is called an **ad hominem fallacy**. Such persuaders try to avoid issues by calling the opposition derogatory names. For example, during an environmental dispute, one side charged that its opponents were "little old ladies in tennis shoes" and "outside agitators." Not to be outdone, the other side labeled

ad hominem fallacy An attempt to discredit a position by attacking the people who favor it.

their antagonists as "rapists of public parkland."[34] Senator Zell Miller recently laced into *New York Times* columnist Maureen Dowd, a major critic of the Bush administration and of the religious right, in the following way: "The more Maureen Loud [sic] gets on 'Meet the Press' and writes those columns, the redder these states get. I mean, they don't want some highbrow hussy from New York City explaining to them that they're idiots and telling them that they're stupid." Miller also suggested "that red-headed woman at the *New York Times*" should not mock anyone's religion: "You can see horns just sprouting up through that Technicolor hair." Dowd responded: "I'm not a highbrow hussy from New York. I'm a highbrow hussy from Washington. Senator, pistols or swords?"[35] Presumably, the public was not much enlightened by this exchange.

Proof by ethos also can be abused when speakers overuse it—when they try to intimidate listeners by citing an overwhelming list of authorities while neglecting to present information or good reasons for accepting their claims.

Finally, speakers neglect their responsibility to prove their points when they merely assert what they have not proved, thereby **begging the question**. Those who beg the question usually rely on colorful language to disguise the inadequacy of their proofs so that the words themselves *seem* to establish the conclusion. Critics who shout, "It's amazing how much money we're wasting on education these days" suggest wild and excessive spending without really proving the allegation. A similar abuse may occur when the speaker taps into the mythos of the audience without adequate justification or preparation. A conclusion such as "Be *patriotic*! Support the *American way of life*! Speak out against gun control!"—tacked onto a speech without further explanation—begs the question, because the speaker has not proved that being against gun control is a form of patriotism.

Defective Patterns of Reasoning

Major fallacies may infest the basic patterns of reasoning in persuasion. It is unethical to commit them purposely, irresponsible to commit them accidentally. In your role as critical listener, be on guard against them at all times.

Errors of Reasoning from Principle.   Reasoning from principle can be only as good as the underlying premise on which it is built. In the **shaky principle fallacy**, the premise is not sound. *If the principle is faulty, the entire argument may crumble.* We once heard a student begin a line of argument with the following statement of principle: "College athletes are not really here to learn." She was instantly in trouble. When her speech was over, the class assailed her with questions: How did she define *athletes*? Was she talking about intercollegiate or intramural athletes? How about the tennis team? How did she define learning? Was she aware of the negative stereotype at the center of her premise? Wasn't she being unfair, not to mention arrogant? It's safe to say that the speaker did not persuade many people that day. To avoid such a fiasco, be sure that you can defend each word in the principle that underlies your reasoning.

Omitted qualifiers, another fallacy common to reasoning from principle, occur when a persuader claims too much, in effect confusing probability with certainty. The logic of everyday life is rarely certain. Suppose a friend from the Tau Beta fraternity calls you to set up a blind date. If the principle "Tau Betas are handsome" holds about 90 percent of the time in your experience, and if you are

---

begging the question   Assuming that an argument has been proved without actually presenting the evidence.

shaky principle fallacy   A reasoning error that occurs when an argument is based on a faulty premise.

omitted qualifiers   A reasoning error that occurs when a persuader claims too much, confusing probability with certainty.

about 90 percent certain that your blind date is a Tau Beta, then your conclusion that your date will be attractive is an assumption qualified by at least two factors of uncertainty. It is better to say: "There is a *good chance* that my date will be handsome." If you point out the uncertainty factor in advance through proper qualification, you may not lose the audience's trust if a prediction does not come true.

Errors of Reasoning from Reality.

An error common to reasoning from reality is *assuming that if something happens after an event, it was caused by the event.* This **post hoc fallacy** confuses association with causation. It is the basis of many superstitious beliefs. The same people who wear their lucky boots and shirts to ball games may also argue that we should have a tax cut because the last time we had one we avoided war, increased employment, or reduced crime. One of our students fell into the post hoc trap when she argued that low readership of certain books in areas where the books are banned in public schools proves that the bans are effective. There may be many reasons why people don't read books—banning them in school libraries may or may not be among those reasons. It is just as likely that the book bans themselves are simply symptoms of deeper cultural conditions and that the bans might actually create curiosity about their objects of censure, resulting in more readership than might otherwise have happened. A speaker must demonstrate that events are causally connected, not just make the assumption on the basis of association.

Another error common to such reasoning is a **hasty generalization** that is based on insufficient or nonrepresentative observations. Suppose a student reasoned, "My big sister in Alpha Chi got a D from Professor Osborn. The guy who sits next to me in history got an F from her. I'm struggling to make a C in her class. Therefore, Professor Osborn is a tough grader." To avoid hasty generalization, you would need to know what Professor Osborn's grade distribution looks like over an extended period of time and across courses, plus how her grades compare with other professors teaching the same courses.

Finally, an error common to both reasoning from principle and reasoning from reality is the **non sequitur fallacy**. It occurs when the principle and the reality discussed don't really relate to each other, when the conclusion does not follow from the relationship between them, or when the evidence presented is irrelevant. Former Speaker of the House Newt Gingrich, lecturing on why men are more suited than women to traditional military combat roles, provided a remarkable example that appears to fit all the conditions of non sequitur reasoning:

> If combat means living in a ditch, females have biological problems staying in a ditch for 30 days because they get infections. . . . [Moreover,] males are biologically driven to go out and hunt for giraffes.

Former Representative Pat Schroeder responded to this wisdom as follows: "I have been working in a male culture for a very long time, and I haven't met the first one who wants to go out and hunt a giraffe."[36]

And then there is the cockeyed non sequitur logic of the late Marge Schott, an owner of the Cincinnati Reds baseball team. Schott told a Denver radio audience that she would rather see children smoke than take drugs. Her reason? "We smoked a peace pipe with the Indians, right?"[37]

---

post hoc fallacy A deductive error in which one event is assumed to be the cause of another simply because the first preceded the second.

hasty generalization An error of inductive reasoning in which a claim is made based on insufficient or nonrepresentative information.

non sequitur fallacy A deductive error occurring when conclusions do not follow from the premises that precede them.

Defective Analogy. A **faulty analogy** occurs when the things compared are dissimilar in some important way. This fallacy lies at the heart of some of our most serious human problems. It rises out of our tendency to assume that what happened to us on one occasion is a sure indicator of what will happen to others in similar circumstances. A father reasons, "When I was a boy, my father made me work and it was good for me. Therefore, Junior should work." A mother answers, "When I was a girl my mother made me work and I hated every minute of it. Therefore, Junior should not work."

Which line of reasoning should win the argument? Neither. There are simply too many dissimilarities operating here. The times have changed, opportunities and expectations have changed, even the nature of the work may well have changed. And above all, neither Father nor Mother *is* Junior, who apparently has not been consulted.

Until they can expand their research to include many more case studies, enough to satisfy critical listeners, and are able to argue from more sound inductive grounds, these frustrated parents can offer only a clash of faulty arguments from analogy.

Fallacies Related to Particular Designs

In addition to fallacies of evidence, proof, and argument, there are at least two major fallacies related to particular persuasive designs. **Either-or thinking**, sometimes called a *false dilemma*, makes listeners think that they have only two mutually exclusive choices. This fallacy is attractive because it is dramatic: It satisfies our need for conflict and simplicity. It occurs in statements such as, "We can either promote jobs or protect the environment—not both" or "If we pay down the debt, we will sacrifice social security." Either-or thinking blinds listeners to other options, such as compromise or creative alternatives not yet considered. Such thinking often infests problem–solution speeches when speakers oversimplify the choices.

People with gardens sometimes make a "straw man" to scare off crows. As the name suggests, the straw is formed into the likeness of a man (presumably, a "straw woman" would work as well, as far as the crows are concerned). From this practice comes the **straw man fallacy**, creating a "likeness" of an opponent's view that makes it seem trivial, ridiculous, and easy to refute. As you might suspect, the straw man fallacy appears most often in speeches that contend with opposition. It understates and distorts the position of opponents and is unethical. Reducing the movement in favor of the Equal Rights Amendment for women to "an effort to abolish separate restrooms for men and women" or dismissing affirmative action as "a policy designed to give unfair advantage to minorities" are classic cases. As an ethical persuasive speaker, you have an obligation to represent an opposing position fairly and fully, even as you refute it. Only then will thoughtful listeners respect you and your arguments. The straw man fallacy is an implicit admission of weakness or desperation and can damage what may well be a legitimate case.

Persuasion is constantly threatened by flaws and deception. In a world of competing views, we often see human nature revealed in its petty as well as its finer moments. As you plan and present your arguments or listen to the arguments of others, be on guard against fallacies. Figure 15.6 lists and defines the fallacies we have been discussing.

---

faulty analogy A comparison drawn between things that are dissimilar in some important way.

either–or thinking A fallacy that occurs when a speaker suggests that there are only two options, and only one is desirable.

straw man fallacy Understating, distorting, or otherwise misrepresenting the position of opponents for ease of refutation.

Figure 15.6

Gallery of Fallacies

Kind	Nature of the Problem
1. Evidential fallacies	
A. Slippery slope	• Arguing that one bad thing will result in many others
B. Confusing fact with opinion	• Asserting opinions as though they were facts, or discrediting facts as opinions
C. Red herring	• Distracting listeners with sensational, irrelevant material
D. Myth of the mean	• Using an average to hide a problem
E. Flawed statistical comparisons	• Using percentage increases or decreases to distort reality
F. Defective testimony	• Omitting when a statement was made or a speaker's credentials; quoting out of context
G. Inappropriate evidence	• Using facts when examples are needed, or examples when facts are needed, or an intimidating list of authorities as a substitute for information
2. Flawed proofs	
A. Ad hominem	• Attacking the person rather than the point
B. Begging the question	• Assuming as decided what has actually not been proved
3. Defective arguments	
A. Shaky principle	• Basing an argument on an unsound assumption
B. Omitted qualifiers	• Confusing probability with certainty by asserting a conclusion without qualification
C. Post hoc	• Assuming because one event follows another, it was caused by it
D. Non sequitur	• Reasoning in which principles and observations are unrelated to each other or to the conclusion drawn
E. Hasty generalization	• Drawing conclusions based on insufficient or nonrepresentative observations
F. Faulty analogy	• Comparing things that are dissimilar in some important way
4. Persuasive design fallacies	
A. Either-or thinking	• Framing choices so that listeners think they have only two options
B. Straw man	• Belittling or trivializing arguments to refute them easily

In Summary

Persuasion is the art of getting others to consider our point of view fairly and favorably. In contrast with informative speaking, persuasive speaking urges a choice among options and asks for a commitment. Rather than speaking as a teacher, the speaker assumes the role of advocate. Ethical persuasive speaking centers on good reasons based on responsible knowledge. Persuasive speeches rely more on emotional involvement than do informative speeches, and they carry an even heavier ethical burden.

Argumentative Persuasion. Manipulative persuasion evades judgment and reflection by thoughtful listeners and avoids the ethical burden of justification. In contrast, argumentative persuasion displays the rationale for its conclusions in the form of evidence, proofs, and patterns of reasoning.

Developing Evidence and Proofs. When used in persuasion, supporting materials become evidence. Facts and statistics alert us to a situation we must change. Examples move listeners, creating a favorable emotional climate for the speaker's recommendations. Narratives bring a sense of reality and help listeners identify with the issue. Testimony calls on witnesses to support a position. When you use evidence, strive for recent facts and figures, emphasize factual examples, engage listeners through stories that make your point, and rely primarily on expert testimony.

Proofs constitute appeals to our rational nature (logos), appeals to feeling (pathos), appeals to the credibility of speaker and sources cited within the speech (ethos), and appeals to cultural identity (mythos). Appeals to rationality assume that we are thinking creatures who respond to well-reasoned demonstrations. Appeals to feeling affirm that we are also creatures of emotion. Appeals to credibility recognize that we respond to leadership qualities in speakers and to the authority of their sources of evidence. Appeals to cultural identity relate to our nature as social beings who respond to group traditions and values. Argumentative persuasion centers on the logos, but effective persuaders must be able to combine the strengths of these various forms.

Patterns of Reasoning. Persuaders must define the meanings of key terms and concepts early in their speeches. Definitions can also attempt to change perspectives on subjects to make listeners more sympathetic to the arguments that will follow.

In deductive reasoning, speakers argue from accepted principles and values in order to justify their conclusions. Such reasoning originates in a principle (major premise), identifies some condition relevant to the principle (minor premise), and makes some judgment about the condition that seems justified by the principle (conclusion).

In inductive reasoning, speakers establish that their arguments are grounded in reality. Such reasoning from reality draws general conclusions from an inspection of particular related instances. It emphasizes evidence provided by facts, statistics, and expert testimony.

In analogical reasoning, persuaders show how we can deal with a problem by considering a similar situation. Such reasoning from parallel cases can help clarify an abstract problem by relating it to a more concrete model. The legitimacy of such reasoning depends on the adequacy of points of comparison.

Toulmin's model of argument displays how these patterns of reasoning can interact in public controversies.

Avoiding Defective Persuasion. Fallacies are errors in reasoning that can damage a persuasive speech. Evidence is defective when speakers misuse facts, statistics, and testimony. Common errors include the slippery slope fallacy, which assumes that a single instance will establish a trend; the confusion of fact with opinion; and the red herring, using irrelevant material to divert attention from the issue. Statistical fallacies include the myth of the mean, in which averages create illusions that hide reality, and faulty conclusions based on flawed statistical comparisons.

Various defects can reduce the value of proof. Speakers can commit an ad hominem fallacy, attacking the person rather than the argument. When speakers merely assume in their conclusion what they have not proved, they commit the fallacy of begging the question.

Fallacies are also common in the patterns of reasoning. If the principle you rely on is faulty, your entire argument will crumble. Or speakers can confuse association with causation, reasoning that if something happened after an event, it therefore was caused by the event. This is called the post hoc fallacy.

A non sequitur occurs when irrelevant conclusions or evidence are introduced into argument. Another error common to inductive reasoning is the hasty generalization, when conclusions are drawn from insufficient or nonrepresentative observations. Analogical reasoning is defective when important dissimilarities outweigh similarities.

Either-or thinking can be a special problem in speeches calling for action. This fallacy reduces audience options to only two, one advocated by the speaker, the other undesirable. When speeches that contend with opposition understate, distort, or misrepresent an opposing position for the sake of easy refutation, they commit the straw man fallacy.

Explore and Apply the Ideas in This Chapter

1. Examine magazine advertisements and newspaper articles to find "infomercials"—persuasive messages cloaked as information. What alerts you to the persuasive intent? In what respects does such communication possess the characteristics of persuasion and information discussed in this chapter?

2. Bring to class examples of advertisements that emphasize each of the four forms of persuasive proof: logos, pathos, ethos, and mythos. What factors in the product, medium of advertising, or intended audience might explain this emphasis in each example? Do the advertisements combine other forms of proof as well? How effective is each advertisement?

3. Analyze the evidence, proofs, and patterns of reasoning that develop in the speech by Bonnie Marshall, reprinted in Appendix B. How powerful is this overall design of persuasive materials? Might it have been even stronger? How?

4. Look for examples of fallacies in the letters-to-the-editor section of your local newspaper over a week's period of time. Bring these specimens to class for discussion and analysis.

5. Keep a diary for the next three days in which you identify all the moments in which you encounter and practice persuasion. When were you most and least persuaded and most and least persuasive? Why? Did you encounter (or commit) any ethical abuses? Discuss your experiences in class.

6. Find a news story that interests you. Using the information in the story, (1) show how you might use this material as evidence in a persuasive speech, (2) indicate how this evidence might be used to develop a proof, and (3) explain how this proof might function as part of a pattern of reasoning.

7. About fifty years ago, in *The Ethics of Rhetoric*, Richard Weaver observed that frequent controversy over the definitions of basic terms in public discourse are a sign of social and cultural division.

   Look and listen for examples of lively disagreement over the definitions of the following terms in contemporary argument:

   a. preemptive war
   b. faith-based initiatives
   c. gun control
   d. same-sex marriage
   e. terrorism

   Do these disagreements reflect the kind of social division Weaver suggested?

The Secrets of Gun Violence in America
Richard F. Corlin

Dr. Richard Corlin, president of the American Medical Association, presented this controversial persuasive speech in 2001 at the AMA's annual meeting. The speech is a model of argumentative persuasion in that it emphasizes appeals to the reasoning capacity of listeners yet makes full use of what Aristotle described as "all the available means of persuasion."

. . . I grew up in East Orange, New Jersey, in the 1940s and 1950s. My high school was a mosaic of racial and ethnic diversity—equal numbers of blacks and whites, some Puerto Ricans, and a few Asians. We'd fight among ourselves from time to time [but] nobody pulled out a gun—none of us had them and no one even thought of having one. The worst wound anyone had after one of those fights was a split lip or a black eye.

. . . Back then, no parents in that town of mostly lower-middle class blue collar workers had to worry that their children might get shot at school, in the park or on the front stoop at home. But then again, that was also a time when we thought of a Columbine as a desert flower, not a high school in Littleton, Colorado.

. . . Today, it's very different. Guns are so available and violence so commonplace that some doctors now see gunshot wounds every week—if not every day. It's as if guns have replaced fists as the playground weapon of choice. The kids certainly think so. In a nationwide poll taken in March after two students were shot to death at Santana High School near San Diego, almost half of the 500 high school students surveyed said it wouldn't be difficult for them to get a gun. And one in five high school boys said they had carried a weapon to school in the last twelve months. One in five. Frightening, isn't it?

. . . With the preponderance of weapons these days, it comes as no surprise that gun violence—both self-inflicted and against others—is now a serious public health crisis. No one can avoid its brutal and ugly presence. No one. Not physicians. Not the public. And most certainly—not the politicians—no matter how much they might want to.

Let me tell you about part of the problem. In the 1990s, the CDC [Centers for Disease Control] had a system in place for collecting data about the results of gun violence. But Congress took away its funding, thanks to heavy lobbying by the anti–gun control groups. You see, the gun lobby doesn't want gun violence addressed as a public health issue. Because that data would define the very public health crisis that these powerful interests don't want acknowledged. And they fear that such evidence-based data could be used to gain support to stop the violence. Which, of course, means talking about guns and the deaths and injuries associated with them.

We all know that violence of every kind is a pervasive threat to our society. And the greatest risk factor associated with that violence—is access to firearms. Because—there's no doubt about it—guns make the violence more violent and deadlier.

Now my speech today is not a polemic. It is not an attack on the politics or the profits or the personalities associated with guns in our society. It isn't even about gun control. I want to talk to you about the public health crisis itself—and how we can work to address it, in the same way we have worked to address other public health crises such as polio, tobacco, and drunk driving.

◄ In his opening Dr. Corlin builds ethos in a subtle way by suggesting that he came from humble beginnings. He also establishes a contrast between the more innocent past of his youth and the more dangerous present. This contrast sets up an important rhetorical move—his redefinition of gun violence as a "serious public health crisis."

◄ Here Dr. Corlin establishes his agenda, his specific purpose. Because any speech bearing on firearms

in America must inescapably be controversial, he must also establish what are not his motives. He further defines a role for his listeners: As doctors, they are scientists, and they must approach this health crisis as scientists. In American society, science is a positive culturetype and scientists enjoy a positive symbolic identity as truth-seekers.

In this section, Dr. Corlin ▶ makes effective use of statistical evidence and inductive reasoning, consistent with his call for a scientific approach to the issue. He also uses comparison and contrast to highlight the power of the facts he introduces.

In the sections that fol- ▶ low, Dr. Corlin may come close to contradicting his earlier promise not to deliver a polemic against the gun industry. And indeed, if gun violence is a serious health crisis, it's hard to see how he could avoid criticizing those who make guns so readily available and who resist efforts to regulate them.

At the AMA, we acknowledged the epidemic of gun violence when—in 1987—our House of Delegates first set policy on firearms. The House recognized the irrefutable truth that "uncontrolled ownership and use of fire-arms, especially handguns, is a serious threat to the public's health inasmuch as the weapons are one of the main causes of intentional and unintentional injuries and death." In 1993 and 1994, we resolved that the AMA would, among other actions, "support scientific research and objective discussion aimed at identifying causes of and solutions to the crime and violence problem."

Scientific research and objective discussion because we as physicians are—first and foremost—scientists. We need to look at the science of the subject, the data, and—if you will—the micro-data, before we make a diagnosis. Not until then can we agree upon the prognosis or decide upon a course of treatment.

First, let's go straight to the science that we do know. How does this disease present itself? Since 1962, more than a million Americans have died in firearm suicides, homicides, and unintentional injuries. In 1998 alone, 30,708 Americans died by gunfire:

- 17,424 in firearm suicides
- 12,102 in firearm homicides
- 866 in unintentional shootings

Also in 1998, more than 64,000 people were treated in emergency rooms for nonfatal firearm injuries.

This is a uniquely American epidemic. In the same year that more than 30,000 people were killed by guns in America, the number in Germany was 1,164; in Canada, it was 1,034; in Australia, 391; in England and Wales, 211; and in Japan, the number for the entire year was 83.

Next, let's look at how the disease spreads, what is its vector, or delivery system. To do that, we need to look at the gun market today. Where the hard, cold reality is—guns are more deadly than ever. Gun manufacturers—in the pursuit of technological innovation and profit—have steadily increased the lethality of firearms. The gun industry's need for new products and new models to stimulate markets that are already oversupplied with guns—has driven their push to innovate. Newer firearms mean more profits. With the American gun manufacturers producing more than 4.2 million new guns per year—and imports adding another 2.2 million annually—you'd think the market would be saturated.

But that's why they have to sell gun owners new guns for their collections—because guns rarely wear out. Hardly anyone here is driving their grandfather's 1952 Plymouth. But a lot of people probably have their grandfather's 1952 revolver. So gun manufacturers make guns that hold more rounds of ammunition, increase the power of that ammunition, and make guns smaller and easier to conceal.

These changes make guns better suited for crime, because they are easy to carry and more likely to kill or maim whether they are used intentionally or unintentionally. In fact, one of the most popular handgun types today is the so-called "pocket rocket": a palm-sized gun that is easy to conceal, has a large capacity for ammunition and comes in a high caliber.

The *Chicago Tribune* reported that the number of pocket rockets found at crime scenes nationwide almost tripled from 1995 to 1997. It was a pocket rocket in the hands of a self-proclaimed white supremacist that shot five children at the North Valley Jewish Community Center and killed a Filipino-American postal worker outside of Los Angeles in August of 1999.

Now, we don't regulate guns in America. We do regulate other dangerous products like cars and prescription drugs and tobacco and alcohol—but not guns. Gun sales information is not public. Gun manufacturers are exempt by federal law from the standard health and safety regulations that are applied to all other consumer products manufactured and sold in the United States.

No federal agency is allowed to exercise oversight over the gun industry to ensure consumer safety. In fact, no other consumer industry in the United States—not even the tobacco industry—has been allowed to so totally evade accountability for the harm their products cause to human beings. Just the gun industry.

In a similar pattern to the marketing of tobacco—which kills its best customers in the United States at a rate of 430,000 per year—the spread of gun-related injuries and death is especially tragic when it involves our children. Like young lungs and tar and nicotine—young minds are especially responsive to the deadliness of gun violence.

Lieutenant Colonel Dave Grossman, a West Point professor of psychology and military science, has documented how video games act as killing simulators, teaching our children not just to shoot—but to kill. Grossman, who calls himself an expert in "killology," cites as evidence the marksmanship of the two children, aged 11 and 13, in the Jonesboro, Arkansas, shootings in 1998. Both shooters were avid video game players. And just like in a video game—they fired off twenty-seven shots—and hit 15 people. Killing four of their fellow students—and a teacher. Such deadly accuracy is rare and hard to achieve—even by well-trained police and military marksmen.

I want you to imagine with me a computer game called "Puppy Shoot." In this game puppies run across the screen. Using a joystick, the game player aims a gun that shoots the puppies. The player is awarded one point for a flesh wound, three points for a body shot, and ten points for a head shot. Blood spurts out each time a puppy is hit—and brain tissue splatters all over whenever there's a head shot. The dead puppies pile up at the bottom of the screen. When the shooter gets to 1,000 points, he gets to exchange his pistol for an Uzi, and the point values go up.

If a game as disgusting as that were to be developed, every animal rights group in the country, along with a lot of other organizations, would protest, and there would be all sorts of attempts made to get the game taken off the market. Yet, if you just change puppies to people in the game I described, there are dozens of them already on the market—sold under such names as "Blood Bath," "Psycho Toxic," "Redneck Rampage," and "Soldier of Fortune." These games are not only doing a very good business—they are also supported by their own Web sites. Web sites that offer strategy tips, showing players how to get to hidden features like unlimited ammunition, access more weapons, and something called "first shot kill," which enables you to kill your opponent with a single shot.

We do not let the children who play these games drive because they are too young. We do not let them drink because they are too young. We do not let them smoke because they are too young. But we do let them be trained to be shooters at

Dr. Corlin's critique of the gun culture as it embeds itself in the lives of children is especially powerful. He uses authority and example to make his point and a striking analogy ("Puppy Shoot") to imprint it in the minds of listeners. His concrete and colorful language stimulates feeling as well as thought, engaging pathos in the service of logos. Note in particular how his use of parallel construction magnifies the permissiveness of the gun culture.

an age when they have not yet developed their impulse control and have none of the maturity and discipline to safely use the weapons they are playing with. Perhaps worst of all, they do this in an environment in which violence has no consequences. These kids shoot people for an hour, turn off the computer—then go down for dinner and do their homework.

We need to teach our children from the beginning that violence does have consequences—serious consequences—all the time. Gunfire kills ten children a day in America. In fact, the United States leads the world in the rate at which its children die from firearms. The CDC recently analyzed firearm-related deaths in twenty-six countries for children under the age of fifteen—and found that 86 percent of all those deaths—occurred in the United States.

If this was a virus—or a defective car seat or an undercooked hamburger—killing our children, there would be a massive uproar within a week. Instead, our capacity to feel a sense of national shame has been diminished by the pervasiveness and numbing effect of all this violence. . . .

Having created a vivid sense of the seriousness of the problem, Dr. Corlin turns to the question of action. What does he want listeners to do and not do? He calls for aggressive data collection concerning the issue, again making use of comparative statistics. He defines carefully the scope of such a research program, and uses argument by analogy—to the motor vehicle fatalities crisis—to suggest the feasibility and effectiveness of such research. He works to build listener confidence in the course of action he proposes.

The question remains, what are we—the physician community—going to do about it? I can tell you first what we're not going to do. We're not going to advocate changing or abolishing the Second Amendment to the Constitution. . . . Our mission is not to abolish all guns from the hands of our fellow citizens. We're not advocating any limitations on hunting or the legitimate use of long guns, or for that matter, any other specific item of gun control. And we won't even be keeping a scorecard of legislative victories against guns in Congress and in the statehouses.

Why not? Because all these well-intentioned efforts have been tried by good people—and they have not met with success. Instead, they have been met with a well-organized, aggressive protest against their efforts by powerful lobbies in Washington and at the state and community levels. We—the American Medical Association—are going to take a different route—not just calls for advocacy—but for diplomacy and for statesmanship and for research as well. And make no mistake about this: We will not be co-opted by either the rhetoric or the agendas of the public policy "left" or "right" in this national debate about the safety and health of our citizens.

One of the ways we will do this is—to help assemble the data. Current, consistent, credible data are at the heart of epidemiology. What we don't know about violence—and guns—is literally killing us. And yet, very little is spent on researching gun-related injuries and deaths.

A recent study shows that for every year of life lost to heart disease, we spend $441 on research. For every year of life lost to cancer, we spend $794 on research. Yet for every year of life lost to gun violence, we spend only $31 on research—less than the cost of a taxi ride here from the airport.

That's bad public policy. It's bad fiscal policy. And it certainly is bad medical policy. If we are to fight this epidemic of violence, the Centers for Disease Control must have the budget and the authority to gather the data we need. As I mentioned earlier, the CDC's National Center for Injury Prevention and Control researched the causes and prevention of many kinds of injuries. But in the mid-90s the gun lobby targeted the NCIPC—and scored a bull's eye when Congress eliminated its funding. It wasn't a lot of money—just $2.6 million—budget dust to the federal government. But it meant the difference between existence and extinction for that project.

Just think—gun injuries cost our nation $2.3 billion dollars in medical costs each year—yet some people think $2.6 million dollars is too much to spend on tracking them. Every dollar spent on this research has the potential to reduce medical costs by $885.

The CDC is intent on doing its job and is now heading up the planning for a National Violent Death Reporting System—coordinated and funded at the federal level—and collecting data at the state level. Because knowing more about the who, what, when, where, why, and how of violent homicides, suicides, and deaths—will help public health officials, law enforcement, and policymakers prevent unnecessary deaths.

We must further insist that such a system be expanded to cover data about non-fatal gunshot injuries so that we can prevent these as well. Such a system of data collection and analysis has already helped us address another national epidemic—motor vehicle fatalities. Prompting preventive measures like mandatory seat belt laws, air bags, improved highway signage, and better designed entry and exit ramps—not the confiscation of cars. The establishment of a National Violent Death and Injury Reporting System would help us establish similar preventive measures against violence. And help us fill in all the blanks about violent death and injury in America. Including such basics as:

■ How do kids with guns get their weapons?

■ Do trigger locks work?

■ What can we do to reduce accidental, self-inflicted gun injuries?

■ What are the warning signs of workplace or school shootings?

■ During which hours of the week and in what specific parts of town (down to individual blocks—not just neighborhoods) do the shootings occur?

■ Do we need to work with police departments to change patrolling patterns based on these data?

■ And finally, the realization that the answers to these questions are apt to be different from one town to the next.

Today, we can't answer these questions—because we are not allowed to collect the data. Collecting and considering the facts isn't a matter of opinion or politics, it's essential. It's a matter of working with other committed leaders to get the job done.

The good news is that we have HELP—the Handgun Epidemic Lowering Plan—with membership of 130 organizations including the AMA and, among others, the Rehabilitation Institute of Chicago, and the Minnesota Department of Health. We also have the Surgeon General's National Strategy for Suicide Prevention, released last month, which also supports the National Violent Death Reporting System.

We will not advocate any changes at all based on urban legend, anecdote or hunch. We will only base our conclusions on evidence-based data and facts. It's just good, common sense—the kind of solid epidemiology that has been brought to bear on other public health hazards—from Legionnaire's disease to food-borne illnesses to exposure to dioxin or DDT. Trustworthy science that can help us prevent harm before it happens. For, as we physicians know, prevention is usually the best cure.

One of the giants of American medicine, Dr. William Osler, proposed using preventive medicine against serious public health threats like malaria and yellow fever. And the tools he advocated—education, organization, and cooperation—sound like a pretty good definition of diplomacy to me. We will put these same tools to use in removing the threat of gun violence from our society.

As we have in the past, we have already sought the cooperation of the American Bar Association—and we are grateful that our invitation has been accepted. We will be working with the ABA on their Forum on Justice Improvements, taking place this October in Washington, D.C. The forum, set up by their Justice Initiatives Group, will focus on gun violence.

We are being advised by a panel of physicians and other experts, who have worked long and hard in tackling the many-headed monster of gun violence and its grisly outcomes. They have welcomed our involvement in this issue and look forward to a newly configured playing field with allies that command such clout as the ABA and the AMA.

People have told me that this is a dangerous path to follow. That I am crazy to do it. That I am putting our organization in jeopardy. They say we'll lose members. They say we'll be the target of smear campaigns. They say that the most extremist of the gun supporters will seek to destroy us. But I believe that this is a battle we cannot not take on.

While there are indeed risks—the far greater risk for the health of the public, for us in this room, and for the AMA, is to do nothing. We, as physicians, and as the American Medical Association, have an ethical and moral responsibility to do this—as our mission statement says—"to promote the science and art of medicine and the betterment of public health." If removing the scourge of gun violence isn't bettering the public health—what is?

As physicians, we are accustomed to doing what is right for our patients—and not worrying about our comfort, ease or popularity. Our goal is to help cure an epidemic, not to win a victory over some real or imagined political enemy. Anyone who helps us in this fight is an ally—anyone.

We don't pretend to have all the answers. Nor do we expect the solution to be quick—and we certainly don't expect it to be easy. In fact, I am certain that we will not reach the solution during my term as your president. But, together as the American Medical Association—guided by our stated mission—we recognize our obligation to contribute our voice, our effort, and our moral imperative to this battle. And we will.

Almost a century ago, in his book *Confessio Medici*, Stephen Paget, the British physician and author, referred to medicine as a divine vocation. This is part of what he said:

"Every year young people enter the medical profession . . . and they stick to it . . . not only from necessity, but from pride, honor, and conviction. And Heaven,

Dr. Corlin acknowledges ▶ the risks of his program for action but appeals to the morality of his listeners and to the mythos of their organization. As doctors, they are obligated to help their patients overcome illness, in this case, the epidemic of gun violence. He suggests even that this may be a divine mission. His listeners can use this sacred principle as the deductive premise, the warrant, that justifies their acceptance of his proposal.

sooner or later, lets them know what it thinks of them. This information comes quite as a surprise to them . . . that they were indeed called to be doctors. . . . Surely a diploma . . . obtained by hard work . . . cannot be a summons from Heaven. But it may be. For, if a doctor's life may not be a divine vocation, then no life is a vocation, and nothing is divine."

We are here today as the guardians of that divine vocation and as such are dedicated to do what is right, whether or not it is comfortable, whether or not it is easy, and whether or not it is popular. Stephen Paget, you can rest well tonight. Your divine vocation is in good hands. We will guard it well. We will live up to our mission—we will do what is right.

Thank you.

16 Persuasive Speaking: Process, Challenges, and Designs

This chapter will help you

- learn the types and functions of persuasive speaking
- understand the persuasive process
- adapt persuasive messages to different audiences
- select appropriate designs for your persuasive speeches

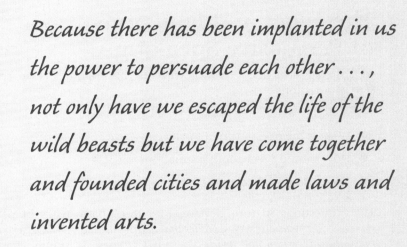

Because there has been implanted in us the power to persuade each other . . . , not only have we escaped the life of the wild beasts but we have come together and founded cities and made laws and invented arts.

—Isocrates

O kay," said practical Linda. "I think I understand proofs and how to build sound arguments. But tell me more about what persuasion can do in real-life situations. Tell me how it can influence people who may not want to change, or who are hard to change, or who are too comfortable to change. Tell me how to build effective persuasive speeches."

In Chapter 15, we put the emphasis on ethical persuasion, how to build arguments that respect rational listeners and that are free from fallacies. But it is one thing to know how to build sound, ethical arguments; it is quite another to use them effectively in speeches to specific audiences. In his recent book *The Assault on Reason,* Al Gore suggests that prolonged television exposure over the last fifty years has made people more passive recipients of messages and more often the targets of persuasive manipulation. People may have lost some of their capacity to generate effective persuasive messages, even when the situation cries out for ethical persuaders. It is important to recover this capacity for persuasion if people are to function as responsible citizens in a free society.

Therefore, practical Linda's questions are right on the money, and this chapter is written for her. We need to learn the types and functions of persuasive messages, how to engage the process of persuasion, how to adapt persuasion to different audiences and situations, and how to design successful persuasive messages. We need, in short, to learn how to make argumentative persuasion an effective force in the marketplace of contending ideas and interests.

The Types and Functions of Persuasive Speaking

*P*ersuasion helps us deal with the uncertainties reflected in the following questions:

- What is the true state of affairs?
- How should I feel about a situation?
- What should I do about it?

These questions in turn develop into three basic types of persuasive speaking: *speeches that focus on facts; speeches that address attitudes, beliefs, and values; and speeches that advocate action and policy.* These basic types, including what they do and how they work, are summarized in Figure 16.1.

Speeches That Focus on Facts

People argue constantly over what the true state of affairs was, is, and will be. Such arguments generate **speeches that focus on facts**. Uncertainty can surround questions of past, current, and future facts.

Past Facts. Did something actually happen? Did the celebrity commit murder? Did the CEO defraud her stockholders? Was the political candidate once actually convicted of marijuana possession? Persuaders argue questions of past facts before juries in courtrooms and on newspaper editorial pages as well as the public platform. Speeches concerning past facts try to shape the perceptions and memories of people and events. They will be successful if they do the following:

- **Present facts that confirm what they claim.** In the text of his speech "Global Burning," reprinted in Appendix B, note how Josh Logan uses charts

speeches that focus on facts Speeches designed to establish the validity of past or present information or to make predictions about what is likely to occur in the future.

Figure 16.1

The Work of Persuasive Speeches

Type	Function	Techniques
Speeches that focus on facts	Establish true state of affairs	Strengthen claims of past, present, and future fact by citing expert testimony and supporting factual and statistical evidence. Create lively pictures of the contested facts through narratives and images that lend them the aura of reality.
Speeches that address attitudes, beliefs, and values	Harmonize attitudes with beliefs, and beliefs with values	Reawaken appreciation for values through stories, examples, and vivid words. Inform listeners about situations that invite the application of these values, encouraging audience to form attitudes and beliefs that will make the values operational.
Speeches that advocate action and policy	Propose programs to remedy problems and put values into action	Show that the program of action will solve the problem by mentioning previous successes in similar situations. Prove that the plan is practical and workable. Picture audience enacting the plan of action. Show the consequences of acting and not acting. Visualize success.

and statistics to confirm the growth of greenhouse gases over the past thousand years.

■ **Present supporting testimony from respected expert sources.** To support his factual claims about global warming, Josh cites the "United Nations Intergovernmental Panel on Climate Change, reporting during the early part of this year." He describes this study as an "authoritative, thousand-page report, which correlates and tests the work of hundreds of environmental scientists from countries all around the globe."

Note the subtle implications as Josh establishes the authority of his source: The UNIPCC is *international*, not biased by national interests. Its work is *recent*, having reported "during the early part of this year." The work is *massive and exhaustive* ("thousand-page report"), and it escapes any possible *error or bias* that might result if it relied too heavily on any single scientist or program of research. Instead, it synthesizes "the work of hundreds of environmental scientists around the globe." Follow Josh's example as you introduce supporting sources into your persuasive speeches.

Speeches that focus on fact may need visual supporting materials to function as evidence for their claims.

■ **Re-create a dramatic, credible narrative of how events in a dispute may have happened.** The renowned Roman orator Cicero, who was also one of the greatest courtroom lawyers who ever lived, was superb in creating narratives of past events that seemed to establish their reality. For an especially spicy example, which also implies the moral depravity of many people in the Rome of several thousand years ago, see his forensic speech, *Pro Caelius.*[1]

Successful speeches concerning past facts develop a compelling case that their versions of events are correct and reliable.

Current Facts. What is actually going on? Is the new medicine a boon or a threat to humankind? Is a certain rogue nation developing weapons of mass destruction? Questions involving current facts are incredibly important to the fate of nations and individuals. On the basis of our perceptions of current facts, we develop value judgments and plans of action. Policymakers in the Bush administration decided that Iraq was vitally engaged in efforts to develop weapons of mass destruction. That perception of current facts confirmed their conclusion that Saddam Hussein was an intolerable threat to the security of the United States. That conclusion, in turn, led to their policy decision to invade Iraq and to remove Hussein from power. Clearly, persuasive speeches on current facts can start a chain reaction of important events.

At times, questions of past and current facts turn not on whether something happened or is happening, but on the *definition* of events. Yes, sexual activity occurred in the encounter between the sports star and the woman, but the sex was "consensual, not rape." A person has died, but the death resulted from "self-defense, not murder." Yes, Nation X possesses the alleged weapons, but they exist "for mass protection, not for mass destruction." To control the definitions of events is to control the feelings that people have about their meaning.

Future Facts. What will the future bring? And how should we plan for it? Persuasive speeches regarding future facts are **predictions** based on readings of the past and present. Therefore, they often depend on prior persuasion about past and current facts. Should we invest in a certain company? That depends on predictions of the company's future earning potential. One persuader may argue that the past record of earnings justifies a strong vote of confidence in the future. Another persuader may answer that much of this past success occurred under different leadership and that current management has yet to prove itself. The first offers an enthusiastic "buy" recommendation; the second advises caution. As a potential investor, you must consider these contending positions carefully, weighing the evidence and testing the soundness of the reasoning.

predictions Forecasts of what we can expect in the future, often based on projections of trends from past occurrences.

Current and future facts were a central issue for Josh Logan's speech, "Global Burning." Josh *says* that the question of whether global warming actually exists is no longer an issue. But the amount of time he spends discussing the problem suggests he suspects his listeners are uninformed, unconvinced, or in denial about the problem. Therefore, his challenge is to create a vivid sense of current facts in their minds. On the basis of this heightened appreciation of danger, he offers a grim prediction of the future unless these trends are altered by changes in the policies of nations and the practices of individuals. His companion speech, also reprinted in Appendix B, offers his recommendations for changes.

Speeches That Address Attitudes, Beliefs, and Values

The world of uncertainty in which we live often underlies **speeches that address attitudes, beliefs, and values**. As we noted in Chapter 5, at the heart of our *attitudes* are feelings we have developed toward certain subjects. For example, Cherie's intense dislike for "ethnic cleansing"—the removal and persecution of entire populations on the basis of religious faith or ethnic affiliation—represents an attitude. *Beliefs* represent what we know or think we know about the world. Cherie's belief that ethnic cleansing is widely practiced in the world gives urgency to her attitude about it. *Values* are underlying principles that support our attitudes and beliefs. Cherie's attitude and belief both rise out of her commitment to a world in which people tolerate, respect, and appreciate one another's differences.

Ideally, our attitudes, beliefs, and values should be in harmony, creating a coherent worldview. However, these elements are sometimes undeveloped, disconnected, or even opposed to one another, leaving that inner world fragmented or confused. When we become aware of this inner disarray, we experience what psychologists call **cognitive dissonance**, the discomfort we feel (or should feel) because of conflict among our attitudes, beliefs, and values. Persuasive speakers have the opportunity to create or restore consistency and harmony for us by recommending appropriate changes in attitude and belief. For example, if Cherie suspects that her listeners are indifferent to ethnic cleansing, even though they strongly value tolerance, she has the opportunity to encourage appropriate feelings and awareness about ethnic cleansing through an effective persuasive speech. By exposing her audience to evidence and powerful proofs, she can expand their moral universe and restore its harmony.[2]

In a similar case, Sam sensed a disconnection—even a contradiction—among the attitudes, beliefs, and values of some classmates toward capital punishment. He sensed that many of them intensely disliked those accused of violent crimes. On the basis of that attitude, they strongly favored capital punishment. Sam felt that this position was inconsistent with the religious values many of them held and with other values of fairness and respect for life. In his persuasive speech, Sam appealed to these values in an effort to change the attitudes of his listeners.

Because values are an integral part of our personality, deep changes in them can have a real impact on how we live. Therefore, we don't change values as readily as we change attitudes and beliefs. Speeches that attempt to change values may seem radical and extreme. For this reason, such speeches are rare, usually occurring only in desperate times and situations. In such moments, speakers often focus more on whether policies serve or betray basic values. The Great Depression of the 1930s, the civil rights struggle of the 1960s, the Vietnam War of the 1960s and 1970s, and the

---

speeches that address attitudes, beliefs, and values Speeches designed to modify these elements and help listeners find harmony among them.

cognitive dissonance The discomfort we feel because of conflict among our attitudes, beliefs, and values.

Iraqi conflict have all inspired persuasive speeches critical either of American values or of policies that relate to them.

Speeches That Advocate Action

Speeches that advocate action often build on earlier speeches that affirm facts or activate values. Therefore, in addition to bringing harmony to our inner world of attitudes, beliefs, and values, persuasive speeches can promote coherence between what we say and what we do. Persuasive speakers remind us that we should practice what we preach.

Such was the goal of Amanda Miller, who presented a powerful indictment of the Western Hemisphere Institute for Security Cooperation, better known as the "School of the Americas." Amanda argued that this institute, conducted for many years at Fort Benning, Georgia, under U.S. sponsorship, had been "implicated in gross human rights violations in Latin America." The school, she said, trained its students in "techniques for torture, false imprisonment, extortion, and intimidation" and had been "responsible for the deaths of many thousands of people and countless acts of terrorism." Amanda painted a vivid picture of the contradiction between American values and American actions, and she urged her listeners to "support the cause" of shutting down the Institute. In the process, they would be restoring coherence to the world of morality and action.

The actions proposed by such speeches can be simple and direct, or they can involve complex policy plans, depending on the nature of the problem. To meet the complex challenge of global warming, Josh Logan developed an elaborate solution that called for listeners' direct personal action as well as their political support for changes in governmental policy. On a less complex issue, Bonnie Marshall asked her listeners to act individually to ensure their right to die with dignity. She urged them to draw up a living will, to assign durable power of attorney to a trusted friend or family member, and to let their personal physicians know their wishes.

Speeches that advocate action encourage listeners to respond to a situation and put into effect the values that they profess.

When a speech advocates group action, the audience must see itself as having a common identity and purpose. As we noted in Chapter 12, the speaker can reinforce group identity by using inclusive pronouns (*we, our, us*), by telling stories that emphasize group achievements, and by referring to common heroes, opponents, or martyrs. Anna Aley used an effective appeal to group identity as she proposed specific actions:

> What can one student do to change the practices of numerous Manhattan landlords? Nothing, if that student is alone. But just think of what we could accomplish if we got all 13,600 off-campus students involved in this issue! Think what we could accomplish if we got even a fraction of those students involved!

By identifying and uniting them as victims of unscrupulous landlords, Anna encouraged her listeners to act as members of a group.

speeches that advocate action Speeches that encourage listeners to change their behavior either as individuals or as members of a group.

Speeches advocating action usually involve risk. Therefore, you must present good reasons to overcome your audience's natural caution. The consequences of acting and not acting must be clearly spelled out. Your plan must be practical and reasonable, and your listeners should be able to see themselves enacting it successfully.

The world of uncertainty in which we live is also a world of controversy. People often see the world differently, develop different value priorities, and therefore respond differently to proposals for action. It is not unusual to hear several competing points of view on the same subject.

As you persuade, you should justify your position and explain why you find other views less persuasive. This clash of ideas can be instructive, providing listeners with a richer sense of alternatives. It can help reveal weak spots in the opposing positions. This verbal "trial by fire" becomes a **debate** when opponents confront each other directly. As listeners witness and evaluate the clash of ideas, they may come closer to the truth of a situation. We talk more about debate strategies when we discuss the refutative design of persuasive speaking later in this chapter.

The Persuasive Process

*T*o function effectively as speakers and listeners, we must understand how persuasion works. William J. McGuire, professor of psychology at Yale University, suggested that successful persuasion is a process involving up to twelve phases.[3] For our purposes, these phases may be grouped into five stages: awareness, understanding, agreement, enactment, and integration (see Figure 16.2). Familiarity with these stages helps us see that persuasion is not an all-or-nothing proposition. A persuasive message can be successful if it moves people through the process toward a goal.

Awareness

The first stage in the persuasive process is **awareness**, knowing about a problem and paying attention to it. This phase is sometimes called *consciousness raising*. Informative speaking can build such awareness and prepare us for persuasion.[4] In her persuasive speech indicting the School of the Americas, Amanda Miller shocked her audience into awareness with her introduction:

> "If any government sponsors the outlaws and killers of innocents, they have become outlaws and murderers themselves, and they will take that lonely path at their own peril." President Bush spoke these words to the world, shortly after the attacks on the World Trade Towers, as he began the fight against terrorism.
>
> But we Americans have been training terrorists ourselves for many years right here in our own country, at a place known until just recently as the School of the Americas.

Creating awareness is especially important when people do not believe that there actually is a problem. For example, before advocates could change the way females were depicted in children's books, they had to convince listeners that

---

debate The clash of opposing ideas, evaluations, and policy proposals on a subject of concern.

awareness This first stage in the persuasive process includes knowing about a problem and paying attention to it.

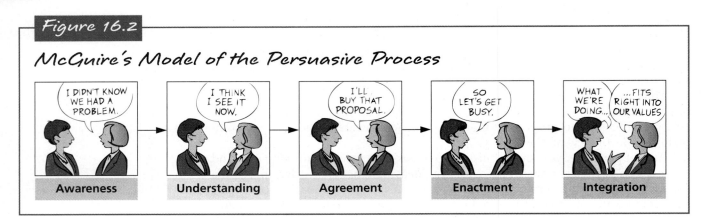

Figure 16.2

McGuire's Model of the Persuasive Process

| Awareness | Understanding | Agreement | Enactment | Integration |

always showing boys in active roles and girls in passive roles created a serious situation. They had to demonstrate that this imbalance could thwart the development of self-esteem or ambition in young girls.[5]

Beyond acquainting listeners with a problem, persuasive messages aimed at building awareness must demonstrate that the problem is important and show listeners how it affects them directly. Josh Logan's speech "Global Burning" had the task of raising awareness of the environmental threat posed by global warming. Persuasive speakers must raise such awareness before moving on to the next stage in the process.

Understanding

The second phase of the persuasive process is **understanding**. Listeners must grasp what you are telling them and know how to carry out your proposals. Amanda Miller encouraged understanding of her School of the Americas message by citing a number of examples:

> In El Salvador, the United Nations Truth Commission found that of twelve officers responsible for the massacre of nine hundred villagers at El Mozote, ten of them were graduates of the School of the Americas.
>
> I wish this were a solitary case. According to an Inter-American Commission on Human Rights, School of the Americas graduate Raphael Samundio Molina led a massacre at the Colombian Palace of Justice, and three years later was inducted into the School of the Americas hall of fame. In the same country, an International Human Rights Tribunal found that of two hundred and forty-six officers cited for various crimes, one hundred and five of them were School of the Americas graduates.
>
> Finally, the School has produced at least twelve Latin American dictators, in countries such as Peru, Bolivia, Argentina, and Ecuador. This is the distinguished record of the School of the Americas that we continue to fund with our taxpayer dollars.

To facilitate understanding, Anna Aley used an "inside-outside" approach in her persuasive speech. She took listeners inside the housing problem in

understanding This second phase in the persuasive process requires that listeners grasp the meaning of the speaker's message.

Manhattan, Kansas, by vividly describing her basement apartment. Then she took listeners outside the problem by showing them the total picture of substandard student housing in the city: the number of students involved and the causes of the problem. Ethical persuasion expands our understanding, demonstrating how some arguments are stronger than others and providing evidence to support a position.[6]

Finally, the audience must understand how to put the speaker's proposals into effect. In her persuasive speech, reprinted in Appendix B, Bonnie Marshall clearly spelled out the steps she wanted her listeners to take, numbering them as she presented them.

Agreement

The third stage in the persuasive process is **agreement**, the acceptance by listeners of your position. As they listen to you, audience members should go through a series of *affirmations*, such as: "He's right, this is a serious problem. . . . That's striking evidence; I didn't know about that. . . . I see how this can affect my life. . . . I've got to do something about this. . . . This plan makes sense. I believe it will work." These affirmations should build on each other, developing momentum toward agreement at the end of the speech. Any doubt, any hesitation over the validity of a claim or the soundness of evidence or the accuracy of reasoning, will weaken the process of agreement.

Speakers themselves become important models for agreement. When Amanda Miller stood to speak against the School of the Americas, audience members were surprised to see this previously mild-mannered person so powerfully committed to a position. "If Amanda is this passionate about it," some of them reasoned, "there must really be something wrong here." As she laid out her evidence, listeners were impressed by her research: "Amanda really knows what she's talking about," they concluded. As she painted vivid word-pictures of the abuse of human rights, her listeners shared her indignation. Her decisive gestures, emphatic voice, and eye contact all engaged her audience and convinced them that Amanda's cause truly deserved their agreement. In these ways, Amanda had provided them with a model for their own commitment to her cause. When you speak as a persuader, you must also become a model for what you are asking of listeners.

Agreement can range from small concessions to total acceptance. Lesser degrees of agreement could represent success, especially when listeners have to change their attitudes, beliefs, or values or risk a great deal by accepting your ideas. During the Vietnam War, we often heard classroom speeches attacking or defending our involvement in that conflict. Feelings about the war ran so high that just to have a speech listened to without interruption was an accomplishment. If a reluctant listener were to nod agreement or concede, "I guess you have a point," then one could truly claim victory.

Enactment

The fourth stage in the persuasive process is **enactment**. It is one thing to get listeners to accept what you say. It is quite another to get them to act on it. If you invite listeners to sign a petition, raise their hands, or voice agreement, you give them a way to enact agreement. When they enact their agreement, listeners make a

---

agreement The third stage in the persuasive process, which requires that listeners accept a speaker's recommendations and remember their reasons for doing so.

enactment The fourth stage of the persuasive process in which listeners take appropriate action as the result of agreement.

Persuasive speakers must often entice a reluctant audience to action, remove barriers to commitment and move listeners to participate.

commitment. The student speaker who mobilized his audience against a proposed tuition increase

- brought a petition to be signed.
- distributed the addresses of local legislators to contact.
- urged listeners to write letters to campus and local newspapers.

He channeled their agreement into constructive action.

Converting agreement to action may require the use of emotional appeals. Stirring stories and examples, vivid images, and colorful language can arouse sympathy. As she told the story of Harry Smith, who died an agonizing death because he had not signed a living will, Bonnie Marshall moved her listeners to act on behalf of themselves and their loved ones. Anna Aley's concluding story of her neighbor's accident helped motivate her audience to take action against substandard student housing. In an especially interesting use of narrative technique, Beth Tidmore asked her listeners to imagine themselves helping as volunteers for a Special Olympics weekend. As she told them the heartwarming story of what they would experience, she in effect invited them to transform this imaginative adventure into reality.

Integration

The final stage in the persuasive process is the **integration** of new commitments into the listeners' previous beliefs and values. For a persuasive speech to have lasting effect, listeners must see the connection between what you propose and their important values. Your ideas must fit comfortably within their belief system. As she presented her case for living wills, Bonnie Marshall anchored her appeals in the right to control one's own destiny. Anna Aley tied her attack on housing conditions to the values of fair treatment and safe living conditions. In the second of his two related persuasive speeches, "Cooling the World's Fever," Josh Logan urged listeners not just to accept his recommendations but to *become* the solution he advocated. He asked for total integration of attitudes, beliefs, values, and actions.

All of us seek consistency between our values and behaviors. For example, it would be inconsistent for us to march against substandard housing on Monday and contribute to a landlord's defense fund on Tuesday. This is why people sometimes seem to agree with a persuasive message and then change their minds. It dawns on them later that this new commitment means that they must rearrange other cherished beliefs and attitudes.

To avoid a delayed counterreaction, try to anticipate such problems as you design your speech. Don't attempt too much persuasion in a single message. Remember that dramatic change may require a campaign of persuasion in which

integration Final stage of the persuasive process in which listeners connect new attitudes and commitments with previous beliefs and values to ensure lasting change.

Speaker's Notes 16.1

Applying McGuire's Model to Persuasive Speeches

Here are some ways you might apply McGuire's model to your persuasive speeches:

1. Arouse attention with your introduction.

2. Relate your message to your listeners' interests and needs.

3. Define complex terms, use concrete examples, and organize your material clearly.

4. Emphasize facts, statistics, and expert testimony to gain acceptance of your position.

5. Present a clear plan of action.

6. Use vivid language to make your message memorable.

7. Ask listeners to make a public commitment.

8. Relate your proposal to your audience's values.

any single speech plays a small but vital role. Be content if you can move listeners just a small distance in a desirable direction.

To conclude, persuasion can be a complicated process. Any persuasive message must focus on the stage at which it can make its most effective contribution: raising awareness, building understanding, seeking agreement, encouraging action, or promoting the integration of beliefs, attitudes, and values. To determine where to focus your persuasive efforts, you must consider the challenges of the specific situation.

The Challenges of Persuasive Speaking

*T*he challenges that persuaders face range from confronting a reluctant audience to preparing messages that meet the most demanding ethical tests. As you plan a persuasive speech, you must consider the audience's position on the topic, how listeners might react to you as an advocate, and the situation in which the speech will be presented. The information and techniques concerning audience analysis that we introduced in Chapter 5 are crucial to success.

Begin preparing your speech by determining where your listeners stand on the issue. Do they hold differing attitudes about the topic, or are they united? If listeners are divided, you might hope to unify them around your position. If listeners are already united—but in opposition—you might try to divide them and attract some toward your position. Also consider how your listeners regard you as a speaker on the subject. If you do not have their respect, trust, and goodwill, use supporting testimony from sources they trust to enhance your ethos and improve your chances for success. Evaluating the relationships among the audience, the topic, and you as the speaker will point you to strategies for effective persuasion.

Enticing a Reluctant Audience to Listen

If you face an audience that opposes your position, you should be happy with small achievements, such as simply getting thoughtful attention. One way to handle a reluctant audience is to adopt a **co-active approach**, which seeks to bridge the

co-active approach A way of approaching reluctant audiences in which the speaker attempts to establish goodwill, emphasizes shared values, and sets modest goals for persuasion.

differences between you and your listeners.[7] The major steps in this approach are as follows:

1. *Establish identification and goodwill early in the speech.* Emphasize experiences, background, beliefs, and values that you share with listeners. Communication consultant Larry Tracy suggests you should try to meet with or telephone key members of your audience before you speak, establishing personal contact and seeking their advice. Then you should mention them favorably as you speak: "Nothing is so sweet to the human ear as the sound of his or her name, especially if it is mentioned positively before others."[8]

2. *Start with areas of agreement before you tackle areas of disagreement.* Otherwise, listeners may simply "turn off and tune out" before you have a chance to state your position.

3. *Emphasize explanation over argument.* By explaining your position more than refuting theirs, you avoid provoking defensive behavior and invite listeners to consider the merits of your position. As Tracy notes, "You cannot persuade people to change their mind; they must persuade themselves." Help them by providing the information they need.

4. *Cite authorities that the audience will respect and accept.* If you can find statements by such authorities that are favorable, you can gain "borrowed ethos" for your case. When he spoke before the Harvard Law School Forum, Charlton Heston, president of the National Rifle Association, attempted to disarm a chilly audience by citing his high regard for Dr. Martin Luther King Jr. and mentioning his attendance at King's "I Have a Dream" speech.[9]

5. *Set modest goals for change.* Don't try to push your audience too far, too fast. If reluctant listeners have listened to you—if you have raised their awareness and built a basis for understanding—you have accomplished a good deal.

6. *Make a multisided presentation that compares your position with others in a favorable way.* Show respect for opposing positions and understanding for why others might have supported them. Then reveal how these positions may not merit such support. Your attitude should be not to challenge listeners but to help them see the situation in a new light.

Let's consider how you might apply these steps in a speech against capital punishment before an audience of reluctant listeners. You could build identification by pointing out the values you share with the audience, such as, "We all respect human life. We all believe in fairness." It might also help to take an indirect approach in which you sketch your reasoning before you announce your purpose.

> What if I were to tell you that we are condoning unfairness, that we are condemning people to death simply because they are poor and cannot afford a good lawyer? What if I were to show you that we are sanctioning a model of violent behavior in our society that encourages more violence and more victims in return?

As you present evidence, cite authorities that your audience will respect and accept—for example, "FBI statistics tell us that if you are poor and black, you are three times more likely to be executed for the crime of murder."

Keep your goals modest. Ask only for a fair hearing. Be aware that reluctant listeners may not *want* to give you a fair hearing. Such listeners may distort your message so that it seems to fit what they already believe. Or they may simply deny or dismiss it, saying that it doesn't apply to them. Or they may discredit a source you cite in your speech, believing that any message that relies on *that* source cannot be taken seriously. Remember also that if you propose too much change, you may create a **boomerang effect** in which the audience reacts by opposing your position even more strongly.[10]

For all these reasons, to hope for a major change on the basis of any single persuasive effort is what McGuire calls the **great expectation fallacy**.[11] Be patient with reluctant listeners. Try to move them a step at a time in the direction you would like them to go. Give them information that may eventually change their minds:

> I know that many of you may not like to hear what I'm saying, but think about it. If capital punishment does not deter violent crime, if indeed it may encourage more violent crime, isn't it time we put capital punishment itself on trial?

Make a **multisided presentation**. Acknowledge the arguments in favor of capital punishment, showing that you respect and understand that position, even though you do not accept it.

> I know that the desire for revenge can be strong. If someone I love had been murdered, I would want the killer's life in return. I wouldn't care if capital punishment wasn't fair. I wouldn't care that it condones brutality. I would just want an eye for an eye. But that doesn't mean you should give it to me. It doesn't mean that society should base its policy on my anger and hatred.

A multisided approach helps make those you do persuade resistant to later counterattacks, because you show them how to answer such arguments. This is called an **inoculation effect**, because you "inject" your listeners with a milder form of the arguments they may hear later in more vehement forms from others.[12]

When you acknowledge and then refute arguments, you also help your credibility in two ways. First, you enhance your trustworthiness by showing respect for your opposition. You suggest that their position deserves consideration, even though you have a better option. Second, you enhance your competence by showing your knowledge of the opposing position—both of the reasons that explain why people may find it attractive and the reasons that reveal how it is defective.

After your speech, you should continue to show respect for the audience. Even if some listeners want to argue or heckle, keep your composure. To help you through such difficult moments, rehearse your speech before friends who pepper you with tough questions after your presentation. Try to anticipate these questions and prepare for them. Listeners may be impressed by your self-control and may be encouraged to rethink their position in light of your example.

There may be times when you and your audience are so far apart that you decide simply to acknowledge your disagreement. You might say that although you do not agree with some people, you respect their right to their position and hope that they will respect yours. Such openness may help establish the beginnings of trust. Even if audience members do not see you as an ally, they may at least start to see you as an honest, committed opponent and give you a hearing. If you emphasize that you will not be asking them to change their minds but simply to hear you out and to

---

boomerang effect A possible audience's reaction to a speech that advocates too much change.

great expectation fallacy The mistaken idea that major change can be accomplished by a single persuasive effort.

multisided presentation A speech in which the speaker's position is compared favorably to other positions.

Persuasive speeches often must arouse strong feelings to move people to action.

listen to the reasons you believe as you do, you may have your day in court. And you may slightly erode their disagreement!

We once heard a student speak against abortion to a class that was sharply divided on that issue. She began with a personal narrative, the story of how her mother had been given a drug that was later found to induce birth defects. Her mother was then faced with a decision on terminating the pregnancy. The student concluded by saying that if her mother had chosen the abortion option, she would not be there speaking to them that day. She paused, smiled, and said, "Although I know some of you may disagree with my views, I must say I am glad that you are here to listen and that I am here to speak. Think about it." If your reasons are compelling and your evidence is strong, you may soften the opposition and move waverers toward your position.

Do not worry if the change you want does not show up immediately. There often is a delayed reaction to persuasion, a **sleeper effect** in which change shows up only after listeners have had time to think about and integrate the message into their belief systems.[13] Even if no change is apparent, your message may sensitize your listeners to the issue and make them more receptive to future persuasion.[14]

Finally, there is one special technique that can sometimes create identification between speakers and reluctant, even hostile, audiences. That technique is laughter. The French philosopher Henri Bergson has pointed out that shared laughter can be the beginnings of community. The late Ann Richards, former governor of Texas, told a story that illustrates how this technique can work. After she had been elected early in her career to the Travis County Commission, Ann paid a visit to a road maintenance crew at their worksite. As she entered the crew office, Ann noticed a particularly ugly dog stretched across the front door. She proceeded to make her presentation to a group of men whose popular male boss she had just defeated. After her speech, no one responded when she asked for questions. As she told the story:

> Finally, just to break the ice and get them talking, I asked them about their dog. Texas men will always talk about their dogs. Nothing. No one said a word. There was some shuffling of feet. I thought, "There must be something unseemly about the dog's name, it's the only answer." I looked around the room and they were ducking my gaze. "Let me tell you," I said, "that I am the only child of a very rough-talking father. So don't be embarrassed about your language. I've either heard it or I can top it. So what's the dog's name?"
>
> An old hand in the back row with a big wide belt and big wide belt buckle sat up and said in a gravel bass, "Well, you're gonna find out sooner or later." He looked right at me. "Her name is Ann Richards." I laughed. And when I laughed they roared. And a little guy in the front row who was a lot younger and smarter than most, said in a wonderfully hopeful tenor, "But we call her Miss Ann!" From then on those guys and I were good friends.[15]

inoculation effect Preparing an audience for an opposing argument by answering it before listeners have been exposed to it.

sleeper effect A delayed reaction to persuasion.

Figure 16.3

Audience Considerations for Persuasive Speeches

Audience Type	Strategies
Reluctant to listen, possibly hostile	Seek common ground and establish good will. Quote sources they respect. Explain more than you argue. Limit your goals: try for a fair hearing, and ask little from listeners. Try to weaken their resistance. Acknowledge opposing arguments, but show tactfully why you have a different commitment.
Uncommitted, even uninterested	Provide information needed to arouse their interest and encourage their commitment. Connect their values with your position. Become a model of commitment for them to follow.
Friendly, but not yet committed	Remind them of what is at stake. Show them why action is necessary now. Give them clear instructions and help them take the first step. Picture them undertaking this action successfully.

Facing a reluctant audience is never easy. But you can't predict what new thoughts your speech might stimulate among listeners or what delayed positive reactions to it there might be. The various kinds of audiences you may confront and the major strategies for dealing with them are summarized in Figure 16.3.

Removing Barriers to Commitment

Listeners may be undecided because

- they need more information on an issue;
- they do not yet see the connection between the issue and their values and vital interests; and/or
- they may not feel certain they can trust your judgment.

Provide Needed Information.   Often, a missing fact or unanswered question stands in the way of commitment. "I know that many of you agree with me but are asking, 'How much will this cost?'" Anticipating reservations and supplying the necessary information can help move listeners toward your position.

Affirm and Apply Values.   Persuasive speeches that threaten audience values are not likely to be effective. You must show listeners that your proposal agrees with their principles. For example, if your listeners resist an educational program for the financially disadvantaged because they think that people ought to take care of themselves, you may have to show them that your program represents "a hand up, not a handout." Show them that your proposal will lead to other favorable outcomes, such as reductions in crime or unemployment.

As we noted earlier, values are resistant to change. If you can reason from the perspective of your listeners' values, using them as the basis for your arguments, you will encourage their commitment to your position.

Strengthen Your Credibility. When audiences hesitate because they question your credibility, you can "borrow ethos" by citing expert testimony. Call on sources that your listeners trust and respect. Uncommitted audiences will scrutinize both you and your arguments carefully. Reason with such listeners, leading them gradually and carefully to the conclusion you would like them to reach and providing supporting material each step of the way. Adopt a multisided approach in which you consider all options fairly to confirm your ethos as a trustworthy and competent speaker.

When addressing uncommitted listeners, don't overstate your case. Let your personal commitment be evident through your sincerity and conviction, but be careful about using overly strong appeals to guilt or fear. Such appeals might cause cautious listeners to resist, resent, and reject both you and your message.[16] Don't push uncommitted listeners too hard. Help them move in the desired direction, but let them take the final step themselves.

Moving from Attitude to Action

Just as opponents may be reluctant to listen, sympathetic audiences may be reluctant to act. It is one thing to agree with a speaker and quite another to accept the inconvenience and risk that action may require. Listeners may believe that the problem does not affect them personally. They may not know what they should do or how they should do it.[17]

To move people to action, you must give them reasons to act. You may have to arouse their enthusiasm, remind them of their beliefs, demonstrate the need for their involvement, present a clear plan of action, and make it easy for them to comply.

Spark Their Enthusiasm. To move people to action, you may have to arouse feelings. Announce your own commitment, and ask listeners to join you. Once people have voiced their commitment, they are more likely to follow through on it.[18] In her speech inviting listeners to become Special Olympics volunteers, Beth Tidmore anticipated that her listeners already agreed with her—*in principle*. But she had not yet won their hearts. Beth decided that the best way to arouse enthusiasm

Speaker's Notes 16.2

Encouraging Uncommitted Listeners

To remove barriers that may block your audience from committing to your position, try the following:

1. Provide missing information that will help listeners decide in your favor.

2. Show how your proposal meets listeners' needs and strengthens their values.

3. Borrow ethos by citing authorities they respect.

4. Do not overstate your case or rely too heavily on emotional appeals.

would be to help listeners imagine themselves enacting her proposal. Here is the way she approached this challenge:

> I've had so many great experiences, but these are hard to describe without overworking words like "fulfilling" and "rewarding." So I'm going to let you experience it for yourself. I want everybody to pack your bags—we're going to the Special Olympics summer games in Georgia! . . .
>
> Some of the athletes will be a little bit scared—it will be their first time away from home. All you've got to do is smile and reassure them that they'll have a great time—and you know they will. . . .
>
> Now we'll go to opening ceremonies. You walk onto a big field, and there's a huge tent, and they're playing loud music. All of the kids start dancing—they've never had such a moment! After that, each county marches by with a banner, and when your county comes by, you'd better be up and cheering.
>
> And then you hear something in the distance: a siren. Police cars and fire engines . . . and it's getting louder and louder. Soon it comes into the court-yard, and you catch your first glimpse of the Olympic torch runner. And as the runner gets closer, the Special Olympics theme blares louder on the speakers, and the sirens are just absolutely piercing. They make a final hand-off, and one chosen athlete will light the cauldron. And the flame goes up in this huge whoosh. It's just incredible. All of the athletes cheer, and they're so proud to be part of this moment. . . . Then the athletes get very serious, because they know it's time to take the Special Olympics oath. . . .
>
> After the games are over, you get to see them all on the podium, because everyone gets a medal or a ribbon, everyone places. And it's great, because they're smiling and they're so proud, and there are flashbulbs going off, and the anthem is playing. And they turn and they congratulate their fellow competitors. . . .
>
> Sunday is a sad time, because you have to send them back home to their parents. But when they run off the buses to show their parents their medals, and their parents walk up to you, their simplest "thank you" is a great reward. And in the end your vocal chords are shot, you have a second degree sunburn on most of your body. Your feet hurt, your back aches, and you feel like you could sleep for a week. But you just can't stop smiling, because you know that you've just taken part in something that is very special.

When Beth distributed commitment cards to her listeners at the end of her speech, it was clear that she had moved her listeners to action.

Revitalize Shared Beliefs and Values.   When speakers and audiences celebrate shared beliefs and values, the result is often a renewed sense of commitment. Such occasions may involve telling stories that resurrect heroes and heroines, giving shared beliefs new meaning.[19] At political conventions, Jefferson, Lincoln, Roosevelt, Kennedy, and Reagan are often invoked in speeches. These symbolic heroes can help bridge audience diversity by bringing different factions together.

In her speech, Beth Tidmore relied on and revitalized the values of benevolence, generosity, and magnanimity—those large-hearted virtues that come into play when we reach out to those who do not share all of our blessings. Beth's narrative did not appeal directly and explicitly to such values—she simply assumed that they already existed in those who would respond to her story.

Demonstrate the Need for Involvement. Show your listeners how the quality of their lives depends on action, and demonstrate that the results will be satisfying. It often helps if you can associate the change with a vision of the future. In his final speech, Martin Luther King Jr. said, "I may not get there with you, but I can see the Promised Land." King's vision of the Promised Land helped justify the sacrifice called for in his plan of action.

Beth Tidmore's speech implied the need for listener involvement. If listeners did not show up to fill the roles she had described for them, the promise of the story would remain unfulfilled.

Present a Clear Plan of Action. Listeners may exaggerate the difficulty of enacting a proposal or insist that it is impossible. To overcome such resistance, tell them how others have been successful using the same approach. Develop examples or narratives that show them completing the project successfully. Stress that "we can do it, and this is how we can do it." A speaker urging classmates to defeat a proposed tuition raise said:

> How many of you are ready to help defeat this plan to raise tuition? Good! I see your heads nodding. Now, if you're willing to sign this petition, hold up your hands. Good again! Now, I'm going to pass around this petition, and I want each of you to sign it. If we act together, we can make a difference.

Be Specific in Your Instructions and Make It Easy to Comply. Your plan must show listeners what to do and how to do it. Instead of simply urging listeners to write their congressional representatives, provide them with addresses and telephone numbers, a petition to sign, or preprinted and addressed postcards to complete and return. Beth Tidmore passed out information and cards at the end of her speech to help listeners confirm their commitment.

The Challenge of Ethical Persuasion

Ours is a skeptical and cynical age, made more so by large-scale abuses of communication ethics. Advertisers assure us that their products will make us sexier or richer, often with no foundation in fact. Persuasive messages disguised as information appear in "infomercials" on television. They try to slip into our minds under the radar of critical listening. So-called "think tanks" try to bribe experts into supporting their points of view, thereby contaminating a major source of responsible knowledge.[20] Public officials may present suspicious statistics, make dubious

Speaker's Notes 16.3

Moving People to Action

To move listeners to action, follow these guidelines:

1. Remind listeners of what is at stake.

2. Provide a clear plan of action.

3. Use examples and stories as models for action.

4. Visualize the consequences of acting and not acting.

5. Demonstrate that you practice what you preach.

6. Ask for public commitments.

7. Make it easy for listeners to take the first step.

InterConnections.
LearnMore 16.1

Persuasion

Influence at Work

www.workingpsychology.com/intro.html

> Provides an in-depth but readable introduction to social influence, persuasion, and propaganda; an outstanding Web site developed by Kelton Rhoades, Ph.D., consultant and lecturer at the University of Southern California and the Annenberg School for Communication.

Links to Social Psychology Topics

www.socialpsychology.org/social.htm

> Comprehensive directory that links the study of social psychology to persuasive communication in a number of specific applications. See especially the section on social influence.

Propaganda Analysis

www.propagandacritic.com/

> A discussion of propaganda techniques, with examples from World War II as well as more contemporary applications; prepared by Aaron Delwiche, assistant professor in the Department of Communication, Trinity University.

denials, or dance around questions they really don't want to answer. Little wonder that many people have lost trust in society's major sources of communication.

As a consumer of persuasive messages, you can at least partially protect yourself by applying the thinking skills we discussed in Chapter 4. As a producer of persuasive messages, you can help counter this trend toward unethical communication. Keep three simple questions in mind as you prepare your persuasive speech:[21]

- What is my ethical responsibility to my audience?

- Could I publicly defend the ethics of my message?

- What does this message say about my character?

These questions should light your way along the path of ethical persuasion.

As we noted in Chapter 1, an ethical speech is based fundamentally on respect for the audience, responsible knowledge of the topic, and concern for the consequences of your words.

Ethics Alert! 16.1

Guidelines for Ethical Persuasion

To earn a reputation as an ethical persuader, follow these guidelines:

1. Avoid name calling: Attack problems, proposals, and ideas—not people.

2. Be open about your personal interest.

3. Don't adapt to the point of compromising your convictions.

4. Argue from responsible knowledge.

5. Don't try to pass off opinions as facts.

6. Don't use inflammatory language to hide a lack of evidence.

7. Be sure your proposal is in the best interest of your audience.

8. Remember, words can hurt.

Designs for Persuasive Speeches

*E*vidence, proof, and patterns of reasoning are not effective until they are framed into a design for your speech. Figure 16.4 provides guidelines on when to use these designs.

Many of the designs used for informative speeches are also appropriate for persuasive speeches. Josh Logan used a categorical design when he proposed three categories of technological improvements in his plan to solve global warming. In addition, the sequential design can outline the steps in a plan of action to make it seem practical. The comparative design works well for speeches that concentrate on developing proposals for action. Following this pattern, you might compare the superior features of your proposal with less adequate features of competing proposals.

Three designs, however, are especially suited to persuasive speeches: the problem–solution design, the motivated sequence design, and the refutative design.

Problem–Solution Design

The **problem–solution design** first convinces listeners that there is a problem and then shows them how to deal with it. The solution can involve changing attitudes and beliefs or taking action.

Figure 16.4

Selecting Persuasive Speech Designs

Design	Use When
Categorical	• Your topic invites thinking in familiar patterns, such as proving a plan will be safe, inexpensive, and effective. Can be used to change attitudes or to urge action.
Comparison/ Contrast	• You want to demonstrate why your proposal is superior to another. Especially good for speeches in which you contend with opposing views.
Sequential	• Your speech contains a plan of action that must be carried out in specific order.
Problem-Solution	• Your topic presents a problem that needs to be solved and a solution that will solve it. Good for speeches involving attitudes and urging action.
Motivated-Sequence	• Your topic calls for action as the final phase of a five-step process that also involves, in order, arousing attention, demonstrating need, satisfying need, picturing the results, and calling for action.
Refutative	• You must answer strong opposition on a topic before you can establish your position. The opposing claims become main points for development. Attack weakest points first and avoid personal attacks.

---

problem–solution design A persuasive speech pattern in which listeners are first persuaded that they have a problem and then are shown how to solve it.

It is sometimes hard to convince listeners that a problem exists or that it is serious. People have an unfortunate tendency to ignore problems until they reach a critical stage. You can counteract this tendency by vividly depicting the crisis that will surely occur unless your audience makes a change.

As you focus on the problem, use substantive evidence and combinations of proof to demonstrate that a serious problem exists. Reason from the reality of the situation by using presentation aids, dramatic examples, and colorful imagery to make the problem loom large in the minds of listeners. Reasoning from principle can help justify a solution ("Because better education means a better future for our children, we must pass this tax increase to upgrade the school system"). Analogical reasoning can help convince listeners that a proposed solution will work ("Here's how New Yorkers solved this problem. . . .").

When a problem is complex, you must examine its causes. Doing so enables you to argue that your solution will work because it deals with the underlying causes.

A problem–solution speech opposing a tuition increase at your university might build on the following general design:

Thesis statement: We must defeat the proposed tuition increase.

I. Problem: The proposal to raise tuition is a bad idea!

    A. The increase will create hardships for many students.

        1. Many current students will have to drop out.

        2. New students will be discouraged from enrolling.

    B. The increase will create additional problems for the university and the community.

        1. Decreased attendance means decreased revenue.

        2. Decreased revenue will reduce the university's community services.

        3. Reduced service will mean reduced support from contributors.

        4. The ironic result will be: another tuition increase!

II. Solution: Defeat the proposal to raise tuition.

    A. Sign our petition against the tuition increase.

    B. Write letters to your state legislators.

    C. Write a letter to our local newspaper.

    D. Attend our campus rally next Wednesday and bring your marching shoes!

When the problem can be identified clearly and the solution is concrete and simple, the problem–solution design works well in persuasive speeches.

As you are planning a problem–solution speech, think of **stock issues**, those generic questions that a thoughtful person will ask before agreeing to a change in policies or procedures.[22] Be certain that your speech can answer these questions to the satisfaction of such listeners:

I. Is there a significant problem?

    A. How did the problem originate?

    B. What caused the problem?

stock issues The major general questions a reasonable person would ask before agreeing to a change in policies or procedures.

C. How widespread is the problem?

D. How long has the problem persisted?

E. What harms are associated with the problem?

F. Will these harms continue and grow unless there is change?

II. What is the solution to this problem?

A. Will the solution actually solve the problem?

B. Is the solution practical?

C. Would the cost of the solution be reasonable?

D. Might there be other consequences to the solution?

III. Who will put the solution into effect?

A. Are these people responsible and competent?

B. What role might listeners play?[23]

Motivated Sequence Design

The **motivated sequence design**, first introduced by Professor Alan Monroe in 1935, offers a practical, step-by-step approach when speakers wish to move from the awareness through the enactment phases of the persuasive process in a single speech.[24] The design offers five steps to persuasive success:

1. *Arouse attention.* As in any speech, you begin by stimulating interest in your subject. Vivid stories or examples, surprising claims, striking facts and statistics, eloquent statements from admired speakers—all can arouse the interest of your listeners.

2. *Demonstrate a need.* Show your listeners that the situation you want to change is urgent. Arrange evidence so that it builds in intensity and taps into audience motivations to help listeners see what they have to win and lose with regard to your proposal. By the end of this demonstration, listeners should be eager to hear your ideas for change.

3. *Satisfy the need.* Present a way to satisfy the need you have demonstrated. Set out a clear plan of action and explain how it will work. Show how this plan agrees with audience principles and values. Offer examples that show how your plan has already worked successfully in other situations.

4. *Visualize the results.* Paint verbal pictures that illustrate the positive results listeners can expect. Show them how their lives will be better when they have enacted your plan. A dramatic picture of the future can help overcome resistance to action. You could also paint a picture of what life will be like if listeners don't enact your suggestions. Place these positive and negative verbal pictures side by side to strengthen their impact through contrast.

5. *Call for action.* Your call for action may be a challenge, an appeal, or a statement of personal commitment. The call for action should be short and to the point. Give your listeners something specific that they can do right away. If you can get them to take the first step, the next will come more easily.

motivated sequence design A persuasive speech design that proceeds by arousing attention, demonstrating a need, satisfying the need, visualizing results, and calling for action.

In the following, summarized version of a persuasive speech, we can see how the motivated sequence design works:

1. *Arouse attention:* Have you ever dreamed about being a hero or a heroine? Have you ever wished you could do something that would really make a difference in our world? Well, I'm here to show you how you can by investing only three hours a week.

2. *Demonstrate a need* Our community needs volunteers to help children who are lonely and neglected. Big Sisters and Big Brothers of Omaha have a program for these children, but it takes people to make the program work. Last year they had forty-eight student volunteers. This year only thirty have signed up to help. They need at least thirty more. They need you.

3. *Satisfy the need* Volunteering to be a big brother or a big sister will help keep this vital program going. It will also make you a hero or heroine in the eyes of a child.

4. *Visualize the results* Last year I worked with ten-year-old Kevin two afternoons a week. He needed help with his homework because his grades were just barely passing. But more than school help, he needed someone who cared about him. The first six weeks, his grades went from D's to C's, and I took him to a basketball game. The next six weeks, his grades went up again, and I took him to a movie. This year Kevin is doing well in school. He's making B's and above in all his courses, but we still meet and work together because I couldn't bear not to see him. I guess this is a small contribution to humankind, but not to Kevin. When I look in his eyes, I see a better reflection of myself. Put yourself in my place. There is a Kevin needing you and waiting for you.

5. *Call for action* Won't you make the commitment to become one of the heroines or heroes of our community? Just one or two afternoons a week can make a difference in the life of a child and in our own future. The pay is not good—nothing!—but the rewards are enormous. I've got the applications with me. Let me sign you up now!

The motivated sequence design has helped generations of persuasive speakers achieve success. To use it, first determine where your listeners stand on the issue you wish to discuss; then concentrate on the steps that will carry persuasion forward. For example, if you are speaking to an audience that is already convinced of the need for a change but lacks a plan to make it work, you should spend more time on step 3, "Satisfy the need." However, if you are facing an audience that questions the need, your emphasis should be on step 2, "Demonstrate a need."

Refutative Design

The **refutative design** is appropriate when you need to discredit opposing views. In this design, the speaker raises doubt about a competing position by revealing its inconsistencies and weaknesses. The point of attack may be illogical reasoning, flimsy evidence, self-interest, or hidden agendas. However, you should avoid personal attacks unless credibility issues are central and inescapable. Above all, be fair.

Inductive reasoning from reality can be especially useful in refutative speeches. Such speeches often criticize specific weaknesses in evidence or proof, arguing that opponents have presented a distorted, flawed, or incomplete picture of reality.

There are five steps in developing an effective refutation. These five steps should be followed in sequence for each point you plan to refute.

1. State the point you are going to refute and explain why it is important.

2. Tell the audience how you are going to refute this point.

3. Present your evidence, using facts and figures, examples, and testimony. Cite sources and authorities that the audience will accept as competent and credible.

4. Spell out the conclusion for the audience. Do not assume that listeners will figure out what the evidence means. Tell them directly.

5. Explain the significance of your refutation—show how it discredits or damages the opposing position.

See if you can identify each step in this pattern in the following refutation of an argument opposing sex education in public high schools:

> Our well-intentioned friends would have you believe, and this is their biggest concern, that birth-control information increases teenage sexual activity. I want to share with you some statistical evidence that contradicts this contention—a contention that is simply not supported by the facts.
>
> The latest study on this issue by the Department of Health, Education, and Welfare compared sexual activity rates in sixty high schools across the United States—thirty with sex education programs and thirty without. Their findings show that there are no significant differences in sexual activity rates between these two groups of schools.
>
> Therefore, the argument that access to birth-control information through sex education programs increases sexual activity simply does not hold water. That's typical of the attack on sex education in the schools—to borrow a line from Shakespeare, it's a lot of "sound and fury, signifying nothing."

You can strengthen this design if you follow your refutation by proving a similar point of your own, thus balancing the negative refutation with a positive demonstration. The result gives the audience an alternative belief to substitute for the one you have refuted. Use the same five-step sequence to support your position. For example, you might follow the preceding refutation with the following demonstration:

refutative design A persuasive speech design in which the speaker tries to raise doubts about, damage, or destroy an opposing position.

I'm not going to try to tell you that birth-control information reduces sexual activity. But I want to tell you what it does reduce. It reduces teenage pregnancy. There is reliable evidence that fewer girls become pregnant in high schools with sex education programs. The same study conducted by Health, Education, and Welfare demonstrated that in high schools with sex education programs, the pregnancy rate dropped from one out of every sixty female students to one out of ninety within two years of the program's going into effect.

Therefore, sex education is a good program. It attacks a devastating social problem—the epidemic of children having children.

Any program that reduces unwanted teenage pregnancy is valuable—valuable to the young women involved, valuable to society. We all pay in so many ways for this personal and social tragedy—we should all support a program that works to reduce it. And we should reject the irrational voices that reject the program.

Combinations of designs often work well in persuasive speeches. Amanda Miller's speech urging the close of the School of the Americas developed primarily in a problem–solution pattern, with the school itself constituting the problem and legislative proposals to close it providing the solution. But as she depicted what a serious problem the school had become, Amanda found it necessary to answer those who continued to defend it. In this section of her speech, she developed a refutative pattern within the larger problem–solution design:

Those who argue in favor of the School claim that for many it is their only source of military education. But what kind of education are we providing?

I've already shown you what the textbooks teach—and that does not fit my idea of education. The School began as a line of defense against the U.S.S.R. in the Cold War. And with the Cold War long since completed, I can see little reason to continue spending millions of dollars each year funding a school that produces such negative results. That money might better be spent on education, or health care, or the environment.

A second argument in favor of the School is that the techniques taught are necessary for "self-defense" against civil wars. But what kinds of selves are these people defending? Are they themselves civil? In 1993, an International Human Rights Tribunal revealed that over one hundred School of the Americas graduates had committed war crimes. Among these crimes were heading the concentration camps in Villa Grimaldi in Chile, organizing the Ocosingo Massacre in Mexico, and participating in drug trafficking and assassinations. How exactly do these activities qualify as "self-defense," in any legitimate sense of the word?

Having completed the refutative part of her speech, Amanda was ready to move on to her solution.

In Summary

The Types and Functions of Persuasive Speaking. Persuasion helps listeners resolve uncertainties surrounding the true state of affairs, how they should feel about these things, and what they ought to do about them. Accordingly, the three basic types of persuasive speaking are speeches that focus on facts, speeches that address attitudes, beliefs, and values, and speeches that advocate action.

Speeches that focus on facts concern questions of past fact (whether something actually occurred), current fact (what is actually going on), and future fact (what is likely to occur). Speeches that address attitudes and values strive to help listeners find harmony among these elements. Speeches that advocate action encourage listeners to act as individuals or as members of a group to respond to the reality of a situation and to put into effect the values they profess. Debates occur when competing proposals for action and policy clash directly.

When persuasion is successful, people listen, learn, agree, and change as a result of what they hear. These behaviors parallel McGuire's categories of awareness, understanding, agreement, enactment, and integration of persuasive material. Awareness suggests that we know of a problem and that it commands our serious attention. Understanding implies that we can see the connection between the problem and our lives and that we know how to carry out the speaker's proposals. Agreement implies our acceptance of a speaker's interpretations and recommendations. Enactment suggests our commitment and readiness to carry out the speaker's proposals. Integration involves consolidating the new attitudes and commitments into our overall belief and value system.

The Challenges of Persuasion. Persuading others can pose many challenges. You may have to entice a reluctant audience to listen, remove barriers that block commitment, and move listeners from agreement to action. In any of these situations, you must be scrupulously ethical.

To encourage reluctant listeners, use a co-active approach that seeks to bridge differences and to build identification. Avoid the great expectation fallacy, which asks for more change than one could reasonably expect after a single speech. Make a multisided presentation in which you acknowledge opposing positions in order to refute them.

Remove barriers to commitment by providing vital information, pointing out the relevance to listeners' lives, and building credibility. To move partisan listeners from agreement to action, use vivid language and examples to bring abstract principles to life and to revitalize shared beliefs and values. You should declare your own commitment to encourage the commitment of others and make it easy for listeners to take the first step into involvement.

To be an ethical persuader, be sure that your messages are based on respect for the audience, responsible knowledge of the topic, and concern for the consequences of your words.

Designs for Persuasive Speaking. Three designs in particular serve the needs of persuasive speaking. In a problem–solution design, you must first convince the audience that a problem exists and then advance a solution that corrects it. The motivated sequence design moves from the awareness through the enactment phases of the persuasive process in a single speech. In the refutative design, you state the point you intend to refute, tell how you will refute it, present your evidence, draw a conclusion, and explain the significance of the refutation.

Explore and Apply the Ideas in This Chapter

1. The letters-to-the editor section of the Sunday newspaper is often a rich source for the study of persuasive material. Using a recent Sunday paper, analyze the persuasion attempted in these letters. Which do you think are most and least effective and why?

2. The speech on slum housing that appears at the end of this chapter was prepared for a student audience at Kansas State University. What, if any, changes might you suggest in this speech if it were to be presented to a luncheon meeting of realtors in Manhattan, Kansas? Why?

3. Are there ever times when a speaker should give up trying to persuade a hostile audience and simply confront listeners directly with the position they appear to oppose? Why would a speaker bother to do this? Might speaker and audience gain anything from such a confrontation? Look for an example of such a speech. Do you agree with the strategy used in it? Discuss in class.

4. Apply the stock issues questions to Anna Aley's persuasive speech reprinted here. Does Anna's speech stand up to the challenge of such questions? Does she answer them satisfactorily?

5. Select a controversial subject and summarize the approach you might make in adapting a speech on this topic to

   a. an uncommitted audience.
   b. an audience in agreement.
   c. a reluctant audience.

Discuss and explain these differences in approaches.

We Don't Have to Live in Slums
Anna Aley

Anna Aley was a student as Kansas State University when she presented this persuasive speech. It is noteworthy for its vivid language; its effective use of supporting materials, especially narrative; and the way in which it focuses listeners on a program of action.

Anna's speech follows a problem–solution design. The barrier she had to overcome was the lack of audience awareness of a problem right under their noses. She creates this awareness and engages her listeners by her use of vivid examples drawn from personal experience.

Slumlords—you'd expect them in New York or Chicago, but in Manhattan, Kansas? You'd better believe there are slumlords in Manhattan, and they pose a direct threat to you if you ever plan to rent an off-campus apartment.

I know about slumlords; I rented a basement apartment from one last semester. I guess I first suspected something was wrong when I discovered dead roaches in the refrigerator. I definitely knew something was wrong when I discovered the leaks: the one in the bathroom that kept the bathroom carpet constantly soggy and molding and the one in the kitchen that allowed water from the upstairs neighbor's bathroom to seep into the kitchen cabinets and collect in my dishes.

Then there were the serious problems. The hot water heater and furnace were connected improperly and posed a fire hazard. They were situated next to the only exit. There was no smoke detector or fire extinguisher and no emergency way out—the windows were too small for escape. I was living in an accident waiting to happen—and paying for it.

The worst thing about my ordeal was that I was not an isolated instance; many Kansas State students are living in unsafe housing and paying for it, not only with their money, but their happiness, their grades, their health, and their safety.

Anna uses statistical evidence to convince her listeners that the problem she mentions is not isolated: It may also involve them and their friends. She reasons carefully from this evidence to paint the seriousness of the problem, as she depicts students as victims of unscrupulous landlords.

We can't be sure how many students are living in substandard housing, housing that does not meet the code specifications required of rental property. We can be sure, however, that a large number of Kansas State students are at risk of being caught in the same situation I was. According to the registrar, approximately 17,800 students are attending Kansas State this semester. Housing claims that 4,200 live in the dorms. This means that approximately 13,600 students live off-campus. Some live in fraternities or sororities, some live at home, but most live in off-campus apartments, as I do.

Many of these 13,600 students share traits that make them likely to settle for substandard housing. For example, many students want to live close to campus. If you've ever driven through the surrounding neighborhoods, you know that much of the available housing is in older houses, houses that were never meant to be divided into separate rental units. Students are also often limited in the amount they can pay for rent; some landlords, such as mine, will use low rent as an excuse not to fix anything and to let the apartment deteriorate. Most importantly, many students are young and, consequently, naive when it comes to selecting an apartment. They don't know the housing codes; but even if they did, they don't know how to check to make sure the apartment is in compliance. Let's face it—how many of us know how to check a hot water heater to make sure it's connected properly?

Adding to the problem of the number of students willing to settle for substandard housing is the number of landlords willing to supply it. Currently, the Consumer Relations Board here at Kansas State has on file student complaints against approximately one hundred landlords. There are surely complaints against many more that have never been formally reported.

There are two main causes of the substandard student housing problem. The first—and most significant—is the simple fact that it is possible for a landlord to lease an apartment that does not meet housing code requirements. The Manhattan Housing Code Inspector will evaluate an apartment, but only after the tenant has given the landlord a written complaint and the landlord has had fourteen days to remedy the situation. In other words, the way things are now, the only way the Housing Code Inspector can evaluate an apartment to see if it's safe to be lived in is if someone has been living in it for at least two weeks!

A second cause of the problem is the fact that campus services designed to help students avoid substandard housing are not well known. The Consumer Relations Board here at Kansas State can help students inspect apartments for safety before they sign a lease, it can provide students with vital information on their rights as tenants, and it can mediate in landlord–tenant disputes. The problem is, many people don't know these services exist. The Consumer Relations Board is not listed in the university catalogue; it is not mentioned in any of the admissions literature. The only places it is mentioned are in alphabetically organized references such as the phone book, but you have to already know it exists to look it up! The Consumer Relations Board does receive money for advertising from the student senate, but it is only enough to run a little two-by-three-inch ad once every month. That is not large enough or frequent enough to be noticed by many who could use these services.

Having depicted the dimensions of the problem, Anna moves to identify its causes. She is following a design that moves from depicting the problem to explaining its causes to proposing a solution.

It's clear that we have a problem, but what may not seem so clear is what we can do about it. After all, what can one student do to change the practices of numerous Manhattan landlords? Nothing, if that student is alone. But just think of what we could accomplish if we got all 13,600 off-campus students involved in this issue! Think what we could accomplish if we got even a fraction of those students involved! This is what Wade Whitmer, director of the Consumer Relations Board, is attempting to do. He is reorganizing the Off-Campus Association in an effort to pass a city ordinance requiring landlords to have their apartments inspected for safety before those apartments can be rented out. The Manhattan code inspector has already tried to get just such an ordinance passed, but the only people who showed up at the public forums were known slumlords, who obviously weren't in favor of the proposed ordinance. No one showed up to argue in favor of the ordinance, so the city commissioners figured that no one wanted it and voted it down. If we can get the Off-Campus Association organized and involved, however, the commissioners will see that someone does want the ordinance, and they will be more likely to pass it the next time it is proposed. You can do a great service to your fellow students—and to yourself—by joining the Off-Campus Association.

Anna issues a stirring appeal for action. She makes a convincing case for joining the Off-Campus Association, but she needed to have membership forms ready to distribute and a petition for listeners to sign.

A second thing you can do to help ensure that no more Kansas State students have to go through what I did is sign my petition asking the student senate to increase the Consumer Relations Board's advertising budget. Let's face it—a service cannot do anybody any good if no one knows about it. The Consumer Relations Board's services are simply too valuable to let go to waste.

An important thing to remember about substandard housing is that it is not only distasteful, it is dangerous. In the end, I was lucky. I got out of my apartment with little more than bad memories. My upstairs neighbor was not so lucky. The main problem with his apartment was that the electrical wiring was done improperly; there were too many outlets for too few circuits, so the fuses were always blowing. One day last November, Jack was at home when a fuse blew—as usual. And, as usual, he went to the fuse box to flip the switch back on. When he touched the switch, it delivered such a shock that it literally threw this guy the size of a football player backwards and down a flight of stairs. He lay there at the bottom, unable to move, for a full hour before his roommate came home and called an ambulance.

Anna concludes with a true-life narrative to ensure that listeners will retain her message and integrate it into their belief systems. Her speech ends with a forceful call to action.

Jack was lucky. His back was not broken. But he did rip many of the muscles in his back. Now he has to go to physical therapy, and he is not expected to fully recover.

Kansas State students have been putting up with substandard living conditions for too long. It's time we finally got together to do something about this problem. Join the Off-Campus Association. Sign my petition. Let's send a message to these slumlords that we're not going to put up with this any more. We don't have to live in slums.

17 Ceremonial Speaking

[People] who celebrate . . . are fused with each other and fused with all things in nature.

—Ernst Cassirer

Your college has just concluded an ambitious fundraising campaign to create scholarships and attract outstanding teachers, artists, and scholars. As the leader of student volunteers who spent many hours soliciting contributions, you have been invited to be the master of ceremonies at a banquet celebrating the campaign. At the banquet, you may both present and listen to many kinds of speeches: speeches offering tribute, speeches conferring and accepting awards, speeches introducing featured speakers, speeches evoking laughter, and speeches inspiring listeners. They are all part of what we call ceremonial speaking.

Ceremonial speaking stresses the sharing of identities and values that unite people into communities.[1] The philosopher John Dewey observed that people "live in a community in virtue of the things which they have in common; and communication is the way in which they come to possess things in common. What they must have in common . . . are aims, beliefs, aspirations, knowledge—a common understanding."[2] It is ceremonial speaking that celebrates and reinforces our common aims, beliefs, and aspirations.

From Frederick Douglass's "What to the Slave Is the Fourth of July?" to Ronald Reagan's "Challenger Disaster Address," many of the greatest or most studied speeches in American history were delivered on ceremonial occasions. We remember them because they provide rich portraits of Americans struggling to reconcile a shared sense of purpose with moments of great testing and trial.

Ceremonial speaking addresses four questions of vital importance to any community: Who are we? Why are we? What have we accomplished? and What can we become together? In answering these questions, ceremonial speakers help to create an "ordered, meaningful cultural world."[3] They also establish practical standards for action by promoting principles that justify subsequent arguments and behavior.

Of course, few of us will ever become towering historical figures, but there are many practical benefits of developing your ceremonial speaking skills. As important as informative and persuasive speaking skills are, you are probably more likely to be asked to "say a few words" upon the retirement of a former teacher or mentor, to present an award to an outstanding coworker, to celebrate the memory of a beloved friend, to offer a toast at a wedding reception, or even to act as the master of ceremonies at a banquet. And, as teachers have noted since Aristotle, when you speak successfully on these occasions, it enhances perceptions of your competence, your character, and your leadership potential. As you conduct your college's celebration of its fundraising campaign, audience members might be thinking, "Wouldn't she make a fine student body president?" or "Wouldn't he make a valuable employee of my company or corporation?"

There are as many forms of ceremonial speaking as there are formal ceremonial occasions. They may range from serious or solemn in tone to lighthearted and even humorous. In this chapter, we help you rise to the challenges of ceremonial speaking.

Techniques of Ceremonial Speaking

*T*wo techniques, identification and magnification, are basic to ceremonial speaking.

Identification

Identification occurs when a speech creates the feeling that speaker and listeners share goals, values, emotions, memories, motives, and cultural background. Kenneth Burke, an important communication theorist of our time, suggested that identification was the key term of public speaking.[4] People who *feel* together on issues will also reason and act together. Because ritual and ceremony draw people together, identification is also the heart of ceremonial speaking. Three common and sometimes overlapping strategies for promoting identification in ceremonial speaking are the use of narrative, the recognition of heroes and heroines, and the renewal of group commitment.

ceremonial speaking (ceremonial speech) Speaking that celebrates special occasions, such as speeches of tribute, inspiration, and introduction, eulogies, toasts, award presentations, acceptances,

and after-dinner speeches. Their deeper function is to share identities and reinforce values that unite people into communities.

identification The feeling of closeness between speakers and listeners that may overcome personal and cultural differences.

The Use of Narrative.   According to communication theorist Walter Fisher, storytelling is one of our most effective means of developing moral identification with an audience.[5] For example, if you were preparing a speech for the fundraising celebration mentioned at the beginning of this chapter, you might recall things that happened during those long evenings when student volunteers were making calls. You might remember moments of discouragement, followed by other moments of triumph when the contributions were especially large or meaningful. Your purpose is to draw listeners close together as they remember the shared experience. While you should be careful not to belittle or offend anyone involved, stories that evoke humor are especially effective because laughter itself tends to bring people together:

> I don't think that any of us will forget the night that John tripped over a phone cord carrying a tray full of coffee and shorted out the computer network for the phone bank. Although many contributors got "cut off" by the accident, the returned calls netted the highest contributions of any night of the campaign.

In her student speech printed at the end of this chapter, Ashlie McMillan told the inspiring story of her cousin Tina's accomplishments as a dwarf. In her introduction, she asked listeners to close their eyes and imagine themselves shrinking to help them identify more closely with the challenges Tina faced on a daily basis. This identification prepared the audience to accept Ashlie's eloquent conclusion: "You too may seem too short to grasp your stars, but you never know how far you might reach if you stand upon a dream." We discuss how to design effective narratives in the final section of this chapter.

The Recognition of Heroes and Heroines.   Another strategy for promoting identification in ceremonial speaking is to invoke the words and deeds of our past and present heroes as role models for future action. Depending on the nature and purpose of the celebration, speakers might invoke such heroes as Thomas Jefferson, Martin Luther King Jr., the Biblical Moses, or prominent figures relevant to specific groups, such as Lee Iacocca of the American auto industry or Clara Barton of the American Red Cross.

On occasions such as the fund-raising banquet mentioned earlier, speakers might focus their praise on the outstanding contributions of specific group members. However, you should be careful not to embarrass a specific member (or offend others) by lavishing excessive praise on one person when others are equally deserving of recognition. Save your praise for those truly outstanding, unusual, or representative contributions. You might say, for instance:

> Let me tell you about Mary Tyrer. I think she's typical. All of us have worked hard over the past two months. Day after day on the phone— talking, coaxing, winning friends for our school, and raising thousands of dollars in contributions. I've worked with Mary and can tell you that she's always been there and hard at work when I show up, and she never seemed to leave before me. This is the passion and commitment we all share for our university. This is the reason we met and surpassed all expectations. This is the spirit by which we will no doubt meet and surpass these numbers again next year!

Renewal of Group Commitment.   Ceremonial speaking is a time both for celebrating what has been accomplished and for renewing commitments. Share with your listeners a vision of what the future can be like if their commitment continues. Plead with them not to be satisfied with present accomplishments. Renew their identity as a group moving toward even greater goals.

To reinforce this emphasis on group renewal, ceremonial speakers often depict a challenging present against the backdrop of an idealized past, then create a moral vision to guide listeners through the present into the future. In his "Gettysburg Address," delivered to commemorate the costliest battle of the costliest war in American history, Abraham Lincoln used this technique to substantially redefine America's moral identity as a nation.

Lincoln opened with a clear reference to an idealized past, "Four score and seven years ago our fathers brought forth on this continent, a new nation, conceived in Liberty, and dedicated to the proposition that all men are created equal." He then moved directly to the troubled present: "Now we are engaged in a great civil war, testing whether that nation, or any nation so conceived and so dedicated, can long endure." After expounding on the sacrifices of the "brave men, living and dead, who struggled here," Lincoln closed by offering a stunning vision to guide the American future: "that this nation, under God, shall have a new birth of freedom—and that government of the people, by the people, for the people, shall not perish from the earth."[6]

Magnification

Magnification is a technique commonly used in ceremonial speeches of tribute. In his *Rhetoric*, Aristotle noted that when speakers select certain features of a person or event and then dwell on those qualities, the effect is to magnify them until they fill the minds of listeners.[7] These magnified features come to represent the meaning of the subject for listeners. They focus attention on what is relevant, honorable, and praiseworthy.

For example, imagine that you are preparing a speech honoring Jesse Owens's incredible track and field accomplishments in the 1936 Olympic Games. In your research, you come up with a variety of facts:

- He had a headache the day he won the medal in the long jump.
- He had suffered from racism in America.
- He did not like the food served at the Olympic training camp.

Speaker's Notes   17.1

Promoting Identification

Use the following techniques to promote identification among listeners:

1. Tell stories that remind listeners of shared experiences.

2. Remember, listeners who laugh together identify with one another.

3. Create portraits of heroes and heroines as role models.

4. Revive legends and traditions that remind listeners of their shared heritage and values.

5. Offer goals and visions to inspire listeners to work together.

magnification   A speaker's selecting and emphasizing certain qualities of a subject to stress the values they represent.

InterConnections.
LearnMore 17.1

Identification

The Kenneth Burke Society
www-home.cc.duq.edu/~thames/kennethburke/Default.htm

Gateway to greater understanding of the life and work of communication theorist Kenneth Burke; contains a discussion section and material on conferences on Burke's work; maintained by Professor Richard Thames, Department of English, Duquesne University.

On Kenneth Burke's Concept of Rhetorical Identification
www.libarts.ucok.edu/english/faculty/stein/rhetoric/report/Kenneth_Burke.htm

A brief, interesting explanation of Burke's treatment of identification; authored by Ricki Higdon.

Kenneth Burke and Identification
www.sla.purdue.edu/people/engl/dblakesley/burke/clark.html

Full text of a paper, "Kenneth Burke, Identification, and Rhetorical Criticism," by Professor Gregory Clark of Brigham Young University; presented at the Conference on College Composition and Communication, March 1997; adapts the concept of identification to the teaching of writing.

- He won four gold medals in front of Adolf Hitler, who was preaching the racial superiority of Germans.

- Some of his friends did not want him to run for the United States.

- After his victories, he returned to further discrimination in America.

If you used all this information, your speech might seem rambling and aimless. Which of these items should you emphasize, and how should you proceed? To make your selection, you need to know what themes are best to develop when you are magnifying the actions of a person. These themes include the following:

- Triumph over obstacles

- Unusual accomplishment

- Superior performance

- Unselfish motives

- Benefit to society

As you consider these themes, it becomes clear which items about Jesse Owens you should magnify and how you should do so. To begin, you would stress that Owens had to overcome obstacles such as racism in America to make the Olympic team. Then you would point out that his accomplishment was unusual. No one else had ever won four gold medals in

Jesse Owens was both a great Olympic hero and a great inspirational speaker.

Magnification

Use the following strategies to magnify a person or accomplishment:

1. Show how people have overcome obstacles to success.

2. Point out how unusual the accomplishments are.

3. Underscore superior features of the performance.

4. Emphasize unselfish motives behind the achievement.

5. Show how listeners and society as a whole have benefited.

6. Use the techniques of magnifying language power that are discussed in Chapter 12.

7. Use speech designs—comparison, chronological, causation, and narrative—that promote magnification.

Olympic track and field competition, and his performances set world records that lasted many years. Because Owens received no material gain from his victories, his motives were unselfish, driven solely by personal qualities such as courage and determination. Finally, you would demonstrate that because his victories repudiated Hitler's racist ideology, causing the Nazi leader public humiliation, Owens's accomplishments benefited our society. The overall effect would be to magnify the meaning of Jesse Owens's great performances, both for himself and for his nation.

In addition to focusing on these basic themes, magnification relies on effective uses of language to create dramatic word-pictures, as we saw in Chapter 12. Metaphor and simile can magnify a subject through creative associations, such as "He struck like a lightning bolt that day." Parallel structure, the repetition of key-words and phrases, can also help magnify a subject and embed it in our minds. For example, if you were to say of Mother Teresa, "Whenever there was hurt, she was there. Whenever there was hunger, she was there. Whenever there was desperation, she was there," you would be magnifying her dedication and selflessness.

Magnification also favors certain speech designs over others. Comparison and contrast designs promote magnification by making selected features stand out. For example, you might contrast the purity of Owens's motives with the crassness of those of today's well-paid athletes. Chronological designs used to relate the history of a situation enhance magnification by dramatizing certain events as stories unfold over time. As Ashlie McMillan sketched incidents in the childhood and adulthood of her cousin, she magnified Tina's developing character. The causation design promotes magnification when a person's accomplishments are emphasized as the causes of important effects. For example, a speaker might suggest that Jesse Owens's victories refuted Nazi propaganda for many people. The narrative design, which helps to dramatize events and accomplishments, is a natural for ceremonial speaking.

Whatever designs ceremonial speeches use, it is important that they build to a conclusion. Speakers should save their best materials and language use for the end of the speech. Ceremonial speeches should never dwindle to a conclusion.

Types of Ceremonial Speeches

As we noted earlier, there are ceremonial speeches for all occasions. In this section, we consider the forms you will most likely present in your personal and professional lives: speeches of tribute (award presentations, eulogies, and

Figure 17.1

Types of Ceremonial Speeches

Type	Use When
Tributes	You wish to honor a person, group, occasion, or event. Subtypes include award presentations, eulogies, and toasts.
Acceptance	You need to acknowledge an award or honor.
Introductions	You must introduce a featured speaker in a program.
Inspiration	You want to motivate listeners to appreciate and commit to a goal, purpose, or set of values; this may be religious, commercial, political, or social in nature.
After-Dinner	You want to entertain the audience while leaving a message that can guide future behavior. Here, as elsewhere, brevity is golden.
Master of Ceremonies	You must coordinate a program and see that everything runs smoothly. The master of ceremonies sets the mood for the occasion.

toasts), acceptance speeches, introductory speeches, speeches of inspiration, after-dinner speeches, and speaking as master of ceremonies (see Figure 17.1).

The Speech of Tribute

In magnifying the importance of accomplishments, the **speech of tribute** endorses the values of individual responsibility, striving, and achievement. For example, you might be called on to honor a former teacher at a retirement ceremony, present an award to someone for an outstanding accomplishment, eulogize a person who has died, or propose a toast to a friend who is getting married.

Speeches of tribute can serve several important purposes. If you have presented a series of speeches on related topics in your class, the speech of tribute gives you a chance to extend your efforts at informing and persuading listeners. For example, Holly Carlson chose the banning of books in public schools as the topic area for all her speeches. In her informative speech, she demonstrated how books are banned in schools all over the country, and she listed the books and authors most often targeted. In her persuasive speech, she offered a stirring plea for intellectual freedom, urging her listeners to support the right to read and think for themselves. Then, for her ceremonial speech, she offered a tribute to one of the most frequently banned authors of the twentieth century, J. D. Salinger. Her tribute to Salinger made her listeners want to read his works themselves. It also dramatized how hurtful censorship could be. Thus, all of Holly's speeches were woven into one pattern, which gave focus to her semester's work.

Speeches of tribute blend easily with inspirational speeches. Leslie Eason's tribute to Tiger Woods, reprinted in Appendix B, exhorts listeners to apply his example of integrity to their own lives. Ashlie McMillan's tribute to her cousin Tina offered

speech of tribute A ceremonial speech that recognizes the achievements of individuals or groups or commemorates special events.

The raising of the American flag at Iwo Jima during World War II became an important symbol for courage and fortitude, themes echoed in the similar photograph of the raising of the flag by firefighters over the wreckage of the World Trade Center.

listeners an inspiring model of determination to overcome obstacles to their own achievements.

Praiseworthy accomplishments are usually celebrated for two reasons. First, *they are important in themselves*: The influence of a teacher may have contributed to the success of many of her former students. Second, *they are important as symbols*. The planting of the American flag at Iwo Jima during some of the most intense fighting of World War II came to symbolize the fortitude of the entire American war effort; it represented commitment, and it was more important as a symbol than as an actual event. Sometimes the same event may be celebrated for both actual and symbolic reasons. A student speech honoring the raising of $60,000 for Katrina relief celebrated this achievement both as a symbol of generosity and for the actual help it brought to many people. When you plan a speech of tribute, you should consider both the actual and the symbolic values that are represented.

Developing Speeches of Tribute.

As you prepare a speech of tribute, keep the following guidelines in mind:

- **Do not exaggerate the tribute.** If you are too lavish with your praise or use too many superlatives, you may embarrass the recipient and make the praise unbelievable.

- **Focus on the person being honored, not on yourself.** Even if you know what effort the accomplishment required because you have done something similar, don't mention that at this time. It will come across as conceit when the focus should be on the honoree.

- **Create vivid images of accomplishment.** Speeches of tribute are occasions for illustrating what someone has achieved, the values underlying those achievements, and their consequences. Tell stories that make those accomplishments come to life.

- **Be sincere.** Speeches of tribute are a time for warmth, pride, and appreciation. Your manner should reflect these qualities as you present the tribute.

When you honor a historical figure, your purpose will often be to promote values represented by the person's life. Note how Tommie Albright, a student at Daytona Beach Community College, developed an agenda of values as she spoke at the college's Martin Luther King Jr. Memorial Evening. Notice especially her use of contrast and parallel structure in the following section of her speech:

> Martin Luther King had many dreams for us, each with its own challenge to us.
> Where he dreamed of peace, we must be peaceful and seek peace.
> Where he saw hope, we must provide fulfillment.
> Where he dreamed of equality, we must treat each other as equals.
> Where he dreamed of brotherhood, we must act as brothers and sisters.
> And where he dreamed of justice, we must provide a just society.[8]

Award Presentations.   When you present an award, you often accompany it with a speech of tribute. An **award presentation** recognizes the achievements or contributions of those on whom the award is bestowed. Most award presenters have two main points: they explain the nature of the award, and they applaud what the recipient did to qualify for it.

Unless the award is quite well known, such as an Oscar or Nobel Prize, you should always begin an award presentation by explaining the award:

> Beth Peterson was a graduate assistant in this department who exemplified the best qualities of a teacher: enthusiasm for her subject, the ability to impart it to others, and a real sense of caring for those whom she taught. After her passing, her parents and friends endowed the Beth Peterson award, offered each year to the graduate assistant in our department who best exemplifies the qualities Beth brought so generously to the classroom.

The second and most important part of an award presentation involves explaining why the honoree was chosen to receive the award. In talking about the recipient, you should emphasize the uniqueness, superiority, and benefits of his or her achievements. Provide specific examples that illustrate these accomplishments. Finally, you should name the recipient of the award and offer your congratulations and wishes for continued success.

Eulogies.   Earlier we asked you to imagine yourself preparing a speech to honor Jesse Owens. Following his death in 1980, many such speeches were actually presented. A speech of tribute presented on the death of a person is called a **eulogy.** The following comments by Thomas P. O'Neill Jr., then Speaker of the House of Representatives, illustrate how some of the major techniques we have discussed can work in a eulogy:

> I rise on the occasion of his passing to join my colleagues in tribute to the greatest American sports hero of this century, Jesse Owens. . . . His performances at the Berlin Olympics earned Jesse Owens the title of America's first superstar. . . .
>
> No other athlete symbolized the spirit and motto of the Olympics better than Jesse Owens. "Swifter, higher, stronger" was the credo by which Jesse Owens performed as an athlete and lived as an American. Of his performances in Hitler's Berlin in 1936, Jesse said: "I wasn't running against Hitler, I was running against the world." Owens's view of the Olympics was just that: He was competing against the best athletes in the world without regard to nationality, race, or political view. . . .
>
> Jesse Owens proved by his performances that he was the best among the finest the world had to offer, and in setting the world record in the 100-yard dash, he became the "fast-est human" even before that epithet was fashionable. . . .
>
> In life as well as on the athletic field, Jesse Owens was first an American, and second, an internationalist. He loved his country; he loved the opportunity his country gave him to reach the pinnacle of athletic prowess. In his own quiet, unassuming, and modest way—by example, by inspiration, and by performance—he helped other young people to aim for the stars, to develop their God-given potential . . .
>
> As the world's first superstar, Jesse Owens was not initially overwhelmed by commercial interests and offered the opportunity to become a millionaire

◀ O'Neill's opening highlights the themes of unusual and superior accomplishment. He begins with the actual value of Owens's victories, and then he describes their symbolic value.

◀ These comments magnify the values represented by Owens's life and develop the theme of benefit to the community. That Owens remained a patriotic American in the face of racism and indifference magnifies his character.

award presentation   A speech of tribute that recognizes achievements of the award recipient, explains the nature of the award, and describes why the recipient qualifies for the award.

eulogy   A speech of tribute presented upon a person's death.

overnight. There was no White House reception waiting for him on his return from Berlin, and as Jesse Owens once observed: "I still had to ride in the back of the bus in my hometown in Alabama."

O'Neill's conclusion emphasizes the symbolic, spiritual values of Owens's life. ▶

Can one individual make a difference? Clearly in the case of Jesse Owens, the answer is a resounding affirmative, for his whole life was dedicated to the elimination of poverty, totalitarianism, and racial bigotry; and he did it in his own special and modest way, a spokesman for freedom, an American ambassador of goodwill to the athletes of the world, and an inspiration to young Americans. . . . Jesse Owens was a champion all the way in a life of dedication to the principles of the American and Olympic spirit.[9]

When presented at memorial services, eulogies should also express the pain of loss and offer comfort.[10] Such eulogies are—indeed, must be—highly personal. Therefore, when you are asked to present a eulogy at a funeral or memorial service, you often confront a special challenge. In addition to dealing with natural anxiety about speaking, you must also control your own feelings of grief. Plan your eulogy with these thoughts in mind:

■ While eulogies should acknowledge a shared sense of grief, remember that your primary purpose is to offer comfort to the living. Remind them of how much they meant to the deceased. Try to provide words that will continue to console them in the days, months, and years later.

Attallah Shabaza presented a moving eulogy for Coretta Scott King.

■ Share stories that highlight the humanity of the person. Use gentle humor to recall his or her endearing qualities.

■ Focus on how wonderful it was to have shared the life of the person more than on the pain of the loss. Make the eulogy a celebration of life.

■ Focus on the meaning of the person's life for those who live on.

In the Fall of 1995, Israeli Prime Minister Yitzhak Rabin was assassinated after agreeing to peace talks with the Palestinians. The conclusion to President Bill Clinton's eulogy exemplified the functions of acknowledging a shared sense of loss while comforting the living and of celebrating the life of the deceased as worthy of emulation:

Leah [Rabin's widow] is at this time without you, but the entire nation is with her and the family. I see our people very distressed, a nation with tears in their eyes. The nation also knows that the bullet that murdered you cannot and will not kill the ideas you advocated.

You did not leave us a will, but you left us a path which we will follow with determination and faith. The nation is crying. I hope there will be tears for unity, tears for peace among us, and peace with our neighbors. . . .

Goodbye, my eldest brother, the bringer of peace. We will add and continue to carry this peace, for near and far, that you wanted and expected in your life and death.[11]

Toasts. A **toast** is a ceremonial speech in miniature, offered as a tribute to people and what they have done, as a blessing for their future, or simply as lighthearted enjoyment of the present moment. You might be asked to toast a coworker who has been promoted or a couple at a wedding reception, or simply to celebrate the beginning of a new year. The occasion may be formal or informal, but the message should always be eloquent. It simply won't do to mutter, "Here's to Tony, he's a great guy!" or "Cheers!" As one writer has said, such a feeble toast is "a gratuitous betrayal—of the occasion, its honoree, and the desire [of the audience] to clink glasses and murmur, 'Hear, hear,' in appreciation of a compliment well fashioned."[12]

Whenever you think you might be called on to offer a toast, plan your remarks in advance. Keep your toast brief, and build to a climax. You might toast the "coach of the year" in the following way:

A toast, a ceremonial speech in minature, is offered as a tribute to people, as a blessing for their future, or simply in light-hearted enjoyment of the moment.

> I want to offer a toast to a person who is being honored tonight as "coach of the year." You talk to the young women and to their parents sitting here, and they'll tell you that we should be toasting her as "coach of the century." Friend, confidante, mentor, model, ambassador for the community, and, yes, coach of winning girls' basketball teams year after year, she means so much to so many of us. So here's to Nancy, who will always be our own "coach of the year!"

While a touch of humor is often appropriate, a toast should never embarrass or humiliate the honoree.[13] For example, it would certainly be inappropriate at a wedding reception to say, "Here's to John and Mary. I hope they don't end up in divorce court the way I did!" Although most speeches are best presented extemporaneously, a toast should be memorized. Practice presenting your toast with glass in hand until it flows easily. If you have difficulty memorizing your toast, it is probably too long. Figure 17.2 offers some sample toasts.

The Acceptance Speech

If you are receiving an award or honor, you may be expected to respond with a **speech of acceptance**. A speech of acceptance should express gratitude for the honor and acknowledge those who made the accomplishment possible. It should be humble, should focus on the values the award represents, and should use language that matches the dignity of the occasion.

When Elie Wiesel was awarded the 1986 Nobel Peace Prize for a lifetime of work bringing Nazi war criminals to justice, he began his acceptance speech with these remarks: "It is with a profound sense of humility that I accept the honor you have chosen to bestow upon me."[14] (The complete text of his speech may be found in Appendix B). Follow his lead and accept an award with grace and modesty.

---

toast A short speech of tribute, usually offered at celebration dinners or meetings.

speech of acceptance A ceremonial speech expressing gratitude for an honor and acknowledging those who made the accomplishment possible.

Figure 17.2

Sample Toasts

- May you have warm words on a cold evening, a full moon on a dark night, and a road downhill all the way to your door. (Irish blessing)

- Here's looking at you, kid. (Humphrey Bogart toasting Ingrid Bergman in *Casablanca*)

- I drink to your charm, your beauty, and your brains—Which gives you a rough idea of how hard up I am for a drink. (Groucho Marx)

- To get the full value of joy, you must have someone to divide it with. (Mark Twain)

- May you have the hindsight to know where you've been, the foresight to know where you're going, and the insight to know when you're going too far.

- As you ramble through life, whatever be your goal, keep your eye upon the doughnut, and not upon the hole. (Offered by Sid Pettigrew)*

- May the road rise to meet you.
  May the wind be always at your back.
  May the sun shine warm upon your face.
  And rains fall soft upon your fields.
  And until we meet again,
  May God hold you in the hollow of His hand. (Irish blessing)

* From "Tom's Toasts: Irish Toasts and Blessings," March 1998.
http://zinnia.umfacad.maine.edu/~donaghue/toasts01.html (16 Dec. 1998).

Acceptance speeches should also give credit where credit is due. When Martin Luther King Jr. accepted his Nobel Peace Prize in 1964, he did so in these words:

> I accept this prize on behalf of all men who love peace and brotherhood. . . . Most of these people will never make the headlines and their names will not appear in Who's Who. Yet when years have rolled past . . . men and women will know and children will be taught that we have a finer land, a better people, a more noble civilization—because these humble children of God were willing to suffer for righteousness' sake.[15]

As you accept an award, express your awareness of its deeper meaning. In their acceptance speeches, both Mr. Wiesel and Dr. King stressed the value of freedom and the importance of involvement—of overcoming hatred with loving concern.

Finally, be sure the eloquence of your language fits the dignity of the moment. Wiesel told the story of a "young Jewish boy discovering the kingdom of night" during the Holocaust. This personal, metaphorical narrative was introduced early in the speech and repeated in the conclusion when Mr. Wiesel remarked, "No one is as capable of gratitude as one who has emerged from the kingdom of night." Although you may not be as eloquent as these Nobel Prize winners, you should make a presentation that fits the dignity of the occasion.

Acceptance speeches may seem to follow a simple pattern of development, but creative speakers can introduce interesting variations. When he accepted the 2006

Martin Luther King Jr. Human Rights Award, John Bakke, Professor Emeritus of the University of Memphis, transformed his remarks into a speech of tribute in which he honored Dr. King for the strength and beauty of his ideas and for his courage in a time of crisis. He then resurrected the meaning and value of King's philosophy of nonviolence by redefining it as "full-time citizenship." Quoting Taylor Branch that "every ballot is a piece of nonviolence," Bakke continued:

> It's time to reclaim our democratic processes. It's time to make the democratic processes work in America as we are now trying to make them work for Iraq. That means more than voting. It means informed voting. It means supporting candidates and policies of our choice. It means commitment to the communication processes that give life to democracy. It means thinking of ourselves more as citizens than as just taxpayers. It means full-time citizenship.

Bakke concluded that such citizenship was a necessary part of homeland security in a violent world. "It is nonviolence," he said, "that makes civilization civil and it is through the nonviolent participation in democracy that we can live out the true meaning of our creed." (See the full text of the speech in Appendix B.)

The Speech of Introduction

One of the more common types of ceremonial speeches is the **speech of introduction**, in which you introduce a featured speaker to the audience. The importance of this speech can vary, depending on how well the speaker is already known. At times, a formal introduction may seem quite unnecessary. For example, when Madonna introduced Muhammad Ali at a gathering of New York sports personalities, she simply said:

> We are alike in many ways. We have espoused unpopular causes, we are arrogant, we like to have our picture taken, and we are the greatest.[16]

A good speech of introduction usually does three things: makes the speaker feel welcome, establishes or strengthens the ethos of the speaker, and prepares the audience for the speech that will follow. You make a speaker feel welcome both by what you say and how you say it. Deliver your words of welcome with warmth and sincerity.

As soon as you know you will be introducing someone, find out as much as you can about the person. You might ask the speaker what you might emphasize that would be most helpful to his or her speech. It may seem obvious, but be sure you know how to pronounce the speaker's name. We have heard John Bakke speak many times, and we have heard introducers butcher his name on more than one occasion.

The following guidelines will help you build ethos and lay the groundwork for speaker–audience identification:

- Create respect by magnifying the speaker's main accomplishments.

- Don't be too lavish with your praise. An overblown introduction can be embarrassing and distracting. One featured speaker was so overcome by an excessive introduction that he responded, "If you do not go to heaven for charity, you will certainly go somewhere else for exaggeration or downright prevarication."[17]

speech of introduction A ceremonial speech in which a featured speaker is introduced to the audience.

Introducing Featured Speakers

When you are called on to introduce a featured speaker, keep the following in mind as you prepare your remarks:

1. Be sure you know how to pronounce the speaker's name.

2. Find out what the speaker would like you to emphasize.

3. Focus on aspects of the speaker's background that are relevant to the topic, audience, and occasion.

4. Announce the title of the speech and tune the audience for it.

5. Make the speaker feel welcome. Be warm and gracious.

6. Be brief!

■ Mention achievements that are relevant to the speaker's message, the occasion on which the speech is being presented, or the audience that has assembled.

■ Be selective! If you try to present too many details and accomplishments, you may take up the speaker's time and make listeners weary. Introducers who drone on too long can create real problems for the speakers who must follow them.

The final function of an effective introduction is to tune the audience. In Chapter 5, we discussed how preliminary tuning can establish a receptive mood. You tune the audience when you arouse anticipation for the message that will follow. However, arousing anticipation does not mean that you should attempt to preview the speech. Don't steal the speaker's thunder! Let the speaker present the speech.

The Speech of Inspiration

The **speech of inspiration** arouses an audience to appreciate, commit to, and pursue a goal, purpose, or set of values or beliefs. Speeches of inspiration help listeners see subjects in a new light. They may be religious, commercial, political, or social. When a sales manager introduces a new product to marketing representatives, pointing up its competitive advantages and its glowing market potential, the speech is both inspirational and persuasive. The marketing reps should feel inspired to push that product with great zeal and enthusiasm. Speeches at political conventions that praise the principles of the party, such as keynote addresses, are inspirational in tone and intent. So also is that great American institution, the commencement address. As different as these speech occasions may seem, they have important points in common.

First, *speeches of inspiration are enthusiastic.* Inspirational speakers accomplish their goals through their personal commitment and energy. Both the speaker and the speech must be active and forceful. Speakers must set an example for their audiences through their behavior both on and off the speaking platform. They must practice what they preach. Their ethos must be consistent with their advice.

Second, *speeches of inspiration draw on past successes and frustrations to encourage future accomplishment.* At a Catalyst Awards dinner, Sheila W. Welling, the organization president, evoked vivid memories of what the past was like for women as she urged continued progress toward equality in the workplace in the new millennium:

> One hundred years ago, at the dawn of the last millennium, our bustled Victorian great-grandmothers could not run for a bus, let alone for Congress. If the race—as the Victorian poet claimed—went to the swift, women lost.

speech of inspiration A ceremonial speech directed at awakening or reawakening an audience to a goal, purpose, or set of values.

Girdled, corseted, enveloped in yards of gingham and lace, women were balanced precariously on their pedestals.

. . . Women couldn't vote when my mother was born. Every time I think about it, it startles me: Even as Edith Wharton wrote her novels, as Helen Keller graduated from Radcliffe with honors, even as women manufactured the arms that led to victory in World War I and the nation's move to global primacy, women still could not vote.[18]

Third, *speeches of inspiration revitalize our appreciation for values or beliefs*. Such speeches can strengthen our sense of mythos, the distinctive code of values underlying our society. In the later years of his life, when his athletic prowess had faded, Jesse Owens became known as a great inspirational speaker. According to his obituary in the *New York Times*, "The Jesse Owens best remembered by many Americans was a public speaker with the ringing, inspirational delivery of an evangelist. . . . [His speeches] praised the virtues of patriotism, clean living and fair play."[19] In the speech that follows, Owens stresses the ideals of brotherhood and tolerance, as well as fair competition.

In his inspirational speeches to budding athletes, Jesse Owens frequently talked about his Olympic achievements. The following excerpts, taken from a statement protesting America's withdrawal from the 1980 Summer Olympic Games, illustrate his inspirational style. Jesse Owens was unable to deliver this message personally. He prepared it shortly before his death from cancer.

What the Berlin games proved . . . was that Hitler's "supermen" could be beaten. Ironically, it was one of his blond, blue-eyed, Aryan athletes who helped do the beating.

◀ *Owens's introduction suggests the larger meaning of his victories and sets the stage for identification.*

I held the world record in the broad jump. Even more than the sprints, it was "my" event. Yet I was one jump from not even making the finals. I fouled on my first try, and playing it safe the second time, I had not jumped far enough.

The broad jump preliminaries came before the finals of my other three events and everything, it seemed then, depended on this jump. Fear swept over me and then panic. I walked off alone, trying to gather myself. I dropped to one knee, closed my eyes, and prayed. I felt a hand on my shoulder. I opened my eyes and there stood my arch enemy, Luz Long, the prize athlete Hitler had kept under wraps while he trained for one purpose only: to beat me. Long had broken the Olympic mark in his very first try in the preliminaries.

◀ *Note the use of graphic detail to recapture the immediacy of the moment.*

"I know about you," he said. "You are like me. You must do it all the way, or you cannot do it. The same that has happened to you today happened to me last year in Cologne. I will tell you what I did then." Luz told me to measure my steps, place my towel 6 inches on back of the takeoff board and jump from there. That way I could give it all I had and be certain not to foul.

◀ *Owens's use of dialogue helps listeners feel they are sharing the experience.*

As soon as I had qualified, Luz, smiling broadly, came to me and said, "Now we can make each other do our best in the finals."

And that's what we did in the finals. Luz jumped and broke his Olympic record. Then I jumped just a bit further and broke Luz's new record. We each had three leaps in all. On his final jump, Luz went almost 26 feet, 5 inches, a mark that seemed impossible to beat. I went just a bit over that and set an Olympic record that was to last for almost a quarter of a century.

*This narrative leaves open the ►
meaning of Owens's "inside"
victory: Perhaps it was over self-
doubt or over his own stereotype of Germans. Perhaps it was
over both.*

*This scene presents an inspira- ►
tional model of international
competition.*

*Owens shows how individuals ►
can rise above ideologies, as
Long's final message invites
identification.*

*Owens ends with a metaphor of ►
the "road to the Olympics."*

I won that day, but I'm being straight when I say that even before I made that last jump, I knew I had won a victory of a far greater kind—over something inside myself, thanks to Luz.

The instant my record-breaking win was announced, Luz was there, throwing his arms around me and raising my arm to the sky. "Jazze Owenz!" he yelled as loud as he could. More than 100,000 Germans in the stadium joined in. "Jazze Owenz, Jazze Owenz, Jazze Owenz!"

Hitler was there, too, but he was not chanting. He had lost that day. Luz Long was killed in World War II and, although I don't cry often, I wept when I received his last letter—I knew it was his last. In it he asked me to someday find his son, Karl, and to tell him "of how we fought well together, and of the good times, and that any two men can become brothers."

That is what the Olympics are all about. The road to the Olympics does not lead to Moscow. It leads to no city, no country. It goes far beyond Lake Placid or Moscow, ancient Greece or Nazi Germany. The road to the Olympics leads, in the end, to the best within us.[20]

The After-Dinner Speech

Occasions that celebrate special events or that mark the beginning or end of a course of action often call for special dinners and provide the setting for an **after-dinner speech**. Political rallies, award banquets, the kickoff for a fundraising campaign, or the end of the school year may constitute such occasions.

The after-dinner speech is one of the great rituals of American public speaking and public life. If you are the leader of the group holding the dinner or have won some special recognition that makes people look up to you or simply have the reputation for being an entertaining speaker, you may be invited to give such a speech. As these qualifications suggest, the purpose of such a speech may vary from celebrating group accomplishments and setting new goals to simply enjoying the company of the moment and the laughter that can enrich lives and bond groups more closely together.

Almost all after-dinner speeches, however, share certain features. In keeping with the nature of the occasion, they should not be too difficult to digest. Speakers making these presentations usually do not introduce radical ideas that require listeners to rethink their values or that ask for dramatic changes in belief or behavior. Nor are such occasions the time for anger or negativity. Rather, they are a time for

---

Presenting the Inspirational Speech

Keep the following suggestions in mind as you prepare an inspirational speech:

1. You must seem personally inspired by your own message.

2. Demonstrate sincerity and personal commitment in your presentation.

3. Set forth goals that will challenge listeners but not discourage them.

4. Tell dramatic stories that catch listeners up in the inspiring action and revitalize their values.

5. Draw upon the past to portray a better future that will reward audience commitment and effort.

---

after-dinner speech A brief, often humorous, ceremonial speech, presented after a meal, that offers a message without asking for radical changes.

people to savor who they are, what they have done, or what they wish to do. A good after-dinner speech typically leaves a message that can guide and inspire future efforts.

The Role of Humor.   Humor is appropriate in most after-dinner speeches. In the introduction, humor can place both the speaker and the audience at ease.[21] Enjoying lighter moments can remind us that there is a human element in all situations and that we should not take ourselves too seriously.

Communication scholar Diane Martin has identified a range of functions that humor can serve in speeches.[22] For example, humorous stories can create identification by building an "insider's" relationship between speaker and audience that draws them closer together. In sharing humor, the audience becomes a community of listeners.[23] Another study has discovered that the use of humorous illustrations helps audiences remember the message of the speech.[24]

As we noted in Chapters 8 and 9, however, speakers should play to their strengths, and humor should not be forced on a speech. If you decide to begin with a joke simply because you think a speech should start that way, the humor may seem contrived and flat. Rather, humor should be functional, relevant, and useful in making a point.

The humor in a speech is best developed out of the immediate situation. Dick Jackman, director of corporate communications at Sun Company, opened an after-dinner speech at a National Football Foundation awards dinner by warning those in the expensive seats under the big chandelier that it "had been installed by the low bidder some time ago."[25] Such references are often made more effective by a touch of self-deprecation.[26] In the Spring of 2007, with his approval ratings lower than any sitting President in over 25 years, President George W. Bush used humor to poke fun at himself and his situation as he spoke at an annual dinner for media correspondents:

> Well, where should I start? A year ago, my approval rating was in the 30s, my nominee for the Supreme Court had just withdrawn, and my Vice President had shot someone. [laughter] Ahh, those were the good old days. [laughter and applause][27]

Humor requires thought, planning, and caution to be effective. If it is not handled well, it can be a disaster. For example, religious humor is dangerous, and racist or sexist humor is unacceptable. In general, avoid any anecdotes that are funny at the expense of others.

Developing an After-Dinner Speech.   After-dinner speeches are more difficult to develop than their lightness and short length might suggest. Like any other speech, they should be carefully planned and practiced. They should have an effective introduction that commands attention right away, especially since some audience members may be more interested in talking to table companions than listening to the speaker. After-dinner speeches should be more than strings of anecdotes to amuse listeners. The stories told must establish a mood, convey a message, or carry a theme forward. Such speeches should build to a satisfying conclusion that conveys the essence of the message.

Above all, perhaps, after-dinner speeches should be mercifully brief. Long-winded after-dinner speakers can leave the audience fiddling with coffee cups and drawing pictures on napkins. After being subjected to such a speech, Albert Einstein once murmured: "I have just got a new theory of eternity."[28]

An after-dinner speech should be light and easy to digest.

Master of Ceremonies

Quite often, ceremonial speeches are part of a program of events that must be coordinated with skill and grace if things are to run smoothly. Being the master of ceremonies is no easy task. A speaker who served in such a capacity for a community program once noted:

> Being an MC was sort of like having to stand up and juggle a dozen oranges in front of an audience. I just kept standing there, fumbling everything and waiting for the whole thing to be over with.[29]

It takes at least as much careful planning, preparation, and practice to function effectively as a master of ceremonies as it does to make a major presentation. As the **master of ceremonies**, you will be expected to keep the program moving along, introduce participants, and possibly present awards. You will also set the tone or mood for the program.

If at all possible, you should be involved in planning the program from the beginning. Then you will have a better grasp of what is expected of you, what events have been scheduled, what the timetable is, who the featured speakers are, and what special logistics (such as meal service) you might have to contend with. The following guidelines should help you function effectively as a master of ceremonies:[30]

- **Know what is expected of you.** Why were you chosen to emcee the program? Remember, as emcee, you are not the "star" of the program; rather, you are the one who brings it all together and makes it work.

- **Plan a good opener for the program.** Your opening remarks as an emcee are as important as the introduction to a major presentation. You should gain the attention of the audience and prepare them for the program. Be sure that the mood you set with your opener is consistent with the nature of the occasion.

- **Be prepared to introduce the participants.** Find out all you can about the speakers in advance: Search the Internet, check *Who's Who*, and examine local newspaper clipping files. Ask them what they would like you to emphasize and determine how you might best tune the audience for their speeches. Be sure you know how to pronounce their names.

- **Be sure you know the schedule and timetable so that you can keep the program on track.** Also, be sure that the participants get this information. They need to know how much time has been allotted for them to speak. Review the schedule with them before the program and work out some way to cue them in case they should run overtime. If time restrictions are severe (as in a televised program), be ready to edit and adapt your own planned comments.

- **Make certain that any prizes or awards are kept near the podium.** You shouldn't be left fumbling around looking for a plaque or trophy at presentation time.

master of ceremonies A person who coordinates an event or program, sets its mood, introduces, and, provides transitions.

- **Plan your comments ahead of time.** Develop a key-word outline for each presentation on a running script of the program. Print the name of the person or award in large letters at the top of each outline so that you can keep your place in the program.

- **Practice your presentation.** Although you are not the featured speaker, your words are important (especially to the person you will introduce or who will receive the award you present). Practice your comments the same way you would practice a speech.

- **Make advance arrangements for mealtime logistics.** Speak with the maître d' before the program to be sure the waiters know the importance of "silent service." If you will be speaking while people are still eating, adapt your message to cope with this distraction by using the attention-gaining techniques discussed in Chapters 9 and 14.

- **Be ready for the inevitable glitches.** Despite your best efforts, Murphy's Law (If anything can go wrong, it will) will surely prevail. Be ready for problems like microphones that don't work or that squeal, trays of dishes being dropped, and people wandering in and out during the course of the program. As you respond to these events, keep your cool and good humor.

- **End the program strongly.** Just as a speech should not dwindle into nothingness, neither should a program. Review the suggestions for speech conclusions in Chapter 9. When ending your presentation, thank those who made the program possible, and then leave the audience with something to remember.

Narrative Design

I n Chapters 3 and 8 we discussed how storytelling helps structure and support a speech. Three forms of narrative often play important roles in ceremonial speeches: embedded narratives, vicarious experience narratives, and master narratives. **Embedded narratives**, stories within speeches, provide a vital form of supporting material. In ceremonial speaking, these narratives can create identification and magnify the importance of actions. The other two forms, vicarious experience and master narratives, provide narrative designs that structure the speeches in which they appear.

Vicarious experience narratives invite listeners *into* the speech, asking them to imagine themselves participating in the action as it unfolds. In her tribute to her cousin, Ashlie McMillan invited listeners to experience what it might mean to be a dwarf (see her speech at the end of this chapter). Note also how President Ronald Reagan encouraged listeners to *enter* the story he portrayed in his second inaugural address:

> Hear again the echoes of our past.
>
> A general falls to his knees in the harsh snow of Valley Forge; a lonely President paces the darkened hall and ponders his struggle to preserve the Union; the men of the Alamo call out encouragement to each other; a settler pushes West and sings a song, and the song echoes out forever and fills the unknowing air.
>
> It is the American Sound. It is hopeful, big-hearted, idealistic—daring, decent and fair. That's our heritage. That's our song.[31]

---

embedded narrative Stories inserted within speeches that illustrate the speaker's points.

vicarious experience narrative Speech strategy in which the speaker invites listeners to imagine themselves enacting a story.

In the **master narrative**, the entire speech becomes a story that reveals some important truth. We saw a good example of this as Jesse Owens recounted his experience at the 1936 Olympic games.

The **narrative design** developed in such speeches differs markedly from other speech design formats. Whereas the categorical, causation, problem–solution, and other designs associated with informative and persuasive speaking typically follow a linear pattern, the narrative design follows a dramatic pattern of development. Speeches that build on narrative design do not make points so much as they present selected scenes in a mini-drama. Such design features three major components: prologue, plot, and epilogue.

Prologue

The **prologue** of narrative design sets the scene for what will follow. It is the counterpart of the introduction in other speech designs. The prologue orients listeners to the context of the action so that they can make sense of it. It foreshadows the meaning and importance of the story that will follow. It also introduces the important characters that will enact the story and whose ethos will develop as the story unfolds.

To see these elements in action, let's consider again the prologue to Jesse Owens's speech on the 1936 Olympics:

> What the Berlin games proved . . . was that Hitler's "supermen" could be beaten. Ironically, it was one of his blond, blue–eyed, Aryan athletes who helped do the beating.
>
> I held the world record in the broad jump. Even more than the sprints, it was "my" event. Yet I was one jump from not even making the finals. I fouled on my first try, and playing it safe the second time, I had not jumped far enough.

The first two sentences in this prologue foreshadow the meaning of the story. They help prepare listeners for the actions that will unfold within the plot. They also anticipate the major character who will develop within the speech, Luz Long. The

---

master narrative Form of speaking in which the entire speech becomes a story that reveals some important truth.

narrative design Speech structure that develops a story from beginning to end through a sequence of scenes in which characters interact.

prologue An opening that establishes the context and setting of a narrative, foreshadows the meaning, and introduces major characters.

final four sentences present the context and setting of the story, the fact that Owens held the world record and was favored and the crisis he now had to confront.

Plot

The **plot** functions as the body of a speech organized by narrative design. Within the plot of a successful speech, two important things must happen. First, *the action of the story unfolds in a sequence of scenes designed to build suspense until there is a moment of climax*. Colorful detail, lively dialogue, and graphic imagery help this action come alive for listeners. Second, *the characters that are central to the story gain complexity by the way they participate in the action*. They develop an ethos that often makes them idealized portraits that live on in our memories after the speech is over.

Consider again the Owens speech. The plot develops in a sequence of three closely connected scenes: (1) the moments before the actual competition, (2) a description of the competition, and (3) the aftermath of the competition.

In the first scene, we watch a crisis of self-doubt, as Owens kneels to pray. We are also introduced to the generous spirit of Luz Long, who appears on cue as though he were the answer to Owens's prayer, and who offers the advice Owens needs to qualify for his event. Owens recreates the immediacy of the moment by using actual dialogue as Long speaks.

The second scene, which describes the competition itself, is summarized rather quickly. It might have been quite colorful, had Owens wished to dwell upon it.

But he hurries on to the third scene, the aftermath, because the real business of this speech is to portray the ethos of Luz Long as an Olympic ideal. The fact that Long is German, even that he represents a Nazi ideology, is relevant to this portrait only as irony. Owens's point is that good sportsmanship transcends both national origin and political affiliation and joins people as brothers and sisters. Thus we behold the extraordinary spectacle at the conclusion of the competition when Luz Long raises Owens's arms to the sky as he leads the throng of Germans in chanting "Jazze Owenz."

Epilogue

The **epilogue** of a story reflects on the meaning of the action and offers final comments on the character of those who participated in it. It is the counterpart of the conclusion in other speech designs. When used in ceremonial speeches, the epilogue often conveys a moral lesson for the present audience and situation. Thus, in the Owens example, we see the nobility of Luz Long reaffirmed in the final scene of the story:

> Luz Long was killed in World War II and, although I don't cry often, I wept when I received his last letter—I knew it was his last. In it he asked me to someday find his son, Karl, and to tell him "of how we fought well together, and of the good times, and that any two men can become brothers."

What Owens doesn't quite tell us, but we can infer it from what he says, is that Long and Owens had become good friends, that they corresponded often, and that Long knew that his end was near. These inferences only strengthen the underlying lesson for the audience Owens addressed in 1980:

> That is what the Olympics are all about. The road to the Olympics does not lead to Moscow. It leads to no city, no country. It goes far beyond Lake Placid or Moscow, ancient Greece or Nazi Germany. The road to the Olympics leads, in the end, to the best within us.

---

plot The body of a speech that follows narrative design; unfolds in a sequence of scenes designed to build suspense.

epilogue The final part of a narrative that reflects upon its meaning.

Figure 17.3

Checklist for Developing a Narrative Design

Develop the Prologue

☐ I have described the setting in which my story will play out.
☐ I have established the context in which my story occurs.
☐ I have aroused audience interest by foreshadowing the characters in my story.
☐ I have aroused curiosity by foreshadowing the meaning of my story.

Develop the Plot

☐ I have selected a scene (or scenes) in which the action of my story will unfold.
☐ I have used colorful detail, picturesque language, and lively dialogue to bring the action to life.
☐ I have developed characters who are interesting because of their roles in the action.
☐ I have built suspense to bring my story to a climax.

Develop the Epilogue

☐ I reflect on the meaning of my story so that listeners get the point.
☐ My story leaves listeners with the feeling that they have met an interesting character(s) they will want to remember.
☐ My story teaches an important lesson that listeners can apply.
☐ I have used language skills to help listeners remember the message.

Just as the Olympic spirit could thrive in the bigoted atmosphere of Nazi Germany in 1936, so also could it blossom in the Cold War atmosphere of Moscow in 1980. Owens's speech, apparently commemorating a long past moment and honoring an obscure sports competitor, becomes finally an argument criticizing the action taken by the United States in boycotting the 1980 games.

From this discussion, we can draw a number of guidelines to help you develop a speech using narrative design. Figure 17.3 summarizes these guidelines. We have also devised an outline format to help you plan the structure of a speech using narrative design. Figure 17.4 displays this format.

And in Conclusion

We began our book with a toast wishing you a successful adventure in your public speaking class. Now we end our book with a speech of tribute, offered again to you. Public speaking may not have been easy for you. But it is our hope that you have grown as a person as you have grown as a speaker. Our special wishes, expressed in terms of the underlying vision of our book, are that

■ You have learned to climb the barriers that people sometimes erect to separate themselves from each other and that too often prevent meaningful communication.

■ You have learned to weave words and evidence into eloquent thoughts and persuasive ideas.

Figure 17.4

Outline Format for Narrative Design

I. Prologue _____
  A. Setting and context of story: _____
  B. Foreshadowing characters: _____
  C. Foreshadowing meaning: _____

II. Plot _____
  A. Scene 1: _____
  B. Scene 2: _____
  C. Scene 3: _____

III. Epilogue _____
  A. Final scene: _____
  B. Lessons of the story: _____

Works and People Consulted

- You have learned to build and present speeches that enlighten others in responsible and ethical ways.

- You have come to appreciate public speaking as a force that can shape our destinies.

And so we propose another toast: *May you use your new speaking skills to improve the lives and lift the spirits of all who may listen to you.*

In Summary

Ceremonial speeches serve important social functions. They reinforce the values that hold people together in a community and give listeners a sense of order and purpose in their lives. They place the spotlight on leadership. They also establish principles that can be applied in later arguments.

Major Techniques of Ceremonial Speaking. Two major techniques of ceremonial speaking are identification and magnification. The first creates close feeling, and the second selects and emphasizes those features of a subject that will convey the speaker's message. Speakers build identification by using narratives that remind listeners of shared experiences.

Recognizing heroes and heroines also provides ideal models of conduct to draw listeners and speakers closer together. Finally, appeals to group commitment can remind listeners of the values and goals they share. Themes worthy of magnification include overcoming obstacles, achieving unusual goals, performing in a superior manner, having unselfish motives, and benefiting the community. Eloquent uses of language can also magnify the subjects of ceremonial speeches.

Types of Ceremonial Speeches. Speeches of tribute recognize achievements or commemorate special events and perform an inspirational function. Award presentations should explain the nature of the award and what the recipient has done to merit it. Eulogies are speeches of tribute presented on the death of a person or persons. Toasts are ceremonial speeches in miniature that pay tribute, offer blessings, or celebrate the moment.

Speeches of acceptance should begin with an expression of gratitude and an acknowledgment of others who deserve recognition. They should focus on the values that the honor represents. Speeches of introduction should welcome the speaker, build her or his ethos, and tune the audience for the message that will follow.

Speeches of inspiration help listeners appreciate values and make them want to pursue worthy goals. Such speeches often call on stories of past successes.

After-dinner speeches should be lighthearted, serving up humor and insight at the same time.

The master of ceremonies coordinates a program and sees that things run smoothly. He or she sets the mood of the program, introduces the participants, provides transitions, and sometimes presents awards.

Narrative Design. Speeches that center on a master narrative or that focus on engaging listeners in a vicarious experience utilize narrative design. Such speeches follow a dramatic rather than a logical pattern of development. They feature a prologue, which sets the scene for what will follow; a plot, which develops suspenseful action through a series of scenes; and an epilogue, which reflects on the meaning of the story and draws out its lesson for listeners.

Explore and Apply the Ideas in This Chapter

1. Analyze Ashley Smith's "Three Photographs" (in Appendix B) as a speech built on narrative design. Can you identify the prologue, plot, and epilogue and the major scenes of the speech? Who is the major character developed by the narrative? How might the narrative have been improved?

2. The speeches in Appendix B by John Bakke and Elie Wiesel are ceremonial addresses. How do they relate to the basic questions, Who are we? Why are we? What have we accomplished? and What can we become together? What values do they celebrate?

3. Some might argue that magnification is distortion: that when you select a person's successes and accomplishments to praise in speeches of tribute, you are ignoring his or her failures and shortcom-

ings. The effect is to revise history and to create a false reflection of that person's reality. What is your position on this issue? Is magnification justifiable? Are there moments in which it might not be justifiable? Offer examples in class discussion to defend your position.

4. Select a public figure whom you admire and prepare a speech of tribute honoring that person. Which aspects of your subject's life did you choose to magnify and why?

5. List five heroes or heroines who are often mentioned in ceremonial speeches. Why do speakers refer to them so frequently? What does this tell us about the nature of these admired persons, about the needs of contemporary audiences, and about the ceremonial speech situation? Be prepared to discuss these topics in class.

Reach for the Stars!

Ashlie McMillan

Please close your eyes. Imagine now that you are shrinking. Can you feel your hands and feet getting smaller, your arms being pulled in closer to your shoulders? Can you picture your legs now dangling off the edge of your seat as your legs shrink up closer to your hips? Now you are only three feet tall. But don't open your eyes yet. This is your first day of being a diastrophic dwarf.

You wake up and get out of bed, which is quite a drop because the bed is almost as tall as you are. You go to the bathroom to wash your face and brush your teeth, but you must stand on a trash can because the faucet is out of your reach. Now you go back to your dorm room, and you're ready to put on your clothes. But again you can't reach the clothes hanging in your closet because you're too short. You have to struggle to get dressed.

Now you have errands that you must run. But how are you going to do them? If you walk, it will take you a long time because you must take many short steps. And you can't drive a car because you can't reach the pedals, much less see over the steering wheel. Finally you get to the bank. But it takes you about five minutes to get the teller's attention because she can't see you below the counter. Next you go to the grocery store. This takes forever because you can't push a cart. You're forced to use a carry basket and to find people who will reach high items for you. Frustrated yet? Okay, open your eyes.

In 1968 my cousin, Tina McMillan, was born. Today she's in her twenty-ninth year as a diastrophic dwarf. What does that mean? It means that she'll never be taller than three feet. It means that her hands will never be able to bend this way [gestures] because she will never have joints in her fingers or toes. She'll always have club feet, and she had to have a rod put in her spine because all diastrophic dwarfs are plagued with scoliosis.

So what does her dwarfism mean to my cousin? Nothing. When you first meet Tina, you might be a little shocked at how tiny she is. But after a while you forget her physical size because her personality is so large and her spirit is so bright. Today I want to tell you the story of how this small person is reaching for the stars. Her life is a miracle that should teach us never to let obstacles stand in the way of our goals and dreams.

When my aunt and uncle were told that they were going to have a baby who was a diastrophic dwarf, they prepared themselves. They were ready to tell their child that she would never be able to have a Great Dane dog because it would be three times the size that she was. That she would never be able to ride a horse. That she would never be able to drive a car. And that she might not be able to attend college because the dormitories and other facilities were not built for people three feet tall.

What my aunt and uncle were *not* prepared for was a child with a physical disability who refused to see herself as disabled. I can tell you that growing up with Tina was quite an experience. She was always the ham of the cousins, always the center of attention. I remember going over to her house and playing with her *three* Great Dane dogs in the backyard. I remember every Sunday when my grandpa would take us out to the farm and we would fight over who got to ride the horses. And Tina would even fight my grandfather so she could get up on the horse all by herself. And I remember the day, some time after her sixteenth birthday, that she slid behind the wheel of a car. She had teamed up with some engineers down in Texas to have the pedals extended as well as hand gears made on the steering wheel so that she could

In her speech of tribute to her cousin, Ashlie McMillan makes use of both identification and magnification, the major techniques of ceremonial speaking. She invites identification with Tina by picturing her in simple, everyday situations. By asking her listeners to imagine themselves as dwarfs, Ashlie develops a narrative based on vicarious experience

After introducing her cousin and defining dwarfism, Ashlie begins magnification by selecting incidents that reveal Tina as a spirited, determined fighter who refuses to accept the role of a disabled person. Ashlie's entire speech is built on an inspiring irony: that someone so small in physique should be so large in spirit.

drive herself. But perhaps my proudest and fondest memory was watching my cousin walk across the graduation stage at Texas Christian University in 1991. She not only got her degree in English, but she went on to get a master's degree in anthropology from TCU. After she graduated, the university invited her to come back to teach in the English Department. But by this time Tina had a new challenge: She declined the teaching job so that she could enter politics as campaign manager for the mayor of Dallas.

Tina has never stopped challenging the perception that she is disabled. Next April she will be marrying a person of normal stature, and once again she will defy society's assumption that something must be wrong about such a marriage. And then in the fall she plans on attending the University of Texas law school. Want to bet against her there?

As she nears the conclusion, Ashlie begins to draw lessons from her cousin's life to inspire listeners. The closing sentence suggests an analogy with a point made earlier in the speech: People must stand on dreams to reach distant goals.

Somehow, against the odds, my cousin has led a normal life. To many people, what she has accomplished might not seem that exceptional. To me, however, she is an inspiration. Whenever I think I've got problems that are too much for me, I think of her and of what she has done, this large and vital person stuffed into such a small body. I think of how she refuses to use her disability as a scapegoat or excuse. And I remember how she does not even consider quitting if something stands in her way. She simply views the obstacle, decides the best way to get around it, and moves on. And although she will lose the ability to walk, probably by the age of forty, I believe that she will still find the way to keep moving toward her goals.

The next time a large obstacle stands in your way, remember Tina, my small cousin who has achieved such noteworthy things. You too may seem too short to grasp your stars, but you never know how far you might reach if you stand upon a dream.

Communicating in Small Groups

Many of the important communication interactions in your life happen in small groups. In school you may be assigned to a team working on a special assignment. At work you may be appointed to a committee to plan a project. In your community there may be problems that can only be solved by people working together. All of these situations require effective group communication skills. Moreover, members of a group often make public presentations promoting their recommendations after the group has completed its work.

To understand how groups communicate, we need to consider the nature of a group. Is any gathering of people a group? Not necessarily. For example, a gathering of people waiting for a bus would not be considered a group. *To be considered a* **group,** *a gathering of people must actively interact with one another over a period of time to reach a goal or goals.*

Let's suppose that the same people have been meeting at the bus stop every workday for several months. They may chat with one another while waiting for the bus, but this casual interaction is not enough to make them a group. Now, suppose that the Metropolitan Transit Organization (MTO) announces in the morning paper that it wants to raise fares from $2.00 to $3.00 each way for the trip downtown. That morning when the people get together, they begin to express their outrage about the problem that confronts them. One of them suggests that they gather at her apartment that evening to come up with a plan to persuade the MTO to reconsider its proposal. When these people get together that evening, they will be interacting as a group.

In this appendix we discuss how groups function and how good public communication skills can make you a better participant or leader in groups. We also consider the various types of group presentations that you may be called upon to make.

Advantages and Disadvantages of Group Problem Solving

When we listen to a single speaker, we hear only one version of a situation or problem. That perspective may be biased, based on self-interest, or simply wrong. When an issue is important, we need to minimize the risk of such possibilities. One way to do this is to form a group to consider the situation and come up with recommendations concerning it.

Group problem solving has many advantages over individual efforts. When people share their various ways of seeing a problem, they create a richer picture of the situation. They begin to see the world as others see it. This sharing of perspectives is self-correcting. Misconceptions and bias may come to light as people share their perceptions of a situation. Listening to others' points of view also can stimulate creative thinking about solutions.

group Gathering of people who interact with one another to reach goals.

In well-managed problem-solving groups, people on all sides of an issue have a chance to discuss the similarities and differences of their perspectives. Through such discussions, they may uncover areas of agreement that can help resolve differences. Additionally, when groups are small, people may explore their differences constructively and feel free to explore a variety of solutions. Because of these advantages, businesses often use small groups to work on important internal organizational problems.

Although working in groups has many advantages, some problems may arise that can reduce the effectiveness of group deliberations. **Cultural gridlock,** or communication problems based on profound cultural differences, can occur in groups whose participants have different backgrounds. For example, people in marketing departments and the research and development scientists in an organization may bring different expectations to a meeting. Participants from different social backgrounds may bring different perspectives, agendas, priorities, procedures, ways of communicating, and standards of protocol to meetings. These differences may sidetrack constructive discussions.

Dealing with cultural gridlock is never easy, but the following guidelines will help minimize its impact:

1. Allow time for people to get acquainted before starting to work.
2. Provide enough physical space so that people don't feel crowded.
3. Distribute an agenda in advance of the meeting so people know what to expect.
4. Summarize discussions as the meeting progresses. Post key points of agreement.
5. Avoid using jargon that some participants may not understand.
6. Be sensitive to cultural differences in how people relate to one another and nonverbal communication.[1]

Another problem groups may encounter is **groupthink,** the uncritical acceptance of a position.[2] Groupthink is most likely to occur when participants place a higher value on harmonious interpersonal interactions than on performing effectively. Other factors that contribute to groupthink include a leader's obvious preference for a certain position or the lack of a clear set of procedures for working through problems.

Groupthink can be dangerous because outsiders may assume that a group has deliberated carefully and responsibly when it has not. The problems in decision making that often accompany groupthink may include an inadequate exploration of the problem, slipshod information gathering and analysis, and an incomplete consideration of alternative solutions.

Dealing with groupthink is difficult, but there are some steps that can guard against it. First, groups need to be aware that groupthink can be a problem. The major symptoms of groupthink include pressuring dissidents within the group and censoring their ideas, defending and justifying opinions more than exploring alternate ways of thinking, and asserting the group's own moral righteousness and attacking the character of opposing groups.

Once a group is aware that groupthink is a problem, the leader can take action to minimize its effects. The leader should encourage the group to set standards for investigation and appraisal that discourage uncritical thinking and premature conclusions. The following leadership behaviors can help reduce groupthink problems:

■ Remind participants to evaluate the support behind recommendations.

■ Urge members to delay decisions until all have had a chance to express their views.

---

cultural gridlock   A problem that occurs when the cultural differences in a group are so profound that they create tensions that block constructive discussion.

groupthink   Occurs when a single, uncritical frame of mind dominates group thinking and prevents the full, objective analysis of specific problems.

- Encourage critical questions from participants.
- Bring in outsiders to talk about the issues under consideration.
- Encourage debate of all recommendations.

Group Problem-Solving Techniques

roup deliberations that are orderly, systematic, and thorough help people reach high-quality decisions. To function effectively, problem-solving groups can use a variety of methods, the most common of which is called reflective thinking.

Reflective Thinking and Problem Solving.

The reflective thinking approach used in problem-solving groups is a modification of a technique first proposed by John Dewey in 1910. This systematic approach has five steps: (1) defining the problem, (2) generating potential solutions, (3) evaluating solution options, (4) developing a plan of action, and (5) evaluating the results.

Step 1: Defining the Problem.   Sometimes what the group initially thinks is the problem is actually only a symptom of the problem. A group that starts with what it thinks is a problem of insufficient support for public education may discover that the actual problem is far more complicated. For example, the real problem may involve the lack of clearly articulated educational goals, poor communication with the public about education in the community, or inadequate public participation (parents and others) with the schools. All problem-solving groups should take time to define the problem carefully before looking for solutions. The following guidelines can help a group define the problem it needs to work on:

1. Describe the problem as specifically as possible.
2. Gather enough information to understand the problem.
3. Explore the causes of the problem.
4. Investigate the history of the problem.
5. Determine who is affected by the problem.
6. Consider the consequences if the problem is solved or not solved.

Step 2: Generating Potential Solutions.   Once the problem has been defined, the group can begin looking for solutions. One useful technique for generating potential solutions is **brainstorming**. Brainstorming encourages all group members to contribute their ideas for solutions.[3] During the brainstorming process, members should not attempt to evaluate the solutions or decide which option to follow. The following rules should govern brainstorming sessions:

- Present your ideas enthusiastically.
- Give voice to all your ideas, no matter how outrageous they may seem. The more options the group generates, the more ideas the group has to work with toward a solution.
- Don't evaluate the ideas presented. Keeping the process of exploration free of criticism helps the group generate more and better potential solutions.

brainstorming Technique that encourages the free play of the mind.

- Don't be afraid to combine ideas to come up with additional options.

- Be sure that everyone contributes.

The process of brainstorming proceeds as follows:

1. The leader asks each member in turn to contribute an idea during each round of participation. If a member does not have an idea, he or she may pass. At this stage, the emphasis is on full participation and the number of ideas advanced.

2. A recorder writes all ideas on a flip chart or marker board so everyone can see them.

3. Brainstorming continues until all members have passed. *Do not stop the process until everyone has presented all their ideas!*

4. The suggestions are reviewed for clarification, adding new options, or combining options.

5. The group identifies the most promising ideas.

6. The leader appoints members to research each idea and to bring additional information to a later evaluation meeting.

7. The process of gathering solution possibilities should remain open. Additional ideas may be considered during the next phase of the problem-solving process.

When time is short or when face-to-face participation may initially discourage the open exploration of ideas because of cultural or status differences among group members, an alternative procedure is **electronic brainstorming,** in which participants generate ideas via computer connections before meeting face-to-face.[4] One advantage of these initial electronic explorations is that leaders can encourage participants to bring additional supportive materials to the meetings to clarify options.

Step 3: Evaluating Solution Options.   When the meeting to generate options comes to an end, the group should schedule a subsequent meeting to evaluate the ideas. Between meetings, members can gather information on each option. When the group reconvenes, it should apply the following evaluation criteria to the selected ideas:

- Costs of the option

- Probability of success

- Ease or difficulty of enacting the option

- Time constraints

- Additional benefits that might accrue

- Potential problems that might be encountered

Groups should summarize the evaluation of each option on a flip chart and then post the summaries so that members can refer to them as they compare options. As options are considered, some will seem weak and be dropped, and others may be strengthened and refined. The group also may combine options to generate new alternatives. For example, if the group is caught between option A, which promises improved efficiency, and option B, which promises lower cost, it may be possible to combine the best features of each into option C.

electronic brainstorming   A group technique in which participants generate ideas in computer chat groups or by email.

After all of the options have been considered, the group then ranks the solutions in terms of their acceptability. The option receiving the highest overall rank becomes the proposed solution.

Participants often become personally caught up with their own solutions. During the evaluation phase, the leader must keep the group focused on the ideas advanced and not on personalities. Differences of opinion and conflict are a natural and necessary part of problem solving. Discussing the strengths of an idea before talking about its weaknesses can help take some of the heat out of the process.

Step 4: Developing a Plan of Action.   Once the group has selected a solution, it must determine how the proposal can be implemented. For example, to improve company morale, a group might recommend a three-step plan:

1. better in-house training programs to increase opportunities for promotion,

2. a pay structure that rewards success in training programs, and

3. increased employee participation in decision making.

As the group considers this plan, it should think about what might help or hinder it, what resources will be needed to enact it, and what type of timetable it would follow. If the group cannot develop a plan of action for the solution or if insurmountable obstacles crop up, the group should return to step 3 and reconsider other options.

Step 5: Evaluating Results.   Not only must a problem-solving group plan how to implement a solution, but it must also determine how to evaluate results of the plan's enactment. The group should establish evaluation criteria for success, a schedule of when results are expected, and contingency plans to use if the original plan doesn't work. For example, to monitor the ongoing success of the three-part plan to improve employee morale, the group would have to determine benchmarks of progress for each stage. That way, the company could detect and correct problems as they occur, before they damage the plan as a whole. Having a scheduled sequence of benchmarks provides a way to determine results while the plan is being enacted, rather than having to wait for the entire project to be completed.

Other Approaches to Group Problem Solving

Although the reflective thinking process works well in many situations, at times a different approach may be needed. When a group consists of people from very diverse backgrounds, **collaborative problem solving** may work best.[5] For example, in many urban areas, coalitions of business executives and educators have worked together on plans to train people for jobs in the community. In such situations, the problems are usually important and the resources are typically limited. Because there is no established authority structure and the factions may have different expectations or goals, these diverse participants may have problems working together. To be effective, such groups need to spend time defining the problem and exploring each other's perspectives. This should help them recognize their interdependence while preserving their independence. In such groups, the participants must come to see themselves *not* as members of group A (the executives) or group B (the educators), but as members of group C (the coalition). Leadership can be especially difficult in such groups.

collaborative problem solving   In group communication, an approach that gathers participants from separate areas of public or private sectors for their input on a problem.

One useful approach in such situations is **dialogue groups.** According to William Isaacs, director of the Dialogue Project at the Massachusetts Institute of Technology Center for Organizational Learning, "Dialogue is a discipline of collective thinking and inquiry, a process for transforming the quality of conversation, and, in particular, the thinking that lies beneath it."[6] Such groups stress understanding the different interpretations of the problem that participants bring to the interaction. Their purpose is to establish a dialogue from which common ground and mutual trust can emerge.

The role of the facilitator is critical in dialogue groups. According to Edgar Schein of the MIT Center, the facilitator must take the following steps:

1. Seat the group in a circle to create a sense of equality.

2. Introduce the problem.

3. Ask people to share an experience in which dialogue led to "good communication."

4. Ask members to consider what leads to good communication.

5. Ask participants to talk about their reactions.

6. Let the conversation flow naturally.

7. Intervene only to clarify problems of communication.

8. Conclude by asking all members to comment however they choose.[7]

The dialogue method is not a substitute for other problem-solving techniques, such as the reflective thinking process presented earlier. Instead, the dialogue method may be used as a precursor because deliberation usually works well only when members understand each other well enough to be "talking the same language."

When an organization wants to delve into the feelings or motivations of their customers or clients, they often put together a **focus group.**[8] Focus groups typically consist of six to ten members carefully selected to provide the type of information sought. In a focus group a trained moderator asks questions and encourages all of the participants to respond. Advertisements, brochures, other printed materials, or video clips may also be used to stimulate discussion. Interactions between members of the group often provide the most valuable information. The sessions are recorded on either audiotape or videotape for later analysis. Focus groups are typically face-to-face encounters, but they may also be conducted through telephone conference calls, in Internet chat rooms, or through videoconferencing.

Participating in Small Groups

 o participate successfully in small groups, you must understand your responsibilities as a group member. You should also be prepared to assume leadership of the group.

Working as a Group Member

Becoming an effective group member means you must accept certain responsibilities:

- First, come to meetings prepared to contribute. This means reading background materials and completing any tasks assigned by the group leader.

---

dialogue groups   A group assembled to explore the underlying assumptions of a problem but not necessarily to solve it.

focus group   A small group formed to reveal the feelings or motivations of customers or clients.

■ Second, be willing to learn from others. Try to contribute to rather than dominate discussions. Don't be afraid to admit you are wrong, and don't become defensive when challenged. Willingness to change your views is not a sign of weakness, nor is obstinacy a strength.

■ Third, listen constructively. Don't interrupt others. Object if you feel consensus is forming too quickly. You might save the meeting from groupthink.

Analyzing your group communication skills can help you become more effective in groups. Use the self-analysis form in Figure A.1 to steer yourself toward more constructive group communication behaviors.

As you participate in groups, you should also keep in mind the following questions:

■ What is happening now in the group?

■ What should be happening in the group?

■ What can I do to make this come about?

If you notice a difference between what the group is doing and what it should be doing to reach its goals, you have the opportunity to demonstrate leadership behavior.

Leading Small Groups

For over fifty years, social scientists have been studying leadership by analyzing group communication patterns. This research suggests that two basic types of leadership behaviors emerge in most groups. The first is **task leadership behavior,** which directs the activity of the group toward a specified goal. The second is **social leadership behavior,** which helps build and maintain positive relationships among group members.

Task leaders initiate goal-related communication, including both giving and seeking information, opinions, and suggestions. A task leader might say, "We need more information on just how widespread sexual harassment is on campus. Let me tell you what Dean Johnson told me last Friday." Or the task leader might ask, "Gwen, tell us what you found out from the Affirmative Action Office."

Social leaders express agreement, help the group release tension, and behave in a supportive manner. A social leader looks for chances to give compliments: "I think Gwen has made a very important point. You really helped us by finding that out." Sincere compliments help keep members from becoming defensive and help maintain a constructive communication atmosphere. In a healthy communication climate, the two kinds of leadership behavior support each other and keep the group moving toward its goal. When one person combines both styles of leadership, that person is likely to be highly effective.

Leadership has also been studied in terms of how the leader enacts the task and maintenance functions. An **autocratic leader** makes decisions without consultation, issues orders or gives direction, and controls the members of the group through the use of rewards or punishments. A **participative leader** seeks input from group members and gives them an active role in decision making. A **free-rein leader** lets members decide on their own what to do, how to do it, and when to do it. If you were working in an organization, you would probably say you "worked *for*" an autocratic leader, "worked *with*" a participative leader, and "worked *in spite of*" a free-rein leader.

---

task leadership behavior   A leadership emphasis that directs the attention and activity of a group toward a specified goal.

special leadership behavior   Occurs when leaders focus upon building and maintaining positive, productive relationships among group members.

autocratic leader   A leader who makes decisions without consultation, issues orders or gives direction, and controls the members of the group through the use of rewards or punishments.

Figure A.1

Group Communication Skills Self-Analysis Form

	Need to Do Less	Doing Fine	Need to Do More
1. I make my points concisely.	☐	☐	☐
2. I speak with confidence.	☐	☐	☐
3. I provide specific examples and details.	☐	☐	☐
4. I try to integrate ideas that are expressed.	☐	☐	☐
5. I let others know when I do not understand them.	☐	☐	☐
6. I let others know when I agree with them.	☐	☐	☐
7. I let others know tactfully when I disagree with them.	☐	☐	☐
8. I express my opinions.	☐	☐	☐
9. I suggest solutions to problems.	☐	☐	☐
10. I listen to understand.	☐	☐	☐
11. I try to understand before agreeing or disagreeing.	☐	☐	☐
12. I ask questions to get more information.	☐	☐	☐
13. I ask others for their opinions.	☐	☐	☐
14. I check for group agreement.	☐	☐	☐
15. I try to minimize tension.	☐	☐	☐
16. I accept help from others.	☐	☐	☐
17. I offer help to others.	☐	☐	☐
18. I let others have their say.	☐	☐	☐
19. I stand up for myself.	☐	☐	☐
20. I urge others to speak up.	☐	☐	☐

participative leader　A leader who seeks input from group members and gives them an active role in decision making.

free-rein leader　A leader who leaves members free to decide what, how, and when to act, offering no guidance.

Currently, work on leadership suggests that leadership styles are either transactional or transformational. **Transactional leadership** takes place in an environment based on power relationships and relies on reward and punishment to accomplish its ends. **Transformational leadership** appeals to "people's higher levels of motivation to contribute to a cause and add to the quality of life on the planet."[9] It carries overtones of stewardship instead of management. Transformational leaders have the following qualities:

- They have a vision of what needs to be done.
- They are empathetic.
- They are trusted.
- They give credit to others.
- They help others develop.
- They share power.
- They are willing to experiment and learn.

In short, transformational leaders lead with both their hearts and their heads. According to John Schuster, a management consultant who specializes in transformational leadership training, "The heart is more difficult to develop. It's easier to get smarter than to become more caring."[10] Transformational leadership encourages communication from subordinates because they are less intimidated by their superiors and more willing to ask for advice or help.[11]

Consider how ideal leadership relates to the major components of **ethos** (see the discussion of ethos in Chapter 3). An effective leader is *competent*. This means the leader understands the problem and knows how to steer a group through the problem-solving process. An effective leader has *integrity*. This means the leader is honest and places group success above personal concerns. An effective leader is perceived as a person of *goodwill*, concerned less about the self and more about those whom the group serves. Finally, an effective leader is *dynamic*. Dynamic leaders are enthusiastic, energetic, and decisive.

Don't be intimidated by this idealized portrait of a leader. Most of us have these qualities in varying degrees and can use them when the need for leadership arises. To be an effective leader, remember two simple goals: *Help others be effective* and *get the job done*. Cultivate an open leadership style that encourages all sides to air their views.

Planning for Meetings. In many organizations, meetings are seen as time wasters. This may be because the people who conduct them do not know when to call meetings or how to run them.[12] Meetings should be called when people need to:

- discuss the meaning of information face-to-face.
- decide on a common course of action.
- establish a plan of action.
- report on the progress of a plan, evaluate its effectiveness, and revise it if necessary.

transactional leadership A leadership style based on power relationships that relies on reward and punishment to achieve its ends.

transformational leadership A leadership style based on mutual respect and stewardship rather than on control.

ethos Those characteristics that make a speaker appear honest, credible, powerful, and appealing.

More than just knowing when to call meetings, you need to know how to plan them. The following guidelines should help you plan effective meetings:

- *Have a specific purpose for holding a meeting.* Unnecessary meetings waste time. If your goal is simply to increase interaction, plan a social event rather than a meeting.

- *Prepare an agenda and distribute it to participants before the meeting.* Having an agenda gives members time to prepare and assemble information they might need. Solicit agenda items from participants.

- *Keep meetings short.* After about an hour, groups get tired, and the law of diminishing returns sets in. Don't try to do too much in a single meeting.

- *Keep groups small.* You get more participation and interaction in small groups. In larger groups, people may be reluctant to ask questions or contribute ideas.

- *Select participants who will interact easily with each other.* In business settings, the presence of someone's supervisor may inhibit interaction. You will get better participation if group members come from the same or nearly the same working level in the organization.

- *Plan the site of the meeting.* Arrange for privacy and freedom from interruptions. A circular arrangement contributes to participation because there is no power position. A rectangular table or a lectern and classroom arrangement may inhibit interaction.

- *Prepare in advance.* Be certain that you have the necessary supplies, such as chalk, a flip chart, markers, note pads, and pencils. If you will use electronic equipment, be sure it is in working order.

Conducting an Effective Meeting. Group leaders have more responsibilities than other members. Leaders must encourage deliberations that proceed in good faith toward constructive ends. They should also be well informed on the issues so that they can answer questions and keep the group moving toward its objectives. The following checklist should be helpful in guiding your behavior as a group leader:

- Begin and end the meeting on time.

- Present background information concisely and objectively.

- Lead, don't run the meeting.

- Be enthusiastic.

- Get conflict out in the open so that it can be dealt with directly.

- Urge all members to participate.

- Keep discussion centered on the issue.

- At the close of a meeting, summarize what the group has accomplished.

As a group leader, you may need to present the group's recommendations to others. In this task, you function mainly as an informative speaker. You should

---

Figure A.2

Behaviors That Enhance or Impede Decision Making

Enhancing Behaviors	Impeding Behaviors
Opinions are sought out.	Members express dislike for others.
Creativity is encouraged.	Members personally attack others.
Participation is encouraged.	Members make sarcastic comments.
Opposing views are encouraged.	Leader sets criteria for solution.
Members provide information.	Leader makes the decision.
Group analyzes suggestions.	Leader intimidates members.
Members listen to one another.	Meeting becomes a gripe session.
Members respect others' ideas.	Disagreements are ignored, not aired.
Members support others' ideas.	Disagreement is discouraged.
Problem is thoroughly researched.	Members pursue personal goals.
Group sets criteria for solution.	
Members are knowledgeable on issue.	
Evidence for suggestions is presented.	
Group focuses on task.	

---

present the recommendations offered by the group, along with the major reasons for making these recommendations. You should also mention reservations that may have surfaced during deliberations. Your job in making this report is not to advocate, but to educate. Later, you may join in any following discussion with persuasive remarks that express your personal convictions on the subject.

Finally, as you conduct meetings, keep in mind behaviors that either advance or impede group effectiveness.[13] Better group decisions are made when all group members participate fully in the process; when members are respectful of each other and leaders are respectful of members; and when negative emotional behaviors are kept in check. More specific details of these findings are listed in Figure A.2.

Guidelines for Formal Meetings

The larger a group is, the more it needs a formal procedure to conduct meetings. Also, if a meeting involves a controversial subject, it is often wise to have a set of rules to follow. Having clear-cut guidelines helps keep meetings from becoming chaotic and helps ensure fair treatment for all participants. In such situations, many groups choose to operate by **parliamentary procedure.**

Parliamentary procedure establishes an order of business for a meeting and lays out the way the group initiates discussions and reaches decisions. Under parliamentary procedure, a formal meeting proceeds as follows:

1. The chair calls the meeting to order.

parliamentary procedure   A set of formal rules that establishes an order of business for meetings and encourages the orderly, fair, and full consideration of proposals during group deliberation.

2. The secretary reads the minutes of the previous meeting, which are corrected, if necessary, and approved.

3. Reports from officers and committees are presented.

4. Unfinished business is considered.

5. New business is introduced.

6. Announcements are made.

7. The meeting is adjourned.

Business in formal meetings goes forward by **motions,** or proposals set before the group. Consider the following. The chair asks: "Is there any new business?" A member responds: "I move that we allot $500 to build a Homecoming float." The member has offered a main motion, which proposes an action. Before the group can discuss the motion, it must be seconded. The purpose of a **second** is to ensure that more than one person wants to see the motion considered. If no one volunteers a second, the chair may ask, "Is there a second?" Typically, another member will respond, "I second the motion." Once a motion is made and seconded, it is open for discussion. It must be passed by majority vote, defeated, or otherwise resolved before the group can move on to other business. With the exception of a few technical motions (such as, "I move we take a fifteen-minute recess" or, "Point of personal privilege—can we do anything about the heat in this room?"), the main motion remains at the center of group attention until resolved.

Let us assume that, as the group discusses the main motion in our example, some members believe the amount of money proposed is insufficient. At this point, another member may say: "I move to amend the motion to provide $750 for the float." The **motion to amend** gives the group a chance to modify a main motion. It must be seconded and, after discussion, must be resolved by majority vote before discussion goes forward. If the motion to amend passes, then the amended main motion must be considered further.

How does a group make a decision on a motion? There usually is a time when discussion begins to lag. At this point the chair might say, "Do I hear a call for the question?" A motion to **call the question** ends discussion, and it requires a two-thirds vote for approval. Once the group votes to end discussion, it must then vote to accept or reject the motion. No further discussion can take place until the original or amended original motion is voted on.

Sometimes the discussion of a motion may reveal that the group is confused or sharply divided about an issue. At this point a member may move to **table the motion.** This is a way to dispose of a troublesome motion without further divisive or confused discussion. At other times, the discussion of a motion may reveal that the group lacks information to make an intelligent decision. At that point, we might hear from a member: "In light of the uncertainty over costs, I move we postpone further consideration until next week's meeting." The **motion to postpone consideration** gives the chair a chance to appoint a committee to gather the information needed. The move to adjourn ends the meeting.

These are just some of the important procedures that can help ensure that formal group communication remains fair and constructive (see Figure A.3). For more information on formal group communication procedures, consult the latest edition of *Robert's Rules of Order.*

motions Formal proposals for group consideration.
second A motion must receive a "second" before group discussion can proceed; ensures that more than one member wishes to have the motion considered.

motion to amend A parliamentary move that offers opportunity to modify a motion presently under discussion.
call the question A motion that proposes to end discussion and bring a vote.

table the motion A parliamentary move to suspend indefinitely the discussion of a motion.
motion to postpone consideration A motion that defers discussion until some specified time.

Figure A.3

Guide to Parliamentary Procedure

Action	Requires Second	Can Be Debated	Can Be Amended	Vote Required	Function
Main Motion	Yes	Yes	Yes	Majority	Commits group to a specific action or position.
Second	No	No	No	None	Assures that more than one group member wishes to see idea considered.
Move to Amend	Yes	Yes	Yes	Majority	Allows group to modify and improve an existing motion.
Call the Question	Yes	No	No	Two-thirds	Brings discussion to an end and moves to a vote on the motion in question.
Move to Table the Motion	Yes	No	No	Majority	Stops immediate consideration of the motion until a later unspecified time.
Move to Postpone Consideration	Yes	Yes	Yes	Majority	Stops immediate discussion and allows time for the group to obtain more information on the problem.
Move to Adjourn	Yes	No	No	Majority	Formally ends meeting.

Making Group Presentations

 fter a group has completed its work, it may need to present its findings and recommendations to a larger audience. To plan this presentation, the group leader should:

- Designate which group members will present which parts of the report.

- Assign other duties such as preparing or coordinating presentation aids

- Develop an outline or agenda for the presentation

- Determine who should handle questions and answers

- Schedule and oversee a rehearsal of the group presentation.

Often, a designated spokesperson will simply present an **oral report.** This report is basically an informative speech which follows a specific protocol. The introduction briefly reviews the problem, introduces the members of the group (including their credentials) if they are not well known to the audience, and describes the process used by the group to study the problem. The body of the report

oral report   Presentation that summarizes the deliberations of a small group to inform a larger audience of decision makers.

covers the major findings or recommendations for action. The conclusion summarizes the findings and may make suggestions for further work. The report should be as brief as possible and should allow for questions and answers following the formal presentation.

In addition to a simple oral report, group presentations may follow four other formats: a symposium, a panel discussion, a roundtable presentation, or a forum.

A **symposium** features a moderator and members of the problem-solving group as presenters. This group should be selected on the basis of special competencies and communication skills. The primary role of the moderator is to introduce the topic and speakers at the beginning of the symposium and to summarize the findings as the presentation draws to a close. Each symposium speaker will typically cover one aspect of the topic, making a short (well-prepared and rehearsed) report on the group's findings or recommendations in that area. The moderator enforces time limits and keeps the presentations on track. The symposium is followed typically by a question-and-answer session.

A **panel discussion** is less formal than a symposium. It also has a moderator who introduces the topic and the participants, but it does not feature prepared speeches. Rather, it features a planned pattern of spontaneous conversational exchanges. Following the brief introductions the moderator asks questions of the group. Participants respond with brief impromptu answers. The moderator guides the discussion and keeps the group in focus. He or she should also see that no single participant dominates the discussion and that all panelists actually participate.

Although responses are impromptu, this does not mean that participants are in the dark about what will happen. Advance planning should indicate what questions will be asked so that panelists can prepare with these in mind. Panelists should review what went on in the group and organize their ideas before participating. Panelists should be prepared for tough follow-up questions either from the moderator or from the audience.

A **roundtable** presentation is an interactive way of publicly exchanging information, ideas, or opinions.[14] All members of the group are considered equal and are encouraged to participate openly and fully in the proceedings. There are no formal opening statements or prepared speeches. A facilitator helps generate discussion, makes certain the speakers stay on track and adhere to time limits, and encourages a nonjudgmental dialogue. In late 2006 the Sierra Club conducted a roundtable on the climate crisis that included business and political leaders as well as environmental activists.[15] You can watch these roundtable participants interact at www.sierraclub.org/lpressroom/events/2006-12-14. An abridged transcript of the proceedings is available in the May/June 2007 issue of *Sierra*.

In a **forum** presentation, questions come from the audience rather than from the moderator. The basic job of the moderator of a forum is to keep the discussion on track. The moderator may introduce the topic and participants, and during the course of the forum, he or she recognizes audience members who wish to ask questions. At times, the moderator may also have to actually "moderate"—act as a referee if questions or answers become heated on emotional topics. If the group anticipates controversy, it may wish to arrange for a parliamentarian to help keep the meeting constructive. Participants should follow the guidelines suggested for handling questions and answers in Chapter 13.

symposium   Group presentation in which speakers address different areas of an issue.
panel discussion   A group presentation that features an organized pattern of exchanges among speakers, directed and controlled by a moderator.

roundtable   Interactive way of informally exchanging ideas, information, or opinions within a small group before a larger audience.

forum   Presentational format in which a group of specialists in different areas of a subject respond to questions from an audience.

Speeches for Analysis

Self-Introductory

Sandra Baltz *My Three Cultures*

Marie D'Aniello *Family Gifts*

Ashley Smith *Three Photographs*

Elizabeth Tidmore *Lady with a Gun*

Informative

Marge Anderson *Looking Through Our Window: The Value of Indian Culture*

Stephen Huff *The New Madrid Earthquake Area*

Cecile Larson *The "Monument" at Wounded Knee*

Persuasive

Joshua Logan *Global Burning*

Joshua Logan *Cooling the World's Fever*

Bonnie Marshall *Living Wills: Ensuring Your Right to Choose*

Ceremonial

John Bakke *Remarks on Accepting the Martin Luther King, Jr., Human Rights Award*

Leslie Eason *A Man for the New Age: Tribute to Tiger Woods*

Elie Wiesel *Nobel Peace Prize Acceptance Speech*

Self-Introductory Speeches

My Three Cultures
Sandra Baltz

Sandra Baltz first presented this self-introductory speech many years ago at the University of Memphis. She addressed the themes of cross-culturalism and family values long before these became fashionable. Sandra's deft use of comparison and contrast, and her example of foods illustrating how three cultures can combine harmoniously, are instructive. As her speech developed, she built her ethos as a competent, warm person, highly qualified to give later informative and persuasive speeches on issues involving medical care. Presented at a time when tensions in the Middle East were running high, Sandra's speech served as a gentle reminder that people of goodwill can always find ways to enjoy their differences and to reaffirm their common membership in the human family.

Several years ago I read a newspaper article in the *Commercial Appeal* in which an American journalist described some of his experiences in the Middle East. He was there a couple of months and had been the guest of several different Arab families. He reported having been very well treated and very well received by everyone that he met there. But it was only later, when he returned home, that he became aware of the intense resentment his hosts held for Americans and our unwelcome involvement in their Middle Eastern affairs. The journalist wrote of feeling somewhat bewildered, if not deceived, by the large discrepancy between his treatment while in the Middle East and the hostile attitude that he learned about later. He labeled this behavior hypocritical. When I reached the end of the article, I was reminded of a phrase spoken often by my mother. "Sandra," she says to me, "*respeta tu casa y a todos los que entran en ella, trata a tus enemigos asi como a tus amigos.*"

This is an Arabic proverb, spoken in Spanish, and roughly it translates into "Respect your home and all who enter it, treating even an enemy as a friend." This is a philosophy that I have heard often in my home. With this in mind, it seemed to me that the treatment the American journalist received while in the Middle East was not hypocritical behavior on the part of his hosts. Rather, it was an act of respect for their guest, for themselves, and for their home—indeed, a behavior very typical of the Arabic culture.

Since having read that article several years ago, I have become much more aware of how my life is different because of having a mother who is of Palestinian origin but was born and raised in the Central American country of El Salvador.

One of the most obvious differences is that I was raised bilingually—speaking both Spanish and English. In fact, my first words were in Spanish. Growing up speaking two languages has been both an advantage and a disadvantage for me. One clear advantage is that I received straight A's in my Spanish class at Immaculate Conception High School. Certainly, traveling has been made much easier. During visits to Spain, Mexico, and some of the Central American countries, it has been my experience that people are much more open and much more receptive if you can speak their language. In addition, the subtleties of a culture are easier to grasp and much easier to appreciate.

I hope that knowing a second language will continue to be an asset for me in the future. I am currently pursuing a career in medicine. Perhaps by knowing Spanish I can broaden the area in which I can work and increase the number of people that I might reach.

Now one of the disadvantages of growing up bilingually is that I picked up my mother's accent as well as her language. I must have been about four years old before I realized that our feathered friends in the trees are called "birds" not "beers" and that, in fact, we had a "birdbath" in our backyard, not a "beerbath."

Family reunions also tend to be confusing around my home. Most of my relatives speak either Spanish, English, or Arabic, but rarely any combination of the three. So, as a result, deep and involved conversations are almost impossible. But with a little nodding and smiling, I have found that there really is no language barrier among family and friends.

In all, I must say that being exposed to three very different cultures—Latin, Arabic, and American—has been rewarding for me and has made a difference even in the music I enjoy and the food I eat. It is not unusual in my house to sit down to a meal made up of stuffed grape leaves and refried beans and all topped off with apple pie for dessert.

I am fortunate in having had the opportunity to view more closely what makes Arabic and Latin cultures unique. By understanding and appreciating them I have been able to better understand and appreciate my own American culture. In closing, just let me add some words you often hear spoken in my home—*adios* and *allak konn ma'eck*—goodbye, and may God go with you.

Family Gifts
Marie D'Aniello

As she prepared her self-introductory speech at Vanderbilt University, Marie D'Aniello discovered in her self-analysis inventory that the most defining thing about her was her debt to various family members who had helped shape her character. Her speech is woven artfully around three themes, each connected with a member of her family. Her speech was also noteworthy for its narrative technique, its use of colorful and active language, and the warmth and sincerity of its presentation.

Lorraine, John, John Victor, Christopher, Michael, and Anthony. That's my family. My mom, my dad, and my four brothers—that's my life. Together these people have shaped me as an individual. Growing up in a small town with a large family teaches you a lot, especially if you grow up like I did, with a lot of love, a little money, and a whole lot of gifts. Not tangible gifts like clothes and jewelry (although those are nice, too), but gifts like strength, and glory, and pride, pride not only in myself, but also in them and in my family name. I am Marie D'Aniello . . . a D'Aniello. I belong to them like they belong to me. I'm a little bit like my Mom and a little bit like my Dad. I can work like my brother John and play like Chris. I can dream like Michael and love like Anthony. I'm Marie, exactly like no one but a little bit like everyone.

Every now and then I hear people say things like, "You know, my family just doesn't understand me." Well, yeah, I feel that way too at times. My family's not perfect. We have our hard times and disagreements. But I always walk away from these spats with a little more knowledge about myself. Maybe I learn that I'm stronger than I thought. That strength comes from my Mom.

It takes a strong woman to work a full-time job, hold together a family, and raise five children. But my mom does it all. I can remember when I was little waking up at night and listening to the sound of the vacuum cleaner. My Mom would stay up all night, cleaning the house and making sure everything was ready for the next day. She never complained about the hard work. She just did it because she loved us.

I never realized the influence my mother had on me until I went away. Now that I'm here, a thousand miles away from her, I sometimes see her smiling and working the night away. And when I get a grade and I don't think it reflects my effort, I can hear my Mom saying, "You're worth more than this, Marie. You'll get it next time." My Mom's strength has given me my own strength and my own perseverance. I know these qualities are the keys to glory.

When I think of glory, I have to think of my brother Chris. I'll never forget his championship basketball game. It's the typical buzzer beater story: five seconds to go, down by one, Chris gets the ball and he drives down the court, he shoots, he scores! We all rush the floor, everyone. But Chris doesn't care about anyone else. All he looks for is us, his family. He wanted to share his glory with us. I'll never forget the headline, "D'Aniello saves the game!" D'Aniello, hey, wait, that's me. I'm a D'Aniello. I could do this too. Maybe I can't play basketball like Chris, but I can do other things.

So I started trying harder in school, "applying myself," as they say. And I had my own taste of glory. I became a valedictorian, won a scholarship, and now I'm here at Vanderbilt. Unbelievable. After I watched Chris drive toward the hoop to score the winning basket, I wanted to "drive" toward my future. And you know what? I just might make it!

And even if I don't make it, at least I'll try and I'll have my pride. At least, that's what my Dad always says. He knows about pride. He knows what it's like to be scorned because you don't make as much money as other people or because you don't have an impressive job. My Dad is a small-town mechanic. He couldn't go to school, so he taught himself everything he knows. And he knows a whole lot, not just about cars, but about honor. I hear my Dad all the time, saying, "Marie, whatever you do, just try to put your whole heart into it. Make it count. Take pride in it." Not a day goes by that I don't hear those words. Because of him, I take pride in my work and I take pride in myself.

I practiced my speech in front of one of my friends, and she said, "Marie, are you sure you're really talking about yourself?" Yeah, I am. When I talk about my family, I'm talking about the main sources of myself. They've given me a world, but it's not like I'm trapped in it. I can go anywhere and do anything because of the gifts they've given me. Strength, glory, pride—thank you, John, Chris, Michael, Anthony, Mom, and Dad. You've made me an individual, Marie D'Aniello, a little bit different from each one of you, and a little bit like all of you

---

Three Photographs

Ashley Smith

In her self-introductory speech presented at Vanderbilt University, Ashley Smith used a clever technique—three photographs—to frame her emphasis on personal experience as the defining thing in her life. Her use of examples and contrast are outstanding features of this speech. Throughout, she builds an image of herself as a dedicated and highly competent person, establishing her credibility for later informative and persuasive speeches on customs in foreign countries and our government's policies with regard to these countries.

Photographs often tell stories that only a few can hear. I would like to tell you the story told me by three snapshots that hang in my room in quiet, suburban Jacksonville, Florida. If you saw them, you might think them totally unrelated; together, they tell a powerful tale.

"Ashley, *levantete!*" I heard each morning for the month that I spent in Costa Rica as an exchange student. I would wake up at 5:30 to get ready for school and would stumble off to the one shower that the family of five shared. I had to wash myself in cold water because there was no warm water—that usually woke me up pretty fast! I then got dressed and breakfast would be waiting on the table. Predictably it would be fruit, coffee, and gallo pinto, a black bean and rice dish usually served at every meal.

We would then walk to school and begin the day with an hour and a half of shop class. After shop we would have about 15- to 20-minute classes in what you and I might call "regular" academic subjects: math and Spanish, for example. Those classes had frequent interruptions and were not taken very seriously. The socialization process was quite clear: These children were being prepared for jobs in the labor force instead of for higher education. Each afternoon as we walked home we passed the elite school where students were still busy working and studying. The picture in my room of my Costa Rican classmates painting picnic tables in the schoolyard reminds me of their narrow opportunities.

The second photograph on my wall is of a little girl in Botswana who is not much younger than I. She's nearing the end of her education and has finished up to the equivalent of the sixth grade. She will now return to a rural setting because her family cannot afford to continue her schooling. To add to the problem, the family goat was eaten by a lion, so she had to return to help them over this crisis.

But she didn't miss out on much—most likely, she would have gone on into the city and ended up in one of the shantytowns, one more victim of the unemployment, poverty, even starvation endured by the people. Her lack of opportunity is due not so much to class inequalities as in Costa Rica, but more to the cultural tradition of several hundred years of European exploitation. Recently there has been extensive growth there, but the natives have been left far behind.

The third photograph in my room is of four high school students, taken where I went to school in Jacksonville, Florida. We're all sitting on the lawn outside school, overlooking the parking lot full of new cars that will take us home to warm dinners and comfortable beds and large homes and privileged lives. Many of us—including myself for most of my life—took this world for granted. But now, for me, no more. I may have gained a lot on my travels, but I lost my political innocence.

One thing I gained is an intense desire to become an educator. I want to teach people to succeed on their merits despite the social and economic inequalities that they're faced with.

And I want to learn from them as well. I want to teach the boy who never mastered welding that he could own the factory. And I want him to teach me how to use a rice cooker. I want to teach the girl who is exhausted each afternoon after walking to the river with a jar on her head to gather water that she could design an irrigation system. But I also want her to teach me how to weave a thatched roof. I want to travel and teach and learn.

Three photographs, hanging on my wall. They are silent, mute, and the photographer was not very skillful. But together they tell a powerful story in my life.

Lady with a Gun
Elizabeth Tidmore

Beth Tidmore presented this self-introductory speech to her honors class in oral communication at the University of Memphis. The speech, offered as a tribute to her mother's faith in her, describes her dramatic development as a shooting champion. Beth's speech is noteworthy for its use of narrative design, especially dialogue. Her graphic descriptions, engaging her listeners' senses of sight, sound, touch, and smell, also helped her establish a vital, direct contact with her audience and transported them to the scenes she depicted. In addition, her colorful uses of voice and gesture helped achieve the ideal of integrated communication described in Chapter 13. By the end of the semester, Beth had won the National Junior Olympic Championship Women's Air Rifle competition and had been named to the All-America shooters team.

I'm sure everybody has had an April Fool's joke played on them. My father's favorite one was to wake me up on April first and tell me, "School's been cancelled for the day; you don't have to go," and then get all excited and say "April Fools!" I'd get up and take a shower . . .

Well, on April first 2000, my mother said three words that I was sure weren't an April Fool's joke. She said, "We'll take it." The "it" she was referring to was a brand-new Anschutz 2002 Air Rifle. Now, this is $2,000 worth of equipment for a sport that I'd been in for maybe three months—not long. That was a big deal! It meant that I would be going from a junior-level to an Olympic-grade rifle.

Someone outside of the sport might think, "Eh, minor upgrade. A gun is a gun, right?" No. Imagine a fifteen-year-old who has been driving a used Toyota and who suddenly gets a new Mercedes for her sixteenth birthday. That's how I felt.

And as she was writing the check, I completely panicked. I thought, "What if I'm not good enough to justify this rifle? What if I decide to quit and we have to sell it, or we can't sell it? What if I let my parents down and I waste their money?" So later in the car I said, "Momma, what if I'm not good enough?" She said, "Don't worry about it—it's my money." Okay . . .

So my journey began. Most shooters start out when they're younger, and they move up through different rifles. Most of my peers had at least four years' experience on me. I had to jump right in and get a scholarship. And to get a scholarship I had to get noticed. And to get noticed I had to win, and to win, I had to shoot great scores immediately.

So my journey was filled with eight hours a day practice, five days a week. On weekends I shot matches and I traveled. I had to take my homework with me to complete it before I got back to school. I had to do physical training, I had dietary restrictions. When all my friends were out at parties and at Cancun for Spring Break, I was at the shooting range. My free time—if I had any—was spent lifting weights and running.

At times I really resented my friends, because I thought they must have all the fun. But you know what, it was worth it! My friends don't know what it's like to feel the cold, smooth wood of the cheekpiece against your face. And they don't know the rich smell of Hoppe's No. 9 [oil] when you're cleaning your rifle. And they've never been to the Olympic Training Center in Colorado and seen how they embroider the little Olympic logo on *everything* from the mattresses to the plates. And they don't know the thrill of shooting in a final and having everyone applaud when you shoot a ten or even a center ten, or standing on the podium and having them put a medal around your neck, and being proud to represent your school, your country. . . .

There's a bumper sticker that says, "A Lady with A Gun Has More Fun." After three years in this sport, I have had so much fun! I've been all over the U.S., I've been captain of a high school rifle team, I've been to matches everywhere, I've won medals, I've been to World Cups and met people from all over the world. And I've gotten to experience so many different people, places, and events through my participation in shooting sports.

So not long ago, I asked my mother, "Mom, how did you know?" She said, "Ah, I just knew." I said, "No, Mom—*really*. How did you know that you weren't going to waste your money?" She got very serious and she took me by the shoulders and she squared me up. She looked me right in the eye and she said, "When you picked up that gun, you just looked like you belonged together. I knew there was a sparkle in your eye, and I knew that you were meant to do great things with that rifle."

So, thanks, Mom.

Informative Speeches

Looking Through Our Window: The Value of Indian Culture
Marge Anderson

This presentation by Marge Anderson, chief executive of the Mille Lacs Band of the Ojibwe, shows that one speech can perform multiple general functions. Anderson both celebrates the values of her culture and persuades listeners to engage in a dialogue, which she defines, citing St. Thomas Aquinas, as "the struggle to learn from each other." The even more fundamental function of her speech is to inform her mainstream Minnesota audience of how Native Americans view the world and their relationship to it. From the basis of that understanding, she explains specific accomplishments of her tribe and the rationale behind her people's business decisions. All of us are enriched, she argues, when we are able to look at the world through each other's windows. Therefore, she suggests, her listeners should honor and help preserve the authenticity of the Native American cultural perspective.

Aaniin. Thank you for inviting me here today. When I was asked to speak to you, I was told you are interested in hearing about the improvements we are making on the Mille Lacs Reservation, and about our investment of casino dollars back into our community through schools, health care facilities, and other services. And I do want to talk to you about these things, because they are tremendously important, and I am very proud of them.

But before I do, I want to take a few minutes to talk to you about something else, something I'm not asked about very often. I want to talk to you about what it means to be Indian. About how my people experience the world. About the fundamental way in which our culture differs from yours. And about why you should care about all this.

The differences between Indians and non-Indians have created a lot of controversy lately. Casinos, treaty rights, tribal sovereignty—these issues have stirred such anger and bitterness. I believe the accusations against us are made out of ignorance. The vast majority of non-Indians do not understand how my people view the world, what we value, what motivates us.

They do not know these things for one simple reason: they've never heard us talk about them. For many years, the only stories that non-Indians heard about my people came from other non-Indians. As a result, the picture you got of us was fanciful, or distorted, or so shadowy, it hardly existed at all. It's time for Indian voices to tell Indian stories.

Now, I'm sure at least a few of you are wondering, "Why do I need to hear these stories? Why should I care about what Indian people think, and feel, and believe?"

I think the most eloquent answer I can give you comes from the namesake of this university, St. Thomas Aquinas. St. Thomas wrote that dialogue is the struggle to learn from each other. This struggle, he said, is like Jacob wrestling the angel—it leaves one wounded and blessed at the same time. Indian people know this struggle very well. The wounds we've suffered in our dialogue with non-Indians are well documented; I don't need to give you a laundry list of complaints.

We also know some of the blessings of this struggle. As American Indians, we live in two worlds—ours, and yours. In the 500 years since you first came to our lands, we have struggled to learn how to take the best of what your culture has to offer in arts, science, technology and more, and then weave them into the fabric of our traditional ways.

But for non-Indians, the struggle is new. Now that our people have begun to achieve success, now that we are in business and in the headlines, you are starting to wrestle with understanding us. Your wounds from this struggle are fresh, and the pain might make it hard for you to see beyond them. But if you try, you'll begin to see the blessings as well—the blessings of what a deepened knowledge of Indian culture can bring to you. I'd like to share a few of those blessings with you today.

Earlier I mentioned that there is a fundamental difference between the way Indians and non-Indians experience the world. This difference goes all the way back to the Bible, and Genesis.

In Genesis, the first book of the Old Testament, God creates man in his own image. Then God says, "be fruitful, multiply, fill the earth and conquer it. Be masters of the fish of the sea, the birds of the heaven, and all living animals on the earth." Masters. Conquer. Nothing, nothing could be further from the way Indian people view the world and our place in it. Here are the words of the great nineteenth- century Chief Seattle: "You are a part of the earth, and the earth is a part of you. You did not weave the web of life, you are merely a strand in it. Whatever you do to the web, you do to yourself."

In our tradition, there is no mastery. There is no conquering. Instead, there is kinship among all creation—humans, animals, birds, plants, even rocks. We are all part of the sacred hoop of the world, and we must all live in harmony with each other if that hoop is to remain unbroken.

When you begin to see the world this way—through Indian eyes—you will begin to understand our view of land and treaties very differently. You will begin to understand that when we speak of Father Sun and Mother Earth, these are not new-age catchwords—they are very real terms of respect for very real beings.

And when you understand this, then you will understand that our fight for treaty rights is not just about hunting deer or catching fish. It is about teaching our children to honor Mother Earth and Father Sun. It is about teaching them to respectfully receive the gifts these loving parents offer us in return for the care we give them. And it is about teaching this generation and the generations yet to come about their place in the web of life. Our culture and the fish, our values and the deer, the lessons we learn and the rice we harvest—everything is tied together. You can no more separate one from the other than you can divide a person's spirit from his body.

When you understand how we view the world and our place in it, it's easier to appreciate why our casinos are so important to us. The reason we defend our businesses so fiercely isn't because we want to have something that others don't. The reason is because these businesses allow us to give back to others—to our People, our communities, and the Creator.

I'd like to take a minute and mention just a few of the ways we've already given back:

We've opened new schools, new health care facilities, and new community centers where our children get a better education, where our elders get better medical care, and where our families can gather to socialize and keep our traditions alive.

We've built new ceremonial buildings, and new powwow and celebration grounds.

We've renovated an elderly center, and plan to build three culturally sensitive assisted living facilities for our elders.

We've created programs to teach and preserve our language and cultural traditions.

We've created a Small Business Development Program to help band members start their own businesses.

We've created more than twenty-eight hundred jobs for band members, people from other tribes, and non-Indians.

We've spurred the development of more than one thousand jobs in other local businesses.

We've generated more than fifty million dollars in federal taxes, and more than fifteen million dollars in state taxes through wages paid to employees.

And we've given back more than two million dollars in charitable donations.

The list goes on and on. But rather than flood you with more numbers, I'll tell you a story that sums up how my people view business through the lens of our traditional values.

Last year, the Woodlands National Bank, which is owned and operated by the Mille Lacs Band, was approached by the city of Onamia and asked to forgive a mortgage on a building in the downtown area. The building had been abandoned and was an eyesore on Main Street. The city planned to renovate and sell the building, and return it to the tax rolls.

Although the bank would lose money by forgiving the mortgage, our business leaders could see the wisdom in improving the community. The opportunity to help our neighbors was an opportunity to strengthen the web of life. So we forgave the mortgage.

Now, I know this is not a decision everyone would agree with. Some people feel that in business, you have to look out for number one. But my people feel that in business—and in life—you have to look out for every one.

And this, I believe, is one of the blessings that Indian culture has to offer you and other non-Indians. We have a different perspective on so many things, from caring for the environment, to healing the body, mind and soul.

But if our culture disappears, if the Indian ways are swallowed up by the dominant American culture, no one will be able to learn from them. Not Indian children. Not your children. No one. All that knowledge, all that wisdom, will be lost forever.

The struggle of dialogue will be over. Yes, there will be no more wounds. But there will also be no more blessings.

There is still so much we have to learn from each other, and we have already wasted so much time. Our world grows smaller every day. And every day, more of our unsettling, surprising, wonderful differences vanish. And when that happens, part of us vanishes, too.

I'd like to end with one of my favorite stories. It's a funny little story about Indians and non-Indians, but its message is serious: you can see something differently if you are willing to learn from those around you.

This is the story: Years ago, white settlers came to this area and built the first European-style homes. When Indian People walked by these homes and saw see-through things in the walls, they looked through them to see what the strangers inside were doing. The settlers were shocked, but it makes sense when you think about it: windows are made to be looked through from both sides.

Since then, my people have spent many years looking at the world through your window. I hope today I've given you a reason to look at it through ours.

Mii gwetch.

"Looking Through Our Window: The Value of Indian Culture," by Marge Anderson in *Vital Speeches of the Day*, March 1, 2000. Used by permission of Vital Speeches, City New Publishing and Marge Anderson, Goff & Howard, Inc.

The New Madrid Earthquake Area
Stephen Huff

Stephen Huff's informative speech skillfully relates his subject to his immediate audience at the outset. He makes excellent use of comparison and contrast, of presentation aids, and of vivid description to make his subject come alive. After first establishing a basis of facts, he builds an imaginary disaster narrative to help his audience understand the magnitude of the problem being discussed. Thus he motivates listeners to take seriously his suggestions for earthquake preparation. A more adequate summary at the end of the speech might have made it even more effective.

How many of you can remember what you were doing around seven o'clock on the evening of October 17th? If you're a sports fan like me, you had probably set out the munchies, popped a cold one, and settled back to watch San Francisco and Oakland battle it out in the World Series. Since the show came on at seven o'clock here in Memphis for its pregame hype, you may not have been paying close attention to the TV—until—until—until both the sound and picture went out because of the Bay Area earthquake.

If you're like me, you probably sat glued to the TV set for the rest of the evening watching the live coverage of that catastrophe. If you're like me, you probably started thinking that Memphis, Tennessee, is in the middle of the New Madrid earthquake area and wondering how likely it would be for a large earthquake to hit here. And if you're like me, you probably asked yourself, "What would I do if a major earthquake hit Memphis?"

As I asked myself these questions, I was surprised to admit that I didn't know very much about the New Madrid earthquake area or the probability of a major quake in Memphis. And I was really upset to discover that I didn't have the foggiest idea of what to do if a quake did hit. So I visited the Center for Earthquake Research and Information here on campus; talked with Dr. Arch Johnston, the director; and read the materials he helped me find. Today, I'd like to share with you what I learned about the New Madrid earthquake area, how likely it is that Memphis may be hit by a major quake in the near future, what the effects of such a quake might be, and—most important—what you can do to be prepared.

Let's start with a little history about the New Madrid earthquake area. During the winter of 1811 to 1812, three of the largest earthquakes ever to hit the continental United States occurred in this area. Their estimated magnitudes were 8.6, 8.4, and 8.8 on the Richter scale. [He reveals magnitude chart.] I have drawn this chart to give you some idea of how much energy this involves. To simplify things, I have shown the New Madrid quakes as 8.5. Since a one-point increase in the Richter scale equals a thirtyfold increase in energy release, the energy level of these quakes was over nine hundred times more powerful than the Hiroshima atomic bomb and more than thirty times more powerful than the 7.0 quake that hit San Francisco last October. [He conceals magnitude chart.]

Most of the reports of these early earthquakes come from journals or Indian legends. The Indians tell of the night that lasted for a week and the way the "Father of Waters"—the Mississippi River—ran backwards. Waterfalls were formed on the river. Islands disappeared. Land that was once in Arkansas—on the west bank of the river—ended up in Tennessee—on the east bank of the river. Church bells chimed as far away as New Orleans and Boston. Cracks up to ten feet wide opened and closed in the earth. Geysers squirted sand fifteen feet into the air. Whole forests sank into the earth as the land turned to quicksand. Lakes disappeared and new lakes were formed. Reelfoot Lake—over ten miles long—was formed when the Mississippi River changed its course. No one is certain how many

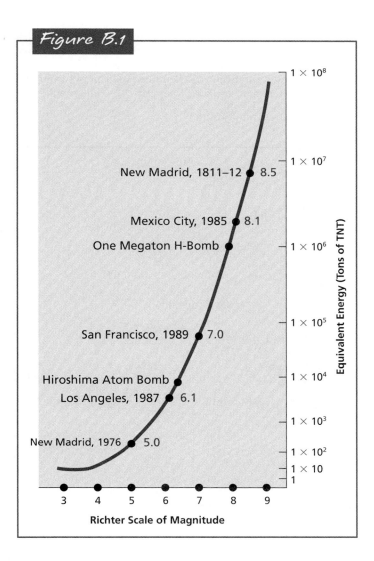

Figure B.1

Equivalent Energy (Tons of TNT)

- 1×10^8
- 1×10^7 — New Madrid, 1811–12 ● 8.5
- Mexico City, 1985 ● 8.1
- One Megaton H-Bomb ● — 1×10^6
- 1×10^5 — San Francisco, 1989 ● 7.0
- 1×10^4 — Hiroshima Atom Bomb ● / Los Angeles, 1987 ● 6.1
- 1×10^3
- New Madrid, 1976 ● 5.0
- 1×10^2
- 1×10
- 1

Richter Scale of Magnitude
3 4 5 6 7 8 9

people died from the quakes because the area was sparsely settled with trappers and Indian villages. Memphis was just an outpost village with a few hundred settlers.

[He shows map of epicenters.] As you can see on this map, Memphis itself is not directly on the New Madrid Fault line. The fault extends from around Marked Tree, Arkansas, northeast to near Cairo, Illinois. This continues to be a volatile area of earthquake activity. According to Robert L. Ketter, director of the National Center for Earthquake Engineering Research, between 1974 and 1983 over two thousand quakes were recorded in the area. About 150 earthquakes per year occur in the area, but only about eight of them are large enough for people to notice. The others are picked up on the seismographs at tracking stations. The strongest quake in recent years occurred here in 1976. [He points to location on map.] This measured 5.0 on the Richter scale.

The New Madrid earthquake area is much different from the San Andreas Fault in California. Because of the way the land is formed, the alluvial soil transmits energy more efficiently here than in California. Although the quakes were about the same size, the New Madrid earthquakes affected an area fifteen times larger than the "great quake" that destroyed San Francisco in 1906.

Although scientists cannot predict exactly when another major quake may hit the area, they do know that the *repeat time* for a magnitude-6 New Madrid earthquake is seventy years, plus or minus fifteen years. The last earthquake of this size to hit the area occurred in 1895 north of New Madrid, Missouri. [He points to epicenter on map.] According to Johnston and Nava of the Memphis Earthquake Center, the probability that one with a magnitude of 6.3 will occur somewhere in the fault area by the year 2010 is 40 to 63 percent. By the year 2035 this probability increases to 86 to 97 percent. The probabilities for larger quakes are lower. They estimate the probability of a 7.6 quake within the next fifty years to be from 19 to 29 percent. [He conceals map of epicenters.]

What would happen if an earthquake of 7.6 hit Memphis? Allan and Hoshall, a prominent local engineering firm, prepared a study on this for the Federal Emergency Management Agency. The expected death toll would top 2,400. There would be at least 10,000 casualties. Two hundred thousand residents would be homeless. The city would be without electricity, gas, water, or sewer treatment facilities for weeks. Gas lines would rup-

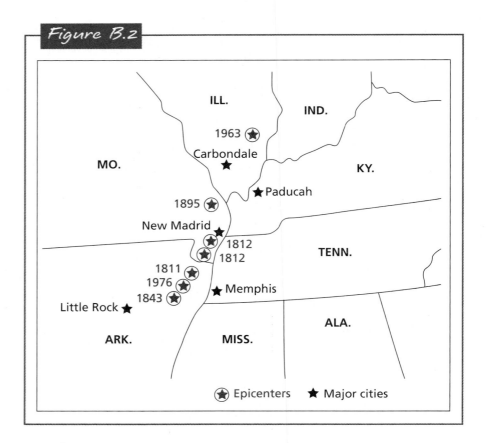

Figure B.2

ture, and fires would sweep through the city. Transportation would be almost impossible, bridges and roads would be destroyed, and emergency supplies would have to be brought in by helicopter. The river bluff, midtown, and land along the Wolfe River would turn to quicksand because of liquification. Buildings there would sink like they did in the Marina area during the San Francisco quake. If the quake hit during daytime hours, at least 600 children would be killed and another 2,400 injured as schools collapsed on them. None of our schools have been built to seismic code specifications.

In fact, very few buildings in Memphis have been built to be earthquake resistant, so it would be difficult to find places to shelter and care for the homeless. The major exceptions are the new hospitals in the suburbs, the Omni Hotel east of the expressway, the Holiday Inn Convention Center, and two or three new office complexes. The only municipal structure built to code is the Criminal Justice Center. The Memphis Pyramid, built by the city and county, which seats over twenty thousand people for the University of Memphis basketball games, was not built to code. I'd hate to be in it if a major quake hit. The prospects are not pretty.

What can we do to prepare ourselves for this possible catastrophe? We can start out by learning what to do if a quake does hit. When I asked myself what I would do, my first reaction was to "get outside." I've since learned that this is not right. The "Earthquake Safety Checklist" published by the Federal Emergency Management Agency and the Red Cross makes a number of suggestions. I've written them out and will distribute them after my speech.

First, when an earthquake hits, if you are inside, stay there. Get in a safe spot: Stand in a doorway, stand next to an inside wall, or get under a large piece of furniture. Stay away from windows, hanging objects, fireplaces, and tall, unsecured furniture until the shaking stops. Do not try to use elevators. If you are outside, get away from buildings, trees, walls, or power lines. If you are in a car, stay in it; pull over and park. Stay away from overpasses and power lines. Do not drive over bridges or overpasses until they have been inspected. If you are in a crowded public place, do not rush for the exit. You may be crushed in the stampede of people.

Figure B.3

Earthquake Preparedness Suggestions

1. If you are inside, stay there. Get in a safe spot: Stand in a doorway, stand next to an inside wall, or get under a large piece of furniture. Stay away from windows, hanging objects, fireplaces, and tall, unsecured furniture until the shaking stops. Do not try to use elevators.

2. If you are outside, get away from buildings, trees, walls, or power lines. If you are in a car, stay in it; pull over and park. Stay away from overpasses and power lines. Do not drive over bridges or overpasses until they have been inspected.

3. If you are in a crowded public place, do not rush for the exit. You may be crushed in the stampede of people.

4. When the shaking stops, check for gas, water, or electrical damage. Turn off the electricity, gas, and water to your home. Do not use electrical switches—unseen sparks could set off a gas fire. Do not use the telephone unless you must report a severe injury. Check to see that the sewer works before using the toilet. Plug drains to prevent sewer backup.

There are also some things you can do in advance to be prepared:

1. Accumulate emergency supplies: At home you should have a flashlight, a transistor radio with fresh batteries, a first-aid kit, fire extinguishers, and enough canned or dried food and beverages to last for 72 hours.

2. Identify hazards and safe spots in your house—secure tall, heavy furniture; don't hang heavy pictures over your bed; keep flammable liquids in a garage or outside storage area—look around each room and plan where you would go if an earthquake hit; conduct earthquake drills with your family.

When the shaking stops, check for gas, water, or electrical damage. Turn off the electricity, gas, and water to your home. Do not use electrical switches—unseen sparks could set off a gas fire. Do not use the telephone unless you must report a severe injury. Check to see that the sewer works before using the toilet. Plug drains to prevent a sewer backup.

There are also some things you can do in advance to be prepared. Accumulate emergency supplies: At home you should have a flashlight, a transistor radio with fresh batteries, a first-aid kit, fire extinguishers, and enough canned or dried food and beverages to last your family for 72 hours. Identify hazards and safe spots in your home—secure tall, heavy furniture; don't hang heavy pictures over your bed; keep flammable liquids in a garage or outside storage area—look around each room and plan where you would go if an earthquake hit. Conduct earthquake drills with your family.

There's one more suggestion that I would like to add. One that is specific to Memphis. Let our local officials know that you are concerned about the lack of preparedness. Urge them to support a building code—at least for public structures—that meets seismic resistance standards.

In preparing this speech, I learned a lot about the potential for earthquakes in Memphis. I hope you have learned something too. I now feel like I know what I should do if an earthquake hits. But I'm not really sure how I would react. Even the experts don't always react "appropriately." In 1971 an earthquake hit the Los Angeles area at about six o'clock in the morning. Charles Richter, the seismologist who developed the Richter scale to measure earthquakes, was in bed at the time. According to his wife, "He jumped up screaming and scared the cat."

The "Monument" at Wounded Knee
Cecile Larson

Cecile Larson's speech informs listeners about a shameful episode in American history. The speech follows a spatial design. Cecile's vivid use of imagery and the skillful contrasts she draws between this "monument" and our "official" monuments create mental pictures that should stay with her listeners long after the words of her speech have been forgotten.

We Americans are big on monuments. We build monuments in memory of our heroes Washington, Jefferson, and Lincoln live on in our nation's capital. We erect monuments to honor our martyrs. The Minuteman still stands guard at Concord. The flag is ever raised over Iwo Jima. Sometimes we even construct monuments to commemorate victims. In Ashburn Park downtown there is a monument to those who died in the yellow fever epidemics. However, there are some things in our history that we don't memorialize. Perhaps we would just as soon forget what happened. Last summer I visited such a place—the massacre site at Wounded Knee.

In case you have forgotten what happened at Wounded Knee, let me refresh your memory. On December 29, 1890, shortly after Sitting Bull had been murdered by the authorities, about 400 half-frozen, starving, and frightened Indians who had fled the nearby reservation were attacked by the Seventh Cavalry. When the fighting ended, between 200 and 300 Sioux had died—two-thirds of them women and children. Their remains are buried in a common grave at the site of the massacre.

Wounded Knee is located in the Pine Ridge Reservation in southwestern South Dakota—about a three-hour drive from where Presidents Washington, Jefferson, Theodore Roosevelt, and Lincoln are enshrined in the granite face of Mount Rushmore. The reservation is directly south of the Badlands National Park, a magnificently desolate area of wind-eroded buttes and multicolored spires.

We entered the reservation driving south from the Badlands Visitor's Center. The landscape of the Pine Ridge Reservation retains much of the desolation of the Badlands but lacks its magnificence. Flat, sun-baked fields and an occasional eroded gully stretch as far as the eye can see. There are no signs or highway markers to lead the curious tourist to Wounded Knee. Even the *Rand-McNally Atlas* doesn't help you find your way. We got lost three times and had to stop and ask directions.

When we finally arrived at Wounded Knee, there was no official historic marker to tell us what had happened there. Instead there was a large, handmade wooden sign—crudely lettered in white on black. The sign first directed our attention to our left—to the gully where the massacre took place. The mass grave site was to our right—across the road and up a small hill.

Two red-brick columns topped with a wrought-iron arch and a small metal cross form the entrance to the grave site. The column to the right is in bad shape: cinder blocks from the base are missing; the brickwork near the top has deteriorated and tumbled to the ground; graffiti on the columns proclaim an attitude we found repeatedly expressed about the Bureau of Indian Affairs—"The BIA sucks!"

Crumbling concrete steps lead you to the mass grave. The top of the grave is covered with gravel, punctuated by unruly patches of chickweed and crabgrass. These same weeds also grow along the base of the broken chainlink fence that surrounds the grave, the "monument," and a small cemetery.

The "monument" itself rests on a concrete slab to the right of the grave. It's a typical, large, old-fashioned granite cemetery marker, a pillar about six feet high topped with an urn—the kind of gravestone you might see in any cemetery with graves from the turn of the century. The inscription tells us that it was erected by the families of those who were killed at Wounded Knee. Weeds grow through the cracks in the concrete at its base.

There are no granite headstones in the adjacent cemetery, only simple white wooden crosses that tell a story of people who died young. There is no neatly manicured grass. There are no flowers. Only the unrelenting and unforgiving weeds.

Yes, Americans are big on monuments. We build them to memorialize our heroes, to honor our martyrs, and sometimes, even to commemorate victims. But only when it makes us feel good.

Persuasive Speeches

Global Burning

Joshua Logan

Josh Logan presented two persuasive speeches on the theme of global warming in his class at the University of Memphis. The texts offered here are adapted from these speeches. Together, the two speeches develop a classic problem-solution design; the first, "Global Burning," focuses on the problem dimension of the design. In terms of the persuasive process discussed in Chapter 16, the speech attempts to arouse awareness, share understanding, and secure agreement. Its strategy is to magnify the reality of global warming and its meaning for listeners. Its challenge is to remove barriers that might stand in the way of their commitment. To achieve his goals, Josh used colorful, graphic language, a presentation aid, and effective examples. His presentation reflected his passion, sincerity, and commitment on this topic.

Ten years ago, five years ago, reasonable people could still argue and even disagree over some tough environmental questions: Is there really such a thing as "global warming"? Is the world really getting hotter at a rapid pace? And is it being fanned by humans? Are we really responsible for environmental conditions?

Now there's little room left for argument. The answer to all these questions is clearly YES. This definitive answer has been provided by the United Nations Intergovernmental Panel on Climate Change, reporting during the early part of 2007. This authoritative report, which correlates and tests the work of hundreds of environmental scientists from countries around the globe, concludes that the process of global warming is now in motion and is accelerating. And the fire is fed largely by humans: the IPCC supports this conclusion at a 90 to 99% level of confidence. The United States especially, with about 4% of the world's population, accounts for 25% of all global warming. We are the ones with our foot on the accelerator.

Today I want to sketch the dimensions of this problem, and what it might mean for you and your children. I will first track the causes of global warming, then trace its recent path and project its future. As recently as 2006, polls tell us that many people in the United States were in denial about global warming: yes, we believe it exists and, yes, we are concerned, but we're not that much concerned. Fifty-four percent of us think global warming is a problem for the future—but not now! Global warming is still something of an abstract, distant problem for us, and we can't see the future all that clearly.

That's the challenge I want to try to meet today. We must recognize global warming for what it is, the monster we are creating by all our action and inaction. We must become scared—really scared! We must be willing to think green and act green, from the personal everyday decisions we make on disposing trash to the big consumer decisions we make on which cars to buy, to the political decisions we make on which candidates to support. We must understand that this hot world is starting to catch fire—and we must be willing to pay the price to help put the flames out. We must be committed to the proposition that global warming must not become global burning.

Global warming begins with greenhouse gases—the tons of carbon dioxide that belch out of our smokestacks and our automobile exhausts; the vast clouds of methane gas that rise from our farms and ranches and landfills; the nitrous oxide from fertilizers, cattle feed lots, and chemical products. The world's forests are supposed to absorb much of this industrial and agricultural output, but guess what? We've also been busy cutting the rainforests and clear-cutting our own forests. We're tying nature's hands behind her back at just the wrong moment. So all these deadly gases mix and accumulate in the atmosphere, where they magnify the heat of the sun.

Now let's gain some perspective on where we now actually stand. I want to show you a chart that traces the human influence on the atmosphere over the past thousand years of history. This chart summarizes the history of greenhouse gases, according to the IPCC's *Summary for Policymakers*. Notice that the bottom border divides the time frame into two-hundred-year periods. The side frame measures the amount of the gas pouring into the atmosphere. Notice that for about eight hundred of these years, this amount is stable and even—almost a straight line. Then as the nineteenth century dawns on the Industrial Revolution, the lines begin to climb, at first gradually, then increasingly steeper until they almost reach the vertical during the past half-century. The dry technical language of the summary, speaking to carbon dioxide alone, carries the message of this chart with sharp clarity: "The atmospheric concentration of carbon dioxide (CO_2) has increased by 31 percent since 1750. The present CO_2 concentration has not been exceeded during the past 420,000 years and likely not during the past 20 million years. The current rate of increase is unprecedented during at least the past 20,000 years."

Now what does all this mean in human terms, especially if these lines continue to climb on the charts of the future? Well get your fans out, because it's going to be hot. Very hot. According to *National Geographic News* of July, 2006, eleven of the last twelve years have been the hottest on record, probably reaching back for at least a thousand years. But that record

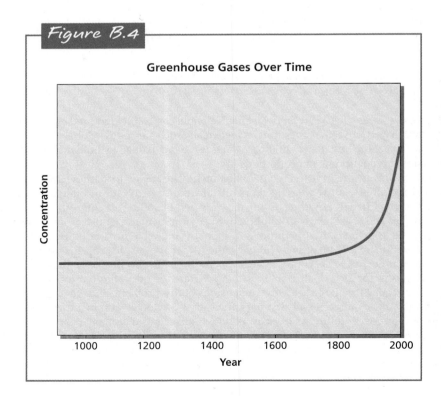

won't last for long. The UN congregation of the world's scientists predicts that the earth's surface temperature could rise at least five degrees over the next hundred years—just in the last generation it has already risen two degrees on average. Can you imagine what it will be like to add five degrees to the average summer day in Memphis?

Beyond that, the world's agriculture will be profoundly changed. Fertile lands will become deserts, and vast populations will be forced to relocate. As you might imagine, and as *Time* magazine of April, 2006 confirms, it is the poorest and least flexible populations—such as those one finds in Africa—who will be hardest hit initially. *Science* magazine adds that major forest fires in the West and South are more numerous and more devastating than they were a generation ago. The average land burned during a given year is more than six times what it was a generation ago.

Moreover, it will soon get more lonely here on planet earth. The latest word is that more than one-third—that's one-third—of all species in several parts of the world could be destroyed over the next fifty years. Chris Leeds, conservation biologist of the University of Leeds, says: "Our analyses suggest that well over a million species could be threatened with extinction as a result of climate change." That's over a million species.

The story becomes more tragic when we contemplate the fate of the oceans. Some scientists had previously discounted global warming because some of the most dire predictions about rising temperatures had not come true. What they forgot was the capacity of the oceans to absorb heat and smother some of the immediate impact of global warming. But a recent issue of *Science* magazine has published reports that—as they put it—"link a warming trend in the upper 3,000 meters of the world's oceans to global warming caused by human activities."

As the oceans grow warmer, especially in the Gulf of Mexico area, the threat of hurricanes grows more ominous. In its summary of conditions in 2006, *Time* reported that over the past thirty-five years, the number of category 4 & 5 hurricanes has jumped 50%. But these reports truly threaten all living creatures. In particular, they confirm the IPCC predictions that most coral reefs will disappear within thirty to fifty years. And as the oceans continue to warm and melt the great ice shelves in the polar regions, the rise in sea level—as much as three feet over the next century and perhaps even more—will wipe out vast lowland areas such as the Sundarbans in India and Bangladesh, the last, best habitat for the Bengal tiger. Large parts of Florida and Louisiana will surrender to the sea—sell your beach property soon! The barrier islands off Mobile Bay, where my parents took me camping as a boy and where I hope to take my own children, will gradually recede into memory. These are just fragments, mere glimpses, of the future global warming has in store for us, our children, and grandchildren.

Well, I hope I have gained your attention today. We have a problem here that threatens the quality of life here on earth. Can we do anything about it? I would like to give you a happy, simple answer to this question, but it is a complex one. It's not like we can just take our foot off the greenhouse accelerator, and bring the bus to a halt. Once it is heated, the ocean does not cool quickly. Once they have accumulated, greenhouse gases can linger for a long time. But there are things we can do to change this scenario. The future is not an either-or proposition, and we can mitigate some of the worst possibilities. We can cool the fires under global warming to prevent it from becoming global burning. In my next speech I hope to show you how.

Cooling the World's Fever

Joshua Logan

In this second of his two speeches on global warming, Josh turns to the solution phase of his overall problem-solution design. He begins by reminding listeners of what he has already proved—the gravity of the problem. He then focuses on the theme of this speech: that his listeners must ultimately provide the solution. He urges their support for three large categories of initiatives developed by local, state, and corporate interests. He then asks them to urge Congress to pass much-needed national legislation. Finally, he asks them to adopt a new environmental lifestyle. Throughout, he draws upon a broad range of factual and statistical evidence, and also relies heavily on expert testimony and example. He concludes with personal reflections on the significance of this issue and on the need for immediate action.

Our world has a fever. And after my last speech, we know the cause of it. Global warming, that threatens to become "global burning." Global burning, that could raise global temperatures by as much as five degrees by the end of this century. Global burning, that could raise ocean levels by three feet all around the globe. Global burning, that could submerge coastal cities, turn fertile lands into deserts, and destroy vast populations of wildlife. Global burning, that threatens many people, especially those in poor areas of the world, with epidemics of disease and hunger and dislocation. In short, global burning that could disrupt civilization and life on this planet.

Scientists around the world, whose work has been collected, tested, and reported by the United Nations Intergovernmental Panel on Climate Change, have confirmed for us that this bleak picture is indeed accurate. *Time* magazine summarizes the gravity of the problem in light of the IPCC report: "Except for nuclear war or a collision with an asteroid, no force has more potential to damage our planet's web of life than global warming."

Now I know you're expecting me to present a solution for this problem. Fair enough, I've got a simple one for you: *you are the solution. You* must support a range of brilliant new strategies that could slow and eventually reverse the mighty engines of global warming. *You* must put the pressure on political decision-makers that are still dragging their feet on much-needed legislation. And *you* must make some fundamental changes in the way you think and live. *You, me, all of us*, must accept responsibility for the fate of Planet Earth.

First, there are many new initiatives and new—often improbable—heroes that deserve our support. In 2005, when the Kyoto Protocol took effect in 141 countries but not the United States, Seattle Mayor George Nickels launched the U. S. Mayors' Climate Protection Agreement. The mayors he led pledged to meet or beat Kyoto's original target for the U. S.—cutting greenhouse-gas emissions to 7% below 1990 levels over the next six years. Portland, Oregon, for example, has already slashed its emissions by 13%. By 2006, 218 mayors had joined the program. And by 2007, this number had almost doubled again to 431 mayors, representing 61 million Americans. These local leaders are doing innovative things—buying hybrid vehicles for the municipal fleet, helping local businesses audit their energy use, imposing higher parking taxes to encourage ride-sharing and use of public transportation, converting traffic lights from incandescents to LEDS, which are 90% more efficient, and rallying public awareness and participation. Says Nickels, "I think this sends a message that there is intelligent life in America."

States have also taken over the leadership role. In 2003 then Governor George Pataki of New York launched the Regional Greenhouse Gas Initiative, a confederation of northeastern and Mid-Atlantic states pledged to reduce greenhouse gas emissions 10% below the current level by 2019. Ten states have already joined this group. Even more dramatically, another Republican governor—Arnold Schwarzenegger of California—signed legislation that commits that huge state to a 25% reduction in greenhouse gases by 2020. California is being sued by automakers who would have to increase fuel efficiency before they could sell cars in that state. If that suit is denied, then California could well have created a *de facto* national standard—taking over in effect the leadership role from a do-nothing national government.

Finally, a number of giant corporations are stepping forward—not because they are treehuggers, but because they've found that energy efficiency and innovation make good sense. General Electric has developed a line of 45 green products, including wind turbines and next-generation jet engines that go easy on the earth. DuPont has cut its greenhouse-gas emissions 72% since 1990. And finally, there's Walmart—yes, Walmart! With its 7,000 stores, 1.8 million employees, and 345 billion dollars in sales, Walmart has become a powerful player in the climate change picture. It has pledged to install solar panels on many of its stores, switch to hybrid vehicles, and conserve water. It has asked its 60,000 suppliers to join its effort to reduce package, waste, and energy use.

And it has joined other large corporate players—including Alcoa, BP America, Duke Energy, Lehman Brothers and Caterpillar—in asking the Federal Government to act aggressively on climate change. After all, where is our national leadership on this issue? Hiding, I'm afraid, somewhere under a rock—or perhaps under a pile of coal or an oil derrick. It's these fossil-fuel oriented industries there are cozying up to Congress and to the Executive branches of government with their aggressive lobbyists.

You need to tell your congressman, your senators, and yes, your president, that enough is enough! Our national government needs to endorse the California initiative to impose new, tough requirements on our automobile makers. They can do a lot better job on fuel efficiency, and it's shameful they haven't done so already. The national leadership needs to follow the state and local leadership in combating greenhouse emissions across a wide spectrum. One really vital thing they can do is to finally pass a law limiting greenhouse emissions.

In 2003 Senators John McCain and Joe Lieberman sponsored a bill that would set limits on industrial greenhouse gases. The bill contained an ingenious proposal: Companies that did better than required would accumulate credits that they could then sell to those that failed to meet their targets. In other words, the dirty company would be penalized, the "clean" company rewarded. And going green would make good monetary sense. It was just this kind of cap-and-trade strategy, as it is called, that was used in the 1990s to curb sulfur dioxide, the leading cause of acid rain (which we haven't heard so much about lately). The legislation worked—there has been a 35% reduction in that kind of pollution. It could also work dramatically to reduce greenhouse gases.

So why was this bill not enacted? What are our national leaders waiting on? Write them, and tell them it's time to get the lead out.

All these grand global plans—all these brilliant initiatives—are great, of course, and long overdue. But in the end, it all comes down to us—to each of us, and our cultivating together a new green lifestyle that will make it possible for us to survive on this planet. We must teach ourselves the values and habits of this new green way of thinking and living. So keep an open mind to the new technologies and how you might make use of them in your everyday life. Instead of always driving your car, walk or ride a bike. You will discover an added benefit—greater health! Instead of driving alone to work, carpool. You may make some new friends or deepen some old friendships. And remember another old friend, trees. Trees cleanse the air of CO_2, and shade our homes, reducing the need for air conditioning in the summer, but letting the sun through in the winter. Join other enlightened people who are working to encourage the wise management of forests.

Figure B.5

How You Can Cool Global Warming
1. Run your dishwasher only when full and use the air-dry option.
2. Clean or replace air conditioner filters regularly.
3. Set your thermostat lower in winter and hgher in summer.
4. Walk, bike, carpool, or use mass transit.
5. Insulate your water heater.
6. Set water heater thermostat below 120°.
7. Install low-flow showerheads.
8. Ask your utility company to conduct a free energy audit of your home.
9. Encourage recycling at school or work.
10. Plant trees next to your home.
11. Wash laundry in cold water.
12. Replace old refrigerators with more energy-efficient models.
13. Reduce garbage by buying reusable products and recycling.
14. Replace standard light bulbs with fluorescent bulbs.
15. When you buy a car, make fuel efficiency a major consideration.
16. When you have your car air conditioner serviced, make sure the coolant is recycled.
17. Install energy-saving windows in your home.
18. Caulk around doors and windows in your home.
19. Insulate all walls and ceilings.
20. If possible, select a utility that does not produce electricity from fossil fuel sources.

SOCM—"Save Our Cumberland Mountains"—is one such local group. These dedicated folks helped save Fall Creek Falls from strip mining, and they are working now to discourage the practice of clear-cutting, the large-scale destruction of forests in West Tennessee. I'm proud to belong to SOCM, and I invite you to join us at our next meeting this Thursday, where we are going to plan some serious environmental action.

You can make a difference in the small everyday choices you make. At the end of my speech I'm going to give you a list of things you can do to help take the red out of global warming. Planting a tree, changing light bulbs to fluorescent, recycling—these may not sound like much, but magnify every little act by a thousand, and then by a million, and then by a thousand million. All around the globe people of good will and good sense, acting together, can make a big difference!

Someday, I hope to take my children, and my grandchildren, to Dauphin Island, Alabama, where they can walk on the sand and swim in the sea and enjoy the wildlife in the Audubon Bird Sanctuary. As I was preparing this speech, I developed an email conversation with Dr. George F. Crozier, executive director of the Sea Lab at Dauphin Island. From that fragile barrier island Dr. Crozier wrote: "We are incorporating the message of global warming into our educational/outreach efforts in hopes that we can get the public's attention before it is too late."

The clock is ticking, but I don't think it's too late. I hope that what I've said in the last two speeches has gained your attention. Get involved! Together we can cool the fever, and turn down the heat under our planet.

Living Wills: Ensuring Your Right to Choose
Bonnie Marshall

Bonnie Marshall was a student at Heidelberg College in Ohio when she made the following persuasive presentation. Her speech is noteworthy for its use of an opening narrative to heighten interest in the problem Bonnie was presenting. The speech is also strong in its use of personal and expert forms of testimony. Clearly, Bonnie had responsible knowledge of her subject. In her conclusion, she makes excellent use of repetition to underscore her message of personal responsibility. She presented the speech with great conviction.

Harry Smith was a cranky, obstinate, old farmer. He loved bowling, Glenn Miller music, and Monday night football. He was also dying from cancer of the esophagus, which had metastasized to his lungs. He didn't like doctors, and he liked hospitals and modern medicine even less. Harry used to say that he remembered when three square meals, mom's mustard plaster, and an occasional house call from Doc Jones was all anyone ever needed to stay healthy. Harry didn't want to live in pain, and he hated being dependent on anyone else; yet like so many others, Harry never expressed his wishes to his family. When Harry's cancer became so debilitating that he could no longer speak for himself, his family stepped in to make decisions about his medical care. Since Harry never told them how he felt, his children, out of a sense of guilt over the things they had done and the love they hadn't expressed, refused to let Harry die. He was subjected to ventilators, artificial feedings, and all the wizardry that modern medicine can offer. Harry did die eventually, but only after months of agony with no hope of recovery.

Harry's doctor, my husband, agonized too over the decisions regarding Harry's care. He knew that the children were acting out of grief and guilt, not for Harry's benefit. Yet because Harry had not documented his wishes, his doctor had no choice but to subject Harry to the senseless torture that he didn't want.

We all know of a similar case that gained national attention. On December 26, 1990, Nancy Cruzan died. The tragic young woman who became the focal point for the right-to-die movement was finally allowed to die after eight long years and a legal battle that reached the hallowed halls of the Supreme Court. Nancy's battle is now over, yet the issue has not been resolved and the need for action is more urgent than ever. Since the Supreme Court ruling on June 25, 1990, public interest in this issue has skyrocketed. From July 1990 to November 1990, the Society for the Right To Die answered 908,000 requests for information. By comparison, in November of 1989, the first month that the Society kept monthly statistics, they answered only 21,000 requests.

Today I would like to explore this problem and propose some solutions that we all can implement.

The *Cruzan* v. *Missouri* decision was significant because it was the first time that the Supreme Court had rendered an opinion on the right-to-die issue. However, the message from the Court is anything but clear and complete. As Justice Sandra Day O'Connor wrote in her concurring opinion, "Today we decide only that one state's practice does not violate the Constitution. . . . The more challenging task of crafting appropriate procedures for safeguarding incompetents' liberty interests is entrusted to the 'laboratory' of the states." So while the Court has for the first time recognized a "constitutionally protected liberty interest in refusing unwanted medical treatment," it has also given the power over this issue back to the states. According to the July 9, 1990, issue of *U.S. News and World Report*, nine states, including Ohio, have no legislation recognizing the legality of living wills. Of the states that do have living will legislation, about one-half do not allow for the withdrawal of nutrition and hydration, even if the will says the patient does not want such treatment, according to Lisa Belken in the June 25th issue of the *New York Times*. Also according to the *Times*, only 33 states have health care proxy laws. Perhaps as a result of all this indecision and inconsistency, desperate patients with terminal illnesses will continue to seek out the "Dr. Deaths" of the medical community, those who, like Dr. Kevorkian of Michigan, are willing to surpass simply allowing the terminally ill to die, to actively bringing about death.

The right-to-die issue may seem far removed from you today, yet the American Medical Association estimates that 80 to 90% of us will die a "managed death." According to an editorial by Anthony Lewis in the June 29, 1990, *New York Times*, "The problem is far more acute and far-reaching than most of us realize. Almost two million people die in the United States every year, and more than half of those deaths occur when some life-sustaining treatment is ended." The decision to provide, refuse, or withdraw medical treatment should be made individually, personally, with the counsel of family, friends, doctors, and clergy, but certainly not by the state.

More and more, however, these personal decisions are being taken away from patients and their families and instead are being argued and decided in courts of law. Perhaps it began with Karen Ann Quinlan. It certainly continued with Nancy Cruzan, and these decisions could be taken away from you, if we do not act now to ensure that our right to refuse medical treatment is protected. And our right to refuse medical treatment includes the right to refuse artificial nutrition and hydration, just as it includes the right to refuse antibiotics, chemotherapy, surgery, or artificial respiration. According to John Collins Harvey, M.D., Ph.D from the Kennedy Institute of Ethics at Georgetown University, "The administration of food and fluid artificially is a medical technological treatment. . . . Utilizing such medical treatment requires the same kind of medical technological expertise of physicians, nurses, and dietitians as is required in utilizing a respirator for treatment of respiratory failure or employing a renal dialysis machine for the treatment of kidney failure. This medical treatment, however, is ineffective, for it cannot cause dead brain cells to regenerate; it will merely sustain biological life and prolong the patient's dying. Such treatment is considered by many physicians and medical ethicists to be extraordinary." Additionally, the Center for Health Care Ethics of St. Louis University, a Jesuit institution, prepared a brief for the Cruzan case which states that "within the Christian foundation, the withholding and withdrawing of medical treatment, including artificial nutrition and hydration, is acceptable."

So what can we do to protect ourselves and assure that our wishes are carried out? My plan is fourfold. First, we in Ohio must urge our legislators to pass living will legislation. Representative Marc Guthrie, from Newark, Ohio, has drafted a living will bill, House Bill 70. We must urge our legislators to pass this bill, since it is more comprehensive than the Senate version and will better protect our rights on this crucial issue.

Second, we must draw up our own living wills stating our philosophy on terminal care. I propose the use of the Medical Directive, a document created by Drs. Linda and Ezekiel Emanuel. This document details twelve specific treatments that could be offered. You can choose different treatment options based on four possible scenarios. You can indicate either that you desire the treatment, do not want it, are undecided, or want to try the treatment, but discontinue it if there is no improvement. This directive, which also includes space for a personal statement, eliminates much of the ambiguity of generic living wills and provides clearer guidelines to your physician and family.

Third, designate a person to make health care decisions for you should you become incompetent. This person should be familiar with your personal philosophy and feelings about terminal care and be likely to make the same decisions that you yourself would make. You should name this person in a Durable Power of Attorney for Health Care, a legal document that is now recognized in the State of Ohio.

Fourth, have a heart-to-heart talk with your doctor and be sure that he or she understands and supports your wishes on terminal care. Have a copy of your living will and Durable Power of Attorney for Health Care placed in your medical file. Finally, for more information on living wills, you can contact: The Society for the Right To Die, 250 West 57th St., New York, NY 10107, or send $1.00 to the Harvard Medical School Health Letter, 164 Longwood Ave., Fourth Floor, Boston, MA 02115 for a copy of the Emanuels' Medical Directive form.

I am interested in this issue because, through my husband, I have seen patients suffer the effects of not having an advance directive. You need to ask yourself how you feel about terminal care, but regardless of your personal response, we all must choose to protect our rights on this issue. WE must choose to pressure our legislators to adopt living will legislation. WE must choose to draw up our own living wills and health care proxies. And most importantly, WE must choose to discuss this most personal and sensitive issue with our families and loved ones, so that in the absence of a legal document, or even with one, they may confidently make the decisions concerning our life and death that we ourselves would make. Not all patients end up like Nancy Cruzan or Harry Smith. Many people are allowed to quietly slip away from the pain and suffering of life. But that can only happen after the careful, painful deliberation of a grieving family, who can at least take comfort in the fact that they are carrying out their loved one's wishes.

Ceremonial Speeches

Remarks on Accepting the Martin Luther King, Jr., Human Rights Award

John Bakke

Professor John Bakke presented this thoughtful speech in 2006 in ceremonies held at the University of Memphis. Dr. Bakke used his acceptance speech to breathe new life into Dr. King's principle of non-violence. Rather than a dated tactic in a long ago Civil Rights struggle, non-violence, by Bakke's interpretation, now demands full participation in the political process and acceptance of one's obligations as a citizen. Thus, what begins as an acceptance speech for an award quickly becomes a speech of tribute to Dr. King and finally a speech of inspiration to his listeners.

Thank you. It seems to me that many acceptance speeches begin with the words, "I've received many awards before, but . . ." Well, the truth is that I have not received many awards before, but of all the awards I have not received, this is the one I always wanted. What is more important in our lives than our rights as human beings? And who in our lifetime has done more to extend human rights than Dr. King? I'm overwhelmed by the honor. So please indulge me for a few minutes while I thank some people who are special to me before I say a few words in honor and memory of the person whom we all have reason to thank today. Dr. Martin Luther King, Jr. gave me the courage to practice what he preached as best I could in and out of academia at critical points in my own life and in the life of this university and our community. And for that I am most thankful. . . .*[Dr. Bakke acknowledges his family and friends, as well as his colleagues at the University of Memphis who shared his values and supported his work.]*

We came to Memphis in 1967 and I was fortunate to be part of a progressive department at a university in a community ready for positive change. It is no accident that four members of that department, then called Speech and Drama, were previous recipients of this Martin Luther King Award. . . . And finally, thanks to all the seekers and holders of elected office who have given me the opportunity to work with them as well as to all the wonderful people whom I have worked with as a partisan in the political process. I got into campaign communication to help good people become more competitive in the campaign arena. I am proud of all these people for what they have done for human rights.

Dr. Martin Luther King Jr. gave to human rights his last full measure of devotion. He was devoted to non-violence as a political strategy and as a personal philosophy because he knew the effects of violence even on those who commit violent acts as a means of necessary self defense or in a just cause. But when King was nearing his last days on earth, as Taylor Branch has recently written, in his commitment to nonviolence, King "found himself nearly alone among colleagues weary of sacrifice."

In 1968 King was increasingly under attack from all sides, by friends and foes alike. He was criticized by the Johnson Administration for opposing the war in Southeast Asia. He was under intense scrutiny by J. Edgar Hoover and the FBI. He was criticized by the white liberal establishment for his proposed Poor People's March. He was criticized by militant Black Power advocates for his non-violent tactics and his coalitions with whites. And many of his closest friends just wanted him to back off for a while and by all means stay out of Memphis where a sanitation workers strike had been going on since February 2nd.

All such criticism came together and reached a crescendo after King's march in Memphis on behalf of the sanitation workers was disrupted by violence. The criticism came from all over, from the *New York Times* and *Washington Post* as well as the *Atlanta Constitution*, the *Dallas Morning News*, and, yes, the local *Memphis Commercial Appeal* and *Press Scimitar* newspapers. In editorials entitled "King's Credibility Gap" and "Chicken a la King," the *Commercial Appeal*, for example, said that "King's pose as the leader of a non-violent movement has been shattered" and "The Real Martin Luther King . . . [is] one of the most menacing men in America today." The *Press-Scimitar* said that King's "rhetoric has lost its spell" and the *Dallas Morning News* called him "a headline hunting high-priest on non-violent violence," "a press agent protester," "a marching militant" willing to "wreck everything for a spot on the evening newscast" and a "peripatetic preacher" who "could not allow the troubled waters to go unfished when there was a chance that the fisher might pick up a little publicity." You can imagine what was being said on the street at the time.

From all corners, the message was clear. "Martin Luther King! Go home! Go back where you came from. Get back in your place! At worst, you're dangerous. At best, you're history." Believe me! James Earl Ray was not the only American who wanted King out of the way. On the eve of April 4, in such a climate of violence in Memphis, Martin Luther delivered his "Mountaintop Speech" at Mason Temple. Like Socrates at his trial, like Jesus before Pilate, like Luther at Worms, King, virtually alone, had to stand up and be who he was: Dr. Martin Luther King, Jr., the true apostle of nonviolent direct action.

I spent much time as a graduate student studying great speeches. I also read many treatises on the nature of eloquence. Thus I can say, personally and professionally, history knows no more eloquent speaker than Martin Luther King, Jr. I never understood what Longinus meant when he wrote that "eloquence was the concomitant of a great soul" until I heard Dr. King in a context in which I knew what he was up against and what he was asking for. His last speech in Memphis was more than speech. It was "eloquence," once described by the great orator Daniel Webster as "action . . . noble, sublime, godlike action."

In the peroration of what became his last speech, King mentioned the threats and uncertainties felt by every person who heard him and said, "I don't know what will happen now. We've got some difficult days ahead. But it doesn't matter with me now. Because I've been to the mountaintop." The spontaneous applause caused King to pause for a moment. Then he went on. "Like anybody," he said, " I would like to live a long life. Longevity has its place." Then, like Jesus had expressed in the Garden of Gethsemane, King said, "I only want to do God's will."

He said that God had allowed him to go up to the mountaintop and to see "the Promised Land." It was a vision of how things would all turn out and reaffirmed the conviction that it had been worth all the pain and years of suffering. After telling his audience that he was not worried and that he had no fear, King chilled their bones and fired their imagination by saying "I may not get there with you. But I want you to know tonight that we as a people will get to the Promised Land."

It was perfect communication. All in his presence were filled with King's conviction and what they felt was his "truth." The striking sanitation workers would get what they deserved and so too would they as a people. That WAS more than speech. It WAS action. In Webster's words: "noble, sublime, manly, godlike action." Martin Luther King, you see, was more than just a "dreamer," more than someone who simply walked on troubled waters turning the other cheek. King was America's conscience and a powerful force for change.

In his *Ethics of Rhetoric*, published in 1953 before King became a national figure, Richard Weaver wrote that the discourse of the noble orator is about "real potentiality or possible actuality," whereas that of the "mere exaggerator" is about "unreal potentiality." In his famous "I Have a Dream" speech, King said—remember it was 1963—that he had a dream that the sons of former slaves and former slave owners would be able to sit down together at the table of brotherhood. Unreal potentiality or possible actuality? He said little black boys and black girls would be able to join hands with little white boys and girls and walk together as sisters and brothers. Possible actuality or unreal potentiality? And he said that his four children would one day live in a nation where they would be judged not by the color of their skin but by the content of their character. A dream? Or real vision? And what about "We as a people will get to the promised land?" What about that one? Where are we on that one today? And if we are not where we want to be, whose fault is it? Certainly not Martin Luther King's nor the legitimacy of his vision.

In the last volume of his great trilogy, *America in the King Years*, Taylor Branch begins with the assertion that today "nonviolence is an orphan among democratic ideas." He says, "It has nearly vanished from public discourse even though the basic element—the vote—has no other meaning." In homage to King and for the good of ourselves, Branch strongly suggests that we commit the same time, energy, and resources to the nonviolent means of change as we now commit to the violent ones. "Every ballot is a piece of nonviolence," he says, "signifying hard-won consent to raise politics above fire power and bloody conquest."

It's time to make that ballot the effect of full democratic participation. It's time to reclaim our democratic processes. It's time to make the democratic processes work in America just as we are trying to make them work for Iraq.

That means more than voting. It means informed voting. It means supporting candidates and policies of our choice. It means commitment to the communication processes that give life to democracy. It means thinking of ourselves more as citizens than as just taxpayers. It means full-time citizenship. If campaigns are now permanent, citizenship cannot be cyclical. Democracy and "the vote" will always be open to criticism if people do not vote or do not know what they are voting for.

I don't care how much we spend on voting technology. I don't care how much we restrict campaign contributions. Special interests will always have special influence as long as we the people are not especially interested. Voting two dead people certainly was bad [in a recent local election], but over 90% of live voters staying home was a whole lot worse.

If we work to make the democratic processes work for us at home as well as around the world, we will be on the true path—the nonviolent path—to the kind of homeland security that will keep us moving toward the Promised Land. It is non-violence that makes civilization civil and it is through the non-violent participation in democracy that we can live out the true meaning of OUR creed. We will be keeping alive the hope of the American dream of our founding fathers and the real potentiality in the vision of Dr. Martin Luther King, Jr.

A Man for the New Age: Tribute to Tiger Woods
Leslie Eason

Leslie Eason's speech of tribute to Tiger Woods illustrates the skillful use of language and good usage of the principles of tribute. Woods' sporting accomplishments are unique and exceptional, and his refusal to accept a racial identity benefits society. Eason argues that the world's way of assigning identity based on race underscores what we are, not who we are. She advises her listeners to create an identity based on character and accomplishment rather than upon skin color.

You're at the Western Open, where Tiger Woods could be Elvis reincarnated. People clap when he pulls out a club. They clap when he hits the ball. They clap no matter where that ball lands. They clap if he smiles. They clap because he is.

Not long ago, when not much else was going on and we were tired of O.J. and very much needed a hero, a young man in a red polo shirt materialized out of nowhere doing magical things with a stick in a sport we usually ignored. He was not just good or even outstanding. He was a miracle. His game all but laughed at records set by men twice his age. Nike threw forty million at him. Rolex threw fifty million at him. American Express lined up to give him millions more.

We started having to pay attention to things like the Masters, and Opens, and Invitationals, and other such things that applied to golf. Other people were playing, but he was all we could see, this young god in a red shirt. Suddenly we had to learn a new language—"fore," "eagle," "birdie," "par," and "bogie"—just to keep up with the latest news about him.

Some people watched him play, and bragged that black people could do just about anything. Then we heard that he was only one-fourth black, and that he did not describe himself as black. Now, in a society that honors the rule that one drop of blood is all it takes to be black, this didn't mean much. We ignored his Thai mother, disregarded the Native American and Chinese and Caucasian he said he had in him, and all we saw was his dark-skinned father, who was always there in the gallery cheering him on.

To us he continued to look a lot like other young black men we knew. Mothers with daughters of a certain age (including my own) said that they wished he was their son-in-law or future son-in-law. Six foot two, a hundred fifty-five pounds, smart—Stanford, remember—clean-cut in his creased khakis, curly hair, gorgeous teeth—gorgeous teeth. Skin the color of what they used to call "suntan" in the Crayola box. And rich—very, very rich.

He's the very opposite of the gangsta boys in the hood—boys who wear their pants hanging below their belt like some people in the penitentiary. Next to them he's prep school and Pepsodent. Some said he put a pretty face on blackness. Others said he couldn't possibly be black.

From the moment the world finally met him at the Nike press conference, people wondered what, not who, he was. He with the almond eyes, the great-colored skin, the photo-op smile. "What are you?" a reporter asked. He didn't seem quite ready for the question, suggesting he wasn't any one thing, but a lot of everything all rolled up into one. Started going into fractions—one-eighth of this, one-fifth of that, a fourth of something else. Told Oprah he didn't feel comfortable being called black. To describe his ethnicity, he came up with the name Cablinasian, combining his Caucasian, Black, Indian, and Asian ethnicities. It seemed both a naive plea for a color-blind, colorless America and a throwback to the quadroon days of old Louisiana when people measured their bloodlines by the teaspoon.

But in actuality, Tiger Woods was something the world needed very much. He transcended the color barrier. Not because he was the first black to do this or do that in golf, but because he refused to be defined by the color of his skin. In the midst of all his fame, fortune, contracts, money, and marriage offers, he had taken the step to destroy the old racist rule, one drop is all it takes. He offered instead a new principle: he was an equal representation of all he came from—Caucasian, Black, Indian, and Asian—but that was not who he was. How does all this help Tiger? Well, to some he's considered the best golfer in the world. Not the best black player, but the best player, period. A perfect example of together and the same, instead of separate but equal. How does this help the rest of us? It shows us that race is just a small part of our identity. Our own personal racial equation does not determine who we are or where we're going. Or even what we can do.

You're back at the Western Open. The fan galleries finally look like America—Asian, white, black, Latino, fathers with sons, mothers pushing baby carriages, people who have been playing golf for years, people who didn't know what golf was before Tiger Woods and now want to try it. Everything revolves around Tiger. Even babies go silent when Tiger's about to swing. Once the ball is hit, people resume their conversation and stampede to the next hole to watch him, leaving the next player to struggle by himself.

So what are we to make of him? His father, Earl Woods, has said that his son would change the course of humanity. You can mark that up to a proud father's hyperbole, but perhaps Tiger has already pointed us in a new direction by his refusal to accept an identity imposed by racist custom. Hopefully one day we will see him as a young man who was simply ahead of his time, instead of viewing him as a naive child trying to escape his heritage.

It's not clear yet who he is, but it's quite clear what he is not. His boundaries are not defined and confined by his complex racial background. Instead, he is what he told us, a complex mixture of heart, talent, dedication, attractiveness of person and personality, and grace under the pressure of constant media attention and tournament competition. The most important ingredient in that mixture is his stubborn refusal to accept the world's ways of limiting identity, and his polite insistence upon leaving himself open to change and growth. He did not inherit a prearranged identity imposed by race; rather, he is responsible for creating who he is and who he will become. Who he is will emerge over time, a product of his character and accomplishments.

As we watch him grow and become himself, we can only celebrate what he means for a nation and world that must become more comfortable with its incredible diversity of race and culture. Tiger Woods, you are a man for the New Age, and we salute you!

Nobel Peace Prize Acceptance Speech
Elie Wiesel

Elie Wiesel delivered the following speech in Oslo, Norway, on December 10, 1986, as he accepted the Nobel Peace Prize. The award recognized his lifelong work for human rights, especially his role as "spiritual archivist of the Holocaust." Wiesel's poetic, intensely personal style as a writer carries over into this ceremonial speech of acceptance. He uses narrative very effectively as he flashes back to what he calls the "kingdom of night" and then flashes forward again into the present. The speech's purpose is to spell out and share the values and concerns of a life committed to the rights of oppressed peoples, in which, as he put it so memorably, "every moment is a moment of grace, every hour an offering."

It is with a profound sense of humility that I accept the honor you have chosen to bestow upon me. I know: your choice transcends me. This both frightens and pleases me.

It frightens me because I wonder: do I have the right to represent the multitudes whc have perished? Do I have the right to accept this great honor on their behalf? I do not. That would be presumptuous. No one may speak for the dead, no one may interpret their mutilated dreams and visions.

It pleases me because I may say that this honor belongs to all the survivors and their children, and through us, to the Jewish people with whose destiny I have always been identified.

I remember: it happened yesterday or eternities ago. A young Jewish boy discovering the kingdom of night. I remember his bewilderment, I remember his anguish. It all happened so fast. The ghetto. The deportation. The sealed cattle car. The fiery altar upon which the history of our people and the future of mankind were meant to be sacrificed.

I remember: he asked his father: "Can this be true? This is the 20th century, not the Middle Ages. Who would allow such crimes to be committed? How could the world remain silent?"

And now the boy is turning to me: "Tell me," he asks. "What have you done with your life?"

And I tell him that I have tried. That I have tried to keep memory alive, that I have tried to fight those who would forget. Because if we forget, we are guilty, we are accomplices.

And then I explained to him how naive we were, that the world did know and remain silent. And that is why I swore never to be silent whenever and wherever human beings endure suffering and humiliation. We must always take sides. Neutrality helps the oppressor, never the victim. Silence encourages the tormentor, never the tormented.

Sometimes we must interfere. When human lives are endangered, when human dignity is in jeopardy, national borders and sensitivities become irrelevant. Wherever men or women are persecuted because of their race, religion or political views, that place must—at that moment—become the center of our universe.

Of course, since I am a Jew profoundly rooted in my people's memory and tradition, my first response is to Jewish fears, Jewish needs, Jewish crises. For I belong to a traumatized generation, one that experienced the abandonment and solitude of our people. It would be unnatural for me not to make Jewish priorities my own: Israel, Soviet Jewry, Jews in Arab lands.

But there are others as important to me. Apartheid is, in my view as abhorrent as anti-Semitism. To me, Andrei Sakharov's isolation is as much a disgrace as Iosif Begun's imprisonment. As is the denial of Solidarity and its leader Lech Walesa's right to dissent. And Nelson Mandela's interminable imprisonment.

There is so much injustice and suffering crying out for our attention: victims of hunger, or racism and political persecution, writers and poets, prisoners in so many lands governed by the left and by the right. Human rights are being violated on every continent. More people are oppressed than free.

And then, too, there are the Palestinians to whose plight I am sensitive but whose methods I deplore. Violence and terrorism are not the answer. Something must be done about their suffering, and soon. I trust Israel, for I have faith in the Jewish people. Let Israel be given a chance, let hatred and danger be removed from her horizons, and there will be peace in and around the Holy Land.

Yes, I have the faith. Faith in God and even in His creation. Without it no action would be possible. And action is the only remedy to indifference: the most insidious danger of all. Isn't this the meaning of Alfred Nobel's legacy? Wasn't his fear of war a shield against war?

There is much to be done, there is much that can be done. One person—a Raoul Wallenberg, an Albert Schweitzer, one person of integrity, can make a difference, a difference of life and death. As long as one dissident is in prison, our freedom will not be true. As long as one child is hungry, our lives will be filled with anguish and shame.

What all these victims need above all is to know that they are not alone: that we are not forgetting them, that when their voices are stifled we shall lend them ours, that while their freedom depends on ours, the quality of our freedom depends on theirs.

This is what I say to the young Jewish boy wondering what I have done with his years. It is in his name that I speak to you and that I express to you my deepest gratitude. No one is as capable of gratitude as one who has emerged from the kingdom of night.

We know that every moment is a moment of grace, every hour an offering; not to share them would mean to betray them. Our lives no longer belong to us alone; they belong to all those who need us desperately.

Thank you Chairman Aarvik. Thank you members of the Nobel Committee. Thank you people of Norway, for declaring on this singular occasion that our survival has meaning for mankind.

Notes

Chapter 1

1. Press Release, National Association of Colleges and Employers, 15 March 2007, www.naceweb.org/press/display.asp?year=2007&prid=254 (accessed 7 May 2007).
2. "Employers Complain about Communication Skills," *Pittsburgh Post-Gazette*, 6 February 2005, www.post-gazette.com/pg/pp/05037/453170.stm (accessed 7 May 2007).
3. Jill J. McMillan and Katy J. Harriger, "College Students and Deliberation: A Benchmark Study," *Communication Education* 51 (2002): 237–253.
4. From Kathleen Peterson, ed., *Statements Supporting Speech Communication* (Annandale, Va.: Speech Communication Association, 1986).
5. See the discussion in James A. Herrick, *The History and Theory of Rhetoric: An Introduction*, 3rd ed. (Boston: Allyn & Bacon, 2005).
6. Pericles, "Funeral Oration," in *Thucydides on Justice, Power, and Human Nature*, ed. and trans. Paul Woodruff (Cambridge, Mass.: Hackett Publishing Company, 1993), p. 42.
7. Aristotle, *On Rhetoric*, trans. George A. Kennedy (New York: Oxford University Press, 1991).
8. Cicero, *De Oratore*, trans. D. W. Sutton and H. Rackham (Cambridge, Mass.: Harvard University Press, 1988).
9. Plato, *Gorgias*, trans. Benjamin Jowett, http://philosophy.eserver.org/plato/gorgias.txt (accessed 8 May, 2007).
10. *The Dialogues of Plato*, trans. Benjamin Jowett, in *Great Books of the Western World*, vol. 7 (Chicago: Encyclopaedia Britannica, Inc., 1952). See also the analysis by Richard M. Weaver, "The *Phaedrus* and the Nature of Rhetoric," in *Language Is Sermonic*, eds. Richard L. Johannesen, Rennard Strickland, and Ralph T. Eubanks (Baton Rouge: Louisiana State University Press, 1970), pp. 57–83.
11. *Quintilian, Institutes of Oratory: Education of an Orator* (12 books), trans. John Selby Watson (London: George Bell & Sons, 1892), http://honeyl.public.iastate.edu/quintilian/index.html (accessed 7 May 2007).
12. Elizabeth Lozano, "The Cultural Experience of Space and Body: A Reading of Latin American and Anglo American Comportment in Public," in *Our Voices: Essays in Culture, Ethnicity, and Communication*, eds. Alberto Gonzalez, Marsha Houston, and Victoria Chen (Los Angeles: Roxbury Publishing, 2004), p. 275.
13. T. Harry Williams, ed., *Abraham Lincoln: Selected Speeches, Messages, and Letters* (New York: Holt, Rinehart and Winston, 1964), p. 148.
14. Claude E. Shannon and Warren Weaver, *The Mathematical Theory of Communication* (Urbana: University of Illinois Press, 1963). Shannon's first classic essay on the subject appeared originally in 1948 in the *Bell System Technical Journal*, and a companion essay appeared in 1949 in *Scientific American*. For an interesting analysis, see Mick Underwood, "The Shannon-Weaver Model," 21 June 2003, www.culsock.ndirect.co.uk/MUHone/cshtml/introductory/sw/html (accessed 4 May 2007).
15. See especially Burke's discussion of identification and consubstantiality in "The Range of Rhetoric," in *A Rhetoric of Motives* (Berkeley: University of California Press, 1969), pp. 3–43.
16. Martin Luther King, Jr., I Have a Dream, www.americanrhetoric.com/speeches/mlkihaveadream.htm (accessed 8 May 2007).
17. Malinda Snow argues that the flight of the children of Israel from Egypt has been a suggestive comparative theme for African Americans since the days of slavery. See her "Martin Luther King's 'Letter from Birmingham Jail' as Pauline Epistle," *Quarterly Journal of Speech* 71 (1985): 318–334.
18. Tom Teepen, "Twisting King's Words to Give His Antagonists Comfort," *Minneapolis Star Tribune*, 14 July 1997, p. 9A.
19. "Quoting Out of Context," *SourceWatch* (Center for Media & Democracy), 4 March 2004, www.sourcewatch.org/index.php?title=Quoting_out_of_context (accessed 6 May 2007).
20. Lawrence M. Hinman, "How to Fight College Cheating," *Washington Post*, 3 Sept. 2004, http://ethics.sandiego.edu/LMH/op-ed/CollegeCheating/index.asp (accessed 29 June 2006).
21. This theme develops in Richard L. Johannesen, *Ethics in Human Communication*, 5th ed. (Long Grove, Ill.: Waveland Press, 2002).
22. Credo of Ethical Communications; National Communication Association. Used by permission of the National Communication Association.

Chapter 2

1. The Gallup Organization, "Snakes Top List of Americans' Fears," 19 Mar. 2001, www.gallup.com/poll/releases/pr010319.asp (accessed 20 Sept. 2003).
2. National Communication Association, "How Americans Communicate" (undated posting), www.natcom.org/research/Roper/how_americans_communicate.htm (accessed 25 June 1999).
3. "Jackson's Comeback Wrecked by Stage Fright," 16 Nov. 2006, http://entertainment.timesonline.co.uk/tol/arts_and_entertainment/article638532.ece, Timesonline (accessed 5 May 2007).
4. "Celebrities' Stage Fright Secrets," 19 Nov. 2003, NCBuy's Worldwide Newsdesk Reporting, www.ncbuy.com/news/2003-11-19/1008286.html (accessed 5 May 2007); and "Famous People" Shyness and Social Anxiety Treatment (undated posting), www.socialanxietyassist.com.au/famous_people.shtml (accessed 5 May 2007).
5. Ed Sherman, "It's Not the Novelty, It's the Challenge," *Chicago Tribune*, 22 May 2003, p. 1. Available online at www.chicagotribune.com.
6. Michael T. Motley, *Overcoming Your Fear of Public Speaking: A Proven Method* (Boston: Houghton Mifflin, 1997).
7. Ralph R. Behnke and Chris R. Sawyer, "Milestones of Anticipatory Public Speaking Anxiety," *Communication Education* 48 (Apr. 1999): 165–172.

8. Jennifer D. Mladenka, Chris R. Sawyer, and Ralph R. Behnke, "Anxiety Sensitivity and Speech Trait Anxiety as Predictors of State Anxiety During Public Speaking," *Communication Quarterly* 46, no. 4 (Fall 1998): 417–429.

9. H. Dennis Beaver, "Got Stage Fright" Resource Library, Graduate School of Banking, University of Wisconsin–Madison, www.gsb.org/articles/Stage_Fright.htm (accessed 15 Feb. 2007).

10. M. B. Stein, J. R. Walker, and D. R. Forde, "Public Speaking Fears in a Community Sample: Prevalence, Impact on Functioning, and Diagnostic Classification," *Archives of General Psychiatry* (February 1996): 169–174 Amy M. Bippus and John A. Daly, "What Do People Think Causes Stage Fright? Naïve Attributions About the Reasons for Public Speaking Anxiety," *Communication Education* 48 (1999): 63–72.

11. Penny Addison, Jaime Ayala, Mark Hunter, Ralph R. Behnke, and Chris R. Sawyer, "Body Sensations of Higher and Lower Anxiety Sensitive Speakers Anticipating a Public Presentation, *Communication Research Reports*, 21 (2004), 284–290.

12. Shannon C. McCullough, Shelly G. Russell, Ralph R. Behnke, Chris R. Sawyer, and Paul L. Witt "Anticipatory Public Speaking State Anxiety as a Function of Body Sensations and State of Mind," *Communication Quarterly*, 54 (2006), 101–109.

13. Harvard University, *Public Speaking Home Page*, http://gseweb.harvard.edu/~westma/pubspeak.htm/ (accessed 28 July 1999).

14. Randolph W. Whitworth and Claudia Cochran, "Evaluation of Integrated Versus Unitary Treatments for Reducing Public Speaking Anxiety," *Communication Education* 45 (1996): 228–235.

15. Melina Gerosa, "Rosie Revealed," *Ladies Home Journal* (Feb. 1999): 118.

16. Joe Ayres and Brian L. Hewett, "The Relationship Between Visual Imagery and Public Speaking Apprehension," *Communication Reports* 10 (1997): 87–94; Joe Ayres, "Performance Visualization and Behavioral Disruption: a Clarification," *Communication Reports*, 18 (2005): 55–63.

17. Joe Ayres, "Speech Preparation Processes and Speech Apprehension," *Communication Education* 45 (1996): 228–235.

18. Whitworth and Cochran, pp. 306–314.

19. Mike Allen, John E. Hunter, and William A. Donohue, "MetaAnalysis of Self-Report Data on the Effectiveness of Public Speaking Anxiety Treatment Techniques," *Communication Education* 38 (1989): 54–76.

Chapter 3

1. John A. Daly, Anita L. Vangelisti, and David J. Weber, "Speech Anxiety Affects How People Prepare Speeches: A Protocol Analysis of the Preparation Processes of Speakers," *Communication Monographs* 62 (1995): 383–397.

2. Donald C. Bryant and Karl R. Wallace, *Fundamentals of Public Speaking*, 4th ed. (New York: Appleton-Century-Crofts, 1969), p. 233.

3. James C. McCroskey and Mason J. Teven, "Goodwill: A Reexamination of the Construct and Its Measurement," *Communication Monographs* 66 (1999): 90–103.

4. Kenneth Burke, *A Rhetoric of Motives* (Berkeley: University of California Press, 1969), pp. 20–23.

5. Barack Obama, "Reclaiming the Promise to the People," *Vital Speeches of the Day* 70 (1 Aug. 2004): 625.

6. James M. Loy, "Proud of What We Do for America," speech to the National Press Club, Washington, D.C., 24 Feb. 2000, *Vital Speeches of the Day* (15 June 2000): 517–520.

7. Obama, pp. 623–24.

Chapter 4

1. Cited in Clifton Fadiman, ed., *The Little, Brown Book of Anecdotes* (Boston: Little, Brown, 1985), pp. 475–476.

2. Thomas L. Means and Gary S. Klein, "A Short Classroom Unit, But a Significant Improvement, in Listening Ability," *Bulletin of the Association for Business Communication* 57 (1994): 13.

3. American Institute of Certified Public Accountants (AICPA), Highlighted Responses from the Association for Accounting marketing survey: Creating the Future Agenda for the Profession—Managing Partner Perspective, www.aicpa.org/pubs/tpcpa/feb2001/hilight/htm (accessed 8 Apr. 2005).

4. "Listening," (2007) www.act.org/workkeys/charts/listen.html (accessed 7 May 2007); and Valerie P. Goby and Justus H. Lewis, "The Key Role of Listening in Business: A Study of the Singapore Insurance Industry," *Business Communication Quarterly* 63 (June 2000): 41–51.

5. R. Bommelje, J. M. Houston, and R. Smither, "Personality Characteristics of Effective Listeners: A Five Factor Perspective," *International Journal of Listening* 17 (2003): 32–46; M. Imhof, "How to Listen More Efficiently: Self-Monitoring Strategies in Listening," *International Journal of Listening* 15 (2001): 2–19.

6. L. A. Janusik, "Teaching Listening: What Do We Know? What Should We Know?" *International Journal of Listening* 16 (2002): 5–39; L. A. Janusik and A. D. Wolvin, "Listening Treatment in the Basic Communication Course Text," in *Basic Communication Course Annual*, ed. D. Sellnow (Boston: American Press, 2002).

7. Richard Bruce Hyde, "Council: Using a Talking Stick to Teach Listening," *Speech Communication Teacher* (Winter 1993): 1–2.

8. Donal Carbaugh, "'Just Listen': 'Listening' and Landscape Among the Blackfeet," *Western Journal of Communication* 63 (1999): 250–270.

9. Luther Standing Bear, Oglala Sioux chief, cited in *Native American Wisdom: Photographs by Edward S. Curtis* (Philadelphia: Running Press, 1993), pp. 58–59.

10. Ronald B. Adler and George Rodman, *Understanding Human Communication*, 5th ed. (Fort Worth, Tex.: Harcourt Brace, 1994), p. 130.

11. C. Glenn Pearce, "Learning How to Listen Empathically," *Supervisory Management* 36 (1991): 11.

12. John Stewart and Carole Logan, "Empathic and Dialogic Listening," in *Bridges Not Walls: A Book About Interpersonal Communication*, ed. John Stewart, 7th ed. (New York: McGraw-Hill, 1999), p. 227.

13. Dave Ellis, *Becoming a Master Student*, 10th ed. (Boston: Houghton Mifflin, 2003), pp. 141–145.

14. Andrew D. Wolvin and Carolyn Gwynn Coakley, *Listening*, 2nd ed. (Dubuque, Iowa: William C. Brown, 1985), p. 177.

15. Larry Barker and Kittie Watson, *Listen Up: How to Improve Relationships, Reduce Stress, and Be More Productive by Using the Power of Listening* (New York: St. Martin's Press, 2000), p. 33.

16. Larry L. Barker and Kittie W. Watson, 21–41; for a synopsis of these listening styles see http://changingminds.org/techniques/listening/listening_styles.htm (accessed 27 Feb. 2007).

17. L. R. Wheeless, "An Investigation of Receiver Apprehension and Social Context Dimensions of Communication Apprehension," *Speech Teacher* 24 (1975): 263.

18. Joe Ayres, A. Kathleen Wilcox, and Debbie M. Ayres, "Receiver Apprehension: An Explanatory Model and Accompanying Research," *Communication Education* 44 (1995): 223–235. Also see Michael J. Beatty, "Receiver Apprehension as a Function of Cognitive Backlog," *Western Journal of Speech Communication* 45 (1981): 277–281; Michael J. Beatty and Steven K. Payne, "Receiver Apprehension and Cognitive Complexity," *Western Journal of Speech Communication* 45 (1981): 363–369; and Raymond W. Preiss, Lawrence R. Wheeless, and Mike Allen, "Potential Cognitive Processes and Consequences of Receiver Apprehension: A Meta-analytic Review," *Journal of Social Behavior and Personality* 5 (1990): 155–172.

19. C. V. Roberts, "A Validation of the Watson-Barker Listening Test," *Communication Research Reports* 3 (1986): 115–119.

20. Anthony J. Clark may have indicated indirectly the value of such exercises when he demonstrated a positive relationship between communication confidence and listening comprehension in "Communication Confidence and Listening Competence: An Investigation of the Relation-ships of Willingness to Communicate, Communication Apprehension, and Receiver Apprehension to Comp-rehension of Content and Emotional Meaning in Spoken Messages," *Communication Education* 38 (1989): 237–248.

21. Richard M. Weaver, "Ultimate Terms in Contemporary Rhetoric," in *Language Is Sermonic: Richard M. Weaver on the Nature of Rhetoric*, eds. Richard L. Johannesen, Rennard Strickland, and Ralph T. Eubanks (Baton Rouge: La., State University Press, 1970), p. 95.

22. Professor Halley discussed this "Triggering Stimuli Assignment" on the Web site of the International Listening Association, www.listen.org, (4 Aug. 1998).

23. "Britain Admits That Much of Its Report on Iraq Came from Magazines," *New York Times* (International), 8 Feb. 2003. www.nytimes.com/2003/02/08/international/europe/08BRIT.html?th. (21 Aug. 2003).

24. "Investigating the President: Media Madness?" transcript of a special report on CNN, 28 Jan. 1998.

25. Nancy Gohring, "Virginia Tech Students Hit Social Sites After Shooting: Spread of Misinformation Raises Questions About the Role of Social Networking Sites in a Crisis," *InfoWorld*, 18 Apr. 2007, www.infoworld.com/ article/07/04/18/HNvatechshooting_1.html (accessed 7 May 2007).

26. Waldo Braden, "The Available Means of Persuasion: What Shall We Do About the Demand for Snake Oil?" in *The Rhetoric of Our Times*, ed. J. Jeffery Auer (New York: Appleton-Century-Crofts, 1969), pp. 178–184.

27. Answers to Explore and Apply the Ideas in this chapter question 5: 1–?, 2–T, 3–?, 4–?, 5–?, 6–?, 7–?, 8–T

Chapter 5

1. *The Rhetoric of Aristotle*, trans. George Kennedy (New York: Oxford University Press, 1992), Book 2, Chs. 11–14, pp. 163–169.

2. The Pew Research Center, "How Young People View Their Lives, Futures, and Politics, 9 Jan. 2007, http://people-press.org/reports/pdf/300.pdf (9 Apr. 2007); Richard E. Petty and Duane T. Wegener, "Attitude Change: Multiple Roles for Persuasion Variables," in *Handbook of Social Psychology*, eds. Daniel T. Gilbert, Susan T. Fiske, and Gardener Lindzey, 4th ed., vol. 1 (Boston: McGraw-Hill, 1998), p. 358; Milton Rokeach, *The Open and Closed Mind* (New York: Basic Books, 1960); and T. R. Tyler and R. A. Schuller, "Aging and Attitude Change," *Journal of Personality and Social Psychology* 61 (1991): 689–697.

3. Cited in Allison Adato and Melissa G. Stanton, "If Women Ran America," *Life* (June 1992): 40.

4. The Pew Research Center, "Trends in Political Values and Core Attitudes: 1987-2007," 22 Mar. 2007, http://people-press.org/reports/print.php3?PageID=1127 (accessed 9 Apr. 2007).

5. "College Gender Gap Widens," *USA Today*, 10 October 2005, www.usatoday.com/news/education/2005-10-19-male-college-cover_x.htm (accessed 11 June 2006).

6. "Women in the Labor Force, 1900–2005" www.infoplease.com/ipa/A0104673.html (accessed 6 Apr. 2007).

7. "Women By the Numbers, From the U.S. Census Bureau," www.infoplease.com/spot/womencensus1.html (accessed 5 Apr. 2007).

8. P. Schonback, *Education and Intergroup Attitudes* (London: Academic Press, 1981); Russell Long, "Prejudice: Its Forms and Causes," (7 Oct. 2006) www.delmar.edu/socsci/rlong/race/far-02.htm (accessed 8 Apr. 2007); K. Stenner, *The Authoritarian Dynamic* (New York: Cambridge University Press, 2005); J. F. Dovido, P. Glick, and L. A. Rudman, eds., *On the Nature of Prejudice: Fifty Years After Allport* (Malden, Mass.: Blackwell, 2005).

9. William McGuire, "Attitudes and Attitude Change," in *Handbook of Social Psychology*, eds. Gardner Lindzey and Eliot Aronson, vol. 2 (New York: Random House, 1985), pp. 271–272.

10. For a detailed analysis of this topic, see Donald R. Kinder, "Opinion and Action in the Realm of Politics," in *Handbook of Social Psychology*, vol. 2, pp. 778–867.

11. Alice A. Eagly and Shelly Chaiken, "Attitude Structure and Function," in *The Handbook of Social Psychology*, vol. 1, pp. 323–390; James M. Olson and Mark P. Zanna, "Attitudes and Attitude Change," *Annual Review of Psychology* 44 (1993): 117–154.

12. Henry A. Murray, *Explorations in Personality* (New York: Oxford University Press, 1938). Interest in Murray's research continues, and the Radcliffe Institute for Advanced Study maintains a Web site for the Murray Research Center at www.radcliffe.edu/.

13. Abraham H. Maslow, *Motivation and Personality*, 2nd ed. (New York: Harper & Row, 1970).

14. North Central Regional Educational Laboratory, "21st Century Skills: Curiosity," www.ncrel.org/enguage/skills/invent3.htm (accessed 18 Apr. 2007).

15. United States Census Bureau, "2005 American Community Survey," http://factfinder.census.gov/servlet/ACSSAFFFacts?_event=&geo_id=01000US&_geoCon (accessed 10 Apr. 2007).

16. Bradley Johnson, "New Census Data Details Major Changes in Language Landscape," *Advertising Age*, 20 Aug. 2006, http://adage.com/print?article_id=111404 (accessed 14 Mar. 2007); Alison Stein Wellner, "Diversity in America," *Supplement to American Demographics* (November 2002): S3.

17. Rushworth M. Kidder, *Shared Values for a Troubled World* (San Francisco: Jossey-Bass, 1994), pp. 1–19. See also the Web site for Kidder's Institute for Global Ethics, www.globalethics.org/ (accessed 20 Apr. 2007).

18. Associated Press, "Gore Promotes Benefits of Good Story-telling," *Memphis Commercial Appeal* (8 Oct. 1995): B2.

19. Sharon S. Brehm and Saul M. Kassin, *Social Psychology*, 3rd ed. (Boston: Houghton Mifflin, 1996), pp. 120–161; Susan T. Fiske, "Stereotyping, Prejudice, and Discrimination," in *Handbook of Social Psychology*, vol. 2, pp. 357–414; Annie Murphy Paul,

"Where Bias Begins: The Truth About Stereotypes," *Psychology Today*, (May/June 1998): 52–55, 82.

20. Humphrey Taylor, "Americans Believe That Over Half the World's Population Speaks English," Harris Poll (November 1998).

Chapter 6

1. Robert J. Kriegel, *If It Ain't Broke . . . Break It!* (New York: Warner, 1991), pp. 167–168.
2. Cited in Judith Humphrey, "Executive Eloquence: A Sevenfold Path to Inspirational Leadership," *Vital Speeches of the Day* 64 (15 May 1998): 469.
3. The concept of mind mapping takes somewhat different directions in books that develop the technique. See, for example, Joyce Wycoff, Steve Cook, and Michael J. Gelb, *Mindmapping: Your Personal Guide to Exploring Creativity and Problem-Solving* (New York: Berkley Publishing Group, 1991), and Tony Buzan and Barry Buzan, *The Mind Map Book: How to Use Radiant Thinking to Maximize Your Brain's Untapped Potential* (New York: Plume Books, 1996).
4. Corporate mind mappers often refer to this space as "landscape." They think of the central concept as a tree and its associated ideas as "branches."
5. Rudyard Kipling, *Just So Stories* (Garden City, N.Y.: Doubleday, 1921), p. 85.
6. Wayne C. Booth, Gregory G. Colomb, and Joseph M. Williams, *The Craft of Research* (Chicago: University of Chicago Press, 1995), p. 42.
7. Ibid., p. 38.

Chapter 7

1. American Library Association, "Introduction to Information Literacy," 21 Mar. 2007, www.ala.org/ala/acrl/acrlissues/acrlinfolit/infolitoverview/introtoinfolit/introinfolit.htm (accessed 27 Apr. 2007).
2. Because of the insidious nature of many of these Web sites, we have refrained from providing URLs for them. For detailed information on misinformation on the Internet, see Anne P. Mintz (ed.), *Web of Deception: Misinformation on the Internet* (Medford, N.J.: CyberAge Books, 2002).
3. Janet E. Alexander and Marsha Ann Tate, *Web Wisdom: How to Evaluate and Create Information Quality on the Web* (Mahwah, N.J.: Lawrence Erlbaum, 1999).
4. Steve Hargreaves, "Exxon Linked to Climate Change Payout," CNNMoney.com, 2 Feb. 2007, http://money.cnn.com/2007/news/companies/Exxon_science/index.htm?cnn=yes (accessed 2 Feb. 2007).
5. Russell Goldman, "Wikiscandal," ABC News, 6 Mar. 2007, http://abcnews.go.com/US/print?id=2928756 (accessed 7 Mar. 2007); Frank Ahrens, "It's on Wikipedia, So It Must Be True," *Washington Post*, 6 Aug. 2006, F07.
6. Alan M. Schlein, *Find It Online* (Tempe, Ariz.: Facts on Demand Press, 2003), p. 381.
7. See Mintz et al. See also Anti-Defamation League, "Hate on Display: A Visual Database of Extremist Symbols, Logos and Tattoos," 2005,. www.adl.org/hate_symbols/.asp (accessed 2 May 2007).
8. For more detailed coverage on interviewing for information, see Joseph A. Devito, *The Interviewing Guidebook* (Boston: Allyn & Bacon, 2008) and Ken Metzler, *Creative Interviewing: The Writer's Guide to Gathering Information by Asking Questions* (Boston: Allyn & Bacon, 1997).
9. Doug Toft (ed.), *Master Student Guide to Academic Success* (Boston: Houghton Mifflin, 2005), pp. 250–251.

Chapter 8

1. Richard Weaver, "Ultimate Terms in Contemporary Rhetoric," in *The Ethics of Rhetoric* (Chicago: Henry Regnery, 1953), pp. 211–232.
2. Cynthia Crossen, *Tainted Truth: The Manipulation of Fact in America* (New York: Simon and Schuster, 1994), p. 36.
3. Reprinted by permission of *World Book Encyclopedia*. This material was brought to our attention by Professor Gray Matthews of the University of Memphis.
4. Anne P. Mintz (ed.), *Web of Deception: Misinformation on the Internet* (Medford, N.J.: CyberAge, 2002), p. 8.
5. Michael J. Fox, Keynote Address to the Bio International Convention, 8 May 2007, www.michaeljfox.org/newsEvents_mjfflnTheNews_article.cfm?ID=179 (accessed 14 May 2007).
6. Richard F. Corlin, "The Secrets of Gun Violence in America," *Vital Speeches of the Day*, 1 Aug. 2001, pp. 610–615.
7. J. Edwin Hill, "Medicine's Challenges in the Post-Katrina Era," *Vital Speeches of the Day*, 15 April 2006, p. 398.
8. John F. Smith Jr., "Eyes on the Road, Hands on the Wheel," *Vital Speeches of the Day*, 15 Nov. 2000, pp. 67–68.
9. Longinus, *On the Sublime*, trans. W. Rhys Roberts, in *The Great Critics: An Anthology of Literary Criticism*, 3rd ed., eds. James Harry Smith and Edd Winfield Parks (New York: W. W. Norton, 1951), p. 82.
10. William L. Benoit and Kimberly A. Kennedy, "On Reluctant Testimony," *Communication Quarterly* 47 (1999): 376–387.
11. Corlin, p. 613.
12. The power of lay testimony is one possible implication of Michael Calvin McGee's "In Search of the People: A Rhetorical Alternative," *Quarterly Journal of Speech* 61 (1975): 235–249.
13. Bill Moyers, "Best of Jobs: To Have and Serve the Public's Trust," keynote address at the PBS Annual Meeting, 23 June 1996, reprinted in *Current*, 8 July 1996.
14. George W. Bush, "The Noblest of Causes: In Loving Memory of America," *Vital Speeches of the Day*, 15 June 2004, p. 519.
15. "On the Campaign Trail," *Reader's Digest*, March 1992, p. 116.
16. Bono, "Remarks to the 2006 National Prayer Breakfast: February 2, 2006," 15 Mar. 2007, http://usliberals.about.com/od/faithinpubliclife/a/BonoSermon.htm (accessed 19 May 2007).
17. Jane Goodall, "Dangers to the Environment," *Vital Speeches of the Day*, 15 Nov. 2003, p. 77.
18. From Norman Mailer, *The Spooky Art*, excerpted in *Newsweek*, 27 Jan. 2003, p. 64.
19. Walter R. Fisher, *Human Communication as Narration: Toward a Philosophy of Reason, Value, and Action* (Columbia: University of South Carolina Press, 1987).

20. Heather Rouston Ettinger, "Shattering the Glass Floor: Women Donors as Leaders of Fundamental Change," *Vital Speeches of the Day*, 15 Sept. 2000, p. 727.
21. Marvin Olasky, "Responding to Disaster: Being Thankful for the Days Without Disaster." *Vital Speeches of the Day*, Nov. 2006, p. 744.
22. Newton Minow, "Campaign Finance Reform: We Have Failed to Solve the Problem," *Vital Speeches of the Day*, 1 July 1997, p. 558.
23. Jimmy Carter, "Excellence Comes from a Repository that Doesn't Change: The True Meaning of Success," *Vital Speeches of the Day*, 1 July 1993, p. 546.
24. Fisher, op. cit.
25. Sam J. Ervin Jr., "Judicial Verbicide: An Affront to the Constitution," presented at Herbert Law Center, Louisiana State University, Baton Rouge, 22 Oct. 1980, in *Representative American Speeches 1980–1981*, ed. Owen Peterson (New York: H. W. Wilson, 1981), p. 62.
26. Olasky, pp. 744–745.
27. Al Gore, "Global Climate Crisis: Making Changes for Our Children," *Vital Speeches of the Day*, May 2007, pp. 182–183.

Chapter 9

1. Patricia Kearney, Timothy G. Plax, Ellis R. Hayes, and Marily J. Ivey, "College Teacher Misbehaviors: What Students Don't Like About What Teachers Say and Do," *Communication Quarterly* 39 (1991): 309–324.
2. Scott E. Caplan and John O. Green, "Acquisition of Message-Production Skill by Younger and Older Adults: Effects of Age, Task Complexity, and Practice," *Communication Monographs* 66 (1999): 31–48.
3. Cited in Michael D. Lemonick and Alice Park, "New Hope for Cancer," *Time*, 28 May 2001, p. 65.
4. Jerry Daniels, "Transforming Aerospace: A Submariner's View," *Vital Speeches of the Day*, 4 Feb. 2002, pp. 249–252.
5. Cited in Arthur M. Schlesinger Jr., *A Thousand Days: John F. Kennedy in the White House* (Boston: Houghton Mifflin, 1965), p. 733.
6. Full text and video of Martin Luther King, Jr.'s "I Have a Dream" speech are available online at www.americanrhetoric.com/speeches/mlkihaveadream.htm.
7. Bob Lannom, "Patience, Persistence, and Perspiration," *Parsons (Tenn.) News Leader*, 20 Sept. 1989, p. 9.
8. Kenneth Burke, *A Rhetoric of Motives* (Berkeley: University of California Press, 1969), pp. 20–23.
9. John Waite Bowers and Michael Osborn, "Attitudinal Effects of Selected Types of Concluding Metaphors in Persuasive Speeches," *Speech Monographs* 33 (1966): 148–155.
10. Melodie Lancaster, "The Future We Predict Isn't Inevitable: Refraining Our Success in the Modern World," *Vital Speeches of the Day*, 1 Aug. 1992, p. 638.
11. Excerpted from Bob Dinneen, "Ethanol: Reducing Greenhouse Gases," *Vital Speeches of the Day*, April 2007, p. 170.

Chapter 11

1. The Academy of Motion Picture Arts and Sciences, 2007 "Winner: Documentary Feature: *An Inconvenient Truth*," www.academyawards.com/oscarnight/winners/?pn=detail&nominee=AnInconvenientTruthDocumentaryFeatureNominee (22 May 2007).
2. Cheryl Hamilton and Cordell Parker, *Communicating for Results*, 6th ed. (Belmont, Calif.: Wadsworth, 2001), p. 396.
3. Robert Heinich, Michael Molenda, and James D. Russell, *Instructional Media and the New Technologies of Instruction*, 4th ed. (New York: Macmillan, 1993), p. 66.
4. See the classic study conducted by Wharton Business School's Applied Research Center and the Management Information Services Department of the University of Arizona, cited by Robert L. Lindstrom, "The Presentation Power of Multimedia," *Sales and Marketing Management*, Sept. 1994.
5. Lisa Collier Cool, "Danger in the Dorm," *Family Circle*, 17 Feb. 2004, p. 15.
6. Cited in Laurence J. Peter, *Peter's Quotations: Ideas for Our Time* (New York: Bantam, 1979), p. 478.
7. An excellent resource on understanding, preparing, and using charts and graphs is Gerald Everett Jones, *How to Lie with Charts*, (Lincoln, Neb.: iUniverse, 2000).
8. Our thanks for this example go to Professor Dave Klope of Trinity Christian College. CRTNET posting #5618, December 12, 2000.
9. Our thanks for this example go to Professor Mary Katherine McHenry, Northwest Mississippi Community College, Senatobia, Mississippi.
10. Rebecca Ganzel, "Power Pointless," *Presentations*, February 2000, pp. 53–58.
11. Ricky Telg and Tracy Irani, "Getting the Most Out of PowerPoint," *Agricultural Education Magazine*, April 2001, p. 11.
12. Dave Paradi, "Survey Shows How to Stop Annoying Audiences with Bad PowerPoint," survey conducted September 2003 www.comunicateusingtechnology.com/articles/pptsurvey_article.htm (14 Mar. 2004).
13. Gerald Everett Jones, *How to Lie with Charts* (Lincoln, Neb.: iUniverse, 2000).
14. Lee Berton, "Deloitte Wants More Women for Top Posts in Accounting," *Wall Street Journal*, 28 Feb. 1993, p. B1.
15. Cornelia Brunner, "Teaching Visual Literacy," *Electronic Learning* (November–December 1994): p. 16.
16. Arthur Goldsmith, "Digitally Altered Photography: The New Image Makers," *Britannica Book of the Year: 1995* (Chicago: Encyclopaedia Britannica, 1995), p. 135.
17. Gloria Borger, "The Story the Pictures Didn't Tell," *U.S. News & World Report*, 22 Feb. 1993, pp. 6–7; and John Leo, "Lapse or TV News Preview?" *Washington Times*, 3 Mar. 1993, p. G3.

Chapter 12

1. William Raspberry, "Any Candidate Will Drink to That," *Austin American Statesman*, 11 May 1984, p. A–10.
2. Ollie Reed, "Corsicans, Navajo Weave Ties," Scripps Howard News Service, 3 July 2001. *Commercial Appeal (Memphis)*, www.gomemphis.com (accessed 5 July 2001).
3. Among the most recent of these studies is that reported by Peter A. Andersen and Tammy R. Blackburn, "An Experimental Study of Language Intensity and Response Rate in E-Mail Surveys," *Communication Reports* 17 (no. 2) Summer, 2004, 73–82.

4. Jerry Tarver, "Words in Time: Some Reflections on the Language of Speech," *Vital Speeches of the Day*, 15 Apr. 1988, p. 410.

5. Ibid., pp. 410–412.

6. Winston Churchill, "Dunkirk," in *The World 's Great Speeches*, ed. Lewis Copeland and Lawrence W. Lamm, 3rd ed. (New York: Dover, 1973), p. 439.

7. These powers of language were first explored in Michael Osborn, *Orientations to Rhetorical Style* (Chicago: Science Research Associates, 1976), and are developed further in Michael Osborn, "Rhetorical Depiction," in *Form, Genre, and the Study of Political Discourse*, eds. Herbert W. Simons and Aram A. Aghazarian (Columbia: University of South Carolina Press, 1986), pp. 79–107.

8. Katherine Stout, "Dear Ryan White," Letters About Literature competition, Level II, 2004, sponsored by Humanities Tennessee for the National Endowment for the Humanities.

9. Based on the account in Claire Perkins, "The Many Symbolic Faces of Fred Smith: Charismatic Leadership in the Bureaucracy," *Journal of the Tennessee Speech Communication Association* 11 (1985): 22.

10. Adapted from *The American Heritage Dictionary*, 2nd ed. (Boston: Houghton Mifflin, 1985), p. 92.

11. Nikki Giovanni, "We Are Virginia Tech," 17 April 2007. www.americanrhetoric.com/speeches/nikkigiovannivatech-memorial.htm (accessed 14 May 2007).

12. Listeners whose lives seem dull and unrewarding are especially susceptible to such dramas. See the discussion in Eric Hoffer, *The True Believer: Thoughts on the Nature of Mass Movements* (New York: Harper, 1951).

13. *Newsweek*, January 8, 2007, p. 17.

14. "Presidential Ecospeak," *New York Times*, Editorials/Op-Ed, 18 Oct. 2003, www.truthout.org/cgi-bin/artman/exec/view.cgi/15/2355 (accessed 29 Oct. 2003).

15. Bill Gates, "High Schools Are Obsolete: Teaching Kids What They Need to Know," *Vital Speeches of the Day* 71 (April 15, 2005): 396–397.

16. All quotations are from *USA Today*, 18 Jan. 1996, p. 4A.

17. L. H. "Cotton" Ivy, "Dieting: Pickin's from the Cotton Patch," *The News Leader* (Parsons, Tenn.), May 24, 2006, p. 5A.

18. "Malapropisms Live!" *Spectra*, May 1986, p. 6.

19. Haven E. Cockerham, "Conquer the Isms That Stand in Our Way," *Vital Speeches of the Day*, 1 Feb. 1998, p. 240.

20. Jim VandeHei, "Kerry Drops Ball with Packers Fans," *Washington Post*, 15 Sept. 2004, www.washingtonpost.com/ac2/wp-dyn/A21672-2004Sept14?language=printer (accessed 15 May 2007).

21. Antoinette M. Bailey, "Bow Wave," *Vital Speeches of the Day*, 1 June 2001, p. 502.

22. For additional discussion of such metaphors, see Michael Osborn, "Archetypal Metaphor in Rhetoric: The Light-Dark Family," *Quarterly Journal of Speech* 53 (1967): 115–126, and "The Evolution of the Archetypal Sea in Rhetoric and Poetic," *Quarterly Journal of Speech* 63 (1977): 347–363.

23. George W. Bush, "Inaugural Address," *Vital Speeches of the Day*, 1 Feb. 2001, p. 226.

24. See another side of this image in J. Vernon Jensen, "British Voices on the Eve of the American Revolution: Trapped by the Family Metaphor," *Quarterly Journal of Speech* 63 (1977): 43–50.

25. For an insightful discussion of the metaphors we use to construct our ideas about illness, see Susan Sontag, *Illness as Metaphor* (New York: Vintage Books, 1979), and *AIDS and Its Metaphors* (New York: Farrar, Straus and Giroux, 1988).

26. See Robert Ivie, "Images of Savagery in American Justifications for War," *Communication Monographs* 47 (1980): 279–294.

27. Michael Osborn, "Patterns of Metaphor Among Early Feminist Orators," in *Rhetoric and Community: Studies in Unity and Fragmentation*, ed. J. Michael Hogan (Columbia: University of South Carolina Press, 1998), pp. 10–11.

28. John Thorne, "AT&T: Anti-Investment Policies," *Vital Speeches of the Day*, 70 (May 15, 2004), p. 478.

29. Wendi C. Thomas, "Spaced Out on Budget Priorities," *The Commercial Appeal*, 1 Jan. 2004, www.commercialappeal.com/mca/news_columnists/article/0,1426,MCA_646_2594495,00.html (accessed 22 Jan. 2004).

30. Seth Zuckerman, "Start by Arming Yourself with Knowledge," *Sierra*, September/October 2006, p. 58.

31. "I'm Feeling Like Job," *Newsweek*, 12 Jan. 2004, p. 25.

32. Michael Calvin McGee, "The Origins of Liberty: A Feminization of Power," *Communication Monographs* 47 (1980): 27–45.

33. Osborn, *Orientations to Rhetorical Style*, p. 16.

34. Richard Weaver, "Ultimate Terms in Contemporary Rhetoric," in *The Ethics of Rhetoric* (Chicago: Henry Regnery, 1953), pp. 211–232.

35. Michael Calvin McGee, "The Ideograph: A Link Between Rhetoric and Ideology," *Quarterly Journal of Speech* 66 (1980): 1–16.

36. This example is adapted from Ronald H. Carpenter, *Choosing Powerful Words: Eloquence That Works* (Boston: Allyn & Bacon, 1999), pp. 14–15.

37. Bill Moyers, "Pass the Bread," a baccalaureate address presented at Hamilton College, May 20, 2006.

38. Statement by the President, broadcast from the Treaty Room at the White House, 7 Oct. 2001.

Chapter 13

1. Janet Beavin Bavelas, "Redefining Language: Nonverbal Linguistic Acts in Face-to-Face Dialogue," 1992 Aubrey Fisher Memorial Lecture, presented at the University of Utah, October 1992.

2. Richard Conniff, "Reading Faces," *Smithsonian* 34 (January 2004): 49.

3. Quoted in Ibid., p. 47.

4. James C. McCroskey, *An Introduction to Rhetorical Communication*, 9th ed. (Boston: Allyn & Bacon, 2006).

5. Virginia P. Richmond and James C. McCroskey, *Nonverbal Behavior in Interpersonal Relations*, 5th ed. (Boston: Allyn & Bacon, 2004).

6. Howard Giles and Arlene Franklyn-Stokes, "Communicator Characteristics," in *Handbook of International and Intercultural Communication*, eds. Molefi Kete Asante and William B. Gudykunst (Newbury Park, Calif.: Sage, 1989), pp. 117–144.

7. Jon Eisenson with Arthur M. Eisenson, *Voice and Diction: A Program for Improvement*, 7th ed. (Boston: Allyn & Bacon, 1996).

8. Adapted from Stuart W. Hyde, *Television and Radio Announcing*, 10th ed. (Boston: Houghton Mifflin, 2003).

9. N. Scott Momaday, *The Way to Rainy Mountain* (Albuq-uerque: University of New Mexico Press, 1969), p. 5.

10. Carole Douglis, "The Beat Goes On: Social Rhythms Underlie All Our Speech and Actions," *Psychology Today*, November 1987, p. 36–41.

11. William Price Fox, "Eugene Talmadge and Sears Roebuck Co.," in *Southern Fried Plus Six* (New York: Ballantine Books, 1968), p. 36.

12. Michael L. Hecht, Peter A. Andersen, and Sidney A. Ribeau, "The Cultural Dimensions of Nonverbal Communication," in *Handbook of International and Intercultural Communication*, ed. Molefi Kete Asante and William B. Gudykunst (Newbury Park, Calif.: Sage, 1989), pp. 163–185; Larry A. Samovar, Richard E. Porter, and Edwin R. McDaniel, *Communication Between Cultures*, 6th ed., Wadsworth Series in Communication Studies (2007).

13. Ralph Hillman, *Delivering Dynamic Presentations: Using Your Voice and Body for Impact* (Boston: Allyn & Bacon, 1999).

14. Don Marquis, adapted from "mehitabel and her kittens," in *the lives and times of archy and mehitabel*. Copyright ©1927 by Doubleday and Company, Inc. Reprinted by permission of the publisher.

15. *NBC Handbook of Pronunciation*, 4th ed. (New York: Harper, 1991).

16. William B. Gudykunst et al., "Language and Intergroup Communication," in *Handbook of International and Intercultural Communication*, eds. Molefi Kete Asante and William B. Gudykunst (Newbury Park, Calif.: Sage, 1989), pp. 145–162.

17. Carolanne Griffith-Roberts, "Let's Talk Southern," *Southern Living*, February 1995, p. 82.

18. "Jeff Foxworthy: From Hootenanny to Hoosier," *Satellite TV Week*, 28 July–3 August 1996, p. l.

19. Samovar and Porter, p. 177.

20. Peter A. Andersen, "Nonverbal Immediacy in Interpersonal Communication," in *Multichannel Integrations of Nonverbal Behavior*, eds. A. W. Siegman and S. Feldstein (Mahwah, N.J.: Erlbaum, 1985).

21. Mark L. Knapp and Judith A. Hall, *Nonverbal Communication in Human Interaction*, 5th ed. (Belmont, CA: Wadsworth, 2002), p. 365.

22. Research psychologist Carolyn Copper has found that newscasters influence voters when they smile while speaking of candidates, further evidence of the power of facial expression ("A Certain Smile," *Psychology Today*, January–February 1992, p. 20).

23. Timothy Gura and Charlotte Lee, *Oral Interpretation*, 11th ed. (Boston: Houghton Mifflin, 2005).

24. Edouard Gasarabwe-Laroche, "Meaningful Gestures: Nonverbal Communication in Rwandan Culture," *UNESCO Courier*, September 1993, pp. 31–33.

25. The literature supporting this conclusion is reviewed by Virginia Kidd, "Do Clothes Make the Officer? How Uniforms Impact Communication: A Review of Literature," presented at the Visual Communication Conference at Pray, Montana, 8 July 2000.

26. D. T. Max, "The Making of the Speech," *New York Times*, 7 Oct. 2001, http://select.nytimes.com/search/restricted/article?res=F40714FF39590C748CDDA90994 (accessed 18 May 2007).

27. David E. Sanger and Don Van Natta, Jr., "After the Attacks: The Events; In Four Days, a National Crisis Changes Bush's Presidency," *New York Times*, 16 Sept. 2001, p.7, http://select.nytimes.com/search/restricted/article?res=F30714F63D5F0C758DDDA00894 (accessed 19 May 2007).

28. "Remarks to Police, Firemen, and Rescueworkers at the World Trade Center Site in New York City," *2001 Presidential Documents Online* 14 Sept. 2001, http://frwebgate3.access.gpo.gov/cgi-bin/waisgate.cgi?WAISdocID=54051314900+24+0+ (accessed 18 May 2007).

29. Ken Ringle, "George Bush and the Words of War," *The Washington Post*, 9 Mar. 2003, http://pqasb.pqarchiver.com/washingtonpost/access/303554101.html?dids=303554101:303 (accessed 18 May 2007).

30. These guidelines for handling questions and answers are a compendium of ideas from the following sources: Stephen D. Body, "Nine Steps to a Successful Question-and-Answer Session," *Management Solutions*, May 1988, pp. 16–17; Teresa Brady, "Fielding Abrasive Questions During Presentations," *Supervisory Management*, February 1993, p. 6; J. Donald Ragsdale and Alan L. Mikels, "Effects of Question Periods on a Speaker's Credibility with a Television Audience," *Southern States Communication Journal* 40 (1975): 302–312; Dorothy Sarnoff, *Never Be Nervous Again* (New York: Ballantine, 1987); Laurie Schloff and Marcia Yudkin, *Smart Speaking: Sixty-Second Strategies* (New York: Holt, 1991); and Alan Zaremba, "Q and A: The Other Part of Your Presentation," *Management World*, January–February 1989, pp. 8–10.

31. "South Carolina Democratic Debate transcript," MSNBC, p. 7, 27 April 2007, www.msnbc.msn.com/id/18352397 (accessed 20 May 2007).

32. Adam Nagourney and Jeff Zeleny, "In Mostly Sedate Debate, Democrats Show More Unity than Strife," *New York Times*, 27 April 2007, http://query.nytimes.com/gst/fullpage.html?res=9400E7DD123EF934A15757C0A9619C8 (accessed 19 May 2007).

33. Commentaries, "Hardball with Chris Matthews," CNBC, April 27, 2007.

34. The authors are indebted to Professor Roxanne Gee of the television and film area in the Department of Communication at the University of Memphis for her assistance and suggestions in putting together this advice.

35. Illustrations of major video hand signals may be found in Stuart W. Hyde, *Television and Radio Announcing*, 10th ed. (Boston: Houghton Mifflin, 2003).

36. Ralph R. Behnke and Chris R. Sawyer, "Public Speaking Procrastination as a Correlate of Public Speaking Communication Apprehension and Self-Perceived Public Speaking Competence," *Communication Research Reports* 16 (1999): 40–47.

37. Tony E. Smith and Ann Bainbridge Frymier, "Get 'Real': Does Practicing Speeches Before an Audience Improve Performance?" *Communication Quarterly* 54 (2006): 113.

38. Judith Humphrey, "Taking the Stage," *Vital Speeches of the Day*, 1 May 2001, pp. 435–438.

39. Ibid., p. 436.

Chapter 14

1. Katherine E. Rowan, "Goals, Obstacles, and Strategies in Risk Communication: A Problem-Solving Approach to Improving Communication About Risks," *Journal of Applied Communication Research* 19 (1991): 314.

2. Ibid.

3. Institute for Learning Styles Research, "Seven Perceptual Styles," n.d., www.learningstyles.org (accessed 24 July 2001).

4. Adapted from material supplied by Randy Scott, Department of Communication, Weber State University, Ogden, Utah.

5. Paul Ashdown, "From Wild West to Wild Web," *Vital Speeches of the Day*, 1 Sept. 2000, pp. 699–701.

6. Paul R. Gamble and Clare E. Kelliher, "Imparting Information and Influencing Behavior: An Examination of Staff Briefing Sessions," *Journal of Business Communication* (July 1999): 261.

7. Ancil B. Sparks and Dennis D. Staszak, "Fine Tuning Your News Briefing: Law Enforcement Agency Media Relations," *FBI Law Enforcement Bulletin* (December 2000): 22.

8. Howard Gardner, *Changing Minds: The Art and Science of Changing Our Own and Other People's Minds* (Cambridge, Mass.: Harvard Business School Publishing, 2006).

9. Representative is Timothy J. Koegel, *The Exceptional Presenter* (Austin, Tex.: Greenleaf Book Group Press, 2007).

Chapter 15

1. Mark A. Hamilton and John E. Hunter, "The Effect of Language Intensity on Receiver Attitudes Toward Message, Source, and Topic," in *Persuasion: Advances Through Meta-Analysis*, eds. M. Allen and R. W. Preiss (Beverly Hills, Calif.: Sage, 1998).

2. Al Gore, *The Assault on Reason* (New York: Penguin Press, 2007), pp. 245–246.

3. Franklin J. Boster et al., "The Persuasive Effects of Statistical Evidence in the Presence of Exemplars," *Communication Studies* 51 (2000): 296–306.

4. M. Sean Limon and Dean C. Kazoleas, "A Comparison of Exemplar and Statistical Evidence in Reducing Counter-Arguments and Responses to a Message," *Communication Research Reports* 21 (2004): 291–298.

5. Steve Hargreaves, "Exxon Linked to Climate Change Pay Out," *Fortune (CNN.Money)*, 2 Feb. 2007, http://money .cnn.com/2007/02/02news/companies/exxon_science/index.htm?cnn=yes (accessed 23 May 2007).

6. Ron Reagan, "Remarks at the Democratic convention," *USA Today*, 29 July 2004, www.usatoday.com/news/politicselections/nation/president/2004-07-29-reagan-speech-text_x.htm (accessed 23 May 2007).

7. Bill Gates, "High Schools Are Obsolete: Teaching Kids What They Need to Know," *Vital Speeches of the Day* 71 (April 15 2005): 398.

8. Thomas Hugh Feeley, Heather M. Marshall, and Amber M. Reinhart, "Reactions to Narrative and Statistical Written Messages Promoting Organ Donation," *Communication Reports* 10 (2006): 89–100.

9. Limon and Kazoleas, 291–298.

10. Shelly Chaiken, Wendy Wood, and Alice H. Eagly, "Principles of Persuasion," in *Social Psychology: Handbook of Basic Principles*, eds. E. Tory Higgins and Arie W. Kruglanki (New York: Guilford, 1996), pp. 702–742.

11. Representative of this scholarship is Ernest G. Bormann, "Fantasy and Rhetorical Vision: The Rhetorical Criticism of Social Reality," *Quarterly Journal of Speech* 58 (1972): 396–407; Walter F. Fisher, "Narration as a Human Communication Paradigm: The Case of Public Moral Argument," *Communication Monographs* 51 (1984); 1–22; Michael C. McGee, "In Search of 'The People': A Rhetorical Alternative," *Quarterly Journal of Speech* 61 (1975): 235–249; Michael Osborn, "Rhetorical Depiction," in *Form, Genre and the Study of Political Discourse*, eds. Herbert W. Simons and Aram A. Aghazarian (Columbia: University of South Carolina Press, 1986), pp. 79–107; and Janice Hocker Rushing, "The Rhetoric of the American Western Myth," *Communication Monographs* 50 (1983): 14–32.

12. In recent times the importance of "goodwill" to impressions of ethos has been discounted by many social scientists. An experimental study that restores the importance of the "goodwill" factor is offered by James C. McCroskey and Mason J. Teven, "Goodwill: A Reexamination of the Construct and Its Measurement," *Communication Monographs* 66 (1999): 90–103.

13. The discussion that follows is based on James C. McCroskey, *An Introduction to Rhetorical Communication*, 9th ed. (Boston: Allyn & Bacon, 2006). We use the term *emerging credibility* in place of McCroskey's *derived credibility* to emphasize the dynamic, interactive nature of the process.

14. Peter A. Andersen and Tammy R. Blackburn, "An Experimental Study of Language Intensity and Response Rate in E-Mail Surveys," *Communication Reports* 17 (2004): 73–82.

15. Antonio R. Damasio, *Descartes' Error: Emotion, Reason, and the Human Brain* (New York: Putnam, 1994).

16. From a brochure distributed by Handgun Control, Inc., 1990.

17. Martha Solomon, "The 'Positive Woman's' Journey: A Mythic Analysis of the Rhetoric of STOP ERA," *Quarterly Journal of Speech* 65 (1979): 262–274.

18. Rushing, pp. 14–32.

19. Roderick P. Hart, *The Political Pulpit* (West Lafayette, Ind.: Purdue University Press, 1977).

20. John Fitzgerald Kennedy, "Acceptance Address, 1960," in *The Great Society: A Sourcebook of Speeches*, ed. Glenn R. Capp (Belmont, Calif.: Dickenson 1969), p. 14.

21. Richard F. Corlin, "The Secrets of Gun Violence in America," *Vital Speeches of the Day*, 1 Aug. 2001, p. 611.

22. George W. Bush, "State of the Union," *Washington Post*, 29 Jan. 2003, p. A10.

23. Richard M. Weaver, "Ultimate Terms in Contemporary Rhetoric," in *Language is Sermonic: Richard M. Weaver on the Nature of Rhetoric*, eds. Richard L. Johannesen, Rennard Strickland, and Ralph T. Eubanks (Baton Rouge: Louisiana State University Press, 1970), pp. 92–93.

24. Hargreaves, "Exxon Linked to Climate Change Pay Out."

25. Corlin, p. 611.

26. Ibid., p. 612.

27. Ibid.

28. Lisa M. Ross, "Buckley Says Drug Attack Won't Work," *Commercial Appeal (Memphis)*, 14 Sept. 1989, p. B2.

29. Mortimer B. Zuckerman, "The Enemy Within," *U.S. News & World Report*, 11 Sept. 1989, p. 91.

30. See Toulmin's discussion in *The Uses of Argument* (London: Cambridge University Press, 1958) and in Stephen Toulmin, Richard Rieke, and Allan Janik, *An Introduction to Reasoning*, 2nd ed. (New York: Macmillan, 1984).

31. Corlin, p. 615.

32. Gilbert Cranberg, "Even Sensible Iowa Bows to the Religious Right," *Los Angeles Times*, 17 Aug. 1992, p. B5.

33. George Orwell, *Shooting an Elephant and Other Essays* (London: Secker and Warburg, 1950), p. 97.

34. Michael M. Osborn, "The Abuses of Argument," *Southern Speech Communication Journal* 49 (1983): 1–11.

35. Keith Kennedy, E-mail to the authors, 11 Nov. 2004.

36. *Newsweek*, 30 Jan. 1995, p. 17.

37. *Commercial Appeal (Memphis)*, 6 Sept. 1996, p. C1.

Chapter 16

1. This speech is made available in English translation by the Perseus Digital Library, sponsored by Tufts University, www.perseus.tufts.edu/cgi-bin/ptext?doc=Perseus: text1999.02.0020:text=Cael.:section=1.

2. For a different view, which depicts persuasion in terms of manipulation and domination, see Sonja K. Foss and Cindy L. Griffin, "Beyond Persuasion: A Proposal for an Invitational Rhetoric," *Communication Monographs* 62 (1995): 2–18.

3. William J. McGuire, "Attitudes and Attitude Change," in *The Handbook of Social Psychology*, eds. Gardner Lindzey and Elliot Aronson (New York: Random House, 1985), vol. 1, pp. 258–261.

4. Roger Brown, *Social Psychology: The Second Edition* (New York: Free Press, 1986).

5. Gloria Steinem, *Revolution from Within: A Book of Self-Esteem* (New York: Little, Brown, 1992), p. 120.

6. John C. Reinard, "The Empirical Study of the Persuasive Effects of Evidence: The Status After Fifty Years of Research," *Human Communication Research* 15 (1988): 3–59.

7. Adapted from Herbert W. Simons, *Persuasion: Understanding, Practice, and Analysis*, 2nd ed. (New York: Random House, 1986), p. 138.

8. Larry Tracy, "Taming Hostile Audiences: Persuading Those Who Would Rather Jeer than Cheer," *Vital Speeches of the Day*, 1 Mar. 2005, p. 311.

9. Charlton Heston, "Winning the Cultural War," *Vital Speeches of the Day*, 1 Apr. 1999, pp. 357–359.

10. N. H. Anderson, "Integration Theory and Attitude Change," *Psychological Review* 78 (1971): 171–206.

11. McGuire, p. 260.

12. Mike Allen, "Meta-Analysis Comparing the Persuasiveness of One-Sided and Two-Sided Messages," *Western Journal of Speech Communication* 55 (1991): 390–404; M. Allen et al., "Testing a Model of Message Sidedness: Three Replications," *Communication Monographs* 56 (1990): 275–291; Jerold L. Hale, Paul A. Mongeau, and Randi M. Thomas, "Cognitive Processing of One- and Two-Sided Persuasive Messages," *Western Journal of Speech Communication* 55 (1991): 380–389; Carl I. Hovland, Arthur A. Lumsdaine, and Fred D. Sheffield, "The Effects of Presenting 'One Side' Versus 'Both Sides' in Changing Opinions on a Controversial Subject," in *Experiments on Mass Communication* (Princeton, N.J.: Princeton University Press, 1949), pp. 201–227; and William J. McGuire, "Inducing Resistance to Persuasion," in *Advances in Experimental Social Psychology*, ed. L. Berkowitz (New York: Academic Press, 1964), pp. 191–229.

13. Mike Allen and James B. Stiff, "Testing Three Models for the Sleeper Effect," *Western Journal of Speech Communication* 53 (1989): 411–426; and T. D. Cook et al., "History of the Sleeper Effect: Some Logical Pitfalls in Accepting the Null Hypothesis," *Psychological Bulletin* 86 (1979): 662–679.

14. M. E. McCombs, "The Agenda-Setting Approach," in *Handbook of Political Communication*, eds. D. D. Nimmo and K. R. Sanders (Beverly Hills, Calif.: Sage, 1981), pp. 121–140.

15. As recounted in Diane M. Martin, "Balancing on the Political High Wire: The Role of Humor in the Rhetoric of Ann Richards," *Southern Communication Journal* 69 (2004): 278.

16. Franklin J. Boster and Paul Mongeau, "Fear-Arousing Persuasive Messages," in *Communication Yearbook 8*, ed. R. Bostrom (Beverly Hills, Calif.: Sage, 1984), pp. 330–377; and Richard E. Petty and Duane T. Wegener, "Attitude Change: Multiple Roles for Persuasion Variables," in *The Handbook of Social Psychology*, eds. Daniel T. Gilbert, Susan T. Fiske, and Gardner Lindzey, 4th ed. (Boston: McGraw-Hill, 1998), pp. 353–354.

17. Katherine E. Rowan, "Goals, Obstacles, and Strategies in Risk Communication: A Problem-Solving Approach to Improving Communication About Risks," *Journal of Applied Communication Research* 19 (1991): 322.

18. Michael Osborn, "Rhetorical Depiction," in *Form, Genre, and the Study of Political Discourse*, eds. Herbert W. Simons and Aram A. Aghazarian (Columbia: University of South Carolina Press, 1986), pp. 79–107.

19. R. A. Wicklund and J. W. Brehm, *Perspectives on Cognitive Dissonance* (Hillsdale, N.J.: Erlbaum, 1976).

20. Steve Hargreaves, "Exxon Linked to Climate Change Pay Out," *Fortune (CNN.Money)*, 2 Feb. 2007 http://money.cnn .com/2007/02/02/news/companies/exxon_science/index .htm?cnn=yes (accessed 23 May 2007).

21. Adapted from Richard L. Johannesen, *Ethics in Communi-cation*, 5th ed. (Prospect Heights, Ill.: Waveland, 2001).

22. J. W. Patterson and David Zarefsky, *Contemporary Debate* (Boston: Houghton Mifflin, 1983).

23. The structure of the stock issues design has been adapted from Charles U. Larson, *Persuasion: Reception and Responsibility*, 11th ed. (Belmont, Calif.: Wadsworth, 2007), and Charles S. Mudd and Malcolm O. Sillars, *Public Speaking: Content and Communication* (Prospect Heights, Ill.: Waveland, 1991), pp. 100–102.

24. The motivated sequence design was introduced in Alan Monroe's *Principles and Types of Speech* (New York: Scott, Foresman, 1935) and has been refined in later editions.

Chapter 17

1. Celeste Michelle Condit, "The Functions of Epideictic: The Boston Massacre Orations as Exemplar," *Communication Quarterly* 33 (1985): 284–299; Gray Matthews, "Epideictic Rhetoric and Baseball: Nurturing Community Through Controversy," *Southern Communication Journal* 60 (1995): 275–291; Randall Parrish Osborn, "Jimmy Carter's Rhetorical Campaign for the Presidency: An Epideictic of American Renewal," Southern States Communication Association Convention, Memphis, March 1996; Ch. Perelman and L. Olbrechts-Tyteca, *The New Rhetoric: A Treatise on Argumentation* (South Bend, Ind.: University of Notre Dame Press, 1971), pp. 47–54; and Richard M. Weaver, *The Ethics of Rhetoric* (Chicago: Henry Regnery, 1953), pp. 164–185.

2. John Dewey, *Democracy and Education* (New York: Macmillan, 1916), p. 4.

3. James W. Carey, "A Cultural Approach to Communication," *Communication* 2 (1975): 6.

4. See Burke's discussion in "The Range of Rhetoric," in *A Rhetoric of Motives* (Berkeley and Los Angeles: University of California Press, 1969), pp. 3–43.

5. Walter R. Fisher, *Human Communication as Narration: Toward a Philosophy of Reason, Value, and Action* (Columbia: University of South Carolina Press, 1989).

6. *Selected Speeches and Writings by Abraham Lincoln* (New York: Vintage Books, 1992), 405.

7. See the discussion in *The Rhetoric of Aristotle*, trans. Lane Cooper (New York: Appleton-Century-Crofts, 1932), I.7, I.9, l.14 (pp. 34–44, 46–55, 78–79).

8. Tommie Albright, "Martin Luther King Jr.'s Legacy for Us," *Vital Speeches of the Day*, 1 Mar. 2000, p. 320.

9. *Congressional Record*, 1 Apr. 1980, pp. 7459–7460.

10. For extended primers on preparing and delivering eulogies, see Garry Schaeffer, *A Labor of Love: How to Write a Eulogy*, 2nd ed. (San Diego: GMS Pub., 1998); and Leo Seguin, *How to Write and Deliver a Loving Eulogy* (Toronto: Hushion House, 2000).

11. "Words of Grief and Resolve from Friends and World Leaders," *New York Times*, 7 Nov. 1995, p. A8.

12. Owen Edwards, "What Every Man Should Know: How to Make a Toast," *Esquire*, January 1984, p. 37.

13. The advice that follows is adapted from Jacob M. Braude, *Complete Speaker's and Toastmaster's Library: Definitions and Toasts* (Englewood Cliffs, N.J.: Prentice Hall, 1965), pp. 88–123; and Wendy Lin, "Let's Lift a Glass, Say a Few Words, and Toast 1996," *Commercial Appeal (Memphis)*, 28 Dec. 1995, p. C3.

14. Elie Wiesel, "Nobel Peace Prize Acceptance Speech," *New York Times*, 11 Dec. 1986, p. A8.

15. Martin Luther King Jr., "Nobel Peace Prize Acceptance Statement," in *The Cry for Freedom: The Struggle for Equality in America*, ed. Frank W. Hale Jr. (New York: Barnes, 1969), pp. 374–377.

16. *Commercial Appeal (Memphis)*, 23 Oct. 1995, p. D2.

17. Cited in Morris K. Udall, *Too Funny to Be President* (New York: Holt, 1988), p. 156.

18. Sheila W. Welling, "Working Women: A Century of Change," *Vital Speeches of the Day*, 15 June 1995, pp. 516–517.

19. *Congressional Record*, 1 Apr. 1980, p. 7249.

20. Ibid., p. 7248.

21. Roger Ailes, *You Are the Message* (New York: Doubleday, 1988), pp. 71–74.

22. Diane M. Martin, "Balancing on the Political High Wire: The Role of Humor in the Rhetoric of Ann Richards," *Southern Communication Journal* 69 (2004): 273–288.

23. For more on the social function of laughter, see Henri Bergson, *Laughter: An Essay on the Meaning of the Comic*, trans. Cloudsley Brereton and Fred Rothwell (London: Macmillan, 1911).

24. Robert M. Kaplan and Gregory C. Pascoe, "Humorous Lectures and Humorous Examples: Some Effects upon Comprehension and Retention," *Journal of Educational Psychology* 69 (1977): 61–65.

25. Dick Jackman, "Awards Dinner of the National Football Foundation and the Hall of Fame," *Harper's Magazine*, March 1985.

26. Charles R. Gruner, "Advice to the Beginning Speaker on Using Humor—What the Research Tells Us," *Communication Education* 34 (1985): 142–147; and Christie McGuffee Smith and Larry Powell, "The Use of Disparaging Humor by Group Leaders," *Southern Speech Communication Journal* 53 (1988): 279–292.

27. "President Bush Attends Radio and Television Correspondents' Annual Dinner," 28 March 2007, www.whitehouse.gov/news/releases/2007/03/20070328-6.html (accessed 23 May 2007).

28. *Washington Post*, 12 Dec. 1978.

29. Cited in Joan Detz, *Can You Say a Few Words?* (New York: St. Martins, 1991), p. 77.

30. Adapted from Detz, pp. 77–78.

31. Ronald Reagan, "Second Inauguration Address," *Vital Speeches of the Day* 51 (1 Feb. 1985): 226–228.

Appendix A

1. Adapted from Marc Hequet, "The Fine Art of Multicultural Meetings," *Training* (July 1993): 29–33.

2. For additional insights on groupthink, see the following articles: Judith Chapman, "Anxiety and Defective Decision Making: An Elaboration of the Groupthink Model," *Management Decision*, 2006, vol. 44, 1391–1404; Jack Eaton, "Management Communication: The Threat of Groupthink," *Corporate Communications*, 2001, vol. 6, 183–192; Phillip M. Johnson, "Effects of Groupthink on Tactical Decision Making," *Storming Media*, www.stormingmedia.us/90/9007/A900783.html, 1 Jan. 2001 (accessed 29 June 2007); Christopher P. Neck and Charles C. Manz, "From Groupthink to Teamthink: Toward the Creation of Constructive Thought Patterns in Self-Managed Work Teams," *Human Relations* (August 1994): 929–953; and Steve A. Yetiv, "Groupthink and the Gulf Crisis," *British Journal of Political Science*, 2003, v. 33, 419–442.

3. For more information on the uses of face-to-face brainstorming see J. M. Hender, et.al., "Improving Group Creativity: Brainstorming versus Non-brainstorming Techniques in a GSS Environment," *Proceedings of the 24th Annual Hawaii International Conference on System Sciences, 2001*; Thomas, J. Kramer, Gerard P. Fleming, and Scott M. Mannis, "Improving Face-to-Face Brainstorming Through Modeling and Facilitation," *Small Group Research*, Vol. 32 (2001); Paul B. Paulus, et.al. "Social and Cognitive Influences in Group Brainstorming: Predicting Production Gains and Losses," *European Review of Social Psychology*, vol. 12, (Jan. 2002). and E. L. Santanen, R. O. Briggs, and G. J. de Vreede, "The Cognitive Network Model of Creativity: A New Causal Model of Creativity and a New Brainstorming Technique," *Proceedings of the 33rd Annual International Conference on System Sciences, January 2000*.

4. For additional information on electronic brainstorming see K. L. Dugosh, et.al, "Cognitive Stimulation in Brainstorming," *Journal of Personal and Social Psychology*, vol. 79(5), Nov. 2000, 722–735; Nicolas Michinov and Corine Primois, "Improving Productivity and Creativity in Online Groups Through Social Comparison Process: New Evidence for Asynchronous Electronic Brainstorming," *Computers in Human Behavior* 21 (2005), 11–28, Available online at www.sciencedirect.com; and Rene Ziegler, Michael Diehl, and Gavin Zijlstra, "Idea Production in Nominal and Virtual Groups: Does Computer-Mediated Communication Improve Group Brainstorming?" *Group Processes and Intergroup Relations*, Vol. 3 (2000), 141–158.

5. Roz D. Lasker and Elisa S. Weiss, "Broadening Participation in Community Problem Solving: A Multidisciplinary Model to Support Collaborative Practice and Research," *Journal of Urban Health*, March 2003, 14–47; Nikol Rummel and Hans Spada, "Learning to Collaborate: An Instructional Approach to Promoting Collaborative Problem Solving in Computer-Mediated Settings," *Journal of the Learning Sciences*, Vol. 14 (2005), 201–241; James Allen, Nate Blaylock, and George Ferguson, "A Problem Solving Model for Collaborative Agents," *Proceedings of the First International Joint Conference on Autonomous Agents and Multiagent Systems: Part 2*, 2002, 774–781; Jacqueline Hood, Jeanne M. Logsdon, and Judith Kenner Thompson, "Collaboration for Social Problem Solving: A Process Model," *Business and Society* (Spring 1993): 1–17.

6. William M. Isaacs, "Taking Flight: Dialogue, Collective Thinking, and Organizational Learning," *Organizational Dynamics* (Autumn 1993): 24–39.

7. Edgar H. Schein, "On Dialogue, Culture, and Organizational Learning," *Organizational Dynamics* (Autumn 1993): 40–51. For additional information on dialogue groups see Joseph H. Albeck, Sami Adwan, and Dan Bar-On, "Dialogue Groups: TRT's Guidelines for Working Through Intractable Conflicts by Personal Story Telling," *Peace and Conflict: Journal of Peace Psychology*, Vol. 8 (2002), pp. 301–322; and David Schoem and Sylvia Hurtado (Eds.) *Intergroup Dialogue: Deliberative Democracy in School, College, Community, and Workplace*, (Ann Arbor, MI: University of Michigan Press, 2001).

8. The information on focus groups was synthesized from Carter McNamara, "Basics of Conducting Focus Groups" (undated posting), www.mapnp.org/library/evaluatn/focusgrp.htm (downloaded 6 March 2004); George Silverman, "How to Get Beneath the Surface in Focus Groups" (undated posting), www.mnav.com/bensurf.htm (downloaded 6 March 2004); Townsend International, "How to Run a Focus Group" (undated posting), www.gdaymate.com/customer_service/focusgroup.html (downloaded 6 March 2004); and Thomas L. Greenbaum, "Ten Tips for Running Successful Focus Groups" (14 Sept. 1998), www.groupsplus.com/pages/mn091498.htm (downloaded 6 March 2004). Also see David W. Stewart, Prem N. Shamdasani, and Dennis W. Rook, *Focus Groups: Theory and Practice*, 2nd Ed. (Thousand Oaks, CA: Sage, 2006); Thomas L. Greenbaum, *Moderating Focus Groups: A Practical Guide for Group Facilitation*, (Thousand Oaks, CA: Sage, 2000); and Claudia Puchta and Jonathan Potter, *Focus Group Practice*, (Thousand Oaks, CA: Sage 2004).

9. John P. Schuster, "Transforming Your Leadership Style," *Association Management* (January 1994): 39–43.

10. *Ibid.*

11. Svjetlana Madzar, "Subordinate's Information Inquiry: Exploring the Effect of Perceived Leadership Style and Individual Differences," *Journal of Occupational and Organizational Psychology* (June 2001): 221–232.

12. Much of the material in this section is adapted from Gregorio Billikopf, "Conducting Effective Meetings," www.cnr.berkeley.edu/ucce50/ag-labor/7labor/11.pdf (August 2005) accessed 30 June 2007; Don Clark, "Meetings," www.nwlink.com/~donclark/leader/leadmet.html (20 May 2007) accessed 30 June 2007; and Carter McNamara, "Basic Guide to Conducting Effective Meetings," www.managementhelp.org/misc/mtgmgmnt.htm (copyright 1997–2007) Accessed 30 June 2007.

13. Michael E. Mayer, "Behaviors Leading to More Effective Decisions in Small Groups Embedded in Organizations," *Communication Reports* (Summer 1988): 123–132.

14. "Roundtables," www.sdanys.org/Archive_Round/NYPWAGuidelines.htm. (4 Dec. 2003) accessed 30 June 2007.

15. Marilyn Berlin Snell, "Climate Exchange," *Sierra*, May/June 2007, 44–53. 73–74.

Index

Note: *f* indicates figures.

Photo Credits

Chapter 1: Page 2: Kayte M. Deioma / PhotoEdit; 6: Bob Daemmrich/The Image Works; 8: Jonathan Nourok / PhotoEdit; 9: Alinari; 14: Jacobs Stock Photography/Getty Images; 20: Ryan McVay/Getty Images; **Chapter 2:** Page 24: Jupiter Images; 27: Gary Newkirk/NewSport/Corbis; 28: Chuck Savage/Corbis; 33: Tony Freeman/PhotoEdit; 39: Patrik Giardino/Corbis; **Chapter 3:** Page 44: Barbara Stitzer/PhotoEdit; 49: David Pu'u/Corbis; 50: Courtesy Beth Tidmore; 51: Alex Wong/Getty Images; 59: Bob Daemmrich/Stock Boston; 60: Terry Wild Studio; **Chapter 4:** Page 70: Stockbyte/Getty Images; 73T: Loren Santow; 73B: Lawrence Migdale, www.migdale.com; 76: Deborah Lerme Goodman; 80: Michael Newman/PhotoEdit; 85: Erik Freeland; **Chapter 5:** Page 94: AP/Wide World Photos; 98: Bob Daemmrich/The Image Works; 100: AP/Wide World Photos; 106: Blaine Harrington III/Corbis; 113: Michael Appleton/Corbis; 116: Christy Bowe/Corbis; **Chapter 6:** Page 120: Warren Morgan/Corbis; 123: Joel W. Rogers/Corbis; 131: Jeff Greenberg/The Image Works; 137: Photodisc/Getty Images; **Chapter 7:** Page 142: David Young-Wolff/PhotoEdit; 147: Rob Crandall; 149: Courtesy Google; 152: Courtesy Sierra Club; 153: Courtesy Mayo Clinic; 154: Colin Young-Wolff / PhotoEdit; 160: Ghislain & Marie David de Lossy/Getty Images; 163: Imagesource/Jupiter Images; **Chapter 8:** Page 168: © Paul Andrew Lawrence / Alamy; 172: Corbis; 176: NewSport/Corbis; 178: Scott Wintrow/Getty Images Sport; 185: AP/Wide World Photos; **Chapter 9:** Page 194: © Rachel Epstein / The Image Works; 198: Gary Connor/PhotoEdit; 202: Charles Gupton/Stock Boston; 207: Asahi Shimbum; 211: AP/Wide World Photos; 214: AP/Wide World Photos; 217: Kayte M. Deioma / PhotoEdit; **Chapter 10:** Page 222: Stuart Dee/Getty Images; 232: Frank Clarkson/Getty Images; 243: Getty Images; **Chapter 11:** Page 246: Junko Kimura/Getty Images; 249: AP/Wide World Photos; 253: Michael Newman/PhotoEdit; 260L: Michael Busselle/Corbis; 260R: AP/Wide World Photos; 261: Bosler Visual Works; **Chapter 12:** Page 282: Jim Hollander/epa/Corbis; 286: Hulton-Deutsch Collection Corbis; 290: AP/Wide World Photos; 300: Jeff Greenberg/PhotoEdit; 301: © Flip Schulke/Corbis; **Chapter 13:** Page 310: AP/Wide World Photos; 314: Joel Gordon 1993; 323: Courtesy Tom Osborn; 324: AP/Wide World Photos; 326: AP/Wide World Photos; 328: Reuters/Corbis; 332: Ghislain & Marie David de Lossy/Getty Images; **Chapter 14:** Page 340: Stan Honda/Getty Images; 345: © James Caldwell / Alamy; 349: Steve Rubin/The Image Works; 353: Fabrice Coffrini/Getty Images; **Chapter 15:** Page 368: AP/Wide World Photos; 372: Frederick Brown/Getty Images; 376: AP/Wide World Photos; 378: Rick Friedman/Corbis; 380: *American Progress*, John Gast, oil on canvas, 1987. Museum of the American West collection, Autry National Center; 383: AP/Wide World Photos; 392: Stockbyte/Getty Images; **Chapter 16:** Page 408: © Janusz Wrobel / Alamy; 412: Charles Gupton/Corbis; 414: Barry Rosenthal/Getty Images; 418: Bob Daemmrich/The Image Works; 422: Peter Turnley/Corbis; **Chapter 17:** Page 438: © Richard B. Levine; 443L: James Burke/Getty Images; 443R: Hulton-Deutsch Collection/Corbis; 446T: Alan Goldstein/Folio; 446B: © 2001 The Record (Bergen County, NJ); 448: AP/Wide World Photos; 449: Stewart Cohen/Getty Images; 456: AP/Wide World Photos